Lecture Notes in Computer Science　　　13643

Founding Editors

The series Lecture Notes in Computer Science (LNCS), including its subseries Lecture Notes in Artificial Intelligence (LNAI) and Lecture Notes in Bioinformatics (LNBI), has established itself as a medium for the publication of new developments in computer science and information technology research, teaching, and education.

LNCS enjoys close cooperation with the computer science R & D community, the series counts many renowned academics among its volume editors and paper authors, and collaborates with prestigious societies. Its mission is to serve this international community by providing an invaluable service, mainly focused on the publication of conference and workshop proceedings and postproceedings. LNCS commenced publication in 1973.

Jean-Jacques Rousseau · Bill Kapralos
Editors

Pattern Recognition, Computer Vision, and Image Processing

ICPR 2022 International Workshops and Challenges

Montreal, QC, Canada, August 21–25, 2022
Proceedings, Part I

 Springer

Editors
Jean-Jacques Rousseau 🆔
York University
Toronto, ON, Canada

Bill Kapralos 🆔
Ontario Tech University
Oshawa, ON, Canada

ISSN 0302-9743   ISSN 1611-3349 (electronic)
Lecture Notes in Computer Science
ISBN 978-3-031-37659-7   ISBN 978-3-031-37660-3 (eBook)
https://doi.org/10.1007/978-3-031-37660-3

This Springer imprint is published by the registered company Springer Nature Switzerland AG
The registered company address is: Gewerbestrasse 11, 6330 Cham, Switzerland

Foreword

The organizers of the 26th International Conference on Pattern Recognition (ICPR 2022) are delighted to present the Proceedings of the event. The conference took place at Palais des Congrès de Montréal in Montreal, Canada, and we are thrilled to share the outcomes of this successful event.

We would like to express our heartfelt gratitude to the International Association for Pattern Recognition (IAPR) for sponsoring the conference, which allowed us to bring together a diverse group of researchers and experts in this field. Without their support, this conference would not have been possible.

We also want to extend our special thanks to the Workshop Chairs who provided excellent leadership in organizing the workshops. We appreciate the tireless efforts they put into making the workshops a success. We would also like to acknowledge the authors and presenters of the articles and workshops for their contributions. The high quality of their work and presentations enriched the conference.

Finally, we would like to thank the attendees for their participation, which made ICPR 2022 a truly collaborative and inspiring event. We hope that the Proceedings will serve as a valuable resource for those interested in pattern recognition and inspire future research in this field.

August 2022

Henrik I. Christensen
Michael Jenkin
Cheng-Lin Liu

Preface

The 26th International Conference on Pattern Recognition Workshops (ICPRW 2022) were held at the Palais des congrès de Montréal in Montreal, Quebec, Canada on Sunday August 21, 2022, one day earlier than the main ICPR conference. 27 workshop submissions were received and were carefully reviewed by the IAPR Conferences and Meetings committee and the workshop chairs. Considering their decisions and anticipated attendance, 24 workshops were selected and 21 workshops actually took place. Many of these workshops received a sponsorship or endorsement from the International Association for Pattern Recognition (IAPR).

ICPR 2022 marked the return of the conference to its in-person format (although workshops had the option of being held in person or remotely). This meant meeting colleagues face to face again, and making new connections to support scientific collaborations and (perhaps) even new friendships. The purpose of publishing the proceedings of a scientific conference such as ICPR 2022 include to:

- Establish a permanent record of the research presented;
- Report on the current research concerns and accomplishments of the conference participants;
- Make new research visible to scientific and other publics to promote collaboration, innovation, and discovery;
- Disseminate the latest research findings to a wider audience, in support of researchers, academics, industry, and other practitioners; and,
- Support the shared goal of staying up to date with developments in the fast moving field of artificial intelligence.

These volumes constitute the refereed proceedings of the twenty-one (21) workshops that were held in conjunction with ICPR 2022. The wide range of topics that it contains is a testament to the ever-widening concerns of AI researchers as they creatively find ways to apply artificial intelligence to domains further from its historical concerns. ICPR 2022 workshops covered domains related to pattern recognition, artificial intelligence, computer vision, and image and sound analysis. Workshop contributions reflected the most recent applications related to healthcare, biometrics, ethics, multimodality, cultural heritage, imagery, affective computing, and de-escalation. The papers included in these proceedings span four volumes and stem from the following workshops:

Volume I:

T-CAP 2022: Towards a Complete Analysis of People: From Face and Body to Clothes
HBU: 12th International Workshop on Human Behavior Understanding
SSL: Theories, Applications, and Cross Modality for Self-Supervised Learning Models
MPRSS 2022: Multimodal Pattern Recognition for Social Signal Processing in Human-Computer Interaction
FAIRBIO: Fairness in Biometric Systems

AIHA: Artificial Intelligence for Healthcare Applications
MDMR: Multimodal Data for Mental Disorder Recognition

Volume II:

MANPU 2022: 5th International Workshop on coMics ANalysis, Processing and Understanding
FOREST: Image Analysis for Forest Environmental Monitoring
MMFORWILD: MultiMedia FORensics in the WILD
IMTA: 8th International Workshop on Image Mining, Theory and Applications
PRHA: Pattern Recognition in Healthcare Analytics
IML: International Workshop on Industrial Machine Learning

Volume III:

PatReCH: 3rd International Workshop on Pattern Recognition for Cultural Heritage
XAIE: 2nd Workshop on Explainable and Ethical AI
PRRS: 12th Workshop on Pattern Recognition in Remote Sensing
CVAUI: Computer Vision for Analysis of Underwater Imagery
UMDBB: Understanding and Mitigating Demographic Bias in Biometric Systems

Volume IV:

AI4MFDD: Workshop on Artificial Intelligence for Multimedia Forensics and Disinformation Detection
AI4D: AI for De-escalation: Autonomous Systems for De-escalating Conflict in Military and Civilian Contexts
AMAR: 3rd International Workshop on Applied Multimodal Affect Recognition

Writing this preface, we were acutely aware of our special responsibilities towards those who will access the Proceedings for future reference. Unlike us and the contributors to these volumes, future readers will not have the benefit of having lived through the moment in which the research was conducted and presented. As background, leading to August 2022, there were two overarching meta-stories in the news: the COVID pandemic and social justice. COVID restrictions were lifted in piecemeal fashion leading to the conference dates, and began the long tail of the end of the pandemic. For conference attendees, wearing face masks was a live issue since masks indoors remained strongly recommended. International travel was still heavily impacted by COVID restrictions, with some participants being unable to travel either due to their COVID status or to the difficulty in meeting the range of COVID testing and inoculation requirements required. The public health theme continued with a new virus called 'Monkeypox' appearing on the scene.

On social justice, the May 25, 2020 murder of George Floyd by Minneapolis police officers continued to cast its shadow. During the summer of 2022, there continued to be protests and other actions to demand an end to anti-Black racism. In parallel, in Canada, Indigenous communities led protests and actions to demand an end to anti-Indigenous racism, and to acknowledge the historical circumstances that explain the discoveries of remains of children in unmarked burial sites at former residential schools. As conference attendees and participants, we lived through this cultural moment and were marked by it. However, future readers may need to supplement these volumes with research into the circumstances in which the research was conceptualized, conducted, and received. Philosophers of science make a relevant distinction here. Since Karl Popper, they speak of the context of discovery and the context of justification. Justification in science is relatively well understood, as it relates to the collection and analysis of data in pursuit of evidence for evaluating hypotheses in conformity with norms referenced to as the 'scientific method'. However, where do the initial questions or leaps of insights come from? The context of discovery is not as well understood. Still, it is widely believed that the social and personal conditions of researchers play an active role. We included a reference to the COVID-19 pandemic and social justice movements as widely shared preoccupations at the time of ICPR 2022 to aid a future reader who may wonder about the context of discovery of what is reported.

We acknowledge that future readers will no doubt enjoy benefits that we cannot enjoy. Specifically, they may be able to better assess which lines of research presented in the Proceedings proved the more beneficial. There are also concrete things: as we write, we do not know whether we are in a COVID pandemic hiatus or at its end; future readers will know the answer to this question.

The organization of such a large conference would not be possible without the help of many people. Our special gratitude goes to the Program Chairs (Gregory Dudek, Zhouchen Lin, Simone Marinai, Ingela Nyström) for their leadership in organizing the program. Thanks go to the Track Chairs and Area Chairs who dedicated their time to the review process and the preparation of the program. We also thank the reviewers who have evaluated the papers and provided authors with valuable feedback on their research work.

Finally, we acknowledge the work of conference committee members (Local Arrangements Chair and Committee Members, Finance Chairs, Workshop Chairs, Tutorial Chairs, Challenges Chairs, Publicity Chairs, Publications Chairs, Awards Chair, Sponsorship and Exhibition Chair) who strongly contributed to make this event successful. The MCI Group, led by Anjali Mohan, made great efforts in arranging the logistics, which is highly appreciated.

August 2022
Jean-Jacques Rousseau
Bill Kapralos

Organization

General Chairs

Henrik I. Christensen — UC San Diego, USA
Michael Jenkin — York University, Canada.
Cheng-Lin Liu — Institute of Automation of Chinese Academy of Sciences, China

Program Committee Co-chairs

Gregory Dudek — McGill University, Canada
Zhouchen Lin — Peking University, China
Simone Marinai — University of Florence, Italy
Ingela Nyström — Swedish National Infrastructure for Computing, Sweden

Invited Speakers Chairs

Alberto Del Bimbo — University of Firenze, Italy
Michael Brown — Canada
Steven Waslander — University of Toronto, Canada

Workshop Chairs

Xiang Bai — Huazhong University of Science and Technology, China
Giovanni Farinella — University of Catania, Italy
Laurence Likforman — Télécom Paris, France
Jonathan Wu — Canada

Tutorial Chairs

David Clausi   University of Waterloo, Canada
Markus Enzweiler   Esslingen University of Applied Sciences,
                                        Germany
Umapada Pal   Indian Statistical Institute, India

Local Arrangements Chair

Ioannis Rekleitis   University of South Carolina, USA

Finance Chairs

Rainer Herpers   Hochschule Bonn-Rhein-Sieg, Germany
Andrew Hogue   Ontario Tech University, Canada

Publication Chairs

Jean-Jacques Rousseau   York University, Canada
Bill Kapralos   Ontario Tech University, Canada

Awards Chair

Johana Hansen   McGill University, Canada

Sponsorship and Exhibition Chair

Hong Zhang   China

Challenges Chairs

Marco Bertini   University of Florence, Italy
Dimosthenis Karatzas   Universitat Autónoma de Barcelona, Spain

Track 1: Artificial Intelligence, Machine Learning for Pattern Analysis

Battista Biggio	Università degli Studi di Cagliari, Italy
Ambra Demontis	Università degli Studi di Cagliari, Italy
Gang Hua	Wormpex AI Research, University of Washington, USA
Dacheng Tao	University of Sydney, Australia

Track 2: Computer Vision and Robotic Perception

Olga Bellon	Universidade Federal do Parana, Brazil
Kosta Derpanis	York University, Canada
Ko Nishino	Kyoto University, Japan

Track 3: Image, Speech, Signal and Video Processing

Ana Fred	University of Lisbon, Portugal
Regina Lee	York University, Canada
Jingdong Wang	Baidu, China
Vera Yashina	Russian Academy of Sciences, Russian Federation

Track 4: Biometrics and Human-Computer Interaction

Kevin Bowyer	University of Notre Dame, USA
Kerstin Dautenhahn	University of Waterloo, Canada
Julian Fierrez	Universidad Autónoma de Madrid, Spain
Shiqi Yu	Southern University of Science and Technology, China

Track 5: Document Analysis and Recognition

Alexandra Branzan Albu	University of Victoria, Canada
Alicia Fornes	Universitat Autònoma de Barcelona, Spain
Koichi Kise	Osaka Prefecture University, Japan
Faisal Shafait	National University of Sciences and Technology, Pakistan

Track 6: Biomedical Imaging and Informatics

Hamid Abbasi   Auckland Bioengineering Institute, New Zealand
Ismail Bey Ayed   Ecole de Technologie Superieure (ETS), Canada
Lukas Käll   KTH Royal Institute of Technology, Sweden
Dinggang Shen   ShanghaiTech University, China

ICPR 2022 Workshops: Volume I

Towards a Complete Analysis of People: From Face and Body to Clothes (T-CAP)

Mohamed Daoudi   IMT Lille Douai, France
Roberto Vezzani   University of Modena and Reggio Emilia, Italy
Guido Borghi   University of Bologna, Italy
Marcella Cornia   University of Modena and Reggio Emilia, Italy
Claudio Ferrari   University of Parma, Italy
Federico Becattini   University of Florence, Italy
Andrea Pilzer   NVIDIA AI Technology Center, Italy

12th International Workshop on Human Behavior Understanding (HBU)

Albert Ali Salah   Utrecht University, The Netherlands
Cristina Palmero   University of Barcelona, Spain
Hugo Jair Escalante   National Institute of Astrophysics, Optics and
                           Electronics, Mexico
Sergio Escalera   Universitat de Barcelona, Spain
Henning Müller   HES-SO Valais-Wallis, Switzerland

Theories, Applications, and Cross Modality for Self-Supervised Learning Models (SSL)

Yu Wang   NVIDIA, USA
Yingwei Pan   JD AI Research, China
Jingjing Zou   UC San Diego, USA
Angelica I. Aviles-Rivero   University of Cambridge, UK
Carola-Bibiane Schönlieb   University of Cambridge, UK
John Aston   University of Cambridge, UK
Ting Yao   JD AI Research, China

Multimodal Pattern Recognition of Social Signals in Human-Computer-Interaction (MPRSS 2022)

Mariofanna Milanova   University of Arkansas at Little Rock, USA
Xavier Alameda-Pineda   Inria, University of Grenoble-Alpes, France
Friedhelm Schwenker   Ulm University, Germany

Fairness in Biometric Systems (FAIRBIO)

Philipp Terhörst	Paderborn University, Germany
Kiran Raja	Norwegian University of Science and Technology, Norway
Christian Rathgeb	Hochschule Darmstadt, Germany
Abhijit Das	BITS Pilani Hyderabad, India
Ana Filipa Sequeira	INESC TEC, Portugal
Antitza Dantcheva	Inria Sophia Antipolis, France
Sambit Bakshi	National Institute of Technology Rourkela, India
Raghavendra Ramachandra	Norwegian University of Science and Technology, Norway
Naser Damer	Fraunhofer Institute for Computer Graphics Research IGD, Germany

2nd International Workshop on Artificial Intelligence for Healthcare Applications (AIHA 2022)

Nicole Dalia Cilia	Kore University of Enna, Italy
Francesco Fontanella	University of Cassino and Southern Lazio, Italy
Claudio Marrocco	University of Cassino and Southern Lazio, Italy

Workshop on Multimodal Data for Mental Disorder Recognition (MDMR)

Richang Hong	Hefei University of Technology, China
Marwa Mahmoud	University of Glasgow, UK
Bin Hu	Lanzhou University, China

ICPR 2022 Workshops: Volume II

5th International Workshop on coMics ANalysis, Processing and Understanding (MANPU 2022)

Jean-Christophe Burie	University of La Rochelle, France
Motoi Iwata	Osaka Metropolitan University, Japan
Miki Ueno	Osaka Institute of Technology, Japan

Image Analysis for Forest Environmental Monitoring (FOREST)

Alexandre Bernardino	Instituto Superior Técnico, Portugal
El Khalil Cherif	Instituto Superior Técnico, Portugal
Catarina Barata	Instituto Superior Técnico, Portugal
Alexandra Moutinho	Instituto Superior Técnico, Portugal
Maria João Sousa	Instituto Superior Técnico, Portugal
Hugo Silva	Instituto Superior de Engenharia do Porto, Portugal

MultiMedia FORensics in the WILD (MMFORWILD 2022)

Mauro Barni	University of Siena, Italy
Sebastiano Battiato	University of Catania, Italy
Giulia Boato	University of Trento, Italy
Hany Farid	University of California, Berkeley, USA
Nasir Memon	New York University, USA

Image Mining: Theory and Applications (IMTA-VIII)

Igor Gurevich	Federal Research Center Computer Science and Control of the Russian Academy of Sciences, Russian Federation
Davide Moroni	Institute of Information Science and Technologies, National Research Council of Italy, Italy

| Maria Antonietta Pascali | Institute of Information Science and Technologies, National Research Council of Italy, Italy |
| Vera Yashina | Federal Research Center Computer Science and Control of the Russian Academy of Sciences, Russian Federation |

International Workshop on Pattern Recognition in Healthcare Analytics (PRHA 2022)

Inci Baytas	Bogazici University, Turkey
Edward Choi	Korea Advanced Institute of Science and Technology, South Korea
Arzucan Ozgur	Bogazici University, Turkey
Ayse Basar	Bogazici University, Turkey

International Workshop on Industrial Machine Learning (IML)

Francesco Setti	University of Verona, Italy
Paolo Rota	University of Trento, Italy
Vittorio Murino	University of Verona, Italy
Luigi Di Stefano	University of Bologna, Italy
Massimiliano Mancini	University of Tübingen, Germany

ICPR 2022 Workshops: Volume III

3rd International Workshop on Pattern Recognition for Cultural Heritage (PatReCH 2022)

Dario Allegra	University of Catania, Italy
Mario Molinara	University of Cassino and Southern Lazio, Italy
Alessandra Scotto di Freca	University of Cassino and Southern Lazio, Italy
Filippo Stanco	University of Catania, Italy

2nd Workshop on Explainable and Ethical AI (XAIE 2022)

Romain Giot	Univ. Bordeaux, France
Jenny Benois-Pineau	Univ. Bordeaux, France
Romain Bourqui	Univ. Bordeaux, France
Dragutin Petkovic	San Francisco State University, USA

12th Workshop on Pattern Recognition in Remote Sensing (PRRS)

Ribana Roscher	University of Bonn, Germany
Charlotte Pelletier	Université Bretagne Sud, France
Sylvain Lobry	Paris Descartes University, France

Computer Vision for Analysis of Underwater Imagery (CVAUI)

Maia Hoeberechts	Ocean Networks Canada, Canada
Alexandra Branzan Albu	University of Victoria, Canada

Understanding and Mitigating Demographic Bias in Biometric Systems (UMDBB)

Ajita Rattani	Wichita State University, USA
Michael King	Florida Institute of Technology, USA

ICPR 2022 Workshops: Volume IV

AI for De-escalation: Autonomous Systems for De-escalating Conflict in Military and Civilian Contexts (AI4D)

Victor Sanchez   University of Warwick, UK
Irene Amerini   Sapienza University of Rome, Italy
Chang-Tsun Li   Deakin University, Australia
Wei Qi Yan   Auckland University of Technology, New Zealand
Yongjian Hu   South China University of Technology, China
Nicolas Sidere   La Rochelle Université, France
Jean-Jacques Rousseau   York University, Canada

3rd Workshop on Applied Multimodal Affect Recognition (AMAR)

Shaun Canavan   University of South Florida, USA
Tempestt Neal   University of South Florida, USA
Saurabh Hinduja   University of Pittsburgh, USA
Marvin Andujar   University of South Florida, USA
Lijun Yin   Binghamton University, USA

Contents – Part I

Towards a Complete Analysis of People: From Face and Body to Clothes (T-CAP)

Uncalibrated, Unified and Unsupervised Specular-Aware Photometric Stereo 7
   Pablo Estevez and Antonio Agudo

Appearance-Independent Pose-Based Posture Classification in Infants 21
   Xiaofei Huang, Shuangjun Liu, Michael Wan, Nihang Fu,
   David Li Pino, Bharath Modayur, and Sarah Ostadabbas

Emotion, Age and Gender Prediction Through Masked Face Inpainting 37
   Md Baharul Islam and Md Imran Hosen

A Masked Face Classification Benchmark on Low-Resolution Surveillance Images 49
   Federico Cunico, Andrea Toaiari, and Marco Cristani

Lightweight Human Pose Estimation Using Loss Weighted by Target Heatmap 64
   Shiqi Li and Xiang Xiang

BYTEv2: Associating More Detection Boxes Under Occlusion for Improved Multi-person Tracking 79
   Daniel Stadler and Jürgen Beyerer

Fast and Effective Detection of Personal Protective Equipment on Smart Cameras 95
   Antonio Greco, Stefano Saldutti, and Bruno Vento

Towards an Accurate 3D Deformable Eye Model for Gaze Estimation 109
   Chenyi Kuang, Jeffery O. Kephart, and Qiang Ji

2D-Pose Based Human Body Segmentation for Weakly-Supervised Concealed Object Detection in Backscatter Millimeter-Wave Images 124
   Lawrence Amadi and Gady Agam

Toward Surroundings-Aware Temporal Prediction of 3D Human Skeleton Sequence 139
   Tomohiro Fujita and Yasutomo Kawanishi

MTGR: Improving Emotion and Sentiment Analysis with Gated Residual
Networks   152
   Rihab Hajlaoui, Guillaume-Alexandre Bilodeau, and Jan Rockemann

**12th International Workshop on Human Behavior Understanding
(HBU)**

A Computational Approach for Analysing Autistic Behaviour During
Dyadic Interactions   167
   Oya Celiktutan, Weiyang Wu, Kai Vogeley, and Alexandra L. Georgescu

Region-Based Trajectory Analysis for Abnormal Behaviour Detection:
A Trial Study for Suicide Detection and Prevention   178
   *Xun Li, Ryan Anthony de Belen, Arcot Sowmya, Sandersan Onie,
   and Mark Larsen*

Automated Behavior Labeling During Team-Based Activities Involving
Neurodiverse and Neurotypical Partners Using Multimodal Data   193
   *Abigale Plunk, Ashwaq Zaini Amat, D. Mitchell Wilkes,
   and Nilanjan Sarkar*

Emergence of Collaborative Hunting via Multi-Agent Deep Reinforcement
Learning   210
   Kazushi Tsutsui, Kazuya Takeda, and Keisuke Fujii

Computational Multimodal Models of Users' Interactional Trust
in Multiparty Human-Robot Interaction   225
   Marc Hulcelle, Giovanna Varni, Nicolas Rollet, and Chloé Clavel

An Exploratory Study on Group Potency Classification from Non-verbal
Social Behaviours   240
   *Nicola Corbellini, Eleonora Ceccaldi, Giovanna Varni,
   and Gualtiero Volpe*

Multi-Channel Time-Series Person and Soft-Biometric Identification   256
   *Nilah Ravi Nair, Fernando Moya Rueda, Christopher Reining,
   and Gernot A. Fink*

To Invest or Not to Invest: Using Vocal Behavior to Predict Decisions
of Investors in an Entrepreneurial Context   273
   Ilona Goossens, Merel M. Jung, Werner Liebregts, and Itir Onal Ertugrul

Theories, Applications, and Cross Modality for Self-Supervised Learning Models (SSL)

Enhancing the Linear Probing Performance of Masked Auto-Encoders 289
  Yurui Qian, Yu Wang, and Jingyang Lin

Involving Density Prior for 3D Point Cloud Contrastive Learning 302
  Fuchen Long and Zhaofan Qiu

Joint Masked Autoencoding with Global Reconstruction for Point Cloud
Learning 313
  Qi Cai

Understanding the Properties and Limitations of Contrastive Learning
for Out-of-Distribution Detection 330
  Nawid Keshtmand, Raul Santos-Rodriguez, and Jonathan Lawry

Multimodal Pattern Recognition of Social Signals in Human-Computer-Interaction (MPRSS 2022)

Deep Learning Architectures for Pain Recognition Based on Physiological
Signals 349
  Patrick Thiam, Hans A. Kestler, and Friedhelm Schwenker

Egocentric Hand Gesture Recognition on Untrimmed Videos Using State
Activation Gate LSTMs 359
  Tejo Chalasani and Aljosa Smolic

Representation Learning for Tablet and Paper Domain Adaptation in Favor
of Online Handwriting Recognition 373
  *Felix Ott, David Rügamer, Lucas Heublein, Bernd Bischl,
  and Christopher Mutschler*

Active Learning Monitoring in Classroom Using Deep Learning
Frameworks 384
  Afsana Mou, Mariofanna Milanova, and Mark Baillie

Pain Detection in Biophysiological Signals: Transfer Learning
from Short-Term to Long-Term Stimuli Based on Signal Segmentation 394
  *Tobias B. Ricken, Peter Bellmann, Steffen Walter,
  and Friedhelm Schwenker*

Leveraging Sentiment Analysis Knowledge to Solve Emotion Detection
Tasks 405
   Maude Nguyen-The, Soufiane Lamghari,
   Guillaume-Alexandre Bilodeau, and Jan Rockemann

Analyzing the Prosodic and Lingual Features of Popular Speakers 417
   Bhavin Jethra, Rahul Golhar, and Ifeoma Nwogu

Fairness in Biometric Systems (FAIRBIO)

Evaluating Proposed Fairness Models for Face Recognition Algorithms 431
   John J. Howard, Eli J. Laird, Rebecca E. Rubin, Yevgeniy B. Sirotin,
   Jerry L. Tipton, and Arun R. Vemury

Disparate Impact in Facial Recognition Stems from the Broad
Homogeneity Effect: A Case Study and Method to Resolve 448
   John J. Howard, Eli J. Laird, and Yevgeniy B. Sirotin

The Influence of Gender and Skin Colour on the Watchlist Imbalance
Effect in Facial Identification Scenarios 465
   Jascha Kolberg, Christian Rathgeb, and Christoph Busch

Fairness Index Measures to Evaluate Bias in Biometric Recognition 479
   Ketan Kotwal and Sébastien Marcel

**2nd International Workshop on Artificial Intelligence for Healthcare
Applications (AIHA 2022)**

Class-Balanced Affinity Loss for Highly Imbalanced Tissue Classification
in Computational Pathology 499
   Taslim Mahbub, Ahmad Obeid, Sajid Javed, Jorge Dias,
   and Naoufel Werghi

Hybrid Approach for the Design of CNNs Using Genetic Algorithms
for Melanoma Classification 514
   Luigi Di Biasi, Fabiola De Marco, Alessia Auriemma Citarella,
   Paola Barra, Stefano Piotto Piotto, and Genoveffa Tortora

Transfer Learning in Breast Mass Detection on the OMI-DB Dataset:
A Preliminary Study 529
   Marya Ryspayeva, Mario Molinara, Alessandro Bria,
   Claudio Marrocco, and Francesco Tortorella

On the Applicability of Prototypical Part Learning in Medical Images:
Breast Masses Classification Using ProtoPNet 539
    Gianluca Carloni, Andrea Berti, Chiara Iacconi,
    Maria Antonietta Pascali, and Sara Colantonio

Deep Learning for Remote Heart Rate Estimation: A Reproducible
and Optimal State-of-the-Art Framework 558
    Nelida Mirabet-Herranz, Khawla Mallat, and Jean-Luc Dugelay

Automatic Bowel Preparation Assessment Using Deep Learning 574
    Mahmood Salah Haithami, Amr Ahmed, Iman Yi Liao,
    and Hamid Jalab Altulea

A Hierarchical 3D Segmentation Model for Cone-Beam Computed
Tomography Dental-Arch Scans 589
    Francesco Rundo, Carmelo Pino, Riccardo E. Sarpietro,
    Concetto Spampinato, and Federica Proietto Salanitri

SARS-CoV-2 Induced Pneumonia Early Detection System Based on Chest
X-Ray Images Analysis by Jacobian-Regularized Deep Network 602
    Francesco Rundo, Carmelo Pino, Riccardo E. Sarpietro,
    and Concetto Spampinato

SERCNN: Stacked Embedding Recurrent Convolutional Neural Network
in Detecting Depression on Twitter 617
    Heng Ee Tay, Mei Kuan Lim, and Chun Yong Chong

Predicting Alzheimer's Disease: A Stroke-Based Handwriting Analysis
Approach Based on Machine Learning 632
    Nicole Dalia Cilia, Tiziana D'Alessandro, Claudio De Stefano,
    Francesco Fontanella, and Emanuele Nardone

Unsupervised Brain MRI Anomaly Detection for Multiple Sclerosis
Classification 644
    Giovanna Castellano, Giuseppe Placidi, Matteo Polsinelli,
    Gianpiero Tulipani, and Gennaro Vessio

Multimodal Data for Mental Disorder Recognition (MDMR)

Dep-Emotion: Suppressing Uncertainty to Recognize Real Emotions
in Depressed Patients 655
    Gang Fu, Jiayu Ye, and Qingxiang Wang

EEG-Based Joint Semi-supervised Learning for Major Depressive
Disorder Detection 668
   Tao Chen, Tong Zheng, Jinlong Shi, and Yanrong Guo

Subject-Aware Explainable Contrastive Deep Fusion Learning for Anxiety
Level Analysis 682
   Michael Briden and Narges Norouzi

MMDA: A Multimodal Dataset for Depression and Anxiety Detection 691
   Yueqi Jiang, Ziyang Zhang, and Xiao Sun

Author Index 703

Towards a Complete Analysis of People: From Face and Body to Clothes (T-CAP)

Towards a Complete Analysis of People: From Face and Body to Clothes (T-CAP 2022)

In modern times, human-centered data are extremely widespread and are being intensely investigated by researchers belonging to very different fields, including Computer Vision, Pattern Recognition, and Artificial Intelligence. In this context, the ability to collect data and extract knowledge about humans is crucial in order to develop new human-based research, real-world applications, and intelligent systems, despite the presence of technical, social, and ethical problems still open.

The ICPR workshop "Towards a Complete Analysis of People: From Face and Body to Clothes" (T-CAP 2022) aims to address this challenging context, focusing on and collecting works that investigate new approaches and analyze the significant recent advancements related to people. These research efforts are motivated by the several highly-informative aspects of humans that can be investigated, ranging from corporal elements (*e.g.* bodies, faces, hands, anthropometric measurements) to expressions, emotions, and outward appearance (*e.g.* garments and accessories).

The huge amount and the extreme variety of human-related data make the analysis and the use of Artificial Intelligence extremely challenging. For instance, several interesting problems can be addressed, such as the reliable detection and tracking of people, the estimation of the body pose, and the development of new human-computer interaction paradigms based on expression and sentiment analysis. Furthermore, considering the crucial impact of human-centered technologies in many industrial application domains, the demand for accurate models able also to run on mobile and embedded solutions is constantly increasing. For instance, the analysis and manipulation of garments and accessories worn by people can play a crucial role in the fashion business. Also, human pose estimation can be used to monitor and guarantee the safety between workers and industrial robotic arms.

The goal of this workshop is to improve the communication between researchers and companies and to develop novel ideas that can shape the future of this area, in terms of motivations, methodologies, prospective trends, and potential industrial applications. Also, a consideration about the privacy issues behind the acquisition and the use of human-centered data must be addressed for both academia and companies. This year we received a total of 16 submissions, all from different institutions. All papers have been peer-reviewed by three different reviewers from our technical program committee. The review process focused on the quality of the papers, their scientific novelty, and their applicability to human-centered problems. After the review process, 11 high-quality papers have been accepted for oral presentation at the workshop. The acceptance rate was 68%. The first edition of the workshop was held in Lecce, Italy, in conjunction with the 21st International Conference on Image Analysis and Processing (ICIAP 2021). Similarly to this event, the format of the workshop included invited speakers, from both industry and academia, and technical presentations.

The workshop program was completed by two invited talks given by, respectively, Prof. Nicu Sebe (University of Trento, Italy) and Sergey Tulyakov (Principal Research Scientist, Snap Research, United States). A special Issue related to the workshop topics has been organized in partnership with the MDPI Journal of Sensors (IF 3.5).

September 2022

Organization

Workshop Chairs

Mohamed Daoudi	IMT Lille Douai, France
Roberto Vezzani	University of Modena and Reggio Emilia, Italy
Guido Borghi	University of Bologna, Italy
Marcella Cornia	University of Modena and Reggio Emilia, Italy
Claudio Ferrari	University of Parma, Italy
Federico Becattini	University of Florence, Italy
Andrea Pilzer	NVIDIA AI Technology Center, Italy

Technical Program Committee

Michal Balazia	Inria, France
João Baptista Cardia Neto	Unesp, Brazil
Niccolò Biondi	University of Florence, Italy
Tong Chen	Southwest University, China
Andrea Ciamarra	University of Florence, Italy
Matteo Fincato	University of Modena and Reggio Emilia, Italy
Tomaso Fontanini	University of Parma, Italy
Alessio Gallucci	Eindhoven University of Technology, Netherlands
Gabriele Graffieti	University of Bologna, Italy
Yante Li	University of Oulu, Finland
Massimiliano Mancini	University of Tübingen, Germany
Gianluca Mancusi	University of Modena and Reggio Emilia, Italy
Davide Morelli	University of Modena and Reggio Emilia, Italy
Fernando Moya Rueda	TU Dortmund University, Germany
Lorenzo Pellegrini	University of Bologna, Italy
Marko Savic	University of Oulu, Finland
Henglin Shi	University of Oulu, Finland
Alessandro Simoni	University of Modena and Reggio Emilia, Italy
Madhumita Takalkar	University of Technology Sydney, Australia

Thuong Khanh Tran   University of Oulu, Finland
Jichao Zhang   University of Trento, Italy

Sponsor

MDPI Sensors journal cooperated with the workshop as media partner.

Uncalibrated, Unified and Unsupervised Specular-Aware Photometric Stereo

Pablo Estevez[ID] and Antonio Agudo[✉][ID]

Institut de Robòtica i Informàtica Industrial, CSIC-UPC, 08028 Barcelona, Spain
aagudo@iri.upc.edu

Abstract. In this paper we present a variational approach to simultaneously recover the 3D reconstruction, reflectance, lighting and specularities of an object, all of them, from a set of RGB images. The approach works in an uncalibrated, unified and unsupervised manner, without assuming any prior knowledge of the shape geometry or training data to constrain the solution and under general lighting. To this end, the approach exploits a physically-aware image formation model that in combination with a perspective projection one and under spherical harmonics lighting gives a fully interpretable algorithm. Integrability is implicitly ensured as the shape is coded by a depth map rather than normal vectors. As a consequence, a wide variety of illumination conditions and complex geometries can be acquired. Our claims have been experimentally validated on challenging synthetic and real datasets, obtaining a good trade-off between accuracy and computational budget in comparison with competing approaches.

Keywords: Specular-aware · Photometric Stereo · Uncalibrated · Unsupervised · Variational Optimization

1 Introduction

Photometric stereo (PS) is a relevant problem in computer vision and pattern recognition aiming to retrieve both the 3D geometry of an object –probably via its normal vectors– and the reflectance of a scene from multiple images taken at the same viewpoint but under different illumination conditions [23–25]. Frequently, the way to sort out the problem consists in inverting a physically-aware image formation model that assumes a certain control of lighting. Despite providing accurate formulations, lighting control reduces the applicability of these methods to laboratory scenarios where an exhaustive calibration of lighting must be performed. Instead, the uncalibrated counterpart is ill-posed as the underlying normal map is recovered up to a linear ambiguity [5], that decreases to a generalized bas-relief one if integrability is enforced. Differential approaches based on variational formulations were introduced in order to directly retrieve the 3D geometry as a depth map, relaxing the remaining ambiguities [2,16]. The previous works assumed an illumination induced by a single source, limiting strongly their applicability to natural scenarios where general lighting conditions appear. A non-directional illumination model was proposed by [7] to encode natural illumination that was even used in cloudy days [8]. Unfortunately, solving PS for uncalibrated and general lighting is a very challenging task that has been rarely explored. Some exceptions were proposed [15,19] by assuming coarse 3D reconstructions as a prior, spatially-varying

© Springer Nature Switzerland AG 2023
J.-J. Rousseau and B. Kapralos (Eds.): ICPR 2022 Workshops, LNCS 13643, pp. 7–20, 2023.
https://doi.org/10.1007/978-3-031-37660-3_1

Table 1. Qualitative comparison of our approach with respect to competing methods. Our approach is the only one that directly retrieves a depth map (potentially non-integrable surface normals are not estimated) of both Lambertian (L) and non-Lambertian (NL) materials; it is uncalibrated and works under general lighting; and it assumes neither shape priors nor training data with ground truth.

Feat. / Meth.	Integrability	Uncalibrated No	Uncalibrated Yes	Prior Shape	Prior Training	Material L	Material NL
[7,8]		✓				✓	
[15,19]	✓		✓	✓		✓	
[12]			✓			✓	
[11,22,26]	✓				✓	✓	✓
[4]	✓		✓			✓	
Ours	✓		✓			✓	✓

directional lighting models [12], or Lambertian materials [4]. Beyond Lambertian PS, the problem can be even more challenging for non-Lambertian objects as its appearance could contain a mixture of specular and diffuse reflection properties.

In parallel, the use of deep learning has been also applied to PS [9,11,22,26]. These approaches propose end-to-end supervised training methodologies that ignore the underlying physical principle of PS as the model is learned from data. While the obtained results are promising, their lack of physical interpretability prevents them from exploiting the real interactions between surface geometry and specularities, as the last are handled in an implicit manner. However, the previous has not prevented a wider up-taking of these methods. The lack of large-scale real-world training data hinders the progress of data-driven deep PS. It is worth noting that obtaining ground truth – including 3D geometries and lighting– in a natural lab setting is both expensive and laborious, especially for certain object materials where the acquisition could be very hard. In addition to that, these approaches normally assume the light direction as well as the intensity at each illumination instant, i.e., the problem is solved in a calibrated manner. Table 1 summarizes a qualitative comparison in terms of available characteristics and assumptions of our approach and the most relevant competing approaches. As it can be seen, our approach is the only one that has all characteristics without assuming strong priors such as the use of large amounts of training data or a 3D rough geometry.

In this paper we overcome most of the limitations of current methods with a variational algorithm that can solve the PS problem for non-specific objects. Our approach is unified, unsupervised –no ground truth is needed for supervision–, and efficient; as well as being able to handle the problem in an uncalibrated manner under general lighting.

2   Physically-Aware Photometric Stereo

Let us consider a set of observations $\{\mathcal{I}_c^i \subset \mathbb{R}^2\}$ composed of $i = \{1, \ldots, I\}$ images with $c = \{1, \ldots, C\}$ color channels where it appears an object we want to reconstruct in 3D. For that object, we also define $\mathcal{M} \subset \mathcal{I}_c^i$ as its shape segmentation in the image set, i.e., the masked pixel domain. Considering that the object to be captured is Lambertian, the surface reflectance for all P pixel points $\mathbf{p} \in \mathcal{M}$ can be modeled by collecting elementary luminance contributions arising from all the incident lighting directions $\boldsymbol{\omega}$ as:

$$\mathcal{I}_c^i(\mathbf{p}) = \int_{\mathbb{H}^2} \rho_c(\mathbf{p})\, l_c^i(\boldsymbol{\omega})\, \max\{0, \boldsymbol{\omega}^\top \mathbf{n}(\mathbf{p})\}\, d\omega, \tag{1}$$

where $\mathbb{H}^2$ is the unit sphere in $\mathbb{R}^3$, $\rho_c(\mathbf{p})$ and $l_c^i(\boldsymbol{\omega})$ indicate the color-wise albedos and intensity of the incident lights, respectively, and $\mathbf{n}(\mathbf{p})$ the unit-length surface normals at the surface point conjugate to pixel $\mathbf{p}$. The Lambertian surface assumes $\rho_c(\mathbf{p})$ to be always a positive value. The object irradiance or shading component is coded by the max operator. Unfortunately, the previous model cannot handle materials that exhibit a combination of specular and diffuse reflection properties, i.e., non-Lambertian surfaces. To solve that, we can follow the approximation of a Phong reflection model that considers the light at the p-th pixel as the sum of two additive terms: a viewpoint-independent diffuse and a view-dependent specular. In other words, as the model in Eq. (1) is specularity-free diffuse, we consider an additive component $s^i(\mathbf{p})$ for the specular reflection as:

$$\mathcal{I}_c^i(\mathbf{p}) = \int_{\mathbb{H}^2} \rho_c(\mathbf{p})\, l_c^i(\boldsymbol{\omega})\, \max\{0, \boldsymbol{\omega}^\top \mathbf{n}(\mathbf{p})\}\, d\omega + s^i(\mathbf{p}). \tag{2}$$

According to literature [2,23,25], the PS problem in an uncalibrated manner consists in recovering the 3D shape of the object (via its normals $\mathbf{n}(\mathbf{p})$) together with the quantities $\{\rho_c\}$, $\{l_c^i\}$ and $\{s^i\}$, all of them, from the set $\{\mathcal{I}_c^i\}$.

Following [1] the irradiance map can be modeled using a spherical harmonic approximation of general lighting by means of a half-cosine kernel:

$$k(\boldsymbol{\omega}, \mathbf{n}(\mathbf{p})) = \max\{0, \boldsymbol{\omega}^\top \mathbf{n}(\mathbf{p})\}. \tag{3}$$

The general image formation model in Eq. (2) can now be written as:

$$\begin{aligned}
\mathcal{I}_c^i(\mathbf{p}) &= \rho_c(\mathbf{p}) \int_{\mathbb{H}^2} l_c^i(\boldsymbol{\omega})\, k(\boldsymbol{\omega}, \mathbf{n}(\mathbf{p}))\, d\omega + s^i(\mathbf{p}) \\
&= \rho_c(\mathbf{p})\alpha(\boldsymbol{\omega}, \mathbf{p}) + s^i(\mathbf{p}).
\end{aligned} \tag{4}$$

By applying the Funk-Hecke theorem we obtain a harmonic expansion ($N = \infty$) of the term $\alpha(\boldsymbol{\omega}, \mathbf{p})$ as:

$$\alpha(\boldsymbol{\omega}, \mathbf{p}) = \sum_{n=0}^{N} \sum_{m=-n}^{n} (l_{n,m}^{i,c} k_n) h_{n,m}(\mathbf{n}(\mathbf{p})), \tag{5}$$

where $\{h_{n,m}\}$ represents the orthogonal spherical harmonics, and $\{l_{n,m}^{i,c}\}$ and $\{k_n\}$ indicate the expansion coefficients of l_c^i and k with respect to $\{h_{n,m}\}$, respectively. According to [1], most energy in Eq. (5) can be modeled by low-order terms and, therefore, a first- or second-order spherical harmonic approximation can be considered. Particularly, for a distant lighting the 75% of the resulting irradiance is captured for $N = 1$, and the 98% for $N = 2$. Then, higher-order approximations are unnecessary.

As a consequence, the image formation model after including the harmonic expansion is written as:

$$\mathcal{I}_c^i(\mathbf{p}) \approx \rho_c(\mathbf{p}) \, {\mathbf{l}_c^i}^{\top} \mathbf{h}[\mathbf{n}](\mathbf{p}) + s^i(\mathbf{p}), \qquad (6)$$

where $\mathbf{l}_c^i \in \mathbb{R}^9$ and $\mathbf{h}[\mathbf{n}] \in \mathbb{R}^9$ are the second-order harmonic lighting coefficients and images, respectively, with:

$$\mathbf{h}[\mathbf{n}] = [1, \mathbf{n}_1, \mathbf{n}_2, \mathbf{n}_3, \mathbf{n}_1\mathbf{n}_2, \mathbf{n}_1\mathbf{n}_3, \mathbf{n}_2\mathbf{n}_3, \mathbf{n}_1^2 - \mathbf{n}_2^2, 3\mathbf{n}_3^2 - 1]^{\top}. \qquad (7)$$

Without loss of generality, to consider a first-order approximation (i.e., $N = 1$), we could directly use the first four terms in $\mathbf{h}[\mathbf{n}]$.

3   Variational Photometric Stereo Optimization

We propose to use the image formation model introduced in the previous section to recover non-Lambertian objects in 3D. However, the estimation of normal vectors is a non-linear problem and, as a consequence, we first introduce a model to achieve a linear dependency on depth. This section is devoted to describing the details of our variational approach for uncalibrated specular-aware PS.

3.1   Measurement Model

We next describe how the process of observing the 3D surface is modeled. Given the 3D coordinates of a surface point in the camera coordinate system $\mathcal{C}$, $\mathbf{x} = [x, y, z]^{\top}$, and assuming the z-axis aligned with the optical axis of the camera, under a perspective projection the 3D coordinates can be given by:

$$\mathbf{x}(u,v) = z(u,v) \begin{bmatrix} f_u & 0 & u_o \\ 0 & f_v & v_0 \\ 0 & 0 & 1 \end{bmatrix}^{-1} \begin{bmatrix} u \\ v \\ 1 \end{bmatrix}, \qquad (8)$$

where (f_u, f_v) include the focal length values, (u_o, v_o) the principal point coordinates, and $\mathbf{p} = [u, v, 1]^{\top} \in \mathcal{M}$ the 2D observation of the point $\mathbf{x}$ in the image plane coded in homogeneous coordinates.

As our goal is to recover the 3D object, we need a way to parametrize the surface normal vector $\mathbf{n}$ at point $\mathbf{x}(u,v)$ by its depth z. To this end, we first compute a vector pointing to the camera as $\bar{\mathbf{n}}(u,v) \approx \partial_u \mathbf{x}(u,v) \times \partial_v \mathbf{x}(u,v)$. According to [4,13], this normal vector $\bar{\mathbf{n}}[z](u,v)$ is given by:

$$\begin{bmatrix} -\dfrac{z(u,v)\partial_u z(u,v)}{f_v} \\ -\dfrac{z(u,v)\partial_v z(u,v)}{f_u} \\ \dfrac{u-u_0}{f_u}\dfrac{z(u,v)\partial_u z(u,v)}{f_v} + \dfrac{v-v_0}{f_v}\dfrac{z(u,v)\partial_v z(u,v)}{f_u} + \dfrac{z(u,v)^2}{f_u f_v} \end{bmatrix}, \qquad (9)$$

that can be simplified to:

$$\begin{bmatrix} f_u \partial_u z(u,v) \\ f_v \partial_v z(u,v) \\ -(u-u_0)\partial_u z(u,v) - (v-v_0)\partial_v z(u,v) - z(u,v) \end{bmatrix}. \qquad (10)$$

Finally, the unit vector oriented towards the camera is computed as:

$$\mathbf{n}[z](u,v) = \frac{\bar{\mathbf{n}}[z](u,v)}{|\bar{\mathbf{n}}[z](u,v)|}. \tag{11}$$

3.2 Variational Optimization

Considering our final model in Eq. (6) together with the parametrization in Eq. (11), the model parameters can be simultaneously estimated by minimizing a photometric error of all the observed points over all images by means of the following variational cost function $\mathcal{A}(\{\rho_c\}, \{\mathbf{l}_c^i\}, \{s^i\}, z)$:

$$\sum_{i=1}^{I} \sum_{c=1}^{C} \int_{\mathcal{M}} \psi_\lambda \left(\rho_c(u,v)\, \mathbf{l}_c^{i^\top} \mathbf{h}[\mathbf{n}[z]](u,v) + s^i(u,v) - \mathcal{I}_c^i(u,v) \right) du\, dv$$

$$+ \mu \sum_{c=1}^{C} \int_{\mathcal{M}} |\triangledown \rho_c(u,v)|_\gamma\, du\, dv + \mu_s \sum_{i=1}^{I} \int_{\mathcal{M}} |s^i(u,v)|_{\gamma_s}\, du\, dv, \tag{12}$$

where $\triangledown$ is the spatial gradient operator and $|\cdot|_\gamma$ denotes a Huber norm. In the data term we use a Cauchy's M-estimator defined by $\psi_\lambda(q) = \lambda^2 \log(1 + \frac{q^2}{\lambda^2})$, where λ is a scaling coefficient. Unfortunately, the previous problem is non-convex and highly non-linear.

To better condition it, we add two regularization priors to improve the joint solution. The first one consists of a Huber total variation term on each albedo map and it is used to enforce smoothness on the albedo maps $\{\rho_c\}$. To prevent a full explanation of the image as a specularity, we also penalize its use by means of a second Huber-based regularizator. Both regularizators are balanced with the data term by using the weights $\{\mu, \mu_s\} > 0$ that are determined empirically. The Huber loss can be defined as:

$$|q|_\gamma = \begin{cases} |q|^2/(2\gamma) & \text{if } |q| \le \gamma \\ |q| - \gamma/2 & \text{if } |q| > \gamma \end{cases}, \tag{13}$$

where γ is a fixed coefficient.

It is worth noting that thanks to our formulation in Eq. (12), we can directly solve the uncalibrated PS problem in terms of z instead of recovering a set of potentially non-integrable normal vectors. Moreover, that means an improvement in terms of computational efficiency as additional post-processing steps are unnecessary.

3.3 Implementation and Initialization

To numerically solve the problem in Eq. (12), the domain $\mathcal{M}$ is replaced by the number of pixels P, and employing a forward difference stencil to discretize the spatial gradient we can finally obtain discretized vectors to encode our model parameters. Then, the optimization problem can be efficiently solved by means of a lagged block coordinate descent algorithm. Basically, the full problem is tackled by means of partial subproblems independently resolved via least squares strategies. As our variational formulation is non-convex, it is important not to initialize their values at random, and for that reason, we follow a strategy as in [4] to initialize albedos and lighting. In addition to that, we impose null specularity for initialization.

Regarding the depth initialization, we use image silhouette to recover a balloon-like surface by solving a constrained minimal surface problem [14,20,21]. Particularly, the solution is constrained by a volume value κ that is set a priori. Fortunately, as in real-world applications the distance from the camera to the object shape is within reasonable bounds, the relation between shape area and shape volume is always similar, simplifying the search for a volume value κ. We will consider that in the experimental section.

4   Experimental Evaluation

In this section we show experimental results on both synthetic and real image collections providing both qualitative and quantitative comparison with respect to state-of-the-art-solutions. For quantitative evaluation, we consider the mean angular error between ground truth $\mathbf{n}^{GT}[z]$ and estimated $\mathbf{n}[z]$ normals defined as:

$$\text{MAE} = \frac{1}{P} \sum_{p=1}^{P} \tan^{-1}\Big(\frac{|\mathbf{n}^{GT}[z] \times \mathbf{n}[z]|}{\mathbf{n}^{GT}[z] \cdot \mathbf{n}[z]}\Big), \tag{14}$$

where $\times$ and $\cdot$ denote cross and dot products, respectively. In all experiments, we set $\gamma = \gamma_s = 0.1$ and $\lambda = 0.15$. The rest of coefficients will be considered later.

4.1   Synthetic Data

We propose the use of four synthetic shapes with different light conditions for evaluation. Particularly, we consider the challenging shapes *Joyful Yell* provided by [27], and *Armadillo*, *Lucy*, and *ThaiStatue* provided by [10]. To generate the datasets, we employ 25 environment maps l^i from [6] with a white albedo ($\rho_c(\mathbf{p}) = 1$). To render synthetic input images, we use Eq. (1) in combination with a specularity mask ($s^i(\mathbf{p}) \neq 0$) per image. All the environment maps we use are shown in Fig. 1-left, as well as the impact of every incident lighting in combination with specularity over the *Joyful Yell* shape in Fig. 1-right.

First of all, we analyze the effect of the initialization in our approach. It is worth recalling that our variational formulation is non-convex and, as a consequence, it is important to consider initialization of certain parameters. To do that, we have tried three alternatives for the specular term: full specularity ($s^i(\mathbf{p}) = 1$), null specularity ($s^i(\mathbf{p}) = 0$), and the provided by [18]. The last one is based on the fact that the intensity ratios for diffuse pixels are independent of the shape geometry. Figure 2 shows visually the effect of those initializations in comparison with the specular ground truth as well as the estimated 3D shape. As it can be seen, when full specularity is used that component absorbs too much information, which causes a very poor estimation of the depth. For null specularity, both the estimated specular component and the 3D shape are very competitive. Finally, when we use [18] for initialization following the implementation in [17], the 3D shape we obtain is slightly worse than the one obtained by

Fig. 1. Illustration of the synthetic *Joyful Yell* **dataset. Left:** 360-degree spherical environment maps. **Right:** Input images after projecting the *Joyful Yell* mesh with specularity and white albedo. Best viewed in color.

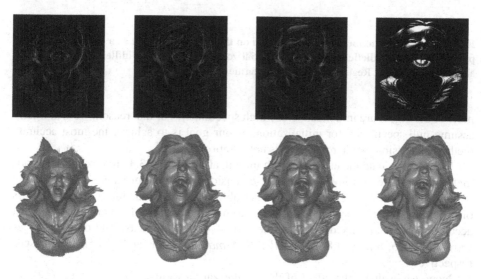

Fig. 2. Effect of specular initialization. In all cases, the figure displays the case of full specularity at initialization, null specularity at initialization, initialization by [17], and ground truth for the *Joyful Yell* shape. **Top:** Specular maps. **Bottom:** Depth estimation.

$(s^i(\mathbf{p}) = 0)$, but it converges faster to the solution. Thus, the estimation obtained by the last initialization could provide the best trade-off between accuracy and efficiency. However, the method fails for images with negligible specular lighting by considering white pixels as points with specularity. This effect is shown in Fig. 3 where some white

Fig. 3. Specular initialization in white areas. Comparison in objects without (on the left) and with specularity (on the right). Odd columns show the initial specular component by [17] and, in the pair ones the albedo-aware ground truth images.

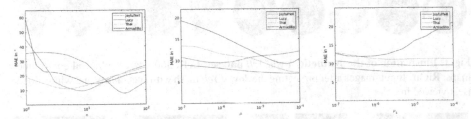

Fig. 4. MAE errors to measure the precision on the estimated depth as a function of tuning parameters for synthetic datasets. Left: Initial volume evaluation. **Middle:** Regularization on albedos by μ. **Right:** Regularization on specularities by μ_s.

parts of the object are initialized with a high specularity. For that reason, we will finally assume null specularity for initialization, as our goal is to achieve the most accurate method as possible while robustness is not compromised.

We next evaluate the effect of depth initialization in Sect. 3.3. To discover the optimal volume values κ for each dataset, we consider the range of values $[10^0, 10^2]$. As it can be seen in Fig. 4-left, the solution is stable for a part of the interval. Without loss of generality, for these synthetic datasets we chose the values which provided the most accurate shapes, and fixed them for the rest of the experiments. The optimal values were 44, 12.25, 8.25 and 8 for *Joyful Yell*, *Armadillo*, *Lucy*, and *ThaiStatue* datasets, respectively.

Now, we evaluate the effect of the regularization weights $\{\mu, \mu_s\}$ in Eq. (12). To this end, we consider for both weights a large range of values for $[10^{-7}, 10^{-4}]$. The MAE error for every dataset is represented as a function of those μ_s and μ values in Fig. 4-right and Fig. 4-middle, respectively. Considering all the datasets, we fix for the rest of experiments $\mu_s = 2 \cdot 10^{-6}$ and $\mu = 3 \cdot 10^{-6}$ despite not being the optimal values for every dataset independently.

Finally, we provide quantitative evaluation and comparison with respect to UPS [4], the most competitive technique in state of the art for our approach according to table 1. This method provided better performance compared to [12, 15, 19] in [4]. The parameters of this method were set in accordance with the original paper. Our results are sum-

Table 2. Reconstruction quantitative comparison. The table reports the MAE results in degrees for UPS [4] and our algorithm. Relative increment is computed with respect to our method, the most accurate solution.

Meth. ＼ Dataset	Joyful Yell	Armadillo	Lucy	ThaiStatue	Average
Ours	7.66	13.63	10.05	10.93	10.66
UPS [4]	13.44	24.83	14.43	23.74	19.11
Relative incre.	1.754	1.822	1.436	2.172	1.793

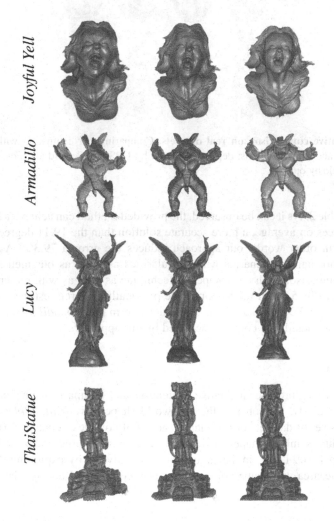

Fig. 5. Qualitative comparison on synthetic datasets. Comparing our estimation with respect to UPS [4] and the ground truth. From left to right it is displayed the UPS [4] estimation, our solution, and ground truth.

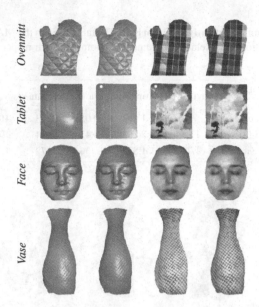

Fig. 6. Qualitative comparison on real datasets. Comparing our estimation with respect to UPS [4]. First and Third columns: depth and albedo by UPS [4]. Second and Fourth columns: depth and albedo by ours.

marized in Table 2. As it can be observed, the provided method can achieve a MAE error of 10.66 degrees on average, a more accurate solution than the 19.11 degrees obtained by UPS [4]. In other words, our approach reduces the error a 79.3%. As expected, UPS [4] cannot handle scenarios with specularities as good as our method does. A qualitative comparison with the competing technique as well as with the ground truth can be seen in Fig. 5. Both methods provide physically coherent estimations, but the differences of the 3D reconstructions are noticeable in the *Armadillo* and *ThaiStatue* datasets as more details are correctly acquired by our approach.

4.2 Real Data

In this section, we provide qualitative evaluation and comparison on four different datasets. Particularly, we consider the real-world shapes *Ovenmitt*, *Tablet*, *Face*, and *Vase* [3]. This set of datasets offers a large variety of complex geometries (nearly planar, smooth and wrinkled shapes) and albedos and was captured under daylight and a freely moving LED. Depth initialization was manually set by exploiting the relation between shape area and shape volume, as it was commented above. The results are

displayed in Fig. 6. As it is showed, our approach visually obtains better 3D representations, especially for *Ovenmitt*, *Tablet*, and *Vase* datasets, by recovering more spatial
details as well as achieving a global consistency. In addition to that, reflectance seems
to be slightly more accurate, as it can be seen in the *Vase* dataset. Similar results with
respect to UPS [4] are obtained in the *Face* dataset, as the specular component is low.
In this line, we consider that our method outperforms UPS [4] for the *Vase* dataset due
to the specular component in this set of images being bigger and, as a consequence,
our method can handle it better and produce more accurate joint solutions. This can be
easily observed in Fig. 7, where we show our specular estimations for one particular
image of several datasets. Fortunately, our approach can capture properly the specular
component, making more robust the joint estimation of depth, albedo, and specularity.
For instance, our method can capture some specularities that are not clearly a diffuse
component, as it can be seen for the nose in the *Face* dataset (see Fig. 7, third row).
Regarding computational complexity, as our method can provide more complete estimations, the computation time is slightly larger than the provided by UPS [4]. A summary of those results (in non-optimized Matlab code) on a commodity laptop Intel Core
i7-8700 3.20GHz CPU are reported in Table 3 for real datasets. Despite increasing the
computational time a 13.5%, the trade-off between accuracy and computation time is
very competitive for our approach as it can accurately solve the problem with a small
increase in computation.

Table 3. Computation time quantitative comparison. The table reports the computation time
results in seconds for UPS [4] and our algorithm. Relative increment is computed with respect to
UPS [4], the most efficient solution.

Meth. \ Dataset	Vase	Tablet	Ovenmitt	Face2	Average
Ours	705.32	884.62	765.34	295.88	662.79
UPS [4]	627.45	783.24	667.16	257.62	583.86
Relative incre.	1.124	1.129	1.147	1.148	1.135

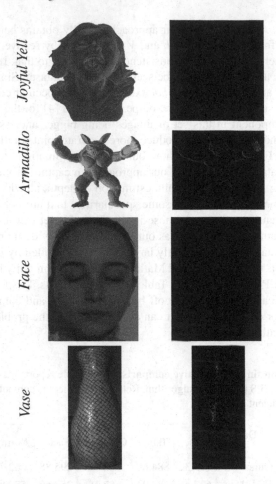

Fig. 7. Specular Recovery. Some input images for synthetic and real images (left columns) together with the specular estimations (right column) obtained by our method.

5   Conclusion

The uncalibrated PS problem under general lighting has been approached by a variational and unified method. The proposed algorithm can jointly retrieve reflectance, 3D reconstruction, lighting and specularities of the object, all of them, from a set of RGB images and without assuming any training data at all. To this end, we have presented a physical-aware image formation model that, in combination with a perspective projection one and under spherical harmonics lighting, gives a fully interpretable algorithm. Thanks to our formulation, we can handle a large variety of complex geometries and illumination conditions without needing any knowledge prior. We have experimentally evaluated our approach both on synthetic and real datasets. While our approach provides a full and interpretable model capable of generating competitive joint 3D and lighting reconstructions with respect to competing techniques, the computational cost slightly increases. An interesting avenue for future research would be to validate our formulation for articulated objects where strong shadows could appear due to self-occlusions.

Acknowledgments. This work has been partially supported by the Spanish Ministry of Science and Innovation under project MoHuCo PID2020-120049RB. The authors wish to thank B. Haefner for fruitful discussions.

References

1. Basri, R., Jacobs, D., Kemelmacher, I.: Photometric stereo with general, unknown lighting. Int. J. Comput. Vision **72**(5), 239–257 (2007)
2. Chandraker, M., Bai, J., Ramamoorthi, R.: On differential photometric reconstruction for unknown, isotropic BRDFs. IEEE Trans. Pattern Anal. Mach. Intell. **35**(12), 2941–2955 (2013)
3. Haefner, B., Peng, S., Verma, A., Queau, Y., Cremers, D.: Photometric depth super-resolution. IEEE Trans. Pattern Anal. Mach. Intell. **42**(10), 2453–2464 (2019)
4. Haefner, B., Ye, Z., Gao, M., Wu, T., Quéau, Y., Cremers, D.: Variational uncalibrated photometric stereo under general lightings. In: IEEE International Conference on Computer Vision (2019)
5. Hayakawa, H.: Photometric stereo under a light source with arbitrary motion. J. Opt. Soc. Am. A **11**(11), 3079–3089 (1994)
6. HDRLabs: sIBL archive. http://www.hdrlabs.com/sibl/archive.html
7. Hold-Geoffroy, Y., Gotardo, P., Lalonde, J.: Deep photometric stereo on a sunny day. arXiv preprint 1803.10850 (2018)
8. Hold-Geoffroy, Y., Zhang, J., Gotardo, P., Lalonde, J.: What is a good day for outdoor photometric stereo? In: International Conference on Computational Photography (2015)
9. Ikehata, S.: CNN-PS: CNN-based photometric stereo for general non-convex surfaces. In: European Conference on Computer Vision (2018)
10. Levoy, M., Gerth, J., Curless, B., Pull, K.: The Stanford 3D scanning repository (2005)
11. Li, J., Robles-Kelly, A., You, S., Matsushita, Y.: Learning to minify photometric stereo. In: IEEE Conference on Computer Vision and Pattern Recognition (2019)
12. Mo, Z., Shi, B., Lu, F., Yeung, S., Matsushitae, Y.: Uncalibrated photometric stereo under natural illumination. In: IEEE Conference on Computer Vision and Pattern Recognition (2018)
13. Munda, G., Balzer, J., Soatto, S., Pock, T.: Efficient minimal-surface regularization of perspective depth maps in variational stereo. In: IEEE Conference on Computer Vision and Pattern Recognition (2015)
14. Oswald, M.R., Toeppe, E., Cremers, D.: Fast and globally optimal single view reconstruction of curved objects. In: IEEE Conference on Computer Vision and Pattern Recognition (2012)
15. Peng, S., Haefner, B., Queau, Y., Cremers, D.: Depth super-resolution meets uncalibrated photometric stereo. In: IEEE International Conference on Computer Vision Workshops (2017)
16. Queau, Y., Wu, T., Lauze, F., Durou, J., Cremers, D.: A non-convex variational approach to photometric stereo under inaccurate lighting. In: IEEE Conference on Computer Vision and Pattern Recognition (2017)
17. Ramos, V.: SIHR: a MATLAB/GNU octave toolbox for single image highlight removal. J. Open Source Softw. **5**(45), 1822 (2020)
18. Shen, H.L., Zheng, Z.H.: Real-time highlight removal using intensity ratio. Appl. Opt. **52**, 4483–4493 (2013)

19. Shi, B., Inose, K., Matsushita, Y., Tan, P., Yeung, S., Ikeuchi, K.: Photometric stereo using internet images. In: 3D Vision (2014)
20. Toeppe, E., Oswald, M.R., Cremers, D., Rother, C.: Silhouette-based variational methods for single view reconstruction. In: Video Processing and Computational Video (2010)
21. Vicente, S., Agapito, L.: Balloon shapes: reconstructing and deforming objects with volume from images. In: 3D Vision (2013)
22. Wang, X., Jian, Z., Ren, M.: Non-lambertian photometric stereo network based on inverse reflectance model with collocated light. IEEE Trans. Image Process. **29**, 6032–6042 (2020)
23. Woodham, R.: Photometric method for determining surface orientation from multiple images. Opt. Eng. **19**(1), 191139 (1980)
24. Wu, L., Ganesh, A., Shi, B., Matsushita, Y., Wang, Y., Ma, Y.: Robust photometric stereo via low-rank matrix completion and recovery. In: Asian Conference on Computer Vision (2010)
25. Wu, T., Tang, C.: Photometric stereo via expectation maximization. IEEE Trans. Pattern Anal. Mach. Intell. **32**(3), 546–560 (2007)
26. Yao, Z., Li, K., Fu, Y., Hu, H., Shi, B.: GPS-net: graph-based photometric stereo network. In: Conference on Neural Information Processing Systems (2020)
27. Yell, T.J.: http://www.thingiverse.com/thing:897412

Appearance-Independent Pose-Based Posture Classification in Infants

Xiaofei Huang[1], Shuangjun Liu[1], Michael Wan[1,2], Nihang Fu[1], David Li Pino[3],
Bharath Modayur[3], and Sarah Ostadabbas[1(✉)]

[1] Northeastern University, Boston, MA, USA
ostadabbas@ece.neu.edu
[2] Roux Institute, Portland, ME, USA
[3] Early Markers, Seattle, WA, USA

Abstract. Disruption of motor development in infancy is a risk indicator for a host of developmental delays and disabilities, but screening for such disruptions currently requires expert assessment. Automated assessment of motor development by advanced computer vision algorithms would yield objective screening tools that are inexpensive, highly scalable, and virtually accessible from anywhere. To this end, we present an appearance-independent posture classification framework based on the 2D or 3D poses of the infants. The framework uses pose information extracted with our previously developed models and classifies infant poses into four major postures. Our method is data and label efficient and can work with small amounts of infant pose and posture data. We trained and compared the performance of the infant posture classification model on input RGB images as well as input 2D and 3D posed of our publicly available synthetic and real infant pose (SyRIP) dataset. When applied to a fully novel dataset of images of infants recorded in their interactive natural environments, the infant posture classification performance achieves a classification accuracy of 80.1% with the 2D pose-based inputs and 83.2% with the 3D pose-based inputs (SyRIP dataset and infant posture classification model code available at https://github.com/ostadabbas/Infant-Posture-Estimation.).

Keywords: Data Efficient Machine Learning · Motor Development Screening · Infant Pose Estimation · Posture Classification

1 Introduction

Motor activities are among the earliest signals observable in infant development prior to the onset of communication and social skills [25]. Disruptions in infant motor development have been associated with speech and language impairment [14] and intellectual disability [15], and are considered prodromal signs for conditions such as cerebral palsy [5], developmental coordination disorder [17], and autism spectrum disorder (ASD) [1]. For instance, atypical motor development has been widely observed in infants who were later diagnosed with ASD [24,29].

© Springer Nature Switzerland AG 2023
J.-J. Rousseau and B. Kapralos (Eds.): ICPR 2022 Workshops, LNCS 13643, pp. 21–36, 2023.
https://doi.org/10.1007/978-3-031-37660-3_2

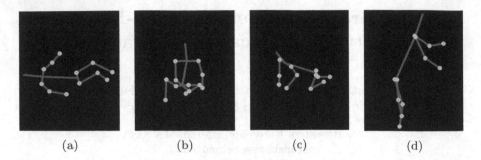

(a)   (b)   (c)   (d)

Fig. 1. Examples of body infant body poses, configured in four postures: (a) supine, (b) sitting, (c) prone, and (d) standing.

Standardized observation-based tests for motor deficits exist [3,22], but they must be conducted by trained professionals during valuable clinic time, so the development of artificial intelligence (AI) guided alternatives for monitoring and assessment of videos shot at home would yield significant gains in efficiency and availability.

Towards this goal, we present work in the AI analysis of infant poses and postures, features which lie at the heart of the motor assessment. In our terminology, infant body *poses* consist of 12 body joint landmark locations, in 2D or 3D coordinates; the *postures* considered are the supine, prone, sitting, and standing postures, which are critical in standardized motor evaluation paradigms [22]. See Fig. 1 for illustrations of example poses in each of the four postures. Our technical contributions can be summarized as follows.

1. We introduce a novel deep neural network classifier of infant posture, based on an input 2D or 3D poses. The use of appearance-independent poses rather than pixel-level features as input allows for privacy-respecting and bandwidth-efficient applications.
2. We combine our previous 2D infant pose estimation model [12] with our new posture classifier to obtain a 2D-based pipeline for posture estimation from infant images, achieving a classification accuracy as high as 90.0% on our publicly-available synthetic and real infant pose (SyRIP) dataset [12], and as high as 80.1% on the novel clinically-purposed modeling infant motor movement (MIMM) dataset.
3. We introduce a 3D-based pipeline for posture estimation from infant images as follows. First, we retrain our 3D infant pose estimation model [20] on newly released 3D ground truth poses for the SyRIP dataset [13], and then combine this pose estimation with a 3D pose-based posture classifier, again trained with the 3D SyRIP data. This pipeline achieves a classification accuracy as high as 89.0% on the SyRIP test set, and as high as 83.3% on the novel MIMM dataset. This pipeline offers improved performance over the 2D pipeline because our pose estimation model takes advantage of depth data during training, even though the final posture classification system only requires flat RGB images as input.

2   Related Work

Here we review computer vision based approaches to pose estimation designed specifically for infants, as adult body methods generally struggle when applied directly to the distinct bodies of infants. Early work in [11] uses random ferns to estimate the 3D body pose of infants from depth images for motion analysis purposes. In [10], the authors present a statistical learning method called 3D skinned multi-infant linear (SMIL) model using incomplete low-quality RGB-D sequence of freely moving infants. Their training dataset is provided by [8], where researchers map real infant movements to the SMIL model with natural shapes and textures, and generated RGB and depth images with 2D and 3D joint positions. This line of work generally requires both RGB and depth data in image or video form as input.

Our lab has actively explored the complementary problem of infant pose estimation and analysis from still RGB images. These efforts include the fundamental 2D and 3D pose estimation algorithms described earlier [12,20]; quantification of bilateral postural symmetry in infants [13] based on 2D and 3D poses; and facial landmark estimation for infant faces [26]. Other computer vision approaches to pose estimation and developmental assessment exist as well. In [2], an efficient infant posture recognition method is proposed to process video sequence of Hammersmith Infant Neurological Examinations (HINE), which includes assessment of posture, cranial nerve functions, tone, movements, reflexes and behaviour for assessment of neurological development in infants. In [21], the authors use pose estimation to measure detect infants turning over in bed. In [4], the authors develop an automated infant neuromotor risk assessment based on quantitative measures from widely-available sources, such as videos recorded on a mobile device. The authors in [7] evaluate the localization performance of four types of convolutional neural networks which were fine-tuned on a novel infant pose dataset collected from a clinical international community for assessment of infant spontaneous movement. Most of these other approaches focus on a limited range of poses, often infants lying on their backs in plain settings with unobstructed front-on camera views. Our research deals with infants in a variety of postures and in natural environments aims to broaden the applicability of work in this area.

3   Methodology

We propose a two-phase pipeline as shown in Fig. 2, which estimates infant posture in an interactive setting using infant pose as its low-dimensional features. In Phase I, we use an infant pose estimation model to extract infant pose from infant video or image source. Then in Phase II, the estimated infant joints are directly fed into a data efficient posture estimation network to predict the infant posture.

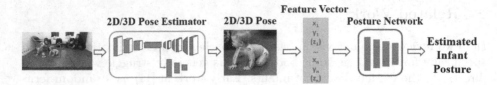

Fig. 2. An overview architecture of our infant pose-based posture recognition pipeline, composed of two phases: 2D or 3D pose extraction by utilizing our previously developed pose estimation networks (Phase I), and posture recognition using 2D or 3D pose data as its features (Phase II). x_i, y_i, and z_i represent the 2D or 3D coordinates for each body joints based on the definition of the pose. In our study, $n = 12$ is considered as the number of infant's body joints.

3.1   2D Pose Feature Extraction

Considering the limitations of the infant data mentioned above, we first employed 2D pose features as a high-level descriptor for infant posture classification. An advanced 2D infant pose estimator, fine-tuned domain-adapted infant pose (FiDIP) [12] previously developed in our lab, is adopted to generate 2D pose features. The strategy of FiDIP method is to transfer the pose learning of the existing adult pose estimation models into the infant poses. The FiDIP network is trained on an infant hybrid synthetic and real infant pose (SyRIP) dataset built based on a cross-domain inspired augmentation approach presented in [12]. In this way, we simultaneously achieved two transfer learning tasks: transferring from adult pose domain into the infant pose domain, and transferring from synthetic image domain into the real image domain.

As the FiDIP framework can be integrated with any existing encoder-decoder 2D pose estimation model, we trained our FiDIP model with several state-of-the-art (SOTA) pose estimation networks, including SimpleBaseline-50 [27], DarkPose [28], and MobileNetV2 [23]. Following the Microsoft COCO annotation format [19], the predicted 2D pose is formed by 17 joints, which includes several joints on head. To reduce redundant information, we only select 12 joints and concatenate their 2D geometric information as the pose features representing human body postures.

3.2   3D Pose Feature Extraction

Another type of features we use to classify infant postures is 3D joint locations, which are also high-level representations with more critical spatial information. In order to extract reliable 3D pose features, we first developed a robust infant 3D pose estimator as our 3D feature extractor. Due to the particularity of the infant group, the datasets built for this group are very limited and usually not publicly available, especially with regards to the 3D pose data that needs to be collected using the motion capture (MoCap) technology. Considering that there is only small-scale infant RGB-D data available, we draw on the previously proposed heuristic weakly supervised 3D human pose estimation (HW-HuP) approach

[20] proposed in our lab. We will refer to the model mentioned in Sect. 4.6 of [20], which uses the 3D skinned multi-infant linear (SMIL) body model [9] and trains on infant data, as *HW-HuP-Infant*, to distinguish it from other models of HW-HuP built on adult human body models and data.

An overview of the HW-HuP-Infant framework is shown in Fig. 3, which includes two networks: (1) a 3D regression network F to estimate pose and shape parameters of 3D human bodies, and camera parameters from 2D image input; and (2) a differentiable neural renderer to generate the predicted depth and mask from the predicted infant 3D mesh. HW-HuP-Infant learns partial pose priors from public 3D adult pose datasets and uses easy-to-access observations from the target domain (RGB-D videos of infants) to iteratively estimate 3D infant pose and shape in an optimization and regression hybrid cycle.

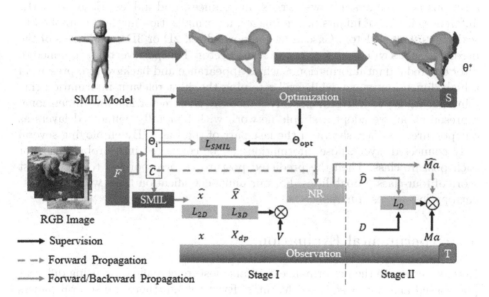

Fig. 3. HW-HuP-Infant [20] framework. HW-HuP-Infant learns from known priors in the source domain (S) and new observations from the target domain (T), iteratively from a coarse to fine manner in two stages. The skinned multi-infant linear body model, SMIL [10], is applied to represent infant 3D body. F is the 3D pose regression network, and NR is the differentiable neural renderer. x stands for the 2D pose, X_{dp} for 3D pose from depth-based proxy, V for the joint visibility, D for depth, Ma for the infant body mask, all extracted from observations in T domain. C stands camera parameters. All hat versions ˆ stand for their estimated counterparts. In each iteration of Stage I, from the initial 3D pose and shape Θ_i, Θ_{opt} is estimated under the source priors to explain the observation in T domain, while the detailed depth supervision comes in the Stage II.

3.3 Posture Classification

The well-child visits for infants under one year of age involve screening for 4 basic infant postures (i.e. Supine, Prone, Sitting, Standing) to identify children who should receive more intensive assessment and intervention [6]. These assessments often involve comprehensive evaluation with direct observation-based, standardized tests [22] that take time and clinical expertise, however many of them are well suited for video-based automation. Here, we present 2D and 3D pose-based infant posture classifiers, which principally can aid parent-led administration of motor assessment at home, to detect four basic postures.

The 2D and 3D pose information generated by FiDIP and HW-HuP-Infant is inputted as the extracted feature vector into the posture classifier. For posture network, we only focus on information of body's 12 joints, which are the bilateral locations of shoulders, elbows, wrists, hips, knees, and ankles. Because of the differences in size of infants in the images, a normalization method is applied to scale the infant skeleton. Cascading the normalized 2D or 3D coordinates of the predicted joints will result in a pose feature vector. This pose vector is assumed to filter out redundant information, such as appearance and background, present in a high-dimension image, while still retaining the most relevant information (i.e. joints locations) to learn the posture. Since the pose vector is a low-dimensional representation, we adopt a simple network with four fully connected layers as our posture classifier, shown in the last part of the Fig. 2. By employing several fully connected layers, pose information can be converted into probabilities for each posture class. Then the predicted posture is corresponded to the highest score of four-class probabilities. For our multi-classification task, we apply cross entropy loss as cost function.

4 Experimental Evaluation

Here, we compare the performance of infant posture classification using different pose-based and non-pose-based features. Even though there are several papers related to the infant pose estimation or posture classification, none of them are reproducible for fair comparison due to (1) unreleased sources of their algorithms or infant models and data, or (2) different categories of infant posture classification task. Hence, we are only able to provide the performances of our models on our accessible datasets.

4.1 Evaluation Datasets

Synthetic and Real Infant Pose (SyRIP) Dataset. In a previous work [12], we built this publicly available infant pose dataset including 700 real images from YouTube videos and Google Images and 1000 synthetic images generated using algorithms presented in [12], which display infants with various poses. All SyRIP pose images are fully annotated with 2D keypoint body joints in the Microsoft COCO format and its real images are tagged for four postures. For training the 2D pose estimator, SyRIP dataset is split into one training set and two test sets. The training part includes 200 real and 1000 synthetic infant images. The first test set (Test500) has 500 real infant images with general poses and the second test dataset (Test100) has 100 complex pose images that are typically seen in infants, selected from Test500. Test100 has more poses with folded limbs or occluded joints, which makes the poses hard to be recognized by SOTA pose estimation models trained on adult datasets. When training the 2D pose-based posture network, we keep the Test100 set as the test set, and employ the remaining 600 real infant images (including Test500) for posture network training.

We also make use of the 3D ground truth labels for keypoint body joints in SyRIP images, produced subsequently by our lab in [13]. These labels were obtained by manually correcting 3D keypoint predictions from our 3D pose estimation model [20]. The correction process involves estimating 3D positions from 2D images while maintaining alignment of the projected 2D positions with the 2D ground truth pose, using an interactive tool from [18]. This process relies on human judgement of 3D pose from 2D information, so it can be only considered as imperfect, *weak ground truth of 3D pose*. Given the scarcity of full ground truth 3D infant pose data, we feel it is reasonable to train and test with this weaker data for applied purposes.

Modeling Infant Motor Movement (MIMM) Dataset. MIMM was collected by our collaborator, Early Markers company (as part of an NIH funded study) and contains RGB-D video recordings of motor assessment sessions from 68 infants under one year of age in an interactive setting with their caregivers and clinical assessors using the Microsoft Kinect device. MIMM data is manually annotated for 2D pose and postures. As for infant body pose, 12 joints and head centroid were annotated. As for postures, labels for four classes of supine, prone, standing, and sitting was added to each image. To verify the accuracy and generalizability of the our pose-posture pipeline, we selected 10 subjects from their dataset to form the mini-MIMM dataset containing 1050 infant GRB and depth images as part of the farthest neighbor set with frames that were maximally separated in terms of visual information for training purposes. In the 2D pose and posture classification models, we used the entire mini-MIMM as a fully novel dataset to evaluate both pose and posture networks. However, in the 3D pose-based posture classification, we split mini-MIMM dataset into training and test sets. After filtering out the non-detected images that the postures do not belong to any of the four posture categories (e.g. transition postures), the size of training and test sets of mini-MIMM for 3D pose-based posture classification is 826 images (from 8 subjects out of 10 subjects) and 191 images (from the other 2 subjects), respectively.

The posture distributions of both datasets are shown in Fig. 4. According to these histograms, the number of images of infants standing are much less than those of other postures, which is in line with the actual situation of the activities of babies under one year old. It is a fact that very young babies are mostly in lying

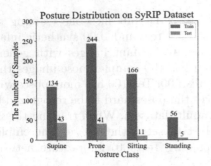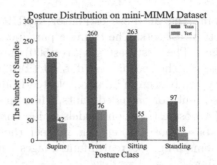

Fig. 4. The posture distributions of both SyRIP and mini-MIMM datasets used in our posture network training and testing. The size of training and test sets of SyRIP dataset is 600 and 100 images, respectively. The number of images in the training and test sets of mini-MIMM dataset is 826 and 191, respectively.

position, and when start the sitting and crawling, they also attempt standing and cruising around.

4.2 Posture Network Using 2D Poses

Implementation Details. For the pose estimation phase, 2D infant poses are inferred by our FiDIP model. At posture phase, We train 2D pose-based posture network with batch size of 50 and 400 epochs. The learning rate of Adam optimizer is 0.00006.

2D Pose-Based Posture Classification Performance. As illustrated in the Fig. 2, to recognize infant posture using 2D pose estimated based on the FiDIP model, the predicted 2D keypoint locations are the input vector into our 2D pose-based posture classifier trained on ground truth poses. The implementation details and performance of FiDIP are given in [12]. The evaluation baseline, which is the performance of our posture model on test dataset with ground truth pose vector as its feature is given in Table 1. It also lists the accuracy in recognizing each posture category based on predicted poses from different models and compares it with the network performance when directly applied on cropped infant RGB images.

Due to the small size of available data, the simple neural network trained on high-dimensional (224 × 224 pixels) image data does poorly for posture classification with accuracy of 37.85%, as shown in Table 1. The accuracy of the best performing FiDIP-based model could reach to 90% on SyRIP Test100 dataset. This observation shows that our 2D pose-based posture classification model has a certain degree of fault tolerance for pose errors, which is a key factor of the model robustness.

For the performance of model on entire mini-MIMM data, compared to the other three posture classes, the accuracy of predicting sitting posture is lower, mostly due to the fact that it covers more transitional poses, where the infant was transitioning from one canonical pose to another. In many cases, it is difficult

Table 1. Posture recognition performance of our 2D pose-based posture recognition model trained on SyRIP dataset and tested on both SyRIP Test100 and entire 1050 mini-MIMM images, compared to posture estimation when RGB image is given as input instead of 2D pose vector. This table also shows when input to the posture network is ground truth pose vs. predicted pose based on FiDIP applied on SimpleBaseline [27], DarkPose [28], and Pose-MobileNet [23] as its baseline models.

Input	Test Dataset	Average	Supine	Prone	Sitting	Standing
Ground Truth	SyRIP Test100	87.00	83.72	92.68	81.82	80.00
	mini-MIMM	**77.93**	73.09	82.20	73.49	88.70
Cropped RGB Image	SyRIP Test100	54.00	39.53	73.17	54.55	20.00
	mini-MIMM	37.85	18.88	70.03	26.20	18.26
DarkPose + FiDIP Pred.	SyRIP Test100	**90.00**	88.37	92.68	90.91	80.00
	mini-MIMM	77.44	72.69	81.60	72.29	90.43
SimpleBaseline + FiDIP Pred.	SyRIP Test100	88.00	81.40	95.12	90.91	80.00
	mini-MIMM	75.22	71.49	81.90	66.57	88.70
Pose-MobileNet + FiDIP Pred.	SyRIP Test100	87.00	83.72	90.24	90.91	80.00
	mini-MIMM	69.11	72.29	74.78	58.13	77.39

Fig. 5. Visualized examples of our 2D pose-based posture recognition performance on mini-MIMM dataset. Each column exhibits one posture class (from left to right): supine, prone, sitting, and standing. The predicted skeletons are overlaid on images and clearly displayed at right-bottom corner as well. The confidence score of each posture is listed at left-bottom corner in order. The posture with highest score is the predicted result. If the prediction is correct, it is green, otherwise, it is red. (Color figure online)

to judge which classes these transitional poses belong to. In Fig. 5, we visualized the performance of our 2D pose-based posture classifier on mini-MIMM dataset. Interestingly, in row 2, column 4 of Fig. 5 even though the prediction is wrong (displayed in red), the transition posture from sitting to standing is getting a confidence score of 0.55 for sitting and the score of 0.44 for standing. In Fig. 6, we demonstrate a pair of posture predictions based on the ground truth 2D pose input, which leads to a wrong predicted posture, and FiDIP-based predicted 2D pose input, which results in predicting posture correctly. This may be caused by the fact that by only looking at the ground truth pose it could be difficult to judge whether the infant is sitting or in transitioning to prone position. In

Fig. 6. Comparing posture predictions between models with inputs as groundtruth 2D pose (the left figure) and predicted 2D pose based on FiDIP (the right figure). The confidence score of each posture is listed at left-bottom corner in order. The posture with highest score is the predicted result. If the prediction is correct, it is green, otherwise, it is red. (Color figure online)

contrast, the wrong predicted pose has made it easy for the network to call it a sitting position with high confidence.

Meanwhile, even if the maximum accuracy of 2D pose-based posture classification can reach to 90%, the lack of 3D spatial information of poses could make it difficult for the network to identify postures in specific camera angles. For example, as shown in Fig. 7, a baby is lying in one image, but when we obtain his predicted 2D pose and remove all the background/shape information to just keep the skeleton, it is difficult even for the naked eyes to tell whether infant is sitting, standing, or lying, let alone our trained posture classification network. Hence, for our appearance-independent pose-based posture classifier, adding extra spatial information seems to be necessary to improve the performance of the posture classification model.

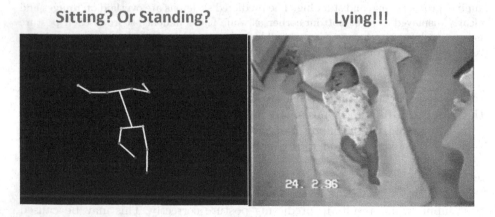

Fig. 7. An example to illustrate shortcomings of the posture recognition only based on 2D pose as input. Left side displays a 2D groundtruth skeleton, while right one is corresponding raw RGB image.

4.3   Posture Network Using 3D Poses

Implementation Details. At the pose estimation phase, we employ the HW-HuP-Infant model to get 3D predicted infant pose. At posture phase, the learning rate is 0.00006 for Adam optimizer. We train posture network with batch size of 50 and 50 epochs on SyRIP 3D pose training set.

3D Infant Pose Estimation Performance. HW-HuP-Infant, introduced in [20], will be to our knowledge the first publicly released trained model attempting to solve the infant 3D pose estimation problem for infants. The model we experiment with in this paper is trained on SyRIP 1600 images (600 real images + 1000 synthetic images) and test on Test100. The split train and test sets of mini-MIMM are also applied for HW-HuP-Infant evaluation. We initialize HW-HuP-Infant with the pre-trained model presented by [16]. MPJPE (Mean Per Joint Position Error), which is L2 distance averaged over all joints, is employed as the main metric. The aligned depth error on mini-MIMM is 42.0mm and the MPJPE of results is 220.53mm, but this MPJPE can be only viewed as a reference since mini-MIMM does not have the true 3D annotations and we can only compute the MPJPE based on its depth information.

Original HW-HuP

HW-HuP-Infant*

HW-HuP-Infant

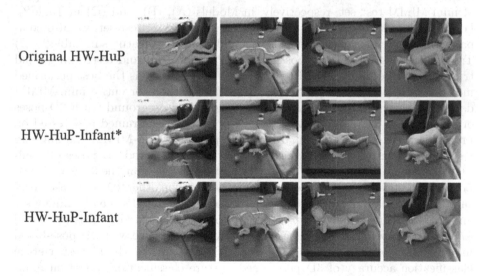

Fig. 8. A qualitative comparison among the original HW-HuP, HW-HuP-Infant*, and HW-HuP-Infant for infant shape and 3D pose estimation.

We display qualitative results of three models, the original HW-HuP trained on the adult dataset, the HW-HuP that only replaces the adult body model with the infant body model (called HW-HuP-Infant*), and our HW-HuP-Infant, in the Fig. 8. Compared to the first two models, HW-HuP-Infant has the ability to achieve better 3D pose and shape estimation performance, which almost fits the input image and has quite high joints fit degree.

Table 2. Performance of our pose-based posture recognition algorithm based on different types of input features on SyRIP and mini-MIMM datasets.

Model	Training Set	Testing Set	Average	Supine	Prone	Sitting	Standing
A	SyRIP 3D GT	SyRIP 3D GT	89.00	86.05	90.24	100.00	80.00
B	SyRIP 3D GT	SyRIP 3D Predictions	87.00	83.72	95.12	81.82	60.00
C	SyRIP 3D GT	mini-MIMM 3D Predictions	83.25	76.19	94.74	67.27	100.00
D	SyRIP 2D GT	mini-MIMM 2D GT	80.10	73.81	89.47	65.45	100.00
E	mini-MIMM 2D GT	mini-MIMM 2D GT	87.96	85.71	94.74	76.36	100.00
F	mini-MIMM Proxy 3D	mini-MIMM Proxy 3D	89.00	83.33	98.68	80.00	88.89
G	mini-MIMM 3D Predictions	mini-MIMM 3D Predictions	**91.62**	88.10	98.68	81.82	100.00

3D Pose-Based Posture Classification Performance. After producing the reliable predicted 3D poses by employing HW-HuP-Infant model, the predicted 3D keypoint locations are processed as the input feature vector into our 3D pose-based posture classifier. To identify the optimal choice of low-dimensional features for the input of pose-based posture classification component, in Table 2, we compared performances of pose-based posture classification models trained based on different types of input features. We trained the 3D pose-based network on our SyRIP 3D weak ground truth poses and tested it on 3D weak ground truth poses and predicted 3D poses of SyRIP test set, and 3D predicted pose of mini-MIMM test set, respectively, in Models (A), (B), and (C) in Table 2). For exploring the network performances on mini-MIMM test set, we also compared different experimental models with different input features in Table 2: (D) Trained on 2D ground truth poses of SyRIP training set and tested on ground truth 2D poses of mini-MIMM test set. This combination is the best performed model for 2D pose-based posture classification method for entire mini-MIMM dataset as shown in Table 1. (E) Trained and tested on ground truth 2D poses of mini-MIMM training and test sets, respectively. (F) Trained and tested on proxy 3D poses (depth + ground truth 2D poses) of mini-MIMM training and test sets, respectively. (G) Trained and tested on predicted 3D poses of mini-MIMM training and test sets, respectively. It is obvious that the 3D pose-based posture classification models perform much better than other 2D pose-based posture models for almost all classes. Even though the limited scale of training set and more amount of network parameters, the 3D pose-based models (89% and 87% in accuracy in Table 2) have comparative performance with 2D pose-based models (90% and 87% in Table 1) on SyRIP dataset. And the highest average classification accuracy of 3D pose-based posture classification model on mini-MIMM dataset can reach 91.62%. By analyzing their corresponding confusion matrices, as shown in Fig. 9, we observe that the most classification failure cases in mini-MIMM data are the sitting postures that are recognized as supine due to the ambiguity of infant transition poses.

In Fig. 10, we exhibit some predictions of 2D pose-based posture classification model compared against the 3D pose-based posture classification model on mini-MIMM test set. These examples show that even without sensitive appearance information, some postures which are difficult to recognize in 2D space are easily identifiable in 3D space.

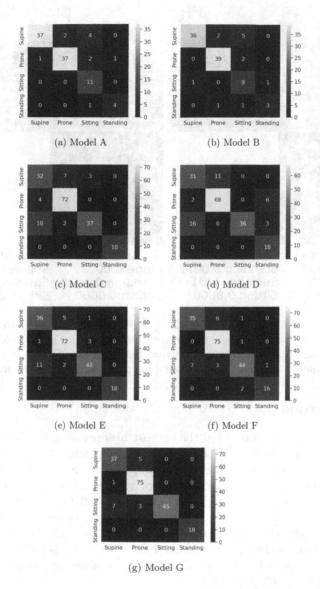

Fig. 9. Confusion Matrix of posture models listed in Table 2. (a) Model A: 3D pose-based posture model trained on SyRIP training set and tested on ground truth of SyRIP test set, (b) Model B: 3D pose-based posture model trained on SyRIP training set and tested on prediction of SyRIP test set, (c) Model C: 3D pose-based posture model trained on SyRIP training set and tested on prediction of mini-MIMM test set, (d) Model D: 2D pose-based posture model trained on SyRIP training set, (e) Model E: 2D pose-based posture model trained on mini-MIMM training set, (f) Model F: proxy 3D pose-based model trained on mini-MIMM training set, and (g) Model G: predicted 3D pose-based model trained on mini-MIMM training set.

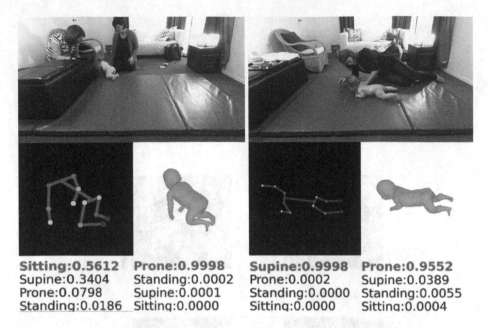

Sitting:0.5612	Prone:0.9998	Supine:0.9998	Prone:0.9552
Supine:0.3404	Standing:0.0002	Prone:0.0002	Supine:0.0389
Prone:0.0798	Supine:0.0001	Standing:0.0000	Standing:0.0055
Standing:0.0186	Sitting:0.0000	Sitting:0.0000	Sitting:0.0004

Fig. 10. Exemplar failure cases of our 2D pose-based posture recognition compared against our 3D pose-based posture recognizer. In each image, The left side presents the predicted 2D skeleton with predicted posture based on the 2D pose, while right side shows the predicted 3D body with predicted posture based on the 3D pose.

5   Conclusion

Gross motor activities are one of the earliest observable signals of development in infants and automatic early screening for motor delays could improve infant development in a wide spectrum of domains. With such applications in mind, we present a two-phase data efficient and privacy-preserving pose-based posture classification framework. Our pipeline first produces 2D or 3D poses using algorithms we previously developed, and then feeds those poses into a posture classification network, which predicts one of four infant posture classes. We evaluate our classification algorithm with complete ablation analysis on two fully diverse infant datasets and achieve high estimation accuracies for the infant postures, especially with the 3D pose framework.

References

1. Ali, J.B., Charman, T., Johnson, M.H., Jones, E.J.: Early motor differences in infants at elevated likelihood of autism spectrum disorder and/or attention deficit hyperactivity disorder. J. Autism Dev. Disord. **50**(12), 4367–4384 (2020)
2. Ansari, A.F., Roy, P.P., Dogra, D.P.: Posture recognition in HINE exercises. In: Raman, B., Kumar, S., Roy, P.P., Sen, D. (eds.) Proceedings of International Conference on Computer Vision and Image Processing. AISC, vol. 460, pp. 321–330. Springer, Singapore (2017). https://doi.org/10.1007/978-981-10-2107-7_29

3. Bayley, N.: Bayley scales of infant and toddler development. PsychCorp, Pearson (2006)
4. Chambers, C., et al.: Computer vision to automatically assess infant neuromotor risk. IEEE Trans. Neural Syst. Rehabil. Eng. **28**(11), 2431–2442 (2020)
5. Centers for Disease Control and Prevention: Data and statistics for cerebral palsy: prevalence and characteristics (2012)
6. Frankenburg, W.K.: Developmental surveillance and screening of infants and young children. Pediatrics **109**(1), 144–145 (2002)
7. Groos, D., Adde, L., Støen, R., Ramampiaro, H., Ihlen, E.A.: Towards human-level performance on automatic pose estimation of infant spontaneous movements. Comput. Med. Imaging Graph. **95**, 102012 (2022)
8. Hesse, N., Bodensteiner, C., Arens, M., Hofmann, U.G., Weinberger, R., Sebastian Schroeder, A.: Computer vision for medical infant motion analysis: state of the art and RGB-D data set. In: Leal-Taixé, L., Roth, S. (eds.) ECCV 2018. LNCS, vol. 11134, pp. 32–49. Springer, Cham (2019). https://doi.org/10.1007/978-3-030-11024-6_3
9. Hesse, N., Pujades, S., Black, M., Arens, M., Hofmann, U., Schroeder, S.: Learning and tracking the 3D body shape of freely moving infants from RGB-D sequences. IEEE Trans. Pattern Anal. Mach. Intell. (2019)
10. Hesse, N., et al.: Learning an infant body model from RGB-D data for accurate full body motion analysis. In: Frangi, A.F., Schnabel, J.A., Davatzikos, C., Alberola-López, C., Fichtinger, G. (eds.) MICCAI 2018. LNCS, vol. 11070, pp. 792–800. Springer, Cham (2018). https://doi.org/10.1007/978-3-030-00928-1_89
11. Hesse, N., Schröder, A.S., Müller-Felber, W., Bodensteiner, C., Arens, M., Hofmann, U.G.: Body pose estimation in depth images for infant motion analysis. In: 2017 39th Annual International Conference of the IEEE Engineering in Medicine and Biology Society (EMBC), pp. 1909–1912. IEEE (2017)
12. Huang, X., Fu, N., Liu, S., Ostadabbas, S.: Invariant representation learning for infant pose estimation with small data. In: IEEE International Conference on Automatic Face and Gesture Recognition (FG), 2021, December 2021
13. Huang, X., Wan, M., Luan, L., Tunik, B., Ostadabbas, S.: Computer vision to the rescue: infant postural symmetry estimation from incongruent annotations. To appear in Winter Conference on Applications of Computer Vision 2023 (2023). http://arxiv.org/abs/2207.09352
14. Iverson, J.M.: Developing language in a developing body: the relationship between motor development and language development. J. Child Lang. **37**(2), 229 (2010)
15. Kim, H., Carlson, A.G., Curby, T.W., Winsler, A.: Relations among motor, social, and cognitive skills in pre-kindergarten children with developmental disabilities. Res. Dev. Disabil. **53-54**, 43–60 (2016). https://doi.org/10.1016/j.ridd.2016.01.016, https://www.sciencedirect.com/science/article/pii/S0891422216300166
16. Kolotouros, N., Pavlakos, G., Black, M.J., Daniilidis, K.: Learning to reconstruct 3d human pose and shape via model-fitting in the loop. In: Proceedings of the IEEE/CVF International Conference on Computer Vision, pp. 2252–2261 (2019)
17. Koutsouki, D., Asonitou, K.: Cognitive processes in children with developmental coordination disorder. In: Cognition, Intelligence, and Achievement, pp. 267–289. Elsevier (2015)
18. Li, S., Ke, L., Pratama, K., Tai, Y.W., Tang, C.K., Cheng, K.T.: Cascaded deep monocular 3D human pose estimation with evolutionary training data. In: The IEEE/CVF Conference on Computer Vision and Pattern Recognition (CVPR), June 2020

19. Lin, T.-Y., et al.: Microsoft COCO: common objects in context. In: Fleet, D., Pajdla, T., Schiele, B., Tuytelaars, T. (eds.) ECCV 2014. LNCS, vol. 8693, pp. 740–755. Springer, Cham (2014). https://doi.org/10.1007/978-3-319-10602-1_48

20. Liu, S., Huang, X., Fu, N., Ostadabbas, S.: Heuristic weakly supervised 3D human pose estimation in novel contexts without any 3D pose ground truth. arXiv preprint arXiv:2105.10996 (2021). https://doi.org/10.48550/ARXIV.2105.10996, https://arxiv.org/abs/2105.10996

21. Okuno, A., Ishikawa, T., Watanabe, H.: Rollover detection of infants using posture estimation model. In: 2020 IEEE 9th Global Conference on Consumer Electronics (GCCE), pp. 490–493. IEEE (2020)

22. Piper, M.C., Darrah, J., Maguire, T.O., Redfern, L.: Motor Assessment of the Developing Infant, vol. 1. Saunders Philadelphia (1994)

23. Sandler, M., Howard, A., Zhu, M., Zhmoginov, A., Chen, L.C.: Mobilenetv 2: inverted residuals and linear bottlenecks. In: Proceedings of the IEEE Conference on Computer Vision and Pattern Recognition, pp. 4510–4520 (2018)

24. Teitelbaum, P., Teitelbaum, O., Nye, J., Fryman, J., Maurer, R.G.: Movement analysis in infancy may be useful for early diagnosis of autism. Proc. Natl. Acad. Sci. **95**(23), 13982–13987 (1998)

25. Tonelli, M., et al.: Recommendations on screening for developmental delay. CMAJ (2016)

26. Wan, M., et al.: InfAnFace: bridging the infant-adult domain gap in facial landmark estimation in the wild. To appear in 26th International Conference on Pattern Recognition (ICPR 2022) (2022)

27. Xiao, B., Wu, H., Wei, Y.: Simple baselines for human pose estimation and tracking. In: Ferrari, V., Hebert, M., Sminchisescu, C., Weiss, Y. (eds.) ECCV 2018. LNCS, vol. 11210, pp. 472–487. Springer, Cham (2018). https://doi.org/10.1007/978-3-030-01231-1_29

28. Zhang, F., Zhu, X., Dai, H., Ye, M., Zhu, C.: Distribution-aware coordinate representation for human pose estimation. In: Proceedings of the IEEE/CVF Conference on Computer Vision and Pattern Recognition, pp. 7093–7102 (2020)

29. Zwaigenbaum, L., Bryson, S., Rogers, T., Roberts, W., Brian, J., Szatmari, P.: Behavioral manifestations of autism in the first year of life. Int. J. Dev. Neurosci. **23**(2–3), 143–152 (2005)

Emotion, Age and Gender Prediction Through Masked Face Inpainting

Md Baharul Islam[1,2]([⊠]) [iD] and Md Imran Hosen[1] [iD]

[1] Department of Computer Engineering, Bahcesehir University, Istanbul, Turkey
bislam.eng@gmail.com
[2] College of Data Science and Engineering, American University of Malta,
Cospicua, Malta

Abstract. Prediction of gesture and demographic information from the face is complex and challenging, particularly for the masked face. This paper proposes a deep learning-based integrated approach to predict emotion and demographic information for unmasked and masked faces, consisting of four sub-tasks: masked face detection, masked face inpainting, emotion, age, and gender prediction. The masked face detector module provides a binary decision on whether the face mask is available or not by applying pre-trained MobileNetV3. We use the inpainting module based on U-Net embedding with ImageNet weights to remove the face mask and restore the face. We use the convolutional neural networks to predict emotion (e.g., happy, angry). Besides, VGGFace-based transfer learning has been used to predict demographic information (e.g., age, gender). Extensive experiments on five publicly available datasets: AffectNet, UTKFace, FER-2013, CelebA, and MAFA, show the effectiveness of our proposed method to predict emotion and demographic identification through masked face reconstruction.

Keywords: Face detection · Face Inpainting · Emotion Prediction

1 Introduction

Automatically predicting emotion and demographic information such as age and gender has gained a lot of attraction and becoming increasingly significant for its wide application such as health-care, surveillance, business, self-driving, and so on [7,22]. Some methods have been reported in the literature, while machine learning/ deep learning-based methods [3,13,17,19] achieved promising outcomes in predicting emotion, gender, and age. One of the earliest approaches proposed by Tang [22] used a support vector machine instead of a softmax layer to analyze human emotion from faces. He used margin-based loss instead of cross-entropy loss. Happy & Routray [7] applied the feature of salient facial patches to automatic facial expression recognition. Their method analyzed only prominent facial patches based on the facial landmarks point, which directly contribute to facial expression classification. However, these methods were limited to only emotion prediction on the unmasked faces. In [3], dealt with age,

© Springer Nature Switzerland AG 2023
J.-J. Rousseau and B. Kapralos (Eds.): ICPR 2022 Workshops, LNCS 13643, pp. 37–48, 2023.
https://doi.org/10.1007/978-3-031-37660-3_3

Input   GT   Output

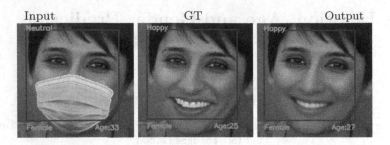

Fig. 1. An example of emotion, age, and gender prediction through masked face inpainting using our method. Our method achieves almost the same projection as the Ground Truth (GT).

gender, and emotion prediction problem by applying Convolutional Neural Networks (CNN) with a guided back-propagation visualization technique. However, it achieved promising performance on gender classification but lower performance on emotion prediction. To address the issue, Seregil & Ozpinar [19] introduced a HyperExtended light face model based on the VGG-Face model. A similar process is implemented in [17]. Although all these methods provided a satisfactory performance for predicting emotion, age, and gender for unmasked faces, the performance dropped significantly for masked faces. Recently, Mukherjee et al., [13] proposed an approach, namely MaskMTL, that jointly estimated heterogeneous attributes such as age, gender, and ethnicity from a single masked facial image. In MaskMTL, the encoder consists of a standard module and three convolution layers. Though their approach prevented a significant drop in performance for masked faces, they achieved comparatively lower performance in the unmasked faces.

Due to the infectious COVID-19 pandemic, people have been forced to wear face masks, especially indoor settings. Since a significant face portion, including a highly informative area such as the nose and mouth, is covered with the face mask, reducing the crucial feature points. Thus, the existing emotion, gender, and age prediction model's performance are significantly reduced for the masked face data. Image inpainting can be handy to solve this problem by restoring the face information covered by the face mask. Besides, an efficient masked face detection model is required to identify both masked and unmasked faces. The main goal of our proposed method is to identify masked and unmasked faces, remove the face mask and restore the mask area before predicting the emotion, age, and gender. An example has been shown in Fig. 1 using our proposed method. The major contributions are summarized below.

– An emotion and demographic information prediction model using deep learning has been proposed to predict the emotion, gender, and age for both masked and unmasked faces.

– A masked face detection model is proposed based on pre-trained MobileNetV3
[9] with a fully connected (FC) head. It is lightweight without sacrificing
performance.
– We propose a novel face inpainting model to remove the face mask and automatically restore the information using U-Net embedding with ImageNet
weights.
– Extensive experiments on different datasets: AffectNet [12], UTKFace [24],
FER-2013 [6], CelebA [10] and MAFA [11] show the effectiveness of our
method.

2   Proposed Method

The overall architecture of the proposed model has been presented in Fig. 2.
Our model works in four sub-tasks: masked face detection, mask removal and
face inpainting, emotion prediction, and demographic information prediction.
Firstly, the masked face detection module checks whether a face is covered with
a mask or not. The intermediary face inpainting module restores the face mask
area before the emotion and demographic information prediction module. We
use transfer learning for masked face detection, age, and gender prediction.

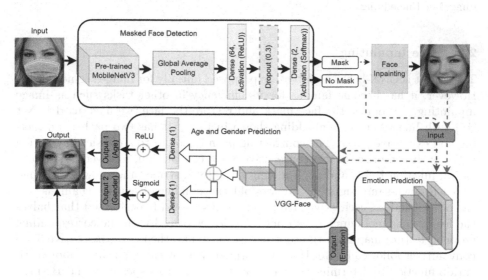

Fig. 2. The overall architecture of the proposed model works in four major sub-
modules: masked face detection, automatic face inpainting, emotion prediction, and
age and gender prediction.

2.1   Masked Face Detection

To accomplish masked face detection, we have used a transfer learning that
utilizes the MobileNetV3 [9] pre-trained model. In the fine-tuning process, the

last layer of MobileNetV3 (small) has been chopped, and a fully connected (FC) new head has been added to the earlier model. Moreover, the weight of the MobileNetV3 architecture has not been updated during the training. The FC head consists of an average pooling layer of pool size 7 × 7. A dense layer with ReLU activation function of 128 neurons, a dropout of 0.3, and a final dense layer with SoftMax activation as shown in Fig. 2 (masked face detection module).

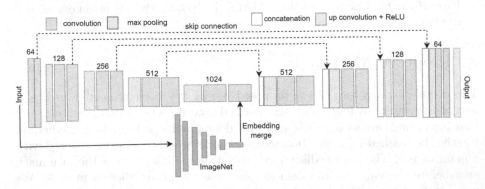

Fig. 3. The architecture of our masked face inpainting module based on U-Net with ImageNet Embedding.

2.2 Face Inpainting

The U-Net is CNN-based architecture proposed initially for image segmentation. However, it has become famous for its efficiency in other tasks such as image inpainting. To remove the face mask and restore the face, we have used U-Net [15] with ImageNet [18] embedding shown in Fig. 3. It has two paths: contracting and expansive paths. The contracting path is similar to a classic convolution network. It comprises of two consecutive 3 × 3 convolution, followed by an activation function ReLU and max-pooling (size 2 × 2, stride 2) for down-sampling. At each down-sampling step, we two-fold the number of feature channels. On the other hand, at each expansive path, an upsampled is performed that halves the feature channel numbers. A concatenation is placed with the corresponding cropped feature map from the contracting path, and then two consecutive 3 × 3 convolutions followed by ReLU are performed. We have applied the sigmoid activation function to determine the validity of the pixel to a specific point. Besides, we have concatenated the U-Net bottleneck layer with ImageNet embedding, which adds more information and helps the up-sampling part perform better.

2.3 Emotion Prediction

Our emotion prediction model consists of four convolution layers, and each is followed by a Batch Normalization, an activation(ReLU), and a max-pooling $(2, 2)$ layer. The convolution layer of the different kernels $[64, 128, 256, 256]$ with

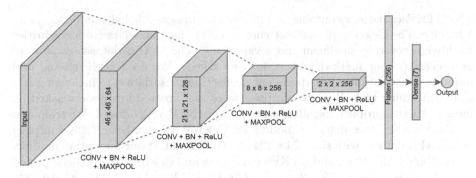

Fig. 4. The architecture of the emotion prediction model (4-layers of CNN architecture).

3×3 filter size is used to calculate the element-wise matrix-multiplication and add them to turn into feature maps. The activation function makes the non-linearity effect on those summations of feature maps. The max-pooling layer lessens the dimension of the images. After four convolution operations, we have applied a flatten operation followed by three dense layers $(128, 64, 7)$. The flattened layer flattens the previous layer's input and makes a one-dimensional vector. Finally, dense layers are placed for classification purposes. A softmax function converts the output into prediction among seven classes: neutral, happy, angry, sad, fear, surprise, and disgust. Figure 4 shows the summary of the emotion prediction model.

2.4   Age and Gender Prediction

For the age and gender, we defined a combined model shown in Fig. 2 (Age and Gender Prediction). We utilized transfer learning and fine-tuned the VGGFace [14] for the face recognition task. The last seven layers of the model have been frozen, and three new layers have been added for each age and gender prediction. Since age is a linear regression problem, we have used the mean square error as a loss function and linear activation function. For gender prediction, binary cross-entropy and sigmoid functions have been used as loss and activation functions.

3   Dataset and Experimental Setup

3.1   Dataset

We use five publicly available datasets, including AffectNet [12], UTKFace [24], FER-2013 [6], CelebA [10] and MAFA [11] for experiment and testing different modules of our method. AffectNet dataset contains around 440K large scale facial expression (e.g. Happy, Surprise, Neutral, Sad, Anger, Fear, Contempt, Disgust) images that are manually labeled. On the other hand, the FER-2013 [6] dataset contains around 32K annotated face images, including seven facial expressions.

The UTKFace dataset contains about 20K face images labeled gender, age, and ethnicity. The CelebA [10] dataset contains 200k face-free data from celebrities worldwide covering significant pose variations. The MAFA dataset consists of 6k images (3k for masked and 3k for unmasked). We need both masked and unmasked face data for the experiment. Collecting these data is a challenging and time-consuming task. We have cropped faces and created synthetic masked [2] faces to fix this problem for all datasets except the MAFA dataset. We train and test our masked face detector module on CelebA [10] synthetic (20K samples) and MAFA dataset with size 224×224. To train and test our inpainting module, we combined AffectNet, and UTKFace datasets and CelebA [10] synthetic paired datasets with a size of 200×200. The AffectNet [12] and FER-2013 [6] datasets have been used for the training emotion module with 48×48 and UTKFace for the age and gender module with 200×200. We have followed the standard data split rules. First, we separate 10% data for testing. The remaining data have been split into 80% for training and 20% for validation (except the inpainting module on the CelebA [10] dataset).

3.2 Experimental Setup

We have used Python, Keras, and Tensorflow environments to process data, train, and test our model. We use a workstation with Windows 10 OS, core i9, 32 GB RAM, and an NVIDIA Geforce RTX 2070 GPU for the experiment. We run the face masked detector module for 10 epochs with batch size 16 and binary_cross entropy as a loss function. To train the inpainting module, we run the module for 35 epochs with SSIM loss and batch size 12. We run the emotion, age, and gender modules for 100 epochs with categorical cross-entropy loss, binary loss, and mse loss, respectively. Adam optimizer and learning rate 0.0001 are constant for all the experiments.

3.3 Evaluation Matrix

To assess the effectiveness of our proposed model, we use different performance measurement metrics such as Structure Similarity Index Method (SSIM), Peak Signal to Noise Ratio (PSNR), and Mean Absolute Error (MAE). The PSNR computes the correlation between the obtained output and the original input. A higher PSNR value indicates better quality in the performance. The SSIM measures the similarity between output and input images.

4   Results and Discussion

In this section, we demonstrate the performance of our model in terms of masked face detection, face inpainting/restoring, emotion, age, and gender prediction on different datasets.

Input   GT   Yu et al.[23]   Din et al. [5]   Ours

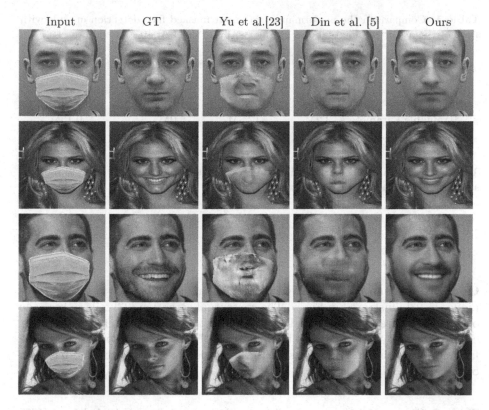

Fig. 5. Qualitative comparison of our results with state-of-the-art methods on the CelebA [10] dataset.

4.1 Masked Face Detection Performance

The performance of our masked face detection module is competitive, lightweight, and requires less prediction time. Table 1 shows the comparison of our results with different pre-trained models on the synthetic masked of CelebA [10] dataset. The RestNet50 [8] achieved slightly better performance than ours. However, our fine-tuned MobileNetV3 is much more lightweight in terms of parameters and latency and requires less prediction time. We have also compared our model with state-of-the-art recent methods [1,4,20] on MAFA [11] dataset. Table 2 shows the comparison result. Our method achieves the highest accuracy at 99.30% while Ahmed et al. [1] are close to our results at 98.20%.

4.2 Face Inpainting Performance

Quantitative Performance. The quantitative comparison of our model with state-of-the-art methods on CelebA dataset (1000 samples) is shown in Table 3. Our method has demonstrated better performance in terms of SSIM and PSNR. It indicates that our approach maintains the similarity of the original face structure and image intensity.

Table 1. Comparison the performance of the our masked face detection module with state-of-the art pre-trained models on the synthetic CelebA [10] paired dataset.

Architecture	VGG19 [21]	Resnet50 [8]	MobileNetV2 [16]	Ours
Accuracy	96.85%	99.03%	97.04%	99%
Total Parameters	23.2M	36.4M	10.2M	1.1M
Trainable Parameters	3.2M	12.8M	8.0M	0.13M
Latency	0.0623s	0.0322s	0.0126s	0.0035s

Table 2. Comparison the performance of the our masked face detector with state-of-the art methods on the MAFA [11] dataset.

Model	Borut et al., [4]	Sethi et al., [20]	Ahmed et al., [1]	Ours
Accuracy	98.18%	98.20%	93.94%	**99.30%**

Qualitative Performance. We compare our model with state-of-the-art techniques [5, 23] illustrated in Fig. 5. The contextual attention [23] fails to keep the original structure of faces, while Din et al. [5] method suffers in maintaining color consistency and structure of the inpainted face. However, our model restores the face similar to the original face structure and maintains the color and intensity of the ground truth.

Table 3. Quantitative Comparison of our inpainting module on CelebA dataset (1000 samples).

Method	Yu et al., [23]	Din et al., [5]	Ours
SSIM	0.89	0.87	**0.92**
PSNR	31	30	**33**

4.3   Emotion Prediction Performance

In Table 4, we report the performance of our emotion prediction module and compare it with state-of-the-art methods on FER [6] and AffectNet [12] datasets. While state-of-the-art methods achieved promising performance on unmasked data, their performance dropped significantly for the masked dataset. For instance, Arriaga et al., [3] acquired 66.0% accuracy on emotion prediction, but their performance dropped around 14% for masked face emotion prediction on the FER [6] dataset. Additionally, Savchenko et al. [17] received 66.3% accuracy on Affectnet [12], and their performance also decreased significantly on the masked face data. Our module performance boosted around 8–10% through inpainting for masked face data. On the other hand, we achieve 63.3% and 65.1% accuracy on FER and AffectNet datasets for unmasked data, respectively.

Table 4. Comparison of our emotion prediction results with state-of-the-art methods on different datasets.

Methods	Dataset	Accuracy (Unmask)	Accuracy (mask)
Yichuan [22]	FER	67.0%	–
Arriaga et al., [3]	FER	66.0%	51.6%
Serengil et al., [19]	FER	57.4%	41.8%
Savchenko [17]	AffectNet	66.3%	52.1%
Ours	FER	63.3%	48.7%
Ours (with inpaint)	Affectnet	65.1%	60.2%

Table 5. Comparison of our Age and Gender prediction results with state-of-the-art methods on UTKFace [24] dataset.

–	Unmasked		Masked	
Methods	Gender	Age (MAE)	Gender	Age (MAE)
Savchenko [17]	93.7%	5.7	87.3%	13.4
Mukherjee et al., [13]	89.6%	11.5	89.1%	12.1
Ours (with inpaint)	93.4%	5.6	91.3%	8.7

However, the performance of the emotion module decreased slightly, which is not significant.

4.4   Age and Gender Prediction Performance

Table 5 shows the performance of our age and gender prediction module compared with the state-of-the-art methods. Savchenko [17] achieved 93.7% accuracy and 5.7 MAE for gender and age prediction for the unmaked faces, while the performance significantly dropped to 87.3% and 13.4 MAE for the masked faces. Mukherjee et al. [13] received better performance for both masked and unmasked faces. On the other hand, our age and gender prediction module achieved 5.6 MAE, and 93.4% accuracy, close to Savchenko [17] for unmasked faces. However, our module performs better than the state-of-the-art methods for the masked faces.

Table 6. Effect of different architectures and network depths in the inpainting module.

Model	Layers	Kernel	Params.	Accuracy
UNet	64, 128, 128, 256, 512	7, 7, 7, 3, 3, 3	19.41M	88.23%
ResUNet	64, 128, 128, 256, 512	7, 7, 7, 3, 3, 3	53.58M	91.04%
ResUNet	64, 128, 256, 512	7, 7, 3, 3	41.04M	90.07%
ResUNet	64, 128, 256, 512	3, 3, 3, 3	23.67M	89.14%
Ours	64, 128, 128, 256, 512	7, 7, 7, 3, 3, 3	19.41M	93.01%

Table 7. Effect of different pre-trained models in the age and gender prediction module.

Architecture	MobileNetV1	MobileNetV2	VGG16	VGGFace
Accuracy (Gender)	92.7%	91.4%	91.0%	93.4%
MAE (Age)	5.7	7.2	6.4	5.6

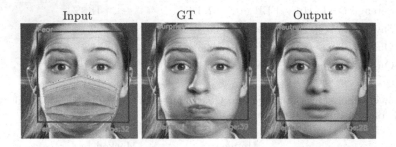

Fig. 6. An example of failure case using our method.

4.5 Ablation Study

More convolution layers and deep networks suffer higher parameters and training costs. We investigated different architecture depths to better the performance and balance between performance and training cost. For face inpainting, we have tested various network architectures and depth, as shown in Table 6. Our U-Net with ImageNet weights achieved the best performance (93.01%) with minimum trainable parameters of 19.4M. To predict emotion, we investigated different architectures with different datasets and hyperparameters. For example, we used 3- and 4-layers CNN architecture on FER and AffectNet datasets. We received around 59.4% and 63.3% accuracy for 3- and 4-layers, respectively, on the FER dataset. On the other hand, our module received around 65.1% accuracy for 4-layers CNN architecture on the AffectNet dataset. Furthermore, we have found 32 batch sizes as an efficient choice. For the age and gender prediction, we investigated with and without a backbone. We noticed that the backbone boosted the performance significantly. We have tried different pre-trained models shown in Table 7 for age and gender prediction, and we found the VGGFace was an efficient choice.

5 Conclusion

This paper presented a method that automatically predicts emotion and demography information for masked and unmasked faces. We used pre-trained MobileNetV3 (small) to detect the masked face, while U-Net embedding with ImageNet weights for mask removal and face restoration. We used CNN for emotion, age, and gender prediction. Extensive experiments on the publicly available dataset demonstrated our method's efficacy and competitiveness performance.

Although our approach shows competitive performance to predict the emotion and demographic information, however, it may fail to predict correctly when the inpainting module can not restore faces accurately, as shown in an example in Fig. 6. Content-aware inpainting method may overcome this limitation before predicting the emotion and demographic information.

Acknowledgements. This work is supported by the Scientific and Technological Research Council of Turkey (TUBITAK) under 2232 Outstanding Researchers program, Project No. 118C301.

References

1. Ahmed, A.E.A., Azim, N., Mahmood, M., Alshammari, H.: A deep learning model for face mask detection. Int. J. Comput. Sci. Netw. Secur. (IJCSNS) **2**, 101–107 (2021). https://doi.org/10.22937/IJCSNS.2021.21.10.13
2. Anwar, A., Raychowdhury, A.: Masked face recognition for secure authentication. arXiv preprint arXiv:2008.11104 (2020)
3. Arriaga, O., Valdenegro-Toro, M., Plöger, P.: Real-time convolutional neural networks for emotion and gender classification. arXiv preprint arXiv:1710.07557 (2017)
4. Batagelj, B., Peer, P., Štruc, V., Dobrišek, S.: How to correctly detect face-masks for COVID-19 from visual information? Appl. Sci. **11**(5), 2070 (2021)
5. Din, N.U., Javed, K., Bae, S., Yi, J.: A novel GAN-based network for unmasking of masked face. IEEE Access **8**, 44276–44287 (2020)
6. Goodfellow, I.J., et al.: Challenges in representation learning: a report on three machine learning contests. In: Lee, M., Hirose, A., Hou, Z.-G., Kil, R.M. (eds.) ICONIP 2013. LNCS, vol. 8228, pp. 117–124. Springer, Heidelberg (2013). https://doi.org/10.1007/978-3-642-42051-1_16
7. Happy, S., Routray, A.: Automatic facial expression recognition using features of salient facial patches. IEEE Trans. Affect. Comput. **6**(1), 1–12 (2014)
8. He, K., Zhang, X., Ren, S., Sun, J.: Deep residual learning for image recognition. In: Proceedings of the IEEE Conference on Computer Vision and Pattern Recognition, pp. 770–778 (2016)
9. Howard, A., et al.: Searching for mobilenetv3. In: Proceedings of the IEEE/CVF International Conference on Computer Vision, pp. 1314–1324 (2019)
10. Liu, Z., Luo, P., Wang, X., Tang, X.: Deep learning face attributes in the wild. In: Proceedings of International Conference on Computer Vision (ICCV), December 2015
11. mask dataset (MAFA), F.: Kaggle.com (2020). https://www.kaggle.com/andrewmvd/face-mask-detection
12. Mollahosseini, A., Hasani, B., Mahoor, M.H.: AffectNet: a database for facial expression, valence, and arousal computing in the wild. IEEE Trans. Affect. Comput. **10**(1), 18–31 (2017)
13. Mukherjee, P., Kaushik, V., Gupta, R., Jha, R., Kankanwadi, D., Lall, B.: MaskMTL: attribute prediction in masked facial images with deep multitask learning. arXiv preprint arXiv:2201.03002 (2022)
14. Parkhi, O.M., Vedaldi, A., Zisserman, A.: Deep face recognition. British Machine Vision Association (2015)

15. Ronneberger, O., Fischer, P., Brox, T.: U-net: convolutional networks for biomedical image segmentation. In: Navab, N., Hornegger, J., Wells, W.M., Frangi, A.F. (eds.) MICCAI 2015. LNCS, vol. 9351, pp. 234–241. Springer, Cham (2015). https://doi.org/10.1007/978-3-319-24574-4_28

16. Sandler, M., Howard, A., Zhu, M., Zhmoginov, A., Chen, L.C.: Mobilenetv 2: inverted residuals and linear bottlenecks. In: Proceedings of the IEEE Conference on Computer Vision and Pattern Recognition, pp. 4510–4520 (2018)

17. Savchenko, A.V.: Facial expression and attributes recognition based on multi-task learning of lightweight neural networks. In: 2021 IEEE 19th International Symposium on Intelligent Systems and Informatics (SISY), pp. 119–124. IEEE (2021)

18. Schroff, F., Kalenichenko, D., Philbin, J.: Facenet: a unified embedding for face recognition and clustering. In: Proceedings of the IEEE Conference on Computer Vision and Pattern Recognition, pp. 815–823 (2015)

19. Serengil, S.I., Ozpinar, A.: Hyperextended lightface: a facial attribute analysis framework. In: 2021 International Conference on Engineering and Emerging Technologies (ICEET), pp. 1–4. IEEE (2021)

20. Sethi, S., Kathuria, M., Kaushik, T.: Face mask detection using deep learning: an approach to reduce risk of coronavirus spread. J. Biomed. Inform. **120**, 103848 (2021)

21. Simonyan, K., Zisserman, A.: Very deep convolutional networks for large-scale image recognition. arXiv preprint arXiv:1409.1556 (2014)

22. Tang, Y.: Deep learning using linear support vector machines. arXiv preprint arXiv:1306.0239 (2013)

23. Yu, J., Lin, Z., Yang, J., Shen, X., Lu, X., Huang, T.S.: Generative image inpainting with contextual attention. arXiv preprint arXiv:1801.07892 (2018)

24. Zhang, Z., et al.: Age progression/regression by conditional adversarial autoencoder. In: IEEE Conference on Computer Vision and Pattern Recognition (CVPR). IEEE (2017)

A Masked Face Classification Benchmark on Low-Resolution Surveillance Images

Federico Cunico[1]($\boxtimes$) (iD), Andrea Toaiari[1] (iD), and Marco Cristani[2] (iD)

[1] Department of Computer Science, University of Verona, Verona, Italy
{federico.cunico,andrea.toaiari}@univr.it
[2] Department of Engineering for Innovation Medicine, University of Verona, Verona, Italy
marco.cristani@univr.it

Abstract. We propose a novel image dataset focused on tiny faces wearing face masks for mask classification purposes, dubbed *Small Face MASK* (SF-MASK), composed of a collection made from 20k low-resolution images exported from diverse and heterogeneous datasets, ranging from 7×7 to 64×64 pixel resolution. An accurate visualization of this collection, through counting grids, made it possible to highlight gaps in the variety of poses assumed by the heads of the pedestrians. In particular, faces filmed by very high cameras, in which the facial features appear strongly skewed, are absent. To address this structural deficiency, we produced a set of synthetic images which resulted in a satisfactory covering of the intra-class variance. Furthermore, a small subsample of 1701 images contains badly worn face masks, opening to multi-class classification challenges. Experiments on SF-MASK focus on face mask classification using several classifiers. Results show that the richness of SF-MASK (real + synthetic images) leads all of the tested classifiers to perform better than exploiting comparative face mask datasets, on a fixed 1077 images testing set. Dataset and evaluation code are publicly available here: https://github.com/HumaticsLAB/sf-mask.

Keywords: Masked face dataset · Low resolution dataset · COVID-19 · Synthetic data · Masked face classification · Surveillance

1 Introduction

The COVID-19 epidemic has posed great challenges to the world. The World Health Organization has provided guidelines on tools to use and protocols to adopt to fight this disease [45]. Among these, distancing and masks have proven to be effective in preventing the spread of the epidemic. In particular, face masks have become the bulwark of COVID-19 prevention, trapping the droplets exhaled from infected individuals [15]. Masks are crucial especially when distancing cannot be easily held, *e.g.* in small indoor environments or on public transportation [11]. The numbers are impressive: 52 billion disposable face masks were produced in 2020, with a market size which is expected to reach USD 2.1 billion

© Springer Nature Switzerland AG 2023
J.-J. Rousseau and B. Kapralos (Eds.): ICPR 2022 Workshops, LNCS 13643, pp. 49–63, 2023.
https://doi.org/10.1007/978-3-031-37660-3_4

by 2030 [2]. It follows that face masks have become a cultural norm [26], and will probably be part of the "new normal" after the pandemic will definitely end. Actually, coronavirus is expected to stay with us in the future, in the form of an endemic disease - meaning that it will continue to circulate in pockets of the global population for years to come [29].

Fig. 1. Example of small bounding box classification using a ResNet-50 trained on SF-MASK with synthetic augmentation. (Color figure online)

Face masks are effective in the measure with which they are worn by everyone and in a consistent way [12,14,18,27]: for this reason, non-collaborative monitoring to ensure proper use of the face mask seems to be a very effective solution, resulting in an obvious clash between privacy and safety [30,32,37]. We are not discussing this issue here, focusing instead on the challenge of detecting face masks from a computer vision point of view. Actually, if the privacy and ethical issues were resolved, there would still remain a fundamental problem for video surveillance, namely that automatically identifying face masks is difficult, especially in selected scenarios.

Figure 1 shows an example of this challenge: a crowd of people is captured by a single picture, where each face can be enclosed by a bounding box of few pixels; furthermore, faces can be rotated, subject to occlusion, affected by glares/dark areas. The face masks themselves bring in a new challenge, since they can be of different shapes and colors, patterned or even skin coloured. Finally, there is an underlying chicken-egg problem: capturing the face to check the presence of a mask is made difficult by the mask itself, which covers most of the discriminative features used to detect a face (mouth, nose). For this reason, general approaches for checking the presence of the mask are based on a people detector run in

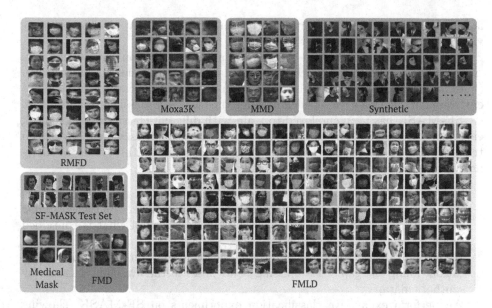

Fig. 2. Composition of SF-MASK dataset, a novel low-resolution masked face dataset. Each box presents a sample of the data extracted from the datasets involved, with the size of the boxes proportional to the portion used. (Color figure online)

advance, where the face is localized thanks to the body layout prior [50]. We assume this pipeline, and specifically to start with an image crop of a face, with the aim of classifying if it wears a mask or not.

Under this scenario, in this paper we present a novel dataset, dubbed *Small Face MASK* (SF-MASK), which serves to train face mask classification systems, supposed to work in a surveillance scenario, with faces captured at a native low resolution. The dataset is composed of 21,675 real-world RGB images with 9,055 images with face masks correctly worn and 12,620 images without face masks. The data collection has span over all the possible datasets containing small faces with masks in the literature, including [1,5,20,34,41,43], with proportions visualized in Fig. 2. One of the main contributions of this paper has been that of first understanding *what is contained* in these datasets in terms of intra-class variability (variation in poses, mask colors, etc.). Since an automatic quantitative analysis is hard (for example, head pose estimation to calculate the variation in pose is itself a tough challenge [21]), we performed a qualitative analysis with the help of the counting grids [28] (CG), a manifold learning approach specifically suited for the image data. The CG allowed us to discover the absence of specific poses: actually, faces filmed by very high cameras, in which the facial features appear strongly skewed, are absent. To address this structural deficiency, we produced a set of 15,481 synthetic images exploiting a pipeline based on Makehuman [7] + Blender [6], where the masked faces are captured in specific poses. This resulted in the satisfactory completion of the intra-class variance, as showed by dimensionality reduction experiments. Additionally, there are 1,701 faces where masks have been incorrectly worn, meaning that the face mask is visible, but is below the nose or the chin.

The dataset is divided into a training and a testing partition. The testing partition has been built from scratch to encapsulate all of the issues discussed above (hard illumination, rotated heads, occlusions) in a real multi-camera surveillance environment, offering a valid benchmark for the face mask classification problem.

SF-MASK has been employed to train with different classifiers a face mask classification system. The results show that the classifiers which have been trained with SF-MASK provide the best performance with respect to alternatives originated by a subset of the whole data.

Summarizing, the contributions of this paper are:

- We collect most of the publicly available datasets on face masks available in the literature, offering a sound qualitative overview of what is contained therein, thanks to the counting grids;
- We crafted SF-MASK, a novel dataset for low-resolution face mask classification, filling the gap of the missing head poses in the available datasets by synthetic data;
- We perform exhaustive classification experiments on SF-MASK, showing that it works as an effective training set for the masked face classification task.

2   Related Works

In this work, we define *face mask classification* as the task of individuating the presence of a face mask, or its absence, on a test image that tightly encloses a face. With *face mask detection* we indicate a system that, given an image, provides as output the bounding boxes of faces, where each bounding box is associated with a label indicating the presence or absence of a face mask. In this literature review, we consider datasets used for both applications. On the contrary, we do not consider all those references which deal with face mask recognition, that individuates a person's identity when they are covered by a face mask. Readers interested in face mask recognition may refer to the survey of [48].

Since the start of the COVID-19 pandemic two years ago, many research contributions have been published in relation to face mask detection and classification [42].

Most of the approaches are based on CNN networks, which require to have large amounts of data available [10,16,31,39].

One of the first public datasets is MAFA [16], explicitly focused on face detection in the presence of occlusions, more or less pronounced. It contains around 35,000 annotated faces collected from Internet, where occlusion elements are of various nature, and not only face masks, such as human body parts, scarfs, hats or other accessories. An extension of MAFA is MAFA-FMD [13], which adds a new wearing state for face masks images, *i.e. incorrect*, and increases the number of low-resolution images. Another example of dataset including improperly worn masks is [20], despite being considerably smaller. In [43], the authors proposed three different datasets: MFDD, RMFRD, SMFRD. The former is indicated for the face mask classification and detection tasks: it contains 24,771 masked face images, derived mainly from the web. RMFRD was generated by searching the web for images of celebrities with and without a mask, and it is specifically suited for the face recognition task. Lastly, SMFRD is a simulated dataset, where real face images are enriched with mask patches.

It is also possible to find small but interesting face mask datasets on the platform Kaggle, such as [41] and [1]. Moxa3K [34] is a fairly small dataset, consisting of data from [41] and other images found online. In this case, most of the faces are relatively small, since the images contain crowds.

Some common practices to create new and more diverse datasets consist in combining pre-existing masked face collections into one consistent set or combining masked face images crawled from the web with popular face detection and face recognition datasets, such as WiderFace [46] and FFHQ [22], which contain many images of faces with various resolutions, lighting conditions and head poses. Some examples of datasets constructed from the combination of previously released collections are LMFD [3,5,39] (MAFA [16] + WiderFace [46]) and [9] (MFDD [43] and SMFRD [43]).

In comparison to these datasets, which report faces at various resolution, we wanted to focus on images of natively low-resolution faces. This is to be compliant with video surveillance scenarios, assuming that the final purpose is to check the crowd at a distance for the presence of masks.

2.1 Synthetic Face Masks Datasets

The idea of crafting synthetical data as proxy for real ones for a better training set is not novel. Some examples of "augmented" datasets are SMFRD [43], which uses custom software to apply mask patches to face images from the LFW [19] and Webface [47] datasets. MFNID [8] is another simulated face mask dataset, based on images from FFHQ [22], created through a mask-to-face deformable model, which exploits multiple face landmarks to position a mask patch in order to simulate different wearing scenarios (correctly worn and three progressive incorrect wearing states). Major problems affecting this kind of approach are the positioning of the masks on faces not facing frontally and the variety of masks in shape and texture. We solved these issues by proposing an algorithm, based on Blender [6] and MakeHuman [7], able to generate a completely synthetic dataset, in which it would be possible to modify at will the orientation of the head, the background, the size of the image and the shape and color of the masks applied to the body.

3   The Dataset

In this section, we show how the SF-MASK dataset has been created and which criteria we adopted to filter the datasets that constitute it.

Table 1. List of datasets considered in the creation of SF-MASK. Faces are considered *Small* if $max(width, height) \leq 64$.

Dataset	Mask	No-Mask	Wrong-Mask	Small
RMFRD [43]	6.664	0	0	1905
MMD [20]	2,855	581	119	986
FMD [1]	768	286	97	532
Medical Mask [41]	3,918	1,319	0	305
FMLD [5]	29,561	43,840	1,531	11,856
Moxa3K [34]	5,380	1,477	0	916
Ours (no synth.)	9,055	12,620	1701	All
Ours	21,384	15,772	1701	All

3.1 Problem Statement

We focused on the face mask classification task on low-resolution images, ascribable to a classic video surveillance scenario. We have therefore selected 64×64 pixel as the maximum size of the faces, and used this to filter out images from all the selected sources. This choice was made with a trade-off between a sufficiently small image size and the number of real images publicly available, besides being a common resolution for analysis on small images, see for instance the Tiny Imagenet Challenge [23]. As reported in Sect. 2 and Table 1, the number of small bounding box faces is limited in every dataset. SF-MASK collect them all, realizing the largest low-resolution face mask dataset to date. This ensemble forms the SF-MASK training set, which will be explained in the following section. In Sect. 3.4 we will detail the SF-MASK testing partition, which has been designed to cover as much as possible the whole intra-class variance of the face mask classification problem. The analysis of the visual domain captured by these partitions will be shown in Sect. 3.5.

3.2 The SF-MASK Training Partition

We collected the images from different datasets, chosen for their peculiarity such as the total number of images (FMLD), challenging environments (Moxa3K), specific types of face masks (Medical Mask, FMD, MMD), and the high number of native low-resolution images w.r.t. the total amount of that specific dataset (MMD, Moxa3K, RMFRD). The cardinality of each dataset is presented in Table 1. All the considered datasets are freely available to academia, as stated by their respective licenses. Other very interesting datasets for our task (*e.g.* MAFA-FMD [13]), although present in literature, are not publicly available or under commercial licences.

We merged the above datasets' training sets into a single set, splitting it into two categories: *Mask* for the faces correctly wearing a face mask, and *No-Mask* otherwise. The resulting size of the merged dataset is:

- *Mask*: 49,227 images
- *No-Mask*: 47,503 images

We removed possible duplicates by analyzing all the images using the structural similarity index measure (SSIM [44]) and then we kept only the images whose size is lesser or equal to 64 × 64 px. As is, the resulting dataset has the following composition:

- *Mask*: 9,055 images
- *No-Mask*: 12,620 images

The distribution of SF-MASK image sizes is reported in Fig. 3. Some dataset also gives the annotation of *Wrong-Mask*, which is the class for face mask incorrectly worn, such as the mask below the nose, or under the chin. This class consists of 1,701 elements.

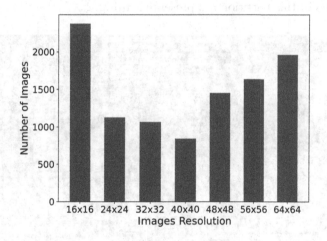

Fig. 3. Distribution of image sizes in SF-MASK (without synthetic data). Each bar represents images of resolution less or equal to that specific tick. The synthetic images are all of the same size and can be produced in any amount.

3.3   Data Processing

Some of the datasets used to compose SF-MASK are already cropped on the full face, showing also the head of the person and not only the eyes, nose, and mouth. Some of the datasets that use bounding box notation, however, do not. FMD, FMLD, MMD, and Moxa3K provide bounding box annotations enabling face extraction. Nonetheless, some of the bounding boxes are tight around the face. In order to obtain the full face of the subject, we enlarged the bounding box on the full face, extending the width and height of the original bounding box by $\frac{1}{6}$ of each respective dimension (width, height).

The dataset RMFRD has been generated by searching the web for images, hence it required manual annotation. In particular, we first ran a face detector [49], then we manually proceeded by removing the false positive detections. During the annotation process, the resulting bounding boxes extension has been performed as well.

3.4   The SF-MASK Testing Partition

In order to test the reliability of the dataset, an additional set of 1077 face images (584 *Mask*, 270 *No-Mask*, and 223 *Wrong-Mask*) has been created from a video sequence acquired with multiple surveillance cameras in the ICE lab[1] of the University of Verona. This dataset is our sample for the video surveillance scenario, and we used it as test set to inspect the actual accuracy of the classifiers trained over SF-MASK. The dataset has been carefully acquired, and manually annotated to have a true example of video surveillance in a real case scenario. A few samples of this partition are presented in Fig. 2.

Fig. 4. The CG approach on the SF-MASK dataset. Here are highlighted different cluster areas in which there are neighborhood similarities. In particular: the top-left green area creates a cluster with a lot of faces facing to the left side, the top-right blue area has many straight-forward looking faces, the bottom right red area contains right-facing faces, and finally, the yellow area contains faces with an angle from below or similar. The full-resolution image will be presented on the dataset web page. (Color figure online)

3.5   Visual Domain Analysis

Not all the datasets contained in SF-MASK present annotations such as head pose, gender, ethnicity or visual attributes of the masks (color, patterned etc.).

---

[1] https://www.icelab.di.univr.it/.

For this purpose, we used an unsupervised method for manifold learning and human information interaction called Counting Grids (CG) [24,28]. The CG assumes the images are represented by an histogram of counts, and provides a torus (usually flattened as a rectangle with wrap-around) where images which are close indicate a smooth transition of some of their histogram's bins. The generative model underlying a CG is not straightforward, and we suggest reading [28] for a strict mathematical analysis.

In our case, we extracted from each image different local descriptions, from quantized multi-level color SIFT descriptors [25] to latent code of variational autoencoders [33] without discovering big differences. In this paper we report the results using 300-dim SIFT codes. Then, we set up a 30 × 60 grid with an overlapping window of 11, essentially indicating the amount of overlap (in bins) where smoothness between adjacent grid locations is required.

In Fig. 4 we report the grid, where we can notice some clear patterns emerging from the dataset, with clusters of similar images and some smooth transitions from one area to another. Specifically, there are visible clusters of masked faces with different illumination conditions, native image resolution, and even similar face orientations. After a careful analysis of the grid (considering also alternative versions obtained with different parameterizations) we discovered very few images representing the typical surveillance scenario where people are observed slightly from above, with angled perspectives. To overcome this limitation we decided to extend our masked face dataset with a novel and dedicated synthetic dataset, presented in the next section.

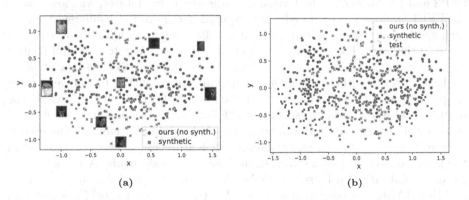

(a)   (b)

Fig. 5. Results of the Kernel PCA algorithm, comparing the SF-MASK training partition, testing partition and the synthetic partition generated as in Sect. 3.6. Fig. 5a shows that the generated data goes to fill an empty portion of the space (at the south). This enforces the idea that the generated fully synthetic data is capable to add variability to the dataset without changing its nature. In Fig. 5b, it can be seen that the test set is actually ranging all over the variance of the training data.

3.6 Synthetic Data Generation

To compensate for the variability in terms of camera viewpoints, as well as people and face masks appearance, we generated a fully synthetic dataset. Artificial human body models, textures, and backgrounds are therefore manageable via a parametric model. It is worth noting that the use of synthetic datasets to train models that cope with real test data has been already investigated, for example in re-identification [4]. Other approaches have tried to extend real masked face datasets [8,43] with custom-created data. Unfortunately, they usually leverage images extracted from large face recognition datasets and automatically apply mask patches on them, meaning that the user can only modify the appearance of the masks, without any control over the characteristics of the faces. We instead developed a generation pipeline based on MakeHuman [7], a tool designed for the prototyping of photo-realistic humanoid models. With this tool and Blender [6], we created over 12000 synthetic human bodies, with different appearances in terms of age, ethnicity, gender, and clothing, and an image size coherent with SF-MASK. We set the generation parameters to balance the gender and ethnicity distributions during the generation.

Starting from these synthetic people, we applied a face mask to 80% of the total, setting them as *Mask* samples, while the remaining 20% is considered *No-Mask*. We collected several texture patterns and randomly apply them to the face masks, in order to obtain variability in terms of face masks colors. Also, random backgrounds collected from the web have been used. The typology of masks is another of the many customisable parameters: from FFP1 (surgical mask) to FFP2 and FFP3. For the first version of this synthetic dataset, we mostly used the FFP1 face mask type. Finally, we acquired one up to three different views of each synthetic human, angled from above, to fill the gap we have discovered with the counting grid. For this task we used Blender, in order to have full control over the image generation (such as illumination conditions, occlusions, etc.).

Examples of synthetic image generation are shown in Fig. 6. The generation scripts will be released along with the dataset at the same link. To assess the usefulness of a synthetic dataset created following these guidelines, we decided to perform an analysis of the distribution of the data. Initially, all the images were resized to a 64 × 64 px resolution and feature maps were extracted with the same ResNet-50 [17] network trained for the experiments. A random sample of the data divided by subset (SF-MASK training partition, synthetic data and SF-MASK test partition) was used. We then applied Kernel PCA [36] with a linear kernel. As visible in Fig. 5b, the two subsets, the SF-MASK training partition and the synthetic one, both contribute to filling different areas of the two-dimensional space. The conjunction of the two then results in a valid representation of the image space, hence providing a suitable training dataset for the classification task. Moreover, from Fig. 5b it is evident that the SF-MASK test partition actually covers almost all the feature space, validating the quality and the variability of the test images.

Fig. 6. Example of some of the images in the SF-MASK synthetic partition. It is possible to notice the variability in ethnicity of the people as well as the different colors, patterns and types of face masks applied on the models.

4 Experiments

Two main experiments have been carried out. In the first one, we validate the expressivity of SF-MASK with and without synthetic data by training several classifiers, and testing on our test set. As a comparison, we trained the same classifiers on each of the datasets that compose SF-MASK.

We used several architectures including VGG19 [38], Resnet-50 [17], MobileNetv2 [35], and EfficientNet [40]. The results in Table 2 show that the classifiers trained on SF-MASK without synthetic data are often performing better, as in the case of MobileNet and EfficientNet. The introduction of the synthetic data gives a general boost, validating the manifold learning analysis and the successive synthetic data generation, which has focused on specific poses, that were missing in the original collection of datasets.

Table 2. Results obtained with different classifiers, trained on the different datasets, and tested with our benchmark acquired in the ICE lab (see Sec. 3.4). Since RMFRD does not have any *No-Mask* images, it was not possible to perform a comparable test.

Dataset	ResNet-50	VGG19	MobileNet	EfficientNet
MMD [20]	0.743	0.848	0.822	0.778
FMD [1]	0.809	0.820	0.834	0.837
Medical Mask [41]	0.837	0.840	0.788	0.849
FMLD [5]	0.842	0.856	0.772	0.857
Moxa3K [34]	0.849	0.835	0.846	0.839
Ours (no synth.)	0.806	0.845	0.855	0.879
Ours	**0.864**	**0.873**	**0.857**	**0.884**

In the second experiment, we performed a leave-one-out pipeline, where we trained with all but one dataset, which was used afterward as an additional testing set, besides the SF-MASK testing partition.

Results are visible in Table 3, showing that the most effective dataset among the pool composing the SF-MASK training partition is indeed the FMLD dataset. This is probably due to the fact that it is the largest dataset. These experiments have been conducted on a ResNet-50 architecture.

Table 3. Leave-one-out experiments on the datasets. The results show that FMLD is the decisive dataset for the leave-one-out strategy, probably due to the large number of images contained in it. As in Table 2, no results on RMFRD are reported here, as it does not contain any image of class *No-Mask*.

Dataset Left Out	Left Out Acc.	Test Set Acc.
MMD [20]	0.982	0.823
FMD [1]	0.961	0.822
Medical Mask [41]	0.960	0.827
FMLD [5]	0.812	0.801
Moxa3K [34]	0.928	0.835

5   Conclusions

In this paper, we present SF-MASK, a novel dataset of native low-resolution images of masked faces, divided into three classes indicating the presence, absence, or incorrect placement of the face masks. We also provide a synthetic data generation method to balance the dataset in terms of the number of images per class and attributes such as gender, ethnicity, face mask variability, illumination conditions, and camera point-of-view. This dataset has proven to be a valid benchmark for surveillance scenarios, in which the people occupy a small portion of the image, and the faces themselves occupy even fewer pixels.

Acknowledgements. This work was partially supported by the Italian MIUR within PRIN 2017, Project Grant 20172BH297: I-MALL - improving the customer experience in stores by intelligent computer vision and the POR FESR 2014-2020 Work Program of the Veneto Region (Action 1.1.4) through the project No. 10288513 titled "SAFE PLACE. Sistemi IoT per ambienti di vita salubri e sicuri".

References

1. Mask dataset. https://makeml.app/datasets/mask
2. Disposable face mask market size: Share & trends analysis report by product (protective, dust, non-woven), by application (industrial, personal), by distribution channel, by region, and segment forecasts, 2022–2030. Res. Mark. **5569707**, 100191 (2022)
3. AIZOO Tech: Aizootech facemaskdetection dataset. https://github.com/AIZOOTech/FaceMaskDetection
4. Barbosa, I.B., Cristani, M., Caputo, B., Rognhaugen, A., Theoharis, T.: Looking beyond appearances: synthetic training data for deep CNNs in re-identification. Comput. Vis. Image Underst. **167**, 50–62 (2018)
5. Batagelj, B., Peer, P., Štruc, V., Dobrišek, S.: How to correctly detect face-masks for COVID-19 from visual information? Appl. Sci. **11**(5) (2021)
6. Blender Online Community: Blender - a 3D modelling and rendering package (2018). http://www.blender.org
7. Briceno, L., Paul, G.: MakeHuman: a review of the modelling framework. In: Bagnara, S., Tartaglia, R., Albolino, S., Alexander, T., Fujita, Y. (eds.) IEA 2018. AISC, vol. 822, pp. 224–232. Springer, Cham (2019). https://doi.org/10.1007/978-3-319-96077-7_23
8. Cabani, A., Hammoudi, K., Benhabiles, H., Melkemi, M.: MaskedFace-net – a dataset of correctly/incorrectly masked face images in the context of COVID-19. Smart Health **19**, 100144 (2021)
9. Dey, S.K., Howlader, A., Deb, C.: MobileNet mask: a multi-phase face mask detection model to prevent person-to-person transmission of SARS-CoV-2. In: Kaiser, M.S., Bandyopadhyay, A., Mahmud, M., Ray, K. (eds.) Proceedings of International Conference on Trends in Computational and Cognitive Engineering. AISC, vol. 1309, pp. 603–613. Springer, Singapore (2021). https://doi.org/10.1007/978-981-33-4673-4_49
10. Draughon, G.T., Sun, P., Lynch, J.P.: Implementation of a computer vision framework for tracking and visualizing face mask usage in urban environments. In: 2020 IEEE International Smart Cities Conference (ISC2), pp. 1–8 (2020)
11. Dzisi, E.K.J., Dei, O.A.: Adherence to social distancing and wearing of masks within public transportation during the COVID 19 pandemic. Transport. Res. Interdisc. Perspect. **7**, 100191 (2020)
12. Esposito, S., Principi, N., Leung, C.C., Migliori, G.B.: Universal use of face masks for success against COVID-19: evidence and implications for prevention policies. Eur. Respir. J. **55**(6) (2020)
13. Fan, X., Jiang, M.: RetinaFaceMask: a single stage face mask detector for assisting control of the COVID-19 pandemic. In: 2021 IEEE International Conference on Systems, Man, and Cybernetics (SMC), pp. 832–837. IEEE (2021)
14. Feng, S., Shen, C., Xia, N., Song, W., Fan, M., Cowling, B.J.: Rational use of face masks in the COVID-19 pandemic. Lancet Respir. Med. **8**(5), 434–436 (2020)
15. Forouzandeh, P., O'Dowd, K., Pillai, S.C.: Face masks and respirators in the fight against the COVID-19 pandemic: an overview of the standards and testing methods. Saf. Sci. **133**, 104995 (2021)
16. Ge, S., Li, J., Ye, Q., Luo, Z.: Detecting masked faces in the wild with LLE-CNNs. In: 2017 IEEE Conference on Computer Vision and Pattern Recognition (CVPR), pp. 426–434. IEEE Computer Society, Los Alamitos, CA, USA (2017)

17. He, K., Zhang, X., Ren, S., Sun, J.: Deep residual learning for image recognition. In: 2016 IEEE Conference on Computer Vision and Pattern Recognition (CVPR), pp. 770–778 (2016)
18. Howard, J., et al.: An evidence review of face masks against COVID-19. Proc. Natl. Acad. Sci. **118**(4) (2021)
19. Huang, G.B., Mattar, M., Berg, T., Learned-Miller, E.: Labeled faces in the wild: a database for studying face recognition in unconstrained environments. In: Workshop on faces in 'Real-Life' Images: Detection, Alignment, and Recognition (2008)
20. Humans in the Loop: Medical mask dataset. https://humansintheloop.org/medical-mask-dataset
21. Jan, Y., Sohel, F., Shiratuddin, M.F., Wong, K.W.: WNet: joint multiple head detection and head pose estimation from a spectator crowd image. In: Carneiro, G., You, S. (eds.) ACCV 2018. LNCS, vol. 11367, pp. 484–493. Springer, Cham (2019). https://doi.org/10.1007/978-3-030-21074-8_38
22. Karras, T., Laine, S., Aila, T.: A style-based generator architecture for generative adversarial networks (2018)
23. Le, Y., Yang, X.: Tiny imagenet visual recognition challenge (2015). https://www.kaggle.com/c/tiny-imagenet
24. Lovato, P., Perina, A., Cheng, D.S., Segalin, C., Sebe, N., Cristani, M.: We like it! Mapping image preferences on the counting grid. In: 2013 IEEE International Conference on Image Processing, pp. 2892–2896. IEEE (2013)
25. Lowe, D.G.: Object recognition from local scale-invariant features. In: Proceedings of the seventh IEEE International Conference on Computer Vision, vol. 2, pp. 1150–1157. IEEE (1999)
26. Malik, S., Mihm, B., Reichelt, M.: The impact of face masks on interpersonal trust in times of COVID-19. Sci. Rep. **11**(1), 1–9 (2021)
27. Mitze, T., Kosfeld, R., Rode, J., Wälde, K.: Face masks considerably reduce COVID-19 cases in Germany. Proc. Natl. Acad. Sci. **117**(51), 32293–32301 (2020)
28. Perina, A., Jojic, N.: Image analysis by counting on a grid. In: CVPR 2011, pp. 1985–1992. IEEE (2011)
29. Phillips, N., et al.: The coronavirus is here to stay-here's what that means. Nature **590**(7846), 382–384 (2021)
30. Pooja, S., Preeti, S.: Face mask detection using AI. In: Khosla, P.K., Mittal, M., Sharma, D., Goyal, L.M. (eds.) Predictive and Preventive Measures for Covid-19 Pandemic. AIS, pp. 293–305. Springer, Singapore (2021). https://doi.org/10.1007/978-981-33-4236-1_16
31. Qin, B., Li, D.: Identifying facemask-wearing condition using image super-resolution with classification network to prevent COVID-19. Sensors **20**(18) (2020)
32. Ram, N., Gray, D.: Mass surveillance in the age of COVID-19. J. Law Biosci. **7**(1), lsaa023 (2020)
33. Ramesh, A., et al.: Zero-shot text-to-image generation. In: International Conference on Machine Learning, pp. 8821–8831. PMLR (2021)
34. Roy, B., Nandy, S., Ghosh, D., Dutta, D., Biswas, P., Das, T.: Moxa: a deep learning based unmanned approach for real-time monitoring of people wearing medical masks. Trans. Indian Natl. Acad. Eng. **5**, 509–518 (2020)
35. Sandler, M., Howard, A.G., Zhu, M., Zhmoginov, A., Chen, L.C.: Mobilenetv 2: inverted residuals and linear bottlenecks. In: 2018 IEEE/CVF Conference on Computer Vision and Pattern Recognition, pp. 4510–4520 (2018)

36. Schölkopf, B., Smola, A., Müller, K.-R.: Kernel principal component analysis. In: Gerstner, W., Germond, A., Hasler, M., Nicoud, J.-D. (eds.) ICANN 1997. LNCS, vol. 1327, pp. 583–588. Springer, Heidelberg (1997). https://doi.org/10.1007/BFb0020217
37. Shorfuzzaman, M., Hossain, M.S., Alhamid, M.F.: Towards the sustainable development of smart cities through mass video surveillance: a response to the COVID-19 pandemic. Sustain. Urban Areas **64**, 102582 (2021)
38. Simonyan, K., Zisserman, A.: Very deep convolutional networks for large-scale image recognition. In: International Conference on Learning Representations (2015)
39. Singh, S., Ahuja, U., Kumar, M., Kumar, K., Sachdeva, M.: Face mask detection using YOLOv3 and faster R-CNN models: COVID-19 environment. Multimedia Tools Appl. **80**(13), 19753–19768 (2021). https://doi.org/10.1007/s11042-021-10711-8
40. Tan, M., Le, Q.: EfficientNet: rethinking model scaling for convolutional neural networks. In: International Conference on Machine Learning, pp. 6105–6114. PMLR (2019)
41. Waghe, S.: Medical mask dataset (kaggle). https://www.kaggle.com/datasets/shreyashwaghe/medical-mask-dataset
42. Wang, B., Zheng, J., Chen, C.L.P.: A survey on masked facial detection methods and datasets for fighting against COVID-19. IEEE Trans. Artif. Intell. 1 (2022)
43. Wang, Z., et al.: Masked face recognition dataset and application (2020)
44. Wang, Z., Bovik, A.C., Sheikh, H.R., Simoncelli, E.P.: Image quality assessment: from error visibility to structural similarity. IEEE Trans. Image Process. **13**(4), 600–612 (2004)
45. World Health Organization, et al.: COVID-19 infection prevention and control living guideline: mask use in community settings, 22 December 2021. Technical report, World Health Organization (2021)
46. Yang, S., Luo, P., Loy, C.C., Tang, X.: Wider face: a face detection benchmark. In: Proceedings of the IEEE Conference on Computer Vision and Pattern Recognition, pp. 5525–5533 (2016)
47. Yi, D., Lei, Z., Liao, S., Li, S.Z.: Learning face representation from scratch. arXiv preprint arXiv:1411.7923 (2014)
48. Zeng, D., Veldhuis, R.N.J., Spreeuwers, L.J.: A survey of face recognition techniques under occlusion. IET Biom. **10**, 581–606 (2021)
49. Zhang, K., Zhang, Z., Li, Z., Qiao, Y.: Joint face detection and alignment using multitask cascaded convolutional networks. IEEE Sig. Process. Lett. **23**(10), 1499–1503 (2016)
50. Zhang, K., Zhang, Z., Wang, H., Li, Z., Qiao, Y., Liu, W.: Detecting faces using inside cascaded contextual CNN. In: Proceedings of the IEEE International Conference on Computer Vision, pp. 3171–3179 (2017)

Lightweight Human Pose Estimation Using Loss Weighted by Target Heatmap

Shiqi Li[iD] and Xiang Xiang[✉][iD]

Key Laboratory of Image Processing and Intelligent Control, Ministry of Education,
School of Artificial Intelligence and Automation,
Huazhong University of Science and Technology, Wuhan 430074, China
xex@hust.edu.cn

Abstract. Recent research on human pose estimation exploits complex structures to improve performance on benchmark datasets, ignoring the resource overhead and inference speed when the model is actually deployed. In this paper, we lighten the computation cost and parameters of the deconvolution head network in SimpleBaseline and introduce an attention mechanism that utilizes original, inter-level, and intra-level information to intensify the accuracy. Additionally, we propose a novel loss function called heatmap weighting loss, which generates weights for each pixel on the heatmap that makes the model more focused on keypoints. Experiments demonstrate our method achieves a balance between performance, resource volume, and inference speed. Specifically, our method can achieve 65.3 AP score on COCO test-dev, while the inference speed is 55 FPS and 18 FPS on the mobile GPU and CPU, respectively.

Keywords: Human pose estimation · Visual attention · Lightweight · Neural networks

1 Introduction

Human pose estimation aims to locate the body joints from image or video data. It has received increasing attention from the computer vision community in the past couple of years and has been utilized in various applications such as animation [12], sports [2,26], and healthcare [13]. Due to the development of deep convolutional neural networks, recent works achieve significant progress on this topic [4,18,21,27].

In order to get higher accuracy, many existing methods usually comprise wide and deep network architectures because they could bring powerful representation capacity. This leads to tremendous parameters and a huge number of floating-point operations (FLOPs). However, the most common operating environments for pose estimation applications are resource-constrained edge devices such as smartphones or robots. The incremental computing cost and parameter memory are crucial barriers to the deployment of pose estimation.

Also with China's Belt & Road Joint Lab on Measur. & Contr. Tech., and National Key Lab of Multi-Spectral Information Intelligent Processing Technology.

J.-J. Rousseau and B. Kapralos (Eds.): ICPR 2022 Workshops, LNCS 13643, pp. 64–78, 2023.
https://doi.org/10.1007/978-3-031-37660-3_5

There is also some work focus on the lightweight human pose estimation method. Lite-HRNet [29] follows High-Resolution Net (HRNet) [21] and reduces its parameters and computation cost. Lite-HRNet achieves extremely low parameters and FLOPs, however, the theoretical lightweight does not always mean fast in practice. The parallelism of the multi-branch structure does not reach the theoretical efficiency and the cross-resolution weight computation also slows down the inference of the model. It is even slower than the HRNet during actual running. Benefit from network architecture search (NAS) technology, ViPNAS [28] reaches a notable balance between accuracy and speed, but its performance while handling picture tasks on the CPU is not satisfactory. Other methods are short in terms of parameter quantity [14]. Research in the lightweight human pose estimation area is still inadequate.

The SimpleBaseline [27] is an elegant and effective method for human pose estimation, they provide the capacity of deconvolution layers in this problem. Based on their successful work, we focus on the design of lightweight and simple network architecture for human pose estimation. First, we use a lightweight network MobileNetV3 [9] as the backbone in our model, rather than the huge ResNet [8]. As the latest model in MobileNet series [9,10,20] MobileNetV3 has shown its performance in many computer vision tasks. Then we analyse the parameters and computation cost in the whole model and notice the deconvolution layers contain the dominant resources. Inspired by the design of the MobileNet series, we change the normal deconvolution layers to a depthwise deconvolution layer following a pointwise convolution layer. To compensate for the performance degradation caused by lightweighting, we introduce an attention mechanism. The attention block utilizes channel, spatial and original information of the input feature maps to enhance the performance. Besides, we observe that Mean Square Error (MSE) loss is widely used by existing methods during the training stage. MSE loss just calculates the average error for different pixels on the heatmaps, without reflecting the inhomogenous from different locations. We propose a novel loss function called heatmap weighting loss to generate weights for every pixel on heatmaps that is used to calculate the final error.

In short, our contribution can be summarized as followed.

- We simplify the deconvolution head network in SimpleBaseline and present an attention mechanism that exploits channel, spatial and global representations to benefit the performance of the lightweight architecture.
- We propose a novel loss function - heatmap weighting loss that explores the information from ground truth heatmaps to improve keypoints localization.

2 Related Work

2.1 Human Pose Estimation

Human posture estimation has been an active research problem in the last decades. Before the rise of deep learning, human pose estimation was mainly based on graph structure models, using picture global features or handcraft filters to detect and localize the keypoints of human body [19]. Since Toshev et al. [23] propose DeepPose, which uses the deep neural network to regress the keypoints locations, the neural network based approach becomes mainstream. Newell et al. [18] propose Hourglass, which consists of multi-stage stacked hourglass networks, it is a milestone on the MPII [1] benchmark dataset. Chen et al. [4] propose Cascaded Pyramid Network (CPN), which is the champion of COCO 2017 keypoint challenge. CPN uses a GlobalNet [4] to estimate simple keypoints and handle complex keypoints with a RefineNet [4]. Xiao et al. [27] propose SimpleBaseline, which is a simple yet effective method composed of a backbone and several deconvolution layers. Sun et al. [21] present a novel High-Resolution Net to maintain high-resolution representation by connecting multi-resolution convolutions in parallel and conducting repeated multi-scale feature map fusion. Cai et al. [3] introduce Residual Steps Network (RSN) to learn more delicate local feature by intra-level information fusion, and propose Pose Refine Machine (PRM) to refine the feature map by attention mechanism. This method is the winner of COCO 2019 keypoint challenge.

2.2 Lightweight Network Design

Design deep neural network architecture for achieving a trade-off between efficiency and accuracy has been an active research topic, especially in industrial research. In recent years, a large number of compact network architectures have been proposed. Xception [5] uses depthwise separable convolution operation to reduce parameters and computation. MobileNets series [9,10,20] are also based on depthwise convolution and pointwise convolution. MobileNetV2 [20] present inverted residual block and MobileNetV3 [9] exploit NAS method searching a optimal structure that has better performance and fewer FLOPs. ShuffleNet [30] proposes a channel shuffle operation for information interaction between feature map groups. ShuffleNetV2 [17] studies the lightweight network design principles and modifies the ShuffleNet according to the proposed guidelines. GhostNet [7] investigates the correlation and redundancy between feature maps and presents a cheap operation to reduce the computation of pointwise convolution. The development of lightweight networks has great significance for our work, on the one hand, we can directly use a more powerful lightweight network as a backbone in our model, on the other hand, we can draw on the idea of compact network design in our downstream tasks.

2.3 Visual Attention Mechanism

Attention mechanism has shown powerful performance in many computer vision tasks such as image classification, scene segmentation, objection detection, and optical character recognition (OCR). Wang et al. [24] propose Non-Local Networks which introduce self-attention to capture long-range dependencies. Hu et al. [11] present Squeeze-and-Excitation Networks (SENet), using weight learned from global information to excite or suppress different channels, which is the champion of ILSVRC 2017. Li et al. [15] expand SENet and propose Selective

Kernel Networks (SKNet), using feature maps generated by multiple kernel sizes to gather attention value. Woo et al. [25] propose Convolutional Block Attention Module (CBAM) to exploit both channel and spatial information to refine the feature map. Most attention modules can be easily embedded in pose estimation network without introducing too much extra computation while improving the performance of the network. In our work, we consider different attention mechanisms and revise the CBAM by simplifying the spatial partition and adding an identity connection to benefit keypoints localization.

3   Methodology

3.1   Lightweight Deconvolution Head Network

Deconvolution head network [27] is a different method to rehabilitate high-resolution feature maps which was introduced in SimpleBaseline. Before that, the combination of upsampling and convolution layer is the dominant technology to generate high-resolution feature maps [4,18]. In the deconvolution head network, a deconvolution layer that could learn the upsampling parameters from input data during training achieves upsampling and convolution parameters in a single operation.

The computational cost of a standard deconvolution layer multiplicatively depends on the size of kernel $D_K \times D_K$, the number of input channels C_{in}, the number of output channels C_{out}, and the size of feature maps $W \times H$. Despite the first layer for channel compression and the last layer for generating output feature maps, the total computation in a l layer deconvolution head network is

$$\sum_i^l D_{K_i} \times D_{K_i} \times C_{in_i} \times C_{out_i} \times W_i \times H_i \qquad (1)$$

Based on the design in MobileNets, we replace the standard deconvolution layer with a depthwise deconvolution layer following a pointwise convolution layer. Figure 1 illustrates the structure of our lightweight deconvolution head network. Depthwise deconvolution applies a single filter on each channel for upsampling and producing the new representations in high-resolution feature maps, while pointwise convolution provides a bridge for information fusion across channels. The influence of the output channels on the parameters and computation is eliminated in depthwise deconvolution, and in pointwise convolution, the kernel size will no longer be a factor. The computation cost of our new deconvolution head network can be written as

$$\sum_i^l D_{K_i} \times D_{K_i} \times C_{in_i} \times W_i \times H_i + C_{in_i} \times C_{out_i} \times W_i \times H_i \qquad (2)$$

The number of parameters is proportional to the computation cost, just remove the size of feature map. Following the setting in SimpleBaseline, we set the layers

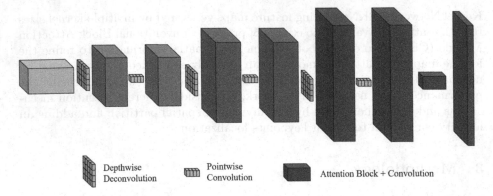

Depthwise
Deconvolution

Pointwise
Convolution

Attention Block + Convolution

Fig. 1. Illustration of lightweight deconvolution head network. Alternating depthwise deconvolutions and pointwise convolutions are stacked for reconstructing high-resolution feature maps. Attention block is applied after the last pointwise convolution.

to 3, kernel size to 4, and the number of channels to 256 in all layers. Thus we can get a reduction in computation cost of

$$
\frac{\sum_i^3 4 \times 4 \times 256 \times W_i \times H_i + 256 \times 256 \times W_i \times H_i}{\sum_i^3 4 \times 4 \times 256 \times 256 \times W_i \times H_i} \tag{3}
$$
$$
= \frac{17}{256} \approx \frac{1}{16}.
$$

3.2   Attention Mechanism

To improve the capacity of our lightweight deconvolution head network, we introduce an attention mechanism. Motivated by the work of SENet, we use an adaptive average pooling to aggregate spatial information in each channel. After generating channel representations, two pointwise convolution layers are used to calculate the correlation between channels. To reduce the parameters, the input feature dimension C is squeezed to C/r after the first convolution, where r is the squeeze ratio. Before finally broadcasting along spatial dimension and multiplying with the original feature map, a hard sigmoid function is utilized to normalize the weight. Define the feature map as f, a convolution layer with p output channels and kernel size of $m \times n$ as $\mathrm{F}_p^{m \times n}$, the hard sigmoid as $\sigma(\cdot)$, the global average pooling as $\mathrm{GAP}(\cdot)$, and the element-wise multiplication as $\odot$. The channel attention $\mathcal{H}_{channel}(\cdot)$ is computed as:

$$
\mathcal{H}_{channel}(f) = f \odot \sigma(\mathrm{F}_C^{1 \times 1}(\mathrm{F}_{C/r}^{1 \times 1}(\mathrm{GAP}(f)))) \tag{4}
$$

Since human pose estimation is a space-sensitive task, a spatial attention mechanism can help to better mine the information in spatial dimension. To converge information in different channels, we apply a pointwise convolution to

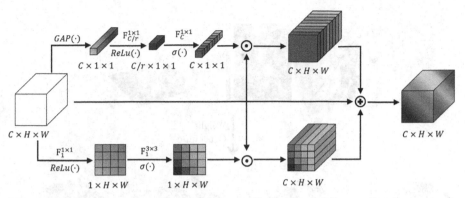

$F_p^{m \times n}$ convolution with m×n kernel p channels $\sigma(\cdot)$ hard sigmoid   ⊙ element-wise multiplication   ⊕ element-wise addition

Fig. 2. Illustration of attention architecture. The upper branch is channel attention, the lower branch is designed for spatial dimension, and the middle branch is an identity connection to keep original information.

get a linearly combined representation. After that, a standard convolution is used to produce the spatial attention map. A hard sigmoid layer is also used to rescale the activation values. Following the definition of the channel portion, the spatial attention $\mathcal{H}_{spatial}(\cdot)$ is written as:

$$\mathcal{H}_{spatial}(f) = f \odot \sigma(F_1^{3\times3}(F_1^{1\times1}(f))) \tag{5}$$

For the arrangement of attention modules, we use a parallel structure, as shown in Fig. 2. Channel attention and spatial attention are applied to the feature map individually and an identity connection is also employed. The identity mapping protects local features from being corrupted by dimensional compression in the attention block. Meanwhile, channel attention exploits inter-level representation to benefit keypoints identification and spatial attention improves keypoints by optimizing spatial information. Finally, the feature maps in three branches are added to get the output feature. Our attention mechanism can be formulated as:

$$f_{out} = f_{in} + \mathcal{H}_{channel}(f_{in}) + \mathcal{H}_{spatial}(f_{in}) \tag{6}$$

3.3 Heatmap Weighting Loss

In the training phase, MSE is commonly used as the loss function [4,18,21,27]. Beyond the previous work, we argue that the weight of the pixels at different locations on the heatmaps should be various. The loss function should focus more on the points with larger values on the heatmaps, which means devoting more attention to those pixels that are closer to the keypoints. Based on this thinking, we propose heatmap weighting loss which generates weight for each

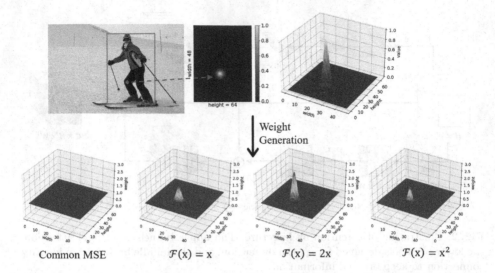

Fig. 3. Proposed heatmap weighting loss. The weight of each pixel is comprised of a value calculated from the label heatmap and a constant.

pixel by adopting the transformation function on the ground truth heatmap, as shown in Fig. 3. Our loss function presents as

$$L = \frac{1}{J} \sum_{j=1}^{J} \left[\mathcal{F}(P_j^{GT}) + 1 \right] \odot \| P_j - P_j^{GT} \|_2 \tag{7}$$

where J is the number of keypoints, P and P^{GT} are predicted heatmap and ground truth heatmap respectively, $\mathcal{F}(\cdot)$ is weight generation function, and $\odot$ denotes element-wise multiplication.

For the selection of weight generation function, in consideration of the target heatmaps are usually sampled from a two-dimensional Gaussian distribution [22]. We select several convex functions on $[0, 1]$ interval such as linear function, power function, and exponential function to generate the weights and evaluate their performance. See Sect. 4.3 for details.

4   Experiments

We evaluate our method on COCO [16] and MPII [1] datasets. Following the two-stage top-down paradigm [21,27], our approach estimates keypoints confidence maps from the detected person boundary box. We report the comparisons with other methods and also conduct inference speed test and ablation studies on these datasets. The project page[1] has been set up with programs available.

---
[1] https://github.com/HAIV-Lab/ICPR22w.

4.1 Experimental Setup

Dataset and Metric. COCO dataset contains over 200K images and 250K person instances with 17 keypoints. Our model is trained on the train2017 set (includes 57K images and 150K person instances) and validated on the val2017 set (includes 5K images). MPII includes around 25K images containing over 40K people with annotated body joints. We adopt object keypoint similarity (OKS) based mean average precision (AP) to evaluate the performance on COCO, for MPII, the standard PCKh (head-normalized percentage of correct keypoints) is used.

Image Cropping. The human box is expanded in height or width to reach a fixed aspect ratio, e.g., height:width = 4:3. Then we crop the box area from the image and finally resize it to a certain resolution such as 256×192 for COCO and 256×256 for MPII.

Data Augmentation. We apply a series of data augmentation operations to make the model learn scale invariance and rotation invariance. Augmentation strategy includes flip, random rotation ($[-80°, 80°]$), random scale ($[0.5, 1.5]$), and half body augmentation which keeps only the upper or the lower body at random for COCO.

Training. We use Adam optimizer mini-batch size 64 to train our network, the initial learning rate is 5e−4 and reduced by a factor of 10 at the 170th and 200th epoch. The training process is terminated within 210 epochs. The warm-up strategy with a liner warm ratio of 0.001 is used in the beginning 500 iterators [6]. Our experiments are conducted on a single NVIDIA 3090 GPU.

Testing. In order to minimize the variance of prediction, following the normal practice [18], we average the heatmaps predicted from the original and flipped images. A quarter of a pixel offset in the direction from the highest response to the second-highest response is applied before the predicted keypoint locations transform back to the original coordinate space of the input image.

4.2 Results

COCO Val. Table 1 reports the comparison results of our method and other state-of-the-art methods. Our method, trained from input resolution with 256×192, achieves a 65.8 AP score. Compared to ShuffleNetV2, our method improves AP by 5.9 points with 42% FLOPs. We use about 35% of the parameters and computational cost while obtaining a gain of 1.2 AP points compared

Table 1. Comparison on COCO val2017 set.

Method	Backbone	Input Size	#Para	GFLOPs	AP	AP^{50}	AP^{75}	AP^M	AP^L	AR
SimpleBaseline	MobileNetV2	256 × 192	9.6M	1.59	64.6	87.4	72.3	61.1	71.2	70.7
SimpleBaseline	MobileNetV2	384 × 288	9.6M	3.57	67.3	87.9	74.3	62.8	74.7	72.9
SimpleBaseline	MobileNetV3	256 × 192	8.7M	1.47	65.9	87.8	74.1	62.6	72.2	72.1
SimpleBaseline	ShuffleNetV2	256 × 192	7.6M	1.37	59.9	85.4	66.3	56.5	66.2	66.4
SimpleBaseline	ShuffleNetV2	384 × 288	7.6M	3.08	63.6	86.5	70.5	59.5	70.7	69.7
ViPNAS [28]	MobileNetV3	256 × 192	2.8M	0.69	67.8	87.2	76.0	64.7	74.0	75.2
Small HRNet	HRNet-W16	256 × 192	1.3M	0.54	55.2	83.7	62.4	52.3	61.0	62.1
Small HRNet	HRNet-W16	384 × 288	1.3M	1.21	56.0	83.8	63.0	52.4	62.6	62.6
Lite-HRNet	Lite-HRNet-18	256 × 192	1.1M	0.20	64.8	86.7	73.0	62.1	70.5	71.2
Lite-HRNet	Lite-HRNet-18	384 × 288	1.1M	0.45	67.6	87.8	75.0	64.5	73.7	73.7
Lite-HRNet	Lite-HRNet-30	256 × 192	1.8M	0.31	67.2	88.0	75.0	64.3	73.1	73.3
Lite-HRNet	Lite-HRNet-30	384 × 288	1.8M	0.70	70.4	88.7	77.7	67.5	76.3	76.2
Ours	MobileNetV3	256 × 192	3.1M	0.58	65.8	87.7	74.1	62.6	72.4	72.1
Ours	MobileNetV3	384 × 288	3.1M	1.30	69.9	88.8	77.5	66.0	76.7	75.5

to MobileNetV2. Our method matches the performance of SimpleBaseline using MobileNetV3 as the backbone, with only 35% FLOPs and 39% parameters. Compared to Small HRNet-W16 [29], we improve 10.6 AP score. Our method also outperforms the Lite-HRNet-18 with 1.0 AP points. There are little gaps (1.3 points and 2.0 points) between our approach and the state-of-the-art methods, Lite-HRNet-30 and ViPNAS, respectively, but our method achieves a much higher inference speed. See Sect. 4.4 for details. It is worth noting that the goal of this work is to introduce a simple lightweight human pose estimation network with high inference speed rather than improving the score of existing SOTA approach on benchmark datasets. For the input size of 384 × 288, our method achieves 69.9 AP score. Some prediction results are visualized in Fig. 4.

COCO Test-Dev. Table 2 reports the comparison results of our models and other lightweight methods. Our networks achieve 65.3 and 69.2 with the input size of 256 × 192 and 384 × 288, respectively. Our approach outperforms other methods except for Lite-HRNet-30 in AP scores, and our method is closer to SOTA with larger input size.

MPII Val. Comprehensive results on MPII are reported in Table 3. Our method achieves 85.9 PCKh with a standard 256 × 256 input size, outperforms the ShuffleNetV2, MobileNetV2 by 3.1 and 0.5 points, respectively.

Fig. 4. Prediction results on COCO val.

Table 2. Comparison on COCO test-dev2017 set.

Method	Backbone	Input Size	#Params	GFLOPs	AP	AP^{50}	AP^{75}	AP^M	AP^L	AR
SimpleBaseline	MobileNetV2	256 × 192	9.6M	1.59	64.1	89.4	71.8	60.8	69.8	70.1
SimpleBaseline	MobileNetV2	384 × 288	9.6M	3.57	66.8	90.0	74.0	62.6	73.3	72.3
SimpleBaseline	ShuffleNetV2	256 × 192	7.6M	1.37	59.5	87.4	66.0	56.6	64.7	66.0
SimpleBaseline	ShuffleNetV2	384 × 288	7.6M	3.08	62.9	88.5	69.4	58.9	69.3	68.9
Small HRNet [29]	HRNet-W16	384 × 288	1.3M	1.21	55.2	85.8	61.4	51.7	61.2	61.5
Lite-HRNet [29]	Lite-HRNet-18	256 × 192	1.1M	0.20	63.7	88.6	71.1	61.1	68.6	69.7
Lite-HRNet	Lite-HRNet-18	384 × 288	1.1M	0.45	66.9	89.4	74.4	64.0	72.2	72.6
Lite-HRNet	Lite-HRNet-30	256 × 192	1.8M	0.31	66.7	88.9	74.9	63.9	71.9	72.7
Lite-HRNet	Lite-HRNet-30	384 × 288	1.8M	0.70	69.7	90.7	77.5	66.9	75.0	75.4
Ours	MobileNetV3	256 × 192	3.1M	0.58	65.3	89.7	73.4	62.6	70.4	71.3
Ours	MobileNetV3	384 × 288	3.1M	1.30	69.2	90.6	76.9	65.8	74.9	74.7

4.3 Weight Generation Function

We experimentally study the influence of heatmap weighting loss. We evaluate different weight generation functions and compare them with the traditional MSE loss. Table 4 reports the results on COCO val with the input size of 256 × 192.

Table 3. Comparison on MPII val set.

Method	Backbone	#Para	GFLOPs	Head	Shld	Elbow	Wrist	Hip	Knee	Ankle	PCKh
SimpleBaseline	MobileNetV2	9.6M	2.12	95.3	93.5	85.8	78.5	85.9	79.3	74.4	85.4
SimpleBaseline	ShuffleNetV2	7.6M	1.83	94.6	92.4	83.0	75.6	82.8	75.9	69.2	82.8
Lite-HRNet [29]	Lite-HRNet-18	1.1M	0.27	96.1	93.7	85.5	79.2	87.0	80.0	75.1	85.9
Lite-HRNet	Lite-HRNet-30	1.8M	0.42	96.3	94.7	87.0	80.6	87.1	82.0	77.0	87.0
Ours	MobileNetV3	3.1M	0.77	95.6	93.9	85.1	79.5	86.3	80.4	75.5	85.9

Table 4. Comparison of different weight generation functions.

Weight Generation Function	AP	AP^{50}	AP^{75}	AR
None	65.56	87.36	73.97	71.65
$\mathcal{F}(x) = x$	65.83	87.70	74.06	72.06
$\mathcal{F}(x) = 2x$	65.59	87.37	74.01	71.90
$\mathcal{F}(x) = x^2$	65.65	87.70	73.96	71.81
$\mathcal{F}(x) = e^x$	65.70	87.66	73.74	71.79

We can find that the AP score got the most significant gain of 0.27 points when using the most simple endomorphism as the weight generation function. When we increase the transformation ratio in linear mapping, the gain becomes negligible (only 0.03 AP score). We also attempt the square and exponential functions that obtain gains of 0.09 and 0.14 points, respectively. Although the gain from our heatmap weighting loss function is not significant now, it provides a new optimization idea for human pose estimation. The notion of our heatmap weighting loss can be considered as a kind of adjustment of the handcrafted two-dimensional Gaussian distribution heatmap to make it approximate the actual distribution of the human keypoint.

4.4   Inference Speed

Operations (OPs) denote the number of computations required for the forward inference of the model and reflect the demand for hardware computational units. While float is the most commonly used data type, FLOPs becomes the general reference for evaluating model size. The actual inference speed on hardware is a complex issue. It is not only affected by the amount of computation, but also by many factors such as the amount of memory access, hardware characteristics, and system environment. For this reason, we study the actual inference speed of different human pose estimation models on an edge device.

Table 5. Comparison of inference speed.

Model	AP	FPS (GPU)	FPS (CPU)	GFLOPs
MobileNetV2 [20]+SBL [27]	64.6	57.6	19.3	1.59
ShuffleNetV2 [17]+SBL	59.9	51.8	20.2	1.37
ViPNAS [28]	67.8	22.6	4.6	0.69
Lite-HRNet18 [29]	64.8	12.8	10.3	0.20
Lite-HRNet30 [29]	67.2	7.5	6.2	0.31
Ours	65.8	55.2	18.3	0.58

Our test platform is a laptop equipped with Intel Core i7-10750H CPU and NVIDIA GTX 1650Ti (Notebooks) GPU. We perform 50 rounds of inference with each model and calculate the average iterations per second. To reduce the error, the initial 5 iterations are not included in the statistics. The time for data pre-processing is eliminated and we keep the same input images from COCO val for each model with 256×192 resolution. We conduct several sets of experiments and calculate the average FPS as the final result. Table 5 and Fig. 5 summarize the results of our speed experiment.

Our experiments confirm that FLOPs do not fully respond to inference speed. The GFLOPs of Lite-HRNet-18 and Lite-HRNet-30 are impressive 0.20 and 0.31, respectively. However, dragged down by the multi-branch parallel convolution architecture, the lite-HRNet series only achieves about 10 FPS on both CPU and GPU platforms. Their inference speed on GPU device is even slower than the speed of MobileNetV2, ShuffleNetV2, and our method on CPU platform. ViPNAS, the most accurate method, reaches 22.6 FPS on the GPU, but less than 5 FPS on the CPU. Our method achieves 55.3 FPS on GPU, which is 7.4 times higher than Lite-HRNet-30 and 2.4 times higher than ViPNAS. On the CPU platform, the FPS of our method is 18.3, about 4 times higher than that of ViPNAS. Our approach achieves higher accuracy while being essentially the same speed as MobileNetV2 and ShuffleNetV2. Inference speed experiments demonstrate that our method is more friendly to the mobile device and better suited to real-world applications.

4.5 Ablation Study

In this part, we validate the improvement of our attention architecture by performing ablation experiments on COCO val set with 256×192 input size, as shown in Table 1. We compare the prior attention mechanism SE-Block, CBAM, and our attention module (Table 6).

Our approach outperforms the other two modules in AP score, which implies trimming the common attention block designed for image classification before applying it to a certain task is necessary.

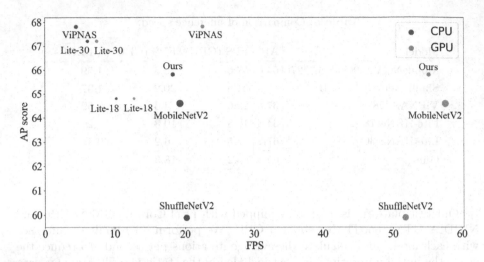

Fig. 5. Speed-accuracy trade-off on COCO val. The circular area represents the number of parameters of the corresponding model.

Table 6. Comparison of different attention blocks.

Attention	AP	AP^{50}	AP^{75}	AR
None	65.29	87.44	73.28	71.53
SE-Block [11]	65.71	87.57	74.10	71.93
CBAM [25]	65.77	87.92	74.19	71.02
Ours	65.83	87.70	74.06	72.06

5   Conclusion

In this paper, we propose a lightweight human pose estimation network with high inference speed by simplifying the deconvolution head network in Simple-Baseline and applying an attention mechanism that exploits channel, spatial and global representations to improve the performance. We also present a novel loss function, heatmap weighting loss, which explores the information from ground truth heatmaps to benefit keypoints localization. Our method achieves a balance between performance, resource volume, and inference speed. We hope that this work gives a new idea for lightweight human pose estimation.

Acknowledgement. This research was supported by HUST Independent Innovation Research Fund (2021XXJS096), Sichuan University Interdisciplinary Innovation Research Fund (RD-03-202108), "Natural Science Fund of Hubei Province (2022Q252)", "Alibaba Inno. Res. program (CRAQ7WHZ11220001-20978282)", and the Key Lab of Image Processing and Intelligent Control, Ministry of Education, China.

References

1. Andriluka, M., Pishchulin, L., Gehler, P., Schiele, B.: 2D human pose estimation: new benchmark and state of the art analysis. In: Proceedings of the IEEE Conference on computer Vision and Pattern Recognition, pp. 3686–3693 (2014)
2. Bridgeman, L., Volino, M., Guillemaut, J.Y., Hilton, A.: Multi-person 3D pose estimation and tracking in sports. In: Proceedings of the IEEE/CVF Conference on Computer Vision and Pattern Recognition (CVPR) Workshops, June 2019
3. Cai, Y., et al.: Learning delicate local representations for multi-person pose estimation. In: Vedaldi, A., Bischof, H., Brox, T., Frahm, J.-M. (eds.) ECCV 2020. LNCS, vol. 12348, pp. 455–472. Springer, Cham (2020). https://doi.org/10.1007/978-3-030-58580-8_27
4. Chen, Y., Wang, Z., Peng, Y., Zhang, Z., Yu, G., Sun, J.: Cascaded pyramid network for multi-person pose estimation. In: Proceedings of the IEEE Conference on Computer Vision and Pattern Recognition, pp. 7103–7112 (2018)
5. Chollet, F.: Xception: deep learning with depthwise separable convolutions. In: Proceedings of the IEEE Conference on Computer Vision and Pattern Recognition, pp. 1251–1258 (2017)
6. Contributors, M.: Openmmlab pose estimation toolbox and benchmark (2020). https://github.com/open-mmlab/mmpose
7. Han, K., Wang, Y., Tian, Q., Guo, J., Xu, C., Xu, C.: Ghostnet: more features from cheap operations. In: Proceedings of the IEEE/CVF Conference on Computer Vision and Pattern Recognition, pp. 1580–1589 (2020)
8. He, K., Zhang, X., Ren, S., Sun, J.: Deep residual learning for image recognition. In: Proceedings of the IEEE Conference on Computer Vision and Pattern Recognition, pp. 770–778 (2016)
9. Howard, A., et al.: Searching for mobilenetv3. In: Proceedings of the IEEE/CVF International Conference on Computer Vision, pp. 1314–1324 (2019)
10. Howard, A.G., et al.: Mobilenets: efficient convolutional neural networks for mobile vision applications. arXiv preprint arXiv:1704.04861 (2017)
11. Hu, J., Shen, L., Sun, G.: Squeeze-and-excitation networks. In: Proceedings of the IEEE Conference on Computer Vision and Pattern Recognition, pp. 7132–7141 (2018)
12. Kumarapu, L., Mukherjee, P.: Animepose: multi-person 3D pose estimation and animation. Pattern Recogn. Lett. **147**, 16–24 (2021)
13. Li, T., et al.: Automatic timed up-and-go sub-task segmentation for Parkinson's disease patients using video-based activity classification. IEEE Trans. Neural Syst. Rehabil. Eng. **26**(11), 2189–2199 (2018). https://doi.org/10.1109/TNSRE.2018.2875738
14. Li, W., et al.: Rethinking on multi-stage networks for human pose estimation. arXiv preprint arXiv:1901.00148 (2019)
15. Li, X., Wang, W., Hu, X., Yang, J.: Selective kernel networks. In: Proceedings of the IEEE/CVF Conference on Computer Vision and Pattern Recognition, pp. 510–519 (2019)
16. Lin, T.-Y., et al.: Microsoft COCO: common objects in context. In: Fleet, D., Pajdla, T., Schiele, B., Tuytelaars, T. (eds.) ECCV 2014. LNCS, vol. 8693, pp. 740–755. Springer, Cham (2014). https://doi.org/10.1007/978-3-319-10602-1_48
17. Jan, Y., Sohel, F., Shiratuddin, M.F., Wong, K.W.: WNet: joint multiple head detection and head pose estimation from a spectator crowd image. In: Carneiro, G., You, S. (eds.) ACCV 2018. LNCS, vol. 11367, pp. 484–493. Springer, Cham (2019). https://doi.org/10.1007/978-3-030-21074-8_38

18. Newell, A., Yang, K., Deng, J.: Stacked hourglass networks for human pose estimation. In: Leibe, B., Matas, J., Sebe, N., Welling, M. (eds.) ECCV 2016. LNCS, vol. 9912, pp. 483–499. Springer, Cham (2016). https://doi.org/10.1007/978-3-319-46484-8_29

19. Pishchulin, L., Andriluka, M., Gehler, P., Schiele, B.: Strong appearance and expressive spatial models for human pose estimation. In: 2013 IEEE International Conference on Computer Vision, pp. 3487–3494 (2013). https://doi.org/10.1109/ICCV.2013.433

20. Sandler, M., Howard, A., Zhu, M., Zhmoginov, A., Chen, L.C.: Mobilenetv 2: inverted residuals and linear bottlenecks. In: Proceedings of the IEEE Conference on Computer Vision and Pattern Recognition, pp. 4510–4520 (2018)

21. Sun, K., Xiao, B., Liu, D., Wang, J.: Deep high-resolution representation learning for human pose estimation. In: Proceedings of the IEEE/CVF Conference on Computer Vision and Pattern Recognition, pp. 5693–5703 (2019)

22. Tompson, J., Goroshin, R., Jain, A., LeCun, Y., Bregler, C.: Efficient object localization using convolutional networks. In: Proceedings of the IEEE Conference on Computer Vision and Pattern Recognition, pp. 648–656 (2015)

23. Toshev, A., Szegedy, C.: Deeppose: human pose estimation via deep neural networks. In: Proceedings of the IEEE Conference on Computer Vision and Pattern Recognition, pp. 1653–1660 (2014)

24. Wang, X., Girshick, R., Gupta, A., He, K.: Non-local neural networks. In: Proceedings of the IEEE Conference on Computer Vision and Pattern Recognition, pp. 7794–7803 (2018)

25. Woo, S., Park, J., Lee, J.-Y., Kweon, I.S.: CBAM: convolutional block attention module. In: Ferrari, V., Hebert, M., Sminchisescu, C., Weiss, Y. (eds.) ECCV 2018. LNCS, vol. 11211, pp. 3–19. Springer, Cham (2018). https://doi.org/10.1007/978-3-030-01234-2_1

26. Xiang, X., Chen, W., Zeng, D.: Intelligent target tracking and shooting system with mean shift. In: 2008 IEEE International Symposium on Parallel and Distributed Processing with Applications, pp. 417–421. IEEE (2008)

27. Xiao, B., Wu, H., Wei, Y.: Simple baselines for human pose estimation and tracking. In: Ferrari, V., Hebert, M., Sminchisescu, C., Weiss, Y. (eds.) ECCV 2018. LNCS, vol. 11210, pp. 472–487. Springer, Cham (2018). https://doi.org/10.1007/978-3-030-01231-1_29

28. Xu, L., et al.: Vipnas: efficient video pose estimation via neural architecture search. In: Proceedings of the IEEE/CVF Conference on Computer Vision and Pattern Recognition, pp. 16072–16081 (2021)

29. Yu, C., et al.: Lite-HrNet: a lightweight high-resolution network. In: Proceedings of the IEEE/CVF Conference on Computer Vision and Pattern Recognition, pp. 10440–10450 (2021)

30. Zhang, X., Zhou, X., Lin, M., Sun, J.: Shufflenet: an extremely efficient convolutional neural network for mobile devices. In: Proceedings of the IEEE Conference on Computer Vision and Pattern Recognition, pp. 6848–6856 (2018)

BYTEv2: Associating More Detection Boxes Under Occlusion for Improved Multi-person Tracking

Daniel Stadler[1,2,3(✉)] and Jürgen Beyerer[1,2,3]

[1] Karlsruhe Institute of Technology, Kaiserstr. 12, 76131 Karlsruhe, Germany
[2] Fraunhofer IOSB, Fraunhoferstr. 1, 76131 Karlsruhe, Germany
{daniel.stadler,juergen.beyerer}@iosb.fraunhofer.de
[3] Fraunhofer Center for Machine Learning, Munich, Germany

Abstract. Most of the multi-person trackers in literature assign only high-confident detections to already tracked targets so the full potential of available detections is not leveraged. Recently, a new association method named BYTE has been proposed that considers also low-confident detections in a second matching step. We think this idea further and additionally utilize heavy-occluded detections in the association which are usually discarded by non-maximum suppression. With our further development termed BYTEv2, the tracking performance under occlusion can be significantly improved. Aiming at a tracking framework that works well under camera motion and is still real-time capable, we built a fast and lightweight model for camera motion compensation based on ORB features. Moreover, a method to terminate inactive tracks under severe camera motion is proposed which further improves the performance. We validate our tracking components with extensive ablative experiments and achieve state-of-the-art results on the two popular benchmarks MOT17 and MOT20.

Keywords: Multi-person tracking · Tracking under occlusion

1 Introduction

The task of multi-person tracking (MPT) can be divided into the two sub-tasks detection and association as done in the tracking-by-detection (TBD) paradigm. The majority of TBD methods sets a score threshold to remove low-confident detections which are likely false positives (FPs) and to keep high-confident detections considered as true positives (TPs) for the association. Obviously, this simple filtering rule is not optimal. Recently, a new association method named BYTE [43] has been proposed that assigns low-confident detections in a second matching step to already tracked targets, while using only high-confident detections for initializing new tracks. With the improved usage of available detections in the association, BYTE achieves state-of-the-art results in MPT.

Besides filtering detections with respect to *confidence*, many modern object detectors [6,11,15,21,22] rely on a non-maximum suppression (NMS) to remove

© Springer Nature Switzerland AG 2023
J.-J. Rousseau and B. Kapralos (Eds.): ICPR 2022 Workshops, LNCS 13643, pp. 79–94, 2023.
https://doi.org/10.1007/978-3-031-37660-3_6

duplicate detections that are produced by design, i.e., since object proposals are distributed densely over the image. This NMS can be regarded as filtering with respect to *overlap*. Similar to the score threshold, the Intersection over Union (IoU) threshold of the NMS determines whether a detection is regarded as FP or TP. Inspired by the idea of BYTE to consider low-confident detections, we argue that detections with high overlaps exceeding the IoU threshold should also be taken into account in the association. Therefore, we propose the advanced association method BYTEv2 that *associates more detection boxes under occlusion.*

The core idea of BYTEv2 is to apply a second NMS with a higher IoU threshold and keep those detections that are not yet included in the standard detection set coming from the first NMS. Then, this second detection set is combined with the low-confident detections and used in the second matching step as in BYTE association. Note that detections kept by the second NMS are only utilized for assignment to already tracked targets and not for initializing new tracks, as done with the low-confident detections. With BYTEv2, the number of detections under severe occlusion (exceeding IoU threshold of first NMS) is increased, not only enhancing detection recall but also improving association accuracy as illustrated in Fig. 1. Combining BYTEv2 with detections of four trackers from literature leads to consistent improvements compared to BYTE showing the effectiveness of the proposed association approach.

With an increased detection set leveraged in the association, an accurate propagation of track positions is desirable. Next to the prediction of the intrinsic motion of targets, considering camera motion is also important. Some trackers [2, 12, 29] hence apply the Enhanced Correlation Coefficient (ECC) maximization [9] for camera motion compensation (CMC). However, this approach is computationally expensive sacrificing real-time capabilities. Therefore, we build a CMC model based on ORB [24] features that can be applied in real-time due to a GPU implementation and achieves even superior results.

Moreover, the transformation matrices of the CMC model are used in a simple method for terminating inactive tracks under severe camera motion. This method prevents wrong motion-based reactivations of tracks and thus further improves the association accuracy of our tracking framework.

We validate the design of our tracking components with ablative experiments and obtain state-of-the-art results on MOT17 [18] and MOT20 [7]. Our contributions are summarized as follows:

- As a further development of BYTE, we propose the advanced association method BYTEv2 that utilizes heavy-occluded detections in the association and thus improves the tracking performance in crowded scenes.
- A fast CMC model based on ORB features is built that greatly improves the performance under camera motion while being applicable in real-time.
- Using the transformation matrices from the CMC model, a method to improve association accuracy by terminating inactive tracks under severe camera motion is introduced.

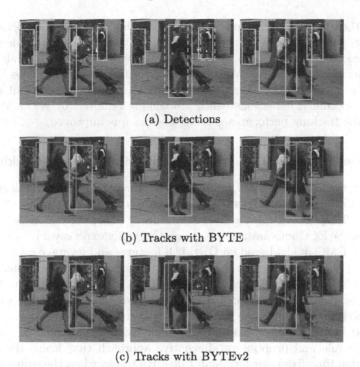

(a) Detections

(b) Tracks with BYTE

(c) Tracks with BYTEv2

Fig. 1. Illustration of BYTEv2 association. (a) Besides standard detections (solid boxes), BYTEv2 also uses detections with high overlaps usually removed by NMS (dashed boxes). (b) A missed detection under severe occlusion introduces an ID switch if the detected box is assigned to the wrong target. Although BYTE takes low-confident detections under occlusion into account, it does not consider occluded detections that exceed the NMS threshold. (c) BYTEv2 utilizes such heavy-occluded detections which simplifies the association task and thus improves the tracking performance under occlusion. Note that these heavy-occluded detections are not used for initializing new tracks.

2 Related Work

2.1 Association Strategies

Most TBD methods follow a simple matching strategy building a distance matrix between detections and tracks and applying the Hungarian method [13] to make all assignments at once [4,27,30,37,39]. Differently, DeepSORT [38] introduces a matching cascade which prioritizes recently detected targets with the motivation that the uncertainty of propagated track locations increases over time. Tracktor [2] uses the regression head of Faster R-CNN [22] to directly regress track boxes in consecutive frames and thus solves the association problem implicitly. While these methods work online, there exist also offline methods that follow a cascaded scheme, where at first short-term tracklets are built that are afterwards linked to long-term trajectories with the help of global information [1,28,33].

Whereas the aforementioned methods only use high-confident detections, the recently proposed association method BYTE [43] considers low-confident detections in a second matching step which improves the utilization of available detections in the tracking process. We think this idea further and propose BYTEv2 that does not only use low-confident detections in the association but also utilizes heavy-occluded detections which are usually removed by NMS. With this strategy, the tracking performance under occlusion is improved.

2.2 Consideration of Camera Motion in Multi-person Tracking

To improve the locations of propagated tracks, some MPT frameworks apply the Enhanced Correlation Coefficient (ECC) maximization [9] to compensate camera motion [2,12,29]. This improves tracking accuracy but greatly increases processing time as the ECC maximisation is computationally expensive. In contrast, we introduce a CMC model based on ORB [24] features and leverage a GPU implementation yielding an accurate model that can be applied in real-time. In spite of using a CMC model, propagated track positions can become inaccurate under severe camera motion. Therefore, MAT [12] introduces a dynamic reconnection context module that limits the time an inactive track can be resumed based on the severity of both camera and target motion. We find that the latter one plays a negligible role and propose an alternative approach that keeps the possible re-connection time fixed but terminates inactive tracks when the camera motion becomes to strong.

3 Method

We first describe our main contribution in Sect. 3.1: BYTEv2, a further development of BYTE, that utilizes heavy-occluded detections in the association. Aiming at a tracking pipeline which works well under camera motion and is also real-time capable, we built a CMC model based on ORB features in Sect. 3.2. A method for terminating inactive tracks under severe camera motion based on the CMC model is introduced in Sect. 3.3.

3.1 BYTEv2

Since our method builds upon the association technique BYTE [43], we briefly describe this pipeline in the following. Let $\mathcal{D}$ denote the set of detections coming from an object detector that depends on NMS as post-processing. To remove duplicate detections, a score threshold s_1 and an IoU threshold o_1 are applied in the NMS yielding the detections $\mathcal{D}_{\mathrm{NMS1}} \subseteq \mathcal{D}$. BYTE splits this detection set into two subsets based on the confidence scores s of the detections and a threshold τ: the high-confident detections $\mathcal{D}_{\mathrm{high}} = \{D|D \in \mathcal{D}_{\mathrm{NMS1}} \wedge s > \tau\}$ and the low-confident detections $\mathcal{D}_{\mathrm{low}} = \{D|D \in \mathcal{D}_{\mathrm{NMS1}} \wedge s \leq \tau\}$. Now let $\mathcal{T}$ be the set of tracks at the current iteration. In a first association step, only the high-confident detections $\mathcal{D}_{\mathrm{high}}$ are utilized as candidates $\mathcal{D}_1$ for matching to the

---

Algorithm 1: Separation of Detections in BYTEv2

Input: Set of detections before NMS $\mathcal{D}$
  Detection threshold τ
  Score and IoU threshold of first NMS s_1, o_1
  Score and IoU threshold of second NMS s_2, o_2 *
Output: Detections for first and second matching $\mathcal{D}_1, \mathcal{D}_2$

1 $\mathcal{D}_{\text{NMS1}} \leftarrow \text{NMS}(\mathcal{D}, s_1, o_1)$ `// first NMS`
2 $\mathcal{D}_{\text{high}} \leftarrow \{D \mid D \in \mathcal{D}_{\text{NMS1}} \wedge s > \tau\}$
3 $\mathcal{D}_{\text{low}} \leftarrow \{D \mid D \in \mathcal{D}_{\text{NMS1}} \wedge s \leq \tau\}$
4 $\mathcal{D}_{\text{NMS2}} \leftarrow \text{NMS}(\mathcal{D}, s_2, o_2)$ `// second NMS` *
5 $\mathcal{D}_{\text{occ}} \leftarrow \mathcal{D}_{\text{NMS2}} \setminus \mathcal{D}_{\text{NMS1}}$ *
6 $\mathcal{D}_1 \leftarrow \mathcal{D}_{\text{high}}$
7 $\mathcal{D}_2 \leftarrow \mathcal{D}_{\text{low}} \cup \mathcal{D}_{\text{occ}}$ *

Differences to BYTE [43] are highlighted with *.

tracks $\mathcal{T}_1 = \mathcal{T}$. In a second association step, the low-confident detections $\mathcal{D}_{\text{low}}$ are taken as candidates $\mathcal{D}_2$ for matching to the unmatched tracks $\mathcal{T}_2 \subseteq \mathcal{T}_1$. As shown in [43], using the low-confident detections $\mathcal{D}_{\text{low}}$ in a second association step leads to a significant improvement of tracking performance.

We argue that besides the low-confident detections, there lies potential in leveraging another set of detections that is usually discarded – detections with heavy occlusion $\mathcal{D}_{\text{occ}}$ filtered by NMS. To make use of those detections, we propose to apply a second NMS with a higher IoU threshold $o_2 > o_1$ and a score threshold s_2 yielding the detections $\mathcal{D}_{\text{NMS2}}$. This detection set includes not only the heavy-occluded detections $\mathcal{D}_{\text{occ}}$ but also detections from $\mathcal{D}_{\text{NMS1}}$. To get the heavy-occluded detections $\mathcal{D}_{\text{occ}}$, we simply subtract the two detection sets: $\mathcal{D}_{\text{occ}} = \mathcal{D}_{\text{NMS2}} \setminus \mathcal{D}_{\text{NMS1}}$. While the first association step is identical to BYTE, we additionally utilize the set of heavy-occluded detections $\mathcal{D}_{\text{occ}}$ in the second association step of BYTEv2: $\mathcal{D}_2 = \mathcal{D}_{\text{low}} \cup \mathcal{D}_{\text{occ}}$. As a consequence, the tracking performance under severe occlusion is improved. The separation of detections in BYTEv2 into low-confident, high-confident, and heavy-occluded detections is summarized in Algorithm 1, whereby differences to BYTE are highlighted.

3.2 Camera Motion Compensation

When facing severe camera motion, a linear motion model as Kalman filter for propagating target locations is not sufficient, especially if the matching between detections and tracks is only based on spatial similarity, for example IoU. Therefore, some multi-person trackers [2,12,29] apply the ECC maximization [9] as CMC model. However, this method is computationally expensive and makes real-time processing at a high frame rate difficult. Therefore, we built an alternative CMC model based on the fast ORB [24] feature detector, which achieves even higher performance with our tracking framework than ECC maximization while running in real-time (see Sect. 4.4 for details). The method works as follows. Let I_{t-1} and I_t be the previous and current image, respectively. For each image, a set of feature points $\mathcal{F}$ is extracted with the ORB detector. Then, the RANSAC algorithm [10] is used to estimate an affine transformation matrix $W_{t-1,t}$ that maps $\mathcal{F}_{t-1}$ to $\mathcal{F}_t$. In our tracking pipeline, $W_{t-1,t}$ is applied on the tracks found in the previous image $\mathcal{T}_{t-1}$ (before propagation with Kalman filter) to get the aligned tracks $\mathcal{T}_t$ that are used for matching to the detections $\mathcal{D}$.

3.3 Termination of Inactive Tracks Under Severe Camera Motion

Since both Kalman filter and CMC model predictions are not optimal, inactive tracks are terminated after a specific number of consecutive frames without assigned detection referred to as inactive patience p_{max}. Here, we follow the argumentation from [12] that the time an inactive track is kept should depend on the complexity of its motion pattern. In [12], a dynamic inactive patience based on both camera and target movement is proposed. However, we find that the influence of target motion on this dynamic inactive patience is negligible and propose an alternative approach for a variable inactive patience when camera motion is present. In each time step t and for each inactive track with last detection at $t - n$, the transformation matrix $W_{t-n,t}$ is approximated as product of the framewise transformation matrices from the CMC model: $W_{t-n,t} = W_{t-n,t-n+1} \cdot W_{t-n+1,t-n+2} \cdots W_{t-1,t}$. Then, the euclidean norm of the transformation matrix $w = ||W_{t-n,t}||_2$ as a measure for the severity of camera motion during the time the track has been inactive is calculated. If w exceeds a predefined threshold w_{max}, the inactive track is terminated, independent from its inactive time. Note that a track is still terminated if its inactive time exceeds p_{max}.

4   Experiments

4.1 Datasets and Performance Measures

We use the two datasets MOT17 [18] and MOT20 [7] from the popular MOTChallenge benchmarks in our experiments. MOT17 includes 14 sequences for multi-person tracking that contain complex scenarios with a large number of occlusions and partly strong camera motions. Since annotations from the 7 test sequences are not publicly available, the 7 sequences of the train split are often divided into two parts, whereby the second halves are used as validation split [34,43,44]. We follow this practice and use MOT17 validation split for all ablative experiments. MOT20 comprises 8 sequences, 4 for train and test each. In comparison to MOT17, the scenes are much more crowded but no severe camera motions are present. We compare our tracker with the state-of-the-art on the test sets of MOT17 and MOT20 by submitting our tracking results to the official evaluation server (https://motchallenge.net/).

For evaluating tracking performance, mainly MOTA [3] and IDF1 [23] are used. While MOTA is dominated by detection accuracy, IDF1 focuses more on association. FP, FN, and number of ID switches (IDSWs) as components of MOTA are also regarded. Moreover, the newly introduced HOTA [17], which balances detection, association, and localization accuracy, is reported in the comparison with the state-of-the-art.

4.2 Implementation Details

For a fair comparison to BYTE, we use the same detection model provided by the authors [43] – a YOLO-X [11] with YOLOX-X backbone trained on a combination of MOT17, CrowdHuman [26], CityPersons [42], and ETH [8]. The model used for ablative experiments was trained on the first half of MOT17 train, while the final model used the complete train split. Differently to MOT17, the model applied on the MOT20 test split was trained on the combination of CrowdHuman and MOT20. Detailed training settings can be found in [43]. Unless otherwise stated, the input size of the network is 1440×800. Our method BYTEv2 introduces two additional parameters for the second NMS that are set to $o_2 = 0.9$ and $s_2 = 0.5$ through ablative experiments. The parameters of BYTE are adopted: IoU threshold of first NMS $o_1 = 0.7$, score threshold of first NMS $s_1 = 0.1$, detection threshold $\tau = 0.6$, initialization threshold for tracks $s_{\text{init}} = 0.7$, matching threshold in first association $m_1 = 0.9$, matching threshold in second association $m_2 = 0.5$. Note that BYTE uses IoU distance $d_2 = 1 - \text{IoU}(D, T)$ for comparing a detection box D to a track box T in the second association and additionally fuses the detection score s in the first association: $d_1 = 1 - \text{IoU}(D, T) \cdot s$, which we also take over. The thresholds related to the termination of inactive tracks are empirically set to $p_{\text{max}} = 60$ and $w_{\text{max}} = 150$.

4.3 Ablation Studies for BYTEv2

IoU Thresholds of the Two NMS. We start the ablation of the proposed association method BYTEv2 by changing the IoU thresholds o_1 and o_2 of the first and second NMS. The results are summarized in Table 1. Without the second NMS, the best results are obtained for $o_1 = 0.7$ leading to 81.4 IDF1 and 77.0 MOTA. Further increasing the IoU threshold o_1 degrades the performance as too many FPs are introduced. However, not all available detections under severe occlusion are false or duplicate detections. Applying a second NMS with $o_2 = 0.9$ and using the heavy-occluded detections $\mathcal{D}_{\text{occ}}$ in the second association of BYTEv2, the performance can be further improved to 82.6 IDF1 and 77.3 MOTA. Moreover, performance gains can be observed for all combinations of o_1 and o_2 indicating a good robustness with respect to the new parameter o_2. Another finding is that if o_1 is set too low, the negative impact can be weakened with BYTEv2: For $o_1 = 0.6$, a gain of +1.4 IDF1 and +1.0 MOTA is achieved.

Score Threshold of Heavy-Occluded Detections. We also ablate the influence of the score threshold s_2 for the heavy-occluded detections $\mathcal{D}_{\text{occ}}$, which can be seen in Table 2. For all values of s_2, the results are better than the baseline

Table 1. Influence of IoU Thresholds o_1 and o_2 in BYTEv2

o_1	o_2	IDF1	MOTA	FP	FN	IDSW
0.6	–	80.5	76.1	**3240**	9506	119
0.6	0.7	80.7 (+0.2)	76.5 (+0.4)	3335	9241	110
0.6	0.8	81.3 (+0.8)	77.0 (+0.9)	3322	8979	106
0.6	0.9	81.9 (+1.4)	77.1 (+1.0)	3339	8909	**99**
0.7	–	81.4	77.0	3458	8833	108
0.7	0.8	81.6 (+0.2)	77.2 (+0.2)	3483	8707	107
0.7	0.9	**82.6** (+1.2)	**77.3** (+0.3)	3487	8642	110
0.8	–	79.4	76.6	3850	8576	173
0.8	0.9	80.8 (+1.4)	76.6 (+0.0)	3909	**8536**	142

Table 2. Influence of Score Threshold s_2 in BYTEv2

s_2	IDF1	MOTA	FP	FN	IDSW
–	81.4	77.0	**3458**	8833	108
0.2	81.6	77.2	3535	8653	107
0.5	**82.6**	**77.3**	3487	**8642**	110
0.8	81.9	77.2	3477	8682	**102**

that does not consider the heavy-occluded detections $\mathcal{D}_{occ}$. Note that this baseline corresponds to BYTE in combination with our modules for dealing with severe camera motion. We find that detections with too low confidence are not reliable, while using only detections with very high confidence does not exploit the full potential of the heavy-occluded detections. The best results are produced with $s_2 = 0.5$.

Assigned Detections Under Severe Occlusion. Although the previous results show a better trade-off between FPs and FNs of BYTEv2 compared to BYTE in total terms, we want to get a deeper understanding of the FP-FN trade-off under occlusion, which is where BYTEv2 aims to make improvements. To achieve this, we calculate the IoU of each false detection box (FP) with all ground truth (GT) boxes and build the maximum denoted as IoU_{max} w/ GT. The same is done for each missed GT box (FN) with the natural exception that the identical GT box is ignored in the IoU calulation. IoU_{max} w/ GT is a measure for the severity of occlusion at the false or missed detection. In Fig. 2, a histogram of FN and FP over different intervals of IoU_{max} w/ GT from decent up to severe occlusion is depicted – both for BYTE and BYTEv2. The strongest differences can be observed for occlusion ratios similar to the IoU threshold $o_1 = 0.7$, where BYTEv2 notably decreases the number of FNs without introducing many FPs.

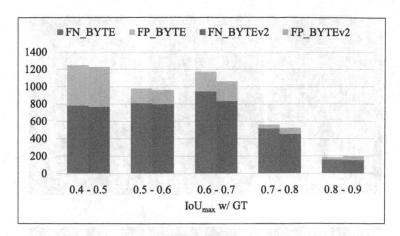

Fig. 2. FN and FP with BYTE and BYTEv2 under severe occlusion. IoU_{max} w/ GT denotes the maximum IoU of a false detection box (FP) with all GT boxes or the maximum IoU of a missed GT box (FN) with all other GT boxes.

Table 3. BYTE and BYTEv2 with Detections of Other Trackers

Method	IDF1	MOTA	Method	IDF1	MOTA
JDE	63.6	60.0	QDTrack	67.8	67.3
JDE_BYTE	66.0	60.6	QDTrack_BYTE	70.9	67.9
JDE_BYTEv2	**67.7**	**62.2**	QDTrack_BYTEv2	**71.6**	**68.1**
CSTrack	**72.3**	68.0	CTracker	60.9	63.1
CSTrack_BYTE	71.7	69.3	CTracker_BYTE	66.7	65.0
CSTrack_BYTEv2	72.2	**69.5**	CTracker_BYTEv2	**68.4**	**65.2**

BYTEv2 with Detections of Other Trackers. To evaluate the generalization ability of BYTEv2, we follow the same strategy as in [43] and apply BYTEv2 on the detections generated by different state-of-the-art trackers, namely JDE [37], QDTrack [19], CSTrack [14], and CTracker [20]. Table 3 lists the results of the original baselines, with association method BYTE, and with BYTEv2. We observe that BYTEv2 achieves consistent improvements both over the baseline methods and also in comparison to BYTE indicating a good robustness with regard to the used detection model that differs among the trackers.

Qualitative Result. BYTEv2 not only enhances MOTA by improving FP-FN trade-off but also improves association accuracy which has been shown quantitatively by a plus of 1.2 IDF1 (Table 1). A qualitative example how BYTEv2 can lead to an improved association accuracy under occlusion is visualized in Fig. 3. In scenarios with missing detections due to severe occlusion, IDSWs easily occur, since the available detections might be ambiguous, i.e., it is not clear to which

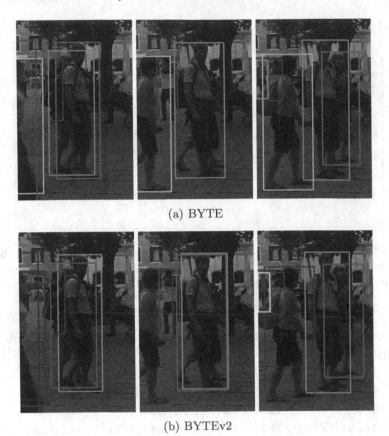

(a) BYTE

(b) BYTEv2

Fig. 3. With BYTEv2, detections of severely occluded targets are leveraged (b), which are typically filtered by NMS (a). Note that this simplifies the association an thus can prevent IDSWs as shown in the example.

targets the detections belong to. BYTEv2 reduces the chance for such ambiguous situations as also heavy-occluded detections are used in the association.

4.4 Experiments Related to Camera Motion

Camera Motion Compensation. We insert two different CMC models into our framework – the ECC [9] maximization and our own model based on ORB [24] features. For both variants, OpenCV [5] implementations are leveraged. While we keep the standard settings for ECC, we experiment with two different configurations of the ORB detector. Next to the default parameters, we apply a light model (ORB_light) that includes only 2 pyramid levels instead of 8 and uses a scale factor of 2.0 instead of 1.2. For ORB_light, we also utilize the available GPU implementation for further acceleration. The processing time of the different CMC models is averaged over 5 runs and a NVIDIA Tesla

Table 4. Comparison of Different CMC Models

Method	Device	IDF1	MOTA	Time in ms
ECC	CPU	81.8	76.7	187.6 ± 2.8
ORB	CPU	82.1	77.2	38.6 ± 0.1
ORB_light	CPU	**82.4**	**77.3**	17.5 ± 0.1
ORB_light	GPU	82.1 ± 0.3	77.3 ± 0.0	$\mathbf{4.3 \pm 0.1}$

V100 is used for the GPU implementation. Table 4 summarizes the results. Note that next to the mean values of the 5 runs the standard deviations are given. Our CMC model built upon the ORB detector is about 5 times faster than ECC and achieves even higher tracking performance. Surprisingly, ORB_light further improves the accuracy while being more than twice as fast as ORB. Finally, the GPU implementation of OpenCV significantly accelerates the calculation yielding a CMC model that runs in about 4.3ms at the input size of 1440×800 and thus can be applied in real-time. However, we find that the GPU implementation of the ORB detector in OpenCV is not deterministic and that the mean IDF1 over 5 runs is 0.3 lower compared to the CPU variant. Certainly, it is possible to implement a deterministic version of the ORB detector on the GPU which we leave for future work and use the CPU version in all other experiments.

Termination of Inactive Tracks. The CMC model is used to determine the severity of camera motion w during the time a track has been inactive. If the camera motion is too strong ($w > w_{max}$), the inactive track is terminated to prevent wrong motion-based reactivations. In addition, an inactive track is kept for at most p_{max} frames without assigned detection. The influence of these parameters can be seen in Table 5. The best performance is obtained for $p_{max} = 60$ which corresponds to approximately 2 s in the MOT17 dataset. However, for scenes with severe camera motion, this inactive patience is too large. When additionally applying $w_{max} = 150$, the association accuracy measured by IDF1 can be increased by 0.2. If w_{max} is set too low, some inactive tracks are terminated too early, whereas the method has no influence if w_{max} is set too high. Note that on sequences with severe camera motion gains up to +1.1 IDF1 are achieved (MOT17-11).

Table 5. Influence of p_{max} and w_{max} for Inactive Tracks

p_{max}	w_{max}	IDF1	MOTA	p_{max}	w_{max}	IDF1	MOTA
40	–	82.3	77.3	60	100	82.4	77.3
60	–	82.4	77.3	60	150	**82.6**	77.3
80	–	82.3	77.3	60	250	82.5	77.3

4.5   Ablations of the Full Tracking Pipeline

The impact of our individual tracking components on the performance are summarized in Table 6. The baseline in the first row is in essence the method Byte-Track [43]. The small deviation in performance compared to [43] (79.3 IDF1, 76.6 MOTA) is attributable to a different setting of p_{max} (60 vs. 30) and potentially small differences in our re-implementation. Inserting our CMC model into the pipeline leads to significant improvements of IDF1 and MOTA. The same holds true for changing the association method from BYTE to BYTEv2. Terminating inactive tracks under severe camera motion further improves the association accuracy. In a post-processing step, we apply linear interpolation to fill the gaps caused by temporally inactive tracks as also done in [43].

Table 7 shows the influence of the maximum gap length that is interpolated. Because of our CMC model and the termination method for inactive tracks under severe camera motion, a large number of frames can be successfully interpolated raising IDF1 to 83.7 and MOTA to 79.3.

Finally, the runtimes of all components are given in Table 8. About 32ms of the total 42ms are spent for detection on an input of size 1440×800. It has been shown in [43] that this time can be greatly reduced using a smaller input size with only a small degradation in performance. Note that BYTEv2 adds only about 1ms to the total processing time which is spent on the second NMS.

Table 6. Influence of Tracking Components

CMC	BYTEv2	Stop Inactive	Interpolate	IDF1	MOTA
✗	✗	✗	✗	79.7	76.5
✓	✗	✗	✗	81.2	77.0
✓	✓	✗	✗	82.4	77.3
✓	✓	✓	✗	82.6	77.3
✓	✓	✓	✓	**83.7**	**79.3**

Table 7. Influence of Maximum Gap Length of Interpolation

Max. gap	IDF1	MOTA	Max. gap	IDF1	MOTA
10	83.1	78.2	40	83.6	79.2
50	**83.7**	**79.3**	60	83.6	79.0

Table 8. Runtime of Detection and Tracking Components

Detection	NMS	CMC	Association	Total
32 ms	2 ms	4 ms	4 ms	42 ms

4.6 Comparison with the State-of-the-Art

A comparison of our method termed *ByteTrackV2* – as further development of ByteTrack [43] – with the state-of-the-art on MOT17 test split can be found in Table 9. ByteTrackV2 ranks first among all methods on MOT17 and achieves the highest values of MOTA, IDF1, and HOTA. Moreover, it has the least number of FNs and IDSWs which indicates the effectiveness of our method BYTEv2 in utilizing heavy-occluded detections in the matching process. The introduced CMC model also benefits association accuracy since some sequences of the MOT17 test set contain camera motion. With respect to ByteTrack, our method increases MOTA, IDF1, and HOTA by 0.3, 1.6, and 0.5 points, respectively, although we do not apply different detection thresholds τ for different sequences of the dataset as done in [43].

Results of the state-of-the-art methods on the more crowded MOT20 test split are depicted in Table 10. With the same settings as used for MOT17, ByteTrackV2 obtains a worse tracking performance than ByteTrack which has the following reasons. For MOT20, ByteTrack uses a larger input size (1920×736 or 1600×896 depending on sequence), a different matching threshold $m_1 = 0.7$, and does not fuse the detection score when calculating the matching distance d_1. Moreover, the detection threshold τ is also tuned for each sequence independently. We try to adopt these settings in a second submission ByteTrackV2* to get a fair comparison. MOTA of ByteTrackV2* is largely increased but still 0.5 points behind ByteTrack, while IDF1 (+0.4) and HOTA (+0.1) are higher. Comparing the MOTA values of the 4 test sequences, we find that MOTA of ByteTrackV2 is higher or on par with ByteTrack on 3 sequences but 3.2 points lower on MOT20-08 which indicates that the detection threshold τ differs. Unfortunately, the exact settings of ByteTrack cannot be found in the pre-print [43] nor derived from the official code which makes a fair comparison on MOT20 test set impossible.

Table 9. State-of-the-Art Methods on MOT17 Test Set

Method	MOTA	IDF1	HOTA	FP	FN	IDSW
CSTrack [14]	74.9	72.6	59.3	**23847**	114303	3567
GRTU [35]	74.9	75.0	62.0	32007	107616	1812
TransTrack [32]	75.2	63.5	54.1	50157	86442	3603
CrowdTrack [30]	75.6	73.6	60.3	25950	109101	2544
TPAGT [25]	76.2	68.0	57.9	32796	98475	3237
CorrTracker [34]	76.5	73.6	60.7	29808	99510	3369
ReMOT [40]	77.0	72.0	59.7	33204	93612	2853
MAATrack [31]	79.4	75.9	62.0	37320	77661	1452
ByteTrack [43]	80.3	77.3	63.1	25491	83721	2196
ByteTrackV2	**80.6**	**78.9**	**63.6**	35208	**73224**	**1239**

Table 10. State-of-the-Art Methods on MOT20 Test Set. A similar parameter setting of our method compared to ByteTrack is denoted by *. See continuous text for details.

Method	MOTA	IDF1	HOTA	FP	FN	IDSW
CSTrack [14]	66.6	68.6	54.0	25404	144358	3196
GSDT [36]	67.1	67.5	53.6	31913	135409	3131
RelationTrack [41]	67.2	70.5	56.5	61134	104597	4243
OUTrack$_{fm}$ [16]	68.6	69.4	56.2	36816	123208	2223
CrowdTrack [30]	70.7	68.2	55.0	**21928**	126533	3198
MAATrack [31]	73.9	71.2	57.3	24942	108744	1331
ReMOT [40]	77.4	73.1	61.2	28351	**86659**	1789
ByteTrack [43]	**77.8**	75.2	61.3	26249	87594	1223
ByteTrackV2	74.5	73.8	59.9	23132	107683	**916**
ByteTrackV2*	77.3	**75.6**	**61.4**	22867	93409	1082

5 Conclusion

We propose a new method BYTEv2 that uses heavy-occluded detections in the association which are usually discarded. It is shown that leveraging these additional detections improves the tracking performance under severe occlusion. Moreover, a real-time capable camera motion compensation model is introduced which, together with a method for terminating inactive tracks under severe camera motion, further improves the performance. With the aforementioned components, our tracking framework ByteTrackV2 achieves state-of-the-art results on the two benchmarks MOT17 and MOT20 and shows a good generalization ability when combined with detections of other trackers from literature.

References

1. Al-Shakarji, N.M., Bunyak, F., Seetharaman, G., Palaniappan, K.: Multi-object tracking cascade with multi-step data association and occlusion handling. In: IEEE International Conference on Advanced Video and Signal Based Surveillance (AVSS) (2018)
2. Bergmann, P., Meinhardt, T., Leal-Taixé, L.: Tracking without bells and whistles. In: International Conference on Computer Vision (ICCV), pp. 941–951 (2019)
3. Bernardin, K., Elbs, A., Stiefelhagen, R.: Multiple object tracking performance metrics and evaluation in a smart room environment. In: European Conference on Computer Vision Workshop (2006)
4. Bewley, A., Ge, Z., Ott, L., Ramos, F., Upcroft, B.: Simple online and realtime tracking. In: IEEE International Conference on Image Processing, pp. 3464–3468 (2016)
5. Bradski, G.: The OpenCV Library. Dr. Dobb's Journal of Software Tools (2000)
6. Cai, Z., Vasconcelos, N.: Cascade R-CNN: delving into high quality object detection. In: IEEE Conference on Computer Vision and Pattern Recognition, pp. 6154–6162 (2018)

7. Dendorfer, P., et al.: Mot20: a benchmark for multi object tracking in crowded scenes. arXiv:2003.09003 (2020)

8. Ess, A., Leibe, B., Schindler, K., Van Gool, L.: A mobile vision system for robust multi-person tracking. In: IEEE Conference on Computer Vision and Pattern Recognition (2008)

9. Evangelidis, G.D., Psarakis, E.Z.: Parametric image alignment using enhanced correlation coefficient maximization. IEEE Trans. Pattern Anal. Mach. Intell. **30**(10), 1858–1865 (2008)

10. Fischler, M.A., Bolles, R.C.: Random sample consensus: a paradigm for model fitting with applications to image analysis and automated cartography. Commun. ACM **24**(6), 381–395 (1981)

11. Ge, Z., Liu, S., Wang, F., Li, Z., Sun, J.: YOLOX: Exceeding YOLO series in 2021. arXiv:2107.08430 (2021)

12. Han, S., Huang, P., Wang, H., Yu, E., Liu, D., Pan, X.: MAT: motion-aware multi-object tracking. Neurocomputing **476**, 75–86 (2022)

13. Kuhn, H.W., Yaw, B.: The Hungarian method for the assignment problem. Naval Res. Logist. Q., 83–97 (1955)

14. Liang, C., Zhang, Z., Lu, Y., Zhou, X., Li, B., Ye, X., Zou, J.: Rethinking the competition between detection and reid in multi-object tracking. arXiv:2010.12138 (2020)

15. Lin, T.Y., Goyal, P., Girshick, R., He, K., Dollár, P.: Focal loss for dense object detection. In: International Conference on Computer Vision (ICCV), pp. 2999–3007 (2017)

16. Liu, Q., et al.: Online multi-object tracking with unsupervised re-identification learning and occlusion estimation. Neurocomputing **483**, 333–347 (2022)

17. Luiten, J., et al.: HOTA: a higher order metric for evaluating multi-object tracking. Int. J. Comput. Vis. **129**(2), 548–578 (2021)

18. Milan, A., Leal-Taixé, L., Reid, I., Roth, S., Schindler, K.: MOT16: a benchmark for multi-object tracking. arXiv:1603.00831 (2016)

19. Pang, J., Qiu, L., Li, X., Chen, H., Li, Q., Darrell, T., Yu, F.: Quasi-dense similarity learning for multiple object tracking. In: IEEE Conference on Computer Vision and Pattern Recognition, pp. 164–173 (2021)

20. Peng, J., et al.: Chained-tracker: Chaining paired attentive regression results for end-to-end joint multiple-object detection and tracking. In: European Conference on Computer Vision (ECCV), pp. 145–161 (2020)

21. Redmon, J., Divvala, S., Girshick, R., Farhadi, A.: You only look once: unified, real-time object detection. In: IEEE Conference on Computer Vision and Pattern Recognition, pp. 779–788 (2016)

22. Ren, S., He, K., Girshick, R., Sun, J.: Faster R-CNN: towards real-time object detection with region proposal networks. IEEE Trans. Pattern Anal. Mach. Intell. **39**(6), 1137–1149 (2017)

23. Ristani, E., Solera, F., Zou, R.S., Cucchiara, R., Tomasi, C.: Performance measures and a data set for multi-target, multi-camera tracking. In: European Conference on Computer Vision Workshop, pp. 17–35 (2016)

24. Rublee, E., Rabaud, V., Konolige, K., Bradski, G.: Orb: an efficient alternative to sift or surf. In: International Conference on Computer Vision, pp. 2564–2571 (2011)

25. Shan, C., Wei, C., Deng, B., Huang, J., Hua, X.S., Cheng, X., Liang, K.: Tracklets predicting based adaptive graph tracking. arXiv:2010.09015 (2020)

26. Shao, S., et al.: CrowdHuman: a benchmark for detecting human in a crowd. arXiv:1805.00123 (2018)

27. Sharma, S., Ansari, J.A., Krishna Murthy, J., Madhava Krishna, K.: Beyond pixels: leveraging geometry and shape cues for online multi-object tracking. In: International Conference on Robotics and Automation, pp. 3508–3515 (2018)
28. Shen, H., Huang, L., Huang, C., Xu, W.: Tracklet association tracker: an end-to-end learning-based association approach for multi-object tracking. arXiv:1808.01562 (2018)
29. Stadler, D., Beyerer, J.: Improving multiple pedestrian tracking by track management and occlusion handling. In: IEEE Conference on Computer Vision and Pattern Recognition. pp. 10953–10962 (2021)
30. Stadler, D., Beyerer, J.: On the performance of crowd-specific detectors in multi-pedestrian tracking. In: IEEE International Conference on Advanced Video and Signal Based Surveillance (2021)
31. Stadler, D., Beyerer, J.: Modelling ambiguous assignments for multi-person tracking in crowds. In: IEEE Winter Conference on Applications of Computer on Vision Works, pp. 133–142 (2022)
32. Sun, P., et al.: Transtrack: multiple object tracking with transformer. arXiv:2012.15460 (2021)
33. Wang, G., Wang, Y., Zhang, H., Gu, R., Hwang, J.N.: Exploit the connectivity: multi-object tracking with trackletnet. In: ACM International Conference on Multimedia (MM), pp. 482–490 (2019)
34. Wang, Q., Zheng, Y., Pan, P., Xu, Y.: Multiple object tracking with correlation learning. In: IEEE Conference on Computer Vision and Pattern Recognition, pp. 3876–3886 (2021)
35. Wang, S., Sheng, H., Zhang, Y., Wu, Y., Xiong, Z.: A general recurrent tracking framework without real data. In: International Conference on Computer Vision, pp. 13219–13228 (2021)
36. Wang, Y., Kitani, K., Weng, X.: Joint object detection and multi-object tracking with graph neural networks. In: International Conference on Robotics and Automation, pp. 13708–13715 (2021)
37. Wang, Z., Zheng, L., Liu, Y., Li, Y., Wang, S.: Towards real-time multi-object tracking. In: European Conference on Computer Vision, pp. 107–122 (2020)
38. Wojke, N., Bewley, A., Paulus, D.: Simple online and realtime tracking with a deep association metric. In: IEEE International Conference on Image Processing, pp. 3645–3649 (2017)
39. Xu, J., Cao, Y., Zhang, Z., Hu, H.: Spatial-temporal relation networks for multi-object tracking. In: International Conference on Computer Vision, pp. 3987–3997 (2019)
40. Yang, F., Chang, X., Sakti, S., Wu, Y., Nakamura, S.: ReMOT: a model-agnostic refinement for multiple object tracking. In: Image and Vision Computing, vol. 106 (2021)
41. Yu, E., Li, Z., Han, S., Wang, H.: Relationtrack: relation-aware multiple object tracking with decoupled representation. arXiv:2105.04322 (2021)
42. Zhang, S., Benenson, R., Schiele, B.: Citypersons: a diverse dataset for pedestrian detection. In: IEEE Conference on Computer Vision and Pattern Recognition, pp. 4457–4465 (2017)
43. Zhang, Y., et al.: Bytetrack: multi-object tracking by associating every detection box. arXiv:2110.06864 (2021)
44. Zhou, X., Koltun, V., Krähenbühl, P.: Tracking objects as points. In: European Conference on Computer Vision (ECCV), pp. 474–490 (2020)

Fast and Effective Detection of Personal Protective Equipment on Smart Cameras

Antonio Greco[1,2]($\boxtimes$) (iD), Stefano Saldutti[3], and Bruno Vento[3]

[1] Department of Information and Electrical Engineering and Applied Mathematics,
University of Salerno, Fisciano, Italy
agreco@unisa.it
[2] A.I. Ready srl, Salerno, Italy
[3] A.I. Tech srl, Salerno, Italy
{stefano.saldutti,bruno.vento}@aitech.vision

Abstract. Worker safety is still a serious problem, as accidents and deaths at work are unfortunately very common, especially in construction sites. To prevent such injuries, there is a great interest in video analysis solutions able to continuously monitor a construction site in order to verify the correct use of PPE by workers. In this paper we propose a method designed for verifying the correct use of helmet and protective vest, optimized to run directly on board of a smart camera, in order to use it also in temporary and mobile construction sites. The proposed approach solves many known problems in PPE verification systems, such as the detection at variable distances, the balancing of the number of samples available for the various classes of interest, a more accurate verification of the presence of the helmet and the management of challenging situations such as bald or hatted heads typically confused with helmets. To this aim, we conducted an ablation study showing the effectiveness of our design choices in terms of dataset preparation and classifier. The detection F-Score of 91.5% in continuous monitoring, up to 94.0% in more controlled access control scenarios, and the PPE recognition accuracy of 93.7%, together with the capability to process 10 to 20 FPS on board of three different smart cameras, demonstrate the suitability of the proposed solution for real construction sites. An example video of the proposed system in action, integrated in a PPE verification product, is online available (https://www.youtube.com/watch?v=-fz25HYcFLo).

Keywords: PPE detection · personal protective equipment · smart camera

1 Introduction

The safety of people is an important aspect for any working reality, as demonstrated by the efforts that each government puts in place to protect the health and safety of workers and the places in which they work [25]. Nonetheless, workplace injuries are still very frequent, especially in sectors where workers interact

J.-J. Rousseau and B. Kapralos (Eds.): ICPR 2022 Workshops, LNCS 13643, pp. 95–108, 2023.
https://doi.org/10.1007/978-3-031-37660-3_7

with machinaries, such as the production chains of the metalworking industries, or on construction sites. According to a recent study by the American Society of Safety Engineers and the European Agency for Safety and Health at Work, the annual cost of accidents at work is approximately 2.680 billion dollars worldwide, of which 476 billion in Europe alone [23]. As for Italy, reports of accidents with a fatal outcome went from 1,205 in 2019 to 1,538 in 2020, with an increase of 27.6% [17]. Although there is great attention to the problem of worker safety, the rules and actions implemented by the companies have as their main limit the objective impossibility of implementing continuous monitoring of risk situations. This control is absolutely necessary to ensure that the safety rules are actually respected by the employers and by the workers, who may underestimate the effectiveness of the personal protective equipment (PPE) to guarantee their own safety [10].

In this regard, video analysis and deep learning [6], which became pervasive in various sectors, from security [11] to retail [14], from smart-cities [16] to intelligent parking management [3], can be very useful since it allows to monitor and analyze environments, systems and people in a non-invasive way using standard video-surveillance cameras [5]. Often these cameras are already installed in the environment to be monitored, without the need for additional sensors or devices [13]. In the field of smart-cities and environmental safety, these technologies have been consolidated for years and, in the recent health emergency, attention has also shifted towards the safety of people, pushing the market towards proposing solutions for the detection of gatherings and PPE verification (mainly the health mask) [15]. These new application contexts have highlighted how the most recent video analysis solutions based on artificial intelligence are now mature and sufficiently reliable to effectively move towards more critical sectors such as personal safety.

It is not a coincidence that various PPE detection products were developed in recent years [29], categorized as follows:

- Application context: construction sites, production lines, access control to areas at risk (e.g. areas in which heavy machinery or chemical agents are present)
- PPE: the equipment may include helmet, goggles, gloves, reflective vest, harness, safety shoes, health mask, headphones, gowns and / or chemical protective clothing
- Monitoring type: continuous in an area of interest (e.g. construction site) or on request for access control
- View of the worker: frontal or from any point of view
- Processing hardware: local server (standard or embedded system), cloud or smart camera.

In this paper, we propose a PPE detection method for constructions sites, which verifies whether the workers wear helmet and reflective vest. The method is independent on the monitoring type, namely it can be used both for continuous monitoring and for access control, and the worker can be framed from any point of view. In addition, differently from most of the existing methods that require servers equipped with GPU and, thus, to send images and/or video streams on the network, our approach is optimized to run in real-time on the edge, directly on board of smart cameras. This is an important feature, since many construction sites are temporary or mobile and it is not easy to guarantee an Internet connection or a private network, effectively limiting the possibility of adopting solutions that require sending the video stream to servers or in the cloud. Furthermore, in some cases these solutions could not be privacy compliant, as they require to transmit the images or the video stream to external systems.

2 Related Works

In contrast to sensor-based techniques [26], which require the installation of a sensor (e.g. RFID) on the worker and/or on each PPE and is more invasive [4], vision-based approaches [7] use cameras to capture images of the construction site, which are analysed to verify that the workers correctly wear the PPE. The task of monitoring PPE compliance inherently involves two subtasks: detection of workers and verification of presence and correct position of PPE.

Various methods have been proposed for detecting helmet and reflective vest in recent years, despite the absence of a standard dataset. In [8] YOLO v3 and Faster R-CNN (with a Feature Pyramid Network and ResNet-50 as backbone) were pre-trained with a synthetic dataset produced with the RAGE engine and then fine-tuned with a small dataset of 100 real images. The method achieved a remarkable accuracy on synthetic images, but it was not able to generalize on a test set with (only) 180 real images collected from the web.

Gong et al. [12] trained YOLO v3, YOLO v4 and YOLO v5 to detect the worker, helmets of four colors and reflective vest on the dataset CHV (Colour Helmet and Vest) [27], collected in real construction sites by combining GDUT-HWD [28] and SHWD (1,330 images and 9,209 instances for training, 133 images for testing). The main drawback of this method is that it detects separately the worker and the PPE, so it may be hard to verify that the protective equipment is correctly worn.

In [2], a nested neural network with two Faster R-CNN models was applied sequentially for verifying the presence of helmet and vest. The former acts as a worker detection module that is applied multiple times to cover near-field, mid-field and far-field workers; the latter is the PPE recognition module and analyzes the upper $1/3$ region to verify the presence of helmet and the lower $2/3$ region to detect the presence of vest. The neural networks were trained with images from CUHK01 [1] and a private dataset, acquired by using cameras installed at a height to frame the whole construction site without occlusions, from a high angle of view. The method has been tested on only 200 images and achieved an accuracy of around 87%. The main problems of this approach are the computational complexity, the aspect ratio not preserved to cover near-, mid- and far-fields and the fact that in case of workers not standing, namely bent or kneeling, the helmet may not be in the upper $1/3$ region and the vest in the lower $2/3$ region.

In [20] a query image is compared with a set of gallery images of workers with different combination of known PPE. Four clusters are defined (W, WH, WV, WHV) at the first level, while other clusters are considered according to the color of the PPE. The features are extracted with ResNet-50, trained with the AlignedReID algorithm [19]. The method achieved 90% accuracy on the Pictor PPE dataset [21], collected through web-mining and crowd-sourcing. The confusion matrices show errors especially in recognizing workers without helmet.

The authors of [27] used their ODPD dataset, collected in an offshore drilling platform, with around 4,000 images of annotated worker (W), worker with helmet (WH), worker with vest (WV) and worker with helmet and vest (WHV), to train a YOLO v3 able to detect workers. Then, they extracted the keypoints of the worker to determine the regions of interest in which a ResNet-50 was applied for recognizing helmet and vest. This method achieved 94.8% accuracy in helmet recognition and 95.6% accuracy in vest recognition.

3   Contribution

In this paper we propose a method to verify that helmet and vest are worn safely by workers. With respect to related works [2, 8, 12, 20, 27], we focus on a solution accurate and efficient, that can be deployed on board of a smart camera, in order to be privacy compliant and to avoid the problem of network connection in temporary or mobile construction sites.

The worker detection is performed with a convolutional neural network (CNN) based on MobileNetv2-SSD, that also provides a first classification of the four considered categories (W, WH, WV, WHV). In addition, our detector can cover near-field, mid-field and far-field workers without the aspect ratio problem reported in [2], since it is possible to define 16:9 areas in which the detector is applied; this choice also allows to increase the receptive field in the regions of interest.

To be more effective in helmet recognition, very critical for the worker safety and a known problem for existing methods [20], we consider an additional level of classification specialized in this task. Unlike other approaches that assume the presence of the helmet in the upper part of the bounding box [2], we carry out the classification on the whole person, as the worker could be kneeling or bent while doing his work. Our experiments demonstrate the effectiveness of this choice.

The detector and the classifier have been trained with a balanced dataset, unlike the state of the art methods that use strongly unbalanced datasets [20]. To achieve this, a grueling activity of semi-automatic or manual annotation of existing datasets (Pictor PPE, VOC2028, CHV) was carried out, along with the collection and annotation of an extensive dataset to balance the number of samples of the various classes.

Finally, for the first time in the literature, we have analyzed and found errors in recognizing the helmet (actually not worn) on people bald and / or wearing hats, as the standard datasets do not include such samples. We demonstrate

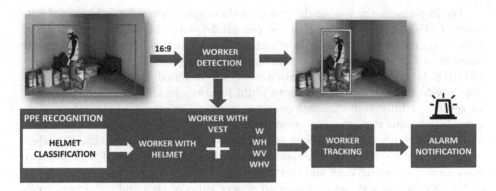

Fig. 1. Architecture of the proposed method. The CNN for worker detection, based on MobileNetv2-SSD, is applied on the 16:9 regions of interest, in order to avoid loosing the aspect ratio and to increase the receptive field in the working areas. In the PPE recognition module, the results of the detection, in terms of bounding boxes and categories (W, WH, WV, WHV), are combined with the results of the binary classifier specialized on helmet recognition. The worker tracking module allows to follow the workers in different frames and to collect information during the time. Finally, the alarm notification module is used to report security risks in access control and continuous monitoring.

that our method is robust to such misclassifications, since our dataset has been augmented with samples of hairless and/or hatted workers; this feature is crucial for a PPE verification system, because such a misclassification error could constitute a serious safety problem for workers.

4   Proposed Method

The architecture of the proposed PPE detection system is depicted in Fig. 1. The application is installed on board of a smart camera, with the additional possibility to use the embedded hardware accelerators (GPU or TPU). The processing pipeline includes worker detection (see Sect. 4.1), PPE recognition (see Sect. 4.2), worker tracking (see Sect. 4.3) and alarm notification (see Sect. 4.4).

4.1   Worker Detection

The worker detection module receives as input the image I_t acquired by the camera at time t and returns a list of bounding boxes $b = \{b_1, ..., b_{|n|}\}$, where $|n|$ is the number of workers detected in I_t. The generic detected worker w_i is represented as a quintuple (x, y, w, h, c), where x and y represent the top-left point, w and h are the width and height of the bounding box surrounding the worker, while c is a category among worker (W), worker with helmet (WH), worker with vest (WV) and worker with helmet and vest (WHV).

We implement the worker detection module with a convolutional neural network (CNN) suitably designed to be compliant with the limited memory and processing resources available on smart cameras. To this aim, we adapt to our purpose a CNN commonly used for embedded devices, namely MobileNetv2-SSD [18,24]. The backbone is based on a streamlined architecture that uses depth-wise separable convolutions to build lightweight CNNs. The basic idea is to replace a fully convolutional operator with a factorized version that splits convolution into two separate layers, one for filtering (depth-wise convolution) and one for combining (point-wise convolution). This factorization has the effect of drastically reducing the number of operations and the model size. To save additional processing time and memory space, we set the network input size to 512×288; in this way, we maintain an aspect ratio of 16:9 and obtain an excellent trade-off between accuracy and computational complexity. The output of the neural network includes, for each detected box, the coordinates $((x, y, w, h))$, a measure of objectness and 4 probabilities, one for each class.

We started the training from the weights pre-trained over the COCO dataset, available on the Tensorflow Model Zoo. We adopted the weighted smooth L1 as localization loss and the weighted sigmoid as classification loss. We chose the RMSProp optimizer, with an initial learning rate equal to 0.004 and an exponential decay with a 0.95 every 200.000 steps. The momentum was set to 0.9 and the batch size to 8. The training was completed in 1.018.699 steps, when we obtained the best checkpoint on the validation set.

In order to avoid the problem of aspect ratio reported in [2], we allow the user to draw one or more 16:9 regions of interest in the image; in each region the detector is applied to localize and classify the workers. In this way, the receptive field of the neural network can be dynamically controlled by the user without loosing the aspect ratio of the image. Similarly to the method proposed in [2], we implement a non-maxima-suppression mechanism based on IoU (≥ 0.5) to discard multiple detections of the same workers; among the overlapping bounding boxes, we choose the one with the maximum objectness value, preserving its class.

4.2 PPE Recognition

The PPE recognition module refines the classification provided by the worker detection module. We have included this further level of classification in the processing pipeline for three reasons: i) not wearing a helmet correctly is a very risky safety problem for workers and deserves more attention; ii) the methods trained with the datasets available in the literature are more effective in recognizing the vest than the helmet and this result is also demonstrated by our preliminary experiments reported in Sect. 6; iii) we observed, for the first time in literature, that the bald or hatted head is confused with the helmet if this case is not considered in the training set; due to the minimum difference among the situations, the detector alone is not able to deal with this challenge (as shown in Sect. 6.2).

(a) WH   (b) W   (c) WV   (d) W

Fig. 2. Examples of challenging images that the proposed PPE recognition module was able to correctly classify, by distinguishing the helmet from a bald or hatted head and a yellow jacket from a vest. (Color figure online)

Therefore, we trained a binary classifier based on MobileNetv2 [24], able to classify the samples among helmet/no helmet taking as input an image crop containing the detected worker entirely. Since a worker can work standing, kneeling or bent, we have chosen a square input size (224×224). To avoid a distortion of the worker image, we have not carried out a simple resize of the bounding box of the worker (which can be rectangular, especially if the worker is standing), but we have cut out the minimum enclosing square around the detected bounding box. In this way, the resize to 224×224 pixels is performed on this square crop and the image of the worker is not distorted.

We adopted a MobileNetv2 model pre-trained over ImageNet and performed 64 epochs of fine tuning, with a batch size equal to 64. We adopted a binary cross-entropy loss function and an Adam optimizer, with an initial learning rate equal to 0.005 and a learning decay factor of 0.5 every 10 epochs. All the parameters were chosen with a grid search on the validation set.

The final worker category (W, WH, WV, WHV) is obtained by combining the results of the detector with those of the classifier. The former allows to determine whether the worker is wearing a vest (V) or not, while the latter verifies the presence of the helmet (H).

4.3 Worker Tracking

The worker tracking module receives the boxes detected at time t $\{b_1, ..., b_{|n|}\}$ and associate them to the people tracked at time $t-1$, to produce a new set of tracked workers $O = \{O_1, ..., O_{|M|}\}$, where $|M|$ is the number of workers tracked at time t. The goal is to assign a unique identifier to each worker, in order to collect the trajectories of the workers and correctly associate the information about the worn PPE. We developed this module as proposed in [9], namely with a one-to-one overlap tracking algorithm, based on a similarity matrix which takes into account the position of the bounding boxes.

Being d_{max} the maximum distance in pixel supposed to be traveled by a worker between two consecutive frames and $d(a, b)$ the Euclidean distance between two points a and b, the similarity s_{ij} between the i-th detected box b_i and the j-th object o_j is computed as follows:

$$s_{ij} = \begin{cases} 1 - \frac{d(b_i,o_j)}{d_{max}} & d(b_i,o_j) < d_{max} \\ 0 & otherwise \end{cases} \tag{1}$$

The points considered in the computation of the distance $d(b_i, o_j)$ are the centroids of b_i and o_j, while the division by d_{max} (set for our experiments to $1/5$ of the image width) is performed to normalize the similarity between 0 and 1. The smaller the distance between b_i and o_j, the higher is their measure of similarity. If the two centroids are farther than d_{max}, the similarity is forced to zero; in this way, the subsequent phase of object matching can discard the associations whose similarity is zero, to avoid wrong associations between different entities. Since the movement of the workers between consecutive frames should be limited in space, this is an effective and efficient solution for the problem at hand.

Workers may be temporarily occluded by other objects or structures on the construction site. To avoid losing track of these workers, we introduce the concept of "ghost" object. In particular, if there is no association between an object o_j with a detected box, we still keep this object (in the ghost state) for a certain configurable time t_g (set in our experiments to 1 s); if the object is not re-associated within a time t_g, then it is deleted from the list.

4.4 Alarm Notification

Our system for PPE verification can be used in two ways: for access control and for continuous monitoring.

In the first case, the camera is placed at the entrance of the construction site and frames the worker, who typically shows himself in collaborative mode, only when he wants to enter the construction site; the system verifies for t_l seconds (user configurable parameter) that the worker is safe and sends a notification (e.g. digital I/O) to unlock the door or the access gate to the construction site only if helmet and vest are correctly worn.

In the other scenario, the camera frames the construction site and the method continuously checks if the workers are wearing helmet and vest; if the system detects for at least t_l seconds the absence of PPE (recognized class other than WHV), it generates an alarm notification, which can be used to order the worker to wear PPE.

In both cases, the temporal analysis in a window of t_l seconds can be done thanks to the worker tracking module, which maintains the history of the worker.

5 Dataset

We composed the dataset used for our experiments by combining the samples of publicly available datasets, such as Pictor PPE [21], VOC2028 [22], CHV [27] and several other images that we acquired in real or simulated construction sites.

(a) Front   (b) Rear   (c) Left   (d) Right

Fig. 3. Examples of images from our PPE dataset. It contains between 2,200 and 3,000 instances for each class, with workers framed from any point of view.

The Pictor PPE dataset consists of 784 images (582 for training, 120 for validation and 152 for testing) and is already annotated for our purposes. We used the images and the annotations of this dataset as they are, but we noticed a strong imbalance. Indeed, the class WV is not represented and there are only 17 samples of the class WHV; WH class is the most represented (517 samples), while the remaining 240 images belong to class W.

We manually labelled the images of VOC2028 and CHV. After this operation, we obtained a dataset of 2,032 images, in which the worker instances are divided as follows: 1232 W W, 2665 WH, 270 WV, 1132 WHV. Therefore, as already found by the analysis of the literature, the publicly available datasets do not contain a balanced number of instances of the 4 classes of interest. In addition, there are a few samples of bald workers and no samples of workers wearing normal hats; since these samples may be challenging for the PPE recognition module and a potential risk for the safety of the workers, it is crucial to fill this gap.

To this aim, we decided to collect our own additional samples in real or simulated construction sites. In our acquisition campaign, we considered the following aspects: balancing the dataset between the 4 classes of interest; collection of samples with differently colored helmets (mainly yellow, orange, red, white, blue); collection of samples with differently colored vests (mainly yellow and orange); acquisition of workers from every point of view (front, rear, left, right) and from different heights (continuous monitoring and access control); collection of bald people or with differently colored hats. Various examples of our PPE dataset are depicted in Fig. 3, while details on its composition are reported in Table 1.

The dataset includes 6,719 images and, to the best of our knowledge, it is the largest benchmark used for this purpose. It is also more balanced than other datasets available in the literature. Indeed, we have between 2,200 and 3,000 instances for each class, for a total of 10,250 worker instances. For our experiments, we divided the dataset into training set (80%), validation set (10%) and test set (10%).

Table 1. Number of images and instances for each category of workers in the PPE dataset used for our experiments, composed of images from Pictor PPE, VOC2028, CHV and collected in real or simulated construction sites.

Number of images	W	WH	WV	WHV	Total
6,719	2,732	2,258	2,343	2,917	10,250

Table 2. Worker detection results achieved by the proposed method in terms of Recall, Precision and F-Score. The performance are reported separately for access control and continuous monitoring scenarios.

Setup	Recall	Precision	F-Score
Access Control	90.4	97.9	94.0
Continuous Monitoring	86.5	97.1	91.5

6   Results

6.1   Worker Detection

We evaluated the performance of our worker detection module in terms of Recall (R), Precision (P) and F-Score (F).

$$R = \frac{TP}{TP + FN}, P = \frac{TP}{TP + FP}, F = \frac{2 * P * R}{P + R} \tag{2}$$

where TP, FN and FP are the number of true positives, false negatives and false positives. A true positive is a detected box whose intersection over union (IoU) with a groundtruth box is higher than 0.5. All the groundtruth elements not associated with detected boxes through this criterion are false negatives, while all the detected boxes not associated with groundtruth elements are false positives.

The results of this evaluation are reported in Table 2. We considered separately the performance achieved in access control scenarios, in which the worker is typically collaborative, and in continuous monitoring, that is substantially more challenging in terms of distance, pose and quality of the image. We achieved a F-Score of 94.0% in a more controlled scenario as the access control and 91.5% in continuous monitoring; this last result is quite impressive considering the challenging conditions of a construction site. To the best of our knowledge, other methods in the literature were not able to exceed 90% and used less samples for the analysis.

6.2   PPE Recognition

We used as performance metric for PPE recognition the accuracy for each class (W, WH, WV, WHV) and the overall accuracy. The accuracy for each class is computed as the ratio between the number of correct classifications and the total number of samples for that class. The overall accuracy is the ratio between the total number of correct classifications and the total number of samples.

The results of the experiment that we carried our for PPE recognition evaluation are reported in Table 3. The proposed method achieves an overall accuracy of 93.7%. We can note a trend that is similar to the literature, namely the performance is higher when the PPE are correctly worn (WHV 98.5%); however, the choice of the classifier and the careful dataset preparation allowed our method to perform successfully even in the other cases (WH 95.6%, W 91.4%, WV 89.3%).

6.3   Ablation Study

To demonstrate the effectiveness of our choices in terms of dataset preparation and design of the classifier, we also carried out an ablation study whose results are reported in Table 3.

Removing the Samples with Bald and Hatted Workers. In this experiment, we trained our binary classifier for helmet/no helmet recognition without using the additional samples of bald and hatted workers. The results show that the overall accuracy reduces to 91.7%, but the analysis of the accuracy for each class gives more insights. In fact, we can note that the accuracy decrease is mainly due to the worst performance on class W (87.4%) and class WV (84.2%); this means that without additional samples of bald and hatted workers, the classifier is less effective in helmet recognition. The slight increase on class WH (96.9%) is an additional clue of the higher sensitivity for the helmet class. This result demonstrates the effectiveness of our augmentation procedure and the necessity to take into account these challenges.

Removing the Classifier. With this experiment, we demonstrate the improvement that the binary classifier for helmet/no helmet recognition allows to obtain with respect to the solution adopting only the detector. In fact, the overall accuracy achieved by the detector only is 91.3%, around 2.5% less than the proposed method. The second classification level allows to improve the accuracy for each class (W 91.4% vs 91.2%, WH 95.6% vs 92.7%, WV 89.3% vs 83.7%, WHV 98.5% vs 97.5%), since the whole system is able to better distinguish workers with or without the helmet and to deal with the challenges related to bald and hatted workers.

Reducing the Input Size of the Classifier. This last experiment allows to motivate the choice of the input size of the proposed binary classifier. We trained, with the same setup described in Sect. 4.2, another classifier with input size 96×96 and used it in the proposed method. The results reported in Table 3 show a substantial overall accuracy decrease (85.5% vs 93.7%), in particular for the classes W (88.2% vs 91.4%) and WV (64.5% vs 89.3%). This result demonstrates that a too small receptive field does not allow to have sufficient information for detecting the presence or absence of the helmet.

Table 3. PPE recognition accuracy for each class and overall achieved by the proposed method and by some of its weakened variants, namely one trained without bald and hatted samples, another using only the detector and the last adopting a classifier with a reduced input size (96×96)

Method	W	WH	WV	WHV	Overall
Proposed	91.4	95.6	89.3	98.5	93.7
No bald and hatted	87.4	96.9	84.2	98.5	91.7
Only detector	91.2	92.7	83.7	97.5	91.3
Classifier 96×96	88.2	92.8	64.5	96.5	85.5

6.4 Processing Time

The proposed solution has been also integrated and tested on three different smart cameras equipped with GPU, namely Panasonic WV-X2251L and Hanwha PNV-A6081R equipped with a GPU and Axis Q1615 Mk III TPU provided. The processing frame rate depends on the computational resources available on the specific cameras, but it varies between 10 and 20 fps, fast enough for continuous monitoring or access control in construction sites. Therefore, the proposed system is ready for being used in real temporary and mobile construction sites both in terms of accuracy and processing time.

7 Conclusion

In this paper, we demonstrated that a careful dataset preparation and targeted design choices allow to realize an effective and efficient method for verifying the correct use of helmet and protective vest.

Unlike other methods recently proposed in the literature, our approach can run directly on board of a smart camera (10-20 FPS) and is also suited for temporary and mobile construction sites (without Internet connection).

In addition, we demonstrated its capability to deal with detection at variable distances and to accurately recognize the presence of the helmet, even in challenging situations such as bald or hatted heads not managed by existing approaches.

The remarkable detection and verification performance and its efficiency make the proposed method reliable and fast enough to be used in a real product for the monitoring of construction sites.

References

1. Ahmed, E., Jones, M., Marks, T.K.: An improved deep learning architecture for person re-identification. In: Proceedings of the IEEE Conference on Computer Vision and Pattern Recognition, pp. 3908–3916 (2015)

2. Akbarzadeh, M., Zhu, Z., Hammad, A.: Nested network for detecting PPE on large construction sites based on frame segmentation. In: Creative Construction e-Conference 2020, pp. 33–38. Budapest University of Technology and Economics (2020)
3. Carletti, V., Foggia, P., Greco, A., Saggese, A., Vento, M.: Automatic detection of long term parked cars. In: 2015 12th IEEE International Conference on Advanced Video and Signal Based Surveillance (AVSS), pp. 1–6. IEEE (2015)
4. Carletti, V., Greco, A., Saggese, A., Vento, M.: A smartphone-based system for detecting falls using anomaly detection. In: International Conference on Image Analysis and Processing, pp. 490–499. Springer (2017)
5. Carletti, V., Greco, A., Saggese, A., Vento, M.: An effective real time gender recognition system for smart cameras. J. Ambient. Intell. Humaniz. Comput. **11**(6), 2407–2419 (2020)
6. D'Arminio, E., Greco, A., Saldutti, S., Vento, B.: Deep learning for edge video analytics solutions: The worldwide successful experience of a universitary spin-off. In: Ital-IA (2022)
7. Delhi, V.S.K., Sankarlal, R., Thomas, A.: Detection of personal protective equipment (ppe) compliance on construction site using computer vision based deep learning techniques. Front. Built Environ. **6**, 136 (2020)
8. Di Benedetto, M., Carrara, F., Meloni, E., Amato, G., Falchi, F., Gennaro, C.: Learning accurate personal protective equipment detection from virtual worlds. Multimedia Tools Appl. **80**(15), 23241–23253 (2021)
9. Di Lascio, R., Foggia, P., Percannella, G., Saggese, A., Vento, M.: A real time algorithm for people tracking using contextual reasoning. Comput. Vis. Image Underst. **117**(8), 892–908 (2013)
10. Ekanayake, B., Wong, J.K.W., Fini, A.A.F., Smith, P.: Computer vision-based interior construction progress monitoring: a literature review and future research directions. Autom. Constr. **127**, 103705 (2021)
11. Elharrouss, O., Almaadeed, N., Al-Maadeed, S.: A review of video surveillance systems. J. Vis. Commun. Image Represent. **77**, 103116 (2021)
12. Gong, F., Ji, X., Gong, W., Yuan, X., Gong, C.: Deep learning based protective equipment detection on offshore drilling platform. Symmetry **13**(6), 954 (2021)
13. Greco, A., Petkov, N., Saggese, A., Vento, M.: AReN: a deep learning approach for sound event recognition using a brain inspired representation. IEEE Trans. Inf. Forensics Secur. **15**, 3610–3624 (2020)
14. Greco, A., Saggese, A., Vento, B.: A robust and efficient overhead people counting system for retail applications. In: International Conference on Image Analysis and Processing (2021)
15. Greco, A., Saggese, A., Vento, M., Vigilante, V.: Performance assessment of face analysis algorithms with occluded faces. In: Del Bimbo, A., et al. (eds.) ICPR 2021. LNCS, vol. 12662, pp. 472–486. Springer, Cham (2021). https://doi.org/10.1007/978-3-030-68790-8_37
16. Greco, A., Saggese, A., Vento, M., Vigilante, V.: Vehicles detection for smart roads applications on board of smart cameras: a comparative analysis. IEEE Transactions on Intelligent Transportation Systems (2021)
17. INAIL: Workplace accidents. http://www.inail.it/cs/internet/comunicazione/news-ed-eventi/news/news-dati-inail-costruzioni-2021.html (2021). Accessed 10 May 2022
18. Liu, W., et al.: SSD: single shot multibox detector. In: Leibe, B., Matas, J., Sebe, N., Welling, M. (eds.) ECCV 2016. LNCS, vol. 9905, pp. 21–37. Springer, Cham (2016). https://doi.org/10.1007/978-3-319-46448-0_2

19. Luo, H., Jiang, W., Zhang, X., Fan, X., Qian, J., Zhang, C.: AlignedReID++: dynamically matching local information for person re-identification. Pattern Recogn. **94**, 53–61 (2019)

20. Nath, N.D., Behzadan, A.H.: Deep learning detection of personal protective equipment to maintain safety compliance on construction sites. In: Construction Research Congress 2020: Computer Applications, pp. 181–190. American Society of Civil Engineers Reston, VA (2020)

21. Nath, N.D., Behzadan, A.H., Paal, S.G.: Deep learning for site safety: Real-time detection of personal protective equipment. Autom. Constr. **112**, 103085 (2020)

22. Peng, D., Sun, Z., Chen, Z., Cai, Z., Xie, L., Jin, L.: Detecting heads using feature refine net and cascaded multi-scale architecture. In: 2018 24th International Conference on Pattern Recognition (ICPR), pp. 2528–2533. IEEE (2018)

23. of Safety Engineers, T.A.S.: The cost of workplace accidents to the company. https://www.axelent.com/media/6547/aw_43_en.pdf (2021). Accessed 10 May 2022

24. Sandler, M., Howard, A., Zhu, M., Zhmoginov, A., Chen, L.C.: Inverted residuals and linear bottlenecks: Mobile networks for classification, detection and segmentation. arXiv (2018)

25. Shin, S.H., Kim, H.O., Rim, K.T.: Worker safety in the rare earth elements recycling process from the review of toxicity and issues. Saf. Health Work **10**(4), 409–419 (2019)

26. Swathi, S., Raj, S., Devaraj, D.: Microcontroller and sensor based smart biking system for driver's safety. In: 2019 IEEE International Conference on Intelligent Techniques in Control, Optimization and Signal Processing (INCOS), pp. 1–5. IEEE (2019)

27. Wang, Z., Wu, Y., Yang, L., Thirunavukarasu, A., Evison, C., Zhao, Y.: Fast personal protective equipment detection for real construction sites using deep learning approaches. Sensors **21**(10), 3478 (2021)

28. Wu, J., Cai, N., Chen, W., Wang, H., Wang, G.: Automatic detection of hardhats worn by construction personnel: a deep learning approach and benchmark dataset. Autom. Constr. **106**, 102894 (2019)

29. Zeng, T., Wang, J., Cui, B., Wang, X., Wang, D., Zhang, Y.: The equipment detection and localization of large-scale construction jobsite by far-field construction surveillance video based on improving yolov3 and grey wolf optimizer improving extreme learning machine. Constr. Build. Mater. **291**, 123268 (2021)

Towards an Accurate 3D Deformable Eye Model for Gaze Estimation

Chenyi Kuang[1]([✉]), Jeffery O. Kephart[2], and Qiang Ji[1]

[1] Rensselaer Polytechnic Institute, Troy, USA
{kuangc2,jiq}@rpi.edu
[2] IBM Thomas J. Watson Research Ctr., Yorktown, USA
kephart@us.ibm.com

Abstract. 3D eye gaze estimation has emerged as an interesting and challenging task in recent years. As an attractive alternative to appearance-based models, 3D model-based gaze estimation methods are powerful because a general prior of eye anatomy or geometry has been integrated into the 3D model hence they adapt well under various head poses and illumination conditions. We present a method for constructing an anatomically accurate 3D deformable eye model from the IR images of eyes and demonstrate its application to 3D gaze estimation. The 3D eye model consists of a deformable basis capable of representing individual real-world eyeballs, corneas, irises and kappa angles. To validate the model's accuracy, we combine it with a 3D face model (without eyeball) and perform image-based fitting to obtain eye basis coefficients The fitted eyeball is then used to compute 3D gaze direction. Evaluation results on multiple datasets show that the proposed method generalizes well across datasets and is robust under various head poses.

Keywords: Eyeball modeling · 3DMM · Gaze estimation

1 Introduction

Eye gaze – an important cue for human behaviour and attention – has been widely explored in recent years by computer vision researchers. As interactive applications such as AR/VR, 3D avatar animation and driver behaviour monitoring [7–9,14] gain more popularity, various 3D gaze methods have been proposed (with much recent emphasis on deep-learning based models). Based on the devices and data they use, 3D gaze estimation methods can be divided into two categories: (1) appearance-based gaze estimation from images/videos; and (2) 3D eye model recovery and model-based gaze estimation. Appearance-based methods usually focus on extracting eye features from web cameras or IR cameras. Such methods can be sensitive to different head poses and illumination conditions; hence their generalization ability can be limited. 3D model-based methods takes a different strategy that entails recovering the anatomical structure of a person's eyeball. Based on the devices and data they require, 3D model-based

© Springer Nature Switzerland AG 2023
J.-J. Rousseau and B. Kapralos (Eds.): ICPR 2022 Workshops, LNCS 13643, pp. 109–123, 2023.
https://doi.org/10.1007/978-3-031-37660-3_8

methods can be further divided into two types: (a) personalized 3D eye model recovery from IR camera systems and (b) 3D eye shape estimation from image features using a pre-constructed deformable eye basis.

The first type (2a) usually requires setting up specific devices and using a complex calculation process to handle light refraction, IR camera calibration, etc. These methods usually build a geometric eye model to represent the anatomical eyeball structure including pupil diameter, 3D pupil center and cornea curvature center. Based on such computation, some wearable devices are offered with a pre-installed and calibrated camera and illumination system for real-time 3D gaze estimation. However, the practicality and accessibility of such methods can be limited. More recently, as 3D morphable face models are successfully applied in accurate 3D face reconstruction and animation, similar experiments have been conducted for constructing a deformable eye model from 3D scans. Wood et al. [32] proposed a 3D deformable eye region model constructed from high-quality 3D facial scans, in which the eye region and the size of iris are parameterized using a PCA basis. Ploumpis et al. [23] constructed a large-scale statistic 3D deformable full head model, including face, ear, eye region and pupil size. Both [23,32] can be applied to eye 3DMM fitting using image feature points for recovering 3D gaze direction. Such statistic eye models provide a parameterized linear space for approximating the size of a new subject's eyeball and can be directly utilized in image-based fitting for gaze estimation.

This paper presents an accurate 3D deformable eye model constructed from recovered geometric parameters of multiple subjects. More specifically, we use the wearable device Tobii pro Glasses2 for data collection and compute individual geometric eyeball parameters through explicit IR camera calibration, pupil & iris detection and glint detection. The eyeball geometry is represented as two intersecting spheres: the eyeball and the cornea, with person-specific parameters for eyeball radius, cornea radius, iris radius and kappa angle. Based on the constructed model, we propose a two-phase framework of 3D gaze estimation for webcam images. In summary, the contributions of this paper include:

– Eye data collection with Tobii pro Glasses2 including 3D gaze direction, 3D gaze point and IR videos of eye region. Then personal eyeball parameters are recovered from data, including eyeball radius, cornea radius, iris radius and kappa angle. PoG (Point of Gaze) error is calculated for evaluating recovered parameters.
– An accurate parameterized 3D eye model with PCA eye basis that represents personal variations in 3D eye geometry.
– Integration of the constructed eye model with a sparse 3D face model, yielding a two-phase gaze estimation framework for monocular webcam images. Experimental results show that our model generalizes well to different benchmark datasets for 3D gaze estimation.

2   Related Works

Our proposed method takes advantage of techniques from 3D eye model recovery using infrared or RGBD cameras combined with model-based gaze estimation. We focus on reviewing related works in these two areas.

2.1   3D Eye Modeling

Infrared-camera based 3D eye model recovery systems are usually paired with pre-calibrated illuminators to generate detectable glints in the IR images [4,13,16]. Through glint tracking and solving for the light reflection equations on cornea surface, the 3D cornea center can be estimated. The 3D pupil center can be solved by ellipse calibration. The IR camera-light system can achieve good accuracy and precision for estimating eyeball geometry, but the setup process is complex. For the convenience of real time gaze estimation, multiple wearable devices have been developed like [12,25–27]. Usually a one-time personal calibration is required by these devices before starting gaze tracking, which is used to recover personal 3D eye model information in advance.

3D eye model recovery methods based on RGB-D-cameras have been proposed as well. Wang et al. [29] recovered subject-dependent 3D eye parameters including eyeball radius, cornea center to eyeball center offset, eyeball center to head center offset and kappa angle using a Kinect camera. Zhou et al. [34] recovered the 3D eyeball center, eyeball radius and iris center using the geometry relationship of two eye models with a Kinect camera. More recently, concurrent with the development of large scale 3D morphable face models [3,11,18,22], researchers are using a similar process to construct a deformable eye region model. Woods et al. [32] constructed a 3D deformable eye model from large scale 3D facial scans. Their model contains a deformable shape basis for the iris, eye socket, eye lid and eye brow. Ploumpis et al. [23] presented a complete 3D deformable model for the whole human head that incorporates eye and eye region models. Compared with [32], their eye model uses finer-grained groups of eyeball, cornea and iris vertices and captures variations in pupil size. We are unaware of prior work that constructs a detailed eye mesh model that focuses simultaneously on modeling the variance of eyeball size, cornea size and iris size.

2.2   Model-based 3D Gaze Estimation

3D gaze estimation methods can be divided into two types: appearance-based methods (which take advantage of image features) and model-based methods, the former type is not discussed in detail and we focus on model-based methods in this paper. Model-based gaze estimation methods have two major advantages over appearance-based methods. First, 3D models are less vulnerable to variations in illumination because it contains a general geometry prior for the 3D eye anatomy that can be fit to different images. Second, 3D models can be rotated arbitrarily by assigning a rotation matrix, making them more robust to head and eye pose variations. Wang et al. [30] exploit a sparse 3D Face-Eye model that can deform in eyeball center position, pupil position and eyeball radius. Based on the face model, 3D head poses can be solved in advance and then eyeball rotation and kappa angle are solved by minimizing eye-landmark error and gaze error. Woods et al. [32] and Ploumpis et al. [23] introduced an "analysis-by-synthesis" framework to fit their 3D eye model to image features. The 3D head pose and eye pose are optimized separately, and eye image texture is utilized to fit the eye pose. They achieved good accuracy in 3D gaze estimation without using gaze labels.

3   3D Deformable Eye Model

The main objective of data collection is to recover anatomically accurate parameters that capture individual eyeball structure. To fully utilize existing resources and tools, we choose a reliable eye tracking device, Tobii Pro Glasses2, which allows us to capture human gaze data in real-world environments in real time. We collected both infrared eye images and true gaze data from Tobii Pro Glasses2, where the former are utilized for computing eye model parameters for each participant and the latter are used as ground-truth to validate our calculation process. In all, we recruited 15 participants, each of whom were involved in multiple data collection experiments to ensure that the training and validation data are both valid. We detail our data collection and processing pipeline in Sect. 3.1.

3.1   Data Collection and Personal Eye Parameter Recovery

Tobii Pro Glasses2 consists of a head unit, a recording unit and controller software. The head unit contains four eye tracking sensors (two for each eye) that take infrared eye region images from different angles to analyze gaze direction and one high-resolution scene camera capturing HD videos of what is in front of the person. Additionally, there are six IR illuminators on each side that generate glints in the eye images due to corneal reflection. For each participant, a pre-calibration before recording is required to ensure that the glass is properly worn and the sensors successfully capture the pupil center of both eyes. We invite each participant to wear the glass and sit in front of a $80\,cm \times 135\,cm$ screen at a distance of 1.5–1.9 m. The participant is asked to track a moving dot in a 3×7 dot array displayed on the screen. During the recording, the participant is allowed to adjust their head orientation in case the gaze angle is too large to be well captured for some corner dots. Each participant is asked to repeat the recording experiment 2–3 times so that we can collect sufficient valid data for generating the model and performing validation. After each recording, four IR eye videos and one scene video as well as a trajectory file documenting 2D and 3D eye gaze information at each time sampling step is saved. We use the eye videos to recover personal 3D eyeball parameters. The scene video and trajectory file are utilized for the validation stage, which will be discussed in Sect. 5.2.

Table 1. 3D Eyeball Parameters

3D parameters	Notation
Eyeball center	O_e
Eyeball radius	r_e
Cornea center	O_c
Cornea radius	r_c
iris& pupil center	O_i
iris radius	r_i
kappa angle	$\theta = [\theta_1, \theta_2]$
optical axis	$\boldsymbol{n}_o$
visual axis	$\boldsymbol{n}_v$

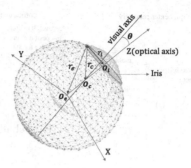

Fig. 1. 3D eye mesh

The personal 3D eye model is defined as a two-sphere system, where the larger sphere represents a 3D eyeball with center O_e and radius r_e and the smaller one represents the cornea with center O_c and radius r_c. The intersection of the two spheres results in a circular plane whose center is defined as iris center O_i. The pupil is assumed to be a concentric circle with the iris circle; hence the pupil center overlaps with the iris center. Geometrically, O_e, O_c, O_i are co-linear points and their connection forms the optical axis. The optical axis can be represented by horizontal and vertical angles (ϕ, γ):

$$
\boldsymbol{n}_o(\phi, \gamma) = \begin{pmatrix} cos(\phi)sin(\gamma) \\ sin(\phi) \\ -cos(\phi)cos(\gamma) \end{pmatrix}
$$

According to eyeball anatomy, the true gaze is defined by a visual axis that connects the fovea center, cornea center and the target object. We define a 2D vector $\boldsymbol{\theta} = [\theta_1, \theta_2]$ to be the Kappa angle representing the calibration term so that visual axis will be $\boldsymbol{n}_v = \boldsymbol{n}_o(\phi + \theta_1, \gamma + \theta_2)$. We summarize the geometric parameters to be recovered in Table 1 and show defined 3D eyeball mesh in Fig. 1. We describe the process of recovering 3D eyeball geometry from Tobii data as below.

3D Pupil Center. We first process eye camera images for pupil ellipse detection, as depicted in Fig. 2(a). Then the 3D pupil center O_i(relative to the reference camera) is recovered through stereo rectification.

3D Cornea Center. With pre-calibrated IR illuminators, We first detect glints $g_{1,1}, g_{1,2}$ caused by light I_1 in two images to calculate the 3D virtual glints v_1, similarly we can obtain another virtual glint v_2 caused by light I_2. The intersection of two light rays l_1, l_2 will be the 3D cornea center O_c. An illustration is shown in Fig. 2(b).

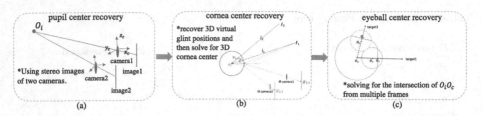

Fig. 2. 3D eyeball recovery process

3D Eyeball Center. We assume that a user's head movement would not cause any position shift of the glass, hence O_e can be considered as a constant vector across one whole recording. As the rotating center of the eyeball, O_e can be estimated by solving for the intersection of O_iO_c (which is the connecting line between O_i and O_c) from multiple frames, as shown in Fig. 2(c).

Eyeball, Cornea and Iris Radius. By referencing the ellipse reconstruction method introduced by Kohlbecher et al. [15] and Chen et al. [5], we can recover the 3D circular function for the iris plane, i.e. the normal vector and iris radius r_i. As in 3D eye geometry we define the iris as the intersection plane of eyeball sphere and cornea sphere, r_e, r_c can be determined by:

$$r_c^2 = r_i^2 + d_{ci}^2$$
$$r_e^2 = r_i^2 + (d_{ci} + d_{ec})^2 \tag{1}$$

where d_{ci} and d_{ec} are the distance from O_c to O_i and O_e to O_c respectively and can be obtained from 3.1,3.1,3.1.

Kappa Angle. According to the accuracy report provided by Tobii Pro Glass2 [12], we extract 3D gaze direction for valid frames of a recording provided by Tobii as the ground truth $\hat{n}_v$ and optimize for the kappa angle by

$$\theta^* = \arg\min_\theta \sum_{m=1}^M \arccos(n_o(\phi^* + \theta_1, \gamma^* + \theta_2), \hat{n}_v) \tag{2}$$

In Table 1, only camera-invariant parameters $p = [r_e, r_c, r_i, \theta_1, \theta_2]$ are selected to construct a personal 3D eye mesh and we manually define O_e to be the origin and O_c, O_i are located on the Z-axis.

3.2 3D Deformable Eye Model Construction

We repeat the process in Sect. 3.1 for each participant and we designate these users as "calibrated users" since their personal eye parameters $p^{5\times1}$ are fully recovered by means of the Tobii device. The calibrated parameter set

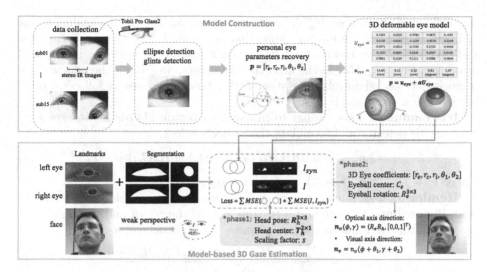

Fig. 3. Overview of our method: including a model construction module and a model-based 3D gaze estimation module.

$P = [p_1, \cdots, p_{15}]^{5 \times 15}$ can be used to construct a linear model that describes variation in eye parameters:

$$\mathcal{M}_{eye} = (\mu_{eye}, U_{eye}) \qquad (3)$$

where $\mu_{eye}^{5 \times 1}$ and $U_{eye}^{5 \times 5}$ are the average 3D eye parameter and an orthogonal PCA basis computed from P. For model-based 3D gaze estimation, we reconstruct p for an "uncalibrated user" by letting $p = \mu_{eye} + \alpha \; U_{eye}$ with the personal coefficient α, rather than repeating the complex data collection and processing procedure using the Tobii device.

We define a fixed eye mesh topology for the two-sphere 3D eye model, where the mesh vertices are divided into different groups, including {Ω_1: "eyeball", Ω_2 "cornea", Ω_3: "iris boundary", Ω_4: "pupil center"}. An average 3D eye mesh can be scaled corresponding to personal eye parameters $[r_e, r_c, r_i]$, resulting in the personal mesh generation process described as: $V^{N \times 3} = f(r_e, r_c, r_i)$.

4   3D Gaze Estimation

We propose a two-phase framework for single-frame based 3D gaze estimation using the constructed 3D eye model, as shown in Fig. 3. This framework can be implemented by an optimization-based fitting or deep-model-based regression scheme. In this section we will discuss the algorithm for 3D gaze estimation through model fitting.

In **phase1**, we solve for a weak-perspective camera viewpoint for the 3D head by fitting a 3D head model [17] to 68 2D facial landmarks of the face image. We implement the SNLS algorithm proposed by Bas te al. [1] and obtain the optimal 3D head pose $R_h^{3\times3}$, head center position $T_h^{2\times1}$ and a scaling factor s. Then, in **phase2**, we use a combination of iris landmark loss, rendering loss and geometrical constraints for left and right eyeball to optimize the eyeball center location $[C_{el}, C_{er}]$ in the head coordinate system (HCS), the personal eye coefficient α and the eyeball rotation $R_e^{3\times3}$. Loss terms are as follows, taking the left eye as an example.

Iris landmark loss: similar to **phase1**, we obtain 2D iris landmarks x_{iris}^{2d} from an iris detector and formulate the projection loss as:

$$L_{iris,l} = \|x_{iris,l}^{2d} - s^* P[R_e R_h^* \{V_i, i \in \Omega_3\} + R_h^* C_{el}] + s^* T_h^*\|^2 \tag{4}$$

where $V = f(p(1), p(2), p(3))$, and $p(\alpha) = \mu_{eye} + \alpha\, U_{eye}$.

Rendering loss: Since optimizing all parameters merely using iris landmarks is an ill-posed problem, we add a texture loss for the sclera and iris regions by projecting the eye mesh to the image frame, which is defined as:

$$L_{img,l} = \frac{\sum_m A_{m,l}\|I - I_{syn}(s^*, \alpha, C_{el}, R_e)\|_2}{\sum_m A_{m,l}} \tag{5}$$

where $A_{m,l}$ is the binary mask for the left eye region generated by 2D eye landmarks.

Geometrical constraints: from **phase1** we can recover 3D eye landmarks x_{eye}^{3d} among the facial landmarks. Since they ought to be very close to the surface of eyeball sphere, we define a regularization term for the eyeball center and radius:

$$L_{geo,l} = \sum_i \|r_e - |x_{eye,l,i}^{3d} - C_{el}|_1\|^2 \tag{6}$$

where $r_e = p(1)$ and $p = \mu_{eye} + \alpha\, U_{eye}$. Equation 4, 5, 6 apply to both eyes. We further constrain the left and right eyeball centers to be symmetric in HCS, i.e., $C_e = [C_{el}(1), C_{el}(2), C_{el}(3)] = [-C_{er}(1), C_{er}(2), C_{er}(3)]$. The resulting overall cost function is:

$$\arg\min_{C_e, \alpha, R_e} \lambda_1(L_{iris,l} + L_{iris,r}) + \lambda_2(L_{img,l} + L_{img,r})$$
$$+ \lambda_3(L_{geo,l} + L_{geo,r}) + \lambda_4\|\alpha\|_2 \tag{7}$$

the last term is used to avoid unreasonable personal eye shapes.

Kappa angle refinement: analysis of the 3D eye basis U_{eye} shows that the kappa angles have very weak correlation with other parameters or, we can consider θ as independent variable from $[r_e, r_i, r_c]$. Hence, we add an optional loss term to refine the 3D eye model parameters when gaze labels are available. The gaze loss is defined as:

$$L_{gaze} = \arccos \langle n_o(\phi_o + \theta_1, \gamma_o + \theta_2), \hat{n}_v \rangle \tag{8}$$

where ϕ_o, γ_o are function of R_e expressed by $n_o = \begin{pmatrix} cos(\phi)sin(\gamma) \\ sin(\phi) \\ -cos(\phi)cos(\gamma) \end{pmatrix} = R_e R_h \begin{bmatrix} 0 & 0 & 1 \end{bmatrix}^T$. Our 3D gaze estimation framework is summarized in Algorithm1.

Algorithm 1. 3D Gaze Estimation Algorithm

1: **phase1: head pose estimation**

2: Input: $\begin{cases} \text{landmarks} : \boldsymbol{x}_{face}^{2d} \\ \text{Deformable face model} : \boldsymbol{B}, \bar{\boldsymbol{B}} \end{cases}$

3: Fitting: weak perspective, SNLS algorithm [1].

4: Output: $[\boldsymbol{R}_h^*, \boldsymbol{T}_h^*, s^*]$.

5: **phase2: 3D Gaze estimation**

6: Input: $\begin{cases} \text{image, landmarks \& eye mask} : I, \boldsymbol{x}_{eye}^{2d}, \boldsymbol{x}_{iris}^{2d}, A_m \\ \text{head pose and scaling factor} : [\boldsymbol{R}_h^*, \boldsymbol{T}_h^*, s^*] \\ \text{3D deformable eye model} : \boldsymbol{U}, \bar{\boldsymbol{u}} \end{cases}$

7: Initialization: $\boldsymbol{R}_e^0 = \text{Identity}(3), \boldsymbol{\alpha}^0 = \boldsymbol{0}, C_e^0$ initialized by face model.

8: Fitting:

9: **if** gaze label $\hat{\boldsymbol{n}}_v$ available **then**

$$C_e^*, \boldsymbol{R}_e^*, \boldsymbol{\alpha}^* = \arg \min_{C_{e}, \boldsymbol{\alpha}, \boldsymbol{R}_e} \lambda_1 (L_{iris,l} + L_{iris,r})$$

$$+ \lambda_2 (L_{img,l} + L_{img,r}) + \lambda_3 (L_{geo,l} + L_{geo,r})$$

$$+ \lambda_4 \|\boldsymbol{\alpha}\|_2 + \lambda_5 L_g$$

10: **else**

$$C_e^*, \boldsymbol{R}_e^*, \boldsymbol{\alpha}^* = \arg \min_{C_{e}, \boldsymbol{\alpha}, \boldsymbol{R}_e} \lambda_1 (L_{iris,l} + L_{iris,r}) + \lambda_4 \|\boldsymbol{\alpha}\|_2$$

$$+ \lambda_2 (L_{img,l} + L_{img,r}) + \lambda_3 (L_{geo,l} + L_{geo,r})$$

11: Output: $[C_e^*, \boldsymbol{R}_e^*, \boldsymbol{\alpha}^*]$

12: **Gaze:** optical axis: $\boldsymbol{n}_o(\phi_o^*, \gamma_o^*) = \boldsymbol{R}_e^* \boldsymbol{R}_h^* \begin{bmatrix} 0 & 0 & 1 \end{bmatrix}^T$
   visual axis: $\boldsymbol{n}_v(\phi_o^* + \boldsymbol{\alpha}^*(4), \gamma_o^* + \boldsymbol{\alpha}^*(5))$

---

5   Experiments

5.1   Experiment Settings

Datasets: We conduct two types of experiments to evaluate the constructed model:

- **Model validation on Tobii recordings.** As mentioned in Sect. 3.1, we collect multiple recordings for each participant and leave one recording out for validation;
- **Benchmark datasets.** We select two datasets with full face images available. Columbia Gaze dataset [24] contains 56 subjects with 21 gaze angles under 5 head poses. EyeDiap [10] contains 16 subjects with different sessions.

   On benchmark datasets, we first perform 2D facial landmark detection using [2] and 2D iris detection using [20]. We use FaceScape [35] as the 3D face shape model to perform head pose estimation in **phase1**.

Table 2. Average 3D gaze error and PoG error on Tobii recordings of 15 participants.

azimuth angle error (in °)	elevation angle error (in °)	PoG error/screen size (in cm)
3.32	3.56	7.64/(80*135)

5.2   Evaluation on Tobii Recordings

For each "calibrated" participant with fully recovered eye parameters p, we perform validation experiments on one of the unused recordings. On the validation IR video, frame-based 3D model fitting is conducted by minimizing the MSE between projected 3D iris vertices and detected 2D iris landmarks. After optimizing for eyeball center O_e and eyeball rotation R_e, the optical axis can be represented as $n_o(\phi_o, \gamma_o) = R_e[0, \ 0, \ 1]^T$ then visual axis can be calculated by $n_v = n_o(\phi_o + \theta_1, \gamma_o + \theta_2)$. Since the visual axis is the unit direction vector connecting cornea center and target object, the point of gaze (PoG) will be the intersection of the left- and right-eye gaze vectors $O_{c,l} + l_1 n_{v,l}$ and $O_{c,r} + l_2 n_{v,r}$, which is computed by solving for l_1 and l_2. In the trajectory file provided by Tobii Pro Glass2, we are able to extract the 3D true gaze vector and the detected 3D target. We validate our model construction procedure in Sect. 3.1 by evaluating angular gaze error and PoG error. Since eyeball is a sphere structure and can be only rotated along two direction, we decompose the 3D gaze vector provided by Tobii into two free rotation angles: horizontal angle $\hat{\phi}_v$ and vertical angle $\hat{\gamma}_v$, then write the gaze vector as $\hat{n}_v(\hat{\phi}_v, \hat{\gamma}_v)$. Comparing the estimated visual axis $\hat{n}_v(\phi_o + \theta_1, \gamma_o + \theta_2)$ with the ground truth $\hat{n}_v(\hat{\phi}_v, \hat{\gamma}_v)$, the angular gaze error can be reflected by a horizontal angle error $\Delta\phi = |\hat{\phi}_v - (\phi_o + \theta_1)|$ and a vertical angle error $\Delta(\gamma) = |\hat{\gamma}_v - (\gamma_o + \theta_2)|$. Results are summarized in Table 2.

5.3   Evaluation on Benchmark Datasets

Evaluations on IR eye videos mentioned in Sect. 5.2 validate that the recovered parameters $p = [r_e, r_c, r_i, \theta_1, \theta_2]$ fit each participant well and can be taken as valid data for constructing our deformable 3D eye model. In addition to that, we evaluated how well the proposed 3D eye model predicts gaze directions for webcam datasets: Columbia Gaze and EyeDiap. For both datasets, we estimate 3D eyeball parameters $[C_e, R_e, \alpha]$ for each subject, under the condition of using 3D gaze labels or not. When no gaze label is involved, i.e., we use step.10 and step.12 in Algorithm.1 to estimate gaze direction for each image. We can also use gaze labels and do step.9 in Algorithm.1 to estimate C_e^* and α^* for a subset of images of one subject and then use the average result as initialization for the remained images of this subject. For the second case, we can get more accurate estimated gaze since C_e^* and α^* are more consistent in terms of subject identity. In all, we designed three experiments with no gaze label(0% column), 5% labels and 10% labels for each subject. We compared our model with SOTA 3D eye

Table 3. Average angular error in under 5 different head angles in Columbia Gaze dataset, **H**: horizontal gaze angle error, **V**: vertical gaze angle error.

Gaze error (H,V)	Percentage of gaze label used		
Head pose	0%	5%	10%
−30°	(8.18,6.80)	(6.80,6.20)	(6.54,6.31)
−15°	(8.20,6.54)	(6.54,6.06)	(6.42,5.89)
0°	(7.80,6.50)	(6.00,5.87)	(6.05,5.64)
15°	(7.90,6.54)	(6.12,5.54)	(6.18,5.32)
30°	(8.24,6.66)	(6.28,5.96)	(6.17,5.88)
Avg.	(8.06,6.61)	(6.35,5.93)	(6.28,5.81)

Table 4. Comparing with state-of-art models on Columbia Gaze, EyeDiap-VGA video and EyeDiap-HD video using different percentage of gaze labels.

Datasets	[33]	[28]	[32]	[30]	**Ours**(with (·)% labels)		
					0%	5%	10%
Columbia Gaze	9.7	10.2	8.9	7.1	9.0	6.5	**6.1**
EyeDiap-VGA	21.2	22.2	**9.44**/21.5	17.3	11.4/19.6	10.2/16.7	9.6/**16.0**
EyeDiap-HD	25.2	28.3	11.0/22.2	16.5	10.5/18.1	9.8/15.4	**9.6/14.7**

modeling methods,including [28,30,32,33], for evaluating our 3D eyeball geometry and fitting algorithm. Most appearance-based gaze estimation models like [6,19,21,31] which usually need full gaze labels and a complex training process to extract deep features from eye images and map to human gaze, rather than estimating 3D geometry and perform 3DMM-fitting. Therefore, we do not compare our model with these methods in this paper. It's worth mentioning that our 3D deformable eye model can be integrated into a deep model framework and combined with appearance-based methods. We'll continue with this part in future research.

The results for Columbia Gaze are shown in Table 3. We use different percentages of gaze labels to get refined kappa angles. Comparing results in Table 3 vertically, our model fits well to different head pose angles, although for larger head angles the gaze estimation accuracy is slightly reduced. From Table 3, it can be seen that our fitting algorithm's estimates of personal 3D eye model parameters and 3D gaze directions improve substantially when the percentage of gaze labels is raised from 0% to 5%, with the angular error decreasing from 9.0° to 6.5°. Increasing the percentage of gaze labels to 10% has only a marginal benefit (angular error 6.1°). Our model outperforms [32] even when we use no gaze labels, and it outperforms [30] (which uses around 14% gaze labels when fitting for their 3D eye model) even when we just use 5% or 10% gaze labels.

On EyeDiap we performed the fitting on VGA images and HD images. We present our results on EyeDiap in the last three columns of Table 4. For fair

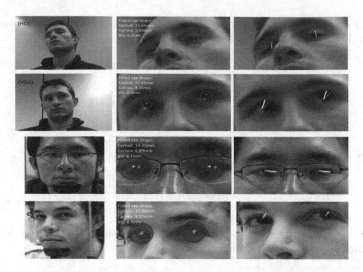

Fig. 4. Example fitting results on EyeDiap [10] and Columbia Gaze [24] datasets. **column 1**: input image. **column2**: projected 3D eyeball vertices(blue), iris vertices (red), eyeball center (yellow) and pupil center (green). Estimated eyeball & cornea & iris radius are displayed upper left. **column3** estimated gaze (white) and ground-truth gaze direction (red). (Color figure online)

comparison, we divide the testing data into ("screen target") / ("floating target") similar to [32] and show the 3D gaze error separately. For [28,30,33] we list the average error on EyeDiap since they do not explicitly split the data. On EyeDiap-VGA videos, event with no gaze labels our model achieves the best gaze estimation results (19.6°) on "floating target" data that exhibit large head pose angles compared to [32] (21.5°). Our gaze estimation performances are further improved when utilizing 10% gaze labels, achieving (9.6°/16.0°). On EyeDiap-HD videos, which have higher resolution than VGA videos, our model outperforms all of the four methods for both "screen target" video and "floating target" video. Fitting examples on Columbia dataset and EyeDiap are visualized in Fig. 4.

To summarize, our 3D model and fitting algorithm achieves state-of-the-art gaze estimation accuracy even when using a small percentage of subject gaze labels. Furthermore, the proposed two-phase fitting algorithm is more robust against large head poses and can still perform well under illumination and image resolution variations.

6   Conclusion

We propose the first 3D eye model with a deformable basis for eyeball radius, cornea radius, iris radius and kappa angle. The 3D eye geometry contains a sphere for eyeball, a smaller sphere for the cornea and the iris plane. The 3D eye geometry is fully parameterized by the eye model coefficients and can be used to approximate the variance in 3D eye shape for different person. We use a wearable device Tobii Pro Glass2 for data collection and preliminary model validation. We present a two-phase fitting algorithm for single-image based 3D gaze estimation using the constructed eye basis. With our 3D eye model and fitting method, personal eye shape parameters and eyeball rotations can be recovered from image pixel feature. Evaluations on benchmark datasets show that our model generalizes well to web-camera images with various head poses, illumination and resolution. The fitting process introduced in our paper can be further transplanted into a deep-model based framework. In the future, we pursue to integrate the 3D eye model into appearance-based deep models for accurate and generalizable 3D gaze estimation.

Acknowledgment. The work described in this paper is supported in part by the U.S. National Science Foundation award CNS 1629856.

References

1. Bas, A., Smith, W.A.: What does 2D geometric information really tell us about 3D face shape? Int. J. Comput. Vis. **127**(10), 1455–1473 (2019)
2. Bulat, A., Tzimiropoulos, G.: How far are we from solving the 2D & 3D face alignment problem? (and a dataset of 230,000 3D facial landmarks). In: International Conference on Computer Vision (2017)
3. Cao, C., Weng, Y., Zhou, S., Tong, Y., Zhou, K.: Facewarehouse: a 3D facial expression database for visual computing. IEEE Trans. Vis. Comput. Graph. **20**(3), 413–425 (2013)
4. Chen, J., Tong, Y., Gray, W., Ji, Q.: A robust 3D eye gaze tracking system using noise reduction. In: Proceedings of the 2008 Symposium on Eye Tracking Research & Applications, pp. 189–196 (2008)
5. Chen, Q., Wu, H., Wada, T.: Camera calibration with two arbitrary coplanar circles. In: Pajdla, T., Matas, J. (eds.) ECCV 2004. LNCS, vol. 3023, pp. 521–532. Springer, Heidelberg (2004). https://doi.org/10.1007/978-3-540-24672-5_41
6. Cheng, Y., Huang, S., Wang, F., Qian, C., Lu, F.: A coarse-to-fine adaptive network for appearance-based gaze estimation. In: Proceedings of the AAAI Conference on Artificial Intelligence, vol. 34, pp. 10623–10630 (2020)
7. Fuhl, W.: From perception to action using observed actions to learn gestures. User Model. User-Adapt. Interact. **31**(1), 105–120 (2021)
8. Fuhl, W., Santini, T., Kasneci, E.: Fast camera focus estimation for gaze-based focus control. arXiv preprint arXiv:1711.03306 (2017)
9. Fuhl, W., et al.: Non-intrusive practitioner pupil detection for unmodified microscope oculars. Comput. Biol. Med. **79**, 36–44 (2016)
10. Funes Mora, K.A., Monay, F., Odobez, J.M.: Eyediap: a database for the development and evaluation of gaze estimation algorithms from RGB and RGB-d cameras. In: Proceedings of the Symposium on Eye Tracking Research and Applications, pp. 255–258 (2014)
11. Gerig, T., et al.: Morphable face models-an open framework. In: 2018 13th IEEE International Conference on Automatic Face & Gesture Recognition (FG 2018), pp. 75–82. IEEE (2018)

12. Glass2, T.P.: Tobii pro eye tracker data quality report (2017). https://www. tobiipro.com/siteassets/tobii-pro/accuracy-and-precision-tests/tobii-pro-glasses-2-accuracy-and-precision-test-report.pdf

13. Hennessey, C., Noureddin, B., Lawrence, P.: A single camera eye-gaze tracking system with free head motion. In: Proceedings of the 2006 Symposium on Eye Tracking Research & Applications, pp. 87–94 (2006)

14. Hutchinson, T.E., White, K.P., Martin, W.N., Reichert, K.C., Frey, L.A.: Human-computer interaction using eye-gaze input. IEEE Trans. Syst. Man Cybernet. **19**(6), 1527–1534 (1989)

15. Kohlbecher, S., Bardinst, S., Bartl, K., Schneider, E., Poitschke, T., Ablassmeier, M.: Calibration-free eye tracking by reconstruction of the pupil ellipse in 3d space. In: Proceedings of the 2008 Symposium on Eye Tracking Research & Applications, pp. 135–138 (2008)

16. Lai, C.C., Shih, S.W., Hung, Y.P.: Hybrid method for 3-D gaze tracking using glint and contour features. IEEE Trans. Circ. Syst. Video Technol. **25**(1), 24–37 (2014)

17. Li, R., et al.: Learning formation of physically-based face attributes (2020)

18. Li, T., Bolkart, T., Black, M.J., Li, H., Romero, J.: Learning a model of facial shape and expression from 4D scans. ACM Trans. Graph. **36**(6), 1–17 (2017)

19. Liu, Y., Liu, R., Wang, H., Lu, F.: Generalizing gaze estimation with outlier-guided collaborative adaptation. In: Proceedings of the IEEE/CVF International Conference on Computer Vision, pp. 3835–3844 (2021)

20. Lugaresi, C., et al.: Mediapipe: a framework for building perception pipelines. arXiv preprint arXiv:1906.08172 (2019)

21. Palmero, C., Selva, J., Bagheri, M.A., Escalera, S.: Recurrent CNN for 3D gaze estimation using appearance and shape cues. arXiv preprint arXiv:1805.03064 (2018)

22. Paysan, P., Knothe, R., Amberg, B., Romdhani, S., Vetter, T.: A 3D face model for pose and illumination invariant face recognition. In: 2009 Sixth IEEE International Conference on Advanced Video and Signal Based Surveillance, pp. 296–301. IEEE (2009)

23. Ploumpis, S., et al.: Towards a complete 3D morphable model of the human head. IEEE Trans. Pattern Anal. Mach. Intell. **43**(11), 4142–4160 (2020)

24. Smith, B.A., Yin, Q., Feiner, S.K., Nayar, S.K.: Gaze locking: passive eye contact detection for human-object interaction. In: Proceedings of the 26th Annual ACM Symposium on User Interface Software and Technology, pp. 271–280 (2013)

25. Song, G., Cai, J., Cham, T.J., Zheng, J., Zhang, J., Fuchs, H.: Real-time 3D face-eye performance capture of a person wearing VR headset. In: Proceedings of the 26th ACM International Conference on Multimedia, pp. 923–931 (2018)

26. Swirski, L., Dodgson, N.: A fully-automatic, temporal approach to single camera, glint-free 3D eye model fitting. In: Proceeding of the PETMEI, pp. 1–11 (2013)

27. Tsukada, A., Kanade, T.: Automatic acquisition of a 3D eye model for a wearable first-person vision device. In: Proceedings of the Symposium on Eye Tracking Research and Applications, pp. 213–216 (2012)

28. Vicente, F., Huang, Z., Xiong, X., De la Torre, F., Zhang, W., Levi, D.: Driver gaze tracking and eyes off the road detection system. IEEE Trans. Intell. Transp. Syst. **16**(4), 2014–2027 (2015)

29. Wang, K., Ji, Q.: Real time eye gaze tracking with kinect. In: 2016 23rd International Conference on Pattern Recognition (ICPR), pp. 2752–2757. IEEE (2016)

30. Wang, K., Ji, Q.: Real time eye gaze tracking with 3D deformable eye-face model. In: Proceedings of the IEEE International Conference on Computer Vision, pp. 1003–1011 (2017)

31. Wang, Y., et al.: Contrastive regression for domain adaptation on gaze estimation. In: Proceedings of the IEEE/CVF Conference on Computer Vision and Pattern Recognition, pp. 19376–19385 (2022)
32. Wood, E., Baltrušaitis, T., Morency, L.-P., Robinson, P., Bulling, A.: A 3D morphable eye region model for gaze estimation. In: Leibe, B., Matas, J., Sebe, N., Welling, M. (eds.) ECCV 2016. LNCS, vol. 9905, pp. 297–313. Springer, Cham (2016). https://doi.org/10.1007/978-3-319-46448-0_18
33. Xiong, X., Liu, Z., Cai, Q., Zhang, Z.: Eye gaze tracking using an RGBD camera: a comparison with a RGB solution. In: Proceedings of the 2014 ACM International Joint Conference on Pervasive and Ubiquitous Computing: Adjunct Publication, pp. 1113–1121 (2014)
34. Zhou, X., Cai, H., Li, Y., Liu, H.: Two-eye model-based gaze estimation from a kinect sensor. In: 2017 IEEE International Conference on Robotics and Automation (ICRA), pp. 1646–1653. IEEE (2017)
35. Zhu, H., et al.: Facescape: 3D facial dataset and benchmark for single-view 3D face reconstruction. arXiv preprint arXiv:2111.01082 (2021)

2D-Pose Based Human Body Segmentation for Weakly-Supervised Concealed Object Detection in Backscatter Millimeter-Wave Images

Lawrence Amadi[✉] [iD] and Gady Agam

Visual Computing Lab, Illinois Institute of Technology, Chicago, IL 60616, USA
lamadi@hawk.iit.edu, agam@iit.edu

Abstract. The detection and localization of anomalies in backscatter images of a person is a standard procedure in airport security screening. Detecting a concealed item on a person and localizing the item to a specific body part requires the ability to recognize and segment distinct body parts. This can be challenging for backscatter images compared with RGB images due to lacking chromaticity cues and the limited availability of annotated backscatter images. To address this problem, we propose a weakly-supervised method for anomaly detection on human body parts which is based on an unsupervised body segmentation procedure that uses keypoints from a pretrained pose estimator to segment backscatter images without significant performance degradation. The paper presents a method for adapting a pretrained RGB pose estimator to segment human body parts in millimeter-wave images. We then train a body part-aware anomaly detection classifier to detect foreign objects on the body part. Our work is applied to TSA's passenger screening dataset containing backscatter millimeter-wave scan images of airport travelers with binary labels that indicate whether a concealed item is attached to a body part. Our proposed approach significantly improves detection accuracy on 2D images from the baseline approach with a state-of-the-art performance of 97% F1-score and 0.0559 log-loss on TSA-PSD test set.

Keywords: Pose refinement · Body segmentation · Object detection

1 Introduction

Backscatter images such as X-ray, MRI, and millimeter-wave scanner images are predominantly used to examine internal organs or beneath the clothing of persons. These images are generated by specialized scanners and are essential for computer-aided medical diagnosis and security screening inspections. Backscatter images are also characterized by very low chromaticity and illumination.

Obtain source code at https://github.com/lawrenceamadi/RaadNet.

© Springer Nature Switzerland AG 2023
J.-J. Rousseau and B. Kapralos (Eds.): ICPR 2022 Workshops, LNCS 13643, pp. 124–138, 2023.
https://doi.org/10.1007/978-3-031-37660-3_9

The low distinctive visibility makes human inspection difficult and also pose a challenge for computer diagnostic software. In the US, the HIPAA Privacy Rule considers these intrusive backscatter images of persons their personal data and protects it against unauthorized inspection. Hence, in the case of airport security screening where full-body backscatter millimeter-wave scan (MWS) images of persons must be inspected to make sure that they do not conceal prohibited or harmful items under their garment, a computer vision algorithm is used to analyze and detect anomalies in the images. When an anomaly is detected, the algorithm must also localize it to a specific body part as it recommends a follow-up pat-down search of the indicated body part. Therefore, localizing anomalies to specific body parts is as important as high precision anomaly detection of concealed items to streamline pat-down searches shorten airport security screening queues. This requirement demands an algorithm capable of recognizing different body parts in backscatter MWS images. Similarly, for medical imaging, there is value in developing an anomaly detection algorithm that is body-organ aware to assist physicians in diagnosis.

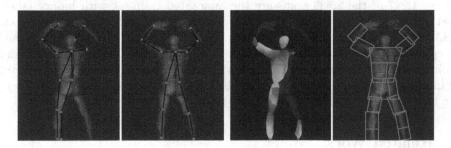

Fig. 1. Example of our refined 2D pose (2th) and unsupervised body segmentation (4th) on MWS images compared to SOTA HRNet 2D pose (1th) [28] and DensePose body segmentation (3th) [14].

Designing a body-aware anomaly detection algorithm for backscatter images is challenging for two reasons. First, unlike RGB images, there are hardly sufficiently large datasets of backscatter MWS images with body part bounding-box or pixel-level annotations to supervise the training of a backscatter body part segmentation deep neural network. Second, as demonstrated in Fig. 1, directly applying pretrained RGB body segmentation models (e.g. DensePose [14]) to MWS images fails to produce meaningful segmentation because of lacking chromatic and illumination cues.

This work makes the following contributions:

1. We introduce an unsupervised procedure for segmenting body parts in MWS images by estimating bounding-polygons for each body part.
2. We then propose a weakly-supervised, RoI-attentive, dual-chain CNN classifier that detects anomalies given multi-view images of a cropped body part.

Our approach leverages multi-view information to refine sub-optimal poses generated by RGB-pretrained human pose estimators. The refined keypoints are then used to estimate bounding-polygons that enclose each body part. Subsequently, the bounding-polygons are used to crop regions of the images that represent each body part and the images are fed to our body-aware anomaly detection neural network.

1.1 TSA Passenger Screening Dataset

Our unsupervised body segmentation method is evaluated on the Transportation Security Administration Passenger Screening Dataset (TSA-PSD) [32] which contains backscatter full-body scans of persons acquired by a High Definition Advanced Imaging Technology (HD-AIT) millimeter wave scanner (MWS). The dataset contains 2,635 scans of airport travelers. Each scan is encoded as a **Projected Image Angle Sequence File** (.*aps*) and contains a sequence of 16 2D images captured from different viewpoints such that the person appears to be spinning from left to right when the images are played back frame by frame. 1,247 of the 2,635 scans are the annotated train-set with binary labels that indicate whether an object is concealed in a body part of the scan subject. TSA outlines 17 body parts of interests. They include right and left forearms, biceps, abdomens, upper and lower thighs, calves, ankles, chest, upper back, and groin. Hence, a scan with 16 images has 17 binary labels. There are no pixel-level or image-level ground-truth annotation of concealed items or body parts. There are also no binary labels per body part, per frame.

2   Related Work

2D pose estimation on RGB images is widely studied in [3,4,16,24,28,30]. However, these models require keypoint annotations to learn proper pose encoding. Similarly, state-of-the-art human body segmentation neural networks [8,10,12,14,15,17,19,20,22,27,33,34,37] rely on bounding-box or pixel-level annotations of body parts.

Anomaly object detection in persons, luggage, cargo containers, and scenes are studied in [1,2,5,13,23,25,29]. A majority of the leading methods are based on deep neural networks. Riffo and Mery [25] propose a shape implicit algorithm for detecting specific threat objects (razor blades, shurikens, and guns) in x-ray images of luggage. Although their method can be modified to detect threat items on the human body, their object-specialized approach is not expected to generalize to unknown objects that are not encountered during training because their algorithm is designed to detect specific items, not general anomalies. A popular approach for detecting threat objects uses AlexNet classifier [2] and predefined fixed region-of-interest (RoI) bounding-boxes to segment body parts. The fixed RoI bounding-boxes do not account for variations of body part size, positioning, and orientation on a per person basis. This limitations makes this approach more suitable for the less mobile torso body parts (e.g. chest, back) and limited viewpoints. Another approach that uses AlexNet for anomaly detection [13] combines 2D and 3D data to segment the body parts and generate threat or benign labels for each cropped image. This enables supervised training of the model using a set of cropped body parts with assigned threat labels. This approach allows for a simpler neural network architecture because of the 1-1 mapping of cropped images and labels. However, generating false labels for cropped images can degrade to the accuracy of the classifier. Note, anomalies in TSA-PSD body parts are typically visible in 6 frames or less.

Other concealed item detection algorithms applied to TSA-PSD are either designed to use 3D volumetric data, or a combination of 3D and 2D images. We give a high-level description of the proprietary TSA-PSD classifiers as reported by the Department of Homeland Security as details of the state-of-the-art classifiers are not released to the public. Jeremy Walthers (1th) approach used an array of deep learning models customized to process images from multiple views. Sergei Fotin (2th) and Oleg Trott (5th) adopted an approach that fuses 2D (10–41 MB per file) and 3D (330 MB per file) data sources to make object and location predictions. Despite their high accuracy, the 1th and 2th approach may be less suitable for real-time use because the inference time for an array of neural networks or very large files can be substantial. David Odaibo and Thomas Anthony (3th) developed an algorithm that uses specialized 3D image-level annotations to train a 2-stage identification model. It is unclear whether the annotations were automated or manually labeled. Location based models (4th), automatic image segmentation with a collection of specialized models trained on cropped body part images (6th), separately trained models with image augmentation (8th), and the use of synthetic data and cross-image analysis (7th) are other techniques used to improve model detection accuracy.

3   Proposed Method

We approach concealed item detection and association to body parts as a two-stage problem. First, we segment the human body parts in the frames of each scan to generate 17 sequences of $n \leq 16$ cropped images (Sect. 3.1). Each sequence corresponds to a body part and contains cropped images of that body part from different viewpoints. Since the presence of a concealed item is often visible in 6 frames or less, never from all viewpoints, we must detect anomalies in body parts on a per image-sequence basis. In the second stage (Sect. 3.2), we train a deep CNN anomaly detector that processes a sequence of cropped images of a body part and classifies it as benign or abnormal when a foreign object is detected in any of the cropped images. Note, a single CNN detector is trained for all body parts. This makes our detector simpler and lightweight compared to other state-of-the-art classifiers that use an array of body part or gender specialized networks. In contrast, our network uses a novel region-attentive architecture that makes it body part aware.

3.1 Body Part Segmentation from 2D Poses

Our approach for adapting an RGB *Human Pose Estimation (HPE)* network to perform unsupervised body segmentation begins with correcting local-optima keypoint locations in confidence map output of a RGB-pretrained 2D pose estimator. The corrected keypoint positions in each frame are further optimized using RANSAC bundle adjustment [35] to consolidate a global-optimum 3D pose. A new set of coherent 2D poses are derived by projecting the global-optimum 3D pose back to the 2D frames. The refined keypoints in each frame are then used to estimate bounding-polygons that segments the body parts in each frame.

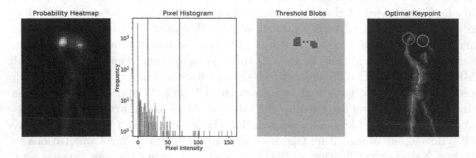

Fig. 2. Outcome of our keypoint selection algorithm for Right Wrist. *A-D* from left-right. *A* depicts the right wrist 2D confidence map. *B* is the histogram of the confidence map. The *red* lines indicate the multi-Otsu thresholds used to segment *A* the confidence map to 3 layers; *blue, orange,* and *brown* (detected blobs) in *C*. *D* shows our algorithm selects the correct position of the right wrist (*green* circle) instead of the location of highest confidence (*red* circle). (Color figure online)

Keypoint Selection from HPE Confidence Maps. Without keypoint annotations to train a pose estimator on the TSA dataset, we use a Deep-HRNet 2D pose estimator [28] pretrained on the COCO dataset [21] to estimate 15 keypoints of persons in MWS images. They include right and left wrists, elbows, shoulders, hips, knees, ankles, head, neck, and pelvis keypoints. Deep-HRNet is preferred to other 2D HPE networks [3,4,24] because of its high-resolution architecture. Compared to the others, it estimates more realistic poses of the subjects in backscatter MWS images. Typically, the position of a keypoint is derived from the corresponding 2D confidence map output of the pose estimator as the pixel location with the highest confidence. We observed that this naive method often produced incorrect keypoint estimates because the Deep-HRNet estimator often generated confidence maps with more than one concentrations of high confidence scores (i.e. blobs) for backscatter MWS images. In such cases, the naive selection will default to the leftmost blob even when the correct keypoint position is in one of the other blobs.

We implement a keypoint selection post-processing procedure that selects the better-positioned blob and keypoint location given the occurrence of multiple blobs in the confidence map. The premise of our keypoint selection algorithm is that the relative positioning (left, center, or right) of joints in each frame is consistent across all scans because subjects assume a standard posture (standing erect with hands raised) when being scanned. And their pose is sustained while each frame is captured from rotating viewpoints. We begin by segmenting the confidence map into three layers using multi-Otsu binarization [36] to determine the confidence threshold for each layer. Using a modified *island-finder* algorithm, we traverse the segmented confidence map (now a 2D matrix with three unique values; 0, 1, 2) to identify all blobs. The blobs are grouped into three clusters by spatial proximity. The cluster nearest to the expected keypoint position (left, center, or right) is selected. We then compute the *argmax* of confidence scores in the chosen blob cluster to retrieve the pixel position of the keypoint. Figure 2 illustrates the outcome of this procedure.

Multi-view Coherent Pose Optimization. We observed that even after refining the 2D pose in each MWS frame, some keypoints may still be sub-optimally estimated in some frames. Subsequently, causing inaccurate segmentation of body parts associated with the keypoint. Therefore, we ought to correct incoherent poses across all frames for each scan. In Algorithm 1 we describe a pose optimization procedure that takes advantage of the multiple viewpoints of TSA-PSD MWS images to reconstruct consistent 2D poses across all frames. The 2D position of each keypoint, across all frames of a scan, are optimized independently using RANSAC bundle adjustment [6,9,11,31,35].

Algorithm 1. Per Keypoint RANSAC Bundle Adjustment

Input: $P \leftarrow \{(x,y) : \forall\ frames\ f_1 \dots f_{16}\}$ ▷ 2D pixel positions of keypoint in each frame
Output: $P^{"}$ ▷ 2D pixel positions of keypoint in each frame after bundle adjustment
1:   $n \leftarrow 0, I \leftarrow \emptyset$
2:   **while** $n \leq 100$ **do**   ▷ iterate over subset of keypoints for 3D bundle adjustment
3:      $R \leftarrow \{(x,y) :\subset P\}$ ▷ randomly selected subset, 1 every 4 consecutive frames
4:      $p^{3D} \leftarrow (x,y,z)_R$ ▷ 3D point is regressed from R via least squares optimization
5:      $P' \leftarrow \{(x',y') : \forall\ frames\}$ ▷ 2D positions after projecting p^{3D} to each frame
6:      $I' \leftarrow \{(x,y) :\subset P\}$ ▷ note inlier points based on Euclidean dist. between P & P'
7:      **if** $|I'| > |I|$ **then**
8:         $I \leftarrow I'$ ▷ retain the largest inlier set
9:      **end if**
10: **end while**
11: $p^{3D} \leftarrow (x,y,z)_I$ ▷ least squares bundle adjusted 3D point regressed from I 2D points
12: $P^{"} \leftarrow \{(x^{"},y^{"}) : \forall\ frames\}$ ▷ final 2D positions after projecting p^{3D} to each frame

---

Estimating Bounding-Polygons for Body Segmentation. After refining the keypoints, we segment the body parts in each frame by defining an oriented bounding-box around each body part. Vertices of the bounding-polygon (a quadrilateral with 4 vertices) are estimated from a subset of keypoints associated with a given body part. We define two types of body parts. *Limb Body Parts* are segmented using a pair of keypoints. They include forearms, biceps, upper and lower thighs, calves, and ankles. We refer to the pair of keypoints used to segment limb body parts as *anchor keypoints*. **Torso Body Parts** are segmented using a set of four keypoints. They include chest, back, abs, and groin. We refer to the keypoints used to segment torso body parts as *pillar keypoints*.

Limb Body Part Segmentation. We begin by computing the angle between the *anchor keypoints* and the y-axis. The image is then rotated by the computed angle so that the limb is vertically aligned. We extract the luminance channel of the rotated image and remove noise with a Gaussian filter. We then sum the pixel intensity along the horizontal axis of a rectangular region enclosing the limb. This produces a *pixel intensity curve*. The rectangular region is vertically bounded by the y-coordinates of the rotated keypoints, and horizontally bounded by a predefined width for each limb. Next, we fit a degree 6 polynomial line to the computed pixel intensity curve and extract the x-coordinates of the rightmost and leftmost local minima of the polynomial line. The x-coordinates of the local minima define the width of an axis-aligned bounding-box around the limb. Similarly, the y-coordinates of the rotated keypoints define the height. The bounding-box is transformed to an oriented bounding-polygon when its vertices are inversely rotated.

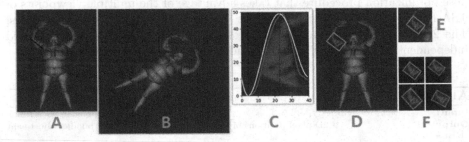

Fig. 3. Visualization of intermediate stages of limb segmentation for the Right Elbow. Black line in *A* links the Right Elbow and Shoulder keypoints. The frame is rotated to vertically align the pillar keypoints in *B*. *C* shows the computed *pixel intensity curve* (red line) and fitted polynomial (white) line. *D* shows the estimated bounding-polygon. *F* are examples of (shift, zoom, rotate) cropped image augmentation (with RoI mask) generated from *E*. (Color figure online)

Torso Body Part Segmentation. Pillar keypoints of torso body parts typically outline a quadrilateral region containing two or more body parts. For example, the right shoulder, neck, pelvis, and right hip keypoints segment the right-Abdomen and half of the upper chest (see image A in Fig. 4). To precisely capture the intended body part, we shift one or more edges of the quadrilateral. The edges that are moved, the direction (horizontally or vertical), and the extent they are shifted is guided by a predefined configuration for each torso body part. The new vertices of the bounding-polygon are computed as the points of intersection of the adjusted quadrilateral edges. This procedure is illustrated in Fig. 4 for the right abdomen.

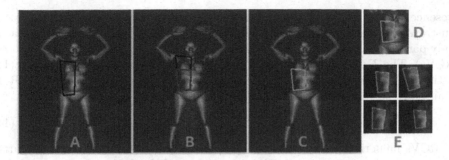

Fig. 4. Visualization of torso segmentation for the Right Abdomen. Vertices of black quadrilateral in A are the Pelvis, Neck, Right Shoulder and Hip keypoints. The top edge of the black quadrilateral in B is shifted downwards, resulting in the blue polygon. The green polygon in C encloses the RoI for the Right Abdomen. E shows examples of (shift, zoom, rotate) randomly generated cropped image augmentation from D, overlaid with RoI mask. (Color figure online)

Each bounding-polygon defines the region-of-interest (RoI) of a body part. The segmented body parts are cropped, in excess, by a standard 160×160 pixel window such that the RoI is contained in the cropped image (see E and F in Fig. 3 and Fig. 4) before down-sampling to 80×80 pixels. This approach preserves the aspect ratio of the body parts in contrast to directly resizing the RoI to the standard size. We found our network performed better at detecting concealed items when the aspect ratio of images are not altered. We have chosen a generous standard size of 160 sq. pixels to accommodate the sizes of all body parts and all subjects, big and small. Another reason for cropping in excess of the RoI is because the demarcation between neighboring body parts is not absolute and when a concealed object spans the boundary of two body parts must only be attributed to one. By over-cropping the RoI and incorporating the RoI mask and our proposed Region Composite Vectors into the network, our model learns to associate concealed objects to the dominant body part. We have designed our network architecture to use the RoI mask to refocus attention on the RoI when detecting anomalies, but only after extracting features from the entire cropped images.

To summarize, given each scan, we compile 17 sequences of cropped images for each body part (from multiple viewpoints). Each sequence contains 12 images because we observed that the maximum number of frames where a body part is visible is 12. Cropped images are re-sampled and augmented to compensate for body parts that are visible in less than 12 frames (as low as 3 for chest and back). Finally, images are downsampled by a factor of 2.

3.2   RaadNet: RoI Attentive Anomaly Detection Network

We design an anomaly object detection network that classifies a sequence of cropped images of a segmented body part as benign or abnormal. Indicating the presence of a concealed item in one or more of the cropped images. The network, illustrated in Fig. 5, takes an input sequence of n=12 cropped images for each body part, their corresponding RoI binary masks, and *Region Composite Vectors* (RCVs). The $\boldsymbol{RCV}$ of a cropped image is a vector of size 17 defined in Eq. (1) as the *intersect-over-union* (IoU) between the body part's RoI I_i and the RoI of all body parts in the given frame I.

$$RCV_i(I) = \langle IoU(I_0, I_i), \ldots, IoU(I_{16}, I_i)\rangle, \quad i \leq 16 \tag{1}$$

RCVs numerically summarize the proportion contribution of the body parts captured in a cropped image. We expect most of the IoU components of the vector will be 0, with only a few having values greater than 0 (as is the case for adjacent body parts). The component corresponding to dominant body part will have the highest value. We found RCVs provide cues to the network that helps it better resolve overlap conflict when a concealed item is partially contained in the RoI. The cropped images pass through feature extraction blocks and the masks are downsampled to match the dimensions of the extracted features. We use the first 5 blocks of MobileNetV2 [26] (pretrained on ImageNet [7]) for feature extraction. The extracted features, downsampled masks, and RCVs are separated into m=4 sub-sequences. Each containing $p=n/m$ contiguous temporal components that are fed to a dual-pipeline, multi-phase sub-network. During each phase, the *Image-pipeline* (*blue path* in Fig. 5) encodes textures of the entire cropped images, while the *RoI-pipeline* (*red path* in Fig. 5) is designed to extract textures precisely from the RoIs in the cropped images. This is achieved by computing

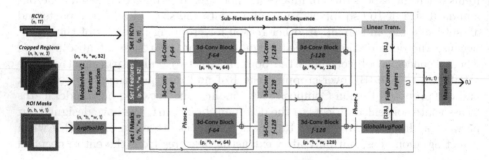

Fig. 5. An instance of RaadNet, our 2-phase, dual-pipeline *(indicated by the blue and red lines)* anomaly detection network that takes as input cropped images of a body part, their RoI masks and RCVs, and outputs the probability that a concealed item is in either of the cropped images. We use $n = 12$ cropped images per body part. $h,w = 80$ are the height and width of the cropped images. $^*h, ^*w = 10$, $p = 3$, $m = 4$. Each sub-sequence of images p is passed through the same sub-network (enclosed in large rectangle). Residual convolution blocks (in dark-blue) contains two 3D convolution layers with *kernel=3* and f filters. Convolutions are accompanied by batch normalization and Re-LU activation. The fully connected block (in light-blue) contains 5 dense layers of sizes 128,64,64,16,1 followed by a sigmoid activation. $\otimes$ and $\oplus$ are element-wise multiplication and addition operations. Notice that a deeper network can be created by increasing the number of phases. (Color figure online)

the element-wise multiplication of the residual convolution block output of the *Image-pipeline* and the convoluted RoI masks. The resulting tensor is passed to the residual block of the *RoI-pipeline*. The dual pipelines ensures the network can detect anomalies that partially appear on the boundary of the body part's RoI and aids the network to decide whether to attribute the detected anomaly to the RoI. This is especially useful when an object is not fully contained in the RoI but well captured in the cropped image. The output of the residual block in the *RoI-pipeline* of the final phase and the RCVs are fed to a fully connected block which outputs the probability that a concealed item is present in one or more of the cropped images in the sub-sequence. The final classification of the body part is the max probability aggregate of the sub-sequences.

Training and Inference with Ensemble Classifiers. Our 2-phase, dual-pipeline network has about $2.47M$ parameters ($5.19M$ flops). We train 3 classifiers on overlapping, equal-sized, subsets of the training set. This is done with a *3-folds* stratified learning scheme where each classifier is trained on 2 subsets and validated on the other subset. Each classifier is trained for 80 epochs with a batch size of 64 using Adam optimizer [18] and a dynamic learning rate starting at $1e-3$ and decreased to $5e-5$ between the 9th and 72th epoch by a non-linear cosine function. During training, we re-sample sequences of cropped images with concealed items and augment all images by moving the cropped window about the RoI, zooming, horizontal flipping, and adjusting image contrast. At inference, the verdict is aggregated as the mean probability of the ensemble classifiers.

4   Experiments and Results

We evaluate the correctness of our 2D-pose refinement procedure in Table 1, the accuracy of our anomaly detection network in Table 2, and compare the performance of our state-of-the-art ensemble classifier to proprietary algorithms and other top detectors applied to TSA-PSD in Fig. 6.

4.1   Evaluation of 2D Pose Refinement for MWS Images

We evaluate our proposed keypoint correction process to show the relevance of our approach that adapts a RGB pretrained pose encoder to estimate more accurate poses on backscatter MWS images without supervision. Table 1 shows the Mean Per Joint Position Error (MPJPE) computed between predicted keypoint positions and manually labeled ground-truth positions. The final stage of our pose refinement (*Coherent-Pose*) decreases the error of estimated keypoints by 68%. We go on to show that this boost in accuracy is carried over to the anomaly detection network when trained with better segmented images. Note, however, that the consolidation of globally optimum coherent poses can sometimes come at the expense of local optima keypoint positions. We observe this consequence in the right and left hip and right knee keypoints where the coherent poses degrade the accuracy of the refined poses. This is because the pixel location of these keypoints are particularly volatile from frame to frame as the viewpoint of the person changes.

Table 1. Accuracy of 2D-poses derived by the naive keypoint selection (*Generic Pose*), our proposed method for guided keypoint selection (*Refined Pose* of Sect. 3.1) and correcting incoherent pose estimation (*Coherent Pose* of Sect. 3.1). Evaluated on the mean L2-norm between manually labelled keypoint locations and estimated keypoint locations of 50 scans (800 images). *R.Sh* refers to Right Shoulder, *L.Ke* Left Knee. *Avg.* is the mean over all keypoints.

mm	R.Sh	R.Eb	R.Wr	L.Sh	L.Eb	L.Wr	R.Hp	R.Ke	R.Ak	L.Hp	L.Ke	L.Ak	Avg.
Generic Pose	115.7	191.5	119.1	100.4	173.4	117.6	88.49	115.3	137.3	79.91	105.8	134.5	123.2
Refined Pose	55.2	36.9	35.2	52.3	44.4	42.6	65.1	38.5	42.9	61.6	36.9	43.6	46.3
Coherent Pose	40.2	32.5	19.9	38.1	31.4	23.6	82.8	38.9	22.4	78.1	35.8	21.0	38.7

4.2 Concealed Item Detection with RaadNet

We conduct ablation experiments on our anomaly detection network trained on different types of segmented body part images and varying inputs. We present a comprehensive evaluation of our methods in comparison to published works on concealed item detection on the TSA dataset in Table 2. Our proposed method of using refined 2D keypoints to segment the human body parts consistently outperforms other published work on 2D concealed item detection in TSA-PSD in all metrics. Our RaadNet detector, trained on body part images segmented by coherent keypoints, RoI masks, and RCVs, performs at an average F1-Score of 98.6% on a disjoint validation-set and 0.0751 log-loss on the test-set. The log-loss ϵ, on the test-set of TSA-PSD is defined in Eq. (2) between predicted

Table 2. Comparison of RaadNet and our proposed body segmentation to relevant published work on TSA-PSD. *Bsl-1* is our baseline network trained with fixed RoI segmented body parts with RoI masks and RCVs. *Bsl-2* is our baseline RaadNet trained with images segmented using original Deep-HRNet keypoints (without refinement), masks, and RCVs. *Abl-1*, *Abl-2* and *Opt.* are our networks trained with body parts segmented using refined keypoints (Sect. 3.1). *Abl-1* is without RoI masks and RCVs, *Abl-2* is without RCVs, and *Opt* is with all three inputs; cropped images of body parts, RoI masks, and RCVs.

Body Part Anomaly Detection Methods	Validation						Test
	Avg.F1 ↑	F1-Sc. ↑	Preci. ↑	Recall ↑	Acc. ↑	L.loss ↓	L.loss ↓
FastNet (*) [23]	.8890	-	-	-	-	-	-
AlexNet-1 (*) [2]	-	-	-	-	-	.0088	-
AlexNet-2 (*) [13]	.9828	-	-	-	-	-	.0913
RaadNet +Fixed RoI Seg. in [2]+Mask+RCV (*Bsl-1*)	.9761	.9555	.9628	.9487	.9723	.0201	.1384
RaadNet +Unrefined-Pose Seg.+Mask+RCV (*Bsl-2*)	.9184	.7526	.8652	.6659	.9108	.1282	.1608
Ours RaadNet +Coherent-Pose Seg. (*Abl-1*)	.9775	.9581	.9655	.9505	.9766	.0143	.0934
Ours RaadNet +Coherent-Pose Seg.+Mask (*Abl-2*)	.9637	.9540	.9550	.9531	.9687	.0131	.0886
Ours RaadNet +Coherent-Pose Seg.+Mask+RCV (*Opt.*)	.9859	.9738	.9941	.9544	.9946	.0097	.0751

threat probabilities $\hat{y}$ and the ground-truth binary label y of all $N=17 \times 1338$ body parts and scan subjects in the test-set. "ln" is natural logarithm.

$$\epsilon = -\frac{1}{N} \sum_{i=1}^{N} [y_i \ln(\hat{y}_i) + (1 - y_i) \ln(1 - \hat{y}_i)] \tag{2}$$

By performing more precise body part segmentation on MWS images using refined 2D keypoints, we improved our network's ability to accurately detect concealed items by 53% (0.0751 test-set log-loss). Outperforming the published state-of-the-art method [13] (at 0.0913 test log-loss) by 17%. This is further extended to a 38% decrease in log-loss by our 3-ensemble classifiers. Note that the methods in the top 3 rows of Table 2 do not directly compare to our results because those works detect anomalies in a small subset of body parts (e.g. chest, thigh, arm, back). Whereas, our method detects concealed items on all body parts and the reported values reflect the cumulative performance on all body parts. To aid comparison with previous works, we show their best results reported for a single body part. Our ablation study highlights the importance of RCV and RoI mask. As expected, the use of masks improves the confidence of classification in *Abl-2* (decrease in log-loss). Although, at the expense of classification accuracy which is recovered by supplying RCVs. This is because RoI masks may exclude parts of objects on the boundary of body parts, whereas, RCVs inform the network how much of the objects are contained in the RoI. Hence, allowing the network to make a better decision of attributing detected concealed objects to body parts.

4.3   Comparison to TSA-PSD Proprietary Classifiers

The anomaly detection accuracy of RaadNet is further improved with 3-ensemble classifiers. Achieving up to 0.05592 mean log-loss on the test-set (7th overall in Fig. 6). Note, mean log-loss is the only evaluation metric reported for the test-set

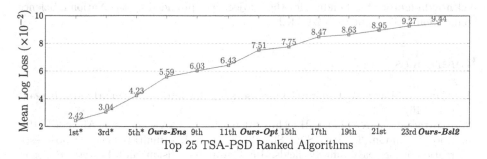

Fig. 6. Top-ranked TSA-PSD algorithms on the Kaggle Leaderboard. (*) indicates algorithms reported to have used 3D image files. Our ensemble RaadNet ranks 7th, placing at topmost proprietary category. Making our method the only published, comprehensive work that places in the top-8.

because the ground-truth labels are private to TSA. This makes our proposed method the only comprehensive, fully-disclosed work that places at the top-8 proprietary category on the TSA Leaderboard. Details of the top-11 algorithms are proprietary and undisclosed to the public. Most of the top-8 methods are reported to use a combination 3D volumetric data (*330 MB* per file) and 2D (*10–41 MB*) image data (1th). Whereas, we use only the smallest 2D image data available (*10 MB, .aps* **files**). RaadNet may be directly compared to the 6th which use 2D data and multiple classifiers specialized for each body part. In contrast, we use only 3-ensemble classifiers, each component classifier trained on a disjoint subset of all body parts. We observed that all our baseline classifiers have a higher rate of false-negatives than false-positives. In other words, Raad-Net is more likely to miss a concealed item than to generate false alarms. The difference narrows and false-negative rates decreases as more precise body part segmentation is used in *Ours-Ens* and *Ours-Opt*. Highlighting the importance of accurate body segmentation in backscatter MWS images.

5   Conclusion

We have shown how improved 2D human pose estimation, and the consequent improvement of body part segmentation can lead to a significant performance boost on body part anomaly detection task. Adapting 2D pose encoders trained on RGB images to estimate the keypoints of persons in backscatter MWS images is non-trivial without ground-truth annotations but, as we show, can be very rewarding when done well. Our keypoint refinement procedure and unsupervised body part segmentation algorithm described in Sect. 3.1 enables us to accurately segment the body parts of persons in MWS images. Subsequently, this allows us to train our anomaly detection network on cropped images of segmented body parts. With precise segmentation of body parts in backscatter MWS, we design a simple and effective body-part-aware neural network architecture that can be trained with weak supervision on all body parts in tandem.

Acknowledgements. Funding for this project was provided by the National Science Foundation, NSF grant BCS 2040422.

References

1. Ajami, M., Lang, B.: Using RGB-d sensors for the detection of unattended luggage (11 2016)
2. Bhattacharyya, A., Lind, C.H.: Threat detection in TSA scans using Alexnet (2018)
3. Cao, Z., Simon, T., Wei, S.E., Sheikh, Y.: Realtime multi-person 2D pose estimation using part affinity fields. In: Computer Vision and Pattern Recognition(CVPR) (2017)
4. Chen, Y., Wang, Z., Peng, Y., Zhang, Z., Yu, G., Sun, J.: Cascaded pyramid network for multi-person pose estimation. In: 2018 IEEE/CVF Conference on Computer Vision and Pattern Recognition, pp. 7103–7112 (2017)

5. Cheng, G., Han, J., Guo, L., Liu, T.: Learning coarse-to-fine sparselets for efficient object detection and scene classification. In: 2015 IEEE Conference on Computer Vision and Pattern Recognition (CVPR), pp. 1173–1181 (2015)
6. CURTIS, A.R., POWELL, M.J.D., REID, J.K.: On the estimation of sparse Jacobian matrices. IMA J. Appl. Math. **13**(1), 117–119 (02 1974). https://doi.org/10.1093/imamat/13.1.117
7. Deng, J., Dong, W., Socher, R., Li, L.J., Li, K., Fei-Fei, L.: ImageNet: a large-scale hierarchical image database. In: CVPR09 (2009). Dataset available at https://image-net.org/index
8. Fang, H., Lu, G., Fang, X., Xie, J., Tai, Y.W., Lu, C.: Weakly and semi supervised human body part parsing via pose-guided knowledge transfer. In: 2018 IEEE/CVF Conference on Computer Vision and Pattern Recognition, pp. 70–78 (2018)
9. Fioraio, N., di Stefano, L.: Joint detection, tracking and mapping by semantic bundle adjustment. In: 2013 IEEE Conference on Computer Vision and Pattern Recognition, pp. 1538–1545 (2013)
10. Gong, K., Liang, X., Li, Y., Chen, Y., Yang, M., Lin, L.: Instance-level human parsing via part grouping network (2018). arXiv: 1808.00157
11. Grisetti, G., Guadagnino, T., Aloise, I., Colosi, M., Corte, B.D., Schlegel, D.: Least squares optimization: from theory to practice. Robotics **9**, 51 (2020)
12. Gruosso, M., Capece, N., Erra, U.: Human segmentation in surveillance video with deep learning. Multimedia Tools Appl. 80 (01 2021). https://doi.org/10.1007/s11042-020-09425-0
13. Guimaraes, A.A.R., Tofighi, G.: Detecting zones and threat on 3D body for security in airports using deep machine learning. In: Computer Vision and Pattern Recognition (2018). ArXiv: 1802.00565
14. Güler, R.A., Trigeorgis, G., Antonakos, E., Snape, P., Zafeiriou, S., Kokkinos, I.: Densereg: fully convolutional dense shape regression in-the-wild. In: 2017 IEEE Conference on Computer Vision and Pattern Recognition (CVPR), pp. 2614–2623 (2017)
15. He, K., Gkioxari, G., Dollár, P., Girshick, R.: Mask R-CNN. Computer Vision and Pattern Recognition (CVPR) (2018)
16. Hidalgo, G., et al.: Single-network whole-body pose estimation. In: 2019 IEEE/CVF International Conference on Computer Vision (ICCV), pp. 6981–6990 (2019)
17. Hynes, A., Czarnuch, S.: Human part segmentation in depth images with annotated part positions. Sensors **18**, 1900 (06 2018). https://doi.org/10.3390/s18061900
18. Kingma, D.P., Ba, J.: Adam: a method for stochastic optimization. CoRR abs/1412.6980 (2014)
19. Li, P., Xu, Y., Wei, Y., Yang, Y.: Self-correction for human parsing. IEEE Trans. Pattern Anal. Mach. Intell. **44**, 3260–3271 (2022)
20. Lin, K., Wang, L., Luo, K., Chen, Y., Liu, Z., Sun, M.T.: Cross-domain complementary learning using pose for multi-person part segmentation. IEEE Trans. Circ. Syst. Video Technol. 1 (05 2020). https://doi.org/10.1109/TCSVT.2020.2995122
21. Lin, T.Y., et al.: Microsoft COCO: common objects in context. In: ECCV (2014), dataset available at https://cocodataset.org/#home
22. Luo, Y., Zheng, Z., Zheng, L., Guan, T., Yu, J., Yang, Y.: Macro-micro adversarial network for human parsing. In: ECCV (2018)
23. Maqueda, I.G., de la Blanca, N.P., Molina, R., Katsaggelos, A.K.: Fast millimeter wave threat detection algorithm. In: 2015 23rd European Signal Processing Conference (EUSIPCO), pp. 599–603 (2015)

24. Newell, A., Yang, K., Deng, J.: Stacked hourglass networks for human pose estimation. In: ECCV (2016)
25. Riffo, V., Mery, D.: Automated detection of threat objects using adapted implicit shape model. IEEE Trans. Syst. Man Cybernet.: Syst. **46**, 472–482 (2016)
26. Sandler, M., Howard, A.G., Zhu, M., Zhmoginov, A., Chen, L.C.: Mobilenetv 2: inverted residuals and linear bottlenecks. In: 2018 IEEE/CVF Conference on Computer Vision and Pattern Recognition, pp. 4510–4520 (2018)
27. Saviolo, A., Bonotto, M., Evangelista, D., Imperoli, M., Menegatti, E., Pretto, A.: Learning to segment human body parts with synthetically trained deep convolutional networks. In: IAS (2021)
28. Sun, K., Xiao, B., Liu, D., Wang, J.: Deep high-resolution representation learning for human pose estimation (2019). arXiv: 1902.09212
29. Thangavel, S.: Hidden object detection for classification of threat, pp. 1–7 (01 2017). https://doi.org/10.1109/ICACCS.2017.8014719
30. Toshev, A., Szegedy, C.: DeepPose: human pose estimation via deep neural networks. In: 2014 IEEE Conference on Computer Vision and Pattern Recognition, pp. 1653–1660 (2014)
31. Triggs, B., McLauchlan, P., Hartley, R., Fitzgibbon, A.: Bundle adjustment - a modern synthesis. In: Workshop on Vision Algorithms (1999)
32. TSA: Passenger screening challenge dataset (2017). https://kaggle.com/c/passenger-screening-algorithm-challenge/data
33. Xia, F., Wang, P., Chen, X., Yuille, A.L.: Joint multi-person pose estimation and semantic part segmentation. In: 2017 IEEE Conference on Computer Vision and Pattern Recognition (CVPR), pp. 6080–6089 (2017)
34. Yang, L., Song, Q., Wang, Z., Jiang, M.: Parsing R-CNN for instance-level human analysis. In: 2019 IEEE/CVF Conference on Computer Vision and Pattern Recognition (CVPR), pp. 364–373 (2019)
35. Yaniv, Z.: Random sample consensus (ransac) algorithm, a generic implementation release. In: Proceedings (2010)
36. Zhang, J., Hu, J.: Image segmentation based on 2D OTSU method with histogram analysis. In: 2008 International Conference on Computer Science and Software Engineering **6**, 105–108 (2008)
37. Zhang, S.H., et al.: Pose2seg: detection free human instance segmentation. In: 2019 IEEE/CVF Conference on Computer Vision and Pattern Recognition (CVPR), pp. 889–898 (2019)

Toward Surroundings-Aware Temporal Prediction of 3D Human Skeleton Sequence

Tomohiro Fujita(✉) [ID] and Yasutomo Kawanishi [ID]

Guardian Robot Project R-IH, RIKEN, Kyoto 619-0288, Japan
{tomohiro.fujita,yasutomo.kawanishi}@riken.jp

Abstract. Temporal prediction of human pose sequence is vital for robot applications such as human-robot interaction and autonomous control of a robot. Recent methods are based on a 3D human skeleton sequence to predict future skeletons. Even if starting motions of two human skeleton sequences are very similar, their future motions may be different because of the surrounding objects of the human; it is difficult to predict the future skeleton sequences only from a given human skeleton sequence. However, don't you think the presence of surrounding objects is an important clue for the prediction? This paper proposes a method of predicting future skeleton sequences by incorporating the surrounding information into the skeleton sequence. We assume that the surrounding condition around a target person does not change significantly within a few seconds and use an image feature around the target person as the surrounding information. Through evaluations on a public dataset, performance improvement is confirmed.

Keywords: Pose prediction · Surroundings information · Image feature

1 Introduction

Prediction of human location and pose in future seconds are very useful for autonomous human support robots. Even if we can predict the future motions of a person only 1 s in advance, it will be possible for robots to provide proactive actions such as avoiding collisions with people or alerting people to dangerous objects. Therefore, we aim to predict the future poses of a target person for about 1 s. The prediction is potentially difficult, so in recent years, Recurrent Neural Network (RNN), which handles temporal information, or Graph Convolutional Network (GCN), which handles graph structure of inputs, have been employed to predict the future poses.

3D human skeleton sequences are often used for modeling human motions because they are robust to the environmental variations such as background, illumination, and clothing of the human. Most existing studies on predicting future pose sequences use only the 3D human skeleton sequences of a target

© Springer Nature Switzerland AG 2023
J.-J. Rousseau and B. Kapralos (Eds.): ICPR 2022 Workshops, LNCS 13643, pp. 139–151, 2023.
https://doi.org/10.1007/978-3-031-37660-3_10

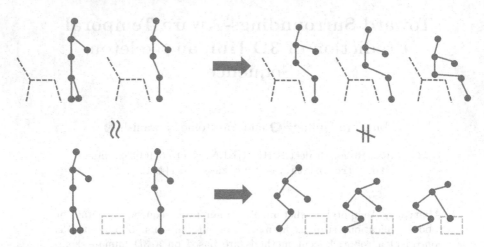

Fig. 1. Example of behaviors that fail to predict. If initial pose sequences are very similar but the future ones are different, it is not enough to use only the 3D pose sequence of initial motion.

person's starting motion as an input. However, starting motions are sometimes similar, even if the future motions are different. Therefore, estimating only from the 3D human skeleton sequence is sometimes difficult. Specific examples include picking up an object or sitting on a chair from a standing position. Figure 1 shows a specific example of a case in which the starting motions are very similar, but the future ones are different. When predicting 3D skeleton sequences such as shown in Fig. 1, an accurate prediction may not be possible if only the 3D skeletal coordinate sequence of the target person's starting motion is used.

Here, when carefully observing human body motions, we can find that human body motions are often affected by surrounding objects, such as handshaking with another person or carrying an object. We humans can somehow predict future motion by looking at the surroundings, even if the starting motions are similar. Based on the observation, this paper proposes a 3D human skeleton prediction model that employs surrounding information.

As for the surrounding information, as a preliminary study, this paper proposes a prediction method of future human skeleton sequences by using an image of human surroundings as an additional information in addition to the 3D skeleton sequence of a starting motion, in order to capture the surrounding features that serve as cues for prediction. To effectively introduce the surrounding information, we also propose a novel feature weighting method, named Image-Assisted Attention for future skeleton prediction (IAA).

Our contributions are summarized as follows:

- We proposed the prediction method of future skeleton sequence by using an image of human surroundings and the new feature weighting method called Image-Assisted Attention for future skeleton prediction (IAA).
- The prediction accuracy is improved by our proposed surroundings-aware human skeleton prediction framework especially in object-related motions.

The rest of this paper is organized as follows: In Sect. 2, recent work on human pose prediction is summarized. In Sect. 3, the details of the proposed surroundings-aware human pose prediction are described. In Sect. 4, experimental results are presented. Finally, we conclude the paper in Sect. 5.

2   Related Work

Early studies on the prediction of 3D skeleton sequence used restricted Boltzmann machine [12], or Gaussian process latent variable models [14]. These methods have difficulty capturing complex human motions; thus, deep learning methods such as Recurrent Neural Network (RNN) and Graph Convolutional Network (GCN) have been widely used in recent years. RNN has several recursive structures inside that allow for processing variable-length input, and they enable the prediction of 3D human skeleton sequences as time-series data [6,11,13], but RNN is generally difficult to learn. On the other hand, since the human body skeleton can be considered a graph structure, recent studies use GCN to predict 3D skeleton sequences [4,8,9].

However, the studies mentioned above use only the short human skeleton sequence of the starting motion of the target person. They do not consider what kind of situation the surroundings are. Therefore, it is difficult to predict if the starting motions of the person are similar. For this problem, several studies proposed an RNN model that considers the locations of the other objects [3], or an RNN model that uses multiple human skeletons and images to consider the contexts [1]. The study by Corona et al. [3] requires to select somehow an object related to the human motion. Also, Adeli et al. [1] use only 13 body joints which are coarse predictions compared to other methods predicting more than 20 joints, and the prediction time is limited.

Besides the above, Chao et al. [2] use only static image to predict 3D skeleton sequence.

3   Surroundings-Aware Prediction of 3D Skeleton Sequence

3.1   Overview of the Proposed Method

Existing methods that use only the 3D skeleton sequence of the starting motion to predict the future skeletons cannot accurately predict where the starting motions are similar but the future motions are different. To deal with this problem, we propose a method for a 3D skeleton prediction framework that takes into account the surrounding information, named surroundings-aware human skeleton prediction. The input of the method is a human 3D skeleton sequence $\mathcal{X}^{\text{in}} = (X_{T_1}, \ldots, X_{T_{\text{in}}})$ and the surrounding information, and the output is the future skeleton sequence $\mathcal{X}^{\text{out}} = (X_{T_{\text{in}}+1}, \ldots, X_{T_{\text{out}}})$ by using a GCN-based Encoder-Decoder model.

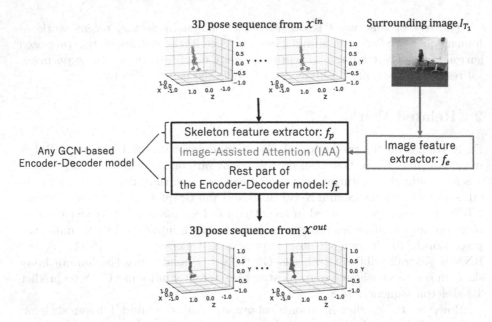

Fig. 2. The proposed surrounding-aware future skeleton prediction framework. In this framework, the skeleton feature is modified using the image feature extracted from an RGB image of around the target person.

In the proposed framework, any existing GCN-based Encoder-Decoder model that processes a skeleton sequence for future skeleton prediction can be used. Generally, an existing GCN-based Encoder-Decoder model predicts the future skeleton sequence $\mathcal{X}^{out}$ from the input $\mathcal{X}^{in}$. The encoder and decoder consists of multiple layers of graph convolution layers; the layers near the input layer can be considered as feature extractors, while the layers near the output layer can be considered as future skeleton reconstructors.

In this paper, we consider to use an image feature as the surroundings information. Here, we assume that the surrounding condition does not change significantly within a few seconds. Based on the assumption, the proposed method use I_{T_1} named the surrounding image, which is a cropped image around the target person at the time T_1. The image is expected to contain objects that affect the motion of the target person, since the view is limited to around the person. To use the information extracted from the surrounding image effectively, we also propose a feature weighting method named Image-Assisted Attention for future skeleton prediction (IAA), which modifies the feature extracted from a skeleton sequence depending on the image feature.

The overall process flow of the proposed framework is visualized in Fig. 2. First, a skeleton feature S is extracted from the input 3D human skeleton sequence $\mathcal{X}^{in}$ via the first layer of the GCN-based encoder. In parallel, a surrounding feature $\mathbf{i}$ is extracted from the surrounding image I_{T_1}. Then, the proposed IAA module modifies the skeleton feature S using the surrounding feature $\mathbf{i}$.

Finally, the modified feature is fed into the rest part of the GCN-based Encoder-Decoder model to predict the future skeletons $\mathcal{X}^{\text{out}}$.

The following sections explain the detail of the proposed method.

3.2 Surrounding Feature Extraction from an Image Around the Target Person

This section explains how to extract the surrounding feature from a cropped image of the surroundings of the target person. The feature extractor that extracts image features should be able to focus on objects in the input image. Therefore, in this study, we used a pre-trained feature extractor, specifically the convolutional layers of EfficientNet [10]. Here, we experimentally used the EfficientNet-B3 model, considering the trade-off between calculation cost and accuracy. This EfficientNet-B3 model is pre-trained on ImageNet [5] by torchvision. The following shows the preprocessing procedure for extracting features from images. The image size is assumed to be $1,280 \times 720$, and the size of a person in the image is less than 200×600 pixels.

1. A 600×600 image centered on a target person was cropped from a $1,280 \times 720$ RGB image. If the cropping position was outside of the original image, it was corrected by moving the center point so that the cropped area did not extend beyond the image.
2. The cropped 600×600 image was scaled down to the EfficientNet-B3 input size of 300×300 using bilinear interpolation.

An image feature is extracted from the image of the person's surroundings obtained by using the feature extractor described above. The parameters of the feature extractor are not updated during training in terms of calculation cost.

3.3 Image-Assisted Attention (IAA) for Future Skeleton Prediction

This section explains the detail of the proposed Image-Assisted Attention for future skeleton prediction (IAA). Figure 3 shows the structure of the proposed IAA.

The inputs to the IAA module are a skeleton feature S extracted via the first layer of the GCN-based Encoder-Decoder model, namely the skeleton feature extractor f_p, and a surrounding feature $\mathbf{i}$ extracted via the image feature extractor f_e consisting of a CNN explained in Sect. 3.2.

$$S = f_p(\mathcal{X}^{\text{in}}) \tag{1}$$

$$\mathbf{i} = f_e(I_{T_1}) \tag{2}$$

Since the skeleton feature S is an output of a graph convolution, it has a graph structure. Therefore, first, the skeleton feature $S \in \mathbb{R}^{m \times n}$ is flattened to a one-dimensional vector $\mathbf{s} \in \mathbb{R}^{mn}$. The inputs $\mathbf{s}$ and $\mathbf{i}$ are converted by fully-connected layers f_s and f_i respectively to be the dimension the same, n-dimensional vectors. Then, these vectors $f_s(\mathbf{s})$ and $f_i(\mathbf{i})$ are added and fed to a

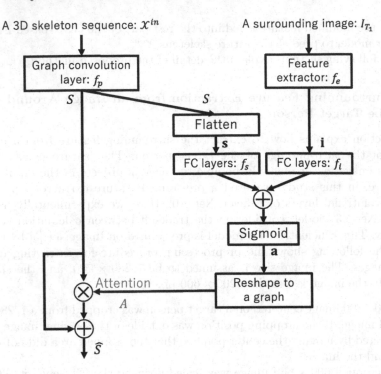

Fig. 3. Structure of the IAA. In IAA, in order to weight skeleton feature, image feature is used to calculate attention for feature elements.

sigmoid function $\sigma(\mathbf{x}) = \frac{1}{1+\exp(-\mathbf{x})}$. Using $\mathbf{s}$ and $\mathbf{i}$, attention vector $\mathbf{a}$ is calculated by Equation (3) as follows:

$$\mathbf{a} = \sigma(f_s(\mathbf{s}) + f_i(\mathbf{i})). \tag{3}$$

The attention vector $\mathbf{a} \in \mathbb{R}^n$ is repeated m times, and the attention matrix $A \in \mathbb{R}^{m \times n}$ is obtained. By using the attention matrix A, the original skeleton feature S is modified as:

$$\widehat{S} = S \circ A + S, \tag{4}$$

where the operator $\circ$ represents the Hadamard product.

As a result, the skeleton feature S of n-dimensional features of m body joints are modified by the attention matrix A, and the modified skeleton feature $\widehat{S}$ is obtained. The above calculation makes the feature values modified using the surrounding information extracted from the image around the target person. This weighting method is different from well-known cross-attention mechanism that use softmax and dot product, etc., but we call it "attention" in this paper because it determines which features are weighted.

In this study, we experimentally use the same vector $\mathbf{a}$ in attention matrix A considering calculation costs.

3.4   Future Skeleton Prediction from the Modified Skeleton Feature

The section explains the final step, future skeleton prediction. The modified skeleton feature $\widehat{S}$ is fed into the rest part of the GCN-based Encoder-Decoder model, f_r. Finally, the future skeleton sequence $\mathcal{X}^{\mathrm{pred}}$ is predicted. In this way, the future skeleton prediction that takes into account human surroundings can be obtained.

$$\mathcal{X}^{\mathrm{pred}} = f_r(\widehat{S}). \tag{5}$$

In the implementation, the IAA layer is inserted between the first and second layers of the GCN-based Encoder-Decoder, and the network except the Efficient-Net is trained in End-to-End manner.

4   Evaluation

4.1   Compared Methods

The objective of this experiment is to confirm the prediction accuracy improvement by our proposed method.

We evaluated the accuracy of the proposed method compared to other prediction methods. Since the proposed method is inserting the IAA module into a GCN-based method, we used the latest GCN-based method [4] and its original method [8] as the existing methods. In this paper, these [4,8] are represented by MSR-GCN and Traj-GCN, respectively. In the evaluation, our proposed method is named with the suffix "with IAA". Here, since we used Traj-GCN and MSR-GCN as a GCN-based Encoder-Decoder model, these methods are comparative methods while Traj-GCN with IAA and MSR-GCN with IAA are the proposed method.

The number of parameters for fully connected (FC) layers in the IAA is shown in Table 1. The other parameters were set following the existing studies. Leaky ReLU with a slope of 0.2 was used as the activation function for the first layer of FC layers f_i that transforms image features. Each learnable parameter except EffcientNet-B3 was learnt by stochastic gradient descent using Adam, with the learning rate of 0.001 and other hyperparameters of PyTorch default setting. Also, the dropout ratio, the number of epochs, and batch size were set to 0.2, 200, and 2,048, respectively. If the loss did not decrease for five epochs, the learning rate was multiplied by 0.1. In addition, if the loss did not decrease for 11 epochs, the training was terminated.

4.2   Dataset

To evaluate the proposed method, a large-scale dataset containing skeleton sequence and images is required. We used a large-scale dataset, NTU RGB+D 120 dataset [7]; this dataset is basically used for evaluating skeleton-based action recognition. This dataset contains 114,480 samples in 120 action classes. In our experiments, we used $1{,}920 \times 1{,}080$ RGB image sequences and 3D skeleton

Table 1. The Number of parameters for fully connected layers (FC layers) in our proposed IAA

FC layers f_s (1 layer): skeleton feature	input	output
Traj-GCN with IAA	16,896 (= 66×256)	256
MSR-GCN with IAA	4,224 (= 66×64)	64
FC layers f_i (2 layers): image feature	input	output
1st layer	1,536	384
2nd layer (Traj-GCN with IAA)	384	256
(MSR-GCN with IAA)	384	64

sequences consisting of 25 joint points in each person. However, 535 samples were excluded because of missing joint data. From this dataset, we generated data for training and evaluation by the following process.

1. Since there are several persons in a video, one person from a video where the variance of the 3D skeleton coordinates using all frames is the largest was selected for each video. This is because some skeletons are misdetections, such as tables and seats.
2. Since the selected data may include the switching of humans and other objects like tables and seats, sections where the sum of distance from "head" to "spine base" and from "spine base" to "left foot" was smaller than 60cm were discarded.
3. To make the system robust to the location of the person, the location is aligned using the locations of "spine base" of the first frame. Also, orientations of skeletons are aligned by rotating them so that hips are orthogonal to the y-z plane.
4. Using a sliding window of 35 frames, multiple subsequences were cropped by shifting the window by one frame from the beginning. The number of joints was also eliminated to adapt the model input (25 joints → 22 joints). Also, we prepared skeletons with 12, 7, and 4 joints by taking the average of the near joints according to the preprocess of the multi-scale joints for MSR-GCN.
5. Each RGB image was resized from $1,920 \times 1,080$ to $1,280 \times 720$ using bilinear interpolation.
6. The subsequences were divided into training set (50%), validation set (25%) and test set (25%) referring to the Cross-Subject evaluation method proposed in the NTURGB+D 120 dataset (dividing such that the same person is not included in different sets).

The number of time steps in the input/output was set to $T_{in} = 10$ and $T_{out} = 35$, following the experiments in the existing studies.

4.3 Evaluation Metric

For the evaluation, Mean Per Joint Position Error (MPJPE), which is the average of all Euclidean distances for each joint in the skeleton, was used as the loss

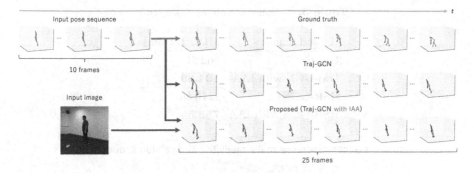

Fig. 4. Example of predicted results (blue) and ground truth (red) in "pick up" action. We can see that the prediction of Traj-GCN with IAA is close to the ground truth by using person's surrounding image. (Color figure online)

Table 2. Prediction result (Average of five times)

Method name	Average MPJPE (mm)
Traj-GCN	99.45 ± 1.11
Traj-GCN with IAA	**98.56 ± 0.60**
MSR-GCN	112.90 ± 3.49
MSR-GCN with IAA	**109.49 ± 2.15**

function and the evaluation metric to evaluate how close the predicted future skeleton sequence is to the ground-truth 3D skeleton sequence. This metric is widely used in 3D pose estimation. Experiment was performed five times by changing initial weights for each method, and the performance of each method were evaluated by the average MPJPE of the five times.

4.4 Result and Discussion

The results of the experiment are shown in Table 2. In the table, the average MPJPE of five times is shown in millimeters. As an example, Table 3 shows the results for the case of the "pick up" class in the dataset. In Table 2 and Table 3, MPJPE are rounded off the third decimal place.

Figure 4 shows an example of the predicted results and the ground truth in the "pick up" class. Figure 5 also shows the predicted future skeleton at the 15th frame in the output. Also, as another prediction example, Fig. 6 shows the results that the predicted skeleton at the 15th frame in a prediction of the "follow other person" class.

As a result, from Table 2, the methods "with IAA" improved the average MPJPE scores and the standard deviations. However, the overall improvement of MPJPE is still small. Looking at the results in detail, even though the actions are the same, there are samples that are contrary to the assumption that the human motion can be predicted by the surround information; in some videos,

Table 3. Action example of "pick up"

Method name	MPJPE (mm)
Traj-GCN	362.81
Traj-GCN with IAA	**194.39**
MSR-GCN	1170.86
MSR-GCN with IAA	**753.55**

15th image corresponding to the predicted 3D skeleton sequence

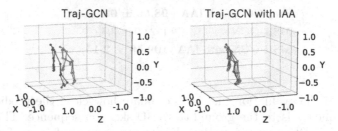

Fig. 5. Example of the 15th frame of a predicted (blue) and ground truth (red) pose in "pick up" action. In the object-related motion, the future skeleton is well predicted by our proposed IAA. (Color figure online)

actors in the video pretended to do an action without objects. In addtion, in most of the RGB images, since there were always objects such as tables and seats that were not directly related to each action, the MPJPE deteriorated in poses like sitting down or standing up from a seats. These factors are considered to be the main cause of the disturbance of the performance improvement.

On the other hand, Table 3, Fig. 4, and Fig. 5 show that our proposed method improves MPJPE over existing methods for the "pick up" action, confirming the effectiveness of using the image of the human surroundings as additional information. Figure 6 also shows that the prediction accuracy has improved for actions related to other person by using our proposed method.

Although MSR-GCN is the newer method than Traj-GCN, our experiment show that the MPJPE of Traj-GCN is better than that of MSR-GCN. In the implementation of the two existing studies, the Traj-GCN has tanh function but the MSR-GCN has Leaky ReLU as activation function of hidden layers.

15th image corresponding to the predicted 3D skeleton sequence

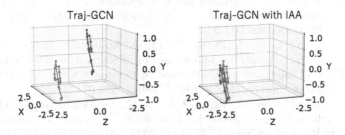

Fig. 6. Example of the 15th frame of a predicted (blue) and ground truth (red) pose in "follow other person" action. In the human-related motion, the future skeleton is well predicted by our proposed IAA. (Color figure online)

We consider that this difference of activation function caused the performance difference between models in experiment using the NTU RGB+D 120.

5 Conclusion

In this study, as a preliminary study, we proposed the method for predicting future human skeleton sequence using surrounding information as additional clue, under the assumption that human motion can be predicted from the surroundings. The surrounding information is extracted from an image around the target person. In the experiment using the NTU RGB+D 120 dataset, it was confirmed that the MPJPE of the future skeleton sequence is improved, especially during the motion involving other objects.

Our proposed method, called IAA, can be applied to any existing GCN-based method. In this paper, we inserted the IAA between the first and second layers of the GCN-based Encoder, but there is still room for debate as to where it should be inserted. It is also possible to change the model that processes the image other than the EfficientNet, and there is a possibility that the accuracy will be improved by updating the parameters of the backbone during training. We will tackle these issues and further improve the MPJPE in future work.

References

1. Adeli, V., Adeli, E., Reid, I., Niebles, J.C., Rezatofighi, H.: Socially and contextually aware human motion and pose forecasting. IEEE Robot. Autom. Lett. **5**(4), 6033–6040 (2020). https://doi.org/10.1109/LRA.2020.3010742
2. Chao, Y.W., Yang, J., Price, B., Cohen, S., Deng, J.: Forecasting human dynamics from static images. In: Proceedings of the IEEE Conference on Computer Vision and Pattern Recognition, pp. 548–556 (Jul 2017). https://doi.org/10.1109/CVPR.2017.388
3. Corona, E., Pumarola, A., Alenya, G., Moreno-Noguer, F.: Context-aware human motion prediction. In: Proceedings of the 2020 IEEE/CVF Conference on Computer Vision and Pattern Recognition, pp. 6990–6999 (Jun 2020). https://doi.org/10.1109/CVPR42600.2020.00702
4. Dang, L., Nie, Y., Long, C., Zhang, Q., Li, G.: MSR-GCN: multi-scale residual graph convolution networks for human motion prediction. In: Proceedings of the 2021 IEEE/CVF International Conference on Computer Vision, pp. 11447–11456 (Oct 2021). https://doi.org/10.1109/ICCV48922.2021.01127
5. Deng, J., Dong, W., Socher, R., Li, L.J., Li, K., Fei-Fei, L.: ImageNet: a large-scale hierarchical image database. In: 2009 IEEE Conference on Computer Vision and Pattern Recognition, pp. 248–255 (Jun 2009). https://doi.org/10.1109/CVPR.2009.5206848
6. Li, M., Chen, S., Zhao, Y., Zhang, Y., Wang, Y., Tian, Q.: Dynamic multiscale graph neural networks for 3D skeleton based human motion prediction. In: Proceedings of the 2020 IEEE/CVF Conference on Computer Vision and Pattern Recognition, pp. 211–220 (Jun 2020). https://doi.org/10.1109/CVPR42600.2020.00029
7. Liu, J., Shahroudy, A., Perez, M., Wang, G., Duan, L.Y., Kot, A.C.: NTU RGB+D 120: a large-scale benchmark for 3D human activity understanding. IEEE Trans. Pattern Anal. Mach. Intell. **42**(10), 2684–2701 (2020). https://doi.org/10.1109/TPAMI.2019.2916873
8. Mao, W., Liu, M., Salzmann, M., Li, H.: Learning trajectory dependencies for human motion prediction. In: Proceedings of the 2019 IEEE/CVF International Conference on Computer Vision, pp. 9488–9496 (Oct 2019). https://doi.org/10.1109/ICCV.2019.00958
9. Sofianos, T., Sampieri, A., Franco, L., Galasso, F.: Space-time-separable graph convolutional network for pose forecasting. In: Proceedings of the 2021 IEEE/CVF International Conference on Computer Vision, pp. 11189–11198 (Oct 2021). https://doi.org/10.1109/ICCV48922.2021.01102
10. Tan, M., Le, Q.: EfficientNet: rethinking model scaling for convolutional neural networks. In: Proceedings of the 36th International Conference on Machine Learning. Proceedings of Machine Learning Research, vol. 97, pp. 6105–6114 (Jun 2019)
11. Tang, Y., Ma, L., Liu, W., Zheng, W.S.: Long-term human motion prediction by modeling motion context and enhancing motion dynamics. In: Proceedings of the Twenty-Seventh International Joint Conference on Artificial Intelligence, IJCAI-18, pp. 935–941 (Jul 2018). https://doi.org/10.24963/ijcai.2018/130
12. Taylor, G.W., Hinton, G.E., Roweis, S.T.: Modeling human motion using binary latent variables. In: Advances in Neural Information Processing Systems, vol. 19 (Sep 2007). https://doi.org/10.7551/mitpress/7503.003.0173

13. Wang, B., Adeli, E., Chiu, H.K., Huang, D.A., Niebles, J.C.: Imitation learning for human pose prediction. In: Proceedings of the 2019 IEEE/CVF International Conference on Computer Vision, pp. 7123–7132 (Oct 2019). https://doi.org/10.1109/ICCV.2019.00722
14. Wang, J., Hertzmann, A., Blei, D.M.: Gaussian process dynamical models. In: Advances in neural information processing systems, vol. 18 (May 2006)

MTGR: Improving Emotion and Sentiment Analysis with Gated Residual Networks

Rihab Hajlaoui[1]([✉]), Guillaume-Alexandre Bilodeau[1], and Jan Rockemann[2]

[1] LITIV Laboratory Polytechnique Montréal, Montréal, Canada
{rihab.hajlaoui,gabilodeau}@polymtl.ca
[2] Airudi, Montréal, Canada
jan.rockemann@airudi.com

Abstract. In this paper, we address the problem of emotion recognition and sentiment analysis. Implementing an end-to-end deep learning model for emotion recognition or sentiment analysis that uses different modalities of data has become an emerging research area. Numerous research studies have shown that multimodal transformers can efficiently combine and integrate different heterogeneous modalities of data, and improve the accuracy of emotion/sentiment prediction. Therefore, in this paper, we propose a new multimodal transformer for sentiment analysis and emotion recognition. Compared to previous work, we propose to integrate a gated residual network (GRN) into the multimodal transformer to better capitalize on the various signal modalities. Our method shows an improvement of the F1 score and the accuracy results on the CMU-MOSI and IEMOCAP datasets compared to the state-of-the-art results.

Keywords: Multimodal fusion · Image and video processing · Natural language processing

1 Introduction

Emotions are expressed differently from one person to another. Most people communicate emotions both verbally (natural language), and non-verbally (facial gestures, tone of voice, etc.) to different degrees depending on circumstances and personalities. Acoustic and visual cues thus can provide additional knowledge to help understand human behaviours and significantly improve the prediction performance of an emotion recognition system. However, combining and integrating different heterogeneous modalities of data into an end-to-end deep learning model is not trivial due to two main reasons:

1. The non-aligned nature of features across modalities. For example, a face gesture at the time step i may relate to a word spoken at another time step j (where $i \neq j$).
2. The heterogeneity of the data across the different modalities. The features of the different modalities are extracted using different tools and with various representations.

© Springer Nature Switzerland AG 2023
J.-J. Rousseau and B. Kapralos (Eds.): ICPR 2022 Workshops, LNCS 13643, pp. 152–163, 2023.
https://doi.org/10.1007/978-3-031-37660-3_11

To address the above issues, prior studies proposed different strategies to fuse different modalities of data. For instance, some of them rely on the early fusion approach to combine the feature vectors of the different modalities [1–3]. Other works used late fusion strategy to combine the results of unimodal classifiers [4,5]. More recently, Multimodal Transformers have been proposed by many researchers and they have shown their effectiveness in dealing with the above issues. Multimodal transformers use a module called crossmodal attention (co-attention). This module will learn the attention across two modalities: the target modality, which is the main input to the model that is used to predict the sentiment/emotion, and the source modality, which is the second input to the model that is used to enhance the features of the target modality. Unlike the self-attention mechanism, the co-attention will compute a new representation for the target modality. This new representation contains information coming from the source modality.

However, we noticed that sometimes the reinforced features contain information from the source modality that might affect negatively the prediction. For example, non-verbal communication sometimes conveys meaning by contradicting verbal communication instead of reinforcing or substituting for it. *Following this observation, we propose to add a GRN (Gated Residual Network) that allows the network to have the flexibility to use or suppress information received from other modalities.*

Therefore, we propose a multimodal transformer with a gated residual network (MTGR) for emotion recognition and sentiment analysis. We use an end-to-end multimodal transformer (MulT) similar to Tsai [6] that uses co-attention, and improved their model by adding a GRN in the multimodal transformer modules. Our proposed architecture allows the multimodal transformer to minimize the contribution of unnecessary information sent from other modalities. The GRN will act as a filtering mechanism that facilitates the flow of information between the layers of the multimodal transformer. Results show that we obtain a significant improvement over the original MulT model for the CMU-MOSI and IEMOCAP datasets.

2   Related Work

The sentiment analysis and emotion recognition fields have observed and confirmed the effectiveness of combining different modalities of data. Many solutions have been proposed to fuse multimodal information and they can be categorized into two types of fusion:

1. **Late fusion (decision-level fusion):** consists in training several classifier networks independently, each classifier being assigned to a single modality. The final decision is obtained by applying, for instance, a weighted sum fusion or a weighted product fusion on the different results [4,5]. Models based on this strategy are not able to learn inter-modality and intra-modality interactions;

2. **Early fusion (feature-level fusion):.** In this strategy, the features of different modalities are merged into a global feature vector. Many early fusion methods can be applied, for instance, a simple concatenation [1–3], an element-wise sum, or an element-wise product [7]. Despite the simplicity of these methods, they are unfortunately not able to explore in-depth both inter-modality and intra-modality interactions.

Recently, more advanced methods were proposed. For example, Li et al. [8] proposed an outer product through the time where all intra- and inter-modality dynamics can be captured. Bagher Zadeh et al. [9] suggested Graph-MFN, which is based on a dynamic fusion graph that can learn crossmodal interactions and can effectively choose the appropriate fusion graph based on the importance of each n-modal dynamic during inference. Wang et al. [10] proposed a Recurrent Attended Variation Embedding Network (RAVEN) that is able to capture the dynamic between words and non-verbal behaviours by shifting the word representations based on non-verbal cues.

However, most of these previous works do not address the problem of feature misalignment between modalities. Other recent methods have explored the use of transformers to learn multimodal representations [6,11] and they have been shown to be effective in dealing with unaligned multimodal language sequences. In Tsai et al. [6] and Delbrouck et al. [11], both of the proposed transformers rely on crossmodal attention (co-attention) that will learn the attention across two modalities. In other words, this module will reinforce the features of a target modality x with those from another source modality y. To do so the key K and the context C of the self-attention are calculated from the features of the modality y instead of those of the modality x. Instead of using only the co-attention, Delbrouck et al. [11] propose the idea of a modular co-attention which consists of calculating the attended features of a primary modality using the self-attention and enhancing the features of a secondary modality by those from the primary modality using the co-attention. The co-attention operation in these proposed methods leads to a new feature representation of the target modality that always contains information coming from other modalities. However, this information might be unnecessary or might contradict the meaning conveyed by the features of the target modality.

3   Methodology

Based on the previous works, we determined that sometimes the reinforced features might contain information from the source modality that is detrimental to the prediction. This motivated us to propose a method with more flexibility to use or suppress information received from other modalities. To do so, we propose to integrate a Gated Residual Network (GRN) [12] after the co-attention operation of a crossmodal transformer, such as the one used in [6].

Figure 1 gives an overview of our proposed method.

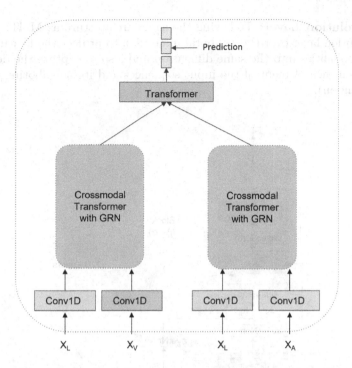

Fig. 1. Overview of the method. The main components of the multimodal transformer are the crossmodal transformers which capture the dynamics between two modalities of data. The outputs of the crossmodal transformers are concatenated and passed through a self-attention transformer to capture temporal information for the prediction.

3.1 Problem Definition

We consider three different modalities of data L (Linguistic), A (Acoustic), and V (Visual). Our goal is to recognize sentiments or emotions based on these three modalities. Given the extracted features of each modality that are denoted as X_l, X_a, and X_v respectively, these feature sequences are going to be the inputs for the multimodal transformer that mainly consists of two crossmodal transformers. Each crossmodal transformer aims to modulate the dynamics between two different modalities of data to improve the prediction for a sentiment analysis or an emotion recognition task. Crossmodal transformers capture these inter-modality interactions by repeatedly reinforcing the characteristics of a target modality X_α with those of another source modality X_β.

3.2 Details of the Proposed Method

In this section we explain the different components of our proposed model (see Fig. 1).

1D Convolution Layer: Following the same architecture as MulT, we use a 1D convolution layer over the temporal dimension to project the features of the different modalities into the same dimension and also to capture the dependencies between each element of the input sequences and its neighboring elements (local attention).

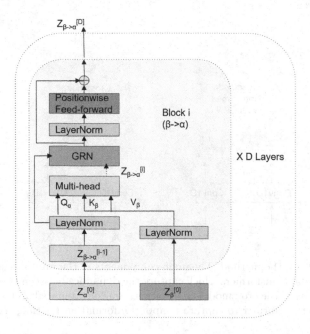

Fig. 2. Crossmodal Transformer Block between two modalities α and β, where α is the target modality and β is the source modality. The main components of the crossmodal transformer are the co-attention operation to calculate the enhanced features for the target modality, and the Gated Residual Network to suppress unnecessary information coming from the source modality.

Crossmodal Transformer with Gated Residual Network: We aim to improve emotion recognition and sentiment analysis by adding a Gated Residual Network (GRN) [12] in multimodal transformers. We decided to add a GRN after the co-attention operation in each crossmodal transformer which will act as a filtering mechanism that will eliminate the unnecessary information calculated by the co-attention operation.

Our new crossmodal transformer block is shown in Fig. 2. In each crossmodal transformer, only two modalities are used: the target modality and the source modality. In our case the target modality is always the language modality because linguistic input usually contains more information that can be used to extract emotions or sentiments. In addition an unimodal transformer that uses textual data usually performs better than an unimodal transformer that uses acoustic or visual data. The crossmodal transformer module aims to enhance the features of the target modality with information coming from the source modality. The layers of the crossmodal transformer consist of multi-headed co-attention that take the feature sequences of two modalities and compute the attention between them. Instead of a simple residual connection, we added a Gated Residual Network that can skip over the multi-head co-attention block. This GRN will learn to combine the features of the target modality (the output from the previous block) and the enhanced features (the output of the co-attention). In this way, the crossmodal transformer will also be able to learn identity mapping. By using GRN, the crossmodal transformer will avoid unnecessary co-attention operations that are used in the architecture.

We selected the model of Tsai et al. [6] for our based multimodal transformer architecture. This model, named MulT, is mainly based on co-attention instead of self-attention in its layers. The co-attention mechanism aims to enhance the features of the target modality with those from the source modality. Given two modalities α and β, the feature sequences extracted from these modalities are denoted by $X_\alpha \in \mathbb{R}^{T_\alpha \times d_k}$ and $X_\beta \in \mathbb{R}^{T_\beta \times d_k}$ respectively, where $T_{()}$ represents the sequence length and $d_{()}$ represents the feature dimension.

Let us suppose that modality α is the target modality and β is the source modality. To compute the co-attention between these two modalities, the queries Q_α will be computed from the target modality and the keys and the values K_β, V_β from the source modality with

$$Q_\alpha = X_\alpha W_{Q_\alpha}, \tag{1}$$

$$K_\beta = X_\beta W_{K_\beta}, \tag{2}$$

and

$$V_\beta = X_\beta W_{V_\beta}, \tag{3}$$

where $W_{Q_\alpha} \in \mathbb{R}^{d_\alpha \times d_k}, W_{K_\beta} \in \mathbb{R}^{d_\beta \times d_k}$ and $W_{V_\beta} \in \mathbb{R}^{d_\beta \times d_v}$ are the weights. For the first block $X_\alpha = Z_\alpha^0$ which is the low-level feature of the target modality, and $X_\beta = Z_\beta^0$ which is the low-level features of the source modality. At each layer of the crossmodal transformer, the low-level features of the modality β are used as the source feature sequences. For an intermediate block i, $X_\alpha = Z_{\beta \to \alpha}^{i-1}$ and $X_\beta = Z_\beta^0$.

The co-attention from β to α is:

$$Y_\alpha = CM_{\beta \to \alpha}(X_\alpha, X_\beta) = softmax(\frac{Q_\alpha Q_\beta^\top}{\sqrt{d_k}})V_\beta. \tag{4}$$

For an intermediate block i, $Y_\alpha = Z_{\beta \to \alpha}^i$ which is the result of the co-attention operation.

The softmax calculates an attention matrix between the two modalities α and β. The output Y_α of co-attention represents the enhanced features that are going to be used as the target modality in the next layer. In addition, a residual

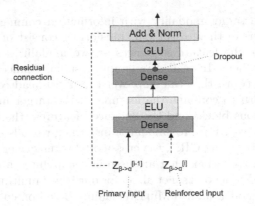

Fig. 3. Gated Residual Network

connection and a feed-forward layer are added to the crossmodal transformer after each co-attention operation.

We modified this base model to include a GRN. This GRN takes a primary input (the features of the target modality, $Z_{\beta \to \alpha}^{i-1}$) and an optional context vector (in our case the context vector is $Z_{\beta \to \alpha}^{i}$, which is the vector resulting from the co-attention operation). Under the assumption that sometimes information sent from other modalities to the target modality may negatively affect the prediction instead of improving it, the GRN will learn to remove unnecessary information sent from other modalities. As shown in Fig. 3, the GRN will produce a vector that can either be the features of the target modality if the model depends only on that modality (the GRN will act as an identity function), or it can combine the features of the target modality with enhanced features that contain information from the source modality. The GRN will also give the crossmodal transformer the flexibility to apply non-linear processing only when necessary. The GRN generates its output as follows:

$$GRN_{\omega}(a, c) = LayerNorm(a + GLU_{\omega}(\eta_1)) \tag{5}$$

$$\eta_1 = W_{1,\omega}\eta_2 + b_{1,\omega} \tag{6}$$

$$\eta_2 = ELU(W_{2,\omega}a + W_{3,\omega}c + b_{2,\omega}) \tag{7}$$

$$GLU_{\omega}(\gamma) = \sigma(W_{4,\omega}\gamma + b_{4,\omega}) \odot (W_{5,\omega}\gamma + b_{5,\omega}) \tag{8}$$

where a is the primary input, c is the context vector, $LayerNorm$ is a layer normalization, η_1 and η_2 are intermediate layers, $W_{()}$ and $b_{()}$ are the weights and biases respectively, ELU is the Exponential Linear Unit activation function, GLU is a Gated Linear Unit, and $\odot$ is en element-wise Hadamard product.

Gated Residual Networks can learn identity mapping more easily than residual connections. If the output of GLU is close to 0, then the entire co-attention module is removed, so feature enhancement will only be applied where it is needed. GRN will remove any co-attention operation from the architecture when it is unnecessary for the given input. If co-attention is applied, then GRN will learn how to combine the reinforced features with the output of the previous layer. In addition, GRNs perform better than residual connections in deeper networks [13].

Self-Attention Transformer: Finally, the outputs of the crossmodal transformers are concatenated together. The resulting feature vector from the concatenation is passed through a self-attention transformer to capture temporal information. Finally, the output of the transformer is passed through a fully connected layer for the prediction.

The loss functions that were used depend on the dataset. For the IEMOCAP dataset we used the Cross Entropy Loss between the inputs and the targets. For CMU-MOSI and CMU-MOSEI datasets we used the L1 Loss function which minimizes the sum of the absolute differences between the inputs and the targets.

4   Experiments

4.1   Datasets and Evaluation Metrics

To evaluate our proposed model, three datasets were used: CMU-MOSI [5], CMU-MOSEI [9] and IEMOCAP [14]. CMU-MOSI is used for multimodal sentiment intensity and subjectivity analysis. It consists of 2,199 online video clips annotated with labels for subjectivity and sentiment intensity at opinion level. CMU-MOSEI dataset is considered as the largest dataset for multimodal emotion recognition and sentiment analysis. This dataset consists of 23,500 sentence utterance video clips from Youtube. CMU-MOSEI is annotated for both sentiment analysis and emotion recognition tasks. Finally, IEMOCAP consists of approximately 12 h of audiovisual data. The dataset contains multiple sessions where in each session two speakers are performing improvisations or scripted scenarios. IEMOCAP is annotated using 9 emotions but only 4 of them are selected for emotion recognition(happy, sad, angry, neutral).

For CMU-MOSI and CMU-MOSEI datasets, the evaluations metrics that are used are: the 7-class accuracy used for the sentiment score classification (acc7), the 5-class accuracy (acc5), the 2-class accuracy (Accuracy), F1 score (F1), mean absolute error (MAE) and the correlation (CC) of model's prediction with true labels. For the IEMOCAP dataset the binary classification accuracy and the F1 score are used to evaluate the model.

4.2   Implementation Details

Features. We trained and evaluated our model using the extracted features from the work of MulT [6]. For the language modality, features were extracted from text using Glove [15] pre-trained for word embedding. The size of an embedding is 300. For the visual modality, Facet [16] was used to extract 35 facial action units from each frame. COVEREP [17] was used to extract features for the acoustic modality.

Hyperprameters. Table 1 shows the different hyperparameters used to train our model and to re-train MulT. For a fair comparison between MulT and our proposed method, we used the same hyperparameters (except the additional one for the GRN).

Table 1. Hyperparameters

Batch Size	24
Number of Epochs	40
Initial Learning Rate	1e-3
Number of Layers	5
Optimizer	Adam
Crossmodal Attention Heads	5
Dropout for Crossmodal Attention Block	0,1
Textual Embedding Dropout	0,25
Dropout for the GRN	0,1
Output Dropout	0,1

4.3 Results and Discussion

In this section, we provide the results of our proposed model (MTGR) and compare these results with the results for state-of-the-art methods on the three datasets. Table 2 gives the results of our method on the CMU-MOSEI dataset. Table 3 gives the results of our method on the CMU-MOSI dataset. Table 4 gives the results of our method on the IEMOCAP dataset.

We recall that our proposed method and MulT were trained in the same way. The results show the effectiveness of the GRN as a filtering mechanism that is able to suppress unnecessary information. If the GRN is always acting like an identity function, it means that the information coming from the source modality is crucial and helps to improve the prediction results.

For the CMU-MOSI and IEMOCAP datasets, the results show that our method performs better than the original Multimodal Transformer. It succeeded to improve all the different metrics that are used for evaluation. For the CMU-MOSEI dataset we can only see some improvements in the 7-class accuracy and the 5-class accuracy metrics.

We also compare our proposed method with several state-of-the-art models on the three benchmark datasets. For CMU-MOSI and CMU-MOSEI datasets, the results on the different metrics show that our method is very competitive and sometimes outperforms state-of-the-art models. For the IEMOCAP dataset, we noticed that our method was able to improve the results of the least present emotions in the dataset (Neutral, Sad and Angry), which shows that our method is also robust to the data imbalance problem compared to other SOTA methods.

Table 2. Results on the CMU-MOSEI Dataset. **Boldface**: best results. ↑: the higher value of the metrics means the better performance of the model. ↓: the lower value of the metrics means the better performance of the model.

	MAE ↓	CC ↑	mult_acc_7 ↑	mult_acc_5 ↑	F1 score ↑	Accuracy ↑
MulT [6]	**0,614**	**0,673**	0,493	0,509	**0,810**	0,808
GraphMFN [9]	0,71	0,54	0,45	-	0,77	0,769
RAVEN [10]	0,614	0,662	0,50	-	0,79	0,79
Transformer-based joint-encoding [18]	-	-	0,45	-	-	**0,82**
MTGR	0,617	0,657	**0,497**	**0,513**	0,794	0,795

Table 3. Results on the CMU-MOSI Dataset. **Boldface**: best results. ↑: the higher value of the metrics means the better performance of the model. ↓: the lower value of the metrics means the better performance of the model.

	MAE ↓	CC ↑	mult_acc_7 ↑	mult_acc_5 ↑	F1 score ↑	Accuracy ↑
MulT [6]	1,030	0,657	0,335	0,384	0,773	0,774
RAVEN [10]	0,915	0,691	0,332	-	0,766	0,78
MTGR	**0,904**	**0,691**	**0,367**	**0,413**	**0,803**	**0,803**

Table 4. Results on the IEMOCAP Dataset. **Boldface**: best results. ↑: the higher value of the metrics means the better performance of the model. ↓: the lower value of the metrics means the better performance of the model.

	Neutral		Happy		Sad		Angry	
	F1 score ↑	Accuracy ↑	F1 score ↑	Accuracy ↑	F1 score ↑	Accuracy ↑	F1 score ↑	Accuracy ↑
MulT [6]	0,690	0,692	0,836	0,859	0,826	0,835	0,851	0,845
RAVEN [10]	0,693	0,697	**0,858**	**0,873**	0,831	0,834	0,8671	**0,873**
MTGR	**0,718**	**0,723**	0.841	0,865	**0,848**	**0,851**	**0,873**	0,869

5 Conclusion

We proposed an improvement to the multimodal transformer (MulT) [6] for sentiment analysis and emotion recognition by adding a Gated Residual Network (GRN) [12] to the original end-to-end architecture. This gives the model more flexibility to use or suppress information received from other modalities. Our method showed an improvement in both F1 score and accuracy metrics for the CMU-MOSI and IEMOCAP datasets compared to MulT. Our method also can compare with, and sometimes outperforms, the state-of-the-art models.

References

1. Morency, L.-P., Mihalcea, R., Doshi. P.: Towards multimodal sentiment analysis: harvesting opinions from the web. In: International Conference on Multimodal Interfaces (ICMI 2011). Alicante, Spain, Nov. (2011)

2. V. Pérez-Rosas, V., Mihalcea, R., Morency, L.-P.: Utterance-level multimodal sentiment analysis. In: Proceedings of the 51st Annual Meeting of the Association for Computational Linguistics (Volume 1: Long Papers). Sofia, Bulgaria: Association for Computational Linguistics, Aug. 2013, pp. 973–982. https://aclanthology.org/P13-1096

3. Poria, S., Chaturvedi, I., Cambria, E., Hussain, A.: Convolutional MKL based multimodal emotion recognition and sentiment analysis. In: 2016 IEEE 16th International Conference on Data Mining (ICDM). (2016), pp. 439–448. https://doi.org/10.1109/ICDM.2016.0055

4. Wang, H., Meghawat, A., Morency, L., Xing, E.P.: Select-Additive Learning: improving cross-individual generalization in multimodal sentiment analysis. In: CoRR abs/1609.05244 (2016). arXiv: 1609.05244

5. Zadeh, A., Zellers, R., Pincus, E., Morency, L.: MOSI: multimodal corpus of sentiment intensity and subjectivity analysis in online opinion videos. In: CoRR abs/1606.06259 (2016). arXiv: 1606.06259

6. Tsai, Y.H., Bai, S., Liang, P.P., Kolter, J.Z., Morency, L., Salakhutdinov, R.: Multimodal transformer for unaligned multimodal language sequences. In: Proceedings of the 57th Conference of the Association for Computational Linguistics, ACL (2019), Florence, Italy, Jul 28- Aug 2, 2019, Volume 1: Long Papers. 2019, pp. 6558–6569. https://doi.org/10.18653/v1/p19-1656

7. Dobrišek, S., Gajšek, R., Mihelic, F., Pavešic, N., Štruc. V.: Towards efficient multimodal emotion recognition. Int. J. Adv. Robot. Syst. **10**.1, 53 (2013)

8. Li, B., Li, C., Duan, F., Zheng, N., Zhao. Q.: TPFN: applying outer product along time to multimodal sentiment analysis fusion on incomplete data. In: Computer Vision - ECCV 2020–16th European Conference, Glasgow, UK, Aug 23–28, 2020, Proceedings, Part XXIV. (2020), pp. 431–447. https://doi.org/10.1007/978-3-030-58586-0_26

9. Zadeh, A., Liang, P.P., Poria, S., Cambria, E., Morency. L.: Multimodal language analysis in the wild: CMU-MOSEI dataset and interpretable dynamic fusion graph. In: Proceedings of the 56th Annual Meeting of the Association for Computational Linguistics, ACL (2018), Melbourne, Australia, Jul 15–20, 2018, Volume 1: Long Papers. 2018, pp. 2236–2246. https://doi.org/10.18653/v1/P18-1208, https://aclanthology.org/P18-1208/

10. Wang, Y., Shen, Y., Liu, Z., Liang, P.P., Zadeh, A., Morency, L.-P.: Words can shift: dynamically adjusting word representations using nonverbal behaviors. In: AAAI, pp. 7216–7223 (2019). https://doi.org/10.1609/aaai.v33i01.33017216

11. Delbrouck, J., Tits, N., Brousmiche, M., Dupont, S.: A transformerbased jointencoding for emotion recognition and sentiment analysis. In: CoRR abs/2006.15955 (2020). arXiv: 2006.15955

12. Lim, B., Arik, S.O., Loeff, N., Pfister, T.: Temporal fusion transformers for interpretable multi-horizon time series forecasting (2020). arXiv:1912.09363 [stat.ML]

13. Savarese, P., Figueiredo, D.: Residual gates: a simple mechanism for improved network optimization. In: Proceedings of the International Conference on Learning Representations (2017)

14. Busso, C., et al.: IEMOCAP: interactive emotional dyadic motion capture database. In: Lang. Resour. Evaluation 42.4 (2008), pp. 335–359. https://doi.org/10.1007/s10579-008-9076-6

15. Pennington, J., Socher, R., Manning, C.D.: Glove: global vectors for word representation. In: Proceedings of the 2014 Conference on Empirical Methods In Natural Language Processing (EMNLP), pp. 1532–1543 (2014)

16. iMotions. https://imotions.com/ (2017)
17. Degottex, G., Kane, J., Drugman, T., Raitio, T., Scherer, S.: COVAREP-A collaborative voice analysis repository for speech technologies. In: IEEE International Conference on Acoustics, Speech And Signal Processing (icassp), vol. 2014, pp. 960–964. IEEE (2014)
18. Delbrouck, J.-B., Tits, N., Brousmiche, M., Dupont, S.: A transformerbased joint-encoding for emotion recognition and sentiment analysis. In: Second Grand-Challenge and Workshop on Multimodal Language (Challenge-HML) (2020). https://doi.org/10.18653/v1/2020.challengehml-1.1

12th International Workshop on Human Behavior Understanding (HBU)

Foreword

The 12th International Workshop on Human Behavior Understanding (HBU) was organized as a virtual event at ICPR 2022. The HBU workshop was first organized in 2010 as a satellite to ICPR, and each year after that, it focused on a different issue in human behavior analysis, and was organized in different conferences, such as AmI, UbiComp, ACM MM, ECCV, FG, and IROS. This year's special theme was clinical settings and tools usable for behavioral scientists.

Our three keynotes reflected the special theme well. Dr. Rich Caruana (Microsoft Research)'s talk entitled "Using Interpretable Machine Learning to Understand Clinical Behavior and Optimize Healthcare" discussed human clinical decision making, surprises that are lurking in clinical data, using glass-box machine learning to optimize healthcare delivery, and methods for protecting privacy and detecting bias. Our second keynote, Dr. Juan Wachs (Purdue University), in his talk "Bridging Fingers - Gestures for Knowledge Gain," discussed the importance of natural physical expression as means for interacting with devices, machines and robots in the healthcare domain, providing insights and findings about the use of gestures to control robots for collaboration with surgeons, for surgical training and for rehabilitation. Finally, Dr. Ehsan Hoque (University of Rochester) asked "Should we deploy our research?", and shared his group's experience of deploying work in the real-world setting, from allowing people to practice public speaking to individuals with movement disorders performing neurological tests - using a computer browser and a webcam.

We have received 15 submissions, each of which received two independent reviews in single blind fashion. Nine papers were accepted, and eight of them are published in this volume. One paper was later withdrawn due to a technical issue. We thank our authors and keynotes for their contributions, the ICPR organization for hosting HBU, and our program committee for their insightful reviews: Carlos Busso, Oya Celiktutan, Anna Esposito, Arya Farkhondeh, Jeffrey Girard, Julio Jacques Junior, Dongmei Jiang, Heysem Kaya, Meysam Madadi, Itir Onal Ertugrul, Luis Pellegrin, Isabella Poggi, Ronald Poppe, Hanan Salam, Giovanna Varni, and Yigeng Zhang.

The workshop was endorsed by IAPR, and financially supported by the ChaLearn Organization and Microsoft Research, for which we are grateful.

August 2022

Albert Ali Salah
Cristina Palmero
Hugo Jair Escalante
Sergio Escalera
Henning Müller

A Computational Approach for Analysing Autistic Behaviour During Dyadic Interactions

Oya Celiktutan[1(✉)], Weiyang Wu[1], Kai Vogeley[2,3],
and Alexandra L. Georgescu[4]

[1] Department of Engineering, King's College London, London WC2R 2LS, UK
oya.celiktutan@kcl.ac.uk
[2] Department of Psychiatry and Psychotherapy, University Hospital of Cologne,
Cologne, Germany
kai.vogeley@uk-koeln.de
[3] Institute of Neuroscience and Medicine, Cognitive Neuroscience (INM-3),
Research Centre Juelich, Juelich, Germany
[4] Department of Psychology, Institute of Psychiatry, Psychology and Neuroscience,
King's College London, London SE1 1UL, UK

Abstract. Successful social encounters crucially depend to a large degree on the smooth exchange of nonverbal cues between two or more interaction partners. Impairments in exchanging nonverbal cues are characteristic of developmental disorders such as autism spectrum disorder (ASD). Thus, modelling nonverbal behaviours is a well-fitting means for developing automatic diagnostic tools. In this paper, we focus on the computational analysis of nonverbal behaviours in dyadic social interactions between two adults (dyads). We studied three dyad types, composed of either two typical individuals, two autistic individuals or one typical and one autistic individual. We extracted both individual features (i.e., head, hand and leg movement) and interpersonal features (i.e., mutual gaze and head, hand and leg synchrony) from videos, which were subsequently used to train two classifiers. Our results show that the proposed approach is able to detect ASD at a performance of 70% and recognise dyad type at a performance of 72% in terms of F-Score, which has implications for minimally invasive autism screening.

Keywords: Nonverbal behaviour analysis · Social interaction · Autism

1 Introduction

The World Health Organization states that autism spectrum disorder (ASD) is one of the most common types of neurodevelopmental conditions, affecting the lives of 1 in 160 people worldwide from childhood to adolescence and adulthood [1]. Prevalence rates are rising alarmingly, due to broadening diagnostic criteria and increasing awareness of the condition [11]. The diagnosis of ASD requires a comprehensive analysis of actual symptoms, medical history data and

© Springer Nature Switzerland AG 2023
J.-J. Rousseau and B. Kapralos (Eds.): ICPR 2022 Workshops, LNCS 13643, pp. 167–177, 2023.
https://doi.org/10.1007/978-3-031-37660-3_12

social functioning by a clinician, which consumes a lot of medical resources and involves long waiting lists [30]. Diagnosis delays however mean delays in accessing essential health care and social support services which significantly contributes to people's mental health comorbidities [6]. Therefore, there has been a significant effort to develop reliable and cost-effective approaches for automating screening and diagnostic practices.

One of the hallmark symptoms of ASD is the difficulty with communication and social interaction, in particular, with the production of nonverbal cues during social encounters. For example, the nonverbal displays of a person with ASD is atypical with respect to the temporal coordination with their own verbal output [25] and with the nonverbal behaviour of their interaction partner [28,31,34,37]. Consequently, atypical nonverbal behavior has been included in the criteria for ASD of the Diagnostic and Statistical Manual of Mental Disorders (DSM-5), a criteria-based classification catalogue for mental disorders published by the American Psychiatric Association [3]. Moreover, reduced interpersonal coordination is also being assessed in standard diagnostic tools, like the Autism Diagnostic Observation Schedule, ADOS [23], and the Autism Diagnostic Interview - Revised, ADI-R [24]. Overall, this suggests that the coordination of nonverbal behaviour is reduced in ASD.

Motivated by this, automatic modelling of nonverbal cues from visual data for building computer-aided or robot-aided therapy systems has become a rapidly growing research area in recent years [14]. However, there are two areas, which have remained underexplored, and this paper aims to fill both gaps. First, to date, most of the proposed approaches have targeted children with ASD [18,35], and little attention has been paid to autistic adults. This is particularly important because of comorbidities and the development of individual coping mechanisms that influence the presentation of autistic persons in adulthood, making diagnosis more challenging and dependent on clinicians' training and experience [17]. Second, most of the proposed techniques have dealt with modelling individual nonverbal cues (e.g., facial expressions) rather than interpersonal cues (e.g. eye contact, mimicry, synchrony). Hence, automatic modelling of interpersonal nonverbal behaviours - not only in the context of autism but in general - are still scarce.

The main goal of this paper is to introduce a method for automatic analysis of autistic behaviour in dyadic interactions between two human adults, which is non-invasive and easily scalable. We use a dataset comprising video recordings of interactions between (1) typical individual vs typical individual (TD-TD); (2) typical individual vs autistic individual (MIXED); and (3) autistic individual vs autistic individual (ASD-ASD). From these recordings, we extract a set of features to model individual cues as well as interpersonal cues, in particular, focusing on head and body movements and mutual attention. We formulate two classification problems: (1) Who has autism? We use the extracted features both singly and jointly to predict whether an individual has autism or not. (2) Which dyad type? A similar approach is applied to predict which of the three dyad types an individual is a part of. This latter classification problem was motivated by research suggesting that the composition of a dyad affects the interpersonal coordination generated during the interaction [8]. Comparing two classical machine learning methods (i.e., support vector machines and random forests), our results show that combining all the features together with random forests achieves a performance of 70% for detecting autism and 72% in terms of F-Score for recognising dyad type.

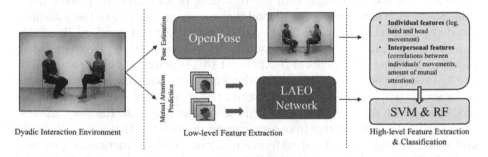

Fig. 1. Automatic analysis of autistic behaviours from nonverbal visual cues in dyadic interactions: We focus on a scenario where two participants (typical or ASD) were engaged in conversations. We used two state-of-the-art networks, namely, OpenPose [4] and LAEO network [26], to estimate body pose and mutual attention from the video clips. These were then used to extract a set of individual and interpersonal features that were fed into classical machine learning methods (i.e., SVM and RF) for detecting whether a participant has autism or not as well as recognising their dyad type (e.g., TD-TD, MIXED or ASD-ASD).

2   Related Work

There are only a handful of attempts that try to classify ASD based on nonverbal behaviour. Crippa *et al.* [7] used a kinematic analysis of upper-limb movements during a simple motor task to classify low-functioning children with ASD. The task involved fifteen children with ASD and fifteen TD children picking up a ball and dropping it into a hole while their movements were recorded using a motion tracker. Seven of the seventeen extracted kinematic parameters were found significant for discrimination. The resulting classification accuracy that distinguished ASD from TD was of 96.7%. In another study on children, the kinematics of simple reach and throw movements of 10 ASD and 10 TD children were quantified and included into a classification algorithm yielding an accuracy of 92.5% [32]. A few recent works have proposed deep learning approaches. Zhang *et al.* [15] developed a framework for automatic mutual gaze detection and investigated the relationship between mutual gaze ratio and social behaviour as a potential assessment tool for autism therapy. Li *et al.* [22] focused on play therapy of children with autism and introduced a multi-task multi-supervision network to simultaneously classify movement scyhrony (i.e., Synchronized, Intermediate, and Asynchronous) between a child and therapist and their activities (i.e., jumping, arm swing, chest expansion, and etc.) as well as predict the quality of action performed by the child.

Although diagnostic tools for children with ASD are relatively well explored, adult assessment methods are less studied. Drimalla *et al.* [10] focused on adults with ASD, and tracked voice parameters, eye gaze and facial expressions during a simulated social interaction with the recording of an actress that asked questions about food experiences. They found that running a classifier on these features can detect ASD accurately and functionally independently of standard diagnostic questionnaires. Finally, Li *et al.* [21] used 40 kinematic parameters from imitative pointing-at-target movements of 16 ASD and 14 TD adult individuals and identified 9 of them to be most significant for discrimination, resulting in a classification accuracy of 93%. These studies demonstrate the potential of using movements as biomarkers with diagnostic value for ASD across development. However, the features used were derived either from simple motor movements that were also staged and therefore highly unnatural, or from simulated social interactions. Given that individuals with ASD have particular difficulties with spontaneous "on-line" social interactions that require fast responses and intuitive decisions [33], this calls for approaches with more external validity. Such approaches can be achieved by using naturalistic nonverbal behaviours as features.

Vision based human motion recognition approaches seem to be very promising for quantifying nonverbal behaviour in general and in ASD in particular. They offer the great advantage of extracting whole-body movements wirelessly. Given the sensory hypersensitivity exhibited by many individuals with ASD, not having to attach any motion tracking equipment to their bodies is of advantage. In [12,13], Georgescu *et al.* investigated a semi-automated motion energy analysis approach that track changes in pixel values through frame differencing. Using Support Vector Machines (SVM), they achieved a performance of 75.9% for classifying ASD vs. TD. In terms of quantifying interpersonal nonverbal behaviour a review paper by Delaherche *et al.* [9] mentions that the most widely used approach is to compute the correlation between each relevant feature of two individuals over time. This has indeed been used in ASD research [31] on interpersonal coordination, where motion energy analysis was applied to head, hand, and trunk individually and correlation was computed to represent the synchrony in movement between a child/adolescent participant with ASD and an experimenter. However, motion energy analysis provides a holistic representation and is prone to noise such as background clutter and subject appearance.

Taken together, there is a gap in the computational assessment of ASD vs. TD nonverbal cues during social interactions beyond motion energy analysis. On the other hand, a review of different methods for human-human interaction recognition, which was performed Stergiou and Poppe recently [36], highlighted that the human skeleton is a useful source of information for learning temporal patterns of interactions, regardless of factors such as luminance, viewpoints, and character appearance. There is indeed previous work in autistic children's individual nonverbal cues (e.g., 3D body pose) [27]. However, we are not aware of any work aiming at analysing autistic adults' behaviours computationally, in particular, within the context of social interaction.

3   Dataset

In this paper, we used a dataset of dyadic interactions to study autistic behaviour, which was introduced and described in [12]. The experimental group consisted of 29 individuals with ASD who were diagnosed through clinical interviews by two physicians according to criteria of the 10th revision of the International Statistical Classification of Diseases and Related Health Problems (ICD), a classification criteria catalogue for mental disorders edited by the World Health Organization (WHO) [1], in the Autism Outpatient Clinic at the Department of Psychiatry of the University Hospital of Cologne in Germany. The typically developed control group was composed of 29 individuals who were students and members of staff at the University of Cologne and the University Hospital of Cologne, Germany and had no mental or neurological disorders histories.

Participants were assigned to one of three dyad groups, made up of either two ASD individuals (ASD-ASD), two typical individuals (TD-TD) or mixed dyads of one ASD individual and one typical individual (MIXED). In total, there were 10 ASD-ASD dyads, 10 TD-TD dyads and 9 MIXED dyads. To achieve optimal matching, dyad assignment was done such that interacting partners would have the same sex and would be not more than +/- 5 years apart in age and +/- 2 standard deviations in intelligence quotient (IQ). Each dyadic interaction took place in a room with standardised artificial lighting where one person sat on the left and the other sat on the right and was recorded using a Sony HD Handycam (Model HDR-XR550) as shown in Fig. 1.

Each dyad was asked to perform five interaction scenarios to investigate a wide range of conversations in both serious and humorous, cooperative and competitive contexts. The order of interaction scenarios was as follows: (1) Desert Island ice breaker task - participants were asked to engage in a long conversation with respect to which five items they would take to a desert island; (2) Two verbal debates: participants were asked to discuss two given topics (one cooperative and one competitive) related to social and political issues; (3) Meal planning task - participants were asked to design a five-course meal composed of dishes and drinks that they both dislike; (4) Joke telling task - participants were asked to tell knock-knock-jokes to each other, involving 6 jokes in total; (5) Role-play task: one participant was randomly assigned to the role of the boss and the other to the employee of a big insurance company. They were then told to enact a meeting, where the boss needed to sanction the employee. This resulted in a total of 6 videos per dyad, where each had a duration of 5 min except for the joke telling task (which lasted for 1 min). To equalise the duration among scenarios, we extracted two short clips (each of 60 s) from the middle of videos except for the joke task. In this way, we obtained 11 short clips for each dyad group, resulting in 317 short clips in total (the competitive debate video was missing for one of the dyads).

Table 1. Autism detection in terms of F-score (×100). Interpersonal features refer to correlation features plus LAEO. The best results are highlighted in bold. (SVM: support vector machines, RF: random forests, ASD: austism spectrum disorder, TD: typical development)

Features	SVM			RF		
	ASD	TD	Ave	ASD	TD	Ave
Individual	0.67	0.49	0.58	0.56	0.59	0.58
Individual+LAEO	0.64	0.63	0.64	0.67	0.67	0.67
Interpersonal	0.66	0.64	0.65	0.68	0.68	0.68
All features	0.67	0.67	**0.67**	0.70	0.69	**0.70**

4   Feature Extraction

We extracted both individual and interpersonal features based on body pose and head orientation (see Fig. 1).

Table 2. Dyad type recognition in terms of F-score (×100). Interpersonal features refer to correlation features plus LAEO. The best results are highlighted in bold. (SVM: support vector machines, RF: random forests, ASD-ASD: two ASD individuals, TD-TD: two typical individuals, mixed: one ASD individual and one typical individual)

Features	SVM				RF			
	ASD-ASD	TD-TD	MIXED	Ave	ASD-ASD	TD-TD	MIXED	Ave
Individual	0.52	0.29	0.11	0.31	0.45	0.48	0.35	0.43
Individual+LAEO	0.57	0.74	0.47	0.60	0.70	0.80	0.49	0.66
Interpersonal	0.64	0.65	0.48	0.59	0.61	0.73	0.47	0.60
All	0.73	0.77	0.67	**0.72**	0.72	0.85	0.60	**0.72**

4.1   Pose Estimation

We used OpenPose [4], a multi-people 2D pose estimation method based on convolutional neural networks. For each frame, we used OpenPose to obtain 2D coordinates of 25 skeleton joints as shown in Fig. 1, from which we computed the amount of body movement. Prior to feature extraction, we normalised each skeleton such that the middle hip joint was centred at the origin and the distance between the neck joint and middle hip joint was set to unit length.

From the normalised skeletons, we computed the following individual features: (1) the total amount of leg movement (i.e., the sum of the distances generated by each adjacent two frames on the knee and ankle joint points of both legs); (2) the total amount of hand movement (i.e., the sum of the distances generated by each adjacent two frames on the wrist joint points of both arms); and (3) the total amount of head movement (i.e., the total moving distance of the nose joint point). Each of the individual features was then aggregated over the whole clip by calculating the average for the duration of 60 s. As highlighted in [9], correlation is the most widely used measure for gauging interactional movement synchrony. Therefore, we defined interpersonal features as the correlation between skeleton joints from two interactions partners for each body region, namely, lower-body, hand and head. Overall, this resulted in a total of 3 individual features and 3 interpersonal features per person.

4.2 Mutual Attention Detection

The human body pose is a rich source of information for interpreting human interactions. To complement the body movement features, we used the Looking-At-Each-Other (LAEO) network [26] to detect whether interacting partners were looking at each other based on the head orientation. In particular, it has been shown that mutual gaze brings infant-adult neural activity into alignment [19] and that it can regulate turn taking during interactions [16]. Nevertheless, individuals with ASD have been found to have atypical mutual gaze or joint attention abilities, i.e., the capacity to coordinate attention using their eyes to communicate intentions [5, 29]. Thus, including this interpersonal feature in the classification models has the potential to be a valuable addition.

LAEO network consists of 3 branches, namely, two head-pose branches and one head-map branch to represent the relative position between two people. A fusion block is used to combine all the branches and delivers the probability of whether people are looking at each other or not for every 10 frames. Finally, we computed the average of the resulting probabilities over the whole clip to model the amount of interaction partners were looking at each other.

5 Experimental Results

We formulated two classification tasks: the detection of autism (i.e., ASD and TD) and the recognition of dyad type (i.e., TD-TD, ASD-ASD, and MIXED), and we presented the classification results respectively.

5.1 Experimental Setup

In our experiments, we compared two classifiers, namely, support vector machines (SVM) and random forests (RF). We used 70% of the data for training and the remaining 30% for testing in a subject-dependent fashion. In other words, the same subjects were not in both training and test sets. The training set was used to select optimal parameters using the grid search method, where we selected the best parameters within the default range of values available in Scikit-learn python toolbox [2].

5.2 Who Has Autism?

In Table 1, we presented the classification results in terms of F-score for detecting whether an individual has autism or not, where RF yielded better classification performance as compared to SVM in general. Looking at the results, we observed the following trend: For both of the classifiers, interpersonal features provided better results as compared to individual features and combining all the features clearly improved the performance. For example, when RF was used for classification, combining all the features outperformed using the individual features by a margin of 12% and using the interpersonal features by a margin of 2%.

5.3   Which Dyad Type?

In Table 2, we presented the classification results in terms of F-score for recognising the dyad type, namely, TD-TD, MIXED and ASD-ASD. While there was no notable difference in terms of performance between the two classifiers, we observed two trends. First, similar to the detection of autism, combining all the features yielded the best classification performance and using individual features resulted in poorer performance. However, in contrast to the detection of autism, using interpersonal features did not improve the performance as compared to using individual features and LAEO. Second, both classifiers were more successful for recognising homogenous dyads (TD-TD and ASD-ASD), while they performed worse in the classification of MIXED dyads. The underlying reason could be that the interaction pattern is consistent from one homogeneous dyad to another, but when the dyad is heterogeneous the intra-class variance is larger and therefore the classifiers perform worse.

6   Conclusion and Future Work

Difficulties of nonverbal communication are characteristic for the entire autistic spectrum, highlighting its potential value as a behavioural biomarker. We propose that (1) vision based human motion recognition approaches, (2) the consideration of interpersonal features in addition to individual ones, and (3) classification algorithms offer the potential for the development of low-cost, highly objective, automated, and non-invasive screening tools that can then help to alleviate bottlenecks in the healthcare system.

In our proof-of-principle study, we demonstrate that it is possible to classify adults with ASD from TD adults on the mere basis of naturalistic nonverbal behaviours in social interactions with an accuracy of over 70%. We also show for the first time that for the classification of ASD, including interpersonal alongside individual features results in improved predictive performance. This validates the notion that, as ASD is a disorder of social interaction, it is essential to start focusing on features that characterise the interaction rather than the individual themselves.

Given our limited sample size (which is common in autism research) and the large phenotypical heterogeneity that is characteristic of ASD, the next steps for future research will need to work with larger data sets, and to investigate categorization of ASD not just by contrast to TD, but also by contrast to other psychiatric disorders that can be classified as disorders of social interaction [20]. Future research should also consider other ways to quantify interpersonal behaviours like window cross-lagged correlation or an analysis of coordination in the frequency rather than time domain (e.g. wavelet analysis). It should also consider a multimodal approach and include a number of different features (fine-grained kinematic analysis of nonverbal features like eye gaze, head and body movements and facial expressions, as well as speech parameters) and clinical data (e.g. questionnaires) in order to improve classification accuracy. Finally, future research should consider increasing the explainability of the models with partial dependence plots or SHAP values.

Acknowledgments. Ethical approval for this study was granted by King's College London's Research Ethics Committee, registration number: LRS/DP-21/22-23235. The work of Oya Celiktutan was supported by the "LISI - Learning to Imitate Nonverbal Communication Dynamics for Human-Robot Social Interaction" Project, funded by Engineering and Physical Sciences Research Council (Grant Ref.: EP/V010875/1).

References

1. Autism spectrum disorders. https://www.who.int/news-room/fact-sheets/detail/autism-spectrum-disorders. Accessed 10 Oct 2019
2. Scikit-learn machine learning in python. http://scikit-learn.org/stable/. Accessed 10 Oct 2019
3. Association, A.P., et al.: Diagnostic and statistical manual of mental disorders (DSM-5®). American Psychiatric Pub (2013)
4. Cao, Z., Simon, T., Wei, S.E., Sheikh, Y.: Realtime multi-person 2D pose estimation using part affinity fields. In: CVPR (2017)
5. Caruana, N., et al.: Joint attention difficulties in autistic adults: an interactive eye-tracking study. Autism **22**(4), 502–512 (2018)
6. Cassidy, S., Bradley, P., Robinson, J., Allison, C., McHugh, M., Baron-Cohen, S.: Suicidal ideation and suicide plans or attempts in adults with Asperger's syndrome attending a specialist diagnostic clinic: a clinical cohort study. Lancet Psych. **1**(2), 142–147 (2014)
7. Crippa, A., et al.: Use of machine learning to identify children with autism and their motor abnormalities. J. Autism Dev. Disord. **45**(7), 2146–2156 (2015)
8. Crompton, C.J., Sharp, M., Axbey, H., Fletcher-Watson, S., Flynn, E.G., Ropar, D.: Neurotype-matching, but not being autistic, influences self and observer ratings of interpersonal rapport. Front. Psychol. **11**, 586171 (2020). https://doi.org/10.3389/fpsyg.2020.586171. https://www.frontiersin.org/articles/10.3389/fpsyg.2020.586171
9. Delaherche, E., Chetouani, M., Mahdhaoui, A., Saint-Georges, C., Viaux, S., Cohen, D.: Interpersonal synchrony: a survey of evaluation methods across disciplines. IEEE Trans. Affect. Comput. **3**(3), 349–365 (2012)
10. Drimalla, H., et al.: Detecting autism by analyzing a simulated social interaction. In: Berlingerio, M., Bonchi, F., Gärtner, T., Hurley, N., Ifrim, G. (eds.) ECML PKDD 2018. LNCS (LNAI), vol. 11051, pp. 193–208. Springer, Cham (2019). https://doi.org/10.1007/978-3-030-10925-7_12
11. Elsabbagh, M., et al.: Global prevalence of autism and other pervasive developmental disorders. Autism Res. **5**(3), 160–179 (2012)

12. Georgescu, A.L., Koeroglu, S., Hamilton, A., Vogeley, K., Falter-Wagner, C.M., Tschacher, W.: Reduced nonverbal interpersonal synchrony in autism spectrum disorder independent of partner diagnosis: a motion energy study. Molecular Autism (2020)
13. Georgescu, A.L., Koehler, J.C., Weiske, J., Vogeley, K., Koutsouleris, N., Falter-Wagner, C.: Machine learning to study social interaction difficulties in ASD. Front. Robot. AI **6**, 132 (2019). https://doi.org/10.3389/frobt.2019.00132. https://www.frontiersin.org/article/10.3389/frobt.2019.00132
14. Grossard, C., Palestra, G., Xavier, J., Chetouani, M., Grynszpan, O., Cohen, D.: ICT and autism care: state of the art. Curr. Opin. Psychiatry **31**(6), 474–483 (2018)
15. Guo, Z., Kim, K., Bhat, A., Barmaki, R.: An automated mutual gaze detection framework for social behavior assessment in therapy for children with autism. In: Proceedings of the 2021 International Conference on Multimodal Interaction, pp. 444–452. ICMI 2021, Association for Computing Machinery, New York, NY, USA (2021). https://doi.org/10.1145/3462244.3479882
16. Jokinen, K., Nishida, M., Yamamoto, S.: On eye-gaze and turn-taking. In: Proceedings of the 2010 workshop on Eye gaze in intelligent human machine interaction, pp. 118–123. ACM (2010)
17. Langmann, A., Becker, J., Poustka, L., Becker, K., Kamp-Becker, I.: Diagnostic utility of the autism diagnostic observation schedule in a clinical sample of adolescents and adults. Research Autism Spectrum Disorders **34**, 34–43 (2017). https://doi.org/10.1016/j.rasd.2016.11.012. https://www.sciencedirect.com/science/article/pii/S1750946716301520
18. Leo, M., et al.: Automatic emotion recognition in robot-children interaction for ASD treatment. In: The IEEE International Conference on Computer Vision (ICCV) Workshops (2015)
19. Leong, V., Byrne, E., Clackson, K., Georgieva, S., Lam, S., Wass, S.: Speaker gaze increases information coupling between infant and adult brains. Proc. Natl. Acad. Sci. **114**(50), 13290–13295 (2017)
20. Leong, V., Schilbach, L.: The promise of two-person neuroscience for developmental psychiatry: Using interaction-based sociometrics to identify disorders of social interaction. British J. Psych. **215**, 1–3 (2018)
21. Li, B., Sharma, A., Meng, J., Purushwalkam, S., Gowen, E.: Applying machine learning to identify autistic adults using imitation: an exploratory study. PLoS ONE **12**(8), e0182652 (2017)
22. Li, J., Bhat, A., Barmaki, R.: Improving the movement synchrony estimation with action quality assessment in children play therapy. In: Proceedings of the 2021 International Conference on Multimodal Interaction, pp. 397–406. ICMI 2021, Association for Computing Machinery, New York, NY, USA (2021). https://doi.org/10.1145/3462244.3479891
23. Lord, C., et al.: The autism diagnostic observation schedule-generic: a standard measure of social and communication deficits associated with the spectrum of autism. J. Autism Dev. Disord. **30**(3), 205–223 (2000)
24. Lord, C., Rutter, M., Le Couteur, A.: Autism diagnostic interview-revised: a revised version of a diagnostic interview for caregivers of individuals with possible pervasive developmental disorders. J. Autism Dev. Disord. **24**(5), 659–685 (1994)
25. de Marchena, A., Eigsti, I.M.: Conversational gestures in autism spectrum disorders: asynchrony but not decreased frequency. Autism Res. **3**(6), 311–322 (2010)

26. Marin-Jimenez, M.J., Kalogeiton, V., Medina-Suarez, P., Zisserman, A.: LAEO-Net: revisiting people looking at each other in videos. In: Proceedings of the IEEE Conference on Computer Vision and Pattern Recognition, pp. 3477–3485 (2019)
27. Marinoiu, E., Zanfir, M., Olaru, V., Sminchisescu, C.: 3D human sensing, action and emotion recognition in robot assisted therapy of children with autism. In: 2018 IEEE/CVF Conference on Computer Vision and Pattern Recognition, pp. 2158–2167 (2018). https://doi.org/10.1109/CVPR.2018.00230
28. Marsh, K.L., et al.: Autism and social disconnection in interpersonal rocking. Front. Integr. Neurosci. **7**, 4 (2013)
29. Mundy, P., Sigman, M., Kasari, C.: Joint attention, developmental level, and symptom presentation in autism. Dev. Psychopathol. **6**(3), 389–401 (1994)
30. Murphy, D.G., Beecham, J., Craig, M., Ecker, C.: Autism in adults. New biologicial findings and their translational implications to the cost of clinical services. Brain Res. **1380**, 22–33 (2011)
31. Noel, J.P., De Niear, M.A., Lazzara, N.S., Wallace, M.T.: Uncoupling between multisensory temporal function and nonverbal turn-taking in autism spectrum disorder. IEEE Trans. Cogn. Develop. Syst. **10**(4), 973–982 (2017)
32. Perego, P., Forti, S., Crippa, A., Valli, A., Reni, G.: Reach and throw movement analysis with support vector machines in early diagnosis of autism. In: 2009 Annual International Conference of the IEEE Engineering in Medicine and Biology Society, pp. 2555–2558. IEEE (2009)
33. Redcay, E., et al.: Atypical brain activation patterns during a face-to-face joint attention game in adults with autism spectrum disorder. Hum. Brain Mapp. **34**(10), 2511–2523 (2013)
34. Romero, V., Fitzpatrick, P., Roulier, S., Duncan, A., Richardson, M.J., Schmidt, R.: Evidence of embodied social competence during conversation in high functioning children with autism spectrum disorder. PLoS ONE **13**(3), e0193906 (2018)
35. Rudovic, O., Utsumi, Y., Lee, J., Hernandez, J., Ferrer, E.C., Schuller, B., Picard, R.W.: CultureNet: a deep learning approach for engagement intensity estimation from face images of children with autism. In: 2018 IEEE/RSJ International Conference on Intelligent Robots and Systems (IROS), pp. 339–346 (2018). https://doi.org/10.1109/IROS.2018.8594177
36. Stergiou, A., Poppe, R.: Understanding human-human interactions: a survey. arXiv preprint arXiv:1808.00022 (2018)
37. Trevarthen, C., Daniel, S.: Disorganized rhythm and synchrony: Early signs of autism and Rett syndrome. Brain Develop. **27**, S25–S34 (2005)

Region-Based Trajectory Analysis for Abnormal Behaviour Detection: A Trial Study for Suicide Detection and Prevention

Xun Li[1] , Ryan Anthony de Belen[1(✉)] , Arcot Sowmya[1] ,
Sandersan Onie[2] , and Mark Larsen[2]

[1] School of Computer Science and Engineering, University of New South Wales,
Sydney, NSW 2052, Australia
{r.debelen,a.sowmya}@unsw.edu.au
[2] Black Dog Institute, University of New South Wales, Sydney, NSW 2031, Australia
mark.larsen@blackdog.org.au

Abstract. We propose a region-based trajectory analysis method to detect abnormal activities in a scene. It provides a self-adapted, location-sensitive and interpretable trajectory analysis method for different scenarios. Our integrated pipeline consists of a pedestrian detection and tracking module to extract density, speed and direction features. In addition, it contains a grid-based feature extraction and clustering module that automatically generates a region map with corresponding feature importance. During testing, the pipeline analyses the segments that fall into the regions, but do not comply with the important features, and clusters trajectories together to detect abnormal behaviours. Our case study of a suicide hotspot proves the effectiveness of such an approach.

Keywords: trajectory analysis · abnormal behavior detection · suicide detection and prevention

1 Introduction

Abnormal behaviour detection has attracted growing interest in recent years due to the advances in video surveillance and wide adoption of closed-circuit television (CCTV). With the popularity of deep learning technology, today's surveillance systems are capable of detecting movements and searching for specific targets in CCTV footage [20]. However, there is still a large gap in the automatic understanding of human behaviours and detection of abnormal activities. Differences in camera angles, depth and resolution make it challenging for a generalised algorithm to fully capture the non-rigid articulated movement of human bodies; moreover, complex background noise and variable illumination conditions add to the challenge.

Researchers in this area generally approach this problem in two different ways: explicit abnormal behaviour recognition and abnormal behaviour detection. The former often requires the explicit modelling of target behaviours and

© Springer Nature Switzerland AG 2023
J.-J. Rousseau and B. Kapralos (Eds.): ICPR 2022 Workshops, LNCS 13643, pp. 178–192, 2023.
https://doi.org/10.1007/978-3-031-37660-3_13

prior identification of target behaviours, as well as behaviour annotations, to supervise the training of the detection model. Previous works [14–16], including ours [22], adopt this approach by first identifying high-risk behaviours, collecting/simulating video footage containing these behaviours and annotating them to train an action recognition model. It requires both expert knowledge in the domain and labour-intensive human annotation. It is also limited by data collected by RGB cameras in good lighting conditions. Abnormal behaviour detection, on the other hand, does not often rely on prior knowledge of the behaviours and is commonly addressed in an unsupervised manner. By collecting sufficient scene footage, normal behaviour patterns may be deduced, and any unusual behaviour can be statistically recognised without any explicit description.

Suicide is a leading cause of death and approximately 30% of suicides occur in public places [23]. There is evidence that individuals in crisis exhibit distinct, identifiable behaviours prior to a suicide attempt [22], and these behaviours may be captured using algorithms that detect abnormal behaviours. While current studies have been able to detect some suicide-related events when they occur [4,14], a more valuable and challenging approach is to detect a human in crisis before a suicide attempt is made, allowing sufficient time for intervention. A key observation of suicide prevention experts is that similar behaviour patterns are present in suicide attempts, such as repetitive movement patterns (e.g., pacing back and forth from the edge of the platform, and staying still for a prolonged time near the railway tracks [19,21]). This demonstrates a close relationship between crisis and location.

In fact, the trajectory and the landscape it covers are highly related factors. However, current literature only uses features universally and with equal importance assigned to every part of the map for abnormal trajectory detection, ignoring the main scene characteristics. In this work, we propose a region-based unsupervised trajectory analysis method to detect abnormal behaviours in location-sensitive applications. As a case study, we analyse CCTV footage for suicide detection and prevention. By using trajectories extracted from normal footage of a suicide hotspot to build a region map of the scene with different feature importance, abnormal trajectories can be detected by unsupervised methods, such as clustering.

2 Related Literature

The trajectory of an object is obtained by tracking its position across time. Trajectory analysis has long been used in the domain of abnormal behaviour detection. In this section, we provide an overview of trajectory extraction and representation, as well as different trajectory clustering algorithms used in the literature (see [2] for a more comprehensive review).

To extract trajectories in a video footage, other works have identified target motion using techniques such as optical flow [1], dense trajectory [33], feature tracking [34] and multi-object tracking [8]. In this work, we use a multi-object detection algorithm combined with a tracking algorithm to produce trajectories of multiple objects in a scene.

A trajectory is mathematically defined by a sequence of location points in the temporal domain and often represented as a collection (x_i, y_i) that denotes x and y positions of points at time t_i. Object tracking algorithms often represent trajectories as bounding boxes containing objects that move through time. Other information, such as density distribution [5,26] and speed profiles [32], are often included in trajectory representation. In this work, we represent trajectories as a combination of different features such as position, speed and direction. A scene usually consists of trajectories of different objects that may appear or disappear within a period of time.

After obtaining object trajectories, clustering algorithms are often employed to detect abnormal behaviours. Trajectory clustering algorithms can be categorised as density-based [9,31], hierarchical [11,13], model-based [12], partitional [6,29] and shrinkage-based [36] methods. Each category has its advantages and disadvantages. It is important to determine a suitable method for the application. Density-based and shrinkage-based methods are sensitive to the number of trajectories available for analysis, making them suitable for clustering a large number of trajectories. Hierarchical-based clustering employs different approaches depending on the dataset. Model-based clustering utilises different features and models that may affect the clustering results. Partitional methods divide the trajectories into similar partitions that resemble clusters. A previous study [30] has shown the effectiveness of joint co-occurrence in classification using image sequence, binary silhouettes, positions and histograms. In this work, we create a multi-dimensional feature space that includes joint co-occurrence of different features for trajectory clustering.

We propose that location and speed are two interconnected elements of a movement pattern. For example, the same speed may be considered normal in one location but abnormal in another. This increases the challenge of identifying abnormal trajectories in complex real-world applications. To address this, a good solution is to introduce a region map using prior knowledge of the scene or deduced using the object trajectories collected from the scene [24]. Using the duration and frequency of a trajectory in a certain region, loitering and suspicious path events are detected. In another work [7], an automatic zone discovery strategy has been proposed. First, the whole scene is abstracted to a grid representation and features of a trajectory point inside each cell form a cell summary, including number, speed and direction. Afterwards, clustering of the grid cell summaries is employed to find regions in the scene that represent distinct motion. It however weights features as equally important factors in each region.

Region-based trajectory analysis is particularly important for location-sensitive abnormal events, as these events are highly correlated with the location. Suicide hotspots are one such location, which are often public sites that provide the means and are associated with a high frequency of suicide. Currently, some hotspots are covered by CCTV cameras but utilise only manual observation or basic visual processing tools to trigger police emergency response when a suicide attempt takes place (e.g. detecting individuals on the wrong side of a safety fence). This is however often too late for suicide prevention. To detect

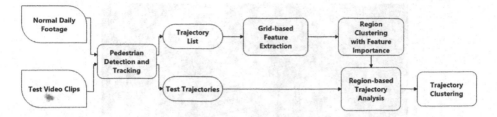

Fig. 1. Proposed trajectory analysis workflow. It consists of a Pedestrian Detection and Tracking module that generates a list of trajectories from a collection of CCTV footage. The Grid-based Feature Extraction module uses the Trajectory List as input and calls upon the Region Clustering with Feature Importance module to identify important features in each identified cluster. The Region-based Trajectory Analysis module analyses a new test clip, computes different features that fall in the important clusters and employs a final clustering algorithm to determine abnormal trajectories

pre-suicide behaviours, our previous work [22] focused on capturing fine-grained human behaviour cues, such as crouching and leaning with head down. As an explicit abnormal behaviour recognition strategy, it requires human analysis by viewing and annotating the footage with behaviour cues. The site however generates a large amount of footage daily. In this study, we propose an unsupervised trajectory clustering approach to make the best use of such information and further automate the detection process.

3   Methodology

In this study, we propose a new abnormal activity detection method for CCTV monitored scenes via region-based trajectory analysis. In Fig. 1, the proposed method is illustrated. Instead of using features universally for every part of a map as in past abnormal detection studies, our approach provides a self-adapted, location-sensitive and interpretable trajectory analysis method for different scenarios. It first uses normal daily footage to perform object detection and tracking using classical deep learning algorithms and generate a 'normal' trajectory list. Then, a grid-based feature extraction strategy [7] is used to obtain a grid cell description of the scene. Region clustering is performed with an interpretation of feature importance, forming different regions of the scene with primary features of their own, which we name as region-based features. With this information, the test videos are entered into the system to generate trajectories and extract region-based features to form a new feature space for each trajectory. A final clustering is performed to discriminate between normal and abnormal activities in the scene. More details of each step are discussed in the following sections.

Fig. 2. Trajectory sample from a normal daily footage. Each pedestrian is represented by its own trajectory in the temporal domain.

3.1 Pedestrian Detection and Tracking

In much of the footage we collected, pedestrians are relatively far away from the cameras and moving through different locations. Therefore, the capability to detect pedestrians at different scales and locations is very important. YOLOv5 [25] is an object detector that uses the most advanced neural network architectures for reduced computation cost without sacrificing accuracy. For our pedestrian detector, we fine-tuned YOLOv5 to suit our camera views.

The output of the pedestrian detector is used as input to the tracking module, for which we use DeepSORT [35], a classical multi-object tracking algorithm. It was selected for its deep appearance embedding into the data association process and consideration of both short-term and long-term occlusions by cascade matching. This approach outperforms many of its counterparts on online multiple object tracking.

We extract and record the whole trajectories generated by all the pedestrians in a given clip scene. An example is shown in Fig. 2. A trajectory is created for each pedestrian in the form of a trajectory point list along with its trajectory id (tid), video id (vid) and pedestrian id (pid). For each point, its corresponding frame ID (fid), timepoint (tp), x and y coordinates as well as human bounding box width and height are recorded. As a result, trajectories are represented as follows:

$$Traj = (tid, vid, pid, [traj\_pt0, traj\_pt1, \cdots, traj\_ptn]) \tag{1}$$

$$traj\_pt = (fid, tp, x, y, bbox_{width}, bbox_{height}) \tag{2}$$

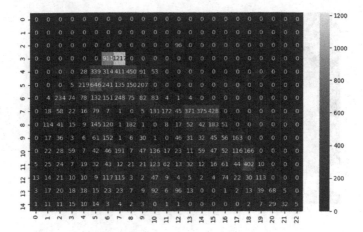

Fig. 3. Point density heat map from normal daily footage collected in the scene. Each value in the grid represents the number of times that point was visited considering all trajectories

3.2 Grid-Based Feature Extraction

After a trajectory summary list is obtained from the collected daily normal footage of the scene, we adopt a grid-based strategy, which is common for road map generation using trajectories [7,27,28]. Our goal is to obtain a general motion pattern description for different scene locations based on normal daily footage. First, a grid is generated to cover the scene with a suitable cell size. Then three types of features are extracted from the trajectories that fall into each cell: point density, speed and directions. Specifically, in the point density calculation, points from all collected trajectories are used as input and the corresponding grid count increases if this point falls into the cell. A point density heat map is generated accordingly (Fig. 3). As can be observed, the area covered by the footpath has a higher trajectory density. Any isolated cell (that contains a positive value but is surrounded by 0 value cells) is likely to be an outlier generated erroneously by the detection or tracking module. Secondly, the speed at each point is calculated. In the corresponding grid cell, all point speeds within that cell are averaged. Thirdly, we analyse the main directions of motion in the scene at various locations. Therefore, 8-direction bins are used with each covering 45°, and bin 0 starts from -22.5° to 22.5°. In the corresponding cell, all directions of motion of points within that cell fall into one of 8 bins. Therefore, the direction description uses 8 dimensions for each cell, recording the number of hits in each bin.

After all the features are extracted, a 10-dimensional feature descriptor is generated for each cell: point density, average speed, and counts in direction bins 0 to 7. Feature normalisation is applied to ensure that the value of each feature has zero mean and unit variance.

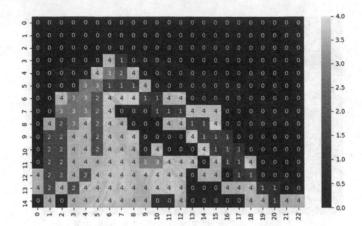

Fig. 4. The region map that was learned from the trajectories captured from the daily normal footage of the scene. Each number in the grid corresponds to regions that our system deduced may contain similar trajectories

3.3 Region Clustering with Feature Importance

We use the 10-dimensional feature descriptor of the cells to perform K-means clustering of the scene (i.e., "region map"). We choose K-means because it is an unsupervised method to group data based on similarity in feature space, and no annotations are required. In addition, we employ a feature importance interpretation of K-means [3,10,18] to understand the most important features that distinguish each region. These features are used to identify normal/abnormal trajectories in any new data. For example, if speed is an important feature for cluster/region K, we obtain an average speed for region K and use it to identify any abnormal speed of a new trajectory that passes through region K in the test videos. Likewise, if the direction of motion plays the key role in forming cluster M, we obtain the direction of motion for region M and use it to identify any abnormal directions of a new trajectory that passes through region M in the test videos. The interpretation method we use is named WCSS (Within-Cluster Sum of Squares) Minimizers [3]. The main idea is to find the dimensions that are responsible for the highest amount of WCSS minimization for each cluster by finding the maximum absolute centroid dimensional movement. The top feature of each region is identified using the feature importance values. The region map of our case study is shown in Fig. 4 with feature importance of region 0 shown in Table 1, which shows the top feature for region 0 is the average speed.

3.4 Region-Based Trajectory Analysis

The region map of the scene is defined by accumulated daily footage. Therefore it defines the "normal" status of the scene, such as the "normal" speed and direction of persons in a certain location. Then new upcoming test videos can

Table 1. Feature importance for cluster 0

Cluster ID	Feature Name	Importance Value
Cluster 0	speed avg	0.62
	direction bin4	0.41
	direction bin0	0.40
	direction bin3	0.37
	direction bin6	0.36
	direction bin7	0.36
	direction bin1	0.35
	direction bin2	0.34
	direction bin5	0.34
	point count	0.29

be used as input to generate "test trajectories" to be analysed. In the analysis module, we propose a novel strategy to capture the full characteristics of trajectories based on the region map. First, we use the top features of each region to detect abnormal "trajectory segments", then we calculate the region distribution of each trajectory. The main idea is to combine these features to form a new feature space for trajectory clustering.

Abnormal speed and direction may only occur in a small part of a trajectory, therefore we define "abnormal segments" with a chosen duration (1-2 s). For each region, a binary mask of the map is generated. Then trajectory segments that fall within the mask are analysed. If the region's top feature is speed, then the average speeds of these segments are calculated. We assume that the speed follows a normal distribution and is always positive. Any segment speed that falls outside of $(\mu\text{-}3\sigma, \mu\text{+}3\sigma)$ is considered abnormal. If the region's top feature is direction, then for each segment that falls into the region, if less than a certain percentage (20% in our case study) of the directions are compliant with this top direction, this segment is considered an abnormal direction.

One important finding of our human coding study is that some persons in crisis may choose to stay at a certain point for a long time, regardless of their gestures/poses during the time. This is a crucial indicator that can be captured by trajectory analysis, without the need for fine-grained action recognition. Therefore, we detect the absence of movement (i.e., "stay points") of pedestrians as proposed and implemented in other works [27,28]. The basic idea is to set up a distance threshold, and if consecutive trajectory points are within this range for a defined duration, then they are considered as stay points. We further modify this distance threshold to normalise it with the human bounding box size so that they are universally consistent in the map scene.

Finally, the overall statistics of each test trajectory in the region map are generated. Specifically, we compute the trajectory point distribution over regions, such as the number of points of trajectory No.1 in region 0, region 1 and so on.

We believe that such information is highly valuable in analysing the trajectory characteristics, as it reflects the regions that a pedestrian visited in the scene and the frequency of visits.

Fig. 5. Total trajectories collected from daily footage.

3.5   Feature Space and Trajectory Clustering

In the previous section, we captured four types of trajectory features: number of abnormal speed and direction segments, number of stay points, and number of trajectory points in each region of the scene. In total, they form an 8-dimensional feature space in which we perform a second K-means clustering, analyse the spatial distribution in feature space of different trajectories and verify if they exhibit normal/abnormal behaviours.

4   Experiments: A Case Study

In this case study, a private dataset collected from CCTV footage recorded at a location frequently used for suicides in Australia was used (the site is not named in line with best practice suicide prevention reporting). This study was approved by the UNSW Human Research Ethics Committee (HC190663). The site includes public parkland, with cliffs adjacent to the ocean. Emergency service call-outs indicate that there are approximately 10 completed suicides and 100 emergency call-outs per year. The site is covered by multiple CCTV cameras. A subset of cameras covers defined regions of interest, and the experiment was conducted in one of these specific regions. Due to the regulation of and restricted access to the actual suicide attempt videos, the experimental dataset contains normal footage collected daily as well as acted footage that simulates both normal and crisis behaviours identified in a companion human coding study [17].

Table 2. Top 3 features for all 5 regions with importance values

Cluster ID	Top 1	Top 2	Top 3
0	speed avg:0.62	direction bin4:0.41	direction bin0:0.40
1	direction bin1:3.14	direction bin5:2.69	direction bin0:1.99
2	direction bin2:3.44	direction bin6:3.16	speed avg:1.03
3	direction bin7:4.17	direction bin3:3.58	direction bin6:1.47
4	speed avg:0.98	direction bin4:0.36	point count:0.33

First, we used the collected normal daily footage to generate the region map of the scene. The data consists of 24 short clips around 1 min in length each, with 1-10 pedestrians in the scene. A total of 163 trajectories were collected. The overall trajectories can be visualised in Fig. 5. With a 30 frames/second rate, trajectory points were sampled every 10 frames. It can be observed that some outliers are generated by false detection by the pedestrian detection and tracking module.

A region map (shown in Fig. 4) was generated using K-means clustering (number of clusters=5). The feature importance was calculated for every region, as shown in Table 2. It can be observed that when the top feature is the direction in this scene, the opposite direction usually gets a similar weight, reflecting bidirectional movement along the path. We consider the top 2 directions as the "normal" directions of the region when "direction" has the highest importance.

Based on both the map and feature importance, regions 0 and 4 are regions with similar speeds - region 4 has very low pedestrian walking speed, while region 0 has no pedestrians visiting it (bushes, or beyond the safety fence). Regions 1, 2 and 3 have similar walking directions and the map shows that they correspond to the footpath areas. We believe that the generated region map is acceptable considering that it was learned in an unsupervised way.

The next step is to use the learned region map to detect any abnormal behaviour in the test videos. In this case study, we created 15 test clips with a mixture of both normal and crisis behaviours identified in the human coding study. Tests 1-10 are clips with normal behaviours (e.g., walking or standing for a short period of time) while Tests 11-15 have abnormal behaviours (e.g., staying at a location for a prolonged time or repetitive behaviour patterns). More details on the data generation and distribution can be found in [17]. The reliability of this simulated data has been thoroughly tested in our previous work [17], which focussed on the action recognition task.

The trajectory segment in this case study was defined as 5 consecutive points, which is approximately 2 s in duration. We used the learned region map to detect the number of abnormal speed or direction segments, as well as the number of stay points, in every trajectory. We also calculated the trajectory point distribution over this region map. More details of the extracted features for each trajectory from test videos can be found in Table 3.

Table 3. Region-based trajectory analysis

traj id	test id	pid	r0	r1	r2	r3	r4	ab speed	ab direct	stay point
0	14	1	1	36	97	136	11	0	0	2
1	1	1	2	55	11	10	32	0	1	0
2	8	2	2	32	15	14	62	0	0	0
3	5	1	8	12	0	0	18	2	0	0
4	7	1	1	26	23	0	65	0	0	0
5	13	1	3	9	19	108	72	0	0	1
6	4	1	1	6	51	42	35	0	1	0
7	9	1	0	0	25	0	34	0	0	0
8	2	1	18	13	4	0	53	2	0	0
9	12	2	28	31	78	98	104	0	3	0
10	11	1	0	35	15	51	656	0	0	1
11	15	1	0	39	82	88	20	0	0	1
12	6	1	18	73	13	13	10	0	0	0
13	3	1	0	27	19	10	67	0	0	0
14	10	1	1	57	28	26	30	0	0	0

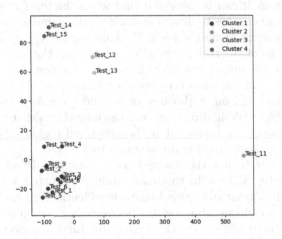

Fig. 6. Two-dimensional PCA visualisation of the K-means clustering results using the 15 test videos. Each point indicates the trajectory obtained in the test clip. Each colour indicates the cluster assignment (Color figure online)

Using the trajectory points in regions 0-4, abnormal speed segments, abnormal directions segments and stay points as an 8-dimensional feature vector, the extracted trajectories from the 15 test videos were clustered.

5   Results and Discussion

By performing a principal components analysis (PCA) for dimensionality reduction, the clustering results using the test trajectories can be visualised (Fig. 6).

Fig. 7. Test trajectories coloured according to their corresponding cluster assignments in Fig. 6. The arrows indicate trajectory directions (Color figure online)

The trajectories extracted from the test videos can also be visualised on the scene itself. They are coloured according to their cluster assignments (Fig. 7). The following observations may be made:

1. **Cluster 1 (blue):** Trajectories from the test clips 1 to 10 are grouped in the left-hand corner of Fig. 6. Their corresponding trajectories (blue arrows in Fig. 7) highlight that these exhibit normal behaviours (e.g., walking along the footpath).
2. **Cluster 2 (orange):** Test clip 11 was the only clip in this cluster. This clip contained a person who had a stay point for a prolonged period (almost 4 min). This trajectory is coloured orange and the stay point can be seen on the left-hand side of Fig. 7. This behaviour can be considered abnormal in the given scene.
3. **Cluster 3 (cyan):** This cluster contains test clips 12&13. Both clips contained trajectories (cyan arrows in Fig. 7) that exhibit back-and-forth movement and several stay points. While these behaviours can be considered normal in certain locations, such as on a platform overlooking a view, the behaviours in these clips were placed in an abnormal location (e.g., the rocky part of the scene).
4. **Cluster 4 (red):** This cluster contains test clips 14&15. Similar to the clips in cluster 2, these clips contained trajectories (red arrows in Fig. 7) with back-and-forth movement and stay points. The main difference is that these trajectories were in different locations.

Analysis of the feature importance output of the region clustering and visualisation of the clustering results help to gain a better understanding of the results of the proposed pipeline. It was found that the generated region map is acceptable and that the clustering results generate trajectory groups that have similarities and are interpretable, proving the effectiveness of the proposed workflow.

6 Conclusion

In this paper, we propose a region-based trajectory analysis method to detect abnormal behaviours in a scene. Instead of using common features like speed and direction with equal importance for trajectory analysis as in past work, this approach first identifies different regions of a scene and their corresponding characteristics described by top feature(s) selected by feature importance. For new test trajectories, the system identifies abnormal trajectory segments that do not comply with the top features in these regions and generates an 8-dimensional feature space where a second clustering is employed to determine abnormal trajectories. Such an approach will be beneficial for abnormal behaviour detection in location-sensitive applications, where crisis behaviours usually take place at highly relevant locations. We conducted a case study on CCTV footage collected in a suicide hotspot and showed the effectiveness of the proposed workflow.

Future work will focus on integrating the proposed trajectory-based abnormal detection with our previous work on fine-grained abnormal behaviour recognition to build a more comprehensive framework for suicide detection and prevention. Furthermore, a more general approach that does not depend on a static viewpoint will be developed to be able to analyse abnormal behaviours in different camera locations. Finally, person re-identification when an individual appears/disappears across different frames and moves to different camera locations will be explored in the future.

Acknowledgment. The authors would like to thank Woollahra Municipal Council for sharing information on the use of CCTV as part of their commitment to self-harm minimization within their local area and the work they are doing with police and emergency response personnel and mental health support agencies. This work was supported by a Suicide Prevention Research Fund Innovation Grant, managed by Suicide Prevention Australia, and the NHMRC Centre of Research Excellence in Suicide Prevention (APP1152952). The contents of this manuscript are the responsibility of the authors, and have not been approved or endorsed by the funders.

References

1. Aggarwal, J.K., Xia, L.: Human activity recognition from 3D data: a review. Pattern Recogn. Lett. **48**, 70–80 (2014)
2. Ahmed, S.A., Dogra, D.P., Kar, S., Roy, P.P.: Trajectory-based surveillance analysis: a survey. IEEE Trans. Circuits Syst. Video Technol. **29**(7), 1985–1997 (2018)
3. Alghofaili, Y.: kmeans feature importance. https://github.com/YousefGh/kmeans-feature-importance (2021)
4. Bouachir, W., Noumeir, R.: Automated video surveillance for preventing suicide attempts. In: 7th International Conference on Imaging for Crime Detection and Prevention (ICDP 2016), pp. 1–6. IET (2016)
5. Breunig, M.M., Kriegel, H.P., Ng, R.T., Sander, J.: LOF: identifying density-based local outliers. In: Proceedings of the 2000 ACM SIGMOD international conference on Management of data, pp. 93–104 (2000)

6. Cai, Y., Wang, H., Chen, X., Jiang, H.: Trajectory-based anomalous behaviour detection for intelligent traffic surveillance. IET Intel. Transport Syst. **9**(8), 810–816 (2015)
7. Coşar, S., Donatiello, G., Bogorny, V., Garate, C., Alvares, L.O., Brémond, F.: Toward abnormal trajectory and event detection in video surveillance. IEEE Trans. Circuits Syst. Video Technol. **27**(3), 683–695 (2016)
8. Deori, B., Thounaojam, D.M.: A survey on moving object tracking in video. Int. J. Inf. Theory (IJIT) **3**(3), 31–46 (2014)
9. Hoeferlin, M., Hoeferlin, B., Heidemann, G., Weiskopf, D.: Interactive schematic summaries for faceted exploration of surveillance video. IEEE Trans. Multimedia **15**(4), 908–920 (2013)
10. Ismaili, O.A., Lemaire, V., Cornuéjols, A.: A supervised methodology to measure the variables contribution to a clustering. In: Loo, C.K., Yap, K.S., Wong, K.W., Teoh, A., Huang, K. (eds.) ICONIP 2014. LNCS, vol. 8834, pp. 159–166. Springer, Cham (2014). https://doi.org/10.1007/978-3-319-12637-1_20
11. Jiang, F., Wu, Y., Katsaggelos, A.K.: A dynamic hierarchical clustering method for trajectory-based unusual video event detection. IEEE Trans. Image Process. **18**(4), 907–913 (2009)
12. Johnson, N., Hogg, D.: Learning the distribution of object trajectories for event recognition. Image Vis. Comput. **14**(8), 609–615 (1996)
13. Kumar, D., Bezdek, J.C., Rajasegarar, S., Leckie, C., Palaniswami, M.: A visual-numeric approach to clustering and anomaly detection for trajectory data. Vis. Comput. **33**(3), 265–281 (2017)
14. Lee, J., Lee, C.-M., Park, N.-K.: Application of sensor network system to prevent suicide from the bridge. Multimedia Tools Appl. **75**(22), 14557–14568 (2015). https://doi.org/10.1007/s11042-015-3134-z
15. Lee, S., et al.: Detection of a suicide by hanging based on a 3-D image analysis. IEEE-Inst Electr. Electron. Eng. Inc **14**(9), 2934–2935 (2014). https://doi.org/10.1109/JSEN.2014.2332070. http://hdl.handle.net/10203/199171
16. Li, T., Sun, Z., Chen, X.: Group-skeleton-based human action recognition in complex events. In: Proceedings of the 28th ACM International Conference on Multimedia (2020). https://doi.org/10.1145/3394171.3416280
17. Li, X., Onie, S., Liang, M., Larsen, M., Sowmya, A.: Towards building a visual behaviour analysis pipeline for suicide detection and prevention. Sensors **22**(12), 4488 (2022)
18. Liu, Y., Li, Z., Xiong, H., Gao, X., Wu, J.: Understanding of internal clustering validation measures. In: 2010 IEEE International Conference on Data Mining, pp. 911–916. IEEE (2010)
19. Mackenzie, J.M., et al.: Behaviours preceding suicides at railway and underground locations: a multimethodological qualitative approach. BMJ Open **8**(4), e021076 (2018)
20. Mileva, M., Burton, A.M.: Face search in CCTV surveillance. Cognitive Res. Principles Implicat. **4**(1), 1–21 (2019)
21. Mishara, B.L., Bardon, C., Dupont, S.: Can CCTV identify people in public transit stations who are at risk of attempting suicide? an analysis of CCTV video recordings of attempters and a comparative investigation. BMC Pub. Health **16**(1), 1–10 (2016)
22. Onie, S., Li, X., Liang, M., Sowmya, A., Larsen, M.E.: The use of closed-circuit television and video in suicide prevention: Narrative review and future directions. JMIR Ment. Health **8**(5), e27663 (2021). https://doi.org/10.2196/27663. https://mental.jmir.org/2021/5/e27663

23. Owens, C., Lloyd-Tomlins, S., Emmens, T., Aitken, P.: Suicides in public places: findings from one English county. Europ. J. Pub. Health **19**(6), 580–582 (2009)
24. Patino, L., Ferryman, J., Beleznai, C.: Abnormal behaviour detection on queue analysis from stereo cameras. In: 2015 12th IEEE International Conference on Advanced Video and Signal Based Surveillance (AVSS), pp. 1–6. IEEE (2015)
25. Redmon, J., Divvala, S., Girshick, R., Farhadi, A.: You only look once: unified, real-time object detection. In: Proceedings of the IEEE Conference on Computer Vision and Pattern Recognition, pp. 779–788 (2016)
26. Roduit, P.: Trajectory analysis using point distribution models. Tech. rep, EPFL (2009)
27. Ruan, S., Li, R., Bao, J., He, T., Zheng, Y.: CloudTP: a cloud-based flexible trajectory preprocessing framework. In: 2018 IEEE 34th International Conference on Data Engineering (ICDE), pp. 1601–1604. IEEE (2018)
28. Ruan, S., et al.: Learning to generate maps from trajectories. In: Proceedings of the AAAI Conference on Artificial Intelligence, vol. 34, pp. 890–897 (2020)
29. Sharma, R., Guha, T.: A trajectory clustering approach to crowd flow segmentation in videos. In: 2016 IEEE International Conference on Image Processing (ICIP), pp. 1200–1204. IEEE (2016)
30. Stauffer, C., Grimson, W.E.L.: Learning patterns of activity using real-time tracking. IEEE Trans. Pattern Anal. Mach. Intell. **22**(8), 747–757 (2000)
31. Tung, F., Zelek, J.S., Clausi, D.A.: Goal-based trajectory analysis for unusual behaviour detection in intelligent surveillance. Image Vis. Comput. **29**(4), 230–240 (2011)
32. Wang, C., Zourlidou, S., Golze, J., Sester, M.: Trajectory analysis at intersections for traffic rule identification. Geo-spatial Information Science **24**(1), 75–84 (2021)
33. Wang, H., Schmid, C.: Action recognition with improved trajectories. In: Proceedings of the IEEE International Conference on Computer Vision, pp. 3551–3558 (2013)
34. Wang, L., Liu, T., Wang, G., Chan, K.L., Yang, Q.: Video tracking using learned hierarchical features. IEEE Trans. Image Process. **24**(4), 1424–1435 (2015)
35. Wojke, N., Bewley, A., Paulus, D.: Simple online and realtime tracking with a deep association metric. In: 2017 IEEE International Conference on Image Processing (ICIP), pp. 3645–3649. IEEE (2017)
36. Xu, H., Zhou, Y., Lin, W., Zha, H.: Unsupervised trajectory clustering via adaptive multi-kernel-based shrinkage. In: Proceedings of the IEEE International Conference on Computer Vision, pp. 4328–4336 (2015)

Automated Behavior Labeling During Team-Based Activities Involving Neurodiverse and Neurotypical Partners Using Multimodal Data

Abigale Plunk[1](✉) ⓘ, Ashwaq Zaini Amat[1] ⓘ, D. Mitchell Wilkes[1] ⓘ,
and Nilanjan Sarkar[1,2] ⓘ

[1] Department of Electrical Engineering and Computer Engineering,
Vanderbilt University, Nashville, TN, USA
abigale.l.plunk@vanderbilt.edu
[2] Department of Mechanical Engineering, Vanderbilt University, Nashville, TN, USA

Abstract. The employment setting for autistic individuals in the USA is grim. Based on reports, individuals with ASD struggle to secure and retain employment due to challenges in communicating and collaborating with others in workplace settings which is often attributed to their social skills deficit. Current programs that support collaborative skills development in vocational settings rely on manual evaluation and feedback by human observers, which can be resource straining and receptive to bias. Using a collaborative virtual environment (CVE) allows neurodiverse individuals to develop teamwork skills by working together with a neurotypical partner in a shared virtual space. An effective CVE system can provide real-time prompts by recognizing the user's behavior to promote teamwork. As such, it is crucial to be able to automatically label both users' behaviors. In this paper, we propose using K-means clustering to automate behavior labeling in a workplace CVE. The results show that K-means clustering enables high accuracy in predicting the user's behavior, therefore, confirming that it can be used in future studies to support real-time prompts to encourage teamwork in a CVE.

Keywords: automated behavior labeling · collaborative virtual environment · clustering · autism spectrum disorder · teamwork training

1 Introduction

Teamwork, which includes skills such as conflict resolution, communication, collaboration, and positive interaction, is highly sought after by employers [50]. Teamwork can fulfill the personal need for social interaction and affiliation leading to increased satisfaction in the workplace and increased productivity for the company [37,55]. However, individuals with autism spectrum disorder[1] (ASD)

---

[1] We are using both identity-first and people-first language to respect both views by interchangeably using the term 'autistic individuals and 'individuals with ASD'. [32].

© Springer Nature Switzerland AG 2023
J.-J. Rousseau and B. Kapralos (Eds.): ICPR 2022 Workshops, LNCS 13643, pp. 193–209, 2023.
https://doi.org/10.1007/978-3-031-37660-3_14

experience core deficits in social interactions such as reduced eye contact, facial expressions, and body gestures that can hinder their ability to work on a team potentially contributing to unemployment [44] and anxiety. Compared to other individuals with disabilities, adults with ASD have the highest unemployment rate between 50–85% [28]. For those with employment, the majority are either underemployed or unable to retain their position due to their perceived deficits in social communication and interaction skills [55]. Studies have shown that unemployment can lead to reduced self-esteem and heightened distress, depression, and anxiety [20,35]. Therefore it is essential to address these deficits as they tend to cast a shadow on the outstanding qualities such as precise technical abilities, high tolerance for repetitive tasks, reliability, and increased concentration for long periods of time that autistic individuals can bring to a team [44,52]. Studies also show that teamwork gives individuals with ASD the opportunity to build upon their social communication skills [18], problem-solving skills [13], and self-confidence [54]. Although existing training and interventions have shown some improvements in teamwork skills in adolescents with ASD, simulating real-world teamwork scenarios can be tedious, resource-straining, and costly, thus limiting the accessibility and reach of the interventions [53]. Computer-based simulators using digital games have been shown to positively impact the training of these skills [33]. However, many digital games lack the structure to scaffold skill learning, do not provide real-time feedback or prompts that could facilitate skill learning, and have no objective means of measuring players' skills improvements. Using a Collaborative Virtual Environment (CVE) to practice, measure, and promote positive social communication skills could be advantageous in preparing autistic individuals for employment while also addressing the pitfalls of simulating real-world teamwork and digital games.

CVEs are virtual environments that allow multiple users to interact with each other and the environment itself in a shared virtual space. CVEs engage the users [17], provide a safe environment for training [41], and provide quantitative measures of the skills they are learning [60]. In addition, they are both reproducible and cost-effective. The CVE discussed in this paper simulates a workplace environment for two users, one with ASD and one who is neurotypical, to work together towards achieving a task that encourages teamwork and collaboration. The CVE is tasked with observing multimodal data (i.e., speech, eye gaze, and controller input), recognizing the behavior of each user, and prompting the system to provide reinforcement or assistance depending on each user's current behavior. However, manually labeling the current behavior of each user is labor-intensive, prone to bias, and inconsistent [25]. In addition, it does not allow for real-time feedback, which is necessary for promoting teamwork in the CVE. To support real-time feedback, an essential criterion involves reliable detection of human behavior in collaborative interactions, which can be achieved through large amounts of labeled data. Therefore, automated labeling is needed for the success of using a CVE for teamwork training. However, the complexity of human behavior and contextual properties make it difficult to recognize human behavior even in constrained domains [48].

Previous solutions for automated labeling include various clustering methods, semi-supervised machine learning algorithms, and unsupervised machine learning algorithms. In this paper, we propose the use of K-means clustering due to its simplicity and efficiency [26] for automated behavior labeling in a CVE-based simulator of workplace scenarios allowing for real-time prompts that encourage collaboration and teamwork between neurodiverse and neurotypical partners. The following section discusses related works that utilize multimodal data in CVEs and different methods used for automated behavior labeling in various applications. Section 3 briefly discusses the experimental design, including the collaborative tasks we employ and the multimodal data captured in our CVE used to represent teamwork. In Sect. 4, we describe the methodology of applying and verifying K-means clustering to automate behavior detection of human behavior followed by an analysis of the results in Sect. 5. Finally, we conclude the paper with a discussion that summarizes our contributions and provides insight for future works.

2 Related Work

Over the last decade, the use of human-computer interaction (HCI) technology has shown promising benefits that can potentially complement conventional ASD interventions by providing engaging interactions and replicable solutions that can minimize costs and provide relatively broader access to users [45]. Additionally, autistic individuals have a natural affinity for technology-based interactions and prefer the consistency that computer-based interactions can offer [46]. Specifically, there have been a number of research that employ VR-based systems intervention tools that are focused on teaching both social skills and technical skills, which include skills such as cooking [6], road safety [47], driving [14], joint attention [62], and emotion recognition [11]. Nonetheless, VR-based systems are limited to single user interaction and are unable to support more natural complex back and forth human-human interactions. Additionally, individuals with ASD might be more comfortable interacting with a virtual avatar compared to a human partner, thus making it less efficient for generalization to the real-world [12,57,59]. Alternatively, CVEs enable users to communicate with each other naturally while performing a task together in the shared virtual environment, in turn minimizing the effect of attachment to virtual avatars. CVE-based systems have been primarily studied to understand the impact of collaborative learning and various aspects of social behavior involved in collaboration for autistic individuals [8,16].

Vocational and technical skills are important aspects of employment and are the main criteria considered for employment [58]. However, interpersonal or professional skills such as teamwork are the core skills needed to secure and retain employment [5]. Recently, the importance of teamwork is reflected in the hiring process of companies like Microsoft and Specialsterne, which employ autistic individuals. They utilize a group assessment process for autistic candidates in place of the conventional interview process. A Lego Mindstorm group project

[2] and Minecraft collaborative tasks [1] were administered to them to assess teamwork skills. Currently, most studies that investigate social skills evaluation rely on qualitative measures of performance and self-reporting questionnaires, which are subjective and prone to bias [9]. Teamwork is a complex social behavior that is not easily assessed since it involves detecting and understanding dynamic social manifestations between individuals. Moreover, some individuals with ASD may present subtle or low manifestations of specific social behaviors due to a deficit in their social reciprocity, making it difficult for their partners or observers to recognize their social cues [15]. Thus, there are potential benefits of capturing objective interaction data from multiple modalities to evaluate these complex skills.

Recently, there has been a growing interest in multimodal data analysis within HCI that uses measurable parameters to assess teamwork objectively and represent the important features of teamwork [38, 43]. Although many studies capture multimodal data in collaborative interactions, there are currently no standardized methods to measure teamwork and collaboration skills in group interactions. A few studies have explored different ways to reliably represent interpersonal behavior using multimodal data in group interactions [24, 27, 42]. In one study, the researchers analyzed multimodal data such as physical locations, speech, movements, and physiological measures to represent different aspects of interpersonal behaviors [24]. Meanwhile, Okada et al. used verbal and non-verbal measures to assess a group's communication skills based on the different types of discussions taking place [42]. In the study, the researchers extracted communication features based on data from speech and head movement information. They compared the analysis against human-coded evaluations of communication skills and found that certain quantitative measures can be analyzed to represent more than one feature. For example, speech data can be used to represent both verbal and non-verbal features in collaborative interactions, while dialogue content can provide social communication features (e.g., intention) and task performance features (e.g., topic/object). In a more recent study, Hayashi conducted a collaborative learning study to systematically evaluate students' learning behavior in a jigsaw-type collaborative task [27]. The researcher used facial expressions together with speech to predict the emotional state of the students and how these emotions influenced their collaborative learning process. The results of these studies can benefit the development of a feedback mechanism in collaborative interaction by generating a reliable evaluation of collaborative behavior. However, they rely heavily on manually labeled data to generate reliable human behavioral models.

Motivated by the limitations of manual data labeling [48], several recent studies have investigated the use of clustering methods and machine learning algorithms to automate behavioral labeling [4, 22, 29, 30, 39, 40, 49, 61]. Current state-of-the-art automated labeling techniques are applied to a wide range of applications such as visual detection [4], human-robot social interaction [29], human actions in video [22], and social signal processing [49]. Hong et al. used a multimodal wearable sensing platform to collect activity data [30]. They then developed a semi-population model that automatically labeled new data based on K-means clustering of selected features using previously collected data to recognize seven different human activities. The semi-population model achieved better accuracy compared to individual and group data. In another study, researchers integrated a K-means clustering method with a decision tree to create an initial transfer learning model [61]. The model was adaptively trained whenever new target data was available. This method managed to reduce complexity and minimize computing power. Furthermore, recent studies have explored the implementation of automated behavior labeling using multimodal data as ground truth in a closed-loop feedback mechanism [39, 40]. In one study, the researchers designed an intelligent mediator that provides dynamic feedback to balance the interactions between participants based on automated labeling of participants' speech [40]. Another study designed a virtual trainer that provided corrective feedback to public speakers based on automated social behavior labeling of speech and body movement of the participant [39].

Motivated by the potential of using various clustering methods and machine learning algorithms to automate human behavior labeling, we believe that the use of K-means clustering can complement manual data labeling without compromising the accuracy of the labeled behavior to evaluate teamwork skills between two individuals interacting together. Additionally, automated labeling can speed up ground truth labeling [56], thus enabling researchers to train a behavior detection model that can be used to provide reliable feedback based on the detected behavior. In the following sections, we will discuss using K-means clustering to automate grouping mutlimodal data into three behaviors. This will be validated using leave-one-out cross-validation with hand-labeled data. The analysis of our automated labeling will be used to develop a feedback mechanism in our CVE that can enhance collaborative interactions, however, it is not within the scope of the current paper.

3   Experimental Design

We conducted a system validation study with 4 pairs of Neurodiverse-Neurotypical participants (N = 8). The study required the participants to work in pairs to complete three collaborative tasks designed to encourage teamwork and collaboration skills. This study was approved by the Institutional Review Board at Vanderbilt University.

3.1   Collaborative Tasks

The collaborative tasks used in this work were presented in our previous work that discussed the design and development of three collaborative tasks to encourage teamwork and collaboration in a workplace setting: a) a PC assembly task, b) a fulfillment center task, and c) a furniture assembly task [7]. These tasks were designed based on stakeholders' inputs and involved one autistic and one neurotypical participant as partners. Although the tasks spread across various domains, the basic elements of teamwork and collaboration were maintained as we incorporated the same collaboration principle across all tasks defined in Meier et al. [21]. The researchers identified 9 features that are related to collaboration which include mutual understanding, dialogue management, information pooling, reaching consensus, task division, time management, reciprocal interaction, technical coordination, and individual task orientation [21]. We designed these tasks in a collaborative virtual environment (CVE) in Unity3D [3], which was connected to various peripheral devices to allow participants to communicate and interact in a shared virtual space with their partners. The system architecture of the workplace CVE was discussed in detail in [7] and is thus omitted here. Figure 1 shows the experiment setup and shows snapshots of all three tasks.

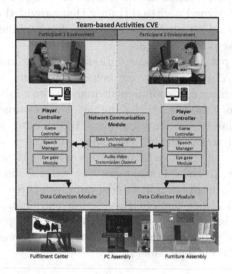

Fig. 1. System setup and snapshots of all three collaborative tasks

3.2   Participants

We recruited 8 individuals (ages: 16–30 years old; mean age: 20.125 years old) to participate in the study. Participants with ASD were recruited from an existing research inventory of individuals previously diagnosed with ASD by licensed clinical psychologists using standard diagnostic tools, such as the Autism Diagnostic Observation Schedule-Second Edition (ADOS-2) [36]. As for the neurotypical participants, they were recruited from the local community through regional advertisement. We also evaluated the current level of ASD symptoms of all participants using the Social Responsiveness Scale, Second Edition (SRS-2) [19]. Table 1 lists the participants' characteristics.

Table 1. Participant Metrics

Metrics	ASD Participants (N=4)	Neurotypical Participants (N=4)
Age Mean (SD)	20 (3.82)	20.25 (5.06)
Gender (% male)	25%	25%
SRS-2 Total Score Mean (SD)	89.73 (23.43)	21.50 (11.90)
SRS-2 T-Score Mean (SD)	70.75 (11.09)	44.50 (3.42)

3.3   Protocol

The CVE system was set up such that each participant sat in a separate experiment room. Since the rooms were inside the same building, all the network connection was running using Vanderbilt University's local connection without any concern for privacy and security.

When participants arrived at the session, they were briefed and given consent forms to sign. Once all the forms were signed, participants were directed to the different rooms. Before starting the experiment, the eye tracker for each participant was calibrated and they both logged on to the shared virtual environment. The experiment lasted approximately 90 min, including briefing, consent form signing, and system set up.

4   Methods

The system consists of three modes of data capture between two participants. Figure 2 summarizes the workflow for multimodal data analysis that includes data collection, pre-processing, K-means clustering, and validation of the participant behavior. The following subsections will further explain the steps of this process.

4.1   Multimodal Data Capture and Decomposition

We used three modes of data capture for each participant using a game controller, a headset, and an eye tracker. We extracted seven binary features portraying aspects of collaboration and attention from these sources and performed classification of human behavior.

As seen in the data decomposition section of the workflow, we decomposed the game controller data into four binary features, the speech data into one binary feature, and the eye gaze data into two binary features. The four features extracted from the game controller were object manipulation, controller activity, movement towards the goal, and movement away from the goal. The object manipulation feature captures the range of interest (ROI) of the participant. If the controller is activated in an area of interest (i.e., on a table component in

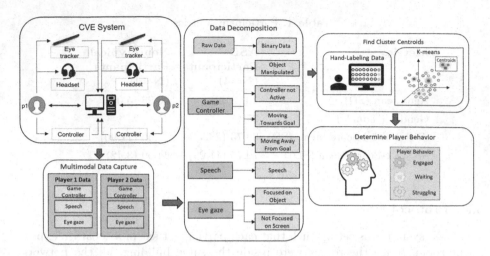

Fig. 2. Workflow for automated labeling

the furniture task) this feature is recorded as '1' otherwise it is recorded as '0'. The controller activity feature is mapped to a '1' if there is no controller input and a '0' if there is controller input. Next, the position of the controller on the screen was extracted to determine in the participant was moving towards the goal or away from the goal. If they were making progress towards achieving the goal, 'moving towards goal' was set to '1'. Alternatively, if they were progressing further from the goal or not progressing at all, 'moving towards goal' was set to '0'. The inverse rules were used to extract the feature 'moving away from goal'. Next, speech data was collected from the headsets. If the participant was speaking, the new binary speech feature was set to '1', otherwise, it was set to '0'. Finally, gaze data was decomposed into two binary features, which can be visualized in Fig. 3: 'focused on object' and 'not focused on screen'. The feature 'focused on object' is set to '1' if the user's scaled gaze fell within the middle 16% of the screen, represented by the green rectangle, as this is the portion of the screen where the collaborative tasks take place. Otherwise, it is set to '0'. The final feature 'not focused on screen' is set to '1' if the user's scaled gaze was negative or fell within the red section of the screen as shown in Fig. 3. After extracting the seven binary features, they were concatenated to form a binary feature vector. All of the features were collected continuously in time with a sampling rate of 1 sample per second.

Using the decomposed multimodal data consisting of the seven binary features established above, K-means clustering was chosen as it is widely used in a variety of domains to group data into clusters based on the similarity of features [34]. Using K-means, we identified the centroids that were used to classify each observation as one of three behaviors: engaged, struggling, or waiting. These three behaviors were chosen as they encapsulate various stages of teamwork allowing the system to provide appropriate feedback. Engaged captures

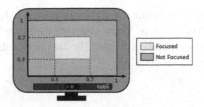

Fig. 3. Definition of focus area for eye gaze

how well the user is involved in the task itself and interacting with their partner allowing the system to provide positive reinforcement [23]. Next, the system needs to identify when the user is either not interacting with the system, not advancing towards the goal, or not engaged with their partner, which is captured by the struggling behavior implying that the system should prompt the users to work together [51]. The final aspect of teamwork and collaboration is taking turns. The waiting behavior captures when a user is waiting for their partner to complete their task [10,29]. The centroids used to classify these behaviors need to be validated as a consistent and accurate form of automated labeling. In the following sub-section, we will discuss the method of finding centroids using leave-one-out cross-validation (LOOCV) with hand-labeled data and K-means clustering. In addition, it will be established how to use the centroids to determine the player's behavior.

4.2   Manual Labeling

As discussed earlier, manual labeling of data is labor-intensive, prone to bias, and could be inconsistent. In addition, it does not allow for real-time feedback. However, to verify the proposed method for automated labeling, it was necessary to hand-label all four sessions of data. In future studies, hand-labeled data will be reduced to only a small subset used for training. To ensure the consistency of hand labeling, a set of coding rules was established beforehand. Bias was mitigated by having two individuals label the four sessions of data separately using the established rules achieving 98% agreement. Of the four labeled sessions the class distributions of the three behaviors were as follows: engaged - 19.9%, waiting - 52.1%, and struggling - 28.0%.

4.3   Determining Player States Using K-Means Centroids

Now that ground-truth labels were set, K-means clustering was applied to the multimodal data. Three clusters were chosen to represent the three behavior: engaged, struggling, or waiting.

We used MATLAB [31] to calculate and analyze the data. The goal of K-means clustering is for each observation to be assigned to the cluster that minimizes the Euclidean distance between the observation and the cluster's centroid. Using an iterative process, the three centroids for each of the four sessions were optimized to have the highest accuracy possible between both the K-means pre-dicted and the ground-truth labels. Once the centroids were optimized, LOOCV was used to verify that they could consistently and accurately be used to predict each player's behavior.

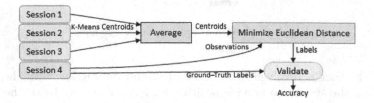

Fig. 4. One Iteration of LOOCV

A flowchart detailing one iteration of LOOCV is shown in Fig. 4. Three of the four hand-labeled sessions were used to generate centroids using K-means, and the final session was used to validate the centroids. After finding the centroids that yielded the highest accuracy using K-means, the centroids from the three sessions were averaged together to create a centroid that is generalized across the training sessions. The test session's labels were computed by minimizing the Euclidean distance between the multimodal data and the optimized centroid. The pseudocode for this calculation is provided in Algorithm 1.

Algorithm 1 Label by Minimizing Euclidean Distance

states = {*engaged, waiting, struggle*}
n = # of samples, m = # of features
for i in n **do**
    for *state* in *states* **do**

$$error(i, state) = \sqrt{\sum_{j=1}^{m}[centroid(state, j) - obs(i, j)]^2}$$

    end for
    label(i) = argmin($error$)
end for

The predicted labels found were then compared with the ground-truth labels for validation. This process was iterated until each session has been used as the validation session with the other sessions used for training. In the next section, the results using this method, an individual model, and a group model are discussed.

5   Results

This section describes the results obtained using our proposed method for automated behavior detection. First, we present the accuracy obtained using LOOCV. This method, which is detailed in the above section, validates the generalizability of centroids found using K-Means on unseen data. The following two subsections will present the results of using an individual model and a group model. These two models are exploratory and do not validate the use of clustering on unseen data. The accuracy presented in the following subsections were calculated with both the typically developing participant and the autistic participant. In addition, the accuracy for each group was calculated separately but showed negligible differences, therefore they are omitted from this discussion.

5.1 LOOCV

To confirm the effectiveness of the proposed method, we analyzed the results using LOOCV. As discussed in the previous section, for this method, the labels of one session were determined using the centroids from the other three sessions. For example, the centroids used to generate labels from Session 1 were the average of the centroids from Sessions 2, 3, and 4. The accuracy for all three behaviors as well as the total accuracy is recorded in Table 2

5.2 Individual Model

In the individual model, the centroids were optimized using K-means clustering iteratively based on the individual session. For this model, we used 80% of the data as a training set to optimize the centroids and the remaining 20% as the test set. This model represents the best case scenario where each session has its own specialized model. This would be ideal if the neurodiverse and neurotypical pairs were to remain constant across multiple sessions. We recorded the average test accuracy across all four sessions using their respective centroids in Table 2.

5.3 Group Model

Finally in the group model, the individualized session centroids that were optimized in the previous subsection were averaged to form one generalized centroid. Using the generalized centroid, we then found the labels that were used to calculate the accuracy on the held out test set for each session. The average accuracy across all four sessions is shown in Table 2.

Table 2. Results across 3 models

State	Accuracy		
	LOOCV	*Individual*	*Group*
Engaged	93.65%	97.70%	100%
Struggle	82.90%	91.23%	83.85%
Waiting	91.10%	90.45%	89.65%
Total	87.38%	91.30%	89.66%

6   Conclusion

Teamwork is a complex social behavior as it involves verbal communication, non-verbal communication, and physical cooperation and coordination between two or more people interacting simultaneously with each other. In this paper, we discussed the use of K-means to complement manual labeling of human behavior based on multimodal data captured in a CVE-based system between individuals with ASD and their neurotypical partners. Although manual labeling can be a reliable source, it can be time-consuming, resource-straining, and susceptible to bias. As such, there is a need for an alternative method to automatically analyze the interpersonal social behavior of the users in team-based tasks. We proposed the use of K-means to complement hand labeling of multimodal data to reduce cost (i.e., resources and time) and minimize bias. The labeled data can then be used to develop and train a prediction model that can reliably predict individual and interpersonal human behavior in real-time. Moving forward, we would like to develop a closed-loop feedback mechanism that can facilitate collaborative interactions between two users by providing a reliable evaluation of the user behavior.

The objective of this study was to analyze collaborative multimodal data using K-means to label users' interpersonal behavior and validate the use of clustering against hand-labeled data. In the previous sections, we presented the procedures we have taken to achieve this and showed that K-means clustering can be used to successfully cluster human behavior. The use of an individual model to cluster user behaviors resulted in an accuracy of 91.30%. However, while this model would be ideal if neurodiverse and neurotypical pairs remained constant across sessions, it is typically not realistic due to the diversity of human behavior. Therefore, we use it to establish a baseline for the other models. In future studies, we plan to use the group model which finds the participant's behavior using the average of the centroids found using the hand-labeled sessions. This model resulted in an accuracy of 89.66% which is very comparable to the individual model. However, this does not verify that the centroids are generalizable to new data. To combat this, we used LOOCV to show that the model did generalize well on unseen data. Using this approach, we achieved an accuracy of 87.38% which, as expected, is slighter lower than both the individual and group models.

While the results discussed above show promise, it is important to highlight the limitations of the study and important targets for future research. First, the sample size was relatively small. Recruiting more participants would allow us to improve the robustness of K-means clustering. However, these preliminary results further support our motivation for the use of K-means to complement manual data labeling. Next, from the analysis, we found that the centroids calculated using K-means clustering were not consistent and can cause misclassification of new data. As such it is important to be able to verify the centroids against a small portion of labeled data before using the centroid to automatically label new data. Although the use of K-means to automatically label human behavior through clustering is not perfect, it serves as one way to further explore the possibility of automating human behavior labeling and has extensive room for further improvements. To our knowledge, this is the first study that systematically evaluates and validates interpersonal behavior using K-means clustering with multimodal data of autistic individuals working together with neurotypical partners. Based on the promising results, future work would include using the labeled data to train machine learning models such as a Markov chain or neural networks to predict user behavior in real-time with a closed-loop feedback mechanism that can enhance user experience and facilitate the development of their teamwork skills.

Acknowledgments. We are grateful for the support provided by NSF grants 1936970 and 2033413 as well as NSF NRT grant DGE 19-22697 for this research. We would also like to thank the Vanderbilt Treatment and Research Institute for Autism Spectrum Disorders (TRIAD) team; Amy Weitlauf and Amy Swanson for their expert advice on interventions for autistic individuals and recruitments for the study. The authors are solely responsible for the contents and opinions expressed in this manuscript.

References

1. Neurodiversity hiring: Global diversity and inclusion at microsoft. https://www.crosoft.com/en-us/diversity/inside-microsoft/cross-disability/neurodiversityhiring
2. Specialsterne: Assessment. https://www.specialisterneni.com/about-us/assessment/
3. Unity website. https://unity3d.com/unity
4. Afsar, P., Cortez, P., Santos, H.: Automatic visual detection of human behavior: a review from 2000 to 2014. Expert Syst. Appl. **42**(20), 6935–6956 (2015). https://doi.org/10.1016/j.eswa.2015.05.023. https://www.sciencedirect.com/science/article/pii/S0957417415003516
5. Agran, M., Hughes, C., Thoma, C., Scott, L.: Employment social skills: What skills are really valued? Career Develop. Trans. Except. Individ. **39**, 111–120 (2014). https://doi.org/10.1177/2165143414546741
6. Almaguer, E., Yasmin, S.: A haptic virtual kitchen for the cognitive empowerment of children with autism spectrum disorder. In: Stephanidis, C., Antona, M. (eds.) HCII 2019. CCIS, vol. 1088, pp. 137–142. Springer, Cham (2019). https://doi.org/10.1007/978-3-030-30712-7_18
7. Amat, A., et al.: Collaborative virtual environment to encourage teamwork in autistic adults in workplace settings, pp. 339–348 (2021). https://doi.org/10.1007/978-3-030-78092-0_22
8. Apostolellis, P., Bowman, D.: C-olive: Group co-located interaction in VEs for contextual learning, pp. 129–130 (2014). https://doi.org/10.1109/VR.2014.6802085
9. Ashton, M.C., Lee, K.: The HEXACO-60: a short measure of the major dimensions of personality. J. Pers. Assess. **91**(4), 340–345 (2009). https://doi.org/10.1080/00223890902935878
10. Basden, B., Basden, D., Bryner, S., Thomas, R.r.: Developing methods for understanding social behavior in a 3D virtual learning environment. J. Exp. Psychol. Learn. Mem. Cogn. **23**(5), 1176–91 (1997). https://doi.org/10.1037//0278-7393.23.5.1176
11. Bekele, E., Zheng, Z., Swanson, A.R., Crittendon, J.A., Warren, Z., Sarkar, N.: Understanding how adolescents with autism respond to facial expressions in virtual reality environments. IEEE Trans. Visual Comput. Graphics **19**, 711–720 (2013)

12. Bernard-Opitz, Vand Ross, K., Tuttas, M.: Computer assisted instruction for autistic children. Ann. Acad. Med. Singap. **19**(5), 611–616 (1990)

13. Bernard-Opitz, V., Sriram, N., Nakhoda, S.: Enhancing social problem solving in children with autism and normal children through computer-assisted instruction. J. Autism Develop. Disord. **31**, 377–84 (2001). https://doi.org/10.1023/A:1010660502130

14. Bian, D., et al.: A novel virtual reality driving environment for autism intervention, pp. 474–483 (2013). https://doi.org/10.1007/978-3-642-39191-0_52

15. Bird, G., Cook, R.: Mixed emotions: the contribution of alexithymia to the emotional symptoms of autism. Transl. Psych. **3**, e285 (2013). https://doi.org/10.1038/tp.2013.61

16. Breland, J., Shiratuddin, M.F.: A study on collaborative design in a virtual environment. Int. J. Learn. **16**, 385–398 (2009). https://doi.org/10.18848/1447-9494/CGP/v16i03/46179

17. Checa, D., Bustillo, A.: A review of immersive virtual reality serious games to enhance learning and training. Multimedia Tools Appl. **79**(9), 5501–5527 (2019). https://doi.org/10.1007/s11042-019-08348-9

18. Chen, W.: Multitouch tabletop technology for people with autism spectrum disorder: a review of the literature. Procedia Comput. Sci. **14**, 198–207 (2012). https://doi.org/10.1016/j.procs.2012.10.023

19. Constantino, J., Gruber, C.: Social responsiveness scale (srs). Western Psychological Services Los Angeles (2005)

20. Creed, P., Macintyre, S.: The relative effects of deprivation of the latent and manifest benefits of employment on the well-being of unemployed people. J. Occup. Health Psychol. **6**, 324–31 (2001). https://doi.org/10.1037/1076-8998.6.4.324

21. Deiglmayr, A., Spada, H., Rummel, N.: A rating scheme for assessing the quality of computer-supported collaboration processes. Int. J. Comput.-Support. Collaborative Learn. **2**(1), 63–86 (2007). https://doi.org/10.1007/s11412-006-9005-x

22. Duchenne, O., Laptev, I., Sivic, J., Bach, F., Ponce, J.: Automatic annotation of human actions in video, pp. 1491–1498 (2009). https://doi.org/10.1109/ICCV.2009.5459279

23. D'Mello, S., Olney, A., Person, N.: Mining collaborative patterns in tutorial dialogues. J. Educ. Data Min. **2**, 1–37 (2010)

24. Echeverria, V., Martinez-Maldonado, R., Buckingham Shum, S.: Towards collaboration translucence: giving meaning to multimodal group data (2019). https://doi.org/10.1145/3290605.3300269

25. Fredriksson, T., Issa Mattos, D., Bosch, J., Olsson, H.: Data Labeling: an Empirical Investigation into Industrial Challenges and Mitigation Strategies, pp. 202–216 (2020). https://doi.org/10.1007/978-3-030-64148-1_13

26. Hanmin, Y., Hao, L., Qianting, S.: An improved semi-supervised k-means clustering algorithm, pp. 41–44 (2016). https://doi.org/10.1109/ITNEC.2016.7560315

27. Hayashi, Y.: Detecting collaborative learning through emotions: an investigation using facial expression recognition, pp. 89–98 (2019). https://doi.org/10.1007/978-3-030-22244-4_12

28. Hendricks, D.: A short review on the current understanding of autism spectrum disorders. J. Vocat. Rehabil. **32**(2), 125–134 (2010)

29. Hoffman, G., Breazeal, C.: Collaboration in human-robot teams. Collection of Technical Papers - AIAA 1st Intelligent Systems Technical Conference 2 (09 2004). https://doi.org/10.2514/6.2004-6434

30. Hong, J.H., Ramos Rojas, J., Dey, A.: Toward personalized activity recognition systems with a semipopulation approach. IEEE Transactions on Human-Machine Systems, pp. 1–12 (2015). https://doi.org/10.1109/THMS.2015.2489688
31. Inc., T.M.: Matlab (2018)
32. Kenny, L., Hattersley, C., Molins, B., Buckley, C., Povey, C., Pellicano, E.: Which terms should be used to describe autism? perspectives from the UK autism community. Autism **20**(4), 442–62 (2016). https://doi.org/10.1177/1362361315588200
33. Kulman, R., Slobuski, T., Seitsinger, R.: Teaching 21st Century, Executive-Functioning, and Creativity Skills with Popular Video Games and Apps, pp. 159–174. ETC Press, Pittsburgh, PA, USA (2014). https://doi.org/10.5555/2811147.2811157
34. Kusumaningrum, R., Farikhin, F.: An automatic labeling of K-means clusters based on chi-square value. J. Phys. Conf. Ser. **801**, 012071 (2017). https://doi.org/10.1088/1742-6596/801/1/012071
35. Litchfield, P., Cooper, C., Hancock, C., Watt, P.: Work and wellbeing in the 21st century †. Int. J. Environ. Res. Public Health **13**, 1065 (2016). https://doi.org/10.3390/ijerph13111065
36. Lord, C., et al.: The autism diagnostic observation schedule-generic: a standard measure of social and communication deficits associated with the spectrum of autism. J. Autism Develop. Disorders **30**, 205–223 (2000). https://doi.org/10.1023/A:1005592401947
37. M. Khawam, A., DiDona, T., S. Hern, B.: Effectiveness of teamwork in the workplace. Int. J. Sci. Basic Appl. Res. (IJSBAR) **32**(3), 267–286 (2017). https://gssrr.org/index.php/JournalOfBasicAndApplied/article/view/7134
38. Martinez-Maldonado, R., Gasevic, D., Echeverria, V., Nieto, G., Swiecki, Z., Buckingham Shum, S.: What do you mean by collaboration analytics? a conceptual model. J. Learn. Analyt. **8**, 126–153 (2021). https://doi.org/10.18608/jla.2021.7227
39. Mihoub, A., Lefebvre, G.: Wearables and social signal processing for smarter public presentations. ACM Trans. Interact. Intell. Syst. **9**, 9 (2018). https://doi.org/10.1145/3234507
40. Müller, P., et al.: Multimediate: multi-modal group behaviour analysis for artificial mediation, pp. 4878–4882 (2021). https://doi.org/10.1145/3474085.3479219
41. Norris, M.W., Spicer, K., Byrd, T.: Virtual reality: the new pathway for effective safety training. Professional Saf. **64**(06), 36–39 (2019)
42. Okada, S., et al.: Estimating communication skills using dialogue acts and nonverbal features in multiple discussion datasets, pp. 169–176 (2016). https://doi.org/10.1145/2993148.2993154
43. Palliya Guruge, C., Oviatt, S., Haghighi, P., Pritchard, E.: Advances in multimodal behavioral analytics for early dementia diagnosis: a review, pp. 328–340 (2021). https://doi.org/10.1145/3462244.3479933
44. Park, H.R., et al.: A short review on the current understanding of autism spectrum disorders. Exper. Neurobiol. **25**, 1 (2016). https://doi.org/10.5607/en.2016.25.1.1
45. Parsons, S., Mitchell, P.: The potential of virtual reality in social skills training for people with autistic spectrum disorders. J. Intell. Disability Res. JIDR **46**, 430–443 (2002). https://doi.org/10.1046/j.1365-2788.2002.00425.x
46. Putnam, C., Chong, L.: Software and technologies designed for people with autism: what do users want? abstract, pp. 3–10 (2008). https://doi.org/10.1145/1414471.1414475

47. Saiano, M., et al.: Natural interfaces and virtual environments for the acquisition of street crossing and path following skills in adults with autism spectrum disorders: a feasibility study. J. Neuroeng. Rehabil. **12**, 17 (2015). https://doi.org/10.1186/s12984-015-0010-z

48. Salah, A., Gevers, T., Sebe, N., Vinciarelli, A.: Challenges of human behavior understanding, vol. 6219, pp. 1–12 (2010). https://doi.org/10.1007/978-3-642-14715-9_1

49. Salah, A., Pantic, M., Vinciarelli, A.: Recent developments in social signal processing, pp. 380–385 (2011). https://doi.org/10.1109/ICSMC.2011.6083695

50. Sanyal, S., Hisam, M.: The impact of teamwork on work performance of employees: a study of faculty members in Dhofar university 20 (2018). https://doi.org/10.9790/487X-2003011522

51. Schmidt, M., Laffey, J., Schmidt, C., Wang, X., Stichter, J.: Developing methods for understanding social behavior in a 3D virtual learning environment. Comput. Human Behav. **28**, 405–413 (2012). https://doi.org/10.1016/j.chb.2011.10.011

52. Scott, M., Falkmer, M., Girdler, S., Falkmer, T.: Viewpoints on factors for successful employment for adults with autism spectrum disorder. PLoS One **6**, 0139281 (2015). https://doi.org/10.1371/journal.pone.0139281

53. Stauch, T.A., Plavnick, J.B.: Teaching vocational and social skills to adolescents with Autism using video modeling. Educ. Treat. Child. **43**(2), 137–151 (2020). https://doi.org/10.1007/s43494-020-00020-4

54. Sung, C., Connor, A., Chen, J., Lin, C.C., Kuo, H.J., Chun, J.: Development, feasibility, and preliminary efficacy of an employment-related social skills intervention for young adults with high-functioning autism. Autism **23**, 136236131880134 (2018). https://doi.org/10.1177/1362361318801345

55. Taylor, J., Seltzer, M.: Employment and post-secondary educational activities for young adults with autism spectrum disorders during the transition to adulthood. J. Autism Dev. Disord. **41**(5), 566–74 (2011). https://doi.org/10.1007/s10803-010-1070-3

56. Vajda, S., Rangoni, Y., Cecotti, H.: Semi-automatic ground truth generation using unsupervised clustering and limited manual labeling: application to handwritten character recognition. Pattern Recogn. Lett. **58**, 23–28 (2015). https://doi.org/10.1016/j.patrec.2015.02.001. https://www.sciencedirect.com/science/article/pii/S0167865515000380

57. Valencia, K., Rusu, C., Quiñones, D., Jamet, E.: The impact of technology on people with autism spectrum disorder: systematic literature review. Sensors **19**(20) (2019). https://doi.org/10.3390/s19204485

58. Walsh, E., Holloway, J., Lydon, H.: An evaluation of a social skills intervention for adults with autism spectrum disorder and intellectual disabilities preparing for employment in ireland: a pilot study. J. Autism Dev. Disord. **48**(5), 1727–1741 (2017). https://doi.org/10.1007/s10803-017-3441-5

59. Williams, C., Wright, B., Callaghan, G., Coughlan, B.: Do children with autism learn to read more readily by computer assisted instruction or traditional book methods?: A pilot study. Autism : Int. Jo. Res. Pract. **6**, 71–91 (2002). https://doi.org/10.1177/1362361302006001006

60. Zhang, L., Warren, Z., Swanson, A., Weitlauf, A., Sarkar, N.: Understanding performance and verbal-communication of children with ASD in a collaborative virtual environment. J. Autism Dev. Disord. **48**(8), 2779–2789 (2018). https://doi.org/10.1007/s10803-018-3544-7

61. Zhao, Z., Chen, Y., Liu, J., Shen, Z., Liu, M.: Cross-people mobile-phone based activity recognition, pp. 2545–2550 (2011). https://doi.org/10.5591/978-1-57735-516-8/IJCAI11-423
62. Zheng, Z., et al.: Impact of robot-mediated interaction system on joint attention skills for children with autism. 2013 IEEE 13th International Conference on Rehabilitation Robotics (ICORR), pp. 1–8 (2013)

Emergence of Collaborative Hunting via Multi-Agent Deep Reinforcement Learning

Kazushi Tsutsui[1(✉)], Kazuya Takeda[1], and Keisuke Fujii[1,2,3]

[1] Nagoya University, Nagoya, Japan
k.tsutsui6@gmail.com
[2] RIKEN, Wako, Japan
[3] PRESTO, Chiyoda, Japan

Abstract. Cooperative hunting has long received considerable attention because it may be an evolutionary origin of cooperation and even our sociality. It has been known that the level of organization of this predation varies among species. Although predator-prey interactions have been studied in multi-agent reinforcement learning domains, there have been few attempts to use the simulations to better understand human and other animal behaviors. In this study, we introduce a predator-prey simulation environment based on multi-agent deep reinforcement learning that can bridge the gap between biological/ecological and artificial intelligence domains. Using this environment, we revealed that organized cooperative hunting patterns with role division among individuals, which is positioned as the highest level of organization in cooperative hunting of animals in nature, can emerge via a simplest form of multi-agent deep reinforcement learning. Our results suggest that sophisticated collaborative patterns, which have often been thought to require high cognition, can be realized from relatively simple cognitive and learning mechanisms and that the close link between the behavioral patterns of agents and animals acquired through interaction with their environments.

Keywords: emergence · collaboration · multi-agent systems · deep reinforcement learning · predator-prey interactions

1 Introduction

Cooperative hunting, that is, where two or more individuals engage in a hunt, has been regarded as one of the most widely distributed forms of cooperation among predatory mammals [36], including humans [23]. This cooperative behavior has thus received considerable attention because it may be an evolutionary origin of animal cooperation and even our sociality [8,29,37]. In cooperative hunting behavior, there are various levels of organization ranging from simply multiple individuals hunting simultaneously to each individual playing a different and complementary role [2,3,6,9,10,14,28,40] (Table 1). Accordingly, comparisons between and within species have focused on behaviors that can potentially distinguish between the different levels of the organization [25]. These observations

© Springer Nature Switzerland AG 2023
J.-J. Rousseau and B. Kapralos (Eds.): ICPR 2022 Workshops, LNCS 13643, pp. 210–224, 2023.
https://doi.org/10.1007/978-3-031-37660-3_15

Table 1. Definitions of the different levels of cooperative hunting [3]

Category	Definition	Variation
Similarity	All hunters concentrate similar actions on the same prey, but without any spatial or time relation between them; however, at least two hunters always act simultaneously	Similar actions are varying elements of pursuing a prey, i.e., stalk or chase ...
Synchrony	Each hunter concentrates in similar actions on the same prey and tries to relate in time to each other's actions	Hunters may begin at the same time or adjust their speed to remain in time
Coordination	Each hunter concentrates in similar actions on the same prey and tries to relate in time and space to each other's actions	Hunters may begin from different directions or adjust their position to remain coordinated
Collaboration	Hunters perform different complimentary actions, all directed towards the same prey	Examples are driving, blocking escape way and encirclement

in nature have established the idea that a cooperative hunting pattern is a consequence of the interaction of various factors both inside and outside the animal, such as the cognitive and motor abilities and its living environment [1]. However, the factors that are crucial in promoting the emergence (or evolution) of organized hunting patterns are not well understood, as there are several challenges in terms of measurement and analysis. For example, correlations between the levels of candidates for crucial factors, such as communication, role differentiation, and food sharing, among the data make it difficult to separate the contribution of each factor [25].

Predator-prey interactions have also been vigorously studied in the multi-agent reinforcement learning (MARL) domain, and recent advances in MARL present potential to overcome the above issues [32]. Nevertheless, most prior research has only used predator-prey environments as a test-bed for MARL algorithms, and there have been few attempts to compare the agent behavior produced by simulation experiments with human and non-human animal behavior for a better understanding. Further, the lack of diversity in behavior patterns among agents, as opposed to real human or non-human animals, is a limitation of existing research and should be addressed in future work [21].

Here, we introduce a predator-prey simulation environment based on multi-agent deep reinforcement learning that can bridge the gap between biological/ecological and artificial intelligence domains and demonstrate that this environment can be a useful tool to better understand human and non-human animal behaviors (Fig. 1). The main contributions of this paper are as follows. (1) We propose a framework of the predator-prey simulation environment, which can

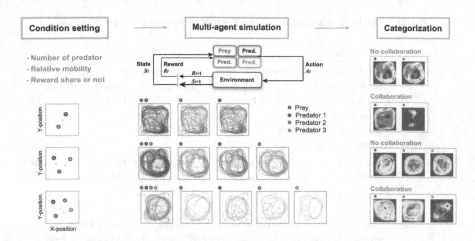

Fig. 1. An overview of our study. In the condition settings (left), three items were selected based on ecological findings. In the multi-agent simulation (middle), the predator and prey were modeled using the framework of independent Q learning, learned (10^6 episodes), and evaluated (100 episodes). The movement trajectory in the figure is an example of predator-prey interactions that overlay ten episodes. In categorization (right), agent behaviors were visualized and classified using heatmaps based on their movement trajectories. For simplicity, we focused on whether collaborative behavior by predator agents is "Collaboration".

identify the crucial factors to emerge certain collective behaviors. (2) We find that a seemingly complex collaborative behavior with role division among agents can be realized via a simplest MARL algorithm, namely individual learning. (3) We show that the collaborative behavior, which is positioned as the highest level of cooperative hunting in animals, is facilitated by a combination of two factors: capture difficulty of solitary hunting and food sharing following capture. In the remainder of this paper, we describe the background of predator-prey interactions and reinforcement learning in Sect. 2, our agent (predator/prey) model implementation in Sect. 3, the environments and results of simulation experiments in Sect. 4, and the conclusions of this paper in Sect. 5.

2 Background

In this section, we first briefly present our rationale for modeling predator-prey interactions using the framework of reinforcement learning and then provide some theoretical background on reinforcement learning and deep reinforcement learning.

2.1 Predator-Prey Interactions

Chase and escape behaviors are crucial for survival in many species, and therefore are fast and robust by necessity, making them incredibly rich subjects to investigate the sensorimotor controls of animals [7,11,35]. As such, numerous studies have been conducted thus far to investigate chase and escape behaviors in a wide range of animal species.

These behaviors are generally thought of as complex phenomena in which two or more agents interact in environments, which change from moment to moment, yet many studies have shown that the rules of behavior (e.g., which direction to move at each time in a given situation) can be described by relatively simple mathematical models consisting of the current state (e.g., positions and velocities) [4,5,12,15,16,18,22,48]. In other words, these behaviors can be modeled by standard reinforcement learning methods for a finite Markov decision process (MDP) in which each sequence is a distinct state.

2.2 Reinforcement Learning

Reinforcement learning addresses the problem of an agent learning to act in an environment to maximize a reward. In this setting, an agent is never directly instructed on the optimal actions to take, but learns them through interaction with the environment.

Agents and Environments. We here considered a sequential decision-making setting in which a single agent interacts with a fully observable environment $\mathcal{E}$ in a sequence of observations, actions, and rewards. At each time-step t, the agent observes a state $s_t \in \mathcal{S}$ and selects an action a_t from a discrete set of actions $\mathcal{A} = \{1, 2, \ldots, |\mathcal{A}|\}$. One time step later, in part as a consequence of its action, the agent receives a reward, $r_{t+1} \in \mathcal{R}$, and moves itself to a new state s_{t+1}. In the MDP, the agent thereby gives rise to a sequence that begins like this: $s_0, a_0, r_1, s_1, a_1, r_2, s_2, a_2, r_3, \ldots$, and let the agents to learn behavioral rules (strategies) that depend upon these sequences.

The goal of the agent is to maximize the expected discounted return over time through its choice of actions [44]. The discounted return R_t was defined as $\sum_{k=0}^{T} \gamma^k r_{t+k+1}$, where $\gamma \in [0, 1]$ is a parameter called the discount rate that determines the present value of future rewards, and T is the time step at which the task terminates. The state-value function, action-value function, and advantage function are defined as $V^\pi(s) = \mathbb{E}_\pi[R_t|s_t = s]$, $Q^\pi(s,a) = \mathbb{E}_\pi[R_t|s_t = s, a_t = a]$, and $A^\pi(s,a) = Q^\pi(s,a) - V^\pi(s)$, respectively, where π is a policy mapping states to actions. The optimal action-value function $Q^\star(s,a)$ is then defined as the maximum expected discounted return achievable by following any strategy, after seeing some state s and then taking some action a, $Q^\star(s,a) = \max_\pi \mathbb{E}[R_t|s_t = s, a_t = a, \pi]$. The optimal action-value function can be computed recursively obeying the Bellman equation:

$$Q^\star(s,a) = \mathbb{E}_{s' \sim \mathcal{E}}[r + \gamma \max_{a'} Q^\star(s', a'|s, a)], \tag{1}$$

where s' and a' are the state and action at the next time-step, respectively. This is based on the following intuition: if the optimal value $Q^\star(s', a')$ of the state s' was known for all possible actions a', the optimal strategy is to select the action a' maximizing the expected value of $r + \gamma \max_{a'} Q^\star(s', a')$. The basic idea behind many reinforcement learning algorithms is to estimate the action-value function by using the Bellman equation as an iterative update; $Q_{i+1}(s, a) = \mathbb{E}[r + \gamma \max_{a'} Q_i(s', a'|s, a)]$. Such value iteration algorithms converge to the optimal action-value function in situations where all states can be sufficiently sampled, $Q_i \to Q^\star$ as $i \to \infty$. In practice, however, it is often difficult to apply this basic approach, which estimates the action-value function separately for each state, to real-world problems. Instead, it is common to use a function approximator to estimate the action-value function, $Q(s, a; \theta) \approx Q^\star(s, a)$.

In the following, we introduce a neural network function approximator referred to as deep Q-network (DQN) and some of its extensions to overcome the limitations of the DQN, namely Double DQN, prioritized experience replay, and dueling network.

Deep Q-networks Deep Q-network is the first deep learning model to successfully learn agents' policies directly from high-dimensional sensory input using reinforcement learning [30, 31]. In a naive manner, a Q-network with weights θ can be trained by minimizing a loss function $\mathcal{L}_i(\theta_i)$ that changes at each iteration i,

$$\mathcal{L}_i(\theta_i) = \mathbb{E}_{s, a \sim \rho(\cdot)}[(y_i - Q(s, a; \theta_i))^2], \qquad (2)$$

where $y_i = r + \gamma \max_{a'} Q(s', a'; \theta_{i-1}|s, a)$ is the target value for iteration i, and $\rho(s, a)$ is a probability distribution over states s and actions a. The parameters from the previous iteration θ_{i-1} are kept constant when optimizing the loss function $\mathcal{L}_i(\theta_i)$. By differentiating the loss function with respect to the weights we arrive at the following gradient,

$$\nabla_{\theta_i} \mathcal{L}_i(\theta_i) = \mathbb{E}_{s, a \sim \rho(\cdot); s' \sim \mathcal{E}} \left[\left(r + \gamma \max_{a'} Q(s', a'; \theta_{i-1}) - Q(s, a; \theta_i) \right) \nabla_{\theta_i} Q(s, a; \theta_i) \right]. \qquad (3)$$

We could attempt to use the simplest Q-learning to learn the weights of the network $Q(s, a; \theta)$ online; However, this estimator performs poorly in practice. In this simplest form, they discard incoming data immediately, after a single update. This causes two issues: (i) strongly correlated updates that break the i.i.d. assumption of many popular stochastic gradient-based algorithms and (ii) the rapid forgetting of possibly rare experiences that would be useful later. To address both of these issues, a technique called experience replay is often adopted [26], in which the agent's experiences at each time-step $e_t = (s_t, a_t, r_{t+1}, s_{t+1})$ are stored into a data-set (also referred to as replay memory) $\mathcal{D} = \{e_1, e_2, \ldots, e_N\}$, where N is the data-set size, for some time. When training the Q-network, instead of only using the current experience as prescribed by standard Q-learning, mini-batches of experiences are sampled from $\mathcal{D}$ uniformly at random to train the network. This enables breaking the temporal correlations by mixing more and less recent experience for the updates, and rare experience will be used for more than just a single update. Another technique called as target-network is also often used for updating to stabilize learning. To achieve this, the target value y_i is replaced by $r + \gamma \max_{a'} Q(s', a'; \theta_i^- | s, a)$, where θ_i^- are the weights frozen for a fixed number of iterations. The full algorithm combining these ingredients, namely experience replay and target-network, is often called a Deep Q-Network (DQN) and its loss function takes the form:

$$\mathcal{L}_i(\theta_i) = \mathbb{E}_{(s,a,r',s' \sim \mathcal{U}(\mathcal{D}))}[(y_i^{DQN} - Q(s, a; \theta_i))^2], \tag{4}$$

where

$$y_i^{DQN} = r + \gamma \max_{a'} Q(s', a'; \theta_i^- | s, a), \tag{5}$$

and $\mathcal{U}(\cdot)$ is an uniform sampling.

Double DQN. It has been known that a Q-learning algorithm performs poorly in some stochastic environments. This poor performance is caused by large over-estimations of action values. These overestimations result from a positive bias that is introduced because Q-learning uses the maximum action value as an approximation for the maximum expected action value. As a method to allevi-ate the performance degradation due to the overestimation, Double Q-learning, which applies the double estimator, was proposed [19]. Double DQN (DDQN) is an algorithm that applies the double Q-learning method to DQN [49]. For the DDQN, the maximum operation in the target is decomposed into action selec-tion and action evaluation, and the target value in the loss function (i.e., Eq. 5) for iteration i is replaced as follows:

$$y_i^{DDQN} = r + \gamma Q(s', \arg\max_{a'} Q(s', a'; \theta_i | s, a; \theta^-). \tag{6}$$

Prioritized Experience Replay. Prioritized experience replay is a method that aims to make the learning more efficient and effective than if all transi-tions were replayed uniformly [39]. For the prioritized replay, the probability of sampling from the data-set for transition i is defined as

$$P(i) = \frac{p_i^\alpha}{\sum_k p_k^\alpha}, \tag{7}$$

where $p_i > 0$ is the priority of transition for iteration i and the exponent α determines how much prioritization is used, with $\alpha = 0$ corresponding to uniform sampling. The priority p_i is determined by $p_i = |\delta_i| + \epsilon$, where δ_i is a temporal-difference (TD) error (e.g., $\delta_i = r + \gamma \max_{a'} Q(s', a'; \theta_i^- | s, a) - Q(s, a; \theta_i)$ in DQN) and ϵ is a small positive constant that prevents the case of transitions not being revisited once their error is zero. Prioritized replay introduces sampling bias, and therefore changes the solution that the estimates will converge to. This bias can be corrected by importance-sampling (IS) weights $w_i = (\frac{1}{N}\frac{1}{P(i)})^\beta$ that fully compensate for the non-uniform probabilities $P(i)$ if $\beta = 1$.

Dueling Network. The dueling network is a neural network architecture designed for value-based algorithms such as DQN [50]. This features two streams of computation, the value and advantage streams, sharing a common encoder, and is merged by an aggregation module that produces an estimate of the state-action value function. Intuitively, we can expect the dueling network to learn which states are (or not) valuable, without having to learn the effect of each action for each state. For the reason of stability of the optimization, the last module of the network is implemented as follows:

$$Q(s,a;\theta,\eta,\xi) = V(s;\theta,\xi) + \left(A(s,a;\theta,\eta) - \frac{1}{|\mathcal{A}|}\sum_{a'} A(s,a';\theta,\eta) \right), \qquad (8)$$

where θ denotes the parameters of the common layers, while η and ξ are the parameters of the layers of the two streams, respectively. Although this loses the original semantics of V and A, subtracting the mean helps with identifiability while preserving the stability of the optimization. In addition, it does not change the relative rank of the A (and hence Q) values, and suffices to evaluate the advantage stream to make decisions. It has been experimentally shown that this module works well in practice.

3   Predator-Prey Model Implementation

Here, we describe the agent (predator/prey) model implementation. We first present the reasons for selecting this model architecture and the definition of its loss function, and then describe the details of model learning.

3.1   Model Architecture

Recently, many attempts to extend success in the single-agent domain of reinforcement learning to multi-agents. In multi-agent reinforcement learning (MARL), multiple agents aim to learn how to interact with others in a shared environment to achieve common or conflicting goals.

We here aimed to construct a biologically plausible (or considered to be more amenable to biological interpretation) simulation environment, and modeled an agent (predator/prey) with independent learning (IL) [45]. The IL is one of the simplest forms of MARL, in which each agent treats the other agents as a part of environment and learns policies that condition only on an agent's local observation history. That is, our method is based on independent end-to-end learning and generalization, resulting in decentralized control within a group. Therefore, in contrast to previous work [13,27,33,34,38,41,43,46], agents do

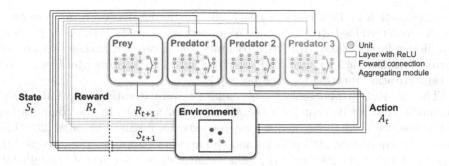

Fig. 2. Model architecture. An agent's policy π is represented by a deep neural network. The state of the environment is given as input to the network. An action is sampled from the network's output, and the agent receives a reward and the subsequent state. The agent learn to select actions in a manner that maximizes cumulative future reward. In this study, each agent learned its policy network independently, that is, each agent treats the other agents as part of the environment. Note that this illustration shows a situation with three predators.

not have access to models of the environment, state of other players, or human policy priors, nor can they communicate with each other outside of the game environment. Specifically, for each agent n, the policy π^n is represented by a neural network and optimized, with the framework of DQN including DDQN, prioritized replay, and dueling architecture (Fig. 2). The loss function of each agent takes the form:

$$\mathcal{L}_i(\theta_i, \eta_i, \xi_i) = \mathbb{E}_{s,a,r',s' \sim \mathcal{P}(\mathcal{D})}[(y_i - Q(s, a; \theta_i, \eta_i, \xi_i))^2], \tag{9}$$

where

$$y_i = r + \gamma Q(s', \arg\max_{a'} Q(s', a'; \theta_i, \eta_i, \xi_i | s, a; \theta_i^-, \eta_i^-, \xi_i^-), \tag{10}$$

and $\mathcal{P}(\cdot)$ is a prioritized sampling. For simplicity, we omitted the agent index n in these equations.

3.2 Training Details

The neural network is composed of four layers. There is a separate output unit for each possible action, and only the state representation is an input to the neural network. The inputs to the neural network are the positions of oneself and others in the absolute coordinate system (x- and y-positions) and the positions and velocities of oneself and others in the relative coordinate system (u- and v-positions and u- and v-velocities), which are determined based on variables used in the chase and escape models in biology [4,5,12,15,16,18,22,48]. We assumed that delays in sensory processing are compensated for by estimation [47] and the current information at each time was used as input as is. The outputs are the acceleration in 12 directions every 30° in the relative coordinate system, which are determined with reference to an ecological study [51]. After the first two hidden layers of the MLP with 64 units, the network branches off into two streams. Each branch has two MLP layers with 32 hidden units. ReLU was used as the activation function for each layer [17].

The network parameters θ^n, η^n, and ξ^n were iteratively optimized via stochastic gradient descent with the Adam optimizer [24]. In the computation of the loss, we used Huber loss to prevent extreme gradient updates [20]. The model was trained for 10^6 episodes and the network parameters were copied to target-network every 2000 episodes. The replay memory size was 10^4, minibatch size during training was 32, and the learning rate was 10^{-6}. The discount factor γ was set to 0.9, and α was set to 0.6.

We used an ε-greedy policy as the behavior policy π^n, which chooses a random action with probability ε or an action according to the optimal Q function $\arg\max_{a \in \mathcal{A}} Q^*(s, a)$ with probability $1 - \varepsilon$. In this study, ε was annealed linearly from 1 to 0.1 over the first 10^4 episodes, and fixed at 0.1 thereafter.

4 Experiments

We focused on predator-prey cooperative and competitive interactions, namely the chase and escape behaviors. In this section, we first describe the environment of our experiment and then present the results obtained by computational experiments.

4.1 Environment

The predator and prey interacted in a two-dimensional world with continuous space and discrete time. This environment was constructed by modifying an environment called the predator-prey in Multi-Agent Particle Environment (MAPE) [27]. The modifications were that the action space (play area size) was constrained to the range of -1 to 1 on the x and y axes, all agent (predator/prey) disk diameters were set to 0.1, landmarks (obstacles) were eliminated, and predator-to-predator contact was ignored for simplicity. The predator(s) was rewarded for capturing the prey (+1), namely contacting the disks, and punished for moving out of the area (-1), and the prey was punished for being captured by the predator or for moving out of the area (-1).

The predator and prey were represented as a red and blue disk, respectively, and the play area was represented as a gray square surrounding them (Fig. 1). The time step was 0.1 s and the time limit in each episode was set to 30 s. The initial position of each episode was randomly selected from a range of -0.5 to 0.5 on the x and y axes. If the predator captured the prey within the time limit, the predator was successful, otherwise the prey was successful. If one side (predators/prey) moved out of the area, the other side (prey/predators) was deemed successful.

4.2   Experimental Condition

We selected the number of predators, relative mobility, and prey (reward) sharing as experimental conditions, based on ecological findings [1,3,25]. For the number of predators, three conditions were set: 1 (One), 2 (Two), and 3 (Three). In all these conditions, the number of preys was 1. For the relative mobility, three conditions were set: 120% (Fast), 100% (Equal), and 80% (Slow) for the acceleration exerted by the predator, based on that exerted by the prey. For the prey sharing, two conditions were set: with sharing (Shared), in which the all predators rewarded when a predator catches the prey, and without sharing (Individual), in which a predator was rewarded only when it catches prey by itself. In total, there were 15 conditions.

4.3   Evaluation

The model performance was evaluated by 100 episodes computational simulation using the trained model in each condition. The initial position and termination conditions in each episode were the same as in training. During the evaluation, ε was set to 0 and each agent was made to take greedy actions. We calculated and analyzed the proportion of successful predation, average episode duration, and predation forms from the data obtained by the simulation experiments.

We first show the proportion of successful predation and average episode duration for each condition (Fig. 3). For the Fast and Equal conditions, the proportion of successful predation was almost 100 %, regardless of the number of predator and the reward sharing. This indicates that in situations where predators were more faster than or equal in speed to their prey, they were successfully

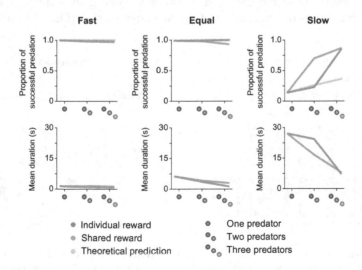

Fig. 3. Proportion of successful predation (top) and episode duration (bottom). Each value is the proportion/mean of 100 episodes of simulation. The theoretical prediction values were calculated based on the proportion of solitary hunts using Eq. 11.

captured in almost all episodes, even when they were alone. Although the mean duration of the episodes decreased with increasing number of predators in both of the Fast and Equal conditions, the difference was small. As a whole, these results indicate that the benefit of multiple predators cooperating in the Fast and Equal conditions is small.

On the other hand, in the Slow condition, a solitary predator was rarely successful, and the proportion of success increased sharply as the number of predators increased. Similarly, the mean duration decreased with increasing number of predators . These results indicate that, under the Slow condition, the benefits of cooperation among multiple predators are significant. Under the Slow conditions, with the exception of the Slow × Two × Individual condition, the increase in proportion of success with increasing number of predators was much greater than the theoretical predictions defined below:

$$H_n = 1 - (1 - H_1)^n \qquad (11)$$

where H_n and H_1 denote the proportion of successful predation when the number of predators is n and 1, respectively. That is, these results suggest that, under these conditions, predation patterns, which qualitatively are different in some respect with solitary, may have emerged rather than simply being a result of increasing the number of predators.

We then analyzed the predation patterns focusing on the Slow condition. Figure 4 shows heatmaps for the predator and prey. The heatmap was made by dividing the play area into 20 by 20 grids and counting the frequency of stay in each grid. The heatmaps were compared between prey and each predator to quantify their predation strategies. In the Individual condition (Fig. 4 left), there were relatively high correlations between the heatmap of the prey and each predator, regardless of the number of predatorspagination (One: $r = 0.96$, Two:

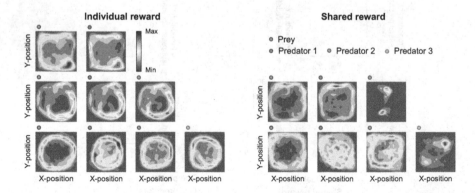

Fig. 4. Heatmaps in individual (left) and shared (right) reward conditions. The heatmap of each agent was made based on the frequency of stay in each position which is cumulative for 100 episodes in each condition.

$r = 0.86, 0.80$, Three: $r = 0.36, 0.58, 0.50$). This suggests that each predator had roughly same behavioral tendencies, namely, each predator pursue its prey without a clear division of roles. In contrast, in the Shared condition (Fig. 4, right), only one predator had a relatively high correlation, while the others had low correlations (Two: $r = 0.68, 0.00$, Three: $r = 0.13, 0.56, 0.01$). As shown in rightmost of the respective rows on the right side of Fig. 4, there were localized concentrations in the heatmaps of certain predators, indicating that they played a different role to the others, namely a strategy such as ambushing their prey.

5 Conclusion

This study introduced a predator-prey model simulation environment based on multi-agent deep reinforcement learning for human and non-human behavioral understanding, and demonstrated its ability to examine the contributions and interactions of the candidate for crucial factors, which has difficulty separating conventional comparisons between and within species in natural observation.

A limitation of the current work, which should be addressed in future work, is the uniformity of mobility among predator agents. In real-world animal groups (e.g., lion packs), it was reported that collaborative predators have physical traits appropriate to their roles [42], suggesting that examining the links between physical characteristics and role differentiation can lead to further understanding of human and other animal behaviors.

Acknowledgment. This work was supported by JSPS KAKENHI (Grant Numbers 20H04075, 21H04892, 21H05300, and 22K17673) and JST PRESTO (JPMJPR20CA).

References

1. Bailey, I., Myatt, J.P., Wilson, A.M.: Group hunting within the Carnivora: physiological, cognitive and environmental influences on strategy and cooperation. Behav. Ecol. Sociobiol. **67**(1), 1–17 (2013)
2. Boesch, C.: Cooperative hunting roles among tai chimpanzees. Hum. Nat. **13**(1), 27–46 (2002)
3. Boesch, C., Boesch, H.: Hunting behavior of wild chimpanzees in the Tai National park. Am. J. Phys. Anthropol. **78**(4), 547–573 (1989)
4. Brighton, C.H., Taylor, G.K.: Hawks steer attacks using a guidance system tuned for close pursuit of erratically manoeuvring targets. Nat. Commun. **10**(1), 1–10 (2019)
5. Brighton, C.H., Thomas, A.L., Taylor, G.K.: Terminal attack trajectories of peregrine falcons are described by the proportional navigation guidance law of missiles. Proc. Natl. Acad. Sci. **114**(51), 13495–13500 (2017)
6. Bshary, R., Hohner, A., Ait-el Djoudi, K., Fricke, H.: Interspecific communicative and coordinated hunting between groupers and giant moray eels in the red sea. PLoS Biol. **4**(12), e431 (2006)
7. Card, G.M.: Escape behaviors in insects. Curr. Opin. Neurobiol. **22**(2), 180–186 (2012)

8. Creel, S., Creel, N.M.: Communal hunting and pack size in African wild dogs, Lycaon Pictus. Anim. Behav. **50**(5), 1325–1339 (1995)
9. De Roy, T., Espinoza, E.R., Trillmich, F.: Cooperation and opportunism in Galapagos sea lion hunting for shoaling fish. Ecol. Evol. **11**(14), 9206–9216 (2021)
10. Ellis, D.H., Bednarz, J.C., Smith, D.G., Flemming, S.P.: Social foraging classes in raptorial birds. Bioscience **43**(1), 14–20 (1993)
11. Evans, D.A., Stempel, A.V., Vale, R., Branco, T.: Cognitive control of escape behaviour. Trends Cogn. Sci. **23**(4), 334–348 (2019)
12. Fabian, S.T., Sumner, M.E., Wardill, T.J., Rossoni, S., Gonzalez-Bellido, P.T.: Interception by two predatory fly species is explained by a proportional navigation feedback controller. J. R. Soc. Interface **15**(147), 20180466 (2018)
13. Foerster, J., Assael, I.A., De Freitas, N., Whiteson, S.: Learning to communicate with deep multi-agent reinforcement learning. Advances in Neural Information Processing Systems 29 (2016)
14. Gazda, S.K., Connor, R.C., Edgar, R.K., Cox, F.: A division of labour with role specialization in group-hunting bottlenose dolphins (Tursiops Truncatus) off cedar key, florida. Proceed. Royal Soc. B Biol. Sci. **272**(1559), 135–140 (2005)
15. Ghose, K., Horiuchi, T.K., Krishnaprasad, P., Moss, C.F.: Echolocating bats use a nearly time-optimal strategy to intercept prey. PLoS Biol. **4**(5), e108 (2006)
16. Gilbert, C.: Visual control of cursorial prey pursuit by tiger beetles (cicindelidae). J. Comp. Physiol. A **181**(3), 217–230 (1997)
17. Glorot, X., Bordes, A., Bengio, Y.: Deep sparse rectifier neural networks. In: Proceedings of the Fourteenth International Conference on Artificial Intelligence and Statistics, pp. 315–323. JMLR Workshop and Conference Proceedings (2011)
18. Haselsteiner, A.F., Gilbert, C., Wang, Z.J.: Tiger beetles pursue prey using a proportional control law with a delay of one half-stride. J. R. Soc. Interface **11**(95), 20140216 (2014)
19. Hasselt, H.: Double q-learning. Advances in Neural Information Processing Systems 23 (2010)
20. Huber, P.J.: Robust estimation of a location parameter. In: Kotz, S., Johnson, N.L. (eds.) Breakthroughs in Statistics, pp. 492–518. Springer Series in Statistics. Springer, NY (1992). https://doi.org/10.1007/978-1-4612-4380-9_35
21. Jaderberg, M., et al.: Human-level performance in 3D multiplayer games with population-based reinforcement learning. Science **364**(6443), 859–865 (2019)
22. Kane, S.A., Fulton, A.H., Rosenthal, L.J.: When hawks attack: animal-borne video studies of goshawk pursuit and prey-evasion strategies. J. Exp. Biol. **218**(2), 212–222 (2015)
23. King, G.E.: Socioterritorial units among carnivores and early hominids. J. Anthropol. Res. **31**(1), 69–87 (1975)
24. Kingma, D.P., Ba, J.: Adam: A method for stochastic optimization. arXiv preprint arXiv:1412.6980 (2014)
25. Lang, S.D., Farine, D.R.: A multidimensional framework for studying social predation strategies. Nature Ecol. Evol. **1**(9), 1230–1239 (2017)
26. Lin, L.J.: Self-improving reactive agents based on reinforcement learning, planning and teaching. Mach. Learn. **8**(3), 293–321 (1992)
27. Lowe, R., Wu, Y.I., Tamar, A., Harb, J., Pieter Abbeel, O., Mordatch, I.: Multi-agent actor-critic for mixed cooperative-competitive environments. Advances in Neural Information Processing Systems 30 (2017)
28. Lührs, M.L., Dammhahn, M.: An unusual case of cooperative hunting in a solitary carnivore. J. Ethol. **28**(2), 379–383 (2010)

29. Macdonald, D.W.: The ecology of carnivore social behaviour. Nature **301**(5899), 379–384 (1983)
30. Mnih, V., et al.: Playing Atari with deep reinforcement learning. arXiv preprint arXiv:1312.5602 (2013)
31. Mnih, V., et al.: Human-level control through deep reinforcement learning. Nature **518**(7540), 529–533 (2015)
32. Mobbs, D., Wise, T., Suthana, N., Guzmán, N., Kriegeskorte, N., Leibo, J.Z.: Promises and challenges of human computational ethology. Neuron **109**(14), 2224–2238 (2021)
33. Moravčík, M., et al.: DeepStack: expert-level artificial intelligence in heads-up no-limit poker. Science **356**(6337), 508–513 (2017)
34. Mordatch, I., Abbeel, P.: Emergence of grounded compositional language in multi-agent populations. In: Proceedings of the AAAI Conference on Artificial Intelligence, vol. 32 (2018)
35. Olberg, R.M.: Visual control of prey-capture flight in dragonflies. Curr. Opin. Neurobiol. **22**(2), 267–271 (2012)
36. Packer, C., Ruttan, L.: The evolution of cooperative hunting. Am. Nat. **132**(2), 159–198 (1988)
37. Rasmussen, G.S., Gusset, M., Courchamp, F., Macdonald, D.W.: Achilles' heel of sociality revealed by energetic poverty trap in cursorial hunters. Am. Nat. **172**(4), 508–518 (2008)
38. Riedmiller, M., Gabel, T.: On experiences in a complex and competitive gaming domain: Reinforcement learning meets RoboCup. In: 2007 IEEE Symposium on Computational Intelligence and Games, pp. 17–23. IEEE (2007)
39. Schaul, T., Quan, J., Antonoglou, I., Silver, D.: Prioritized experience replay. arXiv preprint arXiv:1511.05952 (2015)
40. Scheel, D., Packer, C.: Group hunting behaviour of lions: a search for cooperation. Anim. Behav. **41**(4), 697–709 (1991)
41. Silver, D., et al.: Mastering the game of go without human knowledge. Nature **550**(7676), 354–359 (2017)
42. Stander, P.E.: Cooperative hunting in lions: the role of the individual. Behav. Ecol. Sociobiol. **29**(6), 445–454 (1992)
43. Sukhbaatar, S., Fergus, R., et al.: Learning multiagent communication with back-propagation. Advances in Neural Information Processing Systems 29 (2016)
44. Sutton, R.S., Barto, A.G.: Reinforcement learning: an introduction. MIT press (2018)
45. Tan, M.: Multi-agent reinforcement learning: Independent vs cooperative agents. In: Proceedings of the Tenth International Conference on Machine Learning, pp. 330–337 (1993)
46. Tesauro, G., et al.: Temporal difference learning and TD-gammon. Commun. ACM **38**(3), 58–68 (1995)
47. Tsutsui, K., Fujii, K., Kudo, K., Takeda, K.: Flexible prediction of opponent motion with internal representation in interception behavior. Biol. Cybern. **115**(5), 473–485 (2021). https://doi.org/10.1007/s00422-021-00891-9
48. Tsutsui, K., Shinya, M., Kudo, K.: Human navigational strategy for intercepting an erratically moving target in chase and escape interactions. J. Mot. Behav. **52**(6), 750–760 (2020)
49. Van Hasselt, H., Guez, A., Silver, D.: Deep reinforcement learning with double q-learning. In: Proceedings of the AAAI Conference on Artificial Intelligence, vol. 30 (2016)

50. Wang, Z., Schaul, T., Hessel, M., Hasselt, H., Lanctot, M., Freitas, N.: Dueling network architectures for deep reinforcement learning. In: International Conference on Machine Learning, pp. 1995–2003. PMLR (2016)
51. Wilson, A.M., et al.: Biomechanics of predator-prey arms race in lion, zebra, cheetah and impala. Nature **554**(7691), 183–188 (2018)

Computational Multimodal Models of Users' Interactional Trust in Multiparty Human-Robot Interaction

Marc Hulcelle[1](✉) (ID), Giovanna Varni[1](✉) (ID), Nicolas Rollet[2](ID),
and Chloé Clavel[1](✉)(ID)

[1] LTCI Laboratory, Télécom-Paris, Institut Polytechnique de Paris, 91123 Palaiseau,
France
{marc.hulcelle,giovanna.varni,chloe.clavel}@telecom-paris.fr
[2] 'Institut Interdisciplinaire de l'Innovation' Laboratory, Télécom-Paris, Institut
Polytechnique de Paris, 91123 Palaiseau, France
nicolas.rollet@telecom-paris.fr

Abstract. In this paper, we present multimodal computational models
of interactional trust in a humans-robot interaction scenario. We address
trust modeling as a binary as well as a multi-class classification problem.
We also investigate how early- and late-fusion of modalities impact trust
modeling. Our results indicate that early-fusion performs better in both
the binary and multi-class formulations, meaning that modalities have
co-dependencies when studying trust. We also run a SHapley Additive
exPlanation (SHAP) values analysis for a Random Forest in the binary
classification problem, as it is the model with the best results, to explore
which multimodal features are the most relevant to detect trust or mistrust.

Keywords: HRI · trust · affective computing

1 Introduction

Trust, as a psychological and sociological construct, plays a fundamental role
in the development and maintenance of relationships between individuals [1,22].
Previous work in human-automation interaction (HAI) - the research field on
interactions between robot workers and human operators - shows that trust has
an impact on the robot's acceptance by human users and the performance of the
interaction [28]. Trust research in Human-Robot Interaction (HRI) builds on top
of the foundations laid by the HAI community, with the additional constraint of
managing social interactions.

Trust in HRI is defined as a construct comprising a *cognitive* - the *"self-
efficacy to rely on capabilities and reliabilities of a specific party"* - and an *affective* - the *"self-efficacy on the party based on human affective responses to the
behavior of the party"* - dimension [37]. Studying cognitive trust (CT) requires
investigating task-related processes and functional communication, as was done
in HAI. Studying affective trust (AT) relies on the analysis of multimodal social

© Springer Nature Switzerland AG 2023
J.-J. Rousseau and B. Kapralos (Eds.): ICPR 2022 Workshops, LNCS 13643, pp. 225–239, 2023.
https://doi.org/10.1007/978-3-031-37660-3_16

signals exchanged by participants during an interaction, which impacts their representations and affects. This requires understanding the norms of a social interaction.

Previous definitions of trust rely on a psychological approach that defines it as a state of mind. Since one cannot have access to someone else's state of mind, trust can only be measured through questionnaires that are traditional measurement tools [37,39] generally filled by participants at the end of the interaction. They are, however, an obtrusive and subjective trust measurement tool [7]. Such user's trust assessment at the end of the interaction does not allow studying how trust builds and develops during an interaction.

Most studies on trust in HRI focused on dyadic interactions, and few studies on group interactions exist. But robots mostly face groups during in-the-wild interactions thus requiring to further study team trust in HRI. When participants gather to perform a joint task or achieve common objectives, emergent group states appear due to these continuous interactions, and develop over time [30]. These states regulate the social interactions between members [24]. Team trust is one of these states, and is defined as a *"shared psychological state among team members comprising willingness to accept vulnerability based on positive expectations of a specific other or others"* [13,15]. Team trust also comprises a cognitive and an affective dimension [35].

In this paper we present multimodal computational models of trust in multiparty HRI grounding on a sociological approach. According to sociological theories [12,14,18], we focus on *interactional trust* defined as a state of the participant displaying a form of naturalness - implying that the robot is treated as an interactional partner in the same way as a human partner would be treated -, or fluidity in the interaction [19]. Fluidity relies on several skills from both parties such as linguistic ones, epistemic and empathetic. When interacting with a robot, the participant expects the robot to have a basic set of skills from those previously mentioned to have a meaningful interaction. In this way, interactional trust encapsulates both CT and AT.

To the best of our knowledge, this work is the first to study trust in HRI based on Interactional Sociology theories. We changed the standard approach to model trust in HRI through Psychology to ground this study on Sociology as we aimed to provide a better explanation on how interactional norms shape the participants' trust.

The major contributions of this paper are as follows:

- We present computational models of interactional trust in a mutiparty humans and robot scenario. More specifically, we address the problem of trust classification as a multi-class (trust, mistrust, neutral) and binary one-vs-rest problem.
- We explore how early- and late-fusion of modalities impact trust modeling.
- Starting from the classification results, we investigate which multimodal features can be the most effective to detect trust or mistrust.

2   Background and Related Work

2.1   Trust Definitions

Previous studies in HRI exploit the definitions of trust provided by Psychology that defines it as a construct comprised of two *static* components - the user's propensity to trust, and the other party's trustworthiness - and two *dynamic* ones - the user's CT, and its AT [37]. For instance, when collaborating with a cooking robot holding a knife, CT would be linked to the user's perception of the robot's skills in cutting vegetables, while AT would be linked to the user's feeling of safety. There is extensive research on CT which was shown to be mostly affected by the robot's competence and skills. AT, on the other hand, is mostly affected by social norm violations. The understanding of AT dynamics is still relatively low. In the remainder of this paper, when referring to other work, we will speak of trust on its own only when authors do not specify what type of trust they are referring to.

For this work, we rely on an operational definition of interactional trust from the coding scheme TURIN [19] as a *"form of affiliation and credit characterized by a set of behaviors that are intentional or not, expressive or propositional"*. This definition allows us to interpret behaviors based on the social and competence credit they give to the robot, and recognize human behaviors that include the robot as a putative autonomous participant inside the social interaction as signs of trust. When interacting with a human partner, an individual produces pre-reflexively - i.e. without thinking about them - social behaviors that indicate whether he trusts his partner. It is the pre-reflexive aspect of an individual's behavior that allows fluidity and synchrony to happen during an interaction [9]. When interacting with a robot, these pre-reflexive behaviors convey a stronger sense of trust - even stronger the more anthropomorphic the robot is [23] - since they imply that the robot is treated as a fully autonomous interactional partner in the same way as a human partner. Synchrony and fluidity then become indicators of trust towards the robot. For instance, making a joke with - and not about - the robot is a form of competence credit, i.e. a sign of trust that the robot understands it. Interrupting the robot for a clarification on an explanation is another sign of social credit, as the user trusts the robot to understand the conversational norm violation to provide further explanation.

2.2   Trust Modeling

Research on automated analysis of users' trust dynamics is scarce. Most studies in HRI focus on how the robot's behaviors impact the user's final decision to trust it. Very few studies worked on how participants display trust through their behaviors, for both CT and AT. Lee et al. [27] investigated specific behaviors - posture, smile, and eye - and how they affect the participant's decision to trust its partner in a Prisoner's Dilemma scenario, both in a Human-Human (HH) and in a Human-Robot (HR) interaction. They train Hidden-Markov-Models (HMM) to incorporate the temporal dynamics of trust based on the occurrences of previously identified high trust and low trust signals. One HMM is trained to model interactions resulting in a low trust level and another one for interactions resulting in a high trust level. This separate training revealed different patterns of behaviors for both conditions. This study, however, only focuses on the final decision to trust the partner and does not take into account the evolution of trust through the interaction. While Lee et al. shed light on the temporal sequence of these high-level behaviors relating to trust, research on trust could benefit from further research on the interplay of less specific behaviors.

Khalid et al. [21] studied less specific behaviors of humans by analyzing psycho-physiological correlates to trust in Human-Robot-Human Interaction. The authors model trust through 3 categories - Ability, Benevolence, and Integrity as defined by Mayer [31] - and build a neuro-fuzzy ensemble to classify against the trust categories. They train their model using multimodal features such as facial expressions, heart rate measures, prosody and ethnicity of the participant. While they provide a set of modalities that are relevant to model trust, they did not study the links between modalities and the three categories they used to model trust. This study also focuses on a single evaluation of trust measured only at the end of the interaction.

Some other studies focus on the evolution of trust during a collaborative interaction with a computer or a robot [25,40]. The first work focuses on the degree of reliance on the robot's analysis for an annotation task, whereas the second one studies how proactive the robot should be during the collaboration depending on the user's trust. These studies do not focus, however, on the multimodal behaviors of their users to determine whether their trust increases or decreases, but use proxy performance measures instead.

To the best of our knowledge, this study is the first to model interactional trust in a mixed human-robot team through multimodal features, and investigate how modality fusion impacts trust modeling.

3   Methodology

3.1   Dataset

We chose the Vernissage dataset as our experimental test-bed [20]. It is a multimodal and multiparty dataset, in which 2 humans interact with a NAO robot. The dataset is composed of 10 group interactions. The interactions comprise 3 phases: first, the robot explains paintings hanged at the walls of a room (*vernissage*), then asks the participants to present themselves with more information than simply their name (*self-presentation*), and finally quizzes them on art (*art-quizz*). Since Nao is a highly anthropomorphized robot, participants behave closely to how they would with a human art guide. Vernissage features recordings of the interactions with four video views (three front views including Nao's camera, and a rear view, all captured at 50hz), separate audio files for each user, head-motion for each user captured using a motion-capture Vicon system at 100hz, and logs of the robot's movements.

In this study, we selected the *vernissage* (average length: 3 min 46 s $\pm$ 10.5 s) and the *self-presentation* (average length: 1 min 53 s $\pm$ 17.2 s) steps. We thus have, in total, 10 interactions that last in average 5 min 39 s ($\pm$20.3 s).

3.2   Annotations

We collected annotations using the TURIN coding scheme [19]. As explained in Sect. 2.1, it is the pre-reflexive aspect of behavior production that allows annotators to analyze the participants' social behaviors as observable phenomenon during the annotation process [18]. Indeed, as they are engaged in a social interaction that follows normative rules, participants express pre-reflexive actions and reasonings that can be interpreted by external observers since these follow interactional norms - e.g. when saying hello first, the partner is expected to return the greeting.

The coding scheme therefore unitizes the interaction into segments of coherent trust category and provides three different labels: *Trusting, Neutral,* and *Mistrusting.* The Trusting label is assigned to segments during which participants display interactional trust, friendliness, accept vulnerability, or acknowledge the partner's competence (in our case, the robot). Accepting vulnerability and acknowledging the partner's competence are elements found in Rousseau's and Mayer's definition of trust [31,36]. Friendliness can be seen as a positive expectation of reciprocity from the partner, which is in line with Rousseau's definition. Segments during which the participants display uneasiness, doubt, confusion, aggressiveness, or unwillingness to cooperate are assigned the Mistrusting label. The Neutral label is assigned to all other segments of the interaction. As mentioned in [19], TURIN was validated by two experts in HRI who annotated a subset of Vernissage. The Cohen's Kappa Inter-Rater Agreement (IRA) are as follows: $\kappa = .45$ for "Neutral" (moderate agreement); "Trusting": $\kappa = .64$; "Mistrusting": $\kappa = .79$ (substantial agreement). Given the agreement, one of the experts then annotated the phases of the interaction we decided to focus on.

Some segments are over 20 s long. We decided to divide long segments into several sub-segments to have a better homogeneity when aggregating features over a segment. The new maximum length is thus the average length of segments. Annotated segments are then divided into smaller segments of at most 5 s, segments smaller than 600 milliseconds are dropped out. Such segments are too short and noisy for feature aggregation because of some sensors' sampling frequency. A summary of collected annotations can be found in Table 1, as well as the resulting segments after post-processing. Once done, features are aggregated on the resulting segments.

3.3   Feature Extraction

We automatically and manually extracted features from three modalities: face, body, and voice. We selected features that are generally used to characterize social interactions, e.g. [2,17,21]. We also included other features based on a preliminary analysis of the annotations. Indeed, facial expressions, nods, and

230   M. Hulcelle et al.

Table 1. Summary of annotations collected using TURIN.

Label	Count	Segment length (Avg $\pm std$)
Trusting	193/240	3.7 s $\pm$ 4.9 s/3.0 s $\pm$ 1.5 s
Neutral	260/604	9.5 s $\pm$ 8.8 s/4.1 s $\pm$ 1.4 s
Mistrusting	75/78	2.8 s $\pm$ 2.5 s/2.6 s $\pm$ 1.6 s

Collected   annotations/Annotations   after   sub-segmentation

gesture were the most frequent behavioral cues that were considered relevant during the annotating process.

We extracted features from: (i) each participant (human/robot); (ii) dyads (human-human as well as human/robot); and (iii) the group as a whole (see Fig. 1).

Here in the following we provide details about the features.

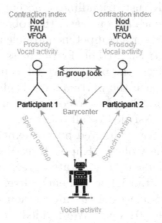

Fig. 1. Model of the group interaction with extracted features.

Face. We extracted Facial Action Units (FAU) using OpenFace [3]. We selected the intensity values of Action Units (AU) 1, 2, 4, 5, 6, 7, 9, 10, 12, 14, 15, 20, and 23. We excluded the FAUs that were not activated at least once during the interactions. FAUs were then filtered using a Savitsky-Golay (SG) filter (window length = 11, polyorder = 3) to reduce noise.

As our working definition of trust is based on the affiliation and credit given to the partner, following the robot's presentation is a sign of trust. The VFOA is therefore an effective cue to study trust. VFOA were manually annotated for both human participants following the labels originally suggested by authors of Vernissage: *left painting, central painting, right painting, Nao, other participant, other, unclear.* VFOA were represented trough a binary indicator of presence or absence of each label during the segment (Bag-Of-Words BOW) for each participant. Then, the time percentage of in-group look was computed, as well as the number of VFOA changes per participant.

Nods were manually annotated for each participant. We then computed the time percentage of nods during a segment.

Body. The dataset provides 3D head poses/rotations of both participants recorded through a Vicon system. We applied an SG filter (window length = 21, polyorder = 3) to reduce noise on the raw signal. We then computed the barycenter of the triangle shaped by both the participants and Nao, and kept the 2D point projected on the floor plane. This gives us the distance between the human participants, and the distance between human participants and the robot.

Skeleton pose extraction by OpenPose [5] resulted in unstable and noisy data. We used more traditional computer-vision-based techniques to extract body movement features. With OpenCV, we extracted the bounding box of each participant and their silhouette to compute their contraction index [4] based on the rear camera view. The contraction index is the ratio between the area of a body's silhouette and its bounding box. Extracted features were cleaned through an SG filter (window length = 11, polyorder = 3).

Voice. The Vernissage dataset provides annotations on all parties' vocal activity. While Nao's annotations are limited to speech and silence, participants' also include laughter. Vocal activity was represented in a BOW similarly to VFOA. Then, the time-percentage of speech overlap between both participants and the robot is computed.

Finally, we computed prosody-related features. We extracted GeMAPS features [10] using OpenSMILE [11], and kept the F0 (normalized for each speaker), loudness, jitter, shimmer, and spectral flux features. Khalid et al. [21] showed that these prosody features are correlated to trust. We reduced the noise of the extracted features using an SG filter (window length = 21, polyorder = 3).

As previously mentioned, we also investigate the interaction between modalities by aggregating features in 2 different manners: early-fusion, and late-fusion. Thus, we aggregated all the extracted features together by computing the mean and standard deviation of the values. This results in a single feature vector having a length equal to 107 to implement early-fusion. Concerning late-fusion, we aggregated together the features belonging to the same modality. This results in 3 separate feature vectors for the face, body, and voice modalities of respective length 70, 8, and 29.

3.4 Model Design

We formulate the trust classification problem in 2 different ways: (i) a One-vs-Rest (OVR) classification task; and (ii) a 3-class classification task. We train the classifiers to predict the label assigned to the segments obtained by the annotation process. Classes correspond to each of the labels from the TURIN coding scheme. Each of these labels correspond to the emergent trust of the group.

Modalities are aggregated in 2 different ways - early-fusion and late-fusion - to study the role of each modality and their co-dependence. We train several machine learning algorithms - Random Forest (RF), Support Vector Machine Classifier (SMV-C), and Multi-Layer Perceptron (MLP) - for both classification tasks, and in early and late-fusion settings. In the late-fusion setting, the outputs for each modality's model are averaged to produce the final output. As SVM doesn't natively support multi-class classification, we trained it as an OVR too. We based our algorithm selection on an explainability criterion. At first, we trained a Ridge classifier. As the results were close to a random vote, hinting that the relations between features are not linear, we included an MLP to study this non-linearity. The SMV-C's learning is based on kernel trick which transforms the data to find an optimal boundary to separate classes. The kernel function choice can generate insight on the input data and the relation between features. The RF's algorithmic design naturally creates interpretability.

4   Results

4.1   Classification Results

We used a leave-3 groups-out (LTGO) cross validation to tune the models' hyper-parameters as well as to evaluate their performances. This enables a reduction of the variance of the performances providing a better overview of the generalization of the models. Since we draw 3 interactions out of a total of 10, this results in 120 rounds of test. The ROC-AUC metric was chosen as it provides a broader view of a model's performance given that it captures the trade-off between precision and recall. We also used the F1 score for the multi-class classification problem. All the models were developed and evaluated using Python's scikit-learn package [34]. As the classes are heavily imbalanced as shown in Table 1, We augmented data using SMOTE [6] to obtain a balanced dataset. Data augmentation was performed after the LTGO division.

Tables 2 and 3 summarize the results.

We conducted a series of statistical tests to compare the classifiers' performance and check for possible statistical differences between them. We used a Kruskal-Wallis test (KW) [26] followed by a post-hoc Dunn test (when needed) [8] to compare all models in either early- or late-fusion, with Bonferroni correction. We conducted a Wilcoxon-Mann-Whitney test (WMW) [41] to compare the performance of a model between early- and late-fusion. For the OVR method, we compared models in a single binary classification task (e.g. trusting-vs-rest for early- against late-fusion, or trusting-vs-rest for RF against MLP against SVM-C). We conducted all of our tests using an alpha value of .05. Figures 2 and 3 sum up all the p-values of our tests.

OVR method: the KW tests point significant differences between the models in early-fusion for Mistrusting-vs-rest, $H = 40.76, p < .001$, Neutral-vs-rest,

Table 2. ROC-AUC test scores of OVR classifiers

Early-fusion	RF	MLP	SMV-C
Trusting-vs-rest	**0.72** ± 0.04	0.70 ± 0.04	**0.74** ± 0.04
Neutral-vs-rest	**0.77** ± 0.04	0.74 ± 0.04	0.75 ± 0.04
Mistrusting-vs-rest	**0.59** ± 0.06	0.54 ± 0.07	**0.58** ± 0.06
Late-fusion			
Trusting-vs-rest	**0.67** ± 0.04	0.60 ± 0.04	**0.66** ± 0.04
Neutral-vs-rest	**0.74** ± 0.04	0.65 ± 0.04	0.70 ± 0.03
Mistrusting-vs-rest	**0.54** ± 0.08	0.48 ± 0.08	0.49 ± 0.10

Table 3. f1 test scores of multi-class classifiers. Rand.: Random Classifier. Maj.: Majority-voting Classifier

Fusion	Rand.	Maj.	RF	MLP	SMV-C
Early	0.38 ± 0.03	0.52 ± 0.05	**0.66** ± 0.04	**0.65** ± 0.04	0.60 ± 0.04
Late	0.38 ± 0.03	0.52 ± 0.05	**0.62** ± 0.03	0.60 ± 0.04	**0.61** ± 0.05

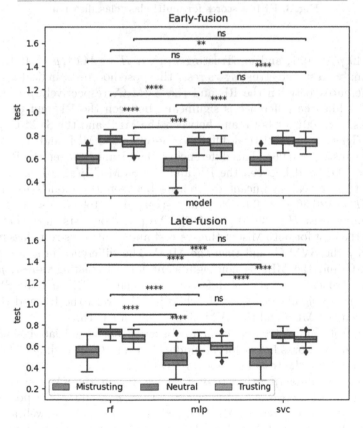

Fig. 2. Boxplot of all models' ROC-AUC test scores in OVR classification. **** $p <$ .0001; *** $p < $.001; ** $p < $.01; * $p < $.05; ns: Non Signficant

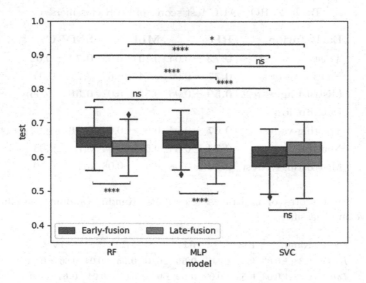

Fig. 3. F1 test scores for multi-class classification.

$H = 28.49, p < .001$, and for Trusting-vs-rest, $H = 44.61, p < .001$. In both Mistrusting-vs-rest and Trusting-vs-rest, the post-hoc tests indicate no significant differences between the RF and the SVM-C, respectively $p = 0.16$ and $p = 0.28$, while the difference is significant between the RF and the MLP in both tasks, $p < .001$ for both, and between the MLP and the SVM-C, $p < .001$ for both. There is no statistical difference between the MLP and the SVM-C in Neutral-vs-rest, $p = 0.065$. This difference is significant between the RF and the MLP, $p < .001$, and between the RF and the SVM-C, $p < .01$ In late-fusion, the KW tests reveal significant differences between the models for Trusting-vs-rest, $H = 126.36, p < .001$, Neutral-vs-rest, $H = 169.65, p < .001$, and for Mistrusting-vs-rest $H = 35.30, p < .001$. The post-hoc tests show that the RF performs the best for both Mistrusting-vs-rest and Neutral-vs-rest classifications, followed by the SVM-C, and then the MLP. The difference in scores between the SVM-C and the MLP is non significant for Mistrusting-vs-rest, $p = .90$. Regarding Trusting-vs-rest, the difference between the RF and the SVM-C is not statistically significant, $p = .24$, while it is between the RF and the MLP, and between the MLP and the SVM-C, $p < .001$ for both.

A series of WMW tests to compare between early and late-fusion reveals that early-fusion works better for all models in every OVR task, $p < .001$ for all models. Results of the tests are shown in Table 4.

Multi-class classification task: for early-fusion, the KW test showed significant difference between models, $H = 104.76, p < .001$. The post-hoc test indicated a difference between MLP and SMV-C, $p < .001$, as well as between RF and SMV-C, $p < .001$, but showed no significant difference between RF and MLP, $p = .54$. For late-fusion, the KW test revealed a difference between models,

Table 4. WMW test results to compare between early and late-fusion for all models in all OVR tasks.

	RF	MLP	SVM-C
Trusting-vs-rest	$U = 2784$	$U = 817$	$U = 1366$
Neutral-vs-rest	$U = 3772$	$U = 986$	$U = 2077$
Mistrusting-vs-rest	$U = 4332$	$U = 4183$	$U = 3101$

For all tests, we have $p < 0.0001$

$H = 25.15, p < .001$. This difference is statistically significant between RF and MLP, $p < .001$, and RF and SMV-C, $p < .05$, but not between MLP and SMV-C, $p = .069$, according to the Dunn test. When comparing between early and late-fusion for each model, a series of WMW test showed that early-fusion yields better results for the RF, $U = 3715, p < .001$, the MLP, $U = 2359, p < .001$, but not for the SMV-C, $U = 6448, p = .081$.

The analysis shows that models perform better in an early-fusion setting. This means that early-fusion captures the interactions between modalities better than late-fusion does, albeit in a simple way. Considering that the RF is the best performing model in the OVR task, we analyzed how each modality's model performs individually in late-fusion. A series of KW tests revealed significant performance difference between modalities for Trusting-vs-rest, $H = 187.48, p < .001$, for Neutral-vs-rest, $H = 288.62, p < .001$, and for Mistrusting-vs-rest, $H = 150.93, p < .001$. For all OVR tasks, the post-hoc Dunn tests showed that the RF trained only on the voice modality performs better, followed by the RF trained on face modality, and finally the RF for the body, $p < .05$ for all (Table 5).

Table 5. ROC-AUC test scores of RF trained separately on the Body, Face, and Voice modalities in OVR classification.

	Body	Face	Voice
Trusting-vs-rest	0.54 ± 0.05	0.62 ± 0.04	**0.65 ± 0.05**
Neutral-vs-rest	0.57 ± 0.03	0.65 ± 0.03	**0.73 ± 0.05**
Mistrusting-vs-rest	0.46 ± 0.08	0.51 ± 0.06	**0.60 ± 0.07**

4.2 Feature Importance

We conducted a SHapley Additive exPlanation (SHAP) [29] values analysis for the random forest with early-fusion, since it gave the best results as shown in Sect. 4.1, to determine the importance of features in the classification task. SHAP values interpret the impact on the model's output of a given feature having a certain value compared to the model's prediction if that feature took some baseline value, e.g. its mean. When there are correlated features, only one of them appears in the SHAP values. We present the analysis' results by modality. About the face modality, participants lower their brows more (higher mean and std of AU4) during mistrusting segments than other segments, talk (higher mean and std of AU10), and change their VFOA more. During trusting segments, participants nod more often, tighten their lid more (higher mean of AU7), while nose wrinkles (higher mean of AU9) plays against classification as trusting. Higher std of the lip corner depressor (AU15) plays against classification as neutral.

Concerning body, the distance of the group to the robot is the most important feature of trust. Greater mean distance to the robot has a positive impact when classifying as mistrusting, while closeness to it has more weight for trusting segments. This result confirms the findings in the literature [32]. When considering between-participants distance, a lower std value has a positive impact for trusting segments. As for the contraction index, its std plays a more important role than its mean value during a segment, with lower std being associated to neutral segments, while higher std are linked to trust.

Regarding the voice, neutral segments are linked to situations where participants are silent. Lower F0 means have a positive impact on classification as trusting, and higher F0 means have more weight for neutral segments. Higher speech overlap time between participants and Nao have a strong impact when classifying as mistrusting.

4.3 Discussion

The SHAP values analysis shows that participants exhibit different behaviors depending on whether they trust the robot or not. Participants in trusting segments tend be closer to the robot, more aligned with the robot's presentation, move and talk more. In mistrusting segments, participants also talk, but they talk more over the robot. They also show signs of doubt through brows lowering, looking around, getting closer together, and being further away from the robot. As for neutral segments, participants are mostly silent and listen to the robot speaking, remain still, and have neutral facial expressions.

The SHAP analysis demonstrated the importance of the participants' distance to the robot. The barycenter feature was shown to be important, while the contraction index feature had a moderate impact on the model's output. However, the series of statistical tests conducted in Sect. 4.1 on the late-fusion OVR task for RF showed that the body modality yields the lowest results. Considering that our set of body features is small, it could be enriched with other features - e.g. deictic gestures - to better model the interaction and improve the computational models' performance.

Our definition of IT is based on concepts of alignment, affiliation and credit [19,38]. During the annotation, annotators focused on social signals to describe the alignment dimension that can also be found in other social phenomenon, in particular engagement [33]. Further investigation on the link between engagement and IT is planned in future work.

5   Conclusion and Future Work

In this paper, we presented computational models of trust whose inputs are multimodal features of a group interaction, and explored how modality fusion impacts the models' performance. The analysis conducted in Sect. 4 shows that the early-fusion setting yields better results than the late-fusion one. In the OVR classification task, the RF had the best performance, while both SVM-C and RF achieved the best performance for the multi-class classification task. For all models in the OVR task, the mistrusting-vs-rest task produced the lowest performances.

We conducted a SHAP value analysis to reveal behaviors exhibited in trusting, mistrusting, and neutral segments. Voice features, specific FAUs, and participants' distance to the robot had the most impact on the classifiers' output. In a future study, we aim to investigate another set of body features.

We plan on improving our computational model of users' trust by integrating the history of the interaction through sequential models based on Deep Learning techniques. In this work, indeed, we modeled the interaction only at the feature level computing them on each segment. We thus focused on social interaction descriptors for interpretability. Although our model achieved fair performances, it takes each segment as independent from other ones. Taking into account a part or the whole history of the interaction will allow us to include the trigger event of the users' mistrust (e.g., the robot's failure) in the prediction. This was previously impossible as mistrusting segments do not systematically include the robot's failure.

Finally, it has been shown that trust depends on the context of the interaction (e.g., its goal and its setup) [16]. As the context changes, so do the participants' behaviors. The Vernissage scenario fosters a multimodal rich dialogue between the robot and humans. Dialogue is an every-day life activity that is at the core of most interactions. However, there are different ways of handling a dialogue: one where the robot takes the lead such as in Vernissage, one where the robot answers questions similarly to home-assistant robots, and a last one in free-form conversation. Further investigation is thus needed to study the generalization of our approach.

Acknowledgment. This work is supported by the Data Science and Artificial Intelligence for Digitalized Industry and Services (DSAIDIS) chair of Télécom Paris, and the European project H2020 ANIMATAS (ITN 7659552).

References

1. Aroyo, A.M., et al.: Overtrusting robots: setting a research agenda to mitigate overtrust in automation. Paladyn, J. Beh. Robot. **12**(1), 423–436 (2021)
2. Atamna, A., Clavel, C.: HRI-RNN: a user-robot dynamics-oriented RNN for engagement decrease detection. In: Proceedings of the Annual Conference of the International Speech Communication Association, INTERSPEECH, vol. 2020-Oct., pp. 4198–4202 (2020)

3. Baltrusaitis, T., Zadeh, A., Lim, Y.C., Morency, L.P.: OpenFace 2.0: facial behavior analysis toolkit. In: 2018 13th IEEE International Conference on Automatic Face and Gesture Recognition (FG 2018), pp. 59–66 (2018)
4. Camurri, A., Mazzarino, B., Volpe, G.: Analysis of expressive gesture: the eyesweb expressive gesture processing library. In: Camurri, A., Volpe, G. (eds.) Gesture-Based Communication in Human-Computer Interaction, pp. 460–467 (2004)
5. Cao, Z., Hidalgo, G., Simon, T., Wei, S.E., Sheikh, Y.: Realtime multi-person 2D pose estimation using part affinity fields. In: Proceedings of the IEEE Conference on Computer Vision and Pattern Recognition (CVPR), pp. 7291–7299 (2017)
6. Chawla, N.V., Bowyer, K.W., Hall, L.O., Kegelmeyer, W.P.: SMOTE: synthetic minority over-sampling technique. J. Artif. Intell. Res. **16**, 321–357 (2002)
7. Chita-Tegmark, M., Law, T., Rabb, N., Scheutz, M.: Can you trust your trust measure? In: Proceedings of the 2021 ACM/IEEE International Conference on Human-Robot Interaction, pp. 92–100 (2021)
8. Dunn, O.J.: Multiple comparisons using rank sums. Technometrics **6**(3), 241–252 (1964)
9. Duranti, A.: The Anthropology of Intentions: Language in a World of Others. Cambridge University Press, Cambridge (2015)
10. Eyben, F., et al.: The Geneva minimalistic acoustic parameter set (gemaps) for voice research and affective computing. IEEE Trans. Affect. Comput. **7**(2), 190–202 (2016)
11. Eyben, F., Wöllmer, M., Schuller, B.: Opensmile: the Munich versatile and fast open-source audio feature extractor. In: Proceedings of the 18th ACM International Conference on Multimedia, pp. 1459–1462 (2010)
12. Ford, C., Thompson, S.: Interactional units in conversation: syntactic, intonational and pragmatic resources. In: Interaction and Grammar, p. 134 (1996)
13. Fulmer, C.A., Gelfand, M.J.: At what level (and in whom) we trust: trust across multiple organizational levels. J. Manag. **38**(4), 1167–1230 (2012)
14. Goodwin, C.: Conversational organization. Interaction between speakers and hearers (1981)
15. Grossman, R., Friedman, S.B., Kalra, S.: Teamwork processes and emergent states. In: The Wiley Blackwell Handbook of the Psychology of Team Working and Collaborative Processes, pp. 243–269. Wiley, March 2017
16. Hancock, P.A., Billings, D.R., Schaefer, K.E., Chen, J.Y.C., de Visser, E.J., Parasuraman, R.: A meta-analysis of factors affecting trust in human-robot interaction. Hum. Fact. J. Hum. Fact. Ergon. Soc. **53**(5), 517–527 (2011)
17. Hemamou, L., Felhi, G., Vandenbussche, V., Martin, J.C., Clavel, C.: HireNet: a hierarchical attention model for the automatic analysis of asynchronous video job interviews. In: Proceedings of the AAAI Conference on Artificial Intelligence, vol. 33, pp. 573–581, July 2019
18. Heritage, J.C.: International accountability: a conversation analytic perspective. Réseaux. Communication-Technologie-Société **8**(1), 23–49 (1990)
19. Hulcelle, M., Varni, G., Rollet, N., Clavel, C.: Turin: a coding system for trust in human robot interaction. In: 2021 9th International Conference on Affective Computing and Intelligent Interaction (ACII), pp. 1–8 (2021)
20. Jayagopi, D.B., et al.: The vernissage corpus: a conversational Human-Robot-Interaction dataset. ACM/IEEE International Conference on Human-Robot Interaction, pp. 149–150 (2013)
21. Khalid, H.M., et al.: Exploring psycho-physiological correlates to trust: implications for human-robot-human interaction. In: Proceedings of the Human Factors and Ergonomics Society Annual Meeting, vol. 60, no. 1, pp. 697–701 (2016)

22. Khavas, Z.R.: A review on trust in human-robot interaction (2021). https://arxiv.org/abs/2105.10045
23. Khavas, Z.R., Ahmadzadeh, S.R., Robinette, P.: Modeling trust in human-robot interaction: a survey. In: Wagner, A.R., et al. (eds.) ICSR 2020. LNCS (LNAI), vol. 12483, pp. 529–541. Springer, Cham (2020). https://doi.org/10.1007/978-3-030-62056-1_44
24. Kozlowski, S.W., Ilgen, D.R.: Enhancing the effectiveness of work groups and teams. Psychol. Sci. Public Interest **7**(3), 77–124 (2006)
25. Kraus, M., Wagner, N., Minker, W.: Modelling and predicting trust for developing proactive dialogue strategies in mixed-initiative interaction. In: Proceedings of the 2021 International Conference on Multimodal Interaction, pp. 131–140 (2021)
26. Kruskal, W.H., Wallis, W.A.: Use of ranks in one-criterion variance analysis. J. Am. Stat. Assoc. **47**(260), 583–621 (1952)
27. Lee, J.J., Knox, B., Baumann, J., Breazeal, C., DeSteno, D.: Computationally modeling interpersonal trust. Front. Psychol. 4 (2013)
28. Lee, J.D., See, K.A.: Trust in automation: designing for appropriate reliance Human Factors. Hum. Factors **46**(1), 50–80 (2004)
29. Lundberg, S.M., Lee, S.I.: A unified approach to interpreting model predictions. In: Advances in Neural Information Processing Systems, vol. 30 (2017)
30. Marks, M.A., Mathieu, J.E., Zaccaro, S.J.: A temporally based framework and taxonomy of team processes. Acad. Manag. Rev. **26**(3), 356–376 (2001)
31. Mayer, R.C., Davis, J.H., Schoorman, F.D.: An integrative model of organizational trust. Acad. Manag. Rev. **20**(3), 709–735 (1995)
32. Mumm, J., Mutlu, B.: Human-robot proxemics: physical and psychological distancing in human-robot interaction. In: HRI 2011 - Proceedings of the 6th ACM/IEEE International Conference on Human-Robot Interaction, pp. 331–338 (2011)
33. Oertel, C., et al.: Engagement in human-agent interaction: an overview. Front. Roboti. AI 7 (2020)
34. Pedregosa, F., et al.: Scikit-learn: machine learning in Python. J. Mach. Learn. Res. **12**, 2825–2830 (2011)
35. Rapp, T., Maynard, T., Domingo, M., Klock, E.: Team emergent states: What has emerged in the literature over 20 years. Small Group Res. **52**, 68–102 (2021)
36. Rousseau, D.M., Sitkin, S.B., Burt, R.S., Camerer, C., Rousseau, D.M., Burt, R.S.: Not So Different After All?: a Cross-Discipline View of Trust. Acad. Manag. Rev. **23**(3), 393–404 (1998)
37. Schaefer, K.E.: The Perception and Measurement of Human-robot Trust. Doctoral Dissertation. University of Central Florida, Orlando (2013)
38. Stivers, T.: Stance, alignment, and affiliation during storytelling: when nodding is a token of affiliation. Res. Lang. Soc. Interact. **41**(1), 31–57 (2008)
39. Syrdal, D.S., Dautenhahn, K., Koay, K.L., Walters, M.L.: The negative attitudes towards robots scale and reactions to robot behaviour in a live human-robot interaction study. In: Adaptive and emergent behaviour and complex systems (2009)
40. Tutul, A.A., Nirjhar, E.H., Chaspari, T.: Investigating trust in human-machine learning collaboration: a pilot study on estimating public anxiety from speech. In: Proceedings of the 2021 International Conference on Multimodal Interaction, pp. 288–296 (2021)
41. Wilcoxon, F.: Individual comparisons by ranking methods. Biomet. Bull. **1**(6), 80–83 (1945)

An Exploratory Study on Group Potency Classification from Non-verbal Social Behaviours

Nicola Corbellini[1]($\boxtimes$) (iD), Eleonora Ceccaldi[1] (iD), Giovanna Varni[2] (iD), and Gualtiero Volpe[1] (iD)

[1] Casa Paganini, InfoMus, DIBRIS, University of Genoa, Genoa, Italy
{nicola.corbellini,eleonora.ceccaldi}@edu.unige.it,
gualtiero.volpe@unige.it
[2] LTCI, Télécom Paris, Institut polytechnique de Paris, S91120 Palaiseau, France
giovanna.varni@telecom-paris.fr

Abstract. Technological research is increasingly focusing on intelligent computer systems that can elicit collaboration in groups made of a mix of humans and machines. These systems have to devise appropriate strategies of intervention in the joint action, a capability that requires them to be able of sensing group processes such as emergent states. Among those, group potency – i.e., the confidence a group has that it can be effective – has a particular relevance. An intervention targeted at increasing potency can indeed increment the overall performance of the group. As an initial step in this direction, this work addresses automated classification of potency from multimodal group behaviour. Interactions by 16 different groups displaying low or high potency were extracted from 3 already existing datasets: AMI, TA2, and GAME-ON. Logistic Regression, Support Vector Machines, and Random Forests were used for classification. Results show that all the classifiers can predict potency, and that a classifier trained with samples from 2 of the datasets can predict the label of a sample from the third dataset. . . .

Keywords: group behaviour · group effectiveness · group potency · emergent states · hybrid intelligence

1 Introduction

In the last decades, social sciences have often focused on groups – as defined in [24] – not only to understand their functioning, but also with the goal of improving their performance. Specific attention has been devoted to a category of psychological constructs: *emergent states* [35]. They are dynamic constructs that emerge from groups members' actions and interactions. Examples of emergent states are: cohesion, group potency and efficacy, and interpersonal trust [42]. Emergent states can have an influence on the group and on its functioning. Group potency, for instance, is a motivational emergent state characterizing the confidence a group has of being effective, independently from the task [17]. Potency

J.-J. Rousseau and B. Kapralos (Eds.): ICPR 2022 Workshops, LNCS 13643, pp. 240–255, 2023.
https://doi.org/10.1007/978-3-031-37660-3_17

can be inferred from different behaviours, such as engagement and commitment in the task or encouraging expressions (e.g., "we can do it!") [17]. Moreover, it is linked to effectiveness and can positively affect group performance (e.g., [16]).

With the advance of human centered technologies and their increasing role in social scenarios, research perspectives are emerging towards the development of intelligent computer systems able to encourage collaboration in groups made by a mix of humans and machines (e.g., [32,46]). To become effective teammates, these systems need to devise appropriate strategies of intervention to participate in a group and improve its performance. A first step to achieve this purpose is to endow them with the capability of sensing group processes and resulting emergent states. In this context, group potency is an ideal candidate to start with: an artificial teammate whose intervention elicits increased group potency can exploit the link with effectiveness to get a positive impact on performance.

This work addresses automated classification of groups displaying low vs high potency from multimodal non-verbal group behaviour such as turn-taking and the kinetic energy of a group as a whole. Our study focuses on high potency scores, since it has been shown that people tend to overestimate their group potency. Specifically, Woodley et al. [52] suggested that people suffer the "better-than-average" bias, having high expectations from their group. They showed that, on average, potency decreases over time (e.g. 6 months), as group members deal with interactions and conflicts, getting an actual understanding of their group capabilities. For this purpose, group interactions were extracted from 3 existing datasets (AMI [39], TA2 [9], and GAME-ON [33]), targeting different tasks, different settings (e.g., seated vs. standing), and different size (from 3 to 4 participants). The interactions were then manually annotated for potency and used for training 3 machine learning techniques, namely Logistic Regression, Support Vector Machine, and Random Forest. Performance were assessed by means of a Leave-One-Group-Out cross-validation. The possible effect of the 3 datasets on the robustness and adaptability of the models was also analyzed through a Leave-One-Dataset-Out cross-validation.

This paper brings the following major contributions: it addresses potency in a multimodal fashion by exploiting speech and movement features; it investigates machine learning models to classify group interactions in terms of low vs. high potency; it runs an in-depth cross-dataset validation to show the robustness of the approach across different datasets.

The paper is organized as follows: Sect. 2 provides theoretical knowledge about group potency and discusses some computational approaches to emergent states; Sect. 3 describes how interactions from the 3 original datasets were collected to build the dataset for the study; Sect. 4 discusses how interactions were annotated, the features that were extracted, and how models were trained and evaluated; Sect. 5 is about the obtained results; finally, in Sect. 6 results are discussed and conclusion drawn.

2   Background and Related Work

2.1   Group Potency

Guzzo and colleagues defined group potency as *"the collective belief in a group that it can be effective"* [17]. As an emergent state [35], it *"originates in the cognition, affect, behaviours, or other characteristics of individuals, is amplified by their interactions, and manifests as a higher-level collective phenomenon"* [23]. Specifically, group potency has 3 main distinguishing features:

- *Task-independence*: group potency is not related to the task the group is involved in; in contrast, it is a generalized belief that the group will be effective in a broad range of situations [16,17]. Given its nature, group potency is reasonably influenced by group interpersonal processes, i.e., *"processes that govern interpersonal activities"*, as described in [35].
- *Motivational construct*: group potency reflects *"the intensity, direction and effort regulation toward team task accomplishment"* [42]. Group potency, together with group efficacy [15], is often referred to as group confidence [42].
- *Group expression*: it is not related to individual beliefs, but it is shared among group members [17]. For instance, one could have low confidence in him/herself, but still be confident that his/her group will be successful. Group potency assessment is often addressed with a *referent-shift composition model* [8]; in other words, the construct is assessed by each individual having the group as referent of the assessment and then averaged between all the members of the group, if and only if a certain amount of agreement exists among them.

As previously mentioned, the group potency-effectiveness link has been documented many times [16,36] as well as many models have been proposed to illustrate the relationship among group potency and its antecedents and consequences. Initially, factors influencing group potency have been divided in *external* and *internal* to the group [17]. The former are mainly those related to the organizational context, such as organizational goal clarity, resources and rewards provided by the organization [17], or management support [21]; the latter are those related to structural characteristics of the group [49] or group processes and interactions. For instance, it has been shown how participation [13], communication. and cooperation, assessed via direct observation and self-report, were positively correlated with group potency as well as charismatic leadership [28]; [51] documents how the leader's mood-group potency link is mediated by the group's affective tone, hence showing the direct link between the last two. Moreover, [26] shows how teams, to develop group potency, need a sense of group identity fostering goals interdependence. This heighten the sense of potency of the group, positively impacting the performance. Sharing a group identity means also to share group norms and strong bonds with other group members. Indeed, [27] shows that cohesion is an antecedent of group potency. Furthermore, de Jong and colleagues suggests that *"each teams may develop a unique set of*

Table 1. Outline of the datasets selected for the study

Name	Description	Setting	Available data
AMI [39]	AMI contains recordings of 2 different meeting scenarios. In the first one volunteers take part in a project and have to design a remote control, in the second one colleagues discuss topics related to their real life.	Seated	Video recordings Audio recordings
TA2 [9]	TA2 contains recordings of people in 2 different rooms playing Battleship and Pictionary while in a video-call. Only videos from one room, during the Battleship game, were selected.	Seated	Video recordings Audio recordings
GAME-ON [33]	GAME-ON contains recordings of people playing a Cluedo inspired game, in an escape-room setting. Players must guess the culprit, motive and weapon of the crime to free themselves.	Standing	Motion capture data Video recordings Audio recordings

shared perceptions or shared mental models regarding the factors that influence potency cognitions [...]" [21]. These mental models, that are *"the knowledge that is common or shared among team members"* [29], are shaped along 3 dimensions, namely *communication, strategy,* and *cooperation* [37]).

Our study focuses on *internal* factors which are easier to operationalize from a computational viewpoint, with emphasis on high potency to overcome group members' biased judgements suffering from the "better-than-average" bias [52].

2.2   Related Work

Group potency has not been deeply investigated by Computational Sciences, so far. One previous work tackled it by training 4 different binary classifiers with 73.33% as best accuracy [6]. That study however focused on one modality only – i.e., verbal behavior – and on compositional characteristics of the groups, such as group size or average GPA (Grade Point Average) of group members. In contrast, this work addresses potency classification from a more embodied perspective, by exploiting the contribution of two other modalities, that is, auditory and body-movement. The methodology adopted to address potency builds on top of a consolidated literature on non-verbal social interaction [14]. Specifically some works have been carried out on the family of emergent states constructs. For instance, in [18] scholars successfully classify high and low level of cohesion exploiting auditory and visual features. Moreover, they show features importance in classifying cohesion with *TotalPauseTime* (the time between two same person turns) being the most performing. [34] extend the previous work by studying the dynamics of cohesion dimensions with a Deep Neural Network, which is able to predict cohesion at a significant higher level than the baseline models. A similar work paved the way towards modeling Transactive Memory System in small groups from audio-visual data, bringing out the need to have more data available for the purpose of studying complex phenomena like the *emergent states* [47].

3   Dataset

Given the task-independent nature of group potency and the lack of datasets specifically designed for the analysis of this emergent state, 3 different existing datasets – AMI [39], TA2 [9], and GAME-ON [33] (see Table 1) – were exploited in this study. Criteria for selection included the following: groups are involved in a task, group members collaborate towards a common goal, and social interaction takes place during different tasks. Moreover, both standing and seated positions are featured, thus providing a diversity of settings.

Data consists of video and audio recordings, as well as motion capture data (see Table 1). Concerning audio, because of the focus on the group rather than on the individuals, mixed tracks were taken when available. For AMI, the *Mix-Headset* audio files were selected. GAME-ON audio data is provided as single tracks hence tracks were mixed together in a single track. TA2 audio files were already mixed together. Regarding videos, the lateral views, when available, were taken for AMI; the frontal view was selected for GAME-ON; the only available view was taken for TA2. Motion capture data available in GAME-ON was also used.

For each dataset, a subset of recordings of different groups was selected by a trained psychologist. Groups showing a strong polarization in at least one of the three dimensions of shared mental models as described in [37] were selected, otherwise were discarded. The final dataset consists of 16 groups, with mean group size of 3.63 people ($SD = 0.90$).

The audio-video recordings of the selected 16 groups were further segmented into 15 s fixed-length non-overlapping windows. Such a window size was suggested by the results from Ambady and colleagues [1] that show how thin slices of behaviours can be enough to form reliable impressions. Furthermore, it has been shown that thin slices of behaviours are reliable also when judging emergent states like cohesion and affective and cognitive trust [43] or team effectiveness [50]. Moreover, 15 s long windows were previously successfully employed for annotation tasks concerning social behaviours [7]. Segmentation yielded 143 segments. 63 segments and 7 groups from AMI, 62 segments and 7 groups from GAME-ON and 18 segments and 2 groups from TA2.

4   Methods

4.1   Manual Annotation

The most common practice to evaluate group potency consists in administering a questionnaire to group members and to aggregate a score for the whole group upon verification of within-agreement among group members [8]. Nevertheless, since this work aims to develop a computational model trained with data mined from cameras and microphone arrays that rather emulate the presence of an external observer, an annotation with an external perspective was deemed more appropriate for generating the ground truth for the study.

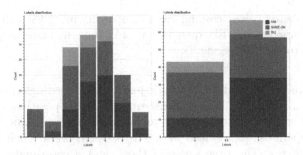

Fig. 1. *Left*: group potency scores across the datasets. *Right*: final label distribution, across datasets, after removal of median scored groups

The 143 segments in the dataset were administered in a random order to a trained psychologist on group potency and the annotator was free to watch them as many time as necessary. After watching each video, the annotator had to answer the 8 items scale developed by Guzzo and colleagues [17] (see Table 2), that has been proven to be a reliable tool [15]. The items were rearranged from a 5-points Likert scale to a 7-points Likert scale (*To no extent* (1) to *To great extent* (7)) as suggested in [21]. Group potency is most often assessed by means of a referent-shift composition model [8], that means that the referent of the assessment is shifted to the group instead of being the individual; this allowed us to keep the original items unchanged, without the need to adapt the items to the perspective of an external observer. The left panel of Fig. 1 displays the obtained distribution of scores.

Table 2. Group potency questionnaire [17]

Items
1. This team has confidence in itself
2. This team believes it can become unusually good at producing high-quality work
3. This team expects to be known as a high-performing team
4. This team feels it can solve any problems it encounters
5. This team believes it can be very productive
6. This team can get a lot done when it works hard
7. No task is too tough for this team
8. This team expects to have a lot of influence around here

4.2 Preprocessing

Audio the initial sampling rate of data was 16 kHz (AMI) and 48 kHz (GAME-ON and TA2), hence all the audio was re-sampled to 44.1 kHz and then converted to mono. Afterwards, audio tracks were filtered with the noise-reduction algorithm in Audacity[1]. Moreover, TA2 audio tracks were previously manually

---

[1] Audacity® software is copyright © 1999–2021 Audacity Team. The name Audacity® is a registered trademark.

processed to silence voices coming from people in the video call. The filtered
audio was trimmed using FFmpeg [48] in 15 s long non-overlapping windows
corresponding to the 143 segments.

Movement since AMI and TA2 provide just video recordings rather than positional motion capture data, a pose consisting of the 2D positions of a collection
of body joints was estimated for each member of the group and at each video
frame using OpenPose [5]. Videos were fed to OpenPose at their native frame-
rates, that is 25 fps. The time series of the x and y coordinates of each joint
were then preprocessed using MATLAB [38] for removing outliers. Specifically,
outliers for the AMI dataset were defined as values having 1.5 Median Absolute
Deviation (MAD) away from neighboring values. The reason for this choice was
that due to the low resolution of the videos (352×288 pixels) and the high number of occlusions occurring, the joints coordinates computed were very noisy,
hence we decided to consider outliers all those points that were outside a static
fence. Detected outliers were replaced with the median value of the segment they
belong to. For TA2, outliers were detected and filled by applying an Hampel filter [30] with default parameters, since pose estimation was more robust. The
cleaned data were smoothed with a Savitzky-Golay filter [44]. Filtering parameters were empirically selected as follows: degree 4 and smoothing factor 0.5 for
AMI, degree 4 and smoothing factor 0.25 for TA2. GAME-ON already provides
cleaned 3D positional data recorded 50 Hz, that was downsampled 25 Hz so to
have the same sampling frequency as positional data from AMI and TA2. No
further preprocessing was needed. The output of the preprocessing step is thus
a set $P = \{\mathbf{p}_1, \mathbf{p}_2, ..., \mathbf{p}_D\}$ of D bidimensional points ($\mathbf{p}_i = [x_i, y_i]^T$), for each
frame of each segment.

4.3   Feature Extraction

Since there are no other works that tackled group potency estimation from acoustic and movement data, this work took inspiration from previous research on
social behaviours and other emergent states that are related to group potency.
For each 15-s segment, a set of 24 multi-modal features characterizing social
interaction was extracted. These are group features only. Statistical functionals
were then computed on most of these features on thin slices of 5 s (overlapping
1 s). This resulted in a set of 81 features (see Table 3), that were standardized
by removing mean and scaling to unit variance.

Acoustic features they consist of prosodic and turn-taking features. Prosodic
features were computed by using OpenSmile [11]. A subset of the features
described in the I09 emotion challenge [45] was selected, as they have been shown
to be relevant in detecting rapport in small groups of people [40]. In particular, the mean and standard deviation values of the Root Mean Square Energy
were mean normalized with the mean values of the recording they were trimmed

from. This was done to mitigate the differences in the recording settings. Turn-taking features are inspired to [18]. Features were computed by using the pre-trained pipeline described in [3]. These are: duration of voice activity (*DurVad*), duration of silence (*Sil*), ratio between duration of voice activity and silence (*VadSil-ratio*), and duration of overlapping speech (*DurOvd*) (see Table 3).

Movement features they reflect the amount of group activity and the degree of involvement in the task and were computed over each set P of bidimensional points.

Mean distance from group's barycenter (MeanDist) this is inspired to [34], that used distance from barycenter as a predictor of cohesion. Given the set of the 2D coordinates of the heads of the group members $P_H = \{\mathbf{p}_{h_1}, \mathbf{p}_{h_2}, ..., \mathbf{p}_{h_N}\}$, $P_H \subset P$, where N is the number of group members, the mean distance from their barycenter was computed as:

$$\overline{d} = \frac{1}{N} \sum_{i=1}^{N} d(\mathbf{p}_{h_i}, \mathbf{q}) = \frac{1}{N} \sum_{i=1}^{N} \|\mathbf{p}_{h_i} - \mathbf{q}\| \tag{1}$$

where d is the Euclidean distance and $\mathbf{q}$ is the barycenter of the group members' heads, i.e.:

$$\mathbf{q} = \left[\frac{1}{N} \sum_{i=1}^{N} x_{h_i}, \frac{1}{N} \sum_{i=1}^{N} y_{h_i} \right]^T \tag{2}$$

Point density of heads and hands (PointsDens) given the set of 2D points representing the positions of the group members' heads and hands, this is the amount of dispersion with respect to their barycenter. It is computed as shown in [41] and it returns an index of the spatial extent of the group around the center of the action.

Kinetic energy of the upper-body during overlapping speech (KinEnOvd) this reflects the extent of involvement, as asserted in [18]. Given the set of 2D points P_U corresponding to the upper body of the group members, kinetic energy was computed just for the frames belonging to the time intervals returned by the algorithm described in [3], that was used to compute *DurOvd*. Masses were set equal to 1, hence assuming equal contribution from every joint.

Ratio between hands and upper-body kinetic energy during overlapping speech (KinEnOvd-ratio) this is used to assess the contribution of hands movements to the overall kinetic energy of the upper bodies of the group members. It is computed as the ratio between the kinetic energy of the hands and the overall energy of the upper body (i.e., *KinEnOvd*).

Hands and heads ellipsoid area ratio sets P_L, P_R, and P_H containing the 2D points corresponding respectively to left hands, right hands, and heads of the groups members are extracted from set P and the smaller ellipses E_1 including all points in $P_L \cup P_R$ and E_2 including all points in P_H are computed. Then the ratio between the area of E_1 and the area of E_2 is calculated. This indicates the extent to which hands are moved forwards, towards the other members of the group.

Mean Hopkins statistic of upper-limbs kinetic energy (KinEnHop) this is defined as the mean value of the Hopkins statistic [25]. The index compares clusters in the original data with clusters of random uniform points and returns a measure of clusterability of the set of values. Given the set of 2D points P_L corresponding to the upper limbs of the group members, the mean kinetic energy for every point over a 5 s window was computed. The Hopkins statistic was then calculated over such set of mean kinetic energies. The statistic was computed 100 times and the mean was taken.

Table 3. Acoustic and movement features. Features with "⋆" are those for which we applied statistical functions (i.e., mean, std, skewness and kurtosis). For features with "*" we computed only the mean value

Modality	Features	Description
Prosodic	$RMSenergy^\star$	Root Mean Square energy of the audio signal
	$ZCR^\star$	Zero Crossing Rate of the audio signal
	$MFCC1 - 12^\star$	Mel-Frequency Cepstral Coefficients from 1st to 12th of the audio signal
Turn-taking	$DurVad$	Duration of Voice Activity
	Sil	Duration of Silence
	$VadSil\text{-}ratio$	Ratio of Voice Activity and Silence
	$DurOvd$	Duration of Overlapping Voice segments
Movement	$MeanDist^\star$	Mean distance from the barycenter of the Heads
	$PointsDens^\star$	Density of the cloud of points composed by the Heads and the Hands
	$KinEnOvd^\star$	Kinetic Energy of the upper-body during overlapping speech segments
	$KinEnOvd\text{-}ratio^\star$	Ratio between hands and upper-body Kinetic Energy during overlapping speech
	$EllipsoidArea^\star$	Ratio between the areas of the minimum ellipsoids enclosing the hands and the heads
	$kinEnHop^*$	Clusterability measure of the Kinetic Energy of the upper limbs points

4.4 Models

Three state-of-the-art Machine Learning (ML) models were selected: Logistic Regression (Log-Reg) with Elastic-Net regularization [12], Support Vector Machine (SVM) with Radial Basis Kernel function (RBF) [2], and Random Forest (RF) [4]. Log-Reg was selected because of its simplicity [22]. SVM models have been shown to be effective when dealing with speech and gestures in human behaviour recognition, even with a small amount of data [20]. RF is an ensemble method that exploits many weak learners, such as Decision Trees (DT) [31] and is shown to be a powerful algorithm, as [10] explains.

For the aim of this study, a binary classification problem was formulated as follows:

$$y = \begin{cases} \text{low, if } p < 4 \\ \text{high, if } p > 4 \end{cases} \tag{3}$$

where y is the label assigned to the segment, and p is the potency score attributed by the annotator and computed as the average of the Likert items rounded to no decimal points. All the segments that resulted having the median score, namely 4, were discarded to get a better polarization of the data. The right panel in Fig. 1 shows the distribution of the binary labels. The final dataset consisted of 448 samples and 81 features. Table 4 summarizes distribution of groups and samples across the 3 datasets. High potency is taken as positive class.

Table 4. Dataset summary

Dataset	# groups	Group size	Segments per group	Samples
AMI	7	4	6.6 ± 2.1	188
GAME-ON	7	3	7.3 ± 2.5	204
TA2	2	3.5 ± 0.5	7.0 ± 1	56

4.5   Model Selection and Evaluation

Models were selected and evaluated by means of a nested cross-validation adopting a *Leave-One-Group-Out* (LOGO) approach, i.e., at each iteration of the external cross-validation, one group was retained for testing and all the other ones were used by the internal cross-validation for training and validation. This approach ensured that the segments of the same group never belong simultaneously to the training, validation, or test set.

To select the best configuration of hyperparameters, a randomized search with a fixed number of 200 iterations was applied, that means that 200 configurations were randomly sampled from every possible configuration of parameters and tested against the validation set. Hyperparameters space was the following:

- Log-Reg:
  - C: 200 values, logarithmic scale from 10^{-3} to 10^2.
  - l1 ratio: 10 values on a linear scale from 0 to 1.
- SVM:
  - C: 200 values, logarithmic scale from 10^{-3} to 10^2.
  - γ: 200 values, logarithmic scale from 10^{-3} to 10^2.
- Random Forest:
  - Criterion: entropy;
  - N. of estimators: integer values from 1 to 800.

- Min samples splits: integer values from 2 to 10.
- Min samples leaf: integer values from 1 to 10.
- Max depth: integer values from 1 to 10.

. F_1 score, precision, recall were selected as metrics.

4.6 Effect of Dataset

To test both the adaptability and the robustness of the models, an in-depth cross-dataset evaluation was carried out. An approach similar to the integrated off-corpus testing described in [19] was chosen. This was implemented trough a *Leave-One-Dataset-Out* (LODO) nested cross-validation: at each iteration of the external cross-validation, all the samples belonging to one of the original datasets were retained for testing and all the other ones were used by the internal cross-validation for training and validation. For estimating hyperparameters, a randomized search with a fixed number of 200 iterations was applied again on the same hyperparameters space.

5 Results

The performance of the models (using LOGO) are reported in Table 5. The 3 ML techniques performed similarly, with an F_1 score of $\cong 0.7 \pm 0.3$ and the Random Forest as the best performing one ($F_1 = 0.68 \pm 0.3$, mean precision = 0.69 and mean recall = 0.78), hence being the one that better classified high potency groups.

In the LODO, the models were trained and validated on 2 out of 3 corpora and then tested on the third one. The best performing algorithm is the SVM with RBF kernel (mean $F_1 = 0.74\pm0.06$, mean precision = 0.63 ± 0.13) and mean recall = 0.93 ± 0.07); followed by the Random Forest (mean $F_1 = 0.71 \pm 0.04$, mean precision = 0.64 ± 0.10) and mean recall = 0.83 ± 0.08) and finally, the Log-Reg with Elastic-Net (mean $F_1 = 0.71 \pm 0.06$, mean precision = 0.60 ± 0.12 and mean recall = 0.92 ± 0.08). Separate performance for every original dataset are summarized in Tables 6, 7, and 8.

Table 5. Leave-One-Group-Out results

Model	F1	Precision	Recall
Log-Reg	0.68 ± 0.31	0.62 ± 0.34	0.88 ± 0.27
SVM	0.69 ± 0.31	0.62 ± 0.34	0.92 ± 0.25
RF	0.68 ± 0.30	0.69 ± 0.35	0.78 ± 0.28

Table 6. Leave-One-Dataset-Out results on AMI

AMI			
	F1	Precision	Recall
Log-Reg	0.77	0.73	0.81
SVM	0.81	0.75	0.88
RF	0.75	0.75	0.75

Table 7. Leave-One-Dataset-Out results on GAME-ON

GAME-ON			
	F1	Precision	Recall
Log-Reg	0.66	0.49	1.00
SVM	0.70	0.55	0.96
RF	0.67	0.57	0.82

Table 8. Leave-One-Dataset-Out results on TA2

TA2			
	F1	Precision	Recall
Log-Reg	0.71	0.57	0.94
SVM	0.72	0.57	0.97
RF	0.72	0.59	0.91

6   Discussion and Conclusion

F1-scores are overall higher than 0.65 for all the models. This is promising, considering the diversity of the 3 original datasets the study grounds on. All the metrics, however, show high standard deviations. This suggests that the models performed excellently on some groups, and quite poorly on others. This is due to the high variance between the groups since every fine-tuned model was tested on a single group. The same behaviour can be noticed in the LODO setting, where strong differences among the 3 datasets emerge.

An important aspect to take into account is the trade-off between precision and recall. Both the LOGO and LODO settings have high recall and smaller precision scores, suggesting that the models are biased towards classifying most of the samples as being high on potency. This behaviour could be explained by the slight class imbalance towards the positive class, after removing groups with median scores. The precision scores for each model in both scenarios resides however above 0.5, with the Random Forest being the most precise and less biased algorithm in all the scenarios.

LODO tested the ability of the models to generalize on completely different scenarios (i.e., each of the 3 original dataset). The best performance is achieved on AMI, secondly TA2, and finally GAME-ON. These results suggest that GAME-ON is the most difficult dataset to classify, in fact all the models were strongly biased towards the positive class. The explanation for this behaviour could rely on the nature of the features, since the strong differences in the recordings setting; indeed, in the GAME-ON dataset, participants are free to walk on a stage, while performing the task. Another possible explanation could be the strong class imbalance that emerges when removing this particular dataset. In fact, when GAME-ON is on the test side, the majority of the samples belongs to AMI and, for the most, they are positive (168 positive vs 76 negative). Results on AMI suggest that this could be the reason. When AMI is on the test side, the training set labels are much more balanced, hence the final results are less biased. These results highlight the difficulty to find suitable examples to investigate a complex emergent state such as group potency.

In this study, a first approach towards building a multimodal computational model of group potency has been presented. Exploiting the task-independent nature of group potency, a dataset was composed from 3 datasets on social interaction. A nested cross-dataset validation was applied to test models ability to generalize. Starting from the obtained results, there is room for improvement. The employed set of features can be extended by taking into consideration the patterns of interaction by means of structural features [49] and the contribution of the individual members. More samples are needed, to span a wider range of scenarios and the models performance can be enhanced by exploiting more sophisticated algorithms.

Acknowledgment. Portions of the research in this paper used the TA2 Dataset made available by the Idiap Research Institute, Martigny, Switzerland. The work of Giovanna Varni has been partially supported by the French National Research Agency (ANR) in the framework of its JCJC program (GRACE, project ANR-18-CE33-0003-01, funded under the Artificial Intelligence Plan).

References

1. Ambady, N., Rosenthal, R.: Thin slices of expressive behavior as predictors of interpersonal consequences: a meta-analysis. Psychol. Bull. **111**(2), 256 (1992)
2. Bishop, C.M., Nasrabadi, N.M.: Pattern Recognition and Machine Learning, vol. 4, pp. 291–357. Springer, New York (2006)
3. Bredin, H., et al.: Pyannote. audio: neural building blocks for speaker diarization. In: ICASSP 2020–2020 IEEE International Conference on Acoustics, Speech and Signal Processing (ICASSP), pp. 7124–7128. IEEE (2020)
4. Breiman, L.: Random forests. Mach. Learn. **45**(1), 5–32 (2001)
5. Cao, Z., Hidalgo Martinez, G., Simon, T., Wei, S., Sheikh, Y.A.: Openpose: real-time multi-person 2D pose estimation using part affinity fields. IEEE Trans. Pattern Anal. Mach. Intell. **43**, 172–186 (2019)
6. Castro-Hernández, A., Swigger, K., Cemile Serce, F., Lopez, V.: Classification of Group Potency Levels of Software Development Student Teams. Polibits (51), 55–62 (2015). 10.17562/PB-51-8, publisher: Instituto Politécnico Nacional, Centro de Innovación y Desarrollo Tecnológico en Cómputo

7. Ceccaldi, E., Lehmann-Willenbrock, N., Volta, E., Chetouani, M., Volpe, G., Varni, G.: How unitizing affects annotation of cohesion. In: 2019 8th International Conference on Affective Computing and Intelligent Interaction (ACII), pp. 1–7. IEEE (2019)

8. Chan, D.: Functional relations among constructs in the same content domain at different levels of analysis: a typology of composition models. J. Appl. Psychol. **83**(2), 234 (1998)

9. Duffner, S., Motlicek, P., Korchagin, D.: The TA2 database - a multi-modal database from home entertainment. Int. J. Comput. Electrical Eng. 670–673 (2012). https://doi.org/10.7763/IJCEE.2012.V4.581

10. D'Amato, V., Volta, E., Oneto, L., Volpe, G., Camurri, A., Anguita, D.: Understanding violin players' skill level based on motion capture: a data-driven perspective. Cogn. Comput. **12**(6), 1356–1369 (2020)

11. Eyben, F., Wöllmer, M., Schuller, B.: Opensmile: the Munich versatile and fast open-source audio feature extractor. In: Proceedings of the 18th ACM international conference on Multimedia, pp. 1459–1462 (2010)

12. Friedman, J., Hastie, T., Tibshirani, R.: Regularization paths for generalized linear models via coordinate descent. J. Stat. Softw. **33**(1), 1 (2010)

13. Gamero, N., Zornoza, A., Peiró, J.M., Picazo, C.: Roles of participation and feedback in group potency. Psychol. Rep. **105**(1), 293–313 (2009). https://doi.org/10.2466/PR0.105.1.293-313

14. Gatica-Perez, D.: Automatic nonverbal analysis of social interaction in small groups: a review. Image Vis. Comput. **27**(12), 1775–1787 (2009). https://doi.org/10.1016/j.imavis.2009.01.004

15. Gibson, C.B., Randel, A.E., Earley, P.C.: Understanding group efficacy: an empirical test of multiple assessment methods. Group Organ. Manag. **25**(1), 67–97 (2000). https://doi.org/10.1177/1059601100251005, publisher: SAGE Publications Inc

16. Gully, S.M., Incalcaterra, K.A., Joshi, A., Beaubien, J.M.: A meta-analysis of team-efficacy, potency, and performance: interdependence and level of analysis as moderators of observed relationships. J. Appl. Psychol. **87**(5), 819–832 (2002). https://doi.org/10.1037/0021-9010.87.5.819

17. Guzzo, R.A., Yost, P.R., Campbell, R.J., Shea, G.P.: Potency in groups: articulating a construct. Br. J. Soc. Psychol. **32**(1), 87–106 (1993). https://doi.org/10.1111/j.2044-8309.1993.tb00987.x

18. Hung, H., Gatica-Perez, D.: Estimating cohesion in small groups using audio-visual nonverbal behavior. IEEE Trans. Multimedia **12**(6), 563–575 (2010). https://doi.org/10.1109/TMM.2010.2055233

19. Hupont, I., Chetouani, M.: Region-based facial representation for real-time action units intensity detection across datasets. Pattern Anal. Appl. **22**(2), 477–489 (2019)

20. Jadhav, N., Sugandhi, R.: Survey on human behavior recognition using affective computing. In: 2018 IEEE Global Conference on Wireless Computing and Networking (GCWCN), pp. 98–103, November 2018. https://doi.org/10.1109/GCWCN.2018.8668632

21. de Jong, A., de Ruyter, K., Wetzels, M.: Antecedents and consequences of group potency: a study of self-managing service teams. Manage. Sci. **51**(11), 1610–1625 (2005). https://doi.org/10.1287/mnsc.1050.0425

22. Kleinbaum, D.G., Dietz, K., Gail, M., Klein, M., Klein, M.: Logistic Regression. Springer, New York (2002)

23. Kozlowski, S., Klein, K.: A multilevel approach to theory and research in organizations: contextual, temporal, and emergent processes. Multi-level theory, research, and methods in organizations: Foundations, extensions, and new directions, October 2012
24. Kozlowski, S.W., Ilgen, D.R.: Enhancing the effectiveness of work groups and teams. Psychol. Sci. Public Interest **7**(3), 77–124 (2006). https://doi.org/10.1111/j.1529-1006.2006.00030.x, publisher: SAGE Publications Inc
25. Lawson, R.G., Jurs, P.C.: New index for clustering tendency and its application to chemical problems. J. Chem. Inf. Comput. Sci. **30**(1), 36–41 (1990)
26. Lee, C., Farh, J.L., Chen, Z.J.: Promoting group potency in project teams: the importance of group identification. J. Organ. Behav. **32**(8), 1147–1162 (2011). https://doi.org/10.1002/job.741
27. Lee, C., Tinsley, C.H., Bobko, P.: An investigation of the antecedents and consequences of group-level confidence1. J. Appl. Soc. Psychol. **32**(8), 1628–1652 (2002). https://doi.org/10.1111/j.1559-1816.2002.tb02766.x
28. Lester, S.W., Meglino, B.M., Korsgaard, M.A.: The antecedents and consequences of group potency: a longitudinal investigation of newly formed work groups. Acad. Manag. J. **45**(2), 352–368 (2002)
29. Levine, J.M., Hogg, M.A. (eds.): Encyclopedia of Group Processes & Intergroup Relations. SAGE Publications, Thousand Oaks, Calif (2010). oCLC: ocn251215605
30. Liu, H., Shah, S., Jiang, W.: On-line outlier detection and data cleaning. Comput. Chem. Eng. **28**(9), 1635–1647 (2004)
31. Maimon, O.Z., Rokach, L.: Data Mining with Decision Trees: Theory and Applications, vol. 81. World scientific (2014)
32. Malone, T.W.: How human-computer' superminds' are redefining the future of work. MIT Sloan Manag. Rev. **59**(4), 34–41 (2018)
33. Maman, L., et al.: GAME-ON: a multimodal dataset for cohesion and group analysis. IEEE Access **8**, 124185–124203 (2020). https://doi.org/10.1109/ACCESS.2020.3005719, conference Name: IEEE Access
34. Maman, L., Likforman-Sulem, L., Chetouani, M., Varni, G.: Exploiting the interplay between social and task dimensions of cohesion to predict its dynamics leveraging social sciences. In: Proceedings of the 2021 International Conference on Multimodal Interaction. ICMI 2021, New York, NY, USA, pp. 16–24. Association for Computing Machinery, October 2021. https://doi.org/10.1145/3462244.3479940
35. Marks, M.A.: A Temporally Based Framework and Taxonomy of Team Processes, p. 22 (2001)
36. Mathieu, J., Maynard, M.T., Rapp, T., Gilson, L.: Team effectiveness 1997–2007: a review of recent advancements and a glimpse into the future. J. Manag. **34**(3), 410–476 (2008). https://doi.org/10.1177/0149206308316061
37. Mathieu, J.E., Heffner, T.S., Goodwin, G.F., Salas, E., Cannon-Bowers, J.A.: The influence of shared mental models on team process and performance. J. Appl. Psychol. **85**(2), 273 (2000)
38. MATLAB: version 7.10.0 (R2010a). The MathWorks Inc., Natick, Massachusetts (2010)
39. Mccowan, I., et al.: The AMI meeting corpus. In: Noldus, L.P.J.J., Grieco, F., Loijens, L.W.S., Zimmerman, P.H. (eds.) Proceedings Measuring Behavior 2005, 5th International Conference on Methods and Techniques in Behavioral Research. Noldus Information Technology, Wageningen (2005)

40. Müller, P., Huang, M.X., Bulling, A.: Detecting low rapport during natural interactions in small groups from non-verbal behaviour. In: 23rd International Conference on Intelligent User Interfaces, pp. 153–164, Tokyo Japan. ACM, March 2018. https://doi.org/10.1145/3172944.3172969

41. Piana, S., Staglianò, A., Camurri, A., Odone, F.: A set of full-body movement features for emotion recognition to help children affected by autism spectrum condition. In: IDGEI International Workshop (2013)

42. Rapp, T., Maynard, T., Domingo, M., Klock, E.: Team emergent states: what has emerged in the literature over 20 years. Small Group Res. **52**(1), 68–102 (2021)

43. Satterstrom, P., Polzer, J.T., Kwan, L.B., Hauser, O.P., Wiruchnipawan, W., Burke, M.: Thin slices of workgroups. Organ. Behav. Hum. Decis. Process. **151**, 104–117 (2019). https://doi.org/10.1016/j.obhdp.2018.12.007

44. Schafer, R.W.: What is a savitzky-golay filter?[lecture notes]. IEEE Signal Process. Mag. **28**(4), 111–117 (2011)

45. Schuller, B., Steidl, S., Batliner, A.: The interspeech 2009 emotion challenge (2009)

46. Seeber, I., et al.: Machines as teammates: a collaboration research agenda (2018)

47. Tartaglione, E., Biancardi, B., Mancini, M., Varni, G.: A hitchhiker's guide towards transactive memory system modeling in small group interactions. In: Companion Publication of the 2021 International Conference on Multimodal Interaction, pp. 254–262 (2021)

48. Tomar, S.: Converting video formats with ffmpeg. Linux J. **2006**(146), 10 (2006)

49. Tröster, C., Mehra, A., van Knippenberg, D.: Structuring for team success: the interactive effects of network structure and cultural diversity on team potency and performance. Organ. Behav. Hum. Decis. Process. **124**(2), 245–255 (2014). https://doi.org/10.1016/j.obhdp.2014.04.003

50. Tsay, C.J.: The vision heuristic: judging music ensembles by sight alone. Organ. Behav. Hum. Decis. Process. **124**(1), 24–33 (2014). https://doi.org/10.1016/j.obhdp.2013.10.003

51. Volmer, J.: Catching leaders' mood: contagion effects in teams. Adm. Sci. **2**(3), 203–220 (2012). https://doi.org/10.3390/admsci2030203, number: 3 Publisher: Molecular Diversity Preservation International

52. Woodley, H.J.R., McLarnon, M.J.W., O'Neill, T.A.: The emergence of group potency and its implications for team effectiveness. Front. Psychol. **10**, 992 (2019). https://doi.org/10.3389/fpsyg.2019.00992

Multi-Channel Time-Series Person and Soft-Biometric Identification

Nilah Ravi Nair[1]([✉])[iD], Fernando Moya Rueda[2][iD], Christopher Reining[1][iD], and Gernot A. Fink[2][iD]

[1] Chair of Material Handling and Warehousing, TU Dortmund University, Dortmund, Germany
{nilah.nair,christopher.reining}@tu-dortmund.de
[2] Pattern Recognition in Embedded Systems Group, TU Dortmund University, Dortmund, Germany
{fernando.moya,gernot.fink}@tu-dortmund.de

Abstract. Multi-channel time-series datasets are popular in the context of human activity recognition (HAR). On-body device (OBD) recordings of human movements are often preferred for HAR applications not only for their reliability but as an approach for identity protection, e.g., in industrial settings. Contradictory, the gait activity is a biometric, as the cyclic movement is distinctive and collectable. In addition, the gait cycle has proven to contain soft-biometric information of human groups, such as age and height. Though general human movements have not been considered a biometric, they might contain identity information. This work investigates person and soft-biometrics identification from OBD recordings of humans performing different activities using deep architectures. Furthermore, we propose the use of attribute representation for soft-biometric identification. We evaluate the method on four datasets of multi-channel time-series HAR, measuring the performance of a person and soft-biometrics identification and its relation concerning performed activities. We find that person identification is not limited to gait activity. The impact of activities on the identification performance was found to be training and dataset specific. Soft-biometric based attribute representation shows promising results and emphasis the necessity of larger datasets.

Keywords: Person Identification · Human Activity Recognition · Soft-Biometrics · Explainable Artificial Intelligence · Deep Neural Network

1 Introduction

Biometrics are physical or behavioural characteristics that can be used to identify an individual [12]. These characteristics need to be universal, distinct, permanent and collectable. For example, fingerprint, signature and gait. Biometrics have gained importance due to security applications. For instance, security footage of individuals in gait motion can be used for their recognition and authentication.

© Springer Nature Switzerland AG 2023
J.-J. Rousseau and B. Kapralos (Eds.): ICPR 2022 Workshops, LNCS 13643, pp. 256–272, 2023.
https://doi.org/10.1007/978-3-031-37660-3_18

However, variation in clothing, multiple subjects in the frame, occlusion and obtrusion are challenges to vision-based gait-based person identification [15]. Using on-body devices (OBDs) can pose a solution to these problems. OBDs, such as smartphones or smartwatches, record gait motion that can facilitate recognition of the individual [8]. Furthermore, OBD recordings can be used to classify individuals based on soft-biometrics, such as age, gender identity and height as given by [26].

HAR, using OBDs, is highly researched due to its applications in industrial environments, clinical diagnosis and activity of daily living (ADL) monitoring [20,21,27]. Real human activity recordings are often required to facilitate process optimisation or real-time HAR. Consequently, the possibility of person identification and soft-biometrics-based classification lead to privacy concerns. [8] raised privacy concerns based on gait-based person identification. [6] concluded that OBD-based identification is not limited to gait; activities such as laying, running, and cleaning can contain an individual's identity. Person identification is particularly interesting for biometric authentication on smartphones [17].

Research on bench-marked datasets is limited due to the unavailability of large, annotated datasets with varying human characteristics and natural body movements. Furthermore, given the case of OBD sensors, the influence of sensor biases needs to be analysed. As a result, this paper serves as a preliminary step towards creating efficient identity protection methods, benchmarked research and motivation for creating large annotated datasets. Thus, we experiment on four benchmark OBD datasets intended for HAR in the context of person identification. Datasets with natural body-movements were preferred. The impact of the activity on identity relations is analysed. Furthermore, the possibility to model soft-biometrics as attribute representation is examined. To avoid manual feature extraction [5], experiments will be performed on Neural Networks, such as Convolutional Neural Networks (CNNs) and Recurrent Neural Networks (RNNs). For the concept of identity protection, methods to either mask or delete identity need to be researched. This process may bring to light the effect of soft-biometrics and the subject's individuality on the HAR dataset and thus, the possibility of enhancing HAR dataset. Explainable Artificial Intelligence (XAI) method is explored to investigate its feasibility.

2   Related Work

Using gait as a biometric is challenging due to its sensitivity to changes in clothing, fatigue and environmental factors [2]. Creating a database template for verification and identification with consideration of these variations is cumbersome. However, gait is one of the most collectable data alongside signature, face thermogram, and hand geometry [12]. The authors in [31] presents a survey of the various methods of person identification using low-resolution video recordings. Silhouette analysis [14] and Gait Energy Image (GEI) [10] are two popular video-based gait-based person identification methods.

Based on gait data acquired from OBDs, [30] mention that the gait parameter study can be extended to person identification and soft-biometrics. The authors in [26] confirmed that a single step recorded from smartphones or smartwatches could be used to reveal soft-biometrics.

Due to the susceptibility of manual feature extraction to subjectivity, [5] performed gait-based person identification using multi-layer sensor fusion-based deep CNN. Furthermore, the late fusion method achieves better accuracy, given a defective OBD amongst a group of sensors. In contrast, the authors in [4] performed gait-based person identification using a simple Neural Network. The authors found that variations in the gait characteristics are based on the subject's height, weight, arm length and personal habits. The authors in [8] attempted person identification on Gated Recurrent Units (GRU) and Long-Short Term Memory (LSTM). The authors concluded that the GRU model performs better than CNN and LSTM. Besides, they identified that the *step* data performed better than the *stride* data. A *step* is defined as the heel strike of one foot followed by the heel strike of the other foot. *Stride* constitutes two heel strikes from one foot. During a typical human walk, the step frequency is between 1– 2 Hz.

In contrast to the previous works, the authors of [6] considered a dataset of 20 daily human activities, such as cleaning, washing dishes, and office-work activities, to perform person identification. Unlike [5], the authors focused on manually extracted features, such as mean, standard deviations (SD) and magnitude. The experiments were performed on classifiers such as Support Vector Machines (SVM), K-Nearest Neighbour (KNN), Neural Network, Decision Tree (DT) and their types. The authors identified that sedentary activities had a higher classification rate. In addition, the authors concluded that all subjects are not equally identifiable. The conclusions derived can be pivotal for research in identity anonymization as found in [16]. Here, the authors used a Convolutional Auto-Encoder to remove the identity information present in the OBD data obtained from a smartphone while maintaining application-specific data, for example, activity recognition and step count. The authors achieved 92% accuracy on activity recognition while reducing user identification accuracy to less than 7%. However, the authors have not considered motionless activities based on their observation that subjects can only be distinguished based on motion activities.

The authors in [25] experimented on person identification using a Deep Neural Network (DNN) and the impact of the sensor noise on the identification. The dataset used consisted of 20 individuals and was annotated with three activity labels, namely, sleep, walk and other. They identified that sleep activity provided the worst person identification, whereas walking activity performed the best. Further, the authors noted that, noise removal methods using Short-Time Fourier Transform (STFT) does not solve sensor dependency issue. However, raw data augmentation helps with achieving sensor independent network. Nevertheless, person identification was achieved at a lesser accuracy rate. [17] experimented with smartphone data UCI-HAR and USC-HAD datasets on CNN, LSTM, CNN-LSTM and ConvLSTM and was able to achieve high accuracy levels for all users. They implemented a sequence of classifiers to perform activity classification followed by user identification. The authors targeted bio-metric user identification based on mobile platforms. These experiments empha-size the importance of large, annotated datasets with varying human character-istics and sensor noise analysis.

The authors of [21, 22] created the Logistic Activity Recognition Challenge (LARa) dataset and annotated the data based on activity classes and attribute representations. Attribute representations describe coarse objects and scenes, as explained in [7,13], and activity classes, as explored in [23,28]. For HAR, linking the body part movement to the activity class helps to describe the class better as well as navigate inter and intra class misclassifications. Given that an individual can be described based on soft-biometrics, it is of interest to extend the idea to person identification by modelling soft-biometrics as attribute representation.

Given the nascent stage of research and variation in experimental approach, person identification using OBDs have conflicting findings. Thus, one needs to experiment on publicly available datasets to ensure reproducible experiments. To investigate the impact of noise and activity, using Explainable Artificial Intel-ligence methods (XAI) may help to verify the observations. For example, [11] experiments on ground reaction forces (GRF) verified that the individual's gait pattern have unique characteristics based on the kinematic and kinetic variables. To verify, the authors used Layer-Wise Relevance Propagation (LRP) [18], a method of XAI. Similarly, LRP method can be used to verify the results of per-son identification using motion information. Research in this direction may show feasibility of noise to signal segregation.

3 Person and Soft-Biometrics Identification

Table 1. Attribute representations are created based on the recording protocol of LARa dataset.

	Recording Protocol					Attribute Representation A_1			
Sub	Gender [F/M]	Age	Weight [kg]	Height [cm]	Handedness [L/R]	Gender [F/M]	Age $\leq 40/> 40$	Weight $\leq 70/> 70$	Height $\leq 170/> 170$
7	M	23	65	177	R	1	0	0	1
8	F	51	68	168	R	0	1	0	0
9	M	35	100	172	R	1	0	1	1
10	M	49	97	181	R	1	1	1	1
11	F	47	66	175	R	0	1	0	1
12	F	23	48	163	R	0	0	0	0
13	F	25	54	163	R	0	0	0	0
14	M	54	90	177	R	1	1	1	1

This work investigates person identification from multi-channel time series recordings of humans performing various activities. Though gait movements are considered to be biometric, body movements performed during activities of daily

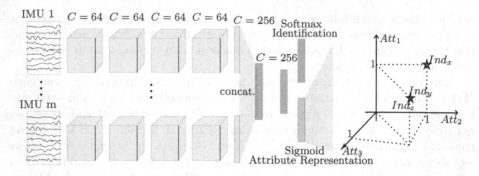

Fig. 1. The tCNN-IMU architecture contains m parallel temporal-convolutional blocks, one per limb. The outputs of the blocks are concatenated and forwarded to a fully connected or 2-LSTM layers according to the network type. Person identification uses softmax in the output layer. Attribute representation uses sigmoid function.

living have not been recognised to be unique. However, classifiers can identify individuals when performing activities following [6]. Here, we attempt to provide a standardised and reproducible set of experiments. Firstly, we explore the impact of channel-normalisation. It is expected that positional bias of the sensors may help improve person identification. Next, we explore the possibility of generalisation of identity over activities. The expectation is that similar activities generalise based on the individual's motion signature. As a result, we employ DNNs on OBD recordings of human activities to attempt at person and soft-biometrics identification. Soft-biometrics identification will be experimented with by modelling soft-biometrics as an attribute representation. Finally, we perform LRP on select dataset to explore the feasibility of XAI to verify person identification.

Table 1 and Fig. 1 briefs the method. Firstly, the OBD data is grouped based on the limb that the OBD is placed on. For example, if the limb *left leg* has two OBDs placed on the ankle and knee respectively, the OBDs will be grouped together. Thus, each limb of the human body with an OBD will be allotted a block of four convolutional layers. This allows extraction of local features. Next the layers are concatenated and followed by two fully connected layers which extract the global features. The final layer is derived based on the required process; person identification using a softmax layer or soft-biometrics using a sigmoid layer. For attribute representation, a person is represented by either a one-hot encoding or a set of soft-biometrics. The attribute representation is created based on the recording protocol.

3.1   Networks

We use the *tCNN-IMU* network [9,20,28]. Here, the late fusion approach is applied using an MLP (*tCNN-IMU$_{MLP}$*) or a two-layered LSTM (*tCNN-IMU$_{LSTM}$*), with a softmax or sigmoid classifier. OBDs from each human limb is allotted a branch of four convolutional layers. The convolutional blocks extract descriptive local features from the input OBD data, while the subsequent layers assimilate the global view of the extracted features. Prior to concatenation, the outputs of each convolutional blocks are processed by a fully connected layer or LSTM layer depending on the network type. Concatenation is followed by a two-layered fully connected MLP and a classifier layer for $tCNN\text{-}IMU_{MLP}$. In the case of $tCNN\text{-}IMU_{LSTM}$, the concatenation is followed by two LSTM layers and a classifier layer.

The networks use a softmax classifier for person identification, whereas a sigmoid layer for soft-biometrics identification [28]. Soft-biometrics of individuals describe or categorise an individual or a group of individuals [30], e.g., Gender Identity, Age, Weight and Height. Attribute representations is a method of describing the data semantically [28]. An attribute vector a represents a set of soft-biometrics. A similar combination of soft-biometrics could represent different persons with similar features. The Nearest Neighbour Approach (NNA) is used for soft-biometrics-based identification. The NNA calculates the distance between a prediction attribute vector a and an attribute representation A, with all the different combinations of soft-biometrics. The person identity is assigned to the one related with the least distance from A. NNA is performed by computing a certain similarity between a A and the vector a from the network; typically, the *cosine* similarity [32] and the *Probabilistic Retrieval Model (PRM)* similarity [29].

Training Procedure. The weights of the network are initialised using the orthogonal initialisation method. The Cross-Entropy Loss function is utilised to calculate person classification loss. In the case of attribute representation, the BCE_{loss} is used. The Root Mean Square Propagation (RMSProp) optimisation is used with a momentum of 0.9 and weight decay of 5×10^{-4}. Gaussian noise with mean $\mu = 0$ and SD $\sigma = 0.01$ is added to the sensor measurements to simulate sensor inaccuracies [9,20]. Dropout of probability $p = 0.5$ was applied on the MLP and LSTM layers of the networks and early-stopping to avoid over-fitting.

4   Experiments and Results

Person identification was performed on four HAR datasets, namely LARa [21], OPPORTUNITY (OPP) [3], PAMAP2 [24], and Order Picking (OrP) [9] using the $tCNN\text{-}IMU_{MLP}$ and $tCNN\text{-}IMU_{LSTM}$. The datasets were selected based on their public availability and prominence in HAR research, thus facilitating comparable and competitive research. Additionally, soft-biometrics identification was performed on the LARa and PAMAP2 datasets using $tCNN\text{-}IMU_{MLP}$; this as its recording protocol is available. To create the training, validation and test set, the recordings of the individuals are split as per $64 - 18 - 18\%$. The split percentages were decided based on the number of recordings available for each individual, while ensuring closeness to standard split percentages.

4.1   Datasets

The datasets of interest are different from each other with respect to the experimental set-up, recording protocol and activities. Table 2 tabulates the differences between the datasets based on the number of subjects, IMUs, channels and activities present in the dataset. Furthermore, the table presents the differences in IMU placement, recording location and activity types. It is to be noted that OrP was recorded from two different warehouses, where one subject was common to both warehouses. Furthermore, the dataset does not have a recording protocol. Unlike laboratory-made LARa and OPP datasets, PAMAP2 requires pre-processing to overcome data loss.

Table 2. Comparison of the features of selected datasets based on number of subjects, IMUs, channels, position of OBDs, and recording environment.

Dataset	MoCap	Mbientlab	Motion Miners	OPP	PAMAP2	OrP
Subject No:	14	8	8	4	9	6
IMU No:	–	5	3	7	3	3
Channel No:	126	30	27	113	40	27
Additional Sensors:	–	–	–	Accelerometers	Heart Monitor	–
Activities No:	7	7	7	Locomotion:4 Gesture:17	12	7
IMU Placement	Chest, wrists, legs	Chest, wrists, legs	Hip, wrists	Chest, wrists, arms, legs	Chest, right wrist right ankle	Chest, wrists
Location	Lab	Lab	Lab	Lab - Kitchen	Outdoor	Warehouses
Act. Type	Logistics	Logistics	Logistics	ADL	ADL	Logistics
Sampling Rate	200 Hz	100 Hz	100Hz	30 Hz	100 Hz	100 Hz

Pre-processing. Sliding window size equivalent to step frequency or duration of 1 s provides better results according to [8]. Consequently, a sliding window size corresponding to the sampling rate was considered for the datasets. LARa-Mbientlab, LARa-MotionMiners and PAMAP2 have a sliding window size of 100 frames and a stride size of 12 frames. OPP was experimented with two sliding window sizes, 24 and 100 frames (~4 s) and a constant stride size of 12 frames. OrP has a fixed window size of 100 frames and stride 1. A zero-mean and unit-SD channel-normalisation is carried out as part of the training procedure from [28], as networks' filters are shared among the channels, independent of their magnitude.

4.2   Person Identification on LARa

Table 3 shows the performance of person identification in terms of Accuracy (Acc) [%] and weighted $F1$ (wF1)[%] on the LARa-Mbientlab and LARa-MotionMiners using the two architectures, $tCNN\text{-}IMU_{MLP}$ and $tCNN\text{-}IMU_{LSTM}$ with three learning rates, $Lr = [10^{-4}, 10^{-5}, 10^{-6}]$, three batch sizes mB size $= [50, 100, 200]$ and 10 epochs. All experimental results are an average of five trial runs (x5) and are presented as percentages. The experiment emphasises the person identification performance on different sensor sets recording similar activities. Both the networks are trained on LARa-Mbientlab and LARa-MotionMiners under similar training conditions. Person identification was found to be feasible for LARa with both five and three OBDs. $tCNN\text{-}IMU_{MLP}$ outperforms $tCNN\text{-}IMU_{LSTM}$. Interestingly, a smaller batch size performs better. Though LARa-MotionMiners have three sensors on the upper body, the accuracy of person identification is comparable to the LARa-Mbientlab with five sensor points. Furthermore, Table 3 presents the performance for LARa-Mocap, considering the human poses as multi-channel time series, using the $tCNN\text{-}IMU_{MLP}$. Person identification performance decreases when using OBDs in comparison to human poses. However, in the best scenario using the $tCNN\text{-}IMU_{MLP}$ for both OBDs sets, the performance decreases only by ~3%; this, as OBDs and human poses are physical related quantities.

Table 3. Person Identification in terms of the average Acc[%] and wF1[%] from five runs (x5) on the LARa-Mbientlab and LARa-MotionMiners using the $tCNN\text{-}IMU_{MLP}$ and $tCNN\text{-}IMU_{LSTM}$ networks and different batches at $Lr = 10^{-4}$ and epoch 10. Here, $*_{MLP}$ and $*_{LSTM}$ represent tCNN-IMU$_{MLP}$ and tCNN-IMU$_{LSTM}$ respectively.

Network	mB	LARa-Mbientlab		LARa-MotionMiners	
		Avg Acc (x5)	Avg wF1 (x5)	Avg Acc (x5)	Avg wF1 (x5)
$*_{MLP}$	50	**93.96 ± 0.03**	**93.84 ± 0.03**	**93.32 ± 0.21**	**93.32 ± 0.22**
	100	92.17 ± 0.003	92.11 ± 0.39	91.36 ± 1.67	91.67 ± 1.67
	200	90.15 ± 0.20	90.01 ± 0.21	88.74 ± 0.92	88.29 ± 0.92
$*_{LSTM}$	50	**90.55 ± 0.57**	**90.41 ± 0.61**	86.19 ± 0.76	86.21 ± 0.76
	100	89.43 ± 0.96	89.22 ± 1.01	**86.43 ± 0.53**	**86.41 ± 0.52**
	200	86.48 ± 0.86	86.08 ± 0.88	84.12 ± 2.09	84.02 ± 2.17

Network	mB	LARa-MoCap	
		Avg Acc (x5)	Avg wF1 (x5)
$*_{MLP}$	100	96.72 ± 0.72	96.71 ± 0.72

Table 3 shows the results using normalised channels; this, as network process sequences time-wise, sharing its filters channel-wise. Consequently, non- and channel-normalised data are compared. This comparison follows the assumption that non-channel-normalised data might provide better person identification performance due to the sensor placement bias. Contrary to expectation, the channel-normalised data provided better identification performance, as shown in Table 4. Similar to Table 3, a smaller batch size provides better performance.

As a preliminary work towards analysing the features that contribute to person identity within HAR data, ϵ-LRP [11,18,19] was attempted on the OBDs

Table 4. Comparison of channel-normalised and non-channel-normalised LARa-Mbientlab on $tCNN\text{-}IMU_{MLP}$. Average Acc[%] and wF1[%] of five runs **(x5)** with $Lr = 10^{-4}$ and epoch 10.

mB	Non-Norm		Norm	
	Avg Acc (x5)	**Avg wF1(x5)**	**Avg Acc (x5)**	**Avg wF1(x5)**
50	90.06 ± 0.65	89.97 ± 0.69	93.96 ± 0.03	93.84 ± 0.03
100	88.59 ± 0.65	88.41 ± 0.73	92.17 ± 0.003	92.11 ± 0.39
200	84.51 ± 0.73	84.06 ± 0.89	90.15 ± 0.20	90.01 ± 0.21

(LARa-Mbientlab) and human poses (LARa-Mocap) per limb with a $tCNN\text{-}IMU_{MLP}$ of one branch for all channels. The ϵ value was fixed at 10^{-9}. Figure 2 shows the root mean square (RMS) of the positive relevances of the limbs (LARa-Mbientlab, LARa-Mocap) of subjects 1 and 6, as mentioned in LARa-Mbientlab protocol, performing the activity "Cart". In this activity, the subjects walk, transporting a Cart with both or one hand. The limbs are represented as left leg (LL), left arm (LA), Neck/Torso (N), right arm (RA) and right leg (RL). For LARa-Mocap, the human limbs contributing to the person identification are related to the "Cart" activity; that is the right and left legs. For LARa-Mbientlab, the Neck/Torso area is relevant for the correct identification. These plots are only a single example of 1 s window of an activity. However, the patterns and variations point that accumulative analysis using tools as mentioned in [1] might help develop methods to either mask or delete the identity data or enhance HAR datasets.

4.3   Person Identification on PAMAP2

While initially experimenting with PAMAP2, each recording of the individuals was split into the train-validation-test (T-V-T) set at 64%–18%–18% without considering the activity being performed in the segmented windows of the recordings. The results on the dataset were similar irrespective of the Lr, mB size, window size and stride at around Acc 50%. The maximum Acc was 57.2% for $Lr = 10^{-4}$, mB size = 50, epoch 50 and without subject 109, as in the recording protocol of PAMAP2.

A new training set was created to investigate whether the poor identification performance was related to the distribution of activities throughout the T-V-T set. The recordings per activity were stacked and then split into [64%–18%–18%] T-V-T sets. Consequently, every activity performed by the individual in the test set would be present in the training, validation and testing set. It was found that the new T-V-T set could perform better and provide better identification performance, as shown in Table 5. The results are an average over five trials **(x5)** and are presented as percentages. The experiment indicates that the network may not generalise features contributing to an individual's identity over activities

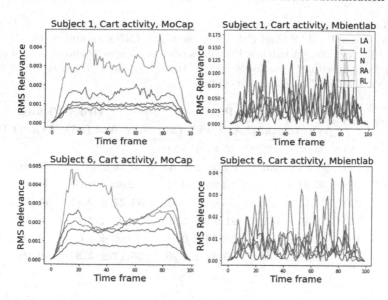

Fig. 2. LRP on LARa dataset with a $tCNN\text{-}IMU_{MLP}$ of one branch for all channels. The plots show the RMS of positive relevance of the sensor channels of Subject 1 and 6 performing the activity "Cart".

that are not present in the training set irrespective of their similarity to the activities. The $tCNN\text{-}IMU_{LSTM}$ shows a better and lesser variable performance than the $tCNN\text{-}IMU_{MLP}$.

4.4 Person Identification on OPPORTUNITY

A $tCNN\text{-}IMU_{MLP}$ was trained on OPP with epochs $= \{5, 10\}$, mB sizes $= \{25, 100\}$, and $Lr = \{10^{-4}, 10^{-5}, 10^{-6}\}$. An Acc and wF1 of 99% was achieved for mB sizes $= \{25, 100\}$, of $Lr = 10^{-4}$ with epochs 5 and 10. Similar to LARa-Mbientlab data, it was noticed that reducing the Lr to 10^{-6} deteriorated the performance of the networks. However, the Acc remained greater than 90%. An average Acc of 96.03% and an average wF1 of 95.84% was achieved five runs (**x5**) of the experiment. The performance of the $tCNN\text{-}IMU_{LSTM}$ was similar to the $tCNN\text{-}IMU_{MLP}$ network.

4.5 Person Identification on Order Picking

OrP is a small dataset created in two real warehouses for HAR. Irrespective of the Lr, mB size and epoch, the Acc failed to improve beyond 55% on both networks. Further, we attempted to find the accuracy on the non-normalised dataset with epoch 15. This resulted in an accuracy level of 57%. Furthermore, we attempted at fine-tuning the dataset using the convolutional layers of the $tCNN\text{-}IMU_{MLP}$ trained on LARa-Mbientlab. However, no improvements in identification were

Table 5. Person Identification in terms of the average Acc[%] and wF1[%] from five runs (x5) on the PAMAP2 and OrP using the $tCNN\text{-}IMU_{MLP}$ and $tCNN\text{-}IMU_{LSTM}$ at $Lr = 10^{-4}$ for different batches. PAMAP2 runs for 10 epochs and OrP for 4 epochs. The original split with "*" was for 50 epochs. Here, $*_{MLP}$ and $*_{LSTM}$ represent tCNN-IMU$_{MLP}$ and tCNN-IMU$_{LSTM}$ respectively.

Network	mB	PAMAP2		Order Picking	
		Avg Acc (x5)	Avg wF1 (x5)	Avg Acc (x5)	Avg wF1 (x5)
O. Split*	50	54.93 ± 4.29	53.84 ± 5.24		
$*_{MLP}$	50	**90.35 ± 0.61**	**90.36 ± 0.61**	52.79 ± 0.98	51.69 ± 0.92
	100	85.03 ± 0.43	84.98 ± 0.43	52.80 ± 0.41	51.71 ± 0.34
	200	75.74 ± 1.45	75.63 ± 1.51	**53.27 ± 2.11**	**51.72 ± 1.58**
$*_{LSTM}$	50	**91.65 ± 0.25**	**91.64 ± 0.25**	49.30 ± 2.83	47.42 ± 3.39
	100	90.31 ± 0.07	90.30 ± 0.08	50.09 ± 1.11	48.56 ± 1.70
	200	87.88 ± 0.89	87.87 ± 0.90	**50.17 ± 1.81**	**49.16 ± 1.85**

achieved. The absence of a recording protocol limits the chances of further experimentation and improvements. Table 5 presents the person identification results on OrP with the two networks. The training was conducted at $Lr = 10^{-4}$ and epoch 4. The values presented are an average of five iterations.

4.6 Impact of Activities

We measured the proportion of activities when an identity is correctly predicted on the test sets; that is $IOA_c^+ = \frac{n_c^+}{n_c^+ + n_c^-}$ for an activity class c. Here, n_c^+ refers to number of windows with correct person identification and n_c^- refers to the number of windows with the activity label that were misclassified.

Table 6 shows the IOA_c^+ for PAMAP2, LARa-Mbientlab, and OPP. For LARa-Mbientlab, the activities that contain gait cycles performed better than activities with upper body movement. The worst performance was showcased by the "Handling down" activity. For OPP, the windows with minimal body movements obtained a higher correct identification rate, similar to the results of [6]. On the other hand, the windows with "Stand" locomotion activity had the least correct window classification. Overall the performance of OPP dataset was good because of the sensor-rich nature of the dataset.

From the four basic activities in PAMAP2 with cyclic body movements, "Cycling" activity shows a poor classification rate. "Nordic walk" and "Walking" perform better than all other activity classes. "Lying", "Sitting" and "Standing" are classified as postures. In general, the classification rate of postures is low. This finding negates the conclusion of [6], that activities with little body movement have high identification accuracy. Identical to the findings in [6], the classification accuracy of "Vacuuming" activity was the worst performance. Activities with tools that cause vibrations impact the sensor data, leading to poor classification accuracy.

Table 6. Impact of activities on PAMAP2, LARa and OPP datasets. The averaged accuracy values are presented as a percentage.

LARa		PAMAP2	
Activity	IOA_c^+	**Activity**	IOA_c^+
Walking	87.67 ± 12.23	Rope Jump	**83.74 ± 6.81**
Cart	**93.37 ± 6.37**	Lying	74.72 ± 26.85
Hand. cen	83.08 ± 8.02	Sitting	75.58 ± 13.97
Hand. down	66.74 ± 22.58	Standing	78.73 ± 14.46
Hand. up	82.187 ± 13.27	Walking	**85.65 ± 19.15**
Standing	**89.21 ± 8.90**	Running	77.41 ± 12.76
Synch	85.02 ± 9.48	Cycling	68.64 ± 22.18
OPP		Nordic Walk	**87.23 ± 13.98**
Activity	IOA_c^+	Asc. Stairs	74.09 ± 22.46
None	98.64 ± 1.68	Des. Stairs	66.64 ± 24.77
Stand	92.42 ± 3.93	Vaccuming	49.39 ± 19.84
Walk	97.69 ± 2.83	Ironing	74.91 ± 22.71
Lie	98.04 ± 5.72	–	–
Sit	98.82 ± 2.53	–	–

One anomaly of the entire dataset is descending stairs activities. Though "Ascending Stairs" has an average performance, "Descending Stairs" has a similar performance to that of "Cycling". It is unclear why two activities that show cyclic body movement showed accuracy rates worse than that of posture activities.

4.7 Soft-Biometrics Identification

Taking inspiration from [23, 26, 28], two sets of attribute representations $[A_1, A_2]$ are created for person identification based on soft-biometrics from the recording protocol of LARa dataset. $A_1 \in \mathbb{B}^4$ contains four binary attributes, which are quantised into two levels. For example, the attribute $A_1^{height} = 0$ when the height is ≤ 170 cm, and $A_1^{height} = 1$ when the height is > 170 cm. $A_2 \in \mathbb{B}^{10}$ contains 10 binary attributes representing the soft-biometrics[1]. Each soft-biometric is divided into three levels, e.g., $A_2^{height[\leq 170, 170-180, > 180]}$. In this case, each level is assigned a binary value, e.g., given an individual of height 163, $A_2^{height[\leq 170]} = 1$, $A_2^{height[170-180]} = 0$ and $A_2^{height[> 180]} = 0$. Given the limited number of subjects in the LARa dataset, we selected the attributes and thresholds such that they contain variations that can facilitate learning. For example, the protocol contains

---

[1] The attribute representation for the two types can be found in https://github.com/nilahnair/Annotation_Tool_LARa/tree/master/From_Human_Pose_to_On_Body_Devices_for_Human_Activity_Recognition/Person_SoftBio_Identification.

information regarding handedness; however, it was not considered an attribute for learning as there were no variations within the subjects, i.e., all subjects were right-handed. Consequently, applying the same attribute representation on a different dataset, for instance, PAMAP2, would not be feasible, as the ranges of the attributes would be different; thus, resulting in a representation with no variation.

Table 7. Leave one out cross-validation (LOOCV) attribute representations using NNA for LARa-Mbientlab, LARa-Motionminers and PAMAP2. M/F refers to Male or Female. L/R refers to handedness left or right. Lr rate= 0.001 and epoch 50. The accuracy values are presented as a percentage.

	A_1			A_2				
	Threshold	Mbientlab	MotionMiners	Threshold	Mbientlab	MotionMiners	Threshold	PAMAP2
Gender	M/F	44.81 ± 24.21	46.03 ± 37.44	M/F	47.19 ± 24.43	44.15 ± 40.54	M/F	81.11 ± 32.17
Handedness	L/R			L/R			L/R	83.82 ± 32.19
Age	≤40/>40	35.11 ± 19.21	64.94 ± 29.84	≤30	44.22 ± 29.11	45.77 ± 34.61	≤25	33.37 ± 15.95
				30–40	66.87 ± 29.43	76.08 ± 42.24	25–30	44.99 ± 21.45
				>40	38.44 ± 22.49	66.55 ± 31.94	>30	56.82 ± 42.11
Weight	≤70/>70	43.82 ± 20.98	58.84 ± 35.83	≤60	46.26 ± 32.27	30.79 ± 35.53	≤70	63.58 ± 34.09
				60–80	55.18 ± 43.92	48.52 ± 42.06	70–80	66.35 ± 31.08
				>80	47.62 ±21.32	59.13 ± 39.83	>80	52.67 ± 19.63
Height	≤170/>170	47.77 ± 30.78	35.82 ± 34.17	≤170	50.89 ± 30.56	33.78 ± 37.00	≤175	50.10 ± 28.86
				170–180	40.83 ± 24.55	31.48 ± 39.44	175–185	44.84 ± 21.75
				>180	65.96 ± 33.17	72.09 ± 42.25	>185	65.45 ± 26.48

An attribute representation $A \in \mathbb{B}^m$ are tabulated following the format presented in [23]. Few subjects have the same attribute representations. For instance, from Table 1, subject 10 and 14 of LARa dataset have the same attribute representation in A_1 as their soft-biometric features fall into the same range. Similarly, subject 12 and 13 have the same attribute representation in A_2 as their soft-biometric features fall into similar ranges. As a result, attribute representations cannot be used to identify a particular individual, rather, a group of individuals with similar soft-biometrics characteristics.

The $tCNN\text{-}IMU_{MLP}$ network was trained eight times by leaving out one subject and testing the network with the left-out subject. The network used epoch 10, $Lr = 10^{-4}$ and mB size = 100. The experiments were conducted using the NNA with the *Cosine* and *PRM* similarities; however, the presented values are using the *Cosine* similarity, as the *PRM* showed the same performance. The average of eight iterations is presented.

Table 7 presents the leave one out cross-validation (LOOCV) average performance of $A_{[1,2]}$ attribute representations of LARa- Mbientlab and Motionminers and A for PAMAP2. For A_1 and A_2, the performance of Gender identity (Gender ID) and Height attributes outperforms that of Weight and Age. As Table 7 shows, in A_2, persons with $A_2^{height[>180]}$ shows a better accuracy for LARa-Mbientlab. However, the improved performance can be attributed to the low amount of variations from the soft-biometrics of the individuals found in the dataset. Hence, the soft-biometrics identification using attribute representation can be said to have potential, provided we have a larger and dedicated dataset.

5 Conclusions

This work explored the possibility of person identification using motion information obtained from OBD data by training DNNs, such as $tCNN\text{-}IMU_{MLP}$ and $tCNN\text{-}IMU_{LSTM}$ using benchmark HAR datasets. Further, the impact of activities on the identification process was analysed. Finally, soft-biometrics identification using attribute representations was deployed. The soft-biometrics were modelled as attribute representations of the individual based on the LARa-Mbientlab dataset recording protocol.

Experiments on the impact of channel-normalisation on $tCNN\text{-}IMU_{MLP}$ using LARa-Mbientlab pointed out that positional bias does not exceed the benefits of channel-normalisation. Based on the experimentation with LARa, OPP, and PAMAP2, person identification is not restricted to gait activity. The impact of activities showed that noise from instruments used could impede identification. Consistent with the research by [6], dormant activities have high classification accuracy in the OPP. However, experiments on PAMAP2 negated the observation.

Attribute representation with higher dimensionality was found to have better performance. Gender identity and height soft-biometrics consistently provided exceptional results. Evidently, the results of attribute representation are relatively poor. Consequently, a larger dataset with soft-biometrics, number of participants, and recording settings are necessary to facilitate attribute representation based transfer learning. This dataset should consider different recording settings for minimising the biases caused by having a single or very few recording set-ups, e.g., sensor position and configuration, per individual. In addition, careful documentation of participants and recording protocols is required. Furthermore, the application of the XAI method- LRP to identify the features that contribute to identity needs to be explored.

Acknowledgment. The work on this publication was supported by Deutsche Forschungsgemeinschaft (DFG) in the context of the project Fi799/10-2 "Transfer Learning for Human Activity Recognition in Logistics".

References

1. Anders, C.J., Neumann, D., Samek, W., Müller, K.R., Lapuschkin, S.: Software for dataset-wide XAI: From local explanations to global insights with zennit, CoRelAy, and ViRelAy. http://arxiv.org/abs/2106.13200
2. Boyd, J.E., Little, J.J.: Biometric gait recognition. In: Tistarelli, M., Bigun, J., Grosso, E. (eds.) Advanced Studies in Biometrics. LNCS, vol. 3161, pp. 19–42. Springer, Heidelberg (2005). https://doi.org/10.1007/11493648_2
3. Chavarriaga, R., Sagha, H., Calatroni, A., Digumarti, S.T., Tröster, G., Millán, J.d.R., Roggen, D.: The opportunity challenge: A benchmark database for on-body sensor-based activity recognition **34**(15), 2033–2042. https://doi.org/10.1016/j.patrec.2012.12.014, https://linkinghub.elsevier.com/retrieve/pii/S0167865512004205

4. Chunsheng, H., De, W., Huidong, Z., Guoli, L.: Human gait feature data analysis and person identification based on IMU. In: 2020 IEEE International Conference on Artificial Intelligence and Computer Applications (ICAICA), pp. 437–442. IEEE. https://doi.org/10.1109/ICAICA50127.2020.9182691, https://ieeexplore.ieee.org/document/9182691/

5. Dehzangi, O., Taherisadr, M., ChangalVala, R.: IMU-based gait recognition using convolutional neural networks and multi-sensor fusion 17(12), 2735. https://doi.org/10.3390/s17122735, http://www.mdpi.com/1424-8220/17/12/2735

6. Elkader, S.A., Barlow, M., Lakshika, E.: Wearable sensors for recognizing individuals undertaking daily activities. In: Proceedings of the 2018 ACM International Symposium on Wearable Computers, pp. 64–67. ACM. https://doi.org/10.1145/3267242.3267245, https://dl.acm.org/doi/10.1145/3267242.3267245

7. Farhadi, A., Endres, I., Hoiem, D., Forsyth, D.: Describing objects by their attributes. In: 2009 IEEE Conference on Computer Vision and Pattern Recognition, pp. 1778–1785. IEEE. https://doi.org/10.1109/CVPR.2009.5206772, https://ieeexplore.ieee.org/document/5206772/

8. Gohar, I., et al.: Person re-identification using deep modeling of temporally correlated inertial motion patterns 20(3), 949. https://doi.org/10.3390/s20030949, https://www.mdpi.com/1424-8220/20/3/949

9. Grzeszick, R., Lenk, J.M., Rueda, F.M., Fink, G.A., Feldhorst, S., ten Hompel, M.: Deep neural network based human activity recognition for the order picking process. In: Proceedings of the 4th International Workshop on Sensor-Based Activity Recognition and Interaction, pp. 1–6. ACM. https://doi.org/10.1145/3134230.3134231, https://dl.acm.org/doi/10.1145/3134230.3134231

10. Han, J., Bhanu, B.: Individual recognition using gait energy image 28(2), 316–322. https://doi.org/10.1109/TPAMI.2006.38, https://ieeexplore.ieee.org/document/1561189/

11. Horst, F., Lapuschkin, S., Samek, W., Müller, K.R., Schöllhorn, W.I.: Explaining the unique nature of individual gait patterns with deep learning 9(1), 2391. https://doi.org/10.1038/s41598-019-38748-8, https://www.nature.com/articles/s41598-019-38748-8

12. Jain, A., Ross, A., Prabhakar, S.: An introduction to biometric recognition 14(1), 4–20. https://doi.org/10.1109/TCSVT.2003.818349, http://ieeexplore.ieee.org/document/1262027/

13. Lampert, C.H., Nickisch, H., Harmeling, S.: Attribute-based classification for zero-shot visual object categorization 36(3), 453–465. https://doi.org/10.1109/TPAMI.2013.140, http://ieeexplore.ieee.org/document/6571196/

14. Wang, L., Tan, T., Ning, H., Hu, W.: Silhouette analysis-based gait recognition for human identification 25(12), 1505–1518. https://doi.org/10.1109/TPAMI.2003.1251144, http://ieeexplore.ieee.org/document/1251144/

15. Liu, L.-F., Jia, W., Zhu, Y.-H.: Survey of gait recognition. In: Huang, D.-S., Jo, K.-H., Lee, H.-H., Kang, H.-J., Bevilacqua, V. (eds.) ICIC 2009. LNCS (LNAI), vol. 5755, pp. 652–659. Springer, Heidelberg (2009). https://doi.org/10.1007/978-3-642-04020-7_70

16. Malekzadeh, M., Clegg, R.G., Cavallaro, A., Haddadi, H.: Mobile sensor data anonymization. In: Proceedings of the International Conference on Internet of Things Design and Implementation, pp. 49–58. ACM. https://doi.org/10.1145/3302505.3310068, https://dl.acm.org/doi/10.1145/3302505.3310068

17. Mekruksavanich, S., Jitpattanakul, A.: Biometric user identification based on human activity recognition using wearable sensors: An experiment using deep learning models **10**(3), 308. https://doi.org/10.3390/electronics10030308, https://www.mdpi.com/2079-9292/10/3/308

18. Montavon, G., Binder, A., Lapuschkin, S., Samek, W., Müller, K.-R.: Layer-wise relevance propagation: An overview. In: Samek, W., Montavon, G., Vedaldi, A., Hansen, L.K., Müller, K.-R. (eds.) Explainable AI: Interpreting, Explaining and Visualizing Deep Learning. LNCS (LNAI), vol. 11700, pp. 193–209. Springer, Cham (2019). https://doi.org/10.1007/978-3-030-28954-6_10

19. Montavon, G., Lapuschkin, S., Binder, A., Samek, W., Müller, K.R.: Explaining nonlinear classification decisions with deep Taylor decomposition **65**, 211–222. https://doi.org/10.1016/j.patcog.2016.11.008, https://linkinghub.elsevier.com/retrieve/pii/S0031320316303582

20. Moya Rueda, F., Grzeszick, R., Fink, G., Feldhorst, S., ten Hompel, M.: Convolutional neural networks for human activity recognition using body-worn sensors **5**(2), 26. https://doi.org/10.3390/informatics5020026, http://www.mdpi.com/2227-9709/5/2/26

21. Niemann, F., et al.: LARa: Creating a dataset for human activity recognition in logistics using semantic attributes **20**(15), 4083. https://doi.org/10.3390/s20154083, https://www.mdpi.com/1424-8220/20/15/4083

22. Reining, C., Rueda, F.M., Niemann, F., Fink, G.A., Hompel, M.T.: Annotation performance for multi-channel time series HAR dataset in logistics. In: 2020 IEEE International Conference on Pervasive Computing and Communications Workshops (PerCom Workshops), pp. 1–6. IEEE. https://doi.org/10.1109/PerComWorkshops48775.2020.9156170, https://ieeexplore.ieee.org/document/9156170/

23. Reining, C., Schlangen, M., Hissmann, L., ten Hompel, M., Moya, F., Fink, G.A.: Attribute representation for human activity recognition of manual order picking activities. In: Proceedings of the 5th intl. Workshop on Sensor-based Activity Recognition and Interaction, pp. 1–10. ACM. https://doi.org/10.1145/3266157.3266214, https://dl.acm.org/doi/10.1145/3266157.3266214

24. Reiss, A., Stricker, D.: Introducing a new benchmarked dataset for activity monitoring. In: 2012 16th International Symposium on Wearable Computers, pp. 108–109. IEEE. https://doi.org/10.1109/ISWC.2012.13, http://ieeexplore.ieee.org/document/6246152/

25. Retsinas, G., Filntisis, P.P., Efthymiou, N., Theodosis, E., Zlatintsi, A., Maragos, P.: Person identification using deep convolutional neural networks on short-term signals from wearable sensors. In: ICASSP 2020–2020 IEEE International Conference on Acoustics, Speech and Signal Processing (ICASSP), pp. 3657–3661. IEEE. https://doi.org/10.1109/ICASSP40776.2020.9053910, https://ieeexplore.ieee.org/document/9053910/

26. Riaz, Q., Vögele, A., Krüger, B., Weber, A.: One small step for a man: Estimation of gender, age and height from recordings of one step by a single inertial sensor **15**(12), 31999–32019. https://doi.org/10.3390/s151229907, http://www.mdpi.com/1424-8220/15/12/29907

27. Rueda, F.M., Fink, G.A.: From human pose to on-body devices for human-activity recognition. In: 2020 25th International Conference on Pattern Recognition (ICPR), pp. 10066–10073. IEEE. https://doi.org/10.1109/ICPR48806.2021.9412283, https://ieeexplore.ieee.org/document/9412283/

28. Rueda, F.M., Fink, G.A.: Learning attribute representation for human activity recognition. In: 2018 24th International Conference on Pattern Recognition (ICPR), pp. 523–528. IEEE. https://doi.org/10.1109/ICPR.2018.8545146, https://ieeexplore.ieee.org/document/8545146/

29. Rusakov, E., Rothacker, L., Mo, H., Fink, G.A.: A probabilistic retrieval model for word spotting based on direct attribute prediction. In: 2018 16th International Conference on Frontiers in Handwriting Recognition (ICFHR), pp. 38–43. IEEE. https://doi.org/10.1109/ICFHR-2018.2018.00016, https://ieeexplore.ieee.org/document/8563223/

30. Shahid, S., Nandy, A., Mondal, S., Ahamad, M., Chakraborty, P., Nandi, G.C.: A study on human gait analysis. In: Proceedings of the Second International Conference on Computational Science, Engineering and Information Technology - CCSEIT 2012, pp. 358–364. ACM Press. https://doi.org/10.1145/2393216.2393277, http://dl.acm.org/citation.cfm?doid=2393216.2393277

31. Singh, J.P., Jain, S., Arora, S., Singh, U.P.: Vision-based gait recognition: A survey **6**, 70497–70527. https://doi.org/10.1109/ACCESS.2018.2879896, https://ieeexplore.ieee.org/document/8528404/

32. Sudholt, S., Fink, G.A.: Attribute CNNs for word spotting in handwritten documents **21**(3), 199–218. https://doi.org/10.1007/s10032-018-0295-0, http://link.springer.com/10.1007/s10032-018-0295-0

To Invest or Not to Invest: Using Vocal Behavior to Predict Decisions of Investors in an Entrepreneurial Context

Ilona Goossens[1], Merel M. Jung[1], Werner Liebregts[2],
and Itir Onal Ertugrul[3(✉)]

[1] Department of Cognitive Science and Artificial Intelligence, Tilburg University,
Tilburg, The Netherlands
{i.goossens,m.m.jung}@tilburguniversity.edu
[2] Jheronimus Academy of Data Science, 's-Hertogenbosch, The Netherlands
w.j.liebregts@tilburguniversity.edu
[3] Department of Information and Computing Sciences, Utrecht University, Utrecht,
The Netherlands
i.onalertugrul@uu.nl

Abstract. Entrepreneurial pitch competitions have become increasingly popular in the start-up culture to attract prospective investors. As the ultimate funding decision often follows from some form of social interaction, it is important to understand how the decision-making process of investors is influenced by behavioral cues. In this work, we examine whether vocal features are associated with the ultimate funding decision of investors by utilizing deep learning methods. We used videos of individuals in an entrepreneurial pitch competition as input to predict whether investors will invest in the startup or not. We proposed models that combine deep audio features and Handcrafted audio Features (HaF) and feed them into two types of Recurrent Neural Networks (RNN), namely Long Short-Term Memory (LSTM) and Gated Recurrent Units (GRU). We also trained the RNNs with only deep features to assess whether HaF provide additional information to the models. Our results show that it is promising to use vocal behavior of pitchers to predict whether investors will invest in their business idea. Different types of RNNs yielded similar performance, yet the addition of HaF improved the performance.

Keywords: vocal behavior · entrepreneurial decision making · deep learning · VGGish · LSTM · GRU

1 Introduction

Entrepreneurial decision-making is at the core of successfully operating within the business sector [37]. It includes all decisions made by entrepreneurs themselves and decisions made by others which have an immediate impact on the entrepreneur. Due to the complex and dynamic environment (e.g., high uncertainty, ambiguity, time pressure, high risks, etc.) that entrepreneurs and associates (e.g., innovators, investors, inventors) are subject to as well as the frequency with which decisions on entrepreneurial tasks and activities have to

© Springer Nature Switzerland AG 2023
J.-J. Rousseau and B. Kapralos (Eds.): ICPR 2022 Workshops, LNCS 13643, pp. 273–286, 2023.
https://doi.org/10.1007/978-3-031-37660-3_19

be made, the entrepreneurial decision-making process often relies on flexible decision-making principles. Previous works [2,13,18,25,39] suggest that when social interactions are involved during the decision-making process, behavioral cues (e.g., physical appearance characteristics, posture and gestures, face and eye movement, and vocal behavior) strongly affect the ultimate decision. Even though many entrepreneurial decisions are made with little to no social interactions, some decisions are heavily based on human-to-human interaction. This is especially true for decisions related to the provision of financial resources by investors in the start-up business environment as entrepreneurial pitch competitions (i.e., events where entrepreneurs convey their start-up business idea to prospective investors) are a common approach to attract financial support. Since these decisions are associated with long-term start-up outcomes, understanding how and to what extent behavioral cues expressed during social interactions influence the decision-making process of investors could benefit entrepreneurs as they could apply this knowledge to increase the effectiveness of their presentation style which, in turn, could lead an increase in funding [5,25,32]. In general, enhancing our understanding of the decision-making process is valuable as decisions have a direct effect on important outcomes for businesses, organizations, institutions, individuals, and societies. Knowledge on how to improve those outcomes would benefit all of these stakeholders [29].

Research on decision-making in the entrepreneurial context is predominantly derived from psychological, sociological, and economic literature. In contrast, research on using machine learning approaches for automated analysis of human behavior to understand the entrepreneurial decision-making process is limited. Previous work focused on applying conventional machine learning methods such as k-Nearest Neighbors (kNN) and support vector machines (SVM) to predict investment based on the visual features including facial actions [28], eye gaze [3], and facial mimicry [19]. Vocal behavior has not been explored in automatically predicting the decisions of investors. Given the superior performance of deep learning-based approaches in several audio classification tasks [17] and the significance of vocal behavior in decision-making process [14], we propose to utilize deep learning methods to model vocal behavior and to predict decisions of investors. This research is conducted on a dataset including video recordings of individuals performing an entrepreneurial pitch about their start-up business idea. They participated in a pitch competition to attract financial resources from potential investors. This study may reveal the importance of vocal characteristics in explaining decisions related to business funding and business growth which have been neglected in research so far [25].

As vocal behavior is derived from speech that has spatiotemporal dynamics, it is crucial to incorporate a deep learning approach with the ability to retain information from previous time points. For that reason, Long Short-Term Memory (LSTM) and Gated Recurrent Unit (GRU) networks, which are two types of Recurrent Neural Network (RNN), are incorporated as their performance on sequence-based tasks and capturing long-term dependencies is well established [7,16]. Besides, LSTM and GRU are both considered to be effective for recognizing vocal characteristics and classifying audio recordings. The RNN architectures are combined with a Convolutional Neural Network (CNN) where the CNN extracts context-aware deep audio features that are fed into the RNN (e.g., [6,26,33]). Combining CNN's capability to learn invariant features with RNN's capability to model temporal dependencies into a single classifier is better known as a Convolutional Recurrent Neural Network (CRNN) [4], and is the current state-of-the-art approach in research on audio classification. In this study, we compare the performance of the models consisting of a CRNN architecture with LSTM or GRU with the proposed models additionally including Handcrafted audio Features (HaF). Introducing HaF into the model can impact the performance as Giannakopoulos et al. [12] reported a significant increase in performance when deep context-aware audio features (i.e., CNN) were combined with HaF. Additionally, Tianyu et al. [40] found that HaF capture complementary information that benefits the RNN.

Considering the literature on entrepreneurial decision-making and the various deep learning approaches across the field of audio classification, this paper explores the fusion of deep context-aware audio features and HaF in combination with the most common architectures for sequence modeling (i.e., LSTM and GRU). Results show that the proposed deep learning models have the ability to detect and recognize vocal patterns which could be used to predict the investor's funding decision. Moreover, this study finds an increase in performance when HaF are introduced into the model, while the impact of the different RNN architectures is negligible as they yielded comparable performances.

2   Related Work

Audio processing based on deep learning approaches is an emerging field due to the promising results these methods produced for tasks such as pitch determination [16], audio and sound classification [34], affective speech classification [23], and audio source separation [27]. As data used for audio processing contains prominent sequential signals, a systematic approach that incorporates the ability to capture spatiotemporal dynamics is required [16]. Recurrent Neural Networks (RNN) are suitable for modeling sequential dependencies and nonlinear dynamics within audio data as it is able to retain information from previous allocation due to the recurrent connections within the network that allow for encoding temporal information [16].

The approach of including a RNN for sequential modeling is widely adopted across audio classification field. For example, Chung et al. [7] compares different types of RNN architectures (i.e., LSTM and GRU) to a traditional Deep Neural Networks (DNN) and reveals that the models including the recurrent units outperform the traditional DNN on classification tasks including music and raw speech signal data.

Recent studies propose a Convolutional Recurrent Neural Network (CRNN) where the RNN, which is highly capable learning temporal context and model sequential data, is used in combination with a Convolutional Neural Network

(CNN). The CNN model has proven to be effective in feature learning as it is able to extract shift invariant high level features which could not be modeled with feature engineering.

Traditionally, feature representations are generated from a feature engineering process which requires domain knowledge and relies heavily on researchers' engineering effort for the task at hand. However, research towards feature learning in deep neural networks, which has been of interest lately as it reduces the required expertise and engineering effort, explored the potential of CNN architectures. Comparing the two approaches, a study by Trigeorgis et al. [41] on speech emotion recognition concluded that feature representations created through an end-to-end deep network significantly outperforms the approach of traditional designed features based on signal processing techniques and shallow processing architectures. They argue that deep networks, especially CNNs, have the ability to extract context-aware effective and robust acoustic features which better suit the task at hand, and therefore, improve the performance of the model. Hershey et al. [17] examines the performances of multiple CNN architectures on audio soundtrack classification by proposing analogs of popular CNN networks (e.g., AlexNet, VGG, Inception, and ResNet-50), which have proven to be effective in image classification. With minor modifications to the models, results show that all CNN architectures yield significant performances on audio classification problems. Comparing the performances of the architectures trained on 70M videos with 3.000 labels based on log-mel spectrogram inputs, the best performing architecture incorporates the Inception-V3 model achieving 0.918 Area Under Curve (AUC) while the worst performing architecture employs the AlexNet model achieving 0.894 AUC. The ResNet-50 and VGGish models report 0.916 AUC and 0.911 AUC, respectively. The findings in this study support that convolutional layers in deep neural networks effectively recognize and preserve modulation patterns while omitting small deviations in pitch and timing by training to extract, regardless of the offset frequency and start time, down- and upward moving spectral patterns.

Lim et al. [26] propose a CRNN for rare sound event detection. They incorporate a CNN model for feature learning, which takes log-amplitude mel-spectrogram extracted from the audio as the input feature and analyzes the audio in chunk-level. The extracted features resulting from the CNN model are fed into a two-layer LSTM network for modeling sequential information. The best performing model report an error rate of 0.13 and a F-score of 0.931.

Sainath et al. [33] propose a Convolutional LSTM Deep Neural Network (CLDNN) which is a unified framework that is trained jointly. In other words, they design an architecture that captures information about the input representation at different levels by combining a CNN, LSTM, and DNN. Here, the CNN is used to reduce spectral variation in the input feature, the LSTM network performs the sequential modeling, and the DNN layers are introduces for the vocabulary tasks. Sainath et al. [33] hypothesize an improvement in performance and output predictions when DNN layers are introduced into the CRNN as the mapping between hidden units and outputs is deeper. Their initial proposed method achieved a word error rate of 17.3, which decreased to 17.0 when uniform random weight initialization was introduced to deal with vanishing gradients. Although their proposed model yields better results, the performance of the CRNN model is with a word error rate of 17.6 considered comparable, yet competitive. They conclude that both the CRNN model and the CLDNN model are able to capture information at different resolutions. Additionally, the performance of the CLDNN model was evaluated on a large dataset resulting in an error rate of 13.1. However, this error rate increases to 17.4 when noise is added.

A similar CRNN configuration to that of [33] is adopted by Cakir et al. [4] for a polyphonic sound event classification task. The main difference between the network as proposed in [33] and applied in [4] is the type of RNN architecture incorporated. Cakir et al. [4] includes a GRU network instead of a LSTM network to model the long-term temporal context in the audio. Other modifications are with regards to the depth of the CNN and LSTM as they increase the number of convolutional layers to four and add one more recurrent layer. They expect their proposed method to outperform established methods in sound event detection. The evaluation results confirm that expectations are met as they show an improvement in performance for the proposed method (i.e., CRNN) compared to previous approaches to sound event detection. Previous approaches, using the same dataset, report error rates between 16.0 to 17.5, while the CRNN achieves an error rate of 11.3.

A CRNN which includes a GRU network as RNN architecture is also used for music classification [6]. They compare the performances of the proposed network to three existing CNN models, and expect that the ability to capture segment structure and the flexibility introduced by the RNN benefits the classification performances. Results show an AUC score of 0.86 for the CRNN, while the AUC scores for the CNN models vary from 0.83 to 0.855. They conclude that the CRNN effectively learns deep features which could be used for prediction tasks such as predicting music tags.

Hence, the CRNN approach provides promising results across various audio classification tasks. However, according to Pishdadian et al. [31] it would be premature to disregard traditional feature representations in favour of exclusively employing deep audio features as the handcrafted features could provide the model with additional information that could not be captured by deep networks. Moreover, Kuncheva et al. [22] argues that combining complementary and diverse features could improve the classification performances of a model. Giannakopoulos et al. [12] provides support for this approach as they find a significant increase in performance for classifying urban audio events and environmental audio sounds when HaF are introduced into the models compared to models that exclusively relied on deep audio features extracted using a CNN. Giannakopoulos et al. [12] apply the different feature representations to similar Support Vector Machine (SVM) architectures to compare their performances, and reports accuracy levels of 44.2% and 52.2% for the model including exclusively deep audio features and the model combining deep audio features with HaF, respectively. They conclude that, based on a simple classification scheme

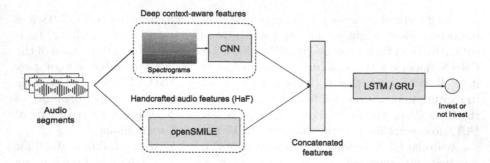

Fig. 1. Pipeline of the proposed approach. Audio segments from the pitcher are used as input to (i) pretrained VGGish network to obtain deep context-aware features and (ii) OpenSMILE to obtain Handcrafted audio Features (HaF). Deep and handcrafted features are concatenated and given as input to a LSTM or a GRU. The model predicts whether the investors will invest in the pitcher's business idea or not.

(i.e., SVM), the contextual knowledge of the input data could be significantly increased when deep audio features are combined with typical HaF. Besides, they recommend that future research should explore a similar approach in the context of a deep learning framework.

This study builds upon the recommendation for future research of Giannakopoulos et al. [12] by introducing HaF into the deep network. To apply the current state-of-the-art approach, this study uses a CRNN architecture. As GRU and LSTM networks are both commonly used in audio classification research, this study compares the performances of these two networks.

3   Method

The proposed network (see Fig. 1) takes a sequence of audio segments as input, extracts deep and handcrafted audio features and concatenates them, finally passes them through a recurrent neural network (LSTM or GRU) to predict whether the startup will get investment or not.

3.1   Feature Extraction

Within this study, two types of features are incorporated: (i) deep context-aware features, and (ii) Handcrafted audio Features (HaF).

Deep Context-Aware Features. The deep context-aware features are extracted with the VGGish architecture which is pre-trained on the YouTube-8M dataset [43]. For the audio input, a short-time Fourier transform with a step size of 10 ms is applied on 25 ms windows to compute the spectrogram. Spectrograms are mapped to 64 Mel-spaced frequency bins and frames with 96×64 pixels are obtained [17]. Finally, log transform is applied to obtain log Mel spectrograms, which are used as input to the pretrained VGGish model.

In this study, the VGGish network with 11 layers is used to extract deep discriminative features. Moreover, the last max-pooling layer and the last group of convolutional layers are dropped, resulting in a VGGish network architecture of four modules [31,43]. The VGGish network outputs a one-dimensional feature vector with 128 extracted features for every ~1-s segment of the input audio.

Handcrafted Audio Features (HaF). The HaF are extracted using the open-source OpenSMILE [9,10] toolkit. OpenSMILE extracts both Low-Level Descriptors (e.g. pitch, energy, Mel Frequency Cepstral Coefficients) as well as their functionals (e.g. extreme values, means, peaks, moments). We used LLDs and functionals in feature set eGeMAPSv02 [8]. Previous work shows the usage potential of the features from OpenSMILE in recognition and classification tasks across multimedia research [9,35,36]. Moreover, the ComParE feature set is applied on various multimedia tasks such as determining emotion from music, speech and sound, and delivered state-of-the-art accuracy [42]). This configuration was shown to be the best performing acoustic feature set for personality impression prediction [15].

3.2 Modeling Long-Term Temporal Information

To model the long-term information in an audio sequence, extracted features are passed through a recurrent neural network. We used two different RNNs namely, LSTM and GRU. GRU contains less parameters compared to LSTM, and generally performs well on limited training data [1] whereas LSTM can remember longer sequences [7]. Our dataset is small in terms of the number of videos and contains rather long sequences. For that reason, we used both GRU and LSTM to model long-term temporal information. We used single-layer GRU and LSTM networks and varied the number of hidden units within the set [64, 128, 256, 512]. The representation obtained from LSTM or GRU is passed to a binary classification layer to predict the investment decision label assigned to the corresponding audio sequence.

4 Experimental Setup

4.1 Dataset

The dataset used in this study was collected for the scientific purpose of investigating how our understanding of the decision-making process, that involves social interactions in the entrepreneurial context, could be advanced by leveraging modern data science techniques [25]. Our data [24] includes video recordings from 43 individuals who perform an entrepreneurial pitch about their start-up business idea and three judges assessing the pitches. From the total of 43 pitches, 26 were performed in an offline setting while 17 were performed in an online environment. The pitchers were all students who took part in the pitch competition as part of their university-level educational program on data science and entrepreneurship. Pitchers had a maximum of three minutes to perform their pitch followed by an interactive Q&A session in which the judges, who were all experienced within the start-up ecosystem, could ask questions to the pitcher for a maximum of ten minutes. For the purpose of this study, only the audio recordings from the pitches are considered.

4.2   Preprocessing of Audio Recordings

Audio recordings from the pitch segments were extracted. As it is preferred to process equally sized inputs to optimize the learning process of deep learning algorithms, audio segments of 150 s are used as input. To this end, the audio segments for pitches shorter than 150 s were (partially) duplicated whereas for the longer pitches the 150 s from the middle of the pitch were selected.

In order to train recurrent neural networks, we segmented audio segments into non-overlapping chunks. In audio processing literature common values of segment size vary from 1 to 10 s [12,20]. Earlier works often adopt a one second time frame when sounds are involved, but prefer a longer time frame (i.e., 2–10 s) when music or speech is involved. In this study, we set the chunk size to 2 s as it is reasonable to assume that speech lasts for at least 2 s [11].

From these 150-s audio segments we created 2-s chunks to approximate the duration of speech [11]. This approach resulted in 75 non-overlapping chunks of 2 s for all 43 pitches which were fed into the feature extractor. The data was split into a training (80%) and test (20%) set to evaluate the performance of the model.

4.3   Outcome Predictor of Investment Decisions

After each pitch, each investor evaluated the performance of the pitcher and assigned a score between 0 and 100 with intermediate steps of 5 indicating the probability of investment. We mapped these scores into binary target labels for each participant consisting of *invest* (i.e., class 1) or *not invest* (i.e., class 0). Although the potential investors (i.e., judges) all had experience within the start-up business environment, their level of experience and expertise with regards to new venture start-ups, new market developments, and new product developments varied. Moreover, the potential investors had various backgrounds (e.g., venture capitalists and business coach) and field of interests (e.g., sustainability, technology, lifestyle, sports, non-profit). According to [30,38], the investment decision-making process, and thereby the ultimate decision, is influenced by the level of experience in the specific type of setting. In other words, two investors with experiences in different markets might evaluate a start-up business differently, resulting in a different decision on whether or not to provide financial resources. These differences in judgment also occur within the dataset as for example one judge evaluated the probability to invest with a score of 80, while another judge assigned a score of 20 to the same pitch. Considering the diverse panel of judges, and thus the differences in evaluations, and by keeping in mind the real-world setting where new ventures are looking for at least one investor, the binary class label *invest* was assigned based on at least one positive evaluation. That is, the label *invest* is assigned when at least one of the potential investors evaluated the pitch with a probability to invest score of 50 or higher, and the label *not invest* is assigned when all scores were lower than 50.

4.4 Models

The proposed models consist of a combination of deep and handcrafted features and a RNN architecture (i.e., GRU or LSTM). In order to see the impact of handcrafted features, we performed an ablation study and used only deep features in combination with LSTM or GRU. We trained the following four models:

Model 1: LSTM with deep context-aware features and HaF (CNN + HaF + LSTM): this model includes a combination of features extracted using VGGish and OpenSMILE and an LSTM for temporal information processing.

Model 2: GRU with deep context-aware features and HaF (CNN + HaF + GRU): this model includes a combination of features extracted using VGGish and OpenSMILE and an GRU for temporal information processing.

Model 3: LSTM with deep context-aware features (CNN + LSTM): this model includes features extracted using VGGish architecture and an LSTM for temporal information processing.

Model 4: GRU with deep context-aware features (CNN + GRU): this model includes features extracted using VGGish architecture and a GRU for temporal information processing.

In general, the process of the four defined models is similar. For each pitch, 75 non-overlapping 2-s audio chunks are sequentially put through the feature extractor(s) which outputs a 2-dimensional feature vector for each pitch. The feature vectors of all pitches are stacked together and form a 3-dimensional input vector for the RNN, which is either the LSTM or the GRU.

We input 2-s audio chunks into VGGish network, which outputs a matrix of size 2×128 for each chunk. The post-processing process flattens the feature vector of the chunk to a 1-dimensional vector of size 1×256, while stacking all chunks together. This iterative process results in a feature matrix of size 75×256 for each pitch. A similar iterative process is defined for all files in the dataset, resulting in the 3-dimensional feature vector which is fed into the RNN (i.e., LSTM or GRU). This process is applied while developing Model 3 and Model 4.

In Model 1 and Model 2, features extracted using VGGish and OpenSMILE are concatenated to capture both deep context-aware features as well as HaF. The OpenSMILE toolkit extracts 113 features (when LLDs and functionals are considered) for each input file resulting in a 1-dimensional feature vector of size 1×113 for each 2-s audio segment. This feature vector is concatenated with the feature vector from the VGGish network into a feature vector of size 1×369 for each chunk. While processing all the chunks, the resulting feature vectors of the chunks are stacked together in a feature matrix of size 75 × 369 for each file. A similar iterative process is defined for all files in the concerned dataset (i.e., training set or test set), resulting in the 3-dimensional feature vector which is fed into the RNN (i.e., LSTM or GRU).

4.5 Training

We performed hyperparameter tuning on each model based on a limited grid search. The explored hyperparameters are number of units (64, 128, 256), dropout rate (0, 0.1, 0.2), learning rate (1e−2, 1e−3, 1e−4), and number of epochs (10, 20, 50). Furthermore, each model includes the Adam optimization algorithm, which is a robust yet computationally efficient stochastic gradient-based optimization that combines the ability to deal with sparse gradient with the ability to deal with non-stationary settings [21]. Moreover, since the models are designed for a binary classification problem, the binary cross-entropy loss function was implemented in all models.

5 Results

We compare the performances of the four models (CNN + HaF + LSTM, CNN + HaF + GRU, CNN + LSTM, and CNN + GRU) to understand the impact of different RNN architectures and to analyze the impact of including HaF on the performance. Table 1 summarizes the performances of the four models.

Table 1. Performances on the test set across the proposed models. The highest performances are presented in **bold**.

	Model	Accuracy	AUC
Model 1	CNN+HaF+LSTM	**0.778**	**0.775**
Model 2	CNN+HaF+GRU	**0.778**	0.750
Model 3	CNN+LSTM	0.667	0.650
Model 4	CNN+GRU	0.667	0.625

5.1 Comparison of Different RNN Architectures

We compare the performances of model pairs containing the same features, but model the temporal information with different RNNs (Model 1 vs. Model 2, and Model 3 vs. Model 4). As shown in Table 1, a similar accuracy of 66.7% is reported for the models containing only deep features regardless of the RNN architecture. Moreover, the proposed models containing a combination of deep and handcrafted features show a similar accuracy of 77.8% regardless of the

RNN architecture. With regards to the AUC score, small differences between the models implementing the LSTM network sequence descriptor and models implementing the GRU network as sequence descriptor are found. The LSTM baseline model yields an AUC value of 0.650 whereas the GRU baseline model results in an AUC value of 0.625. A similar difference is observed for Models 1 and 2 as the LSTM and GRU report AUC values of 0.775 and 0.750 respectively. Hence, while in terms of accuracy scores similar performances between the LSTM and GRU network are found, differences in AUC scores are reported where models implementing the LSTM network appear to perform slightly better than models implementing the GRU network.

5.2   Impact of HaF on Performance

In order to evaluate the impact of HaF, the performances of models with the same RNN, but with different features (with and without HaF) are compared. As shown in Table 1, Model 3 (CNN+LSTM) reports an accuracy score of 66.7% while Model 1 (CNN+HaF+LSTM) yields an accuracy score of 77.8%. A similar increase in performance is found for the models including the GRU network as RNN, where the models without (Model 4) and with (Model 2) HaF report accuracy scores of 66.7% and 77.8%, respectively. In terms of AUC scores, an overall 0.125 increase is reported for models including HaF. Model 3 and Model 1 result in AUC values of 0.650 and 0.775, respectively. Similarly Model 4 yields 0.625 AUC while Model 2 yields 0.750 AUC score. Hence, an increase in both accuracy and AUC scores is found when HaF are introduced into the model irrespective of the type of RNN. This could indicate that the HaF capture complementary information that benefits the model in learning and recognizing acoustic patterns.

6   Conclusion

We aim to examine to what extent an investors' decision to provide financial resources could be predicted based on vocal behavior during entrepreneurial pitches by fusing deep context-aware features and Handcrafted audio Features (HaF) in combination with a Recurrent Neural Network (RNN) architecture, particularly LSTM or GRU. Results show that models that combine deep and HaF outperform the ones without HaF, which indicates that HaF provide the models with additional information that could not be captured by deep features, and that benefits the sequential modeling performance. Moreover, this study shows that GRU and LSTM networks provide comparable performances on audio data.

   This study concludes that it is promising to use vocal behavior to predict an investors' decision on whether or not to provide funding. One limitation is that we used a combined set of offline and online (recorded during the Covid-19 lockdown) pitches to have a larger amount of data to train our deep learning models. Considering the fact that non-verbal behavioral cues such as non-content characteristics of speech could be different in online and offline settings, future work could focus on investigating vocal behavior to predict investment in different settings separately. Another limitation is that we focused on predicting the binary variable reflecting whether the judges would invest in this business idea derived from the probability of investment variable. As judges do not actually make investments at the end of the competition, probability of investment may not necessarily be the most genuine assessment made by them. In future work, additional variables including originality, quality, and feasibility of the business idea could also be predicted to gain a better understanding of decision-making in an entrepreneurial context. Finally, in this work we focused only on vocal behavior. Future research on entrepreneurial decision-making based on deep learning approaches should examine the influence of combining multiple behavioral cues (e.g., facial expressions and body movements) as this could provide us with valuable insights into the way we, as humans, make decisions.

References

1. Bermant, P.C., Bronstein, M.M., Wood, R.J., Gero, S., Gruber, D.F.: Deep machine learning techniques for the detection and classification of sperm whale bioacoustics. Sci. Rep. **9**(1), 1–10 (2019)
2. Bonaccio, S., O'Reilly, J., O'Sullivan, S.L., Chiocchio, F.: Nonverbal behavior and communication in the workplace: a review and an agenda for research. J. Manag. **42**(5), 1044–1074 (2016)
3. de Bont, T.: Social Signal Processing in Entrepreneurial Research: a Pilot Study. Ph.D. thesis, Tilburg University (2020)
4. Cakır, E., Parascandolo, G., Heittola, T., Huttunen, H., Virtanen, T.: Convolutional recurrent neural networks for polyphonic sound event detection. IEEE/ACM Trans. Audio Speech Language Process. **25**(6), 1291–1303 (2017)
5. Carlson, N.A.: Simple acoustic-prosodic models of confidence and likability are associated with long-term funding outcomes for entrepreneurs. In: International Conference on Social Informatics, pp. 3–16 (2017)
6. Choi, K., Fazekas, G., Sandler, M., Cho, K.: Convolutional recurrent neural networks for music classification. In: 2017 IEEE International Conference on Acoustics, Speech and Signal Processing (ICASSP), pp. 2392–2396. IEEE (2017)
7. Chung, J., Gulcehre, C., Cho, K., Bengio, Y.: Empirical evaluation of gated recurrent neural networks on sequence modeling. arXiv preprint arXiv:1412.3555 (2014)
8. Eyben, F., et al.: The Geneva minimalistic acoustic parameter set (gemaps) for voice research and affective computing. IEEE Trans. Affect. Comput. **7**(2), 190–202 (2015)
9. Eyben, F., Weninger, F., Gross, F., Schuller, B.: Recent developments in opensmile, the munich open-source multimedia feature extractor. In: Proceedings of the 21st ACM International Conference on Multimedia, pp. 835–838 (2013)
10. Eyben, F., Wöllmer, M., Schuller, B.: Opensmile: the Munich versatile and fast open-source audio feature extractor. In: Proceedings of 18th ACM International Conference on Multimedia, pp. 1459–1462 (2010)
11. Gallardo-Antolín, A., Montero, J.M.: Histogram equalization-based features for speech, music, and song discrimination. IEEE Signal Process. Lett. **17**(7), 659–662 (2010)

12. Giannakopoulos, T., Spyrou, E., Perantonis, S.J.: Recognition of urban sound events using deep context-aware feature extractors and handcrafted features. In: MacIntyre, J., Maglogiannis, I., Iliadis, L., Pimenidis, E. (eds.) AIAI 2019. IAICT, vol. 560, pp. 184–195. Springer, Cham (2019). https://doi.org/10.1007/978-3-030-19909-8_16

13. Goss, D.: Schumpeter's legacy? Interaction and emotions in the sociology of entrepreneurship. Entrep. Theory Pract. **29**(2), 205–218 (2005)

14. Grahe, J.E., Bernieri, F.J.: The importance of nonverbal cues in judging rapport. J. Nonverbal Behav. **23**(4), 253–269 (1999)

15. Gürpinar, F., Kaya, H., Salah, A.A.: Multimodal fusion of audio, scene, and face features for first impression estimation. In: 2016 23rd International Conference on Pattern Recognition (ICPR), pp. 43–48. IEEE (2016)

16. Han, K., Wang, D.: Neural network based pitch tracking in very noisy speech. IEEE/ACM Trans. Audio Speech Lang. Process. **22**(12), 2158–2168 (2014)

17. Hershey, S., et al.: Cnn architectures for large-scale audio classification. In: 2017 IEEE International Conference on Acoustics, Speech and Signal Processing (ICASSP), pp. 131–135 (2017)

18. Huang, L., Pearce, J.L.: Managing the unknowable: the effectiveness of early-stage investor gut feel in entrepreneurial investment decisions. Adm. Sci. Q. **60**(4), 634–670 (2015)

19. van de Kamp, L.: Predicting Investors' Investment Decisions by Facial Mimicry. Ph.D. thesis, Tilburg University (2020)

20. Kim, H.G., Moreau, N., Sikora, T.: MPEG-7 Audio and Beyond: Audio Content Indexing and Retrieval. Wiley, Chichester (2006)

21. Kingma, D.P., Ba, J.: Adam: a method for stochastic optimization. arXiv preprint arXiv:1412.6980 (2014)

22. Kuncheva, L.I., Whitaker, C.J.: Measures of diversity in classifier ensembles and their relationship with the ensemble accuracy. Mach. Learn. **51**(2), 181–207 (2003)

23. Lee, H., Pham, P., Largman, Y., Ng, A.: Unsupervised feature learning for audio classification using convolutional deep belief networks. Adv. Neural. Inf. Process. Syst. **22**, 1096–1104 (2009)

24. Liebregts, W., Urbig, D., Jung, M.M.: Survey and video data regarding entrepreneurial pitches and investment decisions. Unpublished raw data (2018–2021)

25. Liebregts, W., Darnihamedani, P., Postma, E., Atzmueller, M.: The promise of social signal processing for research on decision-making in entrepreneurial contexts. Small Bus. Econ. **55**(3), 589–605 (2020)

26. Lim, H., Park, J., Han, Y.: Rare sound event detection using 1d convolutional recurrent neural networks. In: Proceedings of the Detection and Classification of Acoustic Scenes and Events 2017 Workshop, pp. 80–84 (2017)

27. Luo, Y., Chen, Z., Hershey, J.R., Le Roux, J., Mesgarani, N.: Deep clustering and conventional networks for music separation: stronger together. In: 2017 IEEE International Conference on Acoustics, Speech and Signal Processing (ICASSP), pp. 61–65. IEEE (2017)

28. van Mil, C.: Improving Your Pitch with Facial Action Units...Is It Possible? Ph.D. thesis, Tilburg University (2020)

29. Milkman, K.L., Chugh, D., Bazerman, M.H.: How can decision making be improved? Perspect. Psychol. Sci. **4**(4), 379–383 (2009)

30. Moritz, A., Diegel, W., Block, J., Fisch, C.: VC investors' venture screening: the role of the decision maker's education and experience. J. Bus. Econ. 1–37 (2021)

31. Pishdadian, F., Seetharaman, P., Kim, B., Pardo, B.: Classifying non-speech vocals: deep vs signal processing representation. In: Proceedings of the Detection and Classification of Acoustic Scenes and Events 2019 Workshop (DCASE2019) (2019)
32. Pollack, J.M., Rutherford, M.W., Nagy, B.G.: Preparedness and cognitive legitimacy as antecedents of new venture funding in televised business pitches. Entrep. Theory Pract. **36**(5), 915–939 (2012)
33. Sainath, T.N., Vinyals, O., Senior, A., Sak, H.: Convolutional, long short-term memory, fully connected deep neural networks. In: 2015 IEEE International Conference on Acoustics, Speech and Signal Processing (ICASSP), pp. 4580–4584. IEEE (2015)
34. Salamon, J., Bello, J.P.: Deep convolutional neural networks and data augmentation for environmental sound classification. IEEE Signal Process. Lett. **24**(3), 279–283 (2017)
35. Schuller, B., et al.: The interspeech 2013 computational paralinguistics challenge: social signals, conflict, emotion, autism. In: Proceedings INTERSPEECH 2013, 14th Annual Conference of the International Speech Communication Association, Lyon, France (2013)
36. Schuller, B.W.: The computational paralinguistics challenge [social sciences]. IEEE Signal Process. Mag. **29**(4), 97–101 (2012)
37. Shepherd, D.A.: Multilevel entrepreneurship research: opportunities for studying entrepreneurial decision making (2011)
38. Slovic, P.: Psychological study of human judgment: implications for investment decision making. J. Financ. **27**(4), 779–799 (1972)
39. Stoitsas, K., Onal Ertugrul, I., Liebregts, W., Jung, M.M.: Predicting evaluations of entrepreneurial pitches based on multimodal nonverbal behavioral cues and self-reported characteristics. In: Companion Publication of the 2022 International Conference on Multimodal Interaction (2022)
40. Tianyu, Z., Zhenjiang, M., Jianhu, Z.: Combining CNN with hand-crafted features for image classification. In: 2018 14th IEEE International Conference on Signal Processing (ICSP), pp. 554–557. IEEE (2018)
41. Trigeorgis, G., et al.: Adieu features? end-to-end speech emotion recognition using deep convolutional recurrent network. In: IEEE International Conference on Acoustics, Speech and Signal Processing, pp. 5200–5204 (2016)
42. Weninger, F., Eyben, F., Schuller, B.W., Mortillaro, M., Scherer, K.R.: On the acoustics of emotion in audio: what speech, music, and sound have in common. Front. Psychol. **4**, 292 (2013)
43. Yu, H., et al.: TensorFlow Model Garden. https://github.com/tensorflow/models (2020)

W02 Theories, Applications, and Cross Modality
for Self-supervised Learning Models (SSL)

Preface

Theories, Applications, and Cross Modality for Self-Supervised Learning Models (SSL)

W03 – Theories, Applications, and Cross Modality for Self-supervised Learning Models (SSL)

Preface

Self-supervised learning has recently seen remarkable processes across various domains. The goal of SSL method is to learn useful semantic features without any human annotations. In the absence of human-defined labels, the deep network is expected to learn richer feature structures explained by the data itself. There are many works across different modalities showing the empirical success of the SSL learning approaches. However, many questions are still lingering: is it possible to view self-supervised learning across different modalities in a unifying view? Is it possible to find the inherent connection between successful vision architectures and NLP architectures? How to interpret these connections? What mechanism essentially matters during the SSL feature learning procedure when we change data modalities? There are recently some emerging works starting to pay attention to these issues. However, the complete answer to the above questions still remains elusive and challenging. This workshop aims to approach the mysteries behind SSL from both theoretical and practical perspectives. We invited experts from different communities and shared their thoughts on how self-supervised learning approaches across different domains were connected and how they can potentially improve each other.

We have in total 5 paper submissions, and 4 out of these submissions were accepted and were presented as oral presentations.

August 2022

Yu Wang
Yingwei Pan
Jingjing Zou
Angelica I. Aviles-Rivero
Carola-Bibiane Schö nlieb
John Aston
Ting Yao

Enhancing the Linear Probing Performance of Masked Auto-Encoders

Yurui Qian[1]($\boxtimes$) (iD), Yu Wang[2], and Jingyang Lin[3]

[1] University of Science and Technology of China, Hefei, China
yuruiqian.ustc@gmail.com
[2] JD AI Research, Beijing, China
[3] Sun Yat-sen University, Guangzhou, China

Abstract. This paper especially investigates the linear probing performance of MAE models. The recent Masked Image Modeling (MIM) approach is shown to be an effective self-supervised learning approach. These models usually mask out some patches of images and require the model to predict specific properties of those missing patches, which can either be raw pixel values or discrete visual tokens learned by pre-trained dVAE. Despite the promising performance on fine-tuning and transfer learning, it is often found that linear probing accuracy of MAE is worse than that of contrastive learning. This is concerning, demonstrating that features out of MAE network may not be linear separable. To investigate this problem, we consider incorporating contrastive learning into the MAE modeling, to examine the mechanism behind linear probing. We design specific head architectures to associate with MAE, which allows us to include additional feature constraints inspired from Barlow Twins method. The motivation behind is our hypothesis that features learned by MIM would focus more on image style and high-frequency details, while features learned by Barlow Twins will focus more on image content. Our motivation then is to select a trade-off between the two types of features in order to improve the linear probing accuracy of MAE without hurting fine-tuning and transfer learning performance. Empirical results demonstrate the effectiveness of our method. We achieve 27.7% top1 accuracy at linear probing with ViT-Tiny as our backbone, which outperforms the MAE protocol under the same settings by 1.6%.

Keywords: Self-supervised learning · Masked Image Modeling · Linear probe

1 Introduction

Recently, unsupervised learning has gain much attention, since tons of text and images are generated on the internet everyday. While annotating data by hand is very expensive and time-consuming, unsupervised learning has the advantage of utilizing large amount of unlabeled data to enhance model's generalization ability to recognize and understand data.

© Springer Nature Switzerland AG 2023
J.-J. Rousseau and B. Kapralos (Eds.): ICPR 2022 Workshops, LNCS 13643, pp. 289–301, 2023.
https://doi.org/10.1007/978-3-031-37660-3_20

In terms of Nature Language Processing (NLP) applications recently, a popular approach in unsupervised learning is Masked Language Modeling (MLM) [9,22]. In BERT [9], random tokens are replaced by a MASK token and the model tries to predict the masked token according to the remaining tokens. Philosophy behind is that once the model figures out the meaning of sentence it would know which token is the most appropriate under such context background. Since BERT has gained great success, a lot attempts have been made to adapt the approach to image recognition [1,15,40].

To adapt the token masking approach in computer vision, many works [1, 11,32] use ViT [12] as their backbone, inspired from NLP applications [31]. ViT models usually treat image patches as tokens and apply similar training technique of BERT. However, image patches are high-dimensional and embed heavy redundancy, which is inherently different from the discrete word tokens in NLP. To this end, [1,11,32] use a pre-trained dVAE [27] to map image patches to discrete visual tokens and models are forced to predict that. People also tried to force the model to predict the pixel value directly [15,33], which proves to be simple but effective. Specifically, MAE [15] uses an autoencoder [17] to predict those missing pixel value during pre-training, and uses the embedding extract from the encoder solely for downstream tasks. MAE has achieved good result on fine-tuning and transfer tasks.

Despite the popularity of MAE, [1,11,15] report that the linear accuracy of the pre-trained feature is often worse than that provided by contrastive learning [5]. It is shown that the feature learned from the MAE encoder is less linear separable than the ones obtained from contrastive and its variants. We assume that as the MIM model aims to reconstruct the pixel value or other high-frequency detail of certain patches, MIM and the likes may ignore the high-level semantic of images. This contradicts with the motivation that model is actually required to learn to understand images and to recognize objects. On the contrary, contrastive learning methods always push apart negative samples and pull together positive samples by ignoring noisy details in the instances. The feature extracted from the pre-trained model therefore can perform well with only a well-trained classifier.

Our method aims to improve the linear accuracy without hurting the performance of fine-tune task based on the MIM method MAE [15]. We employ MAE to build our basic framework, see Fig. 1. We first mask random patches of an image and feed the masked image along with the original image into encoder. The architecture then is followed by a decoder and a head composing of stacks of fully-connected layer and activation layer. With the construction of head, we are able to feed in the embedding of original and masked images together and apply Barlow Twins [36] architecture on the two embeddings. In other words, we treat the two embeddings as different views of a same image and compute cross-correlation matrix of the two views. Then we force the cross-correlation matrix to be identity matrix. For the decoder, we feed in the masked image embedding along with MASK token and the objective of decoder is to reconstruct missing patches. Thus the decoder should only be affected by the masked image. Finally we add together the two losses with a weight coefficient as our optimization objective. In order to achieve a good initialization, we set the weight of Barlow Twins to be zero at early stage of pre-training. Our method improves the linear performance effectively by 1.6% without hurting fine-tune task performance with only an extra head.

We hypothesize that the Barlow Twins loss works as a constraint to the feature. When forcing the cross-correlation matrix to be identity matrix, the cosine similarity of the features of two views is maximized and the correlation between dimensions is minimized. In other words, we hope the model to recognize features of the same image with different augmentation semantic similar by ignoring the noisy augmentation details. In the meanwhile, features should have minimum redundancy [20] along dimension. We conjecture that features from MAE have different properties. Since decoder ought to reconstruct pixel values, encoder also is required to encode every details more than the semantic of an image. To put it simply, Barlow Twins has the objective to recognize image semantic regardless of versatile augmentations, while MAE encoder has to recognize image style together with content. We carefully tune their weight so that Barlow Twins can effectively act as a regularizer on MAE method. This helps the features to be more content identifiable, and thereby become more linear separable.

Although the MIM approaches have achieved good results under fine-tuning. We hope our method and analysis can inspire the community to think more about the linear probing performance of such tasks and investigate the core difference between the MIM tasks and contrastive learning methods.

2   Related Work

2.1   Masked Image Modeling

Existing Masked Image Modeling adopts ViT [12] or Swin Transformer [23] as their backbone and takes image patches as visual tokens. They usually use random masking or block masking [1,29] to decide which patches to be masked. [21] proposes a masking strategy according to patches' attention score. Most works replace all the masked token with a special learnable token before training, which is derived from NLP [9], and set a target for the model to predict. The training targets can be discrete tokens [1,11] learned by a pre-trained dVAE [27], raw pixel values [15,33] or high-dimensional features learned by pre-trained network [32]. [32] investigates five types of target features in detail. The methods relying on pre-trained models to generate targets usually take extra computational cost for the whole training in comparison to those who use pixel values. Specifically, MAE [15] uses an autoencoder to predict pixel values, since in MAE, only the unmasked tokens are fed into the encoder and the decoder in order to predict the masked patches. It narrows the gap between pre-training and downstream tasks since no mask token is used during downstream tasks. Our proposed method also builds upon the MAE structure. However, even if those methods achieve promising score on fine-tune and transfer tasks, it is reported in [15,32] that linear probing accuracy usually lags behind contrastive methods [5]. We are interested

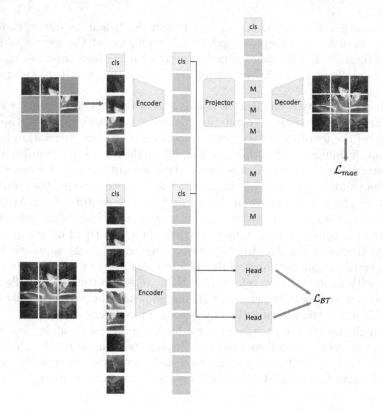

Fig. 1. Our framework. During pre-training, we feed the masked image along with original image into the encoder and get two embeddings. The `cls` token of the two embeddings is used to compute $\mathcal{L}_{BT}$. The masked image embedding with learnable `MASK` token are forwarded into decoder to reconstruct missing patches.

in this phenomenon and we try to improve the linear probing accuracy of the MIM methods. The motivation is that we absorb Barlow Twins [36] loss into the MIM model, in order to force the feature become linear separable. Note that [11] also computes a l_2 loss to make masked and original images more perceptually similar, but they apply this perceptual loss during dVAE pre-training to get better discrete visual tokens. Their method is fundamentally different from ours. We apply Barlow Twins loss during pre-training and the procedure does not involve extra stage to pre-train the target, i.e., we use raw pixel values directly.

2.2 Unsupervised Learning

Unsupervised learning has the advantage of utilizing large amount of unlabeled data to provide model with a better initialization and robustness. Some works modify the data and generate pseudo-label according to the specific modification, so that the model can predict the human generated pseudo-labels, which is called pretext tasks [10, 13, 38, 39]. Contrastive learning [3, 16, 26, 30] sets the goal of the models to separate images having different semantic apart and to pull images having similar semantics closer, which is known respectively as negative and positive pairs. Some approaches recently found that certain architectures without using negative samples [2, 4, 14] are also effective in learning useful features. They usually define the l_2 loss [4, 14] or cross-correlation matrix [36] of two features of the same image to be the penalty objective. These unsupervised methods have different motivation from the MIM methods, and they also behave differently since these contrastive learning based unsupervised methods perform better on linear probing, while MIM performs better on fine-tuning. This motivates us to consider introducing the advantage of these contrastive learning based methods without negative pairs such as Barlow Twins along with the MAE reconstruction loss.

3 Method

We view original image and its masked version as a positive sample pair in the context of contrastive learning. We feed forward two views through an encoder and a head. Then we compute the average cross-correlation matrix to approach the dataset's expected cross-correlation matrix and we force it to be identity matrix. In the meanwhile, we use a decoder to reconstruct the masked patch according to the remaining patch embedding and a learnable MASK token. We then compute the l_2 reconstruction loss between target and the reconstruction. Here only the masked image embedding is used. We add the above two losses together with a hyper-parameter λ to balance their weight.

3.1 Preliminary

Here we briefly introduce the pipeline of MAE [15] and the Barlow Twins [36]. We will then describe how to enhance the linear probing performance of MAE by incorporating the idea of Barlow Twins.

Masked Autoencoder. Following ViT [12], MAE divides image into non-overlapping, fixed-size patches. They randomly remove some patches with a high proportion, denoted as mask ratio. We use x to represent the original image, use *mask* and *remain* to denote the positional index of the corresponding patches. So x_{mask} and x_{remain} represent those masked and remaining patches. MAE's backbone is an autoencoder, composing of a ViT encoder of standard architecture and a lightweight ViT decoder. During pre-training, we append a cls token to x_{remain}, and forward it into encoder to obtain the corresponding patch embedding f_{remain}. We use a projection layer to match the dimension between encoder and decoder. Positional embedding will be added to both encoder and decoder inputs. Then a learnable MASK token will be repeated and appended to f_{remain}, then the patch embeddings should be rearranged to keep align with the original patch order and is fed into decoder to obtain reconstructed image $\hat{x}$. MAE minimizes only the reconstruction distance of the masked patch:

$$\mathcal{L}_{MAE} = ||\hat{x}_{mask} - x_{mask}||^2 \tag{1}$$

The decoder is dropped when the encoder is transferred to downstream tasks. The entire image token will be forwarded into encoder to get image embedding f. Following ViT, we use cls token f^{cls} as image feature.

Barlow Twins Loss. The whole batch image X is first augmented twice to get two views X^A, X^B. They are fed into a backbone *model* and a *head* to compute Z^A, Z^B respectively, where $f = model(x), z = head(f)$. $Z^A, Z^B \in \mathcal{R}^{N \times D}$ is assumed to be normalized along the batch dimension for notation simplification. N is batchsize and D is feature dimension. Then we compute cross-correlation matrix $\mathcal{C} \in \mathcal{R}^{D \times D}$:

$$\mathcal{C} = \sum_{i=1}^{N} z_i^A (z_i^B)^T \tag{2}$$

and Barlow Twins loss :

$$\mathcal{L}_{\mathcal{BT}} = \sum_{i=1}^{D} (\mathcal{C}_{ii} - 1)^2 + \alpha * \sum_{i=1}^{D} \sum_{j \neq i} \mathcal{C}_{ij}^2 \tag{3}$$

α is a hyper-parameter balancing how important the off-diagonal term is. By forcing $\mathcal{C}$ to be identity matrix $\mathcal{I}$, we encourage the two distorted views of the same image to have maximum semantic similarity and minimum redundancy across different dimensions.

3.2   Enhancing the Linear Probing Performance

Our framework is shown in Fig. 1. We first remove random patches away from original image x to get x_{remain}. cls token is appended and cosine positional embedding is added before encoder. Both x and x_{remain} are fed into encoder to get $f = Enc(x)$ and $f_{remain} = Enc(x_{remain})$ respectively. We append MASK token to f_{remain} and send it as a whole into decoder as mentioned in Sect. 3.1 to get $\mathcal{L}_{mae}$. Meanwhile, the cls token of f and f_{remain} are forwarded into a head to get $z^A = head(f^{cls})$, $z^B = head(f_{remain}^{cls})$. $\mathcal{L}_{\mathcal{BT}}$ is computed with Z^A and Z^B. And our objective function is

$$\mathcal{L} = \mathcal{L}_{mae} + \lambda * \mathcal{L}_{\mathcal{BT}} \tag{4}$$

Table 1. Different decoder architecture.

Decoder	fine-tune	linear probing
128d12b	**71.1**	26.1
256d8b	70.3	**28.7**
512d8b	69.7	20.3

We set λ to zero at early stage of pre-training. As mentioned before, the mechanism behind $\mathcal{L}_{mae}$ and $\mathcal{L}_{\mathcal{BT}}$ is different. We are afraid that it may confuse the model at the very start if there are two orthogonal goals for it to pursue. Also, we only want the Barlow Twins loss to act as a regularizer to the MIM method. So we only activate λ at a specific bt_epoch.

4   Experiments

In this section, we empirically evaluate our method and analyze the results. We first introduce our model components and experimental setups. Then we present our results.

4.1   Model Components

Our model primarily involves an autoencoder and a Barlow Twins head.

Autoencoder. Due to computation resource limitation, we choose ViT-T (ViT-Tiny/16) [12] as our encoder. As for decoder, MAE [15] has reported ablation experiments on the decoder width and depth. Since there is no existing published MAE experiments that adopts ViT-T as their encoder, we design a decoder with 12 self-attention blocks [31] and embedding dimension with 128, denoted as 128d12b, in order to match the size of our encoder. The standard decoder size in MAE [15] is 8 self-attention blocks with 512 embedding dimension, denoted as 512d8b, which is too complex for our ViT-T encoder. We speculate that if the decoder's capacity is rich enough, then it can still reconstruct perfectly even with little information learned by the encoder. However, this contradicts with our motivation in terms of training the encoder since only the feature learned by encoder will be used on downstream tasks. On the contrary, if the decoder only has limited capacity, the encoder has to encode good feature to its best to help the decoder reconstruct images well. We confirm our hypothesis empirically. Table 1 performs MAE with different size of decoder and λ is set to zero during the whole pre-training stage. We can see that the linear probing accuracy of decoder 512d8b drops drastically even if the decoder capacity is bigger.

Table 2. Pre-training setting.

config	value
optimizer	AdamW [25]
optimizer momentum	β_1, $\beta_2 = 0.9, 0.95$
base learning rate	1.5e−4
minimum learning rate	0
learning rate schedule	cosine decay [24]
weight decay	0.5
batchsize	4096
batchsize per gpu	128
epochs	100
warm up epochs	5
augmentation	RandomResizedCrop

Barlow Twins Head. In contrastive learning [3], a head is usually appended on the backbone network and is trained along with the backbone during pre-training. The head is dropped when used on downstream tasks. The main reason is that the last several layers may discard some useful information for downstream tasks during pre-training. The head is composed of blocks of linear layer and activation layer with specific depth and dimension. In [36], it is reported that their model's performance saturated when depth is greater than 3. So we adopt depth = 3 in all our experiments. Ablation experiments and discussion about head dimension are in Sect. 4.4.

4.2   Experiments Setups

We use ImageNet-1K [8] as our dataset, which contains 1.2M images in training set and 50,000 in validation set with 1,000 classes. We now briefly describe our default training protocol of pre-training, fine-tuning and linear probing. We follow the protocols defined by MAE to construct our backbone network. All our experiments follow these default settings unless specifically noted. During pre-training, we set α in $\mathcal{L}_{BT}$ to 0.005, which proves to be the best when empirically tested in [36]. We set bt_epoch to be 50 constantly. That means Barlow Twins loss will only be added after 50 epochs. We also set mask ratio to 75% and use random masking strategy to align with MAE. We use 8 GPU for all experiments, and use gradient accumulation to deal with the large batchsize. Our default setting are shown in Table 2, 3 and 4.

4.3   Experiment Results

In our baseline experiment, we forward original image x and masked image x_{remain} together into the encoder, and set λ to zero. This is equivalent to computing $\mathcal{L}_{mae}$ here. The only difference from MAE practice is that the original

Table 3. Fine-tuning setting.

config	value
optimizer	AdamW
optimizer momentum	β_1, $\beta_2 = 0.9,0.999$
base learning rate	3e$-$3
minimum learning rate	1e$-$6
learning rate schedule	cosine decay
layer-wise decay lr decay [6]	0.75
weight decay	0.05
batchsize	1024
batchsize per gpu	128
epochs	100
warm up epochs	5
augmentation	RandAug(9,0.5) [7]
drop path	0.1
mixup [37]	0.8
cutmix [35]	1.0
label smoothing [28]	0.1
drop path [18]	0.1

Fig. 2. Attention map from the last layer of Transformer architecture. Column 1: original image; column 2–4: attention map from the Barlow Twins loss plus MAE; column 5–7: attention map from standard MAE practice.

image is observed by the encoder, but no loss is incurred on it. We can see from Table 5 that our baseline drops a little when compared to the MAE evaluation with ViT-T. We assume that it might be owing to the use of Layer Normalization [19], which functions in every self-attention block. Since the redundant original image goes through the encoder, which has different statistics from the masked image, Layer Normalization will change the whole data statistics and influence feature properties thereby. Our method's linear probing accuracy is higher than both of our baseline and MAE's practice, showing that our method can effectively improve the linear probing performance of the MAE method without hampering fine-tuning. Figure 2 shows that our proposed training mechanism is able to better recognize the important region through self-supervised training.

Table 4. Linear probing setting.

config	value
optimizer	LARS [34]
optimizer momentum	0.9
base learning rate	0.1
minimum learning rate	0
learning rate schedule	cosine decay
weight decay	0
batchsize	16384
batchsize per gpu	256
epochs	90
warm up epochs	10
augmentation	RandomResizedCrop

Table 5. Our method versus baseline.

Method	fine-tune	linear probing
MAE	71.1	26.1
baseline	**71.3**	25.7
our method	71.1	**27.7**

4.4   Ablation Experiments

In this section, we ablate our method on λ and head dimension with default setting in Table 2, 3 and 4.

λ. λ tunes the weight of $\mathcal{L}_{mae}$ and $\mathcal{L}_{BT}$. In our hypothesis, $\mathcal{L}_{BT}$ will force features to learn more about image semantics while features learned by $\mathcal{L}_{mae}$ will focus more on details and style of the image. We hope the $\mathcal{L}_{BT}$ may help the MAE feature pay more attention to semantic information and becomes more linear separable while not interfering with the model in terms of fine tuning. So λ plays a vital role in our objective. Because $\mathcal{L}_{BT}$ is a function of head dimension and the best λ is related to the value of $\mathcal{L}_{mae}$ and $\mathcal{L}_{BT}$. We plot curves about head dimension and λ together in Fig. 3.

Head Dimension. Barlow Twins [36] has reported ablation study against head dimension. We implement similar experiments on different head dimension, results are shown on Fig. 3. The linear probing accuracy grows as head dimension becomes bigger. We observe that $\mathcal{L}_{BT}$ value grows approximately linear with head dimension so different head dimension also have different best λ.

As head dimension grows bigger, it makes sense that the best λ becomes smaller. In such cases, the ratio between $\mathcal{L}_{mae}$ and $\lambda * \mathcal{L}_{BT}$ stays constant.

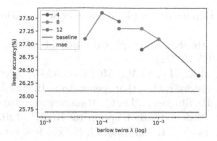

Fig. 3. Linear probing accuracy on different λ and head dimension. We plot λ in log scale. Different curves represent different ratios of head dimension to encoder embedding dimension.

4.5   Attention Map Visualization

In this section, we plot visualization of attention map [2] from the last layer of our encoder. From Fig. 2 we can see that adding the Barlow Twins loss not only can help make our features more linear separable, but also make the `cls` token focus more on salient object on images and have more semantics.

5   Conclusion

The MIM approach masks random patches of images and forces model to reconstruct the missing patches. During the training process, model learns to recognize images so that useful semantics can be learned by encoder. Despite the fact that MIM models show good performance on fine-tuning and transfer learning, the linear probing accuracy of these approaches is worse than that of contrastive learning. This paper particularly investigates this issue and aims to improve the linear probing accuracy without hurting fine-tuning performance by properly incorporating Barlow Twins head with MAE architecture. We hypothesize that features learned by Barlow Twins method will focus more on image content [20] in contrast to the MIM methods that focus more on image style and details. Empirical results have justified part of our hypothesis, that the Barlow Twins loss improves the linear probing accuracy indeed. We plan to investigate what is essentially functioning behind this encoding mechanism after appending the Barlow Twins loss in the future.

References

1. Bao, H., Dong, L., Wei, F.: BEiT: BERT pre-training of image transformers. In: ICLR (2022)
2. Caron, M., et al.: Emerging properties in self-supervised vision transformers. In: ICCV (2021)
3. Chen, T., Kornblith, S., Norouzi, M., Hinton, G.: A simple framework for contrastive learning of visual representations. In: ICML (2020)

4. Chen, X., He, K.: Exploring simple siamese representation learning. In: CVPR (2021)
5. Chen*, X., Xie*, S., He, K.: An empirical study of training self-supervised vision transformers. In: ICCV (2021)
6. Clark, K., Luong, M.T., Le, Q.V., Manning, C.D.: Electra: pre-training text encoders as discriminators rather than generators. In: ICLR (2020)
7. Cubuk, E.D., Zoph, B., Shlens, J., Le, Q.: Randaugment: practical automated data augmentation with a reduced search space. In: NeuIPS (2020)
8. Deng, J., Dong, W., Socher, R., Li, L.J., Li, K., Fei-Fei, L.: Imagenet: a large-scale hierarchical image database. In: CVPR (2009)
9. Devlin, J., Chang, M.W., Lee, K., Toutanova, K.: BERT: pre-training of deep bidirectional transformers for language understanding. In: NAACL (Jun 2019)
10. Doersch, C., Gupta, A., Efros, A.A.: Unsupervised visual representation learning by context prediction. In: ICCV (2015)
11. Dong, X., et al.: PECO: perceptual codebook for BERT pre-training of vision transformers. arXiv:2111.12710 (2021)
12. Dosovitskiy, A., et al.: An image is worth 16x16 words: transformers for image recognition at scale. In: ICLR (2021)
13. Gidaris, S., Singh, P., Komodakis, N.: Unsupervised representation learning by predicting image rotations. In: ICLR (2018)
14. Grill, J.B., et al.: Bootstrap your own latent: a new approach to self-supervised learning. In: NeurIPS (2020)
15. He, K., Chen, X., Xie, S., Li, Y., Dollár, P., Girshick, R.: Masked autoencoders are scalable vision learners. arXiv:2111.06377 (2021)
16. He, K., Fan, H., Wu, Y., Xie, S., Girshick, R.: Momentum contrast for unsupervised visual representation learning. In: CVPR (2019)
17. Hinton, G.E., Zemel, R.: Autoencoders, minimum description length and helmholtz free energy. In: NeuIPS (1993)
18. Huang, G., Sun, Yu., Liu, Z., Sedra, D., Weinberger, K.Q.: Deep networks with stochastic depth. In: Leibe, B., Matas, J., Sebe, N., Welling, M. (eds.) ECCV 2016. LNCS, vol. 9908, pp. 646–661. Springer, Cham (2016). https://doi.org/10.1007/978-3-319-46493-0_39
19. Ba, J.L., Kiros, J.R., Hinton, G.E.: Layer normalization. arXiv:1607.06450 (2016)
20. von Kügelgen, J., et al.: Self-supervised learning with data augmentations provably isolates content from style. In: NeuIPS (2021)
21. Li, Z., et al.: MST: masked self-supervised transformer for visual representation. In: NeurIPS (2021)
22. Liu, Y., et al.: Roberta: a robustly optimized bert pretraining approach. In: arXiv:1907.11692 (2019)
23. Liu, Z., et al.: Swin transformer: hierarchical vision transformer using shifted windows. In: ICCV (2021)
24. Loshchilov, I., Hutter, F.: SGDR: stochastic gradient descent with restarts. In: ICLR (2016)
25. Loshchilov, I., Hutter, F.: Fixing weight decay regularization in ADAM. In: ICLR (2017)
26. van den Oord, A., Li, Y., Vinyals, O.: Representation learning with contrastive predictive coding. arXiv:1807.03748 (2018)
27. Ramesh, A., et al.: Zero-shot text-to-image generation. In: ICML (2021)
28. Szegedy, C., Vanhoucke, V., Ioffe, S., Shlens, J., Wojna, Z.: Rethinking the inception architecture for computer vision. In: CVPR (2016)

29. Tan, H., Lei, J., Wolf, T., Bansal, M.: VIMPAC: video pre-training via masked token prediction and contrastive learning. arXiv:2106.11250 (2021)
30. Tian, Y., Krishnan, D., Isola, P.: Contrastive multiview coding. In: Vedaldi, A., Bischof, H., Brox, T., Frahm, J.-M. (eds.) ECCV 2020. LNCS, vol. 12356, pp. 776–794. Springer, Cham (2020). https://doi.org/10.1007/978-3-030-58621-8_45
31. Vaswani, A., et al.: Attention is all you need. In: NeuIPS (2017)
32. Wei, C., Fan, H., Xie, S., Wu, C., Yuille, A.L., Feichtenhofer, C.: Masked feature prediction for self-supervised visual pre-training. arXiv:2112.09133 (2021)
33. Xie, Z., et al.: SIMMIM: a simple framework for masked image modeling. In: CVPR (2022)
34. You, Y., Gitman, I., Ginsburg, B.: Scaling SGD batch size to 32k for imagenet training. arXiv:1708.03888 (2017)
35. Yun, S., Han, D., Oh, S.J., Chun, S., Choe, J., Yoo, Y.: Cutmix: regularization strategy to train strong classifiers with localizable features. In: ICCV (2019)
36. Zbontar, J., Jing, L., Misra, I., LeCun, Y., Deny, S.: Barlow twins: self-supervised learning via redundancy reduction. In: ICML (2021)
37. Zhang, H., Cissé, M., Dauphin, Y.N., Lopez-Paz, D.: mixup: beyond empirical risk minimization. In: ICLR (2017)
38. Zhang, R., Isola, P., Efros, A.A.: Colorful image colorization. In: Leibe, B., Matas, J., Sebe, N., Welling, M. (eds.) ECCV 2016. LNCS, vol. 9907, pp. 649–666. Springer, Cham (2016). https://doi.org/10.1007/978-3-319-46487-9_40
39. Zhang, R., Isola, P., Efros, A.A.: Split-brain autoencoders: unsupervised learning by cross-channel prediction. In: CVPR (2017)
40. Zhou, J., et al.: ibot: image Bert pre-training with online tokenizer. In: ICLR (2022)

Involving Density Prior for 3D Point Cloud Contrastive Learning

Fuchen Long$^{(\boxtimes)}$ and Zhaofan Qiu

JD Explore Academy, Beijing, China
{longfc.ustc}@gmail.com

Abstract. As a promising scheme of self-supervised learning, contrastive learning has significantly advanced the modeling of image or video in a self-supervised manner, as well as the understanding for 3D point cloud. Nevertheless, normal point cloud contrastive learning methods mainly concentrate on the point-level corresponding matching, ignoring the spatial context in the point cloud 3D space. In this notebook paper, we modify the original point contrastive learning for better 3D modeling, namely Density-Based PointContrast (DBPC), through leveraging the prior knowledge of point cloud density for self-supervised 3D feature optimization. Specifically, we exploit the traditional Density-Based Spatial Clustering of Applications with Noise to cluster the input point cloud to obtain many clusters and each cluster can represent one semantic objective instance. The object-level contrastive loss is employed on the sampled point pairs according to the clustering label to regulate the point-level contrastive learning with richer scene contextual information. Good generalization abilities of the pre-trained model learnt on ScanNet dataset are verified by extensive experiments on the downstream tasks, e.g., point cloud classification, part segmentation and scene semantic segmentation.

1 Introduction

Learning visual features on large-scale annotated datasets is a pre-requisite to obtain good performance in many computer vision tasks such as image recognition [18,41], object detection [7,26], action classification [10,27,28,40,45,50] and temporal action localization [29,30,32,36]. Nevertheless, the annotation processing of the training data for these tasks are very time-consuming and expensive. Recent advances in self-supervised pre-training attract more and more attention to mine the information from data itself for representation learning, which alleviates the cumbersome effort of the data labeling. The data collection and semantic labeling for 3D point cloud data (e.g., bounding box and instance masks) are even more challenging. Unlike images or videos that widely exist on the Internet, collecting real world 3D datasets usually involves traversing the environment in real life and scanning with 3D sensors. Besides, the 3D point cloud labeling needs more complex pipelines [6] and costs more time than image/video annotating. Thus, the 3D point cloud self-supervised learning is an engaged problem in the research community.

© Springer Nature Switzerland AG 2023
J.-J. Rousseau and B. Kapralos (Eds.): ICPR 2022 Workshops, LNCS 13643, pp. 302–312, 2023.
https://doi.org/10.1007/978-3-031-37660-3_21

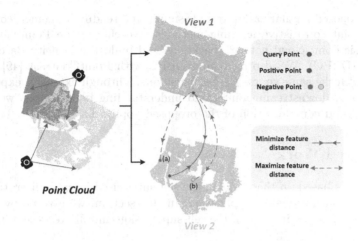

Fig. 1. Illustration of data sampling for the query point, positive point and negative points (i.e., (a) & (b)) through PointContrast [49] as well as the feature optimization direction across different data pairs. Given the query point in the "table" object, both of point (a) and (b) in the different/same object are sampled as negative samples.

Inspired by the great success of contrastive learning [17, 35] in self-supervised image representation learning, a serious point cloud contrastive learning approaches [20, 49, 54] start to be applied in 3D computer vision. The point-level contrastive learning [49] discriminates the point-wise correspondences between different views of a point cloud. The positive pairs are sampled from the 3D neighboring space according to the registration while the negative samples are generated from the far away unmatched ones. Figure 1 conceptually depicts the sampled positive and negative points in different views. Such contrastive learning paradigm, however, ignores the spatial configuration and contexts in a scene, leading to some noise samples during training. For instance, as shown in the figure, there is a "table" covering a large space in the point cloud. Nevertheless, the "far" point (b) of the same "table" is sampled as negative. As such, performing contrastive learning on that positive-negative data pair might be sub-optimal for point cloud information mining.

To alleviate this issue, we propose to involve the density prior of the input point cloud to regulate original point contrast. Technically, we first remove the ground points through height value truncation. Then, the tradition clustering algorithm Density-Based Spatial Clustering of Applications with Noise (DBSCAN) [9] is employed to obtain several clusters according to the point cloud density. Each point cluster can represent one objective instance. In addition to the point-level corresponding matching learning, we also apply the InfoNCE loss [48] on the point pairs sampled from different instance in the same view scene. The optimization objective is combined with a new regularization term to leverage richer context information of the scene for original point contrastive learning.

The proposed regularization term is simple and readily implemented into the existing point contrastive learning methods. We choose the PointNet++ [39] as the basic point cloud network backbone and build the Density-Based Point-Contrast (DBPC). We also compared DBPC with PointContrast [49] through learning with the same sparse ResNet backbone. Through extensive experiments on a series of downstream point cloud understanding benchmarks, we demonstrate the good generalization of the proposed approach.

2   Related Work

Our DBPC is based on the works in the self-supervised learning literature, with 3D point cloud data as an application. In this section, we give an overview of the related advances in both of the self-supervision and 3D representations.

2.1   Self-supervised Learning in Image/Video

Self-supervised learning is a well investigated problem in the traditional computer vision, i.e, image and video representation learning [4,11,16,17,25,31,33, 46]. There are many research directions to mine supervision from data itself and the key is the formulation of pretext task. One of the basic pretext task is the contrastive learning [17,35,48]. It formulates the optimization target as the instance classification of the training data pairs generated from different data augmentation strategy. There is no explicit classifier [48] and the performances are influenced by the negative sampling strategy [17] in a large degree. Our work is based on the InfoNCE [48] for the 3D input formats and the density prior is further incorporated to regulate the model training.

2.2   3D Scene Representation Learning

Research in deep learning on 3D point clouds have been recently shifted from synthetic, single object classification [38,39] to the challenge of large-scale, real-world scene understanding [6]. In the past few years, a variety of algorithms have been proposed for 3D object detection [23,37], semantic segmentation [13,38,44] and instance segmentation [8,19,21,22]. Given the 3D data of real-world scenes, voxelization followed by sparse convolutional networks [5,13] stands out as a promising standard 3D processing approach. Nevertheless, the quantization in voxelization procedure will cause the loss of geometry information. By directly processing the irregular point data without the quantization, the MLP-based backbones [38,39] obtain fairly well accuracy on several point cloud analysis tasks. In this work, we evaluate our self-supervised approach on both of the sparse convolution networks and the MLP-based backbone.

2.3   Self-supervised Learning for 3D Data

Most of the unsupervised point cloud learning approaches formulate the pretext task as the single object classification [1,12,15,24] or instance-level shape reconstruction [14,42,43,51,52]. In these settings, the training data is generated from the synthetic CAD models and the generalization ability is limited by the domain gap between synthetic data and real scenes. PointContrast [49] first demonstrates the effectiveness of self-supervised pre-training on the real-world 3D dataset through point-level contrastive learning. As depicted in Fig. 1, the simple point-level pre-training objective in PointContrast ignores the spatial contexts (e.g., object consistency) which limits the transferability for complex tasks such as instance segmentation.

In summary, our work is a simple refinement of the PointContrast which integrates the density prior to regulate the original contrastive learning. Through pre-training our DBPC on the real-world 3D ScanNet dataset, performance improvements on four downstream datasets are observed.

3 Density-Based PointContrast (DBPC)

In this section, we first briefly revisit the techniques of PointContrast. And then, the upgradation and our proposed Density-based PointContrast is further introduced in detail.

3.1 Revisiting PointContrast

In PointContrast [49], given one scene-level point cloud x, two point clouds x^1 and x^2 from different camera views are generated from x. Through the alignment of the same world coordinates, the point-level correspondence matching M is obtained. If $(i, j) \in M$, then the point x_i^1 and x_j^2 are a pair of matched points. Two geometric transformations (e.g., scaling and rotation) T_1 and T_2 are sampled to transform the x_1 and x_2 as network input, respectively. After feeding the two point clouds into the deep neural networks, a contrastive loss is defined to minimize the distance between matched points and maximize it between unmatched ones. The infoNCE [35] is thus extended as PointInfoNCE for contrastive optimization,

$$L_c = - \sum_{(i,j) \in M} \log \frac{\exp \mathbf{f}_i^1 \cdot \mathbf{f}_j^2 / \tau}{\sum_{(\cdot, k) \in M} \exp \mathbf{f}_i^1 \cdot \mathbf{f}_k^2 / \tau}, \tag{1}$$

where the $\mathbf{f}_i^1$ and $\mathbf{f}_j^2$ represents the output feature of the i-th and j-th point in the x^1 and x^2, respectively. The τ is the temperature parameter. For a matched point pair $(i, j) \in M$, the x_1^i is set as query and x_2^j is set as the only positive key. Meanwhile, all other points x_2^k where $\exists(\cdot, k) \in M$ and $k \neq j$ in x^2 are treated as negative keys.

Although the target of PointContrast is to learn the point *equivariance* with respect to a set of random geometric transformations, the spatial context are not captured since the negative keys could be sampled from the instance having the same semantic meaning in a mini-batch. We believe the relative spatial

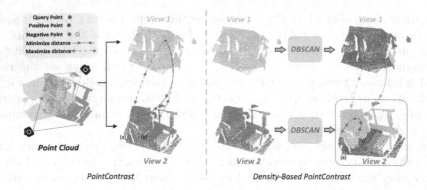

Fig. 2. Illustration of point feature optimization by PointContrast [49] and our Density-Based PointContrast (DBPC). In DBPC, the DBSCAN algorithm [9] first segments the point cloud into several clusters. Each cluster represents one semantic objects. When the positive point and the sampled negative points have the same clustering label in the same view, the negative pair will be removed during training. Furthermore, the clustering labels are also employed for data pair sampling of each view. The contrastive loss minimizes the feature distance between points having the same label while maximizes the distance between points with different labels. Better viewed in original color pdf.

information is pivotal for some complex downstream tasks such as instance segmentation. The unconstrained learning paradigm of PointContrast might result in sub-optimal solution for the point cloud learning.

3.2 Density Prior for Regularization

The traditional unsupervised clustering method DBSCAN [9] progressively enlarges the clustering region according to the local density distribution and finally determines the clusters. Point cloud, as a data format containing rich local geometric information, has been validated [2] to be applicably analyzed by DBSCAN algorithm. In this paper, we exploit DBSCAN to cluster the input scene-level point cloud into several clusters to represent different instances. The clustering label can be treated as the class agnostic instance segmentation mask. Meanwhile, it servers as the density prior with spatial context, and could further guide the point contrastive learning.

Formally, we apply the DBSCAN algorithm [9] to the point cloud to obtain the clustering labels y for each point. The query point, positive and negative points are then sampled as demonstrated in right part of Fig. 2. During contrastive learning, the negative points that have the same clustering label as the positive point will be discarded in loss function for density consistency preserving. Thus, the PointInfoNCE loss for point matching is reformulated as,

$$L_{mc} = - \sum_{(i,j) \in M} \log \frac{\exp \mathbf{f}_i^1 \cdot \mathbf{f}_j^2 / \tau}{\sum_{(\cdot,k) \in M \cap y_k^2 \neq y_j^2} \exp \mathbf{f}_i^1 \cdot \mathbf{f}_k^2 / \tau}, \tag{2}$$

where y_j^2 and y_k^2 denotes the DBSCAN clustering label of the positive point x_j^2 and the negative point x_k^2, respectively.

To further regulate the contrastive learning with the density prior, we sample another set of the training data pairs of each view according to the clustering labels. The InfoNCE loss are then applied on such point set and it can be formulated as the density contrastive loss,

$$L_{dc} = - \sum_{(i,j) \in P} \log \frac{\exp \mathbf{f}_i \cdot \mathbf{f}_j / \tau}{\sum_{(i,k) \in N} \exp \mathbf{f}_i^1 \cdot \mathbf{f}_k^2 / \tau}, \tag{3}$$

where the P and N represents the positive and negative pair sets, respectively. The contrastive loss function L_{dc} enforces the features of the points having the same clustering label close to each other and push the features of the points with different labels far away. The total objective L of our DBPC is computed as

$$L = L_{mc} + \alpha L_{dc}, \tag{4}$$

where α is the loss weight parameter.

4   Experiments

We follow the standard experimental settings in PointContrast [49] and employ the ScanNet [6] as the pre-training dataset. The PointNet++ [39] and Res-UNet [49] are chosen as the network backbone. The model generalization ability are evaluated on ModelNet40 [47] for 3D classification, PartNet [34] and ShapeNet-Part [53] for 3D part segmentation, and S3DIS [3] for 3D scene semantic segmentation.

4.1   Implementation Details

In the pre-training stage with the backbone of Res-UNet, we adopt the same configurations in original PointContrast [49] for training. As for the backbone of PointNet++, we set the basic learning rate as 0.1. The mini-batch size is 32. The learning rate is decreased by a factor of 0.99 every 20 epochs. For all the pre-training settings, the loss weight α is set as 0.5 through cross validation.

In the fine-tuning stage, the experiments on 3D classification are trained with a batch-size of 48 for all 128 epochs. The initial learning rate is 0.01. On the downstream tasks of 3D part segmentation and 3D scene semantic segmentation, the model is fine-tuned by 300 epochs and the basic learning rate is set as 0.1 by cross validation. All the experiments are trained on the parallel 4 NVIDIA P40 GPUs.

4.2   Evaluation on 3D Classification

We first evaluate our DBPC on downstream task of 3D classification on ModelNet40 [47] dataset. Table 1 details the performance comparisons among different methods. "Scratch" denotes the run of random initialization for network

Table 1. Top-1 accuracy on ModelNet40 dataset. We compare DBPC with the training-from-scratch, PointContrast as well as one variant of DBPC (DBPC⁻) which removes the density-based contrastive loss L_{dc} during training.

Initialization	Res-UNet	PointNet++
Scratch	89.5	90.7
PointContrast [49]	90.8	91.8
DBPC⁻	91.1	92.3
DBPC	**92.4**	**93.0**

Table 2. Instance-level mean average IoU (mIoU) on PartNet and ShapeNetPart dataset. We compare DBPC with the training-from-scratch, PointContrast as well as one variant DBPC⁻ which removes the density-based contrastive loss L_{dc} in DBPC during training.

Initialization	PartNet		ShapeNetPart	
	Res-UNet	PointNet++	Res-UNet	PointNet++
Scratch	38.9	43.1	84.7	84.8
PointContrast [49]	40.3	44.0	85.1	85.2
DBPC⁻	42.0	45.6	85.2	85.4
DBPC	**43.5**	**46.1**	**85.5**	**85.7**

parameters. One variant DBPC⁻ is designed for comparison which removes the density-based contrastive loss L_{dc} and only applies the new sampling strategy on PointContrast. With the backbone of Res-UNet and PointNet++, the scratch training has already provided a competitive results, which demonstrates the satisfactory model capacity of the existing convolution-based and MLP-based point cloud networks. Compared to PointContrast, DBPC⁻ boosts the model generalization ability through removing the noise negative samples according to the prior knowledge from point density. Furthermore, through leveraging the clustering label as additional information to regulate contrastive learning, DBPC obtains the highest top-1 accuracy on ModelNet40.

4.3   Evaluation on Part Segmentation

Next, the proposed DBPC is evaluated on the downstream task of part segmentation. Table 2 summarizes the performances on PartNet and ShapeNetPart datasets across different ways of parameter initialization for networks. In particular, the performances of random initialization are much worse on PartNet than those on ShapeNetPart. This might be caused by the fine-grained annotations in PartNet which makes the task more challenging. Even so, our DBPC still makes a mIoU boost by 4.6%/3.0% with the Res-UNet/PointNet++ backbone compared to the training-from-scratch. The performance trade on the ShapeNetPart dataset is similar to that of PartNet and DBPC surpasses the PointContrast baseline by 0.4% and 0.5% on Res-UNet and PointNet++, respectively.

Table 3. Mean average IoU (mIoU) on S3DIS dataset. We compare DBPC with the training-from-scratch, PointContrast as well as one variant DBPC$^-$ which removes the density-based contrastive loss L_{dc} during training.

Initialization	Res-UNet	PointNet++
Scratch	68.2	55.3
PointContrast [49]	70.3	57.2
DBPC$^-$	71.5	59.3
DBPC	**72.0**	**60.4**

4.4   Evaluation on Semantic Segmentation

The density prior of the point cloud mined by DBSCAN algorithm can be represented as different object instances in one scene. As such, the supervision will potentially enhances the networks generalizability to the downstream task which needs more relative information, e.g., scene semantic segmentation. We report the mIoU performances on S3DIS dataset with different pre-training methods in Table 3. The Res-UNet performs much better than the PointNet++ on S3DIS dataset with different model initialization and our DBPC still improves the mIoU from 70.3% to 72.0% compared to PointContrast. The superior results of our DBPC generally demonstrate the advantage of integrating density prior captured by DBSCAN to enable semantic discrimination learning. There is also a 5.1% mIoU gain with the PointNet++ backbone compared to scratch training. Although the network design of PointNet++ is not suit for the scene semantic segmentation, the density prior leveraged by DBPC endows the model ability to capture more relative pose information and eventually obtains better semantic segmentation performances.

5   Conclusions

In this notebook paper, we have presented a simple modification for the point-level contrastive learning. The density prior captured by traditional DBSCAN algorithm is involved as an additional regularization term. The spatial contextual information enhances the model generalizability to different downstream tasks and the good performances verify this claim. Our future works include more in-depth studies of how to learn the correlation between different DBSCAN clusters to boost self-supervised point cloud representation learning.

References

1. Achlioptas, P., Diamanti, O., Mitliagkas, I., Guibas, L.: Learning representation and generative models for 3D point clouds. In: ICML (2018)
2. Ahmed, S.M., Meng, C.C.: Density based clustering for 3D object detection in point clouds. In: CVPR (2020)

3. Armeni, I., et al.: 3D semantic parsing of large-scale indoor space. In: ICCV (2016)
4. Chen, T., Kornblith, S., Norouzi, M., Hinton, G.: A simple framework for contrastive learning of visual representations. In: ICML (2020)
5. Choy, C., Gwak, J., Savarese, S.: 4D spatio-temporal convnets: minkowski convolutional neural networks. In: CVPR (2019)
6. Dai, A., Chang, A.X., Savva, M., Halber, M., Funkhouser, T., Nießner, M.: ScanNet: richly-annotated 3D reconstructions of indoor scenes. In: CVPR (2017)
7. Dai, J., et al.: Deformable convolutional networks. In: ICCV (2017)
8. Engelmann, F., Bokenloh, M., Fathi, A., Leibe, B., Nießner, M.: 3D-MPA: multiproposal aggregation for 3D semantic instance segmentation. In: CVPR (2020)
9. Ester, M., Kriegel, H.P., Sander, J., Xu, X.: A density-based algorithm for discovering clusters in large spatial databases with noise. In: SIGKDD (1996)
10. Feichtenhofer, C., Fan, H., Malik, J., He, K.: SlowFast networks for video recognition. In: ICCV (2019)
11. Feichtenhofer, C., Fan, H., Xiong, B., Girshick, R., He, K.: A large-scale study on unsupervised spatiotemporal representation learning. In: CVPR (2021)
12. Gadelha, M., Wang, R., Maji, S.: Multiresolution tree networks for 3D point cloud processing. In: Ferrari, V., Hebert, M., Sminchisescu, C., Weiss, Y. (eds.) ECCV 2018. LNCS, vol. 11211, pp. 105–122. Springer, Cham (2018). https://doi.org/10.1007/978-3-030-01234-2_7
13. Graham, B., Engelcke, M., van der Maaten, L.: 3D semantic segmentation with submanifold sparse convolution networks. In: CVPR (2018)
14. Han, Z., Wang, X., Liu, Y.S., Zwicker, M.: Multi-angle point cloud-VAE: unsupervised feature learning for 3D point clouds from multiple angles by joint selfreconstruction and half-to-half prediction. In: ICCV (2019)
15. Hassani, K., Haley, M.: Unsupervised multi-task feature learning on point clouds. In: ICCV (2019)
16. He, K., Chen, X., Xie, S., Li, Y., Dollar, P., Girshick, R.: Masked autoencoders are scalable vision learners. In: CVPR (2022)
17. He, K., Fan, H., Wu, Y., Xie, S., Girshick, R.: Momentum contrast for unsupervised visual representation learning. In: CVPR (2020)
18. He, K., Zhang, X., Ren, S., Sun, J.: Deep residual learning for image recognition. In: CVPR (2016)
19. Hou, J., Dai, A., Nießner, M.: 3D-SIS: 3D semantic instance segmentation of RGB-D scans. In: CVPR (2019)
20. Hou, J., Graham, B., Nießner, M., Xie, S.: Exploring data-efficient 3D scene understanding with contrastive scene contexts. In: CVPR (2021)
21. Jiang, H., Yan, F., Cai, J., Zheng, J., Xiao, J.: End-to-end 3D point cloud instance segmentation without detection. In: CVPR (2020)
22. Jiang, L., Zhao, H., Shi, S., Liu, S., Fu, C., Jia, J.: PointGroup: dual-set point grouping for 3D instance segmentation. In: CVPR (2020)
23. Gwak, J.Y., Choy, C., Savarese, S.: Generative sparse detection networks for 3D single-shot object detection. In: Vedaldi, A., Bischof, H., Brox, T., Frahm, J.-M. (eds.) ECCV 2020. LNCS, vol. 12349, pp. 297–313. Springer, Cham (2020). https://doi.org/10.1007/978-3-030-58548-8_18
24. Li, J., Chen, B.M., Lee, G.H.: SO-Net: self-organizing network for point cloud analysis. In: CVPR (2018)
25. Li, J., Zhou, P., Xiong, C., Hoi, S.: Prototypical contrastive learning of unsupervised representations. In: ICLR (2021)
26. Lin, T.Y., Goyal, P., Girshick, R., He, K., Dollar, P.: Focal loss for dense object detection. In: ICCV (2017)

27. Long, F., Qiu, Z., Pan, Y., Yao, T., Luo, J., Mei, T.: Stand-alone inter-frame attention in video models. In: CVPR (2022)
28. Long, F., Qiu, Z., Pan, Y., Yao, T., Ngo, C.W., Mei, T.: Dynamic temporal filtering in video models. In: Avidan, S., Brostow, G., Cissé, M., Farinella, G.M., Hassner, T. (eds.) ECCV 2022. LNCS, vol. 13695. Springer, Cham (2022). https://doi.org/10.1007/978-3-031-19833-5_28
29. Long, F., Yao, T., Qiu, Z., Tian, X., Luo, J., Mei, T.: Gaussian temporal awareness networks for action localization. In: CVPR (2019)
30. Long, F., Yao, T., Qiu, Z., Tian, X., Luo, J., Mei, T.: Learning to localize actions from moments. In: Vedaldi, A., Bischof, H., Brox, T., Frahm, J.-M. (eds.) ECCV 2020. LNCS, vol. 12348, pp. 137–154. Springer, Cham (2020). https://doi.org/10.1007/978-3-030-58580-8_9
31. Long, F., Yao, T., Qiu, Z., Tian, X., Luo, J., Mei, T.: Bi-calibration networks for weakly-supervised video representation learning. arXiv preprint arXiv:2206.10491 (2022)
32. Long, F., Yao, T., Qiu, Z., Tian, X., Mei, T., Luo, J.: Coarse-to-fine localization of temporal action proposals. IEEE Trans. Multimed. (2019)
33. Luo, Z., Peng, B., Huang, D.A., Alahi, A., Fei-Fei, L.: Unsupervised learning of long-term motion dynamics for videos. In: CVPR (2017)
34. Mo, K., et al.: PartNet: a large-scale benchmark for fine-grained and hierarchical part-level 3D object understanding. In: CVPR (2019)
35. van den Oord, A., Li, Y., Vinyals, O.: Representation learning with contrastive predictive coding. In: NeurIPS (2018)
36. Pan, Y., et al.: Smart director: an event-driven directing system for live broadcasting. IEEE Trans. Multimed. Comput. Commun. Appl. (2022)
37. Qi, C.R., Chen, X., Litany, O., Guibas, L.J.: Imvotenet: boosting 3D object detection in point cloud with image votes. In: CVPR (2020)
38. Qi, C.R., Su, H., Mo, K., Guibas, L.J.: Pointnet: deep learning on point sets for 3D classification and segmentation. In: CVPR (2017)
39. Qi, C.R., Yi, L., Su, H., Guibas, L.J.: Pointnet++: deep hierarchical feature learning on point sets in a metric space. In: NeurIPS (2017)
40. Qiu, Z., Yao, T., Mei, T.: Learning spatio-temporal representation with pseudo-3D residual networks. In: ICCV (2017)
41. Russakovsky, O., et al.: ImageNet large scale visual recognition challenge. Int. J. Comput. Vision 115(3), 211–252 (2015). https://doi.org/10.1007/s11263-015-0816-y
42. Sauder, J., Sievers, B.: Self-supervised deep learning on point clouds by reconstructing space. In: NeurIPS (2019)
43. Sun, Y., Wang, Y., Liu, Z., Siegel, J.E., Sarma, S.E.: PointGrow: autoregressively learned point cloud generation with self-attention. In: WACV (2019)
44. Tchapmi, L., Choy, C., Armeni, I., Gwak, J., Savarese, S.: Segcloud: segmentation of 3D point clouds. In: 3DV (2017)
45. Wang, L., et al.: Temporal segment networks: towards good practices for deep action recognition. In: Leibe, B., Matas, J., Sebe, N., Welling, M. (eds.) ECCV 2016. LNCS, vol. 9912, pp. 20–36. Springer, Cham (2016). https://doi.org/10.1007/978-3-319-46484-8_2
46. Wang, X., Gupta, A.: Unsupervised learning of visual representations using videos. In: ICCV (2015)
47. Wu, Z., et al.: 3D ShapeNets: a deep representation for volumetric shape modeling. In: CVPR (2015)

48. Wu, Z., Xiong, Y., Yu, S.X., Lin, D.: Unsupervised feature learning via non-parametric instance discrimination. In: CVPR (2018)
49. Xie, S., Gu, J., Guo, D., Qi, C.R., Guibas, L., Litany, O.: PointContrast: unsupervised pre-training for 3D point cloud understanding. In: Vedaldi, A., Bischof, H., Brox, T., Frahm, J.-M. (eds.) ECCV 2020. LNCS, vol. 12348, pp. 574–591. Springer, Cham (2020). https://doi.org/10.1007/978-3-030-58580-8_34
50. Xie, S., Sun, C., Huang, J., Tu, Z., Murphy, K.: Rethinking spatiotemporal feature learning: speed-accuracy trade-offs in video classification. In: Ferrari, V., Hebert, M., Sminchisescu, C., Weiss, Y. (eds.) ECCV 2018. LNCS, vol. 11219, pp. 318–335. Springer, Cham (2018). https://doi.org/10.1007/978-3-030-01267-0_19
51. Yang, J., Ahn, P., Kim, D., Lee, H., Kim, J.: Progressive seed generation auto-encoder for unsupervised point cloud learning. In: ICCV (2021)
52. Yang, Y., Feng, C., Shen, Y., Tian, D.: FoldingNet: point cloud auto-encoder via deep grid deformation. In: CVPR (2018)
53. Yi, L., et al.: A scalable active framework for region annotation in 3D shape collections. ACM Trans. Graph. (2016)
54. Zhang, Z., Girdhar, R., Joulin, A., Misra, I.: Self-supervised pretraining of 3D features on any point-cloud. In: ICCV (2021)

Joint Masked Autoencoding with Global Reconstruction for Point Cloud Learning

Qi Cai$^{(\boxtimes)}$

University of Science and Technology of China, Hefei, Anhui,
People's Republic of China
cqcaiqi@gmail.com

Abstract. As a new pre-training paradigm, masked autoencoding has significantly advanced self-supervised learning in NLP and computer vision. However, it remains under exploration whether masked autoencoding can be generalized to feature learning in point clouds. In this paper, we present a novel self-supervised learning framework based on Joint Masked Autoencoding with global reconstruction (JMA). The key idea is to randomly mask some patches in the point clouds and use the visible patches to reconstruct the masked ones. In contrast with previous methods based on masked autoencoding, our JMA splits the point clouds into multiple partitions and uses every single partition to predict all other partitions, which involves simultaneous learning of multiple masked autoencoding tasks. Moreover, each partition is supervised to learn the global shape of the point clouds, which enables the model to capture global pictures of the original point clouds. Extensive results demonstrate the advantages of the proposed method on various downstream tasks. Specifically, on the widely used ModelNet40 and the more challenging ScanObjectNN datasets, the pre-trained model achieves consistently improved performances.

Keywords: Self-supervised · Point Cloud · Masked Autoencoding

1 Introduction

Point clouds are an important data format for saving and processing 3D data. There have be tremendous progress in 3D vision built on point cloud data, including 3D classification [1–4], 3D object detection [5–9], and 3D segmentation [10–13]. Most methods developed for point cloud analysis are inspired by 2D image processing and follow a fully-supervised paradigm. A non-eligible drawback is that fully-supervised methods need a large number of human annotations, which is not always available in practice. There have been enormous works aiming at learning image feature representation under data-limited scenarios [14–17]. Given the large collections of unlabeled point clouds, designing a self-supervised algorithm to learn feature representations from the unlabeled data is a promising direction in point cloud analysis.

© Springer Nature Switzerland AG 2023
J.-J. Rousseau and B. Kapralos (Eds.): ICPR 2022 Workshops, LNCS 13643, pp. 313–329, 2023.
https://doi.org/10.1007/978-3-031-37660-3_22

Masked autoencoder [18], which is initially proposed for NLP learning, aims
to recover masked data from unmasked part of the input. Specifically, some words
in a sentence are masked and the other unmasked words are encoded to predict
masked ones. To predict the masked word, the sentences encoder is forced to learn
dependencies between different words and capture high-level semantic features
for sentences. The masked autoencoder has also demonstrated its effectiveness
in computer vision fields [19,20]. The images are divided into grid patches and
a large portion of patched are masked before feeding into a Transformer-based
encoder-decoder network. The encoder-decoder network is required to predict
the raw pixels of masked patches based on their positions.

In principle, the masked autoencoder is also applicable to learning feature
representation for point cloud in a self-supervised way. However compared with
1D sentences or 2D grid images, point clouds are naturally irregular, which
introduces particular challenges for the masked autoencoding framework. Firstly,
the partitions of sentence to word and images to patches are trivial and nearly
cost-free, thanks to the grid representation of sentences and images. For point
cloud, the observed points could appear anywhere in the space and most of the
space is empty, thus making the partition more difficult. Some point cloud models
[1,10] adopt K-NN search to divide point cloud into patches which is computation
heavy. Secondly, the point cloud data has uneven distributions in the space.
Normally each patch only occupies a small portion of space and thus lacks overall
pictures of the objects. Learning the predict each patch will emphasize more local
information and consequently ignore the global information.

Based on the above analysis, in this paper, we extend masked autoencoding
into point cloud analysis with two technical innovations. First, we use furthest
point sampling (FPS) [1] to find K seed points in the original point cloud. The
K seed points are a coarse representation of the point cloud. For each seed point,
K-NN search is employed to find local neighbors in the 3D space, which form a
local patch similar to that in a 2D image. The position encoding is derived from
the absolute position of the seed point. Then we partition the overall patches into
several non-overlap groups. During training, each group of patches is considered
visible patches, and the other groups of patches are masked patches. The visible
patches are processed with a tiny network to get the patch embeddings, which are
further fed into a Transformer-based encoder. The Transformer-based encoder
could build the relations of visible patches with self-attention. Then the position
embeddings of masked patches are padded with visible patch embedding and
then input to the Transformer-based decoder to predict the masked patches.

In this way for each point cloud sample, there are N autoencoding tasks
optimized simultaneously. Besides predicting the local patches, we design a global
prediction branch that takes each visible patch feature as input and predicts the
global shape of the point cloud. Since the original point cloud contains high-
resolution points, which are difficult to predict based on a single visible patch,
we use the K seed points as the targets in the global prediction branch. After
the points encoder is trained, it is transferred to different downstream tasks.

The main contributions can be summarized as follows:

- We propose a novel self-supervised learning framework for point cloud analysis based on a masked autoencoder. In contrast to methods developed for NLP and 2D images, we propose to simultaneously optimize multiple autoencoding tasks for each point cloud sample. In this way, we can make the best of the generated patches.
- We introduce a global shape prediction branch to enforce the model to learn global information. Considering that the original point cloud contains enormous points, we use the seed points as prediction targets which reduces the optimization burden.
- On the widely adopted ModelNet40 and more challenging ScanObjectNN datasets, the proposed method achieves consistent improvements over baseline models.

2 Related Work

The proposed method is inspired by self-supervised masked autoencoding and point cloud feature learning. In this section, we will give a literature review of the aforementioned research topics.

2.1 Self-supervised Learning

In masked language modeling, BERT [18] and its sucessors [21–24] achieve boosted performances on various NLP downstream tasks by predicting masked tokens during the pretraining stage. The core of BERT is masked language modeling (MLM), where a portion of words (15%) is replaced with a [mask] token, and the masked words are to be predicted with a Transfomer-based network. By pre-training on large scale Corpus dataset, BERT achieves remarkable performance boosts across various downstream tasks. In the computer vision field, contrastive learning-based approaches [14, 25–27] learn image features unsupervisedly by distinguishing positive pairs from negative pairs. Contrastive learning [14, 15, 28–30] has dominated self-supervised learning in computer vision until the generative masked image learning approaches [19, 20, 31, 32] start to appear. BeiT [32] follows a similar idea to BERT to predict masked image patches given visible ones. To map the continuous space of image pixels into word-like discrete tokens, BeiT encodes pixels in image patches into discrete tokens and masks a small portion. The remaining patches are fed into the Transformer for predicting the masked tokens. ibot [33] introduces an online tokenizer that is updated during the optimization of the masked autoencoding target. More recently, MAE [19] proposes to directly mask and predict in the image pixel space. Our proposed method takes inspiration from MAE and proposes a masked autoencoder specifically designed for the point cloud data.

2.2 Point Cloud Analysis

Similar to trends in image and video domains [34–36], recently deep learning has advanced point cloud analysis on various tasks, including point cloud classification, point cloud detection, and point cloud segmentation. Among these methods, point-based and projection-based are two representative directions. PointNet [1] is the pioneering architecture for point cloud processing. Each point is processed with MLP networks and then fused with permutation-invariant aggregation operations, for example, max-pooling. PointNet++ [10] improves upon PointNet by introducing local structure modeling. Some subsequent works design more complicated local structure modeling operations including PointCNN [37], PointConv [2], and DGCNN [4]. Recently, Transformer-based models [38,39] demonstrates better performances on point cloud understanding tasks. For projection-based approaches, MVCNN [3] projects point to images from multiple perspectives and perform classification on the projected images. Previous projection-based methods fall behind point-based methods in performance. Recently, SimpleView [40] awakens the power of projection-based methods with residual network design. In this work, we adopt the point-based method due to its effectiveness.

2.3   Self-superivised Point Cloud Analysis

Except for supervised learning on the point cloud, SSL has also been adapted for point cloud analysis. Researchers have proposed various pretext tasks for learning representation from unlabeled point cloud datasets. Rotate [41] learns to predict the rotation angle of the point cloud. OcCo [42] attempts to reconstruct the complete point cloud given occluded ones from camera views. DepthContrast [43] borrows the idea of contrastive learning in 2D images and designs instance discrimination tasks based on augmented point cloud instances. There have also been works using masked autoencoding as a pretext task. Point-Bert [44] trains a point cloud tokenizer to convert local point patches into the discrete token and adopts the MLM tasks in Bert as pretext tasks. Point-Bert shares many similarities with BeiT in the image domain. More recently, Pos-Bert [45] uses a dynamically updated momentum encoder as an online tokenizer which achieves better performances than Point-Bert. Our works also belong to masked autoencoding but consist of technical innovations designed for point cloud data.

3   Method

The proposed method follows an encoder-decoder framework. Specifically, the visible patches are processed with a Transformer based encoder. Then the decoder takes the features of visible patches as well as the position embeddings of masked patches to predict the masked patches. Figure 1 shows the overall framework.

3.1   Patch Generation

Unlike sentences or 2D images, it is nontrivial to divide point clouds into patches due to the irregular nature of point cloud data. We follow the processing method in PointNet++ to group local points and thus divide the whole point cloud into

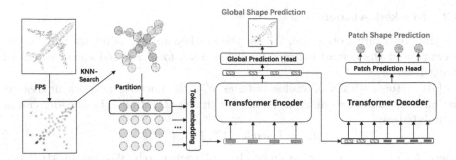

Fig. 1. Framework of the proposed joint masked autoencoding with global reconstruction (JMA). Given a point cloud, FPS is firstly used to find M seed points. For each seed point, K nearest points form a local patch. We partition the patches into G groups and each group is fed into Transformer Encoder, which is further used to predict masked patch shapes. On top of encoded features of visible patches, a global prediction head is appended for global shape prediction.

the sub-point clouds. Given a point cloud of N points, $X \in R^{N \times 3}$, we first use furthest point sampling to get M seed points $S \in R^{M \times 3}$. Then for each seed point, a K-NN search is used to find k nearest neighbors in the original point cloud. The seed point, as well as its k neighbors, form a patch and the overall patches can be represented as $\hat{P} \in R^{M \times k \times 3}$. The patches are normalized with the position of seed points for better convergence. Concretely, the normalized patches are computed as $P = \hat{P} - S$.

Previous works used a random masking ratio to split the patches into visible and masked ones, which ignores the fact that visual patched and masked patches are interchangeable during different training iterations. Instead, we randomly partition the patches into Q parts with equal size: $P = \{P_i | i \in \{1, 2, ..., Q\}\}$ where the size of each part is $P_i \in R^{\frac{M}{Q} \times k \times 3}$. The masking ratio is $1 - 1/Q$. For masking strategy, we select one part P_i as visible patches P_i^v and all other patches are masked patches $P_i^m = \{P_j | j \in \{1, 2, ..., Q\}, j \neq i\}$. Since there are Q parts, for each point cloud sample P, we could construct Q masked autoencoding tasks.

To map the original patch into high-dimensional embeddings, we adopted a lightweight PointNet [1] on each patch. Specifically, PointNet consists of a series of MLPS and max pooling. Given the points in a single patch $\{x_j | j \in \{1, 2, ..., k\}\}$, the embedding F is computed as:

$$f_j = MLP(x_j) \tag{1}$$

$$F = MAXPOOL(\{f_j | j \in \{1, 2, ..., k\}\}) \tag{2}$$

3.2   Masked Autoencoding

For the pre-training objective, We use the masked autoencoding to pre-train the network and the overall network follows a Transformer-based encoder-decoder structure.

Given the features of visible patches F_i^v, the encoder network aggregates the information across different patches with self-attention. The encoder can be formulated as:

$$E_i^v = Encoder(F_i^v, PE_E(P_i^v))$$ (3)

where $PE_E(\cdot)$ is the position embedding of each patch. We use an MLP network to transform the positions of the seed point into high-dimensional position embeddings for the corresponding patch.

For the decoder part, we use a learnable mask embedding E^m to represent the mask tokens. The decoder takes the encoded visual tokens E_i^v and mask embedding E^m and outputs the decoded output:

$$[D_i^v, D_i^m] = Decoder([E_i^v, E^m], PE_D(P_i^v, P_i^m))$$ (4)

where $PE_D(\cdot)$ is the position encoding in the decoding phase.

With the embedding for masked patches D_i^m, a prediction head is appended to generate the point coordinates of the masked patch. For simplification, we use a two-layer MLP as the prediction network. The output dimension of the prediction head is the same as the number of total point coordinates in the masked patch. Then the output is reshaped to match that of point coordinates.

$$O_i^m = Reshape(MLP(D_i^m)), O_i^m \in R^{\frac{M \cdot (Q-1)}{Q} \times K \times 3}$$ (5)

Previous works only take a single visible patch P_i to predict the output O_i^m, which does not take full advantage of generated patches. We use the Q pairs of visile patches $P = \{P_i | i \in \{1, 2, ..., Q\}\}$ to generate the output , $O^m = \{O_i^m | i \in \{1, 2, ..., Q\}\}$. It is worth noting that the size of O_m is $R^{M \cdot Q \times K \times 3}$ and the total number of patches is $R^{M \times K \times 3}$ so there are overlaps in the output O^m. These are patch outputs at the same seed points but are conditioned on different visible patches. We design a consistency regularization to enforce the patch predictions of the same seed points similar as shown in Fig. 2. The conventional masked autoencoding method lacks such consistency regularization and thus fails to capture the dependencies between different visible patches. The consistency regularization can be formulated as:

$$L_c = L_{CD}(\{O_i^m | i \in \{1, 2, ..., Q\}\})$$ (6)

where L_{CD} represents Chamfer Distance [46] between corresponding patch outputs.

3.3   Global Shape Reconstruction

A drawback of reconstructing masked patches is the leak of localization information. To provide the decoder where to reconstruct, the positions of seed points are

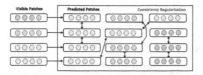

Fig. 2. Joint optimization of multi visible patches of single point cloud. The point cloud is partition into four parts and each part forms a visible patches set to predict patches in other parts. The outputs at same seed points are enccouraged to be consistent.

provided to the decoder. Consequently, the encoder-decode network only needs to model the local structure of the point cloud. Take the point cloud of a "Plane" as an example, the decoder is provided all seed points and dense points in the head. The network could only use the seed points to predict the dense point in the wings in principle. To summarize, the position embedding leaks information about masked patches and provided a shortcut for feature learning. The core reason lies in that point positions contain everything about the point cloud.

Based above analysis, we design a global shape reconstruction target for supervising the network learning. The global prediction head consists of multiple layers of MLP and takes the encoded visible features E_i^v as input and outputs the global shape prediction G_i:

$$G_i = Reshape(MLP(E_i^v)), G_i \in R^{M \times 3} \tag{7}$$

Directly predicting the original point cloud is computation heavy and difficult to converge, as the original point cloud contains many details. Instead, we use the seed points S as the prediction targets which also capture the global structures of the point clouds but with much fewer points.

3.4 Optimization Objective

The overall training objective integrates the masked patch prediction loss, consistency loss, and global shape prediction loss. We choose the Chamfer Distance as the loss function. The Chamfer Distance measures the mismatches between two sets of points and is defined as (Fig. 3):

$$L_{CD}(P^s, P^t) = \frac{1}{2N} \sum_{p_s \in P^s} min_{p_t \in P^t} ||p_s - p_t||_2^2 \tag{8}$$

$$+ \frac{1}{2N} \sum_{p_s \in P^s} min_{p_t \in P^t} ||p_s - p_t||_2^2$$

The final loss function is:

$$L = \frac{1}{Q} \sum_{i \in 1,2,...,Q} (L_{CD}(P_i^m, O_i^m) + L_{CD}(G_i, S)) \tag{9}$$

$$+ L_{CD}(\{O_i^m | i \in \{1, 2, ..., Q\}\}) \tag{10}$$

320   Q. Cai

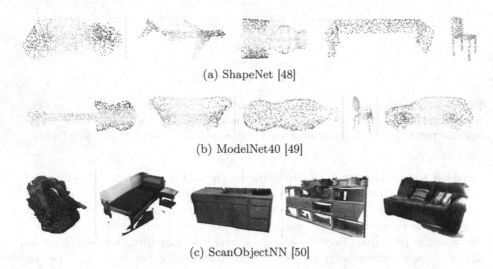

(a) ShapeNet [48]

(b) ModelNet40 [49]

(c) ScanObjectNN [50]

Fig. 3. Point cloud examples of ShapeNet, ModelNet40 and ScanObjectNN datasets.

4 Experiments

In this section, we first describe the experimental settings for evaluating the proposed method. Then we report experiments on several downstream tasks. Finally, we perform ablation studies and analysis experiments to verify each component's effectiveness.

4.1 Dataset

In our experiment, we use ShapeNet [47] as a pre-training dataset and evaluate the proposed method on ModelNet40 [48] and ScanObjectNN [49] datasets.

ShapeNet. ShapeNet [47] contains 57,448 synthetic CAD models distributed among 55 common object categories. To get point cloud data from CAD models, we sample 1,024 points for each object.

ModelNet40. ModelNet40 [48] contains 12,331 synthetic CAD models from 40 categories. It is a popular classification dataset for benchmarking different point cloud models. We sample 1,024 points from each CAD model. We adopt the widely used split to divide the CAD models into 9,843 samples for training and 2,468 samples for testing.

ScanObjectNN. Different from ShapeNet and ModelNet40, SacnObjectNN [49] is a classification dataset captured from the real world with 3D sensors. It contains 2,902 point cloud samples distributed among 15 categories. Compared with point clouds sampled from synthetic CAD models, the points in ScanObjcetNN are more sparse and contain occlusion, jittering, and background noises, thus making it more challenging. We mainly follow [44] and adopt three different evaluation settings, including OBJ-BG and OBJ-ONLY, and PB-T50-RS.

4.2   Experiment Setting

Pre-training. In the pre-training stage, 64 seed points are generated with FPS, and 32 nearest points are searched with K-NN for each seed point. The transformer encoder has 12 layers and 6 heads per layer. To reduce overfitting, we use a 0.1 drop path rate in the transformer encoder. For the transformer decoder layer, the number of layers is 2 and the head number is 6. The number of partition G is set to 4 and the masking ratio is thus 0.25. During training, we use the AdamW [50] optimizer with a learning rate of 0.001, and the learning rate decays following a cosine schedule. The batch size is 16 and trained for 100 epochs. After the pre-training stage, only the encoder is kept for downstream tasks.

Downstream Tasks. For classification on ModelNet40 and ScanObjectNN, 64 seed points are generated with FPS and each seed point is accompanied by 32 neighbors. We mainly compare two different settings: linear classification on frozen features and finetuned setting.

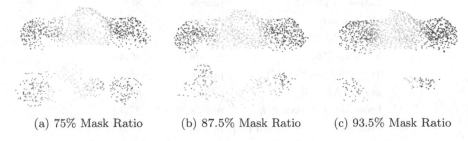

(a) 75% Mask Ratio   (b) 87.5% Mask Ratio   (c) 93.5% Mask Ratio

Fig. 4. Reconstructioned point clouds and masked point clouds with different mask ratios. Top row: reconstructed point clouds. Bottom row: masked point clouds.

4.3   Reconsctruction Results on ShapeNet

To validate the motivation for reconstructing the masked point cloud, we first visualize the reconstructed point cloud on the ShapeNet dataset. It can be seen from Fig. 4 that the point cloud can be well reconstructed under different mask ratios. Although during pre-training we use a 0.75 mask ratio, the reconstructed results at mask ratios of 0.875 and 0.935 also recover the global shape of the original point cloud, proving the effectiveness of the pre-trained model.

4.4   Experimental Results on ModelNet40

We first perform the linear classification on ModelNet40, where the feature extractor is fixed during training and only the last classification layer is trained. Table 1 shows the performance comparisons. Compare with PointNet + Orientation, which uses rotation as a pretext task, our proposed JMA achieves 3.1% improvements, showing the benefits of masked autoencoding. Point-Bert achieves 89.1%, which also uses masked autoencoding, but is still behind JMA. The performance gaps show the advantages of the proposed joint optimization and global shape prediction.

We further study the transferability of the proposed method where the feature extractor is finetuned end to end. The feature extractor uses the pre-trained model parameters as initialization. The results in Table.2 show that our proposed method still achieves competitive performances compared with the most recent work Point-Bert [44].

Table 1. Linear classification accuracy with frozen feature extractor on ModelNet40 dataset.

Method	Input Format	Accuracy
3D-GAN [51]	voxel	83.3
VIP-GAN [52]	views	90.2
Latent-GAN [53]	points	85.7
SO-Net [54]	points	87.3
FoldingNet [55]	points	88.4
MRTNet [56]	points	86.4
3D-PointCapsNet [57]	points	88.9
MAP-VAE [58]	points	88.4
PointNet + Jiasaw [59]	points	87.3
PointNet + Orientation [41]	points	88.6
PointNet + STRL [60]	points	88.3
Point-BERT [61]	points	87.4
PointNet + CrossPoint [62]	points	89.1
JMA(Ours)	points	91.7

4.5   Experimental Results on ScanObjectNN

We then perform experiments on the real-world dataset, ScanObjectNN. Although the pre-training is performed on a synthetic point cloud dataset, we also prove that the learned model can generalize to real-world data. Table 3 shows the results on ScanObjectNN, it can be seen that the proposed method achieves better performances than training from scratch. Compared with the most recent masked autoencoding-based method Point-BERT, the proposed JMA also achieves 1.1% improvement on the hardest PB-T50-RS setting.

Table 2. Classification accuracy on ModelNet40 dataset with end-to-end finetuning.

Method	Acc
PointNet [1]	89.2
PointNet++ [63]	90.5
SO-Net [54]	92.5
PointCNN [37]	92.2
DGCNN [4]	92.9
DensePoint [64]	92.8
RSCNN [65]	92.9
PTC [38]	93.2
NPTC [38]	91.0
Point-Bert [44]	93.2
JMA(Ours)	93.0

Table 3. Classification accuracy on ScanObjectNN dataset. PB-T50-RS is the hardest setting compared with OBJ-BG and OBJ-ONLY.

Methods	OBJ-BG	OBJ-ONLY	PB-T50-RS
PointNet [1]	73.3	79.2	68.0
PointNet++ [10]	82.3	84.3	77.9
DGCNN [4]	82.8	86.2	78.1
PointCNN [37]	86.1	85.5	78.5
GBNet [66]	-	-	80.5
PRANet [67]	-	-	81.0
Transformer [44]	79.86	80.55	77.24
Transformer-OcCo [44]	84.85	85.54	78.79
Point-BERT [44]	87.43	88.12	83.07
JMA(Ours)	**88.47**	**88.25**	**84.28**

4.6 Ablation Studies

In this section, we compare different components in this proposed model. We use the classification on ScanObjectNN as a downstream task for evaluation. The overall training loss includes three parts: patch target loss, consistency loss, and global target loss and we design three different variants. Model A removes the global prediction head. Model B removes the consistency loss and Model C is the full model. Table 4 shows the performance comparisons. It can be seen that combining consistency regularization and global prediction loss achieves the best performances, which aligns with the motivation of joint optimization and learning global features.

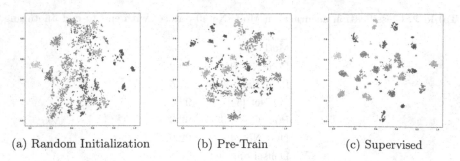

(a) Random Initialization　　　(b) Pre-Train　　　(c) Supervised

Fig. 5. t-SNE visualization of features extracted from ModelNet40 with different feature extractors.

Table 4. Performances on ScanObjectNN PB-T50-RS of different model variants.

Method	Consistency	Global Prediction	Acc
Model A	✓		83.90
Model B		✓	83.65
Model C	✓	✓	**84.28**

4.7 Feature Visualizaton on ModelNet

In this section, we visualize the features on ModelNet40. We compare three models: 1.) random initialized models, 2.) initialized with pre-trained weights proposed in this paper, 3.) initialized with supervised trained weights on ModelNet40. Figure 5 shows the t-SNE visualization of feature distribution. It is clear that features of different categories are more distinct from each other after pre-trained with JMA. Even compared with the fully-supervised setting, the proposed JMA model can learn comparable features. The results demonstrate that the proposed pre-training could learn category semantics even without any supervision information.

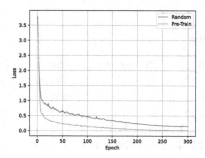

Fig. 6. Loss convergency cruves of Random initialization and Pre-Train initialization with training epochs.

4.8   Convergency Speed

We then compare the convergence speed on downstream tasks. Since the pre-trained model learns semantics among categories, which should speed up the convergence. Figure 6 shows the loss convergency curves of randomly initialized feature extractors and pre-trained model initialized ones. It is clear that pre-training could speed up the loss decrease and finally converges at a lower loss.

5   Conclusion

In this paper, we propose a novel joint masking autoencoder for self-supervised point cloud learning. In contrast to previous methods, we propose to jointly optimize multiple autoencoding tasks and introduce a global shape prediction branch to enforce learning global features. On two popular datasets including Model-Net40 and ScanObjectNN, the proposed method achieves consistent improvements. In the future, we will explore the self-supervised learning on outdoor scenes like Waymo Open Dataset [68] and nuScenes dataset [69].

References

1. Qi, C.R., Su, H., Mo, K., Guibas, L.J.: Pointnet: deep learning on point sets for 3d classification and segmentation. In: Proceedings of the IEEE Conference on Computer Vision and Pattern Recognition, pp. 652–660 (2017)
2. Wu, W., Qi, Z., Fuxin, L.: PointConv: deep convolutional networks on 3D point clouds. In: Proceedings of the IEEE/CVF Conference on Computer Vision and Pattern Recognition, pp. 9621–9630 (2019)
3. Su, H., Maji, S., Kalogerakis, E., Learned-Miller, E.: Multi-view convolutional neural networks for 3d shape recognition. In: Proceedings of the IEEE International Conference on Computer Vision, pp. 945–953 (2015)
4. Wang, Y., Sun, Y., Liu, Z., Sarma, S.E., Bronstein, M.M., Solomon, J.M.: Dynamic graph CNN for learning on point clouds. Acm Trans. Graph. (tog) **38**(5), 1–12 (2019)
5. Qi, C.R., Litany, O., He, K., Guibas, L.J.: Deep hough voting for 3d object detection in point clouds. In: Proceedings of the IEEE/CVF International Conference on Computer Vision, pp. 9277–9286 (2019)
6. Shi, S., et al.: Pv-rcnn: point-voxel feature set abstraction for 3d object detection. In: Proceedings of the IEEE/CVF Conference on Computer Vision and Pattern Recognition, pp. 10 529–10 538 (2020)
7. Liu, Z., Zhang, Z., Cao, Y., Hu, H., Tong, X.: Group-free 3d object detection via transformers. In: Proceedings of the IEEE/CVF International Conference on Computer Vision, pp. 2949–2958 (2021)
8. Cai, Q., Pan, Y., Yao, T., Mei, T.: 3d cascade rcnn: high quality object detection in point clouds. IEEE Trans. Image Process. (2022)
9. Pan, Y., et al.: Silver-bullet-3d at maniskill 2021: learning-from-demonstrations and heuristic rule-based methods for object manipulation. In: ICLR 2022 Workshop on Generalizable Policy Learning in Physical World (2022)

10. Qi, C.R., Yi, L., Su, H., Guibas, L.J.: Pointnet++: deep hierarchical feature learning on point sets in a metric space. In: Advances in Neural Information Processing Systems, vol. 30 (2017)

11. Xu, C., Wu, B., Wang, Z., Zhan, W., Vajda, P., Keutzer, K., Tomizuka, M.: SqueezeSegV3: spatially-adaptive convolution for efficient point-cloud segmentation. In: Vedaldi, A., Bischof, H., Brox, T., Frahm, J.-M. (eds.) ECCV 2020. LNCS, vol. 12373, pp. 1–19. Springer, Cham (2020). https://doi.org/10.1007/978-3-030-58604-1_1

12. Landrieu, L., Simonovsky, M.: Large-scale point cloud semantic segmentation with superpoint graphs. In: CVPR (2018)

13. Vo, A.-V., Truong-Hong, L., Laefer, D.F., Bertolotto, M.: Octree-based region growing for point cloud segmentation. ISPRS J. Photogramm. Remote. Sens. **104**, 88–100 (2015)

14. He, K., Fan, H., Wu, Y., Xie, S., Girshick, R.: Momentum contrast for unsupervised visual representation learning. In: Proceedings of the IEEE/CVF Conference on Computer Vision and Pattern Recognition, pp. 9729–9738 (2020)

15. Chen, T., Kornblith, S., Norouzi, M., Hinton, G.: A simple framework for contrastive learning of visual representations. In: International Conference on Machine Learning. PMLR, pp. 1597–1607 (2020)

16. Cai, Q., Pan, Y., Ngo, C.-W., Tian, X., Duan, L., Yao, T.: Exploring object relation in mean teacher for cross-domain detection. In: Proceedings of the IEEE/CVF Conference on Computer Vision and Pattern Recognition, pp. 11 457–11 466 (2019)

17. Cai, Q., Pan, Y., Yao, T., Yan, C., Mei, T.: Memory matching networks for one-shot image recognition. In: Proceedings of the IEEE Conference on Computer Vision and Pattern Recognition, pp. 4080–4088 (2018)

18. Devlin, J., Chang, M.-W., Lee, K., Toutanova, K.: Bert: pre-training of deep bidirectional transformers for language understanding. arXiv preprint arXiv:1810.04805 (2018)

19. He, K., Chen, X., Xie, S., Li, Y., Dollár, P., Girshick, R.: Masked autoencoders are scalable vision learners. arXiv preprint arXiv:2111.06377 (2021)

20. Chen, X., et al.: Context autoencoder for self-supervised representation learning. arXiv preprint arXiv:2202.03026 (2022)

21. Lan, Z., Chen, M., Goodman, S., Gimpel, K., Sharma, P., Soricut, R.: Albert: a lite bert for self-supervised learning of language representations. arXiv preprint arXiv:1909.11942 (2019)

22. Yang, Z., Dai, Z., Yang, Y., Carbonell, J., Salakhutdinov, R.R., Le, Q.V.: Xlnet: Generalized autoregressive pretraining for language understanding. Advances in neural information processing systems, vol. 32 (2019)

23. Joshi, M., Chen, D., Liu, Y., Weld, D.S., Zettlemoyer, L., Levy, O.: Spanbert: improving pre-training by representing and predicting spans. Trans. Assoc. Comput. Linguist. **8**, 64–77 (2020)

24. Reimers, N., Gurevych, I.: Sentence-bert: sentence embeddings using siamese bert-networks. arXiv preprint arXiv:1908.10084 (2019)

25. Chen, T., Kornblith, S., Swersky, K., Norouzi, M., Hinton, G.: Big self-supervised models are strong semi-supervised learners. arXiv preprint arXiv:2006.10029 (2020)

26. Grill, J.-B., et al.: Bootstrap your own latent-a new approach to self-supervised learning. In: Advances in Neural Information Processing Systems, vol. 33, pp. 21 271–21 284 (2020)

27. Chen, X., Fan, H., Girshick, R., He, K.: Improved baselines with momentum contrastive learning. arXiv preprint arXiv:2003.04297 (2020)

28. Cai, Q., Wang, Y., Pan, Y., Yao, T., Mei, T.: Joint contrastive learning with infinite possibilities. In: Advances in Neural Information Processing Systems, vol. 33, pp. 12 638–12 648 (2020)
29. Wang, Y., et al.: A low rank promoting prior for unsupervised contrastive learning. IEEE Trans. Pattern Anal. Mach. Intell. (2022)
30. Yao, T., Zhang, Y., Qiu, Z., Pan, Y., Mei, T.: Seco: exploring sequence supervision for unsupervised representation learning. In: Proceedings of the AAAI Conference on Artificial Intelligence, vol. 35, no. 12, 2021, pp. 10 656–10 664 (2021)
31. Xie, Z., et al.: Simmim: a simple framework for masked image modeling. arXiv preprint arXiv:2111.09886 (2021)
32. Bao, H., Dong, L., Wei, F.: Beit: bert pre-training of image transformers. arXiv preprint arXiv:2106.08254 (2021)
33. Zhou, J., et al.: ibot: Image bert pre-training with online tokenizer. arXiv preprint arXiv:2111.07832 (2021)
34. Pan, Y., et al.: Smart director: an event-driven directing system for live broadcasting. ACM Trans. Multimed. Comput. Commun. Appl. (TOMM) 17(4), 1–18 (2021)
35. Deng, J., Pan, Y., Yao, T., Zhou, W., Li, H., Mei, T.: Single shot video object detector. IEEE Trans. Multimedia 23, 846–858 (2020)
36. Cai, Q., Pan, Y., Wang, Y., Liu, J., Yao, T., Mei, T.: Learning a unified sample weighting network for object detection. In: Proceedings of the IEEE/CVF Conference on Computer Vision and Pattern Recognition, pp. 14 173–14 182 (2020)
37. Li, Y., Bu, R., Sun, M., Wu, W., Di, X., Chen, B.: Pointcnn: convolution on x-transformed points. In: Advances in neural information processing systems, vol. 31 (2018)
38. Guo, M.-H., Cai, J.-X., Liu, Z.-N., Mu, T.-J., Martin, R.R., Hu, S.-M.: PCT: point cloud transformer. Comput. Visual Media 7(2), 187–199 (2021). https://doi.org/10.1007/s41095-021-0229-5
39. Zhao, H., Jiang, L., Jia, J., Torr, P.H., Koltun, V.: Point transformer. In: Proceedings of the IEEE/CVF International Conference on Computer Vision, pp. 16 259–16 268 (2021)
40. Goyal, A., Law, H., Liu, B., Newell, A., Deng, J.: Revisiting point cloud shape classification with a simple and effective baseline. In: International Conference on Machine Learning. PMLR, pp. 3809–3820 (2021)
41. Poursaeed, O., Jiang, T., Qiao, H., Xu, N., Kim, V.G.: Self-supervised learning of point clouds via orientation estimation. In: 2020 International Conference on 3D Vision (3DV). IEEE, pp. 1018–1028 (2020)
42. Wang, H., Liu, Q., Yue, X., Lasenby, J., Kusner, M.J.: Unsupervised point cloud pre-training via occlusion completion. In: Proceedings of the IEEE/CVF International Conference on Computer Vision, pp. 9782–9792 (2021)
43. Zhang, Z., Girdhar, R., Joulin, A., Misra, I.: Self-supervised pretraining of 3D features on any point-cloud. In: Proceedings of the IEEE/CVF International Conference on Computer Vision, pp. 10 252–10 263 (2021)
44. Yu, X., Tang, L., Rao, Y. , Huang, T., Zhou, J., Lu, J.: Point-bert: pre-training 3d point cloud transformers with masked point modeling. arXiv preprint arXiv:2111.14819 (2021)
45. Fu, K., Gao, P., Liu, S., Zhang, R., Qiao, Y., Wang, M.: Pos-bert: point cloud one-stage bert pre-training. arXiv preprint arXiv:2204.00989 (2022)
46. Fan, H., Su, H., Guibas, L.J.: A point set generation network for 3d object reconstruction from a single image. In: Proceedings of the IEEE Conference on Computer Vision and Pattern Recognition, pp. 605–613 (2017)

47. Chang, A.X., et al.: Shapenet: An information-rich 3d model repository. arXiv preprint arXiv:1512.03012 (2015)

48. Wu, Z., et al.: 3d shapenets: a deep representation for volumetric shapes. In: Proceedings of the IEEE Conference on Computer Vision and Pattern Recognition, pp. 1912–1920 (2015)

49. Uy, M.A., Pham, Q.-H., Hua, B.-S., Nguyen, T., Yeung, S.-K.: Revisiting point cloud classification: A new benchmark dataset and classification model on real-world data. In: Proceedings of the IEEE/CVF International Conference on Computer Vision, pp. 1588–1597 (2019)

50. Loshchilov, I., Hutter, F.: Decoupled weight decay regularization. arXiv preprint arXiv:1711.05101 (2017)

51. Wu, J., Zhang, C., Xue, T., Freeman, B., Tenenbaum, J.: Learning a probabilistic latent space of object shapes via 3D generative-adversarial modeling. In: Advances in Neural Information Processing Systems, vol. 29 (2016)

52. Han, Z., Shang, M., Liu, Y.-S., Zwicker, M.: View inter-prediction GAN: Unsupervised representation learning for 3D shapes by learning global shape memories to support local view predictions. Proceedings of the AAAI Conference on Artificial Intelligence **33**(01), 8376–8384 (2019)

53. Valsesia, D., Fracastoro, G., Magli, E.: Learning localized representations of point clouds with graph-convolutional generative adversarial networks. IEEE Trans. Multimedia **23**, 402–414 (2020)

54. Li, J., Chen, B.M., Lee, G.H.: So-net: self-organizing network for point cloud analysis. In: Proceedings of the IEEE/CVF Conference on Computer Vision and Pattern Recognition, pp. 9397–9406 (2018)

55. Yang, Y., Feng, C., Shen, Y., Tian, D.: Foldingnet: point cloud auto-encoder via deep grid deformation. In: Proceedings of the IEEE/CVF Conference on Computer Vision and Pattern Recognition, pp. 206–215 (2018)

56. Gadelha, M., Wang, R., Maji, S.: Multiresolution tree networks for 3D point cloud processing. In: Ferrari, V., Hebert, M., Sminchisescu, C., Weiss, Y. (eds.) ECCV 2018. LNCS, vol. 11211, pp. 105–122. Springer, Cham (2018). https://doi.org/10.1007/978-3-030-01234-2_7

57. Zhao, Y., Birdal, T., Deng, H., Tombari, F.: 3D point capsule networks. In: Proceedings of the IEEE/CVF Conference on Computer Vision and Pattern Recognition, pp. 1009–1018 (2019)

58. Han, Z., Wang, X., Liu, Y.-S., Zwicker, M.: Multi-Angle Point Cloud-VAE: Unsupervised feature learning for 3D point clouds from multiple angles by joint self-reconstruction and half-to-half prediction. In: Proceedings of the IEEE/CVF International Conference on Computer Vision. IEEE, pp. 10 441–10 450 (2019)

59. Sauder, J., Sievers, B.: Self-supervised deep learning on point clouds by reconstructing space. In: Advances in Neural Information Processing Systems, vol. 32 (2019)

60. Huang, S., Xie, Y., Zhu, S.-C., Zhu, Y.: Spatio-temporal self-supervised representation learning for 3D point clouds. In: Proceedings of the IEEE/CVF International Conference on Computer Vision, pp. 6535–6545 (2021)

61. Yu, X., Tang, L., Rao, Y., Huang, T., Zhou, J., Lu, J.: Point-BERT: pre-training 3D point cloud transformers with masked point modeling. In: Proceedings of the IEEE Conference on Computer Vision and Pattern Recognition (CVPR) (2022)

62. Afham, M., Dissanayake, I., Dissanayake, D., Dharmasiri, A., Thilakarathna, K., Rodrigo, R.: CrossPoint: self-supervised cross-modal contrastive learning for 3D point cloud Understanding. arXiv preprint arXiv:2203.00680 (2022)

63. Qi, C.R., Yi, L., Su, H., Guibas, L.J.: Pointnet++ deep hierarchical feature learning on point sets in a metric space. In: NeurIPS (2017)
64. Liu, Y., Fan, B., Meng, G., Lu, J., Xiang, S., Pan, C.: Densepoint: learning densely contextual representation for efficient point cloud processing. In: ICCV (2019)
65. Rao, Y., Lu, J., Zhou, J.: Global-local bidirectional reasoning for unsupervised representation learning of 3D point clouds. In: Proceedings of the IEEE/CVF Conference on Computer Vision and Pattern Recognition, pp. 5376–5385 (2020)
66. Qiu, S., Anwar, S., Barnes, N.: Geometric back-projection network for point cloud classification. IEEE Trans. Multimed. (2021)
67. Cheng, S., Chen, X., He, X., Liu, Z., Bai, X.: Pra-net: point relation-aware network for 3d point cloud analysis. IEEE Trans. Image Process. **30**, 4436–4448 (2021)
68. Sun, P., et al.: Scalability in perception for autonomous driving: Waymo open dataset. In: Proceedings of the IEEE/CVF Conference on Computer Vision and Pattern Recognition, pp. 2446–2454 (2020)
69. Caesar, H., et al.: nuscenes: a multimodal dataset for autonomous driving. In: Proceedings of the IEEE/CVF conference on computer vision and pattern recognition, pp. 11 621–11 631 (2020)

Understanding the Properties and Limitations of Contrastive Learning for Out-of-Distribution Detection

Nawid Keshtmand[1]([✉]), Raul Santos-Rodriguez[2], and Jonathan Lawry[2]

[1] Department of Aerospace Engineering, University of Bristol, Bristol, UK
yl18410@bristol.ac.uk
[2] Department of Engineering Mathematics, University of Bristol, Bristol, UK
{enrsr,j.lawry}@bristol.ac.uk

Abstract. A recent popular approach to out-of-distribution (OOD) detection is based on a self-supervised learning technique referred to as *contrastive learning*. There are two main variants of contrastive learning, namely instance and class discrimination, targeting features that can discriminate between different instances for the former, and different classes for the latter.

In this paper, we aim to understand the effectiveness and limitation of existing contrastive learning methods for OOD detection. We approach this in 3 ways. First, we systematically study the performance difference between the instance discrimination and supervised contrastive learning variants in different OOD detection settings. Second, we study which in-distribution (ID) classes OOD data tend to be classified into. Finally, we study the spectral decay property of the different contrastive learning approaches and examine how it correlates with OOD detection performance. In scenarios where the ID and OOD datasets are sufficiently different from one another, we see that instance discrimination, in the absence of fine-tuning, is competitive with supervised approaches in OOD detection. We see that OOD samples tend to be classified into classes that have a distribution similar to the distribution of the entire dataset. Furthermore, we show that contrastive learning learns a feature space that contains singular vectors containing several directions with a high variance which can be detrimental or beneficial to OOD detection depending on the inference approach used.

Keywords: OOD detection · Contrastive Learnining

1 Introduction

In recent years, neural networks have been increasingly deployed for prediction tasks. However, they still make erroneous predictions when exposed to inputs from an unfamiliar distribution [17]. This poses a significant obstacle to the deployment of neural networks in safety-critical applications. Therefore, for applications in these domains, it is necessary to be able to distinguish in-distribution (ID) data from data belonging to a different distribution on which the neural network was trained (OOD data). The problem of detecting such inputs is generally referred to as *out-of-distribution* (OOD) detection, outlier detection, or anomaly detection [21].

Recent studies have shown that a type of self-supervised learning referred to as *contrastive learning* can learn a feature space that is able to capture the features of an input

© Springer Nature Switzerland AG 2023
J.-J. Rousseau and B. Kapralos (Eds.): ICPR 2022 Workshops, LNCS 13643, pp. 330–343, 2023.
https://doi.org/10.1007/978-3-031-37660-3_23

x that enable effective OOD detection [1,25,26]. The two main types of contrastive learning approaches are referred to as unsupervised instance discrimination and supervised contrastive learning/supervised class discrimination. The former works by bringing together the features of the different views of the same data point close together in the feature space enabling discrimination between different instances [1]. Instead, supervised contrastive learning brings data points belonging to the same class close together in feature space, which enables discrimination between data points belonging to different classes [10]. In light of the variety of contrastive learning approaches used in practice, it is difficult to ascertain which properties of contrastive learning are beneficial to OOD detection. In this work, we aim to understand the effectiveness and limitations of existing contrastive learning methods for OOD detection. We approach this in 3 ways.

1. We systematically study the performance difference of the instance discrimination and supervised contrastive learning variants in different OOD detection settings (Sect. 4).
2. We investigate which ID classes OOD data tend to be classified into.
3. We analyze the spectral decay property of the different contrastive learning approaches and how it correlates with OOD detection performance. The spectral decay indicates how many different directions of high variance are present in the feature space and is related to the feature space compression [19].

This involves designing a fair training setup, categorizing the difficulty of OOD detection based on whether ID and OOD datasets are semantically similar (near-OOD) or unrelated (far-OOD), as well as comparing the OOD detection performance using established metrics (Sect. 3). Our main findings and contributions are summarized below: The key contributions of the paper are as follows:

- We perform experiments that show unsupervised instance discrimination, in the absence of fine-tuning, is well-suited to far-OOD detection, where it can be competitive with supervised approaches but ineffective at near-OOD detection (Sect. 4).
- We analyze the classification of OOD samples and see that they tend to be classified into classes that have a distribution similar to the distribution of the entire dataset. This suggests that similar to the phenomena seen in deep generative models, discriminative models assign OOD samples to classes where the latent features capture non-class discriminatory information rather than class-discriminatory information [23] (Sect. 5).
- We show that contrastive learning learns a feature space that contains singular vectors containing several directions with a high variance which can be detrimental or beneficial to OOD detection depending on the inference approach used (Sect. 6).

2 Background

Most OOD detection methods use the features obtained from a classification network trained with the supervised cross-entropy loss. These classification networks learn decision boundaries that discriminate between the classes in the training set. However, using a conventional cross-entropy loss does not incentivize a network to learn features beyond the minimum necessary to discriminate between the different classes and therefore may not be well suited for OOD detection. An alternative to using classification networks for learning is contrastive learning [3]. The idea of contrastive learning is to learn an encoder f_θ, where θ denotes the parameters of the encoder, to extract the necessary information to distinguish between similar and other samples. Let x be a query, whilst $\{x_+\}$ and $\{x_-\}$ denote the sets of positive samples of x and negative samples of x respectively. The goal of contrastive loss is to learn features of x, denoted $z = f_\theta(x)$, similar to the features of $\{x_+\}$ denoted $\{z_+\} = f_\theta(\{x_+\})$ whilst also being dissimilar to $\{z_-\} = f_\theta(\{x_-\})$. The most common form of similarity measure between features z and z' is given by the cosine similarity as given in Eq. 1:

$$sim(z, z') = \frac{z \cdot z'}{\|z\| \, \|z'\|} \tag{1}$$

The first type of contrastive loss considered in this paper is the Momentum Contrast (Moco) loss [7], where the objective relates to the task of instance discrimination and utilizes two different encoders, a query encoder f_{θ_q} and a key encoder f_{θ_k}. The parameters of the query encoder are updated using traditional backpropagation, whilst the parameters of the key encoder are an exponentially weighted average of the parameters of the query encoder, shown by Eq. 2:

$$\theta'_k = m\theta_k + (1 - m)\theta_q \tag{2}$$

where m is an encoder momentum hyperparameter, θ_q are parameters of the query encoder, and θ_k and θ'_k are the parameters of the key encoder before and after the update respectively.

The setup for the training process is as follows. Let $\tilde{x}_i^1$ and $\tilde{x}_i^2$ be two independent augmentations of x_i, namely $\tilde{x}_i^1 = T_1(x_i)$ and $\tilde{x}_i^2 = T_2(x_i)$ where T_1, T_2 are separate augmentation operators sampled from the same family of augmentations $\mathcal{T}$. The Moco objective treats each $(\tilde{x}_i^1, \tilde{x}_i^2)$ and $(\tilde{x}_i^2, \tilde{x}_i^1)$ as a query-positive key pair $x^{query}, x^{key_{pos}}$. Query data points are passed through a query encoder to obtain query features $q = f_{\theta_q}(x^{query})$ and key data points are passed through the key encoder to obtain the key features $k_{pos} = f_{\theta_k}(x^{key_{pos}})$. The contrastive loss for Moco, $\mathcal{L}_{moco}$ is then given by Eq. 3:

$$\mathcal{L}_{moco} = -log \frac{q \cdot k_{pos}/\tau}{\sum_{i=0}^{K} exp(q \cdot k_i/\tau)} \tag{3}$$

where k_{pos} is the positive key for each query q, whilst k_i are previous outputs of the key encoder which were saved in a queue and τ refers to a temperature hyperparameter.

The second type of contrastive loss considered in this paper is the Supervised Contrastive (SupCLR) loss [10]. The SupCLR loss is a generalization of the instance discrimination loss which can deal with an arbitrary number of positives samples to enable contrasting samples in a class-wise manner instead of an instance-wise manner. In this case, all the data points in the same class as the query x^{query} are treated as positive samples $x^{key_{pos}}$ whilst data points in a different class than the query are treated as negative samples $x^{key_{neg}}$. The SupCLR loss only requires using a single encoder f_θ to obtain features for the queries q, positive keys k_{pos} and negative keys k_{neg} where $q = f_\theta(x^{query})$, $k_{pos} = f_\theta(x^{key_{pos}})$ and $k_{neg} = f_\theta(x^{key_{neg}})$. The SupCLR contrastive loss is then given by Eq. 4:

$$\mathcal{L}_{SupCLR} = \frac{-1}{|P(q))|} \sum_{pos \in P(q)} log \frac{exp(q \cdot k_{pos}/\tau)}{\sum_{i \in A(q)} exp(q \cdot k_i/\tau)} \tag{4}$$

Here, $P(q)$ is the set of indices of all positives keys of q which are present in the batch, and $|P(q)|$ is its cardinality. $A(q)$ is the set of all indices in the batch excluding q itself, this includes both k_{pos} and k_{neg}. Intuitively, the instance discrimination loss learns the features in each instance which makes it different from other instances whilst also being invariant to data augmentation, whilst the SupCLR loss learns the features in common between different instances of the same class.

3   OOD Experimental Preliminaries

In this section, we discuss the experimental setup that we use throughout this work.
Datasets. We study OOD detection for the following ID dataset (D_{in}) and OOD dataset (D_{out}) pairs. We use both simple grayscale dataset pairs and more complex RGB dataset pairs for the task. For the grayscale dataset case which uses MNIST, FashionM-NIST, and KMNIST, one of the datasets is defined as D_{in} whilst the other datasets are defined as D_{out} [4, 12, 27]. For the RGB datasets, we use CIFAR-10, CIFAR100 as well as SVHN and follows the same procedure where one dataset is defined as D_{in} whilst the others are defined as D_{out} [11, 16].

Similar to Winkens et al, we use the class-wise confusion log probability (CLP) as a measure of the difficulty of an OOD detection task [26]. As described in Winkens et al, CLP is based on the probability of a classifier confusing OOD data with ID data. This involves computing an estimate of the expected probability of a test OOD sample x being predicted to be an ID class k by an ensemble of N classifiers as given by:

$$c_k(x) = \frac{1}{N} \sum_{j=1}^{N} p^j(\widehat{y} = k|x) \tag{5}$$

where $p^j(\widehat{y} = k|x)$ refers to the probability that the jth classifier assigns x as belonging to class k. The class-wise confusion log probability (CLP) of ID class k for $\mathcal{D}_{test}$ becomes:

$$CLP_k(\mathcal{D}_{test}) = log \left(\frac{1}{\mathcal{D}_{test}} \sum_{x \in \mathcal{D}_{test}} c_k(x) \right) \tag{6}$$

We compute the CLP with $\mathcal{D}_{test}$ being the test samples belonging to the OOD dataset. The distance between the dataset pairs is defined by the min-max bounds on the CLP (lowest CLP value to highest CLP value for the dataset pair). In our work, we use 3 Resnet-18 models to calculate $c_k(x)$. For further details on the Confusion Log probability, see Winkens et al. [26], Sect. 4.

Table 1. Class-wise Confusion Log Probability (CLP) min-max bounds for the different ID-OOD dataset pairs.

Datasets	CLP bounds
ID:MNIST, OOD:FashionMNIST	-7.26 to -7.15
ID:MNIST, OOD:KMNIST	-7.29 to -6.88
ID:FashionMNIST, OOD:MNIST	-7.43 to -7.23
ID:FashionMNIST, OOD:KMNIST	-7.31 to -6.54
ID:KMNIST, OOD:MNIST	-6.87 to -6.03
ID:KMNIST, OOD:FashionMNIST	-7.22 to -6.96
ID:CIFAR10, OOD:SVHN	-7.25 to -6.27
ID:CIFAR10, OOD:CIFAR100	-4.80 to -3.53
ID:CIFAR100, OOD:SVHN	-9.08 to -7.52
ID:CIFAR100, OOD:CIFAR10	-7.74 to -4.94

The min-max bounds of the CLP for the different dataset pairs are given in Table 1. For the purpose of categorizing the different dataset pairs, we label pairs that have both values for the bounds of the CLP above 6.5 as a far-OOD dataset pair, below 6.5 as near-OOD dataset pair, and dataset pairs which have bounds that have a value above and below 6.5 as a near & far-OOD dataset pair. The CLP values were chosen by hand so as to separate the datasets and enable comparison.

Metrics. We measure the quality of OOD detection using the established metrics for this task, which are the AUROC, AUPR and the FPR at 95% TPR [9]. For the AUPR, we treat OOD examples as the positive class. Unless otherwise stated, metrics reported in this work are obtained based on 8 repeat readings.

Training Setup. Experiments were conducted using 2 T P100-PCIE-16GB with 28 CPUs using Pytorch Version 1.7.1 and Pytorch Lightning Version 1.2.3 [5, 18]. We adopt a Resnet-50 as the encoder f_θ for all the different models with a fixed-dimensional output dimensionality of 128-D with the outputs being l2 normalized [8]. For the case of the classification network, also referred to as the Cross-Entropy (CE) model, the output of the Resnet-50 encoder is followed by an additional fully connected layer with an output dimensionality equal to the number of classes in the ID training data.

For the case of the Moco model, both the query encoder and the key encoder have the same architecture. All models are trained for 300 epochs with a batch size of 256, using the SGD optimizer with a learning rate of $3e^{-2}$, optimizer momentum of 0.9 and weight decay of $1e^{-4}$, queue size of 4096, and an encoder momentum m of 0.999. Furthermore, both the Moco and SupCLR model use a softmax temperature τ of 0.07 in the loss function.

For data augmentation, we use random crop and resize (with random flip), color distortion (for the RGB datasets), and Gaussian blur.

4   Instance Discrimination Is Effective for Far-OOD Detection

4.1   Hypothesis

We hypothesized that as instance discrimination requires being able to distinguish each individual sample from one another, the model trained using instance discrimination will output features z which retains a large amount of information about the input x. By retaining a large amount of information regarding an input, the Moco model could achieve high OOD performance. This depends on how semantically similar the ID and OOD points are to one another and what information the inference approach focuses on.

4.2   Procedure

To investigate when the instance discrimination loss is effective, we compare the Moco model with the SupCLR and CE model to see the difference when using training labels in the training process. Furthermore, we look at the effect of supervised labels during inference by examining the OOD detection performance of different models across several different dataset pairs using two different inference approaches. The inference approaches used are the Mahalanobis Distance with class-dependent covariance matrices [26] which use class labels, as well as the kernel density estimation (KDE) approach which does not use class labels.

4.3   Results

For the case of the KDE approach, Table 2 shows that the Moco model consistently performed worse. This showed that in the absence of any training labels, the instance discrimination training makes it difficult to group ID data together and therefore leads to poor OOD detection performance. Furthermore, the CE model is generally the highest performing model across the metrics, even outperforming SupCLR. This shows that in the absence of labels during the inference process, the CE model is best able to group the data in the feature space such that the OOD test data are farther than the ID test data from the ID training data points.

For the task of OOD detection using the Mahalanobis Distance inference approach, Table 3 shows that for the grayscale datasets, the Moco model is competitive with the CE model and the SupCLR model achieves the best results. This shows that for the grayscale datasets, the features learned from contrastive learning are able to compete with or outperform the CE model. However, for the case of the RGB datasets, the Moco approach outperforms the CE model on the CIFAR10-SVHN dataset pair and outperforms SupCLR on the CIFAR100-SVHN dataset pair, both of which are categorized as far-OOD. In contrast, for the case of CIFAR10-CIFAR100 (near-OOD) and CIFAR100-CIFAR10 (near & far-OOD), Moco performs significantly worse than both supervised approaches. This suggests that for far-OOD detection tasks, it can be beneficial to use the unsupervised instance discrimination training to perform OOD detection, although, class discriminatory information obtained from supervised training is important for high performance in near-OOD detection settings. Furthermore, it can be seen that using

Table 2. AUROC, AUPR and FPR for different models on different ID-OOD dataset pairs using the KDE approach and * indicates that an approach is better than the CE baseline.

ID	OOD	AUROC	AUPR	FPR
		CE/Moco/SupCLR		
CIFAR10	SVHN	0.950 / 0.574 / **0.962***	0.975 / 0.779 / **0.980***	**0.166** / 0.887 / 0.170
	CIFAR100	**0.883** / 0.576 / 0.882	0.863 / 0.591 / **0.864***	**0.399** / 0.888 / 0.415
	MNIST	**0.939** / 0.462 / 0.900	**0.920** / 0.437 / 0.880	**0.219** / 0.875 / 0.346
	FashionMNIST	**0.955** / 0.514 / 0.943	**0.943** / 0.487 / 0.933	**0.162** / 0.887 / 0.232
	KMNIST	**0.941** / 0.472 / 0.935	0.911 / 0.444 / **0.915***	**0.188** / 0.893 / 0.233
CIFAR100	SVHN	**0.853** / 0.567 / 0.828	**0.907** / 0.767 / 0.897	**0.415** / 0.879 / 0.482
	CIFAR10	0.726 / 0.569 / **0.736***	0.680 / 0.562 / **0.693***	0.784 / 0.881 / **0.722***
	MNIST	**0.646** / 0.307 / 0.594	**0.620** / 0.378 / 0.564	**0.719** / 0.964 / 0.775
	FashionMNIST	**0.851** / 0.522 / 0.841	**0.812** / 0.484 / 0.806	**0.458** / 0.881 / 0.485
	KMNIST	0.757 / 0.403 / **0.769***	0.720 / 0.413 / **0.736***	**0.608** / 0.945 / 0.643
MNIST	FashionMNIST	0.984 / 0.587 / **0.992***	0.979 / 0.621 / 0.99*	0.080 / 0.899 / **0.034***
	KMNIST	0.957 / 0.616 / **0.982***	0.958 / 0.694 / 0.98*	0.218 / 0.899 / **0.077***
FashionMNIST	MNIST	**0.807** / 0.624 / 0.754	**0.818** / 0.606 / 0.804	**0.614** / 0.821 / 0.820
	KMNIST	**0.821** / 0.638 / 0.791	**0.822** / 0.611 / 0.821	**0.576** / 0.771 / 0.738
KMNIST	MNIST	**0.972** / 0.656 / 0.971	**0.970** / 0.712 / 0.966	0.108 / 0.822 / **0.107***
	FashionMNIST	**0.985** / 0.620 / **0.985**	**0.984** / 0.621 / 0.978	**0.056** / 0.818 / 0.056

Table 3. AUROC, AUPR and FPR for different models on different ID-OOD dataset pairs using the Mahalanobis Distance inference approach and * indicates that an approach is better than the CE baseline

ID	OOD	AUROC	AUPR	FPR
		CE/Moco/SupCLR		
CIFAR10	SVHN	0.891 / 0.908* / **0.950***	0.939 / 0.960* / **0.973***	0.283 / 0.408 / **0.187***
	CIFAR100	0.875 / 0.784 / **0.902***	0.851 / 0.778 / **0.892***	0.418 / 0.657 / **0.386***
	MNIST	0.931 / **0.988*** / 0.951*	0.906 / **0.985*** / 0.935*	0.214 / **0.051*** / 0.176*
	FashionMNIST	0.945 / 0.971* / **0.973***	0.926 / **0.971*** / 0.965*	0.180 / 0.143* / **0.111***
	KMNIST	0.929 / 0.952* / **0.956***	0.892 / **0.941*** / 0.933*	0.195 / 0.174* / **0.142***
CIFAR100	SVHN	**0.858** / 0.828 / 0.818	0.900 / **0.908*** / 0.870	0.420 / 0.565 / **0.413***
	CIFAR10	0.731 / 0.614 / **0.746***	0.680 / 0.574 / **0.698***	0.730 / 0.836 / **0.683***
	MNIST	**0.656** / 0.398 / 0.625	**0.623** / 0.467 / 0.604	**0.754** / 0.964 / 0.811
	FashionMNIST	0.886 / 0.895* / **0.902***	0.856 / **0.880*** / 0.877*	0.375 / 0.403 / **0.319***
	KMNIST	0.777 / 0.604 / **0.798***	0.730 / 0.595 / **0.762***	**0.588** / 0.887 / 0.599
MNIST	FashionMNIST	0.988 / **0.997*** / 0.990*	0.985 / **0.995*** / 0.983	0.018 / **0.012*** / 0.028
	KMNIST	0.984 / 0.972 / **0.993***	0.982 / 0.962 / **0.991***	0.061 / 0.108 / **0.030***
FashionMNIST	MNIST	0.921 / **0.980*** / 0.971*	0.933 / **0.980*** / 0.969*	0.456 / **0.105*** / 0.138*
	KMNIST	0.941 / 0.966* / **0.972***	0.950 / 0.965* / **0.969***	0.309 / 0.173* / **0.138***
KMNIST	MNIST	0.973 / 0.957 / **0.991***	0.970 / 0.954 / **0.989***	0.089 / 0.208 / **0.037***
	FashionMNIST	0.962 / 0.982* / **0.984***	0.953 / **0.978*** / 0.973*	0.219 / 0.076* / **0.043***

class labels to group the features during the inference process leads to a larger improvement in the contrastive learning models compared to the CE model as shown by a larger improvement in the contrastive models when using the Mahalanobis Distance inference approach rather than KDE.

5   OOD Samples Are Classified into Classes that Learn Non-class Discriminatory Statistics

5.1   Hypothesis

We hypothesized that the more similar a class distribution is to the distribution of the entire dataset, which we refer to as the overall distribution, the more likely it is that OOD data will be misclassified as that class. The intuition here is that OOD data tends to be misclassified as belonging to the least distinctive class. We believe that the similarity of a class distribution to the overall distribution indicates how much the features of a particular class contain non-class discriminatory information, which indicates how distinctive the class distribution is.

5.2   Procedure

To quantify the dissimilarity of the class distribution to the overall distribution, we approximated the class distribution as well as the overall distribution by Gaussian distributions and calculated the KL divergence between the overall distribution and class distribution, $KL\left(Overall\|Class\right)$. Furthermore, the expected Overall-Class KL as shown by Eq. 7 was calculated for the contrastive models to see whether there was any difference in this metric between the two approaches.

$$\mathbb{E}\left[KL\left(Overall\|Class\right)\right] = \sum_{k}^{K} KL\left(Overall\|Class_k\right) \tag{7}$$

5.3   Results

From Fig. 1, it can be seen that there is a negative correlation between the KL divergence and the class-wise confusion log probability. This supports our hypothesis that the more dissimilar the class distribution is to the overall distribution, the more likely OOD data points will be misclassified into that ID class. This behavior agrees with the phenomena seen in deep generative models where OOD data points are given high likelihoods by arbitrarily having low compressed lengths and being similar to the non-class discriminatory statistics of the data [23].

From Table 4, it can be seen that the Moco model had expected Overall-Class KL values smaller than the SupCLR model. We believe this explains why the Moco model performs poorly on the near-OOD detection pairs such as CIFAR10-CIFAR100 and CIFAR100-CIFAR10. For the case of Moco where there is a small KL divergence between the overall and class distributions, it indicates that the features from Moco capture general non-class discriminatory information which is common in the ID dataset.

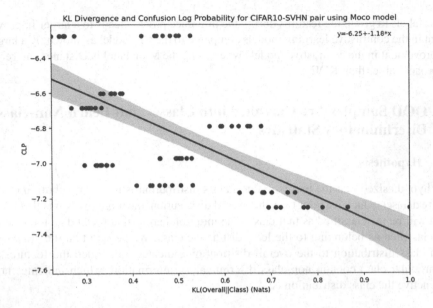

Fig. 1. Scatter plot of the normalized KL divergence between the overall distribution and class distribution, $KL(Overall\|Class)$ (normalized by dividing by the maximum $KL(Overall\|Class)$), and the class-wise confusion log probability (CLP).

Table 4. Expected Overall-Class KL between the overall distribution and class distribution, $\mathbb{E}[KL(Overall\|Class)]$, when using different learning approaches.

Datasets	Moco	SupCLR
MNIST	173.790	567.539
FashionMNIST	249.147	1484.179
KMNIST	122.158	468.819
CIFAR10	44.395	193.645
CIFAR100	96.943	1603.609

This can make near-OOD detection difficult as the OOD dataset is likely to have similar non-class discriminatory statistics in common with the ID dataset. However, in the case of a far-OOD detection situation, the non-class discriminatory statistics are sufficiently different between the two datasets to enable Moco to effectively detect OOD data.

6   Number of Directions of Significant Variance

6.1   Hypothesis

From the OOD detection results (Sect. 4), contrastive learning results in poorer performance in OOD detection than the traditional CE model when using KDE than when using the Mahalanobis Distance approach. We claim that this is, at least in part, due to contrastive learning trained models learn a rich feature space with several different directions of high variance [26].

In the situation where KDE is used for inference, having a feature space with several directions of variance is likely to result in the OOD data having similar features to the ID data, leading to the misclassification of OOD data as ID. However, in the situation where the Mahalanobis Distance inference approach is used, using class labeled data can help to identify which factors of variation are important for class discrimination which can be used to aid in discriminating the ID data from the OOD data.

6.2 Procedure

To quantify how rich a feature space is, we investigated the number of factors of variation in the features by following the procedure taken in Sect. 5 of Roth et al. which involves calculating the spectral decay ρ [19]. This involves computing the singular value decomposition (SVD) of the features of the training data, normalizing the sorted spectrum of singular values, and computing the KL-divergence between a D-dimensional discrete uniform distribution and the sorted spectrum of singular values. Using this metric, lower values of ρ indicate more directions of significant variance.

6.3 Results

From Fig. 2, it can be seen that both contrastive models generally have lower values of ρ than the CE model, with the exception of the CIFAR100 dataset where the CE model has a lower ρ than the SupCLR approach. As the supervised SupCLR model was able to outperform the supervised CE model on all the datasets in which the SupCLR model had a lower ρ value when using the Mahalanobis Distance, this suggests that having a large number of significant directions of variance is an important property for OOD detection. The Moco model consistently has the lowest ρ which indicates its features have the largest number of factors of variation. This is likely due to the difficult task of instance discrimination requiring learning a large number of factors of variation to perform the task. Whereas, the CE and SupCLR models only require learning features needed to discriminate data between different classes resulting in a smaller number of significant factors of variation.

7 Related Work

Recent approaches in OOD detection can be categorized as calibration-based [13,14], density estimation-based [15], and self-supervised learning-based. Self-supervised learning-based approaches can be split into auxiliary pretext task-based [6], contrastive based [26] or approaches that utilize aspects of both auxiliary pretext tasks and contrastive learning [24,25]. The contrastive learning approaches vary significantly and our work also falls in the category of investigating contrastive learning for OOD detection. Some approaches use instance discrimination-based pretraining followed by fine-tuning with a supervised cross-entropy loss [20,26]. Both these papers and ours focus on the

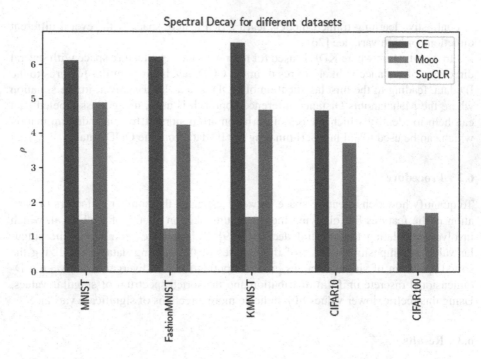

Fig. 2. Spectral decay for the different training datasets using different learning approaches.

instance discrimination contrastive learning task, however, our work focuses on instance discrimination in the absence of fine-tuning with a supervised loss. Other approaches do not use the pretraining followed by fine-tuning paradigm and instead focus on using a supervised contrastive loss for OOD detection when labels are available [2,22,25]. Our work also examines the performance of the supervised contrastive loss for OOD detection, although we use the original supervised contrastive loss for the purpose of analyzing the properties present in contrastive learning which makes it effective for OOD detection. Furthermore, our work differs from all the aforementioned work as it is the first to examine the differences between using a supervised contrastive compared to an instance discrimination approach as well as the effect of different inference methods on OOD detection performance.

8   Conclusion

In this work, we investigated the effectiveness and limitations of two popular contrastive learning approaches for the problem of OOD detection. In our work, we saw that:

– Contrastive learning learns a larger number of factors of variation compared to classification networks. This can be detrimental to OOD detection performance when using KDE (unsupervised inference) but beneficial when using Mahalanobis distance (supervised inference).

- Unsupervised instance discrimination learns a richer feature space with a wide variety of factors of variation compared to supervised contrastive learning as shown by analyzing the spectral decay.
- By having a large number of factors of variation, instance discrimination can be more effective than the Cross-Entropy baseline at far-OOD detection.
- Despite having a larger number of factors of variation than the supervised contrastive Learning, instance discrimination is ineffective at near-OOD detection.
- Instance discrimination is ineffective at near-OOD detection as it leads to a poorer separation between the different classes in the feature space which was shown by having a lower $\mathbb{E}\left[KL\left(Overall\|Class\right)\right]$.

8.1 Limitations and Future Work

We would also like to point out some limitations of our study. Firstly, we focus on two different contrastive learning methods which uses explicit negatives (e.g. MoCo and SupCLR). We chose to focus on these two methods as these methods are quite general contrastive learning approaches where the only significant difference is the use of supervision. Therefore, comparing the results of the two methods should give an indication of the effect of supervision in OOD detection performance. We believe that other methods based on explicit negatives such as the InfoNCE and Triplet losses would also exhibit similar behaviour [1,3]. An avenue of future work could examine the effect of different properties of self-supervised approaches on OOD detection performance. Example of such properties could be whether a self-supervised approach uses explicit negatives or not, as well as the effect of redundancy reduction principle from Barlow Twins [28]. Furthermore, after identifying that OOD samples tend to be allocated to classes that have a distribution similar to the overall distribution, future work could involve investigating whether it is possible to regularise the contrastive loss to prevent each class from being too similar to the overall distribution. This could enable the instance discrimination contrastive loss to learn a rich feature space whilst also learning class-specific semantic features which can improve near-OOD detection.

Acknowledgment. This research was partially funded by an EPRSC PhD studentship as part of the Centre for Doctoral Training in Future Autonomous and Robotic Systems (grant number EP/L015293/1). RSR is funded by the UKRI Turing AI Fellowship EP/V024817/1.

References

1. Chen, T., Kornblith, S., Norouzi, M., Hinton, G.: A simple framework for contrastive learning of visual representations. In: International Conference on Machine Learning, pp. 1597–1607. PMLR (2020)
2. Cho, H., Seol, J., Lee, S.g.: Masked contrastive learning for anomaly detection. arXiv preprint arXiv:2105.08793 (2021)
3. Chopra, S., Hadsell, R., LeCun, Y.: Learning a similarity metric discriminatively, with application to face verification. In: 2005 IEEE Computer Society Conference on Computer Vision and Pattern Recognition (CVPR 2005), vol. 1, pp. 539–546. IEEE (2005)

4. Clanuwat, T., Bober-Irizar, M., Kitamoto, A., Lamb, A., Yamamoto, K., Ha, D.: Deep learning for classical japanese literature. arXiv preprint arXiv:1812.01718 (2018)
5. Falcon, WA, e.a.: Pytorch lightning. GitHub. Note: https://github.com/PyTorchLightning/pytorch-lightning 3 (2019)
6. Golan, I., El-Yaniv, R.: Deep anomaly detection using geometric transformations. arXiv preprint arXiv:1805.10917 (2018)
7. He, K., Fan, H., Wu, Y., Xie, S., Girshick, R.: Momentum contrast for unsupervised visual representation learning. In: Proceedings of the IEEE/CVF Conference on Computer Vision and Pattern Recognition, pp. 9729–9738 (2020)
8. He, K., Zhang, X., Ren, S., Sun, J.: Deep residual learning for image recognition. In: Proceedings of the IEEE Conference on Computer Vision and Pattern Recognition, pp. 770–778 (2016)
9. Hendrycks, D., Gimpel, K.: A baseline for detecting misclassified and out-of-distribution examples in neural networks. arXiv preprint arXiv:1610.02136 (2016)
10. Khosla, P., et al.: Supervised contrastive learning. arXiv preprint arXiv:2004.11362 (2020)
11. Krizhevsky, A., Hinton, G., et al.: Learning multiple layers of features from tiny images (2009)
12. LeCun, Y.: The mnist database of handwritten digits (1998). http://yann.lecun.com/exdb/mnist/
13. Lee, K., Lee, K., Lee, H., Shin, J.: A simple unified framework for detecting out-of-distribution samples and adversarial attacks. Advances in neural information processing systems 31 (2018)
14. Liang, S., Li, Y., Srikant, R.: Enhancing the reliability of out-of-distribution image detection in neural networks. arXiv preprint arXiv:1706.02690 (2017)
15. Malinin, A., Gales, M.: Predictive uncertainty estimation via prior networks. arXiv preprint arXiv:1802.10501 (2018)
16. Netzer, Y., Wang, T., Coates, A., Bissacco, A., Wu, B., Ng, A.Y.: Reading digits in natural images with unsupervised feature learning (2011)
17. Nguyen, A., Yosinski, J., Clune, J.: Deep neural networks are easily fooled: High confidence predictions for unrecognizable images. In: Proceedings of the IEEE Conference on Computer Vision and Pattern Recognition, pp. 427–436 (2015)
18. Paszke, A., et al.: Automatic differentiation in pytorch (2017)
19. Roth, K., Milbich, T., Sinha, S., Gupta, P., Ommer, B., Cohen, J.P.: Revisiting training strategies and generalization performance in deep metric learning. In: International Conference on Machine Learning, pp. 8242–8252. PMLR (2020)
20. Roy, A.G., et al.: Does your dermatology classifier know what it doesn't know? detecting the long-tail of unseen conditions. arXiv preprint arXiv:2104.03829 (2021)
21. Ruff, L., et al.: A unifying review of deep and shallow anomaly detection. Proceedings of the IEEE (2021)
22. Sehwag, V., Chiang, M., Mittal, P.: Ssd: a unified framework for self-supervised outlier detection. arXiv preprint arXiv:2103.12051 (2021)
23. Serrà, J., Álvarez, D., Gómez, V., Slizovskaia, O., Núñez, J.F., Luque, J.: Input complexity and out-of-distribution detection with likelihood-based generative models. arXiv preprint arXiv:1909.11480 (2019)
24. Sohn, K., Li, C.L., Yoon, J., Jin, M., Pfister, T.: Learning and evaluating representations for deep one-class classification. arXiv preprint arXiv:2011.02578 (2020)
25. Tack, J., Mo, S., Jeong, J., Shin, J.: Csi: Novelty detection via contrastive learning on distributionally shifted instances. arXiv preprint arXiv:2007.08176 (2020)
26. Winkens, J., et al.: Contrastive training for improved out-of-distribution detection. arXiv preprint arXiv:2007.05566 (2020)

27. Xiao, H., Rasul, K., Vollgraf, R.: Fashion-mnist: a novel image dataset for benchmarking machine learning algorithms. arXiv preprint arXiv:1708.07747 (2017)
28. Zbontar, J., Jing, L., Misra, I., LeCun, Y., Deny, S.: Barlow twins: self-supervised learning via redundancy reduction. In: International Conference on Machine Learning, pp. 12310–12320. PMLR (2021)

Multimodal Pattern Recognition
of Social Signals
in Human-Computer-Interaction
(MPRSS 2022)

Preface

This book chapter presents the proceedings of the 7th IAPR TC 9 Workshop on *Pattern Recognition of Social Signals in Human-Computer-Interaction (MPRSS 2022)*. The goal of this workshop is to bring together recent research in pattern recognition and human-computer-interaction. Research in the field of intelligent human-computer-interaction has made considerable progress in methodology and applications, however, building intelligent artificial companions capable to interact with humans, in the same way humans interact with each other, remains a major challenge in this field. Pattern recognition and machine learning methodology play a major role in this pioneering field of research.

MPRSS 2022 was held as a satellite workshop of the International Conference on Pattern Recognition (ICPR 2022) in Montreal, Canada, August 21, 2022 as an online event. This workshop would not have been possible without the help of many people and organizations. First of all, we are grateful to all the authors who submitted their contributions to the workshop. We thank the members of the program committee for performing the task of selecting the best papers for the workshop, and we hope that readers may enjoy this selection of papers and get inspired from these excellent contributions.

For the MPRSS 2022 workshop six out of seven papers have been selected for inclusion into this volume, additionally to the regular presentations, the invited talk by Patrick Thiam, Ulm University on *Deep Learning Architectures for Pain Recognition based on Physiological Signals*, has been included to the workshop program, as well as a tutorial session by Mariofanna Milanova entitled *Deep Learning NVIDIA Tutorial*.

MPRSS 2022 has been supported by the International Association for Pattern Recognition (IAPR) and the new IAPR Technical Committee on *Pattern Recognition in Human Computer Interaction* (TC 9).

September 2022

Mariofanna Milanova
Xavier Alameda-Pineda
Friedhelm Schwenker

Organization

General Chairs

Mariofanna Milanova   University of Arkansas at Little Rock, USA
Xavier Alameda-Pineda   Inria, University of Grenoble-Alpes, France
Friedhelm Schwenker   Ulm University, Germany

Program Committee

Anna Espositio   Universita della Campania Luigi Vanvitelli, Italy
Dilana Hazer-Rau   Ulm University, Germany
Mamata S. Kalas   KIT College of Engineering, Kolhapur, India
Steffen Walter   Ulm University, Germany
Xiaojun Wu   Jiangnan University, China

Deep Learning Architectures for Pain Recognition Based on Physiological Signals

Patrick Thiam[1,2](✉) ⓘ, Hans A. Kestler[1] ⓘ, and Friedhelm Schwenker[2] ⓘ

[1] Institute of Medical Systems Biology, Ulm University, Albert-Einstein-Allee 11, 89081 Ulm, Germany
`hans.kestler@uni-ulm.de`
[2] Institute of Neural Information Processing, Ulm University, James-Franck-Ring, 89081 Ulm, Germany
`{patrick.thiam,friedhelm.schwenker}@uni-ulm.de`

Abstract. The overall classification performance as well as generalization ability of a traditional information fusion architecture (built upon so called handcrafted features) is limited by its reliance on specific expert knowledge in the underlying domain of application. The integration of both feature engineering and fusion parameters' optimization in a single optimization process using deep neural networks has shown in several domains of application (e.g. computer vision) its potential to significantly improve not just the inference performance of a classification system, but also its ability to generalize and adapt to unseen but related domains. This is done by enabling the designed system to autonomously detect, extract and combine relevant information directly from the raw signals accordingly to the classification task at hand. The following work focuses specifically on pain recognition based on bio-physiological modalities and consists of a summary of recently proposed deep fusion approaches for the aggregation of information stemming from a diverse set of physiological signals in order to perform an accurate classification of several levels of artificially induced pain intensities.

Keywords: Pain Recognition · Physiological Signals · Deep Learning · Information Fusion

1 Introduction

Traditional information fusion approaches [1] are characterized by two distinct phases: the first phase consists in designing and extracting relevant feature representations from each of the available modalities (or input channels); the second phase consists in designing an appropriate architecture to perform the aggregation of the extracted feature representations, with the specific goal of improving the performance as well as the robustness of the resulting classification system (in comparison to one built upon a single input channel). Therefore, expert knowledge in the domain of application is needed for the extraction of a relevant set of features. Furthermore, since both phases (feature extraction and fusion

© Springer Nature Switzerland AG 2023
J.-J. Rousseau and B. Kapralos (Eds.): ICPR 2022 Workshops, LNCS 13643, pp. 349–358, 2023.
https://doi.org/10.1007/978-3-031-37660-3_24

parameters' optimization) are decoupled from each other, the performance of the designed fusion architectures is tightly bounded to the discriminative performance of the manually extracted feature representations. Moreover, adapting such a system to a different but related domain (sharing several characteristics with the one used to design and optimize the fusion architecture) can be extremely difficult (and in most cases sub-optimal) since the set of features upon which the whole system is built, is relevant for this specific task. In order to improve on these shortcomings, deep fusion approaches [2] enable a combination of feature extraction and selection, as well as information aggregation parameters' optimization into a single optimization process. This specific characteristic of deep fusion approaches leads to some significant improvement of the ability of the inference system to successfully identify, extract and aggregate the most relevant feature representations, resulting in some significant boost of the overall classification performance, with little to no expert knowledge needed in the underlying area of application. Moreover, the hierarchical characteristic of deep neural networks significantly improves the generalization ability of the designed architecture, since specific layers can be optimized and adapted to unseen but related classification tasks. However, such deep neural networks need a huge amount of labeled samples in order to be successfully optimized. Thus, data augmentation approaches are usually designed and applied in cases where such an amount of data is not available. This aspect can further increase the complexity of the designed system as well as the amount of time needed in order to effectively train the entire architecture.

Recently, deep fusion approaches have been successfully applied in different computer vision areas such as in semantic image segmentation [3], gesture recognition [4], or object detection [5], where they also significantly outperform more conventional fusion approaches in most cases. Concerning emotion recognition, several deep fusion approaches have also been proposed and effectively assessed for the aggregation of information stemming from audio-visual channels [6,7], as well as a combination of body posture and movements, additionally to audio-visual channels [8], and also physiological signals [9]. In the current work, a short summary of recent deep fusion approaches proposed for the classification of artificially induced pain intensities based on several physiological signals is provided. A short overview of the pain recognition task is first described in Sect. 2, followed by the description of recent fusion approaches based on deep neural networks in Sect. 3. The work is concluded in Sect. 4, by providing a discussion about the presented approaches as well as a description of potential future works.

2   Pain Recognition

Pain is a very complex phenomenon consisting of a physiological and psychological response to a noxious stimulus. Pain assessment constitutes a very challenging task, due to the inherent subjective nature of pain and the complexity associated with its quantification. Hence, self-reporting tools such as the Visual Analog Scale (VAS) [10] or the Numerical Rating Scale (NRA) [11] constitute the gold standard in clinical settings for pain assessment. However, such tools are unreliable in cases where an individual is unable to effectively assess and report some experienced or observed pain episode. This can be caused by several factors, ranging from physical or psycho-physiological traits, to different types of cognitive impairments impeding with an individual's ability to perceive and share informative insights about a specific pain episode. In such cases, an effective automatic pain assessment system based on measurable behavioral and bio-physiological channels could provide valuable insights regarding the underlying pain episode and therefore help a physician to decide on the best pain relieving therapy to be applied to the corresponding individual.

Recently, this specific area of research have been attracting a lot of interest from the research community. Several researchers have been focusing on the development of an automatic pain assessment system, either based on a single modality [12–15], or a combination of several modalities [16–19]. This is enabled by a constantly increasing amount of studies built around the generation of multi-modal pain related data sets. In most of these studies, data sets are generated by artificially applying different levels of pain elicitation to the participants using different types of stimuli such as thermal stimuli [20,21], electrical stimuli [22,23], or even cold pressure stimuli [24], among others, while recording different types of modalities. The resulting classification task consist of the discrimination between the different levels of pain elicitation based on the recorded behavioral and bio-physiological channels. These modalities mostly consist of: audio signals, video signals, body posture parameters and bio-physiological signals such as Electrocardiography (ECG), Electromyography (EMG), respiration (RSP), Electrodermal Activity (EDA).

The modalities are used in combination with the corresponding levels of pain elicitation (which constitute the classes of the inference task) to design and assess different types of multiple classifier systems (MCS) with the corresponding information fusion approaches. Most of these approaches consist of traditional fusion architectures built upon handcrafted features: one of the most simple and straight forward fusion approach consists of the early fusion technique, where the extracted feature representations are concatenated into a single high-dimensional feature representation and subsequently fed into a subsequent classifier [25–27]; Late fusion approaches consist in training a single classifier on each modality-specific feature representation and optimizing a fusion approach (with fixed or trainable aggregation parameters) to perform the aggregation of the classifiers' outputs [28–30]; Finally, hybrid classifier fusion approaches consist of a combination of both early and late fusion approaches; in this specific case, the modality-specific feature representations are aggregated at different levels of abstraction before a single classifier is trained on each resulting feature set; a fusion approach is subsequently used to aggregate the outputs of the trained models [31,32]. Although such traditional information fusion approaches have yielded promising results, deep learning fusion approaches have proven to be able to reach state-of-the-art classification performances while outperforming the traditional fusion approaches.

3 Deep Physiological Fusion Approaches

The authors in [33] propose several deep fusion approaches characterized by architectures revolving around one-dimensional convolutional neural networks (1-D CNNs). The proposed architectures consist of performing the aggregation of information extracted directly from a set of raw physiological signals (namely ECG, EMG and EDA signals) at different levels of abstraction (see Fig. 1): the early fusion approach (see Fig. 1a) consists of merging the input signals into a single two-dimensional representation that is subsequently fed into a deep neural network; the first late fusion approach (see Fig. 1b) consists of concurrently training channel-specific CNN branches and concatenating the feature representations of the top fully connected layers of the channel-specific branches, before feeding the resulting representation into a classification model; finally, the last late fusion architecture, which is characterized by a trainable aggregation layer (see Fig. 1c), consists of a multi-task architecture, where the output of each channel-

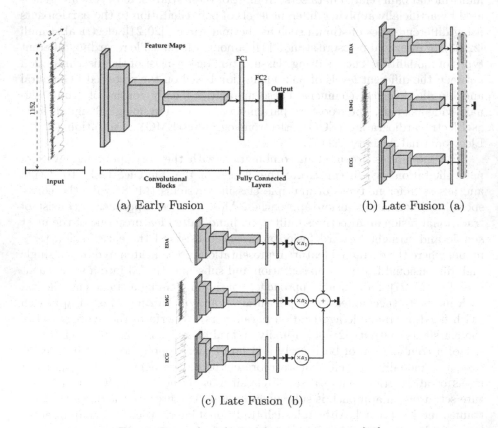

(a) Early Fusion   (b) Late Fusion (a)

(c) Late Fusion (b)

Fig. 1. Deep physiological fusion approaches [33].

specific model is fed into the aggregation layer with trainable parameters in order to generate the final output of the classification system. All approaches are optimized in an end-to-end manner, thus no expert knowledge is required in order to extract relevant feature representations. Moreover, each architecture performs concurrently the optimization of relevant feature representations as well as the optimization of the aggregation parameters in a single optimization process. The performed assessment showed that the proposed approaches are able to attain state-of-the-art classification performances, while significantly outperforming previously proposed approaches based on handcrafted features. Moreover, the late fusion approach with an additional trainable aggregation layer performed best and outperformed the other deep fusion approaches.

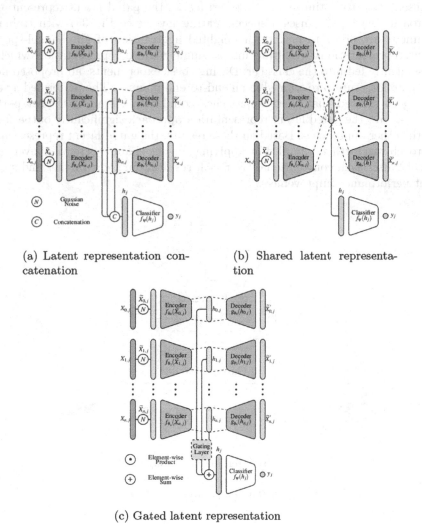

(a) Latent representation concatenation

(b) Shared latent representation

(c) Gated latent representation

Fig. 2. Deep Denoising Convolutional Auto-Encoder (DDCAE) fusion approaches [34].

Furthermore, the authors in [34] experimented with different Deep Denoizing Convolutional Auto-Encoder (DDCAE) fusion approaches. These specific approaches are characterized by the concurrent optimization of a classification branch, as well as several channel-specific auto-encoders. The approaches can be categorized depending on the specific method used to generate the single feature representation used to concurrently optimize the classifier: the concatenated latent representation approach (see Fig. 2a) consists in concatenating the resulting channel-specific latent representations into a single feature representation that is subsequently fed into the classifier; the shared latent representation approach (see Fig. 2b) consists in optimizing a single shared latent representation between all channel-specific auto-encoders and concurrently using this specific representation to optimize the classifier; lastly, the gated latent representation approach (see Fig. 2c) uses a specific gating layer (see Fig. 3a) with trainable parameters in order to perform a weighted aggregation of all channel-specific latent representations, resulting into a single feature representation which is subsequently fed into the classifier. During these experiments, all proposed deep fusion architectures are trained in an end-to-end manner. The performed assessment also showed that these approaches could attain state-of-the-art performances, with the gated latent representation approach significantly outperforming the other approaches. Based on these results, the gated latent representation approach was further extended by applying specific channel attention layers (see Fig. 3b) after each convolutional layer [35], resulting in some further and significant performance improvement.

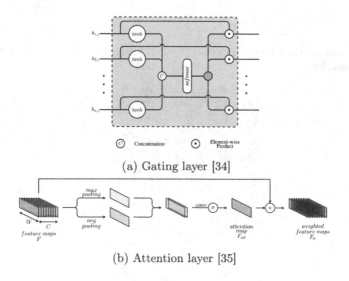

(a) Gating layer [34]

(b) Attention layer [35]

Fig. 3. Gating and attention layers.

4   Summary and Perspectives

The described deep fusion approaches based on bio-physiological signals were able to consistently achieve state-of-the-art pain classification performances, while outperforming (and in most cases significantly) previously proposed fusion approaches based on handcrafted features. Moreover, trainable aggregation methods seem to outperform more straight-forward and less complex fusion approaches. Thus, enabling a classification system to autonomously optimize the channel-specific feature representations as well as the fusion parameters by using deep neural networks can be considered as a sound alternative to manual feature engineering. Additionally, the inherent hierarchical structure of deep neural networks improves the adaptability of such approaches to different but related tasks. However, a huge amount of labeled data is needed in order to effectively optimize such deep neural networks. Thus, data augmentation approaches should be assessed and applied in order to alleviate this specific issue. Of particular interest is the research area consisting of the application of generative adversarial networks (GANs) for the generation of artificial samples that can be used to further improve the performance of a deep fusion network [36].

Acknowledgments. We gratefully acknowledge the support of NVIDIA Corporation with the donation of the Tesla K40 GPU used for this research.

References

1. Kuncheva, L.I.: Combining Pattern Classifiers: Methods and Algorithms. EBL-Schweitzer, Wiley (2014). https://books.google.de/books?id=MZgtBAAAQBAJ
2. Gao, J., Li, P., Chen, Z., Zhang, J.: A survey on deep learning for multimodal data fusion. Neural Comput. **32**(5), 829–864 (2020). https://doi.org/10.1162/neco_a_01273
3. Zhang, Y., Sidibé, D., Morel, O., Mériaudeau, F.: Deep multimodal fusion for semantic image segmentation: a survey. Image Vis. Comput. **105**, 104042 (2021). https://doi.org/10.1016/j.imavis.2020.104042
4. Roitberg, A., Pollert, T., Haurilet, M., Martin, M., Stiefelhagen, R.a.: Analysis of Deep Fusion Strategies for Multi-Modal Gesture Recognition. In: 2019 IEEE/CVF Conference on Computer Vision and Pattern Recognition Workshops (CVPRW), pp. 198–206 (2019). https://doi.org/10.1109/CVPRW.2019.00029
5. Farahnakian, F., Heikkonen, J.: Deep Learning Applications, Volume 3, chap. RGB and Depth Image Fusion for Object Detection Using Deep Learning, pp. 73–93. Springer, Singapore (2022). https://doi.org/10.1007/978-981-16-3357-7_3
6. Zhang, Y., Wang, Z.R., Du, J.: Deep fusion: an attention guided factorized bilinear pooling for audio-video emotion recognition. In: 2019 International Joint Conference on Neural Networks (IJCNN), pp. 1–8 (2019). https://doi.org/10.1109/IJCNN.2019.8851942
7. Praveen, R.G., et al.: A joint cross-attention model for audio-visual fusion in dimensional emotion recognition. In: 2022 IEEE/CVF Conference on Computer Vision and Pattern Recognition Workshops (CVPRW), pp. 2485–2494 (2022). https://doi.org/10.1109/CVPRW56347.2022.00278

8. Nguyen, D., Nguyen, K., Sridharan, S., Dean, D., Fookes, C.: Deep spatio-temporal feature fusion with compact bilinear pooling for multimodal emotion recognition. Comput. Vis. Image Underst. **174**, 33–42 (2018). https://doi.org/10.1016/j.cviu.2018.06.005

9. Li, X., Song, D., Zhang, P., Hou, Y., Hu, B.: Deep fusion of multi-channel neurophysiological signal for emotion recognition and monitoring. Int. J. Data Min. Bioinform. **18**(1), 1–27 (2017). https://doi.org/10.1504/IJDMB.2017.086097

10. Hawker, G.A., Mian, S., Kendzerska, T., French, M.: Measures of adult pain: Visual Analog Scale for Pain (VAS Pain), Numeric Rating Scale for Pain (NRS Pain), McGill Pain Questionnaire (MPQ), Short-Form McGill Pain Questionnaire (SF-MPQ), Chronic Pain Grade Scale (CPGS), Short Form-36 Bodily Pain Scale (SF-36 BPS), and Measure of Intermittent and Constant Osteoarthritis Pain (ICOAP). Arthritis Care Res. **63**(S11), S240–S252 (2011). https://doi.org/10.1002/acr.20543

11. Eckard, C., et al.: The integration of technology into treatment programs to aid in the reduction of chronic pain. J. Pain Manage. Med. **2**(3), 118 (2016). https://www.ncbi.nlm.nih.gov/pmc/articles/PMC5279929/

12. Werner, P., Al-Hamadi, A., Limbrecht-Ecklundt, K., Walter, S., Gruss, S., Traue, H.C.: Automatic pain assessment with facial activity descriptors. IEEE Trans. Affect. Comput. **8**(3), 286–299 (2017). https://doi.org/10.1109/TAFFC.2016.2537327

13. Thiam, P., Kessler, V., Schwenker, F.: Hierarchical combination of video features for personalised pain level recognition. In: 25th European Symposium on Artificial Neural Networks, Computational Intelligence and Machine Learning, pp. 465–470, April 2017. https://www.esann.org/sites/default/files/proceedings/legacy/es2017-104.pdf

14. Thiam, P., Schwenker, F.: Combining deep and hand-crafted features for audio-based pain intensity classification. In: Schwenker, F., Scherer, S. (eds.) MPRSS 2018. LNCS (LNAI), vol. 11377, pp. 49–58. Springer, Cham (2019). https://doi.org/10.1007/978-3-030-20984-1_5

15. Thiam, P., Kestler, H.A., Schwenker, F.: Two-stream attention network for pain recognition from video sequences. Sensors **20**(839) (2020). https://doi.org/10.3390/s20030839

16. Tsai, F.S., Hsu, Y.L., Chen, W.C., Weng, Y.M., Ng, C.J., Lee, C.C.: Toward development and evaluation of pain level-rating scale for emergency triage based on vocal characteristics and facial expressions. In: Interspeech 2016, pp. 92–96 (2016). https://doi.org/10.21437/Interspeech. 2016-408

17. Martinez, D.L., Picard, R.W.: Multi-task neural networks for personalized pain recognition from physiological signals. CoRR abs/1708.08755 (2017). http://arxiv.org/abs/1708.08755

18. Bellmann, P., Thiam, P., Schwenker, F.: Multi-classifier-systems: architectures, algorithms and applications. In: Pedrycz, W., Chen, S.-M. (eds.) Computational Intelligence for Pattern Recognition. SCI, vol. 777, pp. 83–113. Springer, Cham (2018). https://doi.org/10.1007/978-3-319-89629-8_4

19. Bellmann, P., Thiam, P., Schwenker, F.: Using a quartile-based data transformation for pain intensity classification based on the SenseEmotion database. In: 2019 8th International Conference on Affective Computing and Intelligent Interaction Workshops and Demos (ACIIW), pp. 310–316 (2019). https://doi.org/10.1109/ACIIW.2019.8925244

20. Walter, S., et al.: The BioVid heat pain database: data for the advancement and systematic validation of an automated pain recognition system. In: 2013 IEEE International Conference on Cybernetics, pp. 128–131 (2013). https://doi.org/10.1109/CYBConf.2013.6617456
21. Velana, M., et al.: The SenseEmotion database: a multimodal database for the development and systematic validation of an automatic pain- and emotion-recognition system. In: Schwenker, F., Scherer, S. (eds.) MPRSS 2016. LNCS (LNAI), vol. 10183, pp. 127–139. Springer, Cham (2017). https://doi.org/10.1007/978-3-319-59259-6_11
22. Haque, M.A., et al.: Deep multimodal pain recognition: a database and comparison of spatio-temporal visual modalities. In: 2018 13th IEEE International Conference on Automatic Face & Gesture Recognition (FG 2018), pp. 250–257 (2018). https://doi.org/10.1109/FG.2018.00044
23. Gruss, S., et al.: Multi-modal signals for analyzing pain responses to thermal and electrical stimuli. J. Visualized Exp. (JoVE) (146), e59057 (2019). https://doi.org/10.3791/59057
24. Zhang, Z., et al.: Multimodal spontaneous emotion corpus for human behavior analysis. In: 2016 IEEE Conference on Computer Vision and Pattern Recognition (CVPR), pp. 3438–3446 (2016). https://doi.org/10.1109/CVPR.2016.374
25. Werner, P., Al-Hamadi, A., Niese, R., Walter, S., Gruss, S., Traue, H.C.: Automatic pain recognition from video and biomedical signals. In: 2014 22nd International Conference on Pattern Recognition, pp. 4582–4587 (2014). https://doi.org/10.1109/ICPR.2014.784
26. Walter, S., et al.: Automatic pain quantification using autonomic parameters. Psychol. Neurosci. **7**(3), 363–380 (2014). https://doi.org/10.3922/j.psns.2014.041
27. Kächele, M., Werner, P., Al-Hamadi, A., Palm, G., Walter, S., Schwenker, F.: Bio-visual fusion for person-independent recognition of pain intensity. In: Schwenker, F., Roli, F., Kittler, J. (eds.) MCS 2015. LNCS, vol. 9132, pp. 220–230. Springer, Cham (2015). https://doi.org/10.1007/978-3-319-20248-8_19
28. Kächele, M., et al.: Multimodal data fusion for person-independent, continuous estimation of pain intensity. In: Iliadis, L., Jayne, C. (eds.) EANN 2015. CCIS, vol. 517, pp. 275–285. Springer, Cham (2015). https://doi.org/10.1007/978-3-319-23983-5_26
29. Kächele, M., Thiam, P., Amirian, M., Schwenker, F., Palm, G.: Methods for person-centered continuous pain intensity assessment from bio-physiological channels. IEEE J. Sel. Top. Signal Process. **10**(5), 854–864 (2016). https://doi.org/10.1109/JSTSP.2016.2535962
30. Thiam, P., et al.: Multi-modal pain intensity recognition based on the SenseEmotion database. IEEE Trans. Affective Comput. (2019). https://doi.org/10.1109/TAFFC.2019.2892090, 2019 IEEE
31. Thiam, P., Kessler, V., Walter, S., Palm, G., Schwenker, F.: Audio-visual recognition of pain intensity. In: Schwenker, F., Scherer, S. (eds.) MPRSS 2016. LNCS (LNAI), vol. 10183, pp. 110–126. Springer, Cham (2017). https://doi.org/10.1007/978-3-319-59259-6_10
32. Kessler, V., Thiam, P., Amirian, M., Schwenker, F.: Multimodal fusion including camera photoplethysmography for pain recognition. In: 2017 International Conference on Companion Technology (ICCT), pp. 1–4 (2017). https://doi.org/10.1109/COMPANION.2017.8287083
33. Thiam, P., Bellmann, P., Kestler, H.A., Schwenker, F.: Exploring deep physiological models for nociceptive pain recognition. Sensors **4503**(20) (2019). https://doi.org/10.3390/s19204503

34. Thiam, P., Kestler, H.A., Schwenker, F.: Multimodal deep denoising convolutional autoencoders for pain intensity classification based on physiological signals. In: Proceedings of the 9th International Conference on Pattern Recognition Applications and Methods (ICPRAM), vol. 1, pp. 289–296. INSTICC, SciTePress (2020). https://doi.org/10.5220/0008896102890296

35. Thiam, P., Hihn, H., Braun, D.A., Kestler, H.A., Schwenker, F.: Multi-modal pain intensity assessment based on physiological signals: a deep learning perspective. Front. Physiol. **12**, 720464 (2021). https://doi.org/10.3389/fphys.2021.720464

36. Antoniou, A., Storkey, A., Edwards, H.: Data Augmentation Generative Adversarial Networks. arXiv (2017). https://arxiv.org/abs/1711.04340

Egocentric Hand Gesture Recognition on Untrimmed Videos Using State Activation Gate LSTMs

Tejo Chalasani[(✉)] and Aljosa Smolic[(✉)]

Trinity College, Dublin, Ireland
{chalasat,smolica}@tcd.ie

Abstract. Deep Neural Networks have been used for recognising ego-hand gestures in trimmed videos extensively. However, recognising ego-hand gestures from untrimmed videos has been largely unexplored. In this work, we propose the concept of State Activation Gate (StAG) to extend the current LSTM framework and successfully apply it to recognising ego-hand gestures from untrimmed videos. We explore the usage of StAG LSTM combined with 3D convolutional neural networks to compare their performance to the state-of-the-art for two publicly available datasets. In addition, we present an intra-gesture (IG) loss function and a metric that favours continuity of gesture labels called Continuity Favouring Jaccard Index (CFJI). StAG LSTM reduces the need to use heuristics currently employed in ego-hand gesture recognition on untrimmed videos. Using the proposed IG loss function for training, achieves better performance on metrics like Jaccard Index (JI) and AUC scores compared to the state of the art.

Keywords: Egocentric Vision · HCI · Hand Gesture Recognition

1 Introduction

We use hand gestures to communicate effectively in our daily life. With the increasing presence and availability of head-mounted Augmented Reality (AR) and Virtual Reality (VR) devices, it is natural to extend hand gestures as an interface to interact with virtual elements. Hand gestures viewed from the camera of a head-mounted device are called egocentric hand gestures, as they are seen from the wearer's perspective. Recognising such egocentric hand gestures can lead to better interfaces for head-mounted AR and VR.

Research on egocentric hand gesture recognition for a large number of gestures gained popularity recently due to the development of deep learning frameworks and the availability of large-scale datasets these frameworks require [6,27,29]. However, most of these approaches attempt to recognise gestures from trimmed videos [1,5,7]. Ego-hand gesture recognition on trimmed videos can not be used for practical purposes because, the video contains many gestures interlaced with images without gestures. In the untrimmed video scenario, recognising an ego-hand gestures also involves finding frames in the video without and

© Springer Nature Switzerland AG 2023
J.-J. Rousseau and B. Kapralos (Eds.): ICPR 2022 Workshops, LNCS 13643, pp. 359–372, 2023.
https://doi.org/10.1007/978-3-031-37660-3_25

with gestures, adding to the complexity of the problem. This problem has been tackled to a certain extent in action recognition, in terms of action localisation [4,14,18,19] and action recognition in the wild [3,26]. These approaches assume some prior knowledge about the videos which are not applicable to our case. We discuss this in detail in the Background Study section.

Recognition of an ego-hand gesture involves spatial understanding of the position of ego-hands in the scene, their pose and movement. 3D CNNs have proved incredibly useful in recognising actions and gestures in videos [16,20,21], because they can extract and encode features relevant to the recognition task both in spatial and temporal dimensions. 3D CNNs take video clips of predefined size as input, which limits the network capacity to understand temporal relations beyond the clip length. To overcome this limitation, 3D CNNs are connected to a recurrent neural network (RNN) to infer temporal relations beyond the clip size [5,7,15]. In the case of recognising gestures from untrimmed videos, there is an imbalance in the number of frames without a gesture and with a particular gesture. To overcome this imbalance heuristics like using selective part of a video, weighted cross entropy loss, a limited number of frames are used during training. We proposed an additional gate called State Activation Gate to the existing LSTM framework that modulates the flow of input and hidden state depending on the presence or absence of an ego-hand gesture in the current input frame to account for the imbalance mentioned above in the place of heuristics. We used R(2+1)D Net [21] as visual encoder and StAG LSTM as sequence decoder to understand the presence or absence of gesture in a frame and recognise the gesture simultaneously. A new loss function was introduced for training to penalise the difference in labels for consecutive frames. This arises from the fact that when a gesture is being performed, it does not change midway. JI is a widely used metric to measure the similarity of two sequences [22,27]. However, it does not account for continuity of a sequence. To reward continuous labels in comparison to non-continuous labels in a sequence we introduced Continuity Favouring JI. We measured the performance of our network on two datasets, EgoGesture and NVIDIA Gesture beating the state of the art scores on metrics like JI and AUC scores (reported in Sect. 5). Our contributions are summarised below

- StAG LSTM, an LSTM with a proposed state activation gate that can be trained without involving heuristics that are currently used in training LSTMs for ego gesture recognition (Sect. 3.2).
- A new IG loss that penalises if consecutive frames do not have the same label (Sect. 4.2).
- A new metric Continuity Favouring Jaccard Index which also measures the continuity of predicted labels in addition to IOU when compared to the ground truth (Sect. 4.3).

The efficacy of StAG LSTM compared to normal LSTM without using heuristics is empirically shown in Sect. 5.2. Section 5.3 demonstrate the advantages of using IG loss in conjunction with the standard cross entropy loss for non gesture supression and early detection. In the following section we review pertinent ego gesture recognition research.

2   Background Study

2.1   EgoGesture Recognition Trimmed Video

In this section, we reviewed ego gesture recognition networks on trimmed videos since we followed principles from these algorithms to design our network. 3D CNNs are known to extract spatio-temporal features from video data [20,21]. Spatio Temporal Transformer Module (STTM) was proposed by [5]. STTMs were used to estimate spatial transforms between frames, and these transforms are applied to consecutive frames. STTMs, in conjunction with 3D CNNs and LSTMs, were used to compensate for ego-motion and recognise ego gestures in trimmed videos. Approaches like [7,9] proposed using encoder and decoder architecture to extract visual features and LSTM as sequence decoder to recognise gestures from trimmed videos. Zhang et al. [25] proposed deformable 3D convolutions to selectively applying spatiotemporal convolutions. They argued applying spatio-temporal convolutional selectively through their deformable 3D CNN modules yields better focus on hands and their movements, which lead to improved results on the EgoGesture dataset.

2.2   EgoGesture Recognition on UnTrimmed Video

The work in [27] proposed using weakly segmented videos and limiting the length of a video to 120 frames to train and an architecture with 3D CNN + LSTM to recognise ego-hand gestures from untrimmed videos. They segmented the video heuristically to include some frames without gestures along with frames with gestures. They also proposed a different approach that combines [5] and weakly segmented video training for the RGB modality since the earlier approach yields good results only for the depth and RGBD modalities. Our network and training methodology, in contrast, precisely avoids these kinds of heuristics and works well, beating the state-of-the-art across all modalities. We follow the idea of using 3D CNN for encoding spatio-temporal features and using a variation of LSTM we proposed in Sect. 3.2 for recognising the encoded sequence.

A two-stream network structure was proposed by [11], one stream to detect the presence of gesture, and once the gesture presence is detected, the images are queued and sent to the second stream of a classification network. They also employed heuristics in terms of weighted cross entropy loss to account for the uneven number of gesture vs non-gesture frames. The crux of their procedure lies in the post-processing step they proposed. Our network does not employ such heuristics, and when compared to the raw results produced by their network, performs better, which we reported in the experiments and analysis section.

The problem of recognising non-egocentric gestures in untrimmed videos has been tackled by employing gesture spotting, and recognition techniques [2,12,28]. Lee et al. [12] proposed the idea of identifying the start and end of a gesture depending on the human pose (the distance of the hand from the body) and collecting the frames in between start and end to identify the gestures. Zhu et al. [28] proposed a two-stage deep neural network architecture for gesture recognition on untrimmed videos using the framework of 3D Convolutions in tandem with RNNs. The first stage of the network finds the segments in the input video with gestures, and the second stage takes each of these segments as input to recognise the gesture in the segmented video. In [2] Benitez-Garcia et al. proposed a method to spot a gesture depending on the similarities between the start and ending frame of a gesture. After this step, they perform a temporal normalisation of frame features between the boundaries and identify the gesture. However, all these approaches identify the gesture after its performance. Our proposed network is different from these approaches since we recognise the gesture in the video as it is being performed but not after it is finished.

Action recognition in untrimmed videos is similar to ego gesture recognition in untrimmed videos since both of these contain frames with actions or gestures interspersed with background frames. SSTA Detection networks proposed by [3] dealt with this by using 3D CNN as the visual encoder and a semantically constrained recurrent memory module implemented with a Gated Recurrent Unit. However, their network requires the number of actions in a given video as input for their network, not a viable solution for untrimmed gesture recognition. Another untrimmed video action recognition approach proposed by [26] created two different networks, each with feature extraction and self-attention modules. They used untrimmed videos in one network, and trimmed videos in the other, transfer the knowledge from trimmed video network to untrimmed network to improve the classification performance. However, this method assumes only one action per video, which is not the case for our problem. Most recently [17] proposed an framework to recognise, localise and summarise actions in egocentric videos using a combination of random walks performed on graph representation constructed with super pixels as their nodes and a fractional knapsack. This approach also requires the whole video as input to their framework, so it can not be used for our purpose.

3   Architecture and Training Overview

We used a combination of a 3D CNN to encode spatio-temporal features and an RNN to recognise ego-hand gestures from a sequence of encoded spatio-temporal features. We were inspired by various networks proposed in the past for gesture, and action recognition [5,7,8,26]. We described the 3D CNN we choose for our visual encoder and StAG LSTM we proposed for the sequence decoder in the following sections.

3.1   Visual Encoder

There have been several 3D CNN architectures introduced (C3D, P3D, R(2+1)D) [16,20,21]. We use R(2+1)D networks introduced in [21] for the visual encoder. R(2+1)D is a variation of the P3D network, which itself is an extension of ResNet [23] from 2D to 3D space. R(2+1)D networks were empirically shown to be superior to other 3D network architectures even with considerably fewer

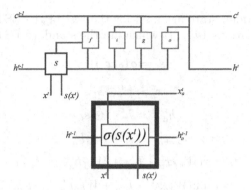

Fig. 1. Stag LSTM. State Activation Gate is added to standard LSTM to modulate the flow of input and hidden state. In addition to the hidden state and cell state, StAG LSTM also outputs the activation mapping for input to optimise the activation function s. For brevity, only the state activation gate is expanded.

layers [21]. We choose R(2+1)D networks for the above reasons. The number of blocks in each layer was set to two, using the shallowest version of R(2+1)D Network.

3.2 StAG LSTM

We append an RNN to the last encoding layer of our visual encoder to discern the temporal relations between video clips to give the network a larger temporal view of the video. Long-Short Term Memory or LSTMs as they are called in short, an improved version of RNNs were proposed by [10] and since have been extensively researched and applied to action and gesture recognition [5,7,8,13,15,24,28]. LSTMs are made of input, forget, output gates represented by equations. These gates influence the current cell state and hidden state deciding what information needs to be remembered, forgotten and to what extent. The hidden state is then connected to a linear filter to generate a gesture label using Softmax classification.

However, in the case of ego gesture recognition on untrimmed videos, the number of frames with a non-gesture label is high compared to frames with one particular gesture. In such a scenario using the entire video for training leads the network to overfit on non-gesture data if plain LSTMs are used, as reported in Sect. 5.2. To avoid this issue, heuristics have been used to select a part of the video for training the RNN [11,27]. The heuristics involved using a particular amount of frames without gestures before and after the gesture is performed [27]. We introduced an additional gate to the LSTM framework to avoid the usage of such heuristics. We call this state activation gate. A state activation gate modulates the activation of input and hidden state depending on the input's current state. The equations $1a, 1b, 1c$ represent the state activation gate and the gate being applied to the input and the hidden state. Figure 1 illustrates the addition of State Activation Gate to LSTM. As it can be seen that the new activated input, hidden state are used for the rest of the LSTM instead of the original states (equations $1d \ldots 1i$ which are the standard LSTM gates).

$$s_t = \sigma(s(x^t)) \tag{1a}$$

$$x_a^t = x^t \odot s_t \tag{1b}$$

$$h_a^{t-1} = h^{t-1} \odot s_t \tag{1c}$$

$$i_t = \sigma(W_{xi}x_a^t + b_{xi} + W_{hi}h_a^{t-1} + b_{hi}) \tag{1d}$$

$$f_t = \sigma(W_{xf}x_a^t + b_{xf} + W_{hf}h_a^{t-1} + b_{hf}) \tag{1e}$$

$$g_t = \tanh(W_{xg}x_a^t + b_{xg} + W_{hg}h_a^{t-1} + b_{hg}) \tag{1f}$$

$$o_t = \sigma(W_{xo}x_a^t + b_{xo} + W_{ho}h_a^{t-1} + b_{ho}) \tag{1g}$$

$$c_t = f_t \odot c_{t-1} + i_t \odot g_t \tag{1h}$$

$$h_t = o_t \odot \tanh(c_t) \tag{1i}$$

The state activation gate maps the input x_t at time t to a value between 0 and 1, such that the gate can selectively modulate the input and hidden state that needs to enter the next gates in LSTM. For our purpose, we choose s to be a linear mapping neural network that infers if the current frame x_t has an ego-hand gesture or not. The output of the function s is used in a binary cross entropy loss function to learn its parameters, along with the loss function back propagated from the hidden state. This allows the network to actively modulate the flow of input and hidden state depending on the presence or absence of a gesture in the current frame, allowing for the parameters in the LSTM to be learnt for gestures instead of the no gesture frames during training. There is no need to modulate the cell state separately, as evident from Eq. 1h, since inputs to this gate are already activated input and hidden states. The following section details the training and evaluation procedure.

4   Training and Evaluation

We formalise the problem of ego-hand gesture recognition. V is a video containing $x_1 \ldots x_t$ frames, $l_1 \ldots l_t$ are the corresponding gesture labels, where $0 \leq l_i \leq n$, n being the number of gestures, 0 label corresponds to no gesture. We need to find a function f that maps $x_1 \ldots x_t$ to $l_1 \ldots l_t$.

4.1   Training

The video is chunked into clips of length c_l frames with a stride c_s. The full length of the encoded video is used as input to StAG LSTM unlike Zhange et al. [27] who uses heuristically segmented videos. We used all the videos in training split in a single batch. StAG LSTM has two outputs, one from the state activation function described in Eq. 1a and the hidden state. Binary cross entropy loss is used for the state activation function. The hidden state is connected to a linear layer with $n + 1$ neuron, n being the number of gestures. The loss function we used for training StAG LSTM is represented by the Eq. 2

$$L = L_{StA} + L_{CE} + L_{IG} \tag{2}$$

where L_{StA} is the state activation loss. As described earlier, we use binary cross entropy to represent this loss. L_{CE} is the standard cross entropy loss, and L_{IG} is the IG loss explained in the following section.

4.2 Intra-Gesture Loss

IG loss is defined by Eq. 3

$$L_{IG}(P||Q) = \sum_{x \in X} \delta_{xl} * P(x) * ln(P(x)/Q(x)) \tag{3}$$

where l is the ground truth label, δ is the Kronecker delta. IG loss is the product of Kronecker delta and Kullback-Leibler distance. In our case, P and Q are the estimated probability distributions between two consecutive gesture frames. The idea of IG loss is to penalise if the distribution of prediction for two consecutive frames is different. However, with Kronecker delta's introduction, this penalty is selectively applied to the gesture label that matches the ground truth.

4.3 Evaluation

JI has been used as an evaluation metric for gesture recognition on untrimmed videos [22, 27]. As indicated by equations $5a, 5b, 5c$, JI measures the relative overlap between the ground truth and predicted sequences.

$$JI(G||P)_{s,i} = \frac{G_{s,i} \bigcap P_{s,i}}{G_{s,i} \bigcup P_{s,i}} \tag{4a}$$

where $G_{s,i}$ is the ground truth part of sequence which has gesture i, similarly $P_{s,i}$ is the predicted part of sequence which has gesture i.

$$JI(G||P)_s = \frac{1}{N} \sum_{i=1}^{N} JI_{s,i} \tag{4b}$$

$$JI(G||P) = \frac{1}{S} \sum_{s=1}^{S} JI_s \tag{4c}$$

where $JI(G||P)_s$ measures the JI between two sequences with N different gestures in it and $JI(G||P)$ is the mean JI of all the sequences in the set with cardinality S. However, the JI does not take the continuity of predicted labels into account. For example if $0, 0, 1, 1, 1, 1, 1, 1, 0, 0$ are ground truth labels

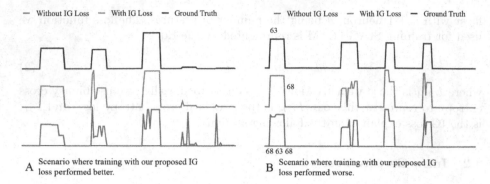

A Scenario where training with our proposed IG loss performed better.

B Scenario where training with our proposed IG loss performed worse.

Fig. 2. (A) Labels predicted for video Subject 14, Scene 3, Task4. The model trained with IG loss showed less variations in predictions compared to those trained without IG loss yielding better JI and CFJI scores. (B) Labels predicted for Subject 11, Scene 2, Task5, even though number of variations are less, but the model trained with IG loss performed worse. The IG loss model predicted wrong label consistently, but the model trained without IG loss intermittently predicted correct labels.

G for a sequence, $0, 0, 1, 0, 1, 0, 1, 0, 0, 0$ is a set of predicted labels P_1, and $0, 0, 0, 0, 0, 1, 1, 1, 0, 0$ is another set of predicted labels P_2, then $JI(G\|P_1) = JI(G\|P_2)$. We would like to device a metric M that would score $M(G\|P_2) > M(G\|P_1)$, since it would be more useful if labels are continuous, instead of segmented. We define a new metric Continuity Favouring Jaccard Index (CFJI) that would favour continuity and also measures the relative overlap between ground truth and predicted labels. CFJI is defined by the following equations

$$CFJI(G\|P)_{s,i} = \begin{cases} \dfrac{N_{s,i}(G)}{N_{s,i}(P)} * \dfrac{G_{s,i} \bigcap P_{s,i}}{G_{s,i} \bigcup P_{s,i}}, \\ \text{if } N_{s,i}(P) \geq N_{s,i}(G) \\\\ \dfrac{N_{s,i}(P)}{N_{s,i}(G)} * \dfrac{G_{s,i} \bigcap P_{s,i}}{G_{s,i} \bigcup P_{s,i}}, \\ \text{if } N_{s,i}(G) > N_{s,i}(P) \\\\ 0, \\ \text{if } N_{s,i}(G) = 0 \text{ or } N_{s,i}(P) = 0 \end{cases} \qquad (5a)$$

where $N_{s,i}$ is the number of continuous segments of gesture i in sequence s. It can be seen that if the number of continuous segments for a gesture is different in predicted sequence labels compared to the ground truth, our metric CFJI decreases the score; if they are the same, it retains the JI value.

$$CFJI(G||P)_s = \frac{1}{N}\sum_{i=1}^{N} CFJI_{s,i} \qquad (5b)$$

$$CFJI(G||P) = \frac{1}{S}\sum_{s=1}^{S} CFJI_s \qquad (5c)$$

5 Experiments and Analysis

We used EgoGesture [5], the biggest ego-hand gesture dataset available publicly, and NVIDIA Gestures [15] to validate our network architecture and training with StAG LSTM.

5.1 Results on EgoGesture Dataset

EgoGesture dataset has 2081 videos with gestures being performed at irregular intervals recorded in different environments with varied lighting conditions and has 83 different gestures performed by 50 subjects. These are split into 1239, 411, 431 videos of training, validation and testing set respectively. We followed the same settings mentioned in [27] to report the results.

After the visual encoder is trained, the feature vectors at the spatio-temporal pooling layer (of length $512 \times n$ where n is the number of clips in the video) are stored. The hidden size in StAG LSTM is set to 128. The activation function is trained for the first 40 epochs by using only the activation function loss. The classifier loss is used from the 41st epoch until the validation error does not improve any more. We assigned the network's output per clip to the slide window to generate full length of video labels to compare with ground truth labels. The metrics scores are reported on the test set. Table 1 compares our network's performance with the state of the art.

RGB modality scores compared to Depth and RGBD are less in both the state-of-the-art and our network. This is attributed to the fact that RGB images have a lot of background signal which needs to be filtered. Depth images can be easily thresholded to extract ego-hands, but they lose some finer details, so they perform better than RGB. RGBD modality outperforms both RGB and depth modalities because it combines the information from these two modalities. Kopuklu et al. [11] is the other network that recognises ego-gestures from untrimmed videos in the EgoGestures dataset. However, the performance of the two-stream network proposed by them is particularly low because their algorithm's crux is a proposed postprocessing step. Their network scored 0.484 on the JI metric without postprocessing. Applying their postprocessing does not output a sequence label for doing a direct comparison. Their network's performance relied on a ResNext [23] network which can not form long term dependencies, and its performance is limited to the size of the clip, which was chosen to be 32 in their case.

Table 1. JI scores for various networks. Heuristics are employed by current methods to adapt networks trained on trimmed videos to untrimmed videos. Our network which uses **StAG LSTM does not employ heuristics** and performs better or similar on various modalities in comparison to existing networks. For networks using simple LSTM without heuristics, the JI metric score is very low. The networks with simple LSTMs trained without heuristics did not converge.

Method	Modality	Heuristics	JI
C3D+STTM	RGB	Yes	0.670
R(2+1)D+LSTM	RGB	No	0.158
R(2+1)D+StAGLSTM	RGB	**No**	**0.684**
C3D+LSTM	Depth	Yes	**0.710**
R(2+1)D+LSTM	Depth	No	0.083
R(2+1)D+StAGLSTM	Depth	**No**	**0.710**
C3D+LSTM	RGBD	No	0.156
C3D+LSTM	RGBD	Yes	0.718
R(2+1)D+LSTM	RGBD	No	0.159
R(2+1)D+StAGLSTM	RGBD	**No**	**0.722**

5.2   Ablation Studies

One of the problems to solve in training deep neural networks for ego gesture recognition on untrimmed video is a large number of training images containing no gestures compared to that with a particular gesture. Methods like [11,27] use heuristics like carefully choosing a part of the training sequence, and using weighted cross entropy loss(weights chosen are another set of heuristics) to deal with this issue. We trained LSTM with the same procedure used to train StAG LSTM. The training loss stopped decreasing much earlier compared to StAG LSTM. The metrics on the validation set also followed the same trend. StAG LSTM lead to better training loss and validation accuracy while eliminating the need for heuristics that are used in [11,27]

Table 2. JI and CFJI metrics for training with and without IG loss. Adding the IG loss component improves both the metrics across modalities.

Loss	Modality	JI	CFJI
$L_{StA} + L_{CE}$	RGBD	0.718	0.676
$L_{StA} + L_{CE} + L_{IG}$	RGBD	0.722	0.681
$L_{StA} + L_{CE}$	Depth	0.706	0.664
$L_{StA} + L_{CE} + L_{IG}$	Depth	0.710	0.665
$L_{StA} + L_{CE}$	RGB	0.682	0.639
$L_{StA} + L_{CE} + L_{IG}$	RGB	0.684	0.642

We can see across all modalities that using IG loss improves both the JI and the CFJI scores as reported in Table 2. In Fig. 2 we report two results, one where using IG loss clearly helps get better CFJI score and the other where it fails to. Gesture 63 (Thumbs Upwards) is confused for gesture 68 (Thumbs Forward), in the case that does not employ IG loss we can see that part of the gesture is labelled as 63, but when IG loss is used the entire gesture is labelled 68 (incorrectly). This could be a potential downside, meaning if a gesture gets labelled incorrectly in the beginning, it could retain the wrong label until the gesture ends. However, this behaviour occurs less in comparison to predicting the correct labels, hence the overall improvement in both JI and CGJI metrics.

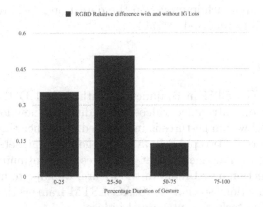

Fig. 3. Early detection with IG loss: The length of each gesture is divided into four buckets: (0–25, 25–50, 50–75, 75–100)%, this graph plots the relative mAP of network trained with IG loss versus without IG loss for each bucket. The most gains of the network trained with IG loss can be seen in the 25–50% bucket, this enables us to perform early detection which in turn can make interactions with virtual elements quicker.

5.3 Early Detection Analysis

Detecting a gesture early can help making the interactions with virtual elements smoother. To analyse early gesture detection performance of training our network with and without IG loss, we divided each gesture in the test set into four equal temporal segments, corresponding to 0–25%, 25–50%, 50–75%, 75–100% of the duration of the gesture. The relative difference in mean average precision (mAP) in each bucket is plotted (Fig. 3), it can be seen that most of the gain in mAP scores using IG loss occurred in the 25–50% and the 0–25% temporal segments of a gesture performance. Using IG loss forces the network score sequential frames with the same gesture label leading to early detection mAP gains.

5.4 Results on NVIDIA Gesture Dataset

NVIDIA Gesture dataset [15] was introduced prior to the EgoGesture dataset. The dataset contains gestures which can be used in user interface scenarios in

Table 3. Our network performs better on the ROC+AUC detection score compared to the state-of-the-art.

Method	Modality	ROC AUC
3D-CNN + CTC [15]	Depth	0.91
R(2+1)D + StaG LSTM	Depth	**0.92**

untrimmed videos, making it a suitable candidate for testing our network and training approach. The number of gestures in this dataset is 25. The batch size for training visual encoder is set to 11 and used the entire batch for training StAG LSTM. Our approach improves on the detection ROC+AUC scores in the state-of-the-art [15] as reported in Table 3.

6   Conclusion

We presented StAG LSTM in conjunction with R(2+1)D that can recognise ego-hand gestures on untrimmed videos. In addition, a new loss that penalises differences in labels within gestures is introduced. Together they perform better than state of the art for two publicly available gesture datasets on various metrics. We introduced a new metric that measures the continuity of a gesture in addition to Intersection over Union. In the future, we hope to find more suitable state activation functions so that the StAG LSTM framework can also be used for more recognition tasks on untrimmed videos.

Acknowledgements. This publication has emanated from research conducted with the financial support of Science Foundation Ireland (SFI) under the Grant Number 15/RP/2776.

References

1. Abavisani, M., Joze, H.R.V., Patel, V.M.: Improving the performance of unimodal dynamic hand-gesture recognition with multimodal training. In: Proceedings of the IEEE Computer Society Conference on Computer Vision and Pattern Recognition (2019)
2. Benitez-Garcia, G., Haris, M., Tsuda, Y., Ukita, N.: Continuous finger gesture spotting and recognition based on similarities between start and end frames. IEEE Trans. Intell. Transp. Syst. (2020)
3. Buch, S., Escorcia, V., Ghanem, B., Fei-Fei, L., Niebles, J.C.: End-to-end, single-stream temporal action detection in untrimmed videos. In: British Machine Vision Conference (2017)
4. Buch, S., Escorcia, V., Shen, C., Ghanem, B., Niebles, J.C.: SST: single-stream temporal action proposals shyamal. In: Computer Vision and Pattern Recognition (2017)
5. Cao, C., Zhang, Y., Wu, Y., Lu, H., Cheng, J.: Egocentric gesture recognition using recurrent 3D convolutional neural networks with spatiotemporal transformer modules. In: International Conference on Computer Vision (2017)

6. Chalasani, T., Ondrej, J., Smolic, A.: Egocentric gesture recognition for head-mounted AR devices. In: Adjunct Proceedings - 2018 IEEE International Symposium on Mixed and Augmented Reality, ISMAR-Adjunct 2018 (2018)

7. Chalasani, T., Smolic, A.: Simultaneous segmentation and recognition: towards more accurate ego gesture recognition. In: International Conference on Computer Vision Workshop (2019)

8. Donahue, J., et al.: Long-Term Recurrent Convolutional Networks for Visual Recognition and Description. Conference on Computer Vision and Pattern Recognition (2015)

9. Fan, D., Lu, H., Xu, S., Cao, S.: Multi-task and multi-modal learning for rgb dynamic gesture recognition. IEEE Sens. J. (2021)

10. Hochreiter, S., Schmidhuber, J.: Long Short-Term Memory. Neural Computation (1997)

11. Köpüklü, O., Gunduz, A., Kose, N., Rigoll, G.: Real-time hand gesture detection and classification using convolutional neural networks. In: International Conference on Automatic Face and Gesture Recognition (2019)

12. Lee, D., Yoon, H., Kim, J.: Continuous gesture recognition by using gesture spotting. In: International Conference on Control, Automation and Systems (2016)

13. Liu, J., Shahroudy, A., Xu, D., Wang, G.: Spatio-temporal lstm with trust gates for 3d human action recognition. European conference on computer vision (2016)

14. Long, F., Yao, T., Qiu, Z., Tian, X., Luo, J., Mei, T.: Gaussian temporal awareness networks for action localization. In: Proceedings of the IEEE Computer Society Conference on Computer Vision and Pattern Recognition (2019)

15. Molchanov, P., Yang, X., Gupta, S., Kim, K., Tyree, S., Kautz, J.: Online detection and classification of dynamic hand gestures with recurrent 3D convolutional neural networks. In: 2016 IEEE Conference on Computer Vision and Pattern Recognition (CVPR) (2016)

16. Qiu, Z., Yao, T., Mei, T.: Learning spatio-temporal representation with pseudo-3D residual networks. In: Proceedings of the IEEE International Conference on Computer Vision (2017)

17. Sahu, A., Chowdary, A.S.: Together recongnizing, localizing and summarizing actions in egocentric videos. IEEE Trans. Image Process. (2021)

18. Shi, B., Dai, Q., Mu, Y., Wang, J.: Weakly-supervised action localization by generative attention modeling. In: Computer Vision and Pattern Recognition (2020)

19. Shou, Z., Wang, D., Chang, S.F.: Temporal action localization in untrimmed videos via multi-stage CNNs. In: Proceedings of the IEEE Computer Society Conference on Computer Vision and Pattern Recognition (2016)

20. Tran, D., Bourdev, L., Fergus, R., Torresani, L., Paluri, M.: Learning spatiotemporal features with 3D convolutional networks. In: Proceedings of the IEEE International Conference on Computer Vision (2015)

21. Tran, D., Wang, H., Torresani, L., Ray, J., Lecun, Y., Paluri, M.: A closer look at spatiotemporal convolutions for action recognition. In: Proceedings of the IEEE Computer Society Conference on Computer Vision and Pattern Recognition (2018)

22. Wan, J., Li, S.Z., Zhao, Y., Zhou, S., Guyon, I., Escalera, S.: ChaLearn looking at people RGB-D isolated and continuous datasets for gesture recognition. In: IEEE Computer Society Conference on Computer Vision and Pattern Recognition Workshops (2016)

23. Wu, S., Zhong, S., Liu, Y.: Deep residual learning for image recognition. CVPR (2016)

24. Xu, M., Gao, M., Chen, Y.T., Davis, L., Crandall, D.: Temporal recurrent networks for online action detection. In: Proceedings of the IEEE International Conference on Computer Vision (2019)
25. Zhang, X.Y., Shi, H., Li, C., Li, P.: Multi-instance multi-label action recognition and localization based on spatio-temporal pre-trimming for untrimmed videos. In: Proceedings of the AAAI Conference on Artificial Intelligence (2020)
26. Zhang, X.Y., Shi, H., Li, C., Zheng, K., Zhu, X., Duan, L.: Learning transferable self-attentive representations for action recognition in untrimmed videos with weak supervision. In: Proceedings of the AAAI Conference on Artificial Intelligence (2019)
27. Zhang, Y., Cao, C., Cheng, J., Lu, H.: EgoGesture: a new dataset and benchmark for egocentric hand gesture recognition. IEEE Trans. Multimed. (2018)
28. Zhu, G., Zhang, L., Shen, P., Song, J., Shah, S.A.A., Bennamoun, M.: Continuous gesture segmentation and recognition using 3dcnn and convolutional lstm. IEEE Trans. Multimed. (2019)
29. Zimmermann, C., Ceylan, D., Yang, J., Russell, B., Argus, M.J., Brox, T.: Frei-HAND: a dataset for markerless capture of hand pose and shape from single rgb images. In: Proceedings of the IEEE International Conference on Computer Vision (2019)

Representation Learning for Tablet and Paper Domain Adaptation in Favor of Online Handwriting Recognition

Felix Ott[1,2]([⊠])([iD]), David Rügamer[2,3]([⊠])([iD]), Lucas Heublein[1]([⊠])([iD]), Bernd Bischl[2]([⊠])([iD]), and Christopher Mutschler[1]([⊠])([iD])

[1] Fraunhofer IIS, Fraunhofer Institute for Integrated Circuits IIS, Erlangen, Germany
{felix.ott,heublels,christopher.mutschler}@iis.fraunhofer.de
[2] LMU Munich, Munich, Germany
{david.ruegamer,bernd.bischl}@stat.uni-muenchen.de
[3] RWTH Aachen, Aachen, Germany

Abstract. The performance of a machine learning model degrades when it is applied to data from a similar but different domain than the data it has initially been trained on. The goal of domain adaptation (DA) is to mitigate this domain shift problem by searching for an optimal feature transformation to learn a domain-invariant representation. Such a domain shift can appear in handwriting recognition (HWR) applications where the motion pattern of the hand and with that the motion pattern of the pen is different for writing on paper and on tablet. This becomes visible in the sensor data for online handwriting (OnHW) from pens with integrated inertial measurement units. This paper proposes a supervised DA approach to enhance learning for OnHW recognition between tablet and paper data. Our method exploits loss functions such as maximum mean discrepancy and correlation alignment to learn a domain-invariant feature representation (i.e., similar covariances between tablet and paper features). We use a triplet loss that takes negative samples of the auxiliary domain (i.e., paper samples) to increase the amount of samples of the tablet dataset. We conduct an evaluation on novel sequence-based OnHW datasets (i.e., words) and show an improvement on the paper domain with an early fusion strategy by using pairwise learning.

Keywords: Online handwriting recognition (OnHW) · sensor pen · domain adaptation (DA) · deep metric learning (DML) · writer-(in)dependent tasks

1 Introduction

HWR can be categorized into offline and online HWR. While offline HWR deals with the analysis of the visual representation, OnHW recognition works on different types of spatio-temporal signals and can make use of temporal information such as writing

Supported by the Federal Ministry of Education and Research (BMBF) of Germany by Grant No. 01IS18036A and by the project "Schreibtrainer", Grant No. 16SV8228, as well as by the Bavarian Ministry for Economic Affairs, Infrastructure, Transport and Technology through the Center for Analytics-Data-Applications within the framework of "BAYERN DIGITAL II".

© Springer Nature Switzerland AG 2023
J.-J. Rousseau and B. Kapralos (Eds.): ICPR 2022 Workshops, LNCS 13643, pp. 373–383, 2023.
https://doi.org/10.1007/978-3-031-37660-3_26

direction and speed [20]. Typically, recording systems make use of a stylus pen together with a touch screen surface [1]. Systems for writing on paper became popular, first prototypical systems were used [4], and recently a novel system enhanced with inertial measurement units (IMUs) became prominant [19]. These IMU-enhanced pens are real-world applicable. While previous work [10,15,16,18,19] used this pen for writing on paper, [17] used this pen for writing on tablet. Figure 1 presents IMU data from a sensor-enhanced pen for writing on paper (left) and tablet (right). Due to the rough paper, the sensor data for writing on paper has more noise than writing on surface. Furthermore, the magnetic field of the tablet influences the magnetometer of the pen. This leads to different distributions of data and a domain shift between both data sources. Previously, tablet and paper data are processed separately, and hence, there is no method that can use both data sources simultaneously and inter-changeably.

Traditional ML algorithms assume training and test datasets to be *independent and identically distributed*. When applied in practice a domain shift appears in test data (here, shift between sensor data from tablet and paper), and hence, this assumption rarely holds in practice [23]. DA [12,25] tries to compensate for this domain shift by transferring knowledge between both data sources. Most techniques transform the

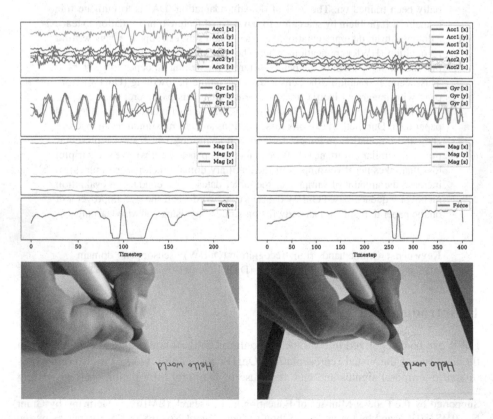

Fig. 1. Comparison of accelerometer (1st row), gyroscope (2nd row), magnetometer (3rd row) and force (4th row) data from a sensor pen [19] on paper (left) and tablet (right).

source data (here, data written on paper) by minimizing the distance to the target data (here, data written on tablet) [23], or by transforming the extracted features of the data sources [16]. To transform features of source domain into the target domain or to compare feature embeddings, higher-order moment matching (HoMM) [2] is often employed. Typically, the maximum mean discrepancy (MMD) [11] (HoMM of order 1) or the kernelized method kMMD [13] between features is evaluated. Correlation alignment (CORAL) [24] is of order 2. A related, yet different, task is pairwise learning. The *pairwise contrastive loss* [3] minimizes the distance between feature embedding pairs of the same class and maximizes the distance between feature embeddings of different classes dependent on a margin parameter. The *triplet loss* [21] defines an anchor and a positive as well as a negative point, and forces the positive pair distance to be smaller than the negative pair distance by a certain margin. While the triplet loss is typically used for image recognition, [9, 15] used this loss for sequence-based learning.

Contributions. We propose a method for OnHW recognition from sensor-enhanced pens for classifying words written on tablet and paper. We address the task of representation learning of features from different domains (i.e., tablet and paper) by using moment matching techniques (i.e., MMD and CORAL). For matching positive and negative samples of paper datasets w.r.t. anchor samples of tablet datasets, we use a triplet loss with dynamic margin and triplet selection based on the Edit distance. We conduct a large evaluation on OnHW [18] datasets. Website: www.iis.fraunhofer.de/de/ff/lv/data-analytics/anwproj/schreibtrainer/onhw-dataset.html.

The remainder of this paper is organized as follows. Section 2 discusses related work followed by our proposed methodology in Sect. 3. The experimental setup is described in Sect. 4 and the results are discussed in Sect. 5. Section 6 concludes.

2 Related Work

In this section, we address related work for OnHW recognition and for pairwise learning in relation to domain adaptation.

OnHW Recognition. The novel sensor-enhanced pen based on IMUs enables new applications for writing on normal paper. First, [19] introduced a character-based dataset from sensor-enhanced pens on paper and evaluated ML and DL techniques. [18] proposed several sequence-based datasets written on paper and tablet and a large benchmark of convolutional, recurrent and Transformer-based architectures, loss functions and augmentation techniques. To enhance the OnHW dataset with an offline HWR dataset, [15] generated handwritten images with ScrabbleGAN [7] and improved the training with cross-modal representation learning between online and offline HWR. [16] proposed a DA approach with optimal transport to adapt left-handed writers to right-handed writers for single characters. [17] reconstructed the trajectory of the pen tip for single characters written on tablet from IMU data and cameras pointing on the pen tip.

Pairwise Learning for DA. Research for pairwise and triplet learning is very advanced in general [3, 21], while the pairwise learning has rarely been used for sequence-based

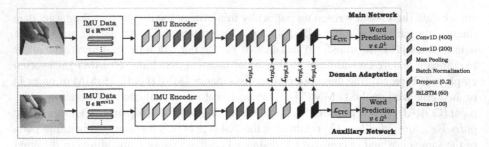

Fig. 2. Detailed method overview: The main network (top pipeline, tablet data) and the auxiliary network (bottom pipeline, paper data) consist of the respective pre-trained architectures with convolutional and bidirectional layers. The weights are fine-tuned with domain adaptation techniques such as the triplet loss at five different fusion points.

learning. [9] use a triplet selection with L_2-normalization for language modeling. While they consier all negative pairs for triplet selection with fixed similarity intensity parameter, our triplet approach dynamically selects positive and negative samples based on ED that is closer to the temporally adaptive maximum margin function by [22] as data is evolving over time. DeepTripletNN [27] also uses the triplet loss on embeddings between time-series data (audio) and visual data. While their method uses cosine similarity for the final representation comparison, we make use of mean discrepancy and correlation techniques.

3   Methodology

We start with a formal definition of multivariate time-series (MTS) classification and an method overview in Sect. 3.1. We propose our sequence-based triplet loss in Sect. 3.2, and finally give details about DML for DA in Sect. 3.3.

3.1   Methodology

MTS Classification. We define the sensor data from pens with integrated IMUs as a MTS $\mathbf{U} = \{\mathbf{u}_1, \ldots, \mathbf{u}_m\} \in \mathbb{R}^{m \times l}$, an ordered sequence of $l \in \mathbb{N}$ streams with $\mathbf{u}_i = (u_{i,1}, \ldots, u_{i,l}), i \in \{1, \ldots, m\}$, where $m \in \mathbb{N}$ is the length of the time-series. The MTS training set is a subset of the array $\mathcal{U} = \{\mathbf{U}_1, \ldots, \mathbf{U}_{n_U}\} \in \mathbb{R}^{n_U \times m \times l}$, where n_U is the number of time-series. Each MTS is associated with $\mathbf{v}$, a sequence of L class labels from a pre-defined label set Ω with K classes. For our classification task, $\mathbf{v} \in \Omega^L$ describes words. We train a convolutional neural network (CNN) in combination with a bidirectional long short-term memory (BiLSTM). We use the connectionist temporal classification (CTC) [8] loss to predict a word $\mathbf{v}$.

Method Overview. Figure 2 gives a method overview. The *main* task (top pipeline) is to classify sensor data represented as MTS with word labels $\mathbf{v}$ written with a sensor-enhanced pen [19] on tablet. The *auxiliary* task (bottom pipeline) is to classify sensor data from the same sensor-enhanced pen written on paper. For optimally combining both datasets, we train a common representation between both networks by using the triplet loss $\mathcal{L}_{\text{trpl},c}$, see Sect. 3.2, with $c \in C = \{1, 2, 3, 4, 5\}$ defines the layer both networks are combined. $c = 1$ represents an intermediate fusion, while $c = 5$ represents a late fusion. With DML techniques, we minimize the distance (or maximizing the similarity) between the distributions of both domains (see Sect. 3.3).

3.2 Contrastive Learning and Triplet Loss

To learn a common representation typically pairs of same class labels of both domains are used. Pairs with similar but different labels can improve the training process. This can be achieved using the triplet loss [21] which enforces a margin between pairs of MTS of tablet and paper sources with the same identity to all other different identities. As a consequence, the feature embedding for one and the same labels lives on a manifold, while still enforcing the distance and thus discriminability to other identities. We define the MTS $\mathbf{U}_i^a$ of the tablet dataset as *anchor*, an MTS $\mathbf{U}_i^p$ of the paper dataset as the *positive* sample, and an MTS $\mathbf{U}_i^n$ of the paper dataset as the *negative* sample. We seek to ensure that the embedding of the anchor $f_c(\mathbf{U}_i^a)$ of a specific label is closer to the embedding of the positive sample $f_c(\mathbf{U}_i^p)$ of the same label that it is to the embedding of any negative sample $f_c(\mathbf{U}_i^n)$ of another label. Thus, we want the inequality

$$\mathcal{L}_{\text{DML}}\big(f_c(\mathbf{U}_i^a), f_c(\mathbf{U}_i^p)\big) + \alpha < \mathcal{L}_{\text{DML}}\big(f_c(\mathbf{U}_i^a), f_c(\mathbf{U}_i^n)\big), \tag{1}$$

to hold for all training samples $\big(f_c(\mathbf{U}_i^a), f_c(\mathbf{U}_i^p), f_c(\mathbf{U}_i^n)\big) \in \Phi$ with Φ being the set of all possible triplets in the training set. α is a margin between positive and negative pairs. The DML loss $\mathcal{L}_{\text{DML}}$ is defined in Sect. 3.3. The *contrastive loss* minimizes the distance of the anchor to the positive sample and separately maximizes the distance to the negative sample. Instead, we can formulate the *triplet loss* as

$$\mathcal{L}_{\text{trpl},c}(\mathbf{U}^a, \mathbf{U}^p, \mathbf{X}^n) = \sum_{i=1}^{N} \max \Big[\mathcal{L}_{\text{DML}}\big(f_c(\mathbf{U}_i^a), f_c(\mathbf{U}_i^p)\big) -$$

$$\mathcal{L}_{\text{DML}}\big(f_c(\mathbf{U}_i^a), f_c(\mathbf{U}_i^n)\big) + \alpha, 0\Big], \tag{2}$$

where N is the number of triplets. To ensure fast convergence, it is necessary to select triplets that violate the constraint from Eq. 1. Computing the loss for all triplet pairs leads to poor training performance as poorly chosen pairs dominate hard ones [5]. We use the triplet selection approach by [15] that uses the Edit distance (ED) to define the identity and select triplets. We define two sequences with an ED of 0 as positive pair, and with an ED larger than 0 as negative pair (between 1 and 10). We use only substitu-

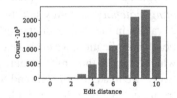

Fig. 3. Number tablet-paper pairs dependent on the ED.

tions for triplet selection. Figure 3 shows the number of triplet pairs for each ED. While there exist 265 samples for $ED = 0$, 3,022 samples for $ED = 1$ and 23,983 samples for

$ED = 2$, the number of pairs highly increase for higher EDs. For each batch, we search in a dictionary of negative sample pairs for samples with $ED = 1 + \lfloor \frac{\max_e - e - 1}{20} \rfloor$ as lower bound for the current epoch e and maximal epochs $\max_e = 200$ [15]. For every pair we randomly select one paper sample. We let the margin α in the triplet loss vary for each batch such that $\alpha = \beta \cdot \overline{ED}$ is depending on the mean ED of the batch and is in the range $[1, 11]$. β depends on the DML loss (see Sect. 3.3).

3.3 Domain Adaptation with Deep Metric Learning

A domain $\mathcal{D}$ consists of a feature space $\mathcal{X}$ with marginal probability $P(\mathcal{X})$. The task is defined by the label space $\mathcal{Y}$. When considering OnHW recognition, there is a source domain (paper dataset) $\mathcal{D}_S = \{\mathcal{U}_S^i, \mathcal{Y}_S^i\}_{i=1}^{\mathcal{N}_S}$ of $\mathcal{N}_S$ labeled samples of $|\mathcal{Y}_S^i|$ categories, and a target domain (tablet dataset) $\mathcal{D}_T = \{\mathcal{U}_T^i, \mathcal{Y}_T^i\}_{i=1}^{\mathcal{N}_T}$ of $\mathcal{N}_T$ labeled samples of $|\mathcal{Y}_T^i|$ categories. DA can mitigate the domain shift and improve the classification accuracy in the target domain by enforcing the distance of target embeddings $f_c(\mathbf{U}_i^a)$ and source domain embeddings $f_c(\mathbf{U}_i^p)$ and $f_c(\mathbf{U}_i^n)$ to be minimal. The embeddings are of size 400×200 for $c = 1$, of size 60×200 for $c = 2$ and $c = 3$, and of size 60×100 for $c = 4$ and $c = 5$. We search for a DML loss $\mathcal{L}_{\text{DML}}(f_c(\mathbf{U}_i^a), f_c(\mathbf{U}_i^p))$, respectively for the negative sample $\mathbf{U}_i^n$, that takes the domain shift into account. To perform domain alignment, we use higher-order moment matching (HoMM) [2]

$$\mathcal{L}_{\text{HoMM}}(f_c(\mathbf{U}_i^a), f_c(\mathbf{U}_i^p)) = \frac{1}{H^p} \left\| \frac{1}{n_s} \sum_{i=1}^{n_s} f_c(\mathbf{U}_i^a)^{\otimes p} - \frac{1}{n_t} \sum_{i=1}^{n_t} f_c(\mathbf{U}_i^p)^{\otimes p} \right\|_F^2, \quad (3)$$

between embeddings $f_c(\mathbf{U}_i^a)$ and $f_c(\mathbf{U}_i^p)$, respectively for $f_c(\mathbf{U}_i^a)$ and $f_c(\mathbf{U}_i^n)$. It holds $n_s = n_t = b$ with the batch size b. $\| \cdot \|_F$ denotes the Frobenius norm, H is the number of hidden neurons in the adapted layer, and $(\cdot)^{\otimes p}$ denotes the p-level tensor power. When $p = 1$, HoMM is equivalent to the linear MMD [25], and when $p = 2$, HoMM is equivalent to the Gram matrix matching. When the embeddings are normalized by subtracting the mean, the centralized Gram matrix turns into the covariance matrix [2], and hence, HoMM for $p = 2$ is equivalent to CORAL [24]. However, the space complexity for calculating the tensor $(\cdot)^{\otimes p}$ reaches $\mathcal{O}(H^p)$. This can be reduced by *group moment matching* that divides the hidden neurons into n_g groups, with each group $\lfloor \frac{H}{n_g} \rfloor$ neurons, and the space complexity reduces to $\mathcal{O}(n_g \cdot \lfloor \frac{H}{n_g} \rfloor^p)$. Furthermore, *random sampling matching* randomly selects T values in the high-level tensor, and only aligns these T values in the source and target domains. The space complexity reduces to $\mathcal{O}(T)$ [2]. For our application, we evaluate orders $p = 1$, $p = 2$ and $p = 3$, and choose $T = 1,000$, which reaches the limits of our training setup of GPUs with 32 GB VRAM. Alternatively, we make use of (Jeff and Stein) CORAL [24]. We choose the hyperparameters β from Sect. 3.2 proposed in Table 1.

4 Experiments

OnHW recognition uses time in association with different types of spatio-temporal signal. The pen in [19] uses two accelerometers (3 axes each), one gyroscope (3 axes),

Table 1. Hyperparameter choices of β for all DML loss functions and fusion points c.

DA Loss	$c = 1$	$c = 2$	$c = 3$	$c = 4$	$c = 5$
kMMD [13] $(p = 1)$	10	100	100	10	10
HoMM [2] $(p = 2)$	0.01	10^5	10^4	100	0.1
HoMM [2] $(p = 3)$	10^{-6}	10^6	10^5	100	10^{-3}
kHoMM [2] $(p = 2)$	10^3	10^6	10^6	10^4	10
kHoMM [2] $(p = 3)$	100	10^6	10^6	10^4	10
CORAL [23]	0.01	10^4	10^4	10	0.01
Jeff CORAL [23]	0.1	100	100	1	0.1
Stein CORAL [23]	1	100	100	10	1

one magnetometer (3 axes), and one force sensor at 100 Hz. One sample of size $m \times l$ represents an MTS of m time steps from $l = 13$ sensor channels. We make use of three sequence-based datasets proposed by [18]: The *OnHW-words500* dataset contains 500 repeated words from 53 writers. The *OnHW-wordsRandom* contains randomly selected words from 54 writers. Both datasets combined represent the (auxiliary task) dataset from source domain written on paper, and contains in total 39,863 samples. The *OnHW-wordsTraj* dataset contains 4,262 samples of randomly selected words from two writers, and represents the (main task) dataset from target domain written on tablet. The challenging task is to adapt on one of the two writers (who collected data on tablet) by utilizing the paper datasets. We make use of 80/20 train/validation splits for writer-dependent (WD) and writer-independent (WI) evaluation.

Language Models (LMs). We apply LMs to the softmax output values of the neural networks. We use the Wikimedia database by the Wikimedia Foundation [26]. We create the n-gram dictionaries with the `nltk` package [14] and exclude punctuation marks. These dictionaries store the probabilities of the order of characters generated from sequences of items. Next, we select the paths (word length $\times$ number of character labels) of the network predictions with the highest softmax values with a softmax threshold of 0.001. For more than $path\_thresh = 512$ available paths, we limit the number of paths to $max\_paths = 50$. Lastly, the n-gram models are applied to these paths.

5   Experimental Results

Hardware and Training Setup. For all experiments we use Nvidia Tesla V100-SXM2 GPUs with 32 GB VRAM equipped with Core Xeon CPUs and 192 GB RAM. We use the vanilla Adam optimizer with a learning rate of 10^{-4}. We pre-train both networks for 1,000 epochs, and adapt for 200 epochs for the contrastive loss and 2,000 epochs for the triplet loss. A metric for sequence evaluation is the character error rate (CER) and the word error rate (WER) defined through the ED (see [18]).

5.1   Baseline Results

Figure 4 presents baseline results for our CNN+BiLSTM architecture compared to InceptionTime (IT) [6] with and without additional BiLSTM layer. Consistently,

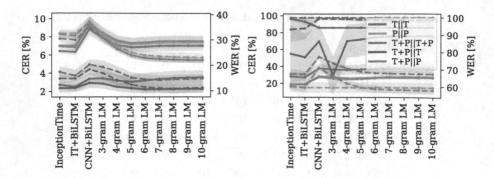

Fig. 4. Baseline results (WER: dashed, CER: solid, in %, averaged over cross-validation splits) for the InceptionTime (IT) [6] and our CNN+BiLSTM architectures and different n-gram LMs. Left: WD task. Right: WI task. Legend (tablet = T, paper = P): First notes training set and second notes validation set of the OnHW datasets [18].

IT+Bi-LSTM outperforms IT, while the CER and WER slightly increases for our CNN+Bi-LSTM model. For all datasets, the WD classification task shows better performance than the WI task. We can improve the CNN+BiLSTM results with the LM from 3.38% to 3.04% CER and from 20.23% to 15.13% WER with 5-gram LM trained on the tablet dataset. While the WER consistently decreases with higher n-gram LM, the CER increases higher than 5-gram LM. This is more notable for the separate tablet (T) dataset as the length of the words are here shorter than for the paper (P) datasets. By simply combining both datasets, the models achieve lower error rates evaluated on the tablet dataset only (from 3.04% CER for T∥T to 2.34% CER for T+P∥T for 5-gram LM), but increases for the model evaluated on the paper dataset only (from 7.21% CER for P∥P to 7.32% CER for T+P∥P for 5-gram LM). We define X∥Y, with X notes training dataset and Y notes validation dataset. This demonstrates the problem that there is a domain shift between tablet and paper data and that the size of the tablet dataset is small.

5.2 Domain Adaptation Results

We train the contrastive and pairwise learning approach by adapting paper data to tablet data with different representation loss functions (HoMM [2] and CORAL [24]) and propose results in Fig. 5. State-of-the-art pairwise learning techniques cannot be applied to our setup as they are typically proposed for single label classification tasks. While the contrastive loss cannot improve the tablet validation results (5a), the validation on paper (5c) does improve (orange and purple curve of Fig. 4). Also for the WI task, the paper validation improves (5d), while the tablet dataset is still a challenging task (5b). The triplet loss is on par with the baseline results for the WD task (5e). We see that early fusion ($c = 1$) leads to consistently low CERs as it is possible to adapt more trainable parameters after this fusion point. Intermediate ($c = 2$ and $c = 3$) and late ($c = 4$ and $c = 5$) fusion is dependent on the representation loss. kHoMM of order $p = 3$ at $c = 3$ leads to the highest significant improvement of 13.45% WER and 2.68% CER.

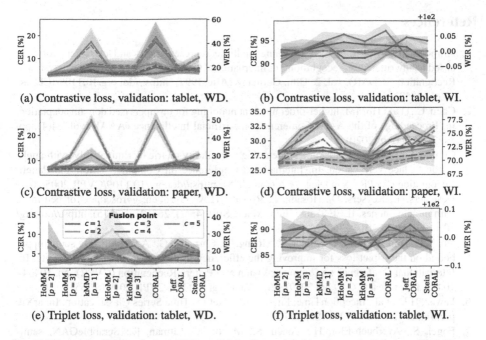

Fig. 5. DA results (WER: dashed, CER: solid, in %, averaged over cross-validation splits) for our CNN+BiLSTM architecture (with a 6-gram LM for tablet trainings, 10-gram for paper trainings respectively, for WD tasks and without LMs for WI tasks). The model is trained with the combined tablet and paper dataset with different representation loss functions at five different fusion points c.

The error rates of Jeff and Stein CORAL are marginally higher. LMs for $c = 4$ and $c = 5$ decrease results as the softmax output values are lower (uncertainty is higher) and the LM often chooses the second largest softmax value. We summarize the main difficulties as following: (1) While the paper dataset is very large, the tablet dataset as target domain is rather small. This leads to a small number of pairs with a small ED (see Fig. 3). (2) Furthermore, as the OnHW-words500 dataset contains the same 500 word labels per writer, the variance of specific positive pairs is small.

6   Conclusion

We proposed a DA approach for online handwriting recognition for sequence-based classification tasks between writing on tablet and paper. For this, contrastive and triplet losses enhance the main dataset and allows a more generalized training process. We evaluated moment matching techniques as DML loss functions. The kernalized HoMM of order 3 at the intermediate fusion layer combined with a n-gram language model provides the lowest error rates.

References

1. Alimoglu, F., Alpaydin, E.: Combining multiple representations and classifiers for pen-based handwritten digit recognition. In: International Conference on Document Analysis and Recognition (ICDAR). vol. 2. Ulm, Germany (Aug 1997). https://doi.org/10.1109/ICDAR.1997.620583
2. Chen, C., et al.: HoMM: higher-order moment matching for unsupervised domain adaptation. In: Proceedings of the AAAI Conference on Artificial Intelligence (AAAI). vol. 34(4), pp. 3422–3429 (Apr 2020)
3. Chopra, S., Hadsell, R., LeCun, Y.: Learning a similarity metric disriminatively, with application to face verification. In: International Conference on Computer Vision and Pattern Recognition (CVPR). San Diego, CA (Jun 2005). https://doi.org/10.1109/CVPR.2005.202
4. Deselaers, T., Keysers, D., Hosang, J., Rowley, H.A.: GyroPen: gyroscopes for pen-input with mobile phones. IEEE Trans. Hum.-Mach. Syst. 45(2), 263–271 (2015). https://doi.org/10.1109/THMS.2014.2365723
5. Do, T.T., Tran, T., Reid, I., Kumar, V., Hoang, T., Carneiro, G.: A theoretically sound upper bound on the triplet loss for improving the efficiency of deep distance metric learning. In: International Conference on Computer Vision and Pattern Recognition (CVPR), pp. 10404–10413. Long Beach, CA (Jun 2019). https://doi.org/10.1109/CVPR.2019.01065
6. Fawaz, H.I., et al.: InceptionTime: Finding AlexNet for Time Series Classification. In: arXiv preprint arXiv:1909.04939 (Sep 2019)
7. Fogel, S., Averbuch-Elor, H., Cohen, S., Mazor, S., Litman, R.: ScrabbleGAN: semi-supervised varying length handwritten text generation. In: International Conference on Computer Vision and Pattern Recognition (CVPR). Seattle, WA (Jun 2020). https://doi.org/10.1109/CVPR42600.2020.00438
8. Graves, A., Liwicki, M., Fernández, S., Bertolami, R., Bunke, H., Schmidhuber, J.: A novel connectionist system for unconstrained handwriting recognition. In: Transactions on Pattern Analysis and Machine Intelligence (TPAMI). vol. 31(5), pp. 855–868 (May 2009). https://doi.org/10.1109/TPAMI.2008.137
9. Guo, D., Tang, S., Wang, M.: Connectionist temporal modeling of video and language: a joint model for translation and sign labeling. In: International Joint Conference on Artificial Intelligence (IJCAI), pp. 751–757 (2019). https://doi.org/10.24963/ijcai.2019/106
10. Klaß, A., et al.: Uncertainty-aware evaluation of time-series classification for online handwriting recognition with domain shift. In: IJCAI-ECAI Workshop on Spatio-Temporal Reasoning and Learning (STRL) (Jul 2022)
11. Long, M., Cao, Y., Wang, L., Jordan, M.I.: Learning Transferable Features with Deep Adaptation Networks. In: International Conference on Machine Learning (ICML). vol. 37, pp. 97–105 (Jul 2015)
12. Long, M., Wang, J., Ding, G., Sun, J., Yu, P.S.: Transfer joint matching for unsupervised domain adaptation. In: International Conference on Computer Vision and Pattern Recognition (CVPR), pp. 1410–1417. Columbus, OH (Jun 2014). https://doi.org/10.1109/CVPR.2014.183
13. Long, M., Zhu, H., Wang, J., Jordan, M.I.: Deep transfer learning with joint adaptation networks. In: International Conference on Machine Learning (ICML). vol. 70, pp. 2208–2217 (Aug 2017)
14. NLTK: Natural Language Toolkit (Jul 2022). https://www.nltk.org/index.html#
15. Ott, F., Rügamer, D., Heublein, L., Bischl, B., Mutschler, C.: Cross-Modal Common Representation Learning with Triplet Loss Functions. In: arXiv preprint arXiv:2202.07901 (Feb 2022)

16. Ott, F., Rügamer, D., Heublein, L., Bischl, B., Mutschler, C.: Domain Adaptation for Time-Series Classification to Mitigate Covariate Shift. In: arXiv preprint arXiv:2204.03342 (Jul 2022)
17. Ott, F., Rügamer, D., Heublein, L., Bischl, B., Mutschler, C.: Joint classification and trajectory regression of online handwriting using a multi-task learning approach. In: Proceedings of the IEEE/CVF Winter Conference on Applications of Computer Vision (WACV), pp. 266–276. Waikoloa, HI (Jan 2022). https://doi.org/10.1109/WACV51458.2022.00131
18. Ott, F., et al.: Benchmarking Online Sequence-to-Sequence and Character-based Handwriting Recognition from IMU-Enhanced Pens. In: arXiv preprint arXiv:2202.07036 (Feb 2022)
19. Ott, F., Wehbi, M., Hamann, T., Barth, J., Eskofier, B., Mutschler, C.: The OnHW Dataset: online handwriting recognition from imu-enhanced ballpoint pens with machine learning. In: Proceedings of the ACM on Interactive, Mobile, Wearable and Ubiquitous Technologies (IMWUT). vol. 4(3), article 92. Cancún, Mexico (Sep 2020). https://doi.org/10.1145/3411842
20. Plamondon, R., Srihari, S.N.: On-line and off-line handwriting recognition: a comprehensive survey. In: Transactions on Pattern Analysis and Machine Intelligence (TPAMI). vol. 22(1), pp. 63–84 (Jan 2000). https://doi.org/10.1109/34.824821
21. Schroff, F., Kalenichenko, D., Philbin, J.: FaceNet: a unified embedding for face recognition and clustering. In: International Conference on Computer Vision and Pattern Recognition (CVPR). Boston, MA (Jun 2015). https://doi.org/10.1109/CVPR.2015.7298682
22. Semedo, D., Magalhães, J.: Adaptive temporal triplet-loss for cross-modal embedding learning. In: ACM International Conference on Multimedia (ACMMM), pp. 1152–1161 (Oct 2020). https://doi.org/10.1145/3394171.3413540
23. Sun, B., Feng, J., Saenko, K.: Correlation Alignment for Unsupervised Domain Adaptation. In: arXiv preprint arXiv:1612.01939 (Dec 2016)
24. Sun, B., Saenko, K.: Deep CORAL: correlation alignment for deep domain adaptation. In: European Conference on Computer Vision (ECCV). vol. 9915, pp. 443–450 (Nov 2016). https://doi.org/10.1007/978-3-319-49409-8_35
25. Tzeng, E., Hoffman, J., Zhang, N., Saenko, K., Darrell, T.: Deep Domain Confusion: Maximizing for Domain Invariance. In: arXiv preprint arXiv:1412.3474 (Dec 2014)
26. Wikimedia Foundation: Wikimedia Downloads (Jul 2022). https://dumps.wikimedia.org/
27. Zeng, D., Yu, Y., Oyama, K.: Deep triplet neural networks with cluster-CCA for audio-visual cross-modal retrieval. In: Transactions on Multimedia Computing, Communications, and Applications (TOMM). vol. 16(3), pp. 1–23 (Aug 2020). https://doi.org/10.1145/3387164

Active Learning Monitoring in Classroom Using Deep Learning Frameworks

Afsana Mou[✉], Mariofanna Milanova, and Mark Baillie

University of Arkansas at Little Rock, Little Rock, Arkansas, USA
{armou,mgmilanova,mtbaillie}@ualr.edu

Abstract. For both teachers and students studying science, technology, engineering, and mathematics (STEM), active learning is more likely to be productive because learners engage in a variety of classroom activities. As instructors are trying different pedagogies in the classroom, it is also important to check the effectiveness of those methods. Our work aims to identify the classroom activities with more accuracy which will help to measure the student involvement in the class. Using automatic audio classification, we can help to improve active learning strategies in the classroom, and it will be cost-effective too. Various deep learning techniques, such as deep neural networks, convolutional neural networks, and long short-term (LSTM) memories, are examined in this study for categorizing classroom audio. We test the models using recordings from our classroom for three different types of tasks labeled "single voice," "multiple voices," and "no voice." To train the model, the audio recording's generated Mel spectrogram is employed. We get the highest accuracy of 98% and an F1 score of .97 with the LSTM with 10-s frames.

Keywords: Active learning · Deep learning · Convolutional Neural network · Long short-term memory · Mel spectrograms

1 Introduction

Active learning pedagogies rather of the standard lecturing in the classroom can help STEM students learn and accomplish more. Active learning can assist students develop their critical thinking abilities and knowledge retention. Thus, numerous students will be drawn to study in the STEM fields. STEM faculty members must be knowledgeable with this method because it is new to this discipline. In order to quantify the success of active learning in the classroom and the advancement thereof, we need specific measurements [1, 2].

In Wang et al. [3], In order to categorize the three activities ("teacher lecturing," "whole class discussion," and "student group work") from classroom audio, the LENA system (Language Environment Analysis system) [9] is utilized. All three tasks are classified using the Random Forest classifier. Later, Owens et al. [4] created the Decibel Analysis for Research in Teaching (DART) program, that is built on machine learning and can evaluate classroom recordings without the aid of a trained eye. With the help

© Springer Nature Switzerland AG 2023
J.-J. Rousseau and B. Kapralos (Eds.): ICPR 2022 Workshops, LNCS 13643, pp. 384–393, 2023.
https://doi.org/10.1007/978-3-031-37660-3_27

of a group of binary decision trees, they attempt to gauge how much time is expended on "single voice" (such as lectures), "multiple voices" (such as pair discussions), and "no voice" (such as clicker question pondering) activities. They examined around 1486 recordings totaling 1720 h of audio and obtained 90% accuracy. A deep and recurrent neural network is employed afterward in Cosbey et al. [5] to improve the DART system. They obtained the frame error rates of 7.1% and 10.1%, correspondingly, for the teachers who had been seen before and those who had not. The instructor and student's participation in the classroom should also be noted. Siamese neural model was proposed by Li et al. [13] to distinguish between the teacher and student during classroom sessions. For extracting features from audio, they employ the log Mel-filter bank. To distinguish between classroom activities, they assessed the model on LSTM, gated recurrent unit (GRU), and attention mechanism. For the goal of detecting classroom activity, they used a different approach [14], utilizing a multimodal attention layer that makes use of an attention-based neural network.

For a 9-way classifier with 5-way and 4-way task generalizations, Slyman et al. [6] evaluate the efficacy of deep fully connected, convolutional, and recurrent neural network models. Their top model can complete the 4-way, 5-way, and 9-way classification tasks with frame-level error rates of 6.2%, 7.7%, and 28.0% when employing Mel-filterbank, OpenSmile, and self-supervised acoustic features. Convolutional neural networks have shown encouraging results for both audio and image classification, according to Hersey et al. [8]. On 5.24 million pieces of data, they analyze a number of models, including fully connected Deep Neural Networks (DNNs), Alex Net, VGG, Inception, and ResNet. Furthermore, Palanisamy et al. [10] suggested an audio classification that used an ensemble of ImageNet pre-trained DenseNet model and achieved an accuracy of 92.89% and 87.42% on the ESC-50 and UrbanSound8K datasets. Rather than employing a fixed frame, the LSTM architecture may record the audio's sequential nature. To better capture long-range feature patterns, a series of memory gates are used [11]. LSTM is employed later in Lezhenin et al. [12] for the classification of environmental sound. The UrbanSound8K dataset's characteristics were extracted using the Mel Spectrogram, and the model was examined using 5-fold cross-validation. In comparison to CNN, LSTM displayed good results. There are many different approaches extracting audio features, including time, frequency, cepstrum, time-frequency, etc. The power modulus of the signal spectrum can be used to obtain MFCCs (Mel Frequency Cepstral Coefficients). To gather additional data in the intermediate stage, the Short Time Fourier Transform or Spectrogram is helpful [7].

The rest of the paper is organized as follows: The methodology is presented in Sect. 2; the experimental setup is elaborated in Sect. 3; Sect. 4 is about the explanation of the experiments and the results are shown and discussed; in Sect. 5 we conclude the paper.

Our contributions are following.

- Create our own dataset with the recording of our two instructors and divided the audio into three classes.
- Evaluating the performance of our recorded classroom activities with two instructors and the extraction of audio features from the Mel spectrograms were compared in this study among Deep neural networks, 2D Convolutional Neural Networks, and the LSTM model.

– Evaluate the impact of different hyperparameters such as window size, hop length, and n_fft in the training processes of models.

2 Methodology

The challenge of categorizing images is where deep learning excels, and it has yielded ground-breaking results across a variety of fields. Deep learning is also showing promise in tasks involving the classification of audio, such as the classification of musical genres and environmental sounds. The paper's proposed pipeline is shown in Fig. 1.

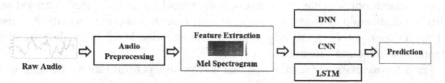

Fig. 1. Pipeline of the proposed method.

The following is a thorough description of the proposed work.

2.1 Mel Spectrogram

As we just stated, there are many ways to obtain features from the annotated audio data for the audio classification task, including Mel filter banks, MFCCs, and Mel Spectrograms. In this study, we employ the Mel spectrogram to extract audio components from recordings made in classrooms. Typically, one of two domains—time or frequency—can be used to define a sound. We can translate the sound from the time domain to the spectrum, also known as the frequency domain, with the aid of Fourier transformations. We mostly hear composite signals for sound. This signal can be divided into its component signals using the Fourier transform. We are unable to obtain the time-localized signal information using the usual Fast Fourier transform. However, by performing a Fast Fourier transform on a tiny fraction of the waveform, the Short-time Fourier transform (STFT) displays changing frequencies over time. STFT can be applied in windows or in small amounts to produce spectrograms. To depict the nonlinearity of human pitch, Mel spectrograms are useful. Normal frequency, f, is transformed to Mel scale, M(f), using the equation:

$$M(f) = 1125 \log\left(1 + \frac{f}{700}\right) \tag{1}$$

Here $M(f)$ denotes the frequencies on the Mel scale measured in Mels and f on the R.H.S denotes normal frequencies measured in Hz.

All the pitches in Mel Scale are equally spaced apart, just as a human ear would perceive them. 1000 mels in Mel scale correspond to 1000 Hz, which is 40 dB over the listener threshold.

2.2 Convolutional Neural Network

A particular subset of deep neural networks is the convolutional neural network (CNN). CNN has produced many state-of-the-art achievements for image recognition and classification tasks. For input into CNN, pixels are used as an array of width, height, and depth. It just transfers the weights from the previous layer to the next layer, rather than moving all the weights from one layer to another. CNN offers better weight management as a result. The Convolutional layer is the initial layer of the CNN architecture. Each layer of the CNN with pixel array extracts various features using a different filter or kernel, such as identification, edge detection, sharpen, box blur, gaussian blur, etc. By limiting the overlapping in the matrices, Stride also aids in the reduction of parameter size. When the kernel slides through the image, part of the information on the edge may not always be caught. In this process, padding can be useful. Additionally, it aids in maintaining image size. For zero padding, the formula is shown in Eq. 3. Down- sampling employs pooling. In most cases, max pooling reduces the image resolution by taking the highest value in a smaller region. Every node in the fully connected layer is connected to both the preceding and the following layer, much like in a standard neural network [16] [15] [19].

The equation for convolutional layer is,

$$f_l^k(\text{p}, \text{q}) = \sum_c \sum_{x,y} i_c(x, y).e_l^k(u, v) \tag{2}$$

Here, $i_c(x, y)$ represents the element of an input image, and $e_l^k(u, v)$ means the index of the element of the kernel. The Convolutional kernel operates by cutting the image into discrete portions, referred to as receptive fields. Extracting feature patterns from a picture is made easier by breaking it up into little pieces. By multiplying its components by the corresponding components of the receptive field, the kernel convolves with the pictures using a particular set of weights.

The equation for zero padding output, O is following:

$$O = 1 + \frac{N + 2P - F}{S} \tag{3}$$

Here, N for input size of image N x N, F for filter size of F x F, P for zero padding layer number, and S for stride. We can avoid network output size from decreasing with depth by using this padding concept.

2.3 Long Short-Term Memory

A unique class of neural networks called the recurrent neural network (RNN) performs incredibly well with sequential input. The primary distinction between RNN and conventional neural networks is how it provides feedback to the input layer to improve feature extraction. However, very long data sequences do not work well with RNNs. The gradient may disappear or explode, for example. To resolve these problems, LSTM can be helpful. An LSTM contains a memory cell that may retain information for a long time and whose input and output can also be controlled by gates [20, 21].

3   Experimental Setup

3.1   Dataset

For our experiment, we did not use any accessible or created data. We use our own classroom recording as the dataset. This dataset is not available to the public yet. The total recording time for the two instructors was 9 h. The software Audacity is free, open source, and simple to use for various operations for audio. It contains many features including recording, importing, exporting, and several editing tools (split, merge, and many more) for audio. Audacity is used to process the recordings, then divided into three classes. A single voice for lecturing by teachers, many voices for collaborative projects, and no voice for classroom assignments. The whole audio sample rate is 44,100 Hz.

3.2   Data Preprocessing

It will be challenging to distinguish the audio if there are many dead spots in it. The audio clips can all be visually similar. The dead space is first removed from the audio data by cleaning it using a signal envelope [25, 26]. The boundaries of a signal are represented by its envelopes, which are fictitious curves. Envelopes include some signal information, even though it is an imaginary curve [27]. The audio is trimmed to remove any section that is under 20 dB. All the audios have the same frame size of 60 s and later 10 s for computational simplicity. We use a training set of 9 h' worth of data and a test set of 3 h' worth of data.

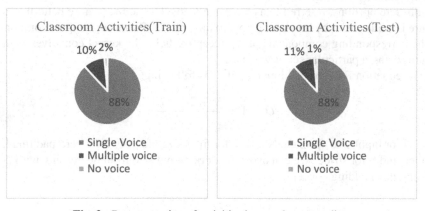

Fig. 2. Representation of activities in one class recording.

For real-time GPU audio feature extraction from Mel spectrograms, Keras Audio Preprocessors (Kapre) [24] are employed. Kapre can optimize signal parameters in real-time and deploying models becomes considerably easier and more reliable. Figure 2, shows the total distribution of instructor lecturing as a single voice, group discussion as multiple voices, and students doing some study as no voice.

4 Results

We ran two experiments utilizing the LSTM algorithm, DNN, 1D CNN, and 2D CNN with Python's TensorFlow framework to assess the classification of classroom activities. In the 2D CNN, we took into account four Max-pooling layers, five convolutional layers, and finally, the dense layer.

Table 1. Comparison of different model (Frame size 60s)

Model	Test 1				Test 2			
	Accuracy	Precision	Recall	F1	Accuracy	Precision	Recall	F1
DNN	0.83	0.81	0.81	0.81	0.81	0.81	0.81	0.81
1D CNN	0.81	0.91	0.73	0.81	0.86	0.86	0.81	0.83
2D CNN	0.97	0.98	0.97	0.97	0.95	0.97	0.97	0.97
LSTM	0.92	0.90	0.94	0.92	0.95	0.94	0.94	0.94

In LSTM, we employ the bidirectional unit and dense layer at the model's conclusion. Adam is employed as the optimizer in all three models. We used the following hyperparameters to extract the features from the Mel spectrograms: 128 Mels, n _fft of 512, window size of 400, 16 kHz sample rate, and hop length of 160. To create the Mel spectrograms, we combine STFT and the Hann window.

Table 2. Comparison of different model (Frame size 10s)

Model	Test 1				Test 2			
	Accuracy	Precision	Recall	F1	Accuracy	Precision	Recall	F1
DNN	0.81	0.81	0.80	0.81	0.79	0.80	0.80	0.79
1D CNN	0.93	0.91	0.93	0.93	0.92	0.92	0.90	0.93
2D CNN	0.96	0.98	0.97	0.97	0.95	0.96	0.94	0.95
LSTM	0.96	0.94	0.94	0.95	0.98	0.97	0.97	0.98

The outcomes of the two tests we ran for 60 s frame are displayed in Table 1. We obtain an accuracy of.83 and an F1 score of.81 for DNN. We obtain an accuracy of .86 and an F1 score of .83 for 1D CNN. The accuracy we obtained with the 2D CNN and f1 score of.97 was the greatest. The classification challenge has also yielded promising results for LSTM. It received an f1 score of.94 and an accuracy of.95. The outcomes of the two tests for 10 s frame we ran are displayed in Table 2. We obtain an accuracy of .81 and an F1 score of .81 for DNN. We obtain an accuracy of .93 and an F1 score of .93 for 1D CNN. The accuracy we obtained with the 2D CNN is 0.96 and an f1 score of.97. The accuracy we obtained with the LSTM is 0.98 and an f1 score of.98 was the greatest.

Table 3. Comparison on effect of different Hyperparameters.

Model				Test 1	Test 2
	W	H	n_fft	Accuracy	Accuracy
1DCNN	300	160	512	0.81	0.80
	350	180	256	0.86	0.85
	400	1024	2048	0.88	0.89
	300	160	512	0.96	0.97
2DCNN	350	180	256	0.92	0.94
	400	1024	2048	0.90	0.89
	300	160	512	0.95	0.98
LSTM	350	180	256	0.96	0.92
	400	1024	2048	0.92	0.81

The outcomes of the two tests we ran for different hyperparameters are displayed in Table 3. We considered 300, 350, and 400 as window length and 160, 180, and 1024 as hop length. We took the n_fft value of 512, 256, and 2048. We got the best result for identifying the accuracy with 300 as window length, 160 as hop length, and 512 as n_fft.

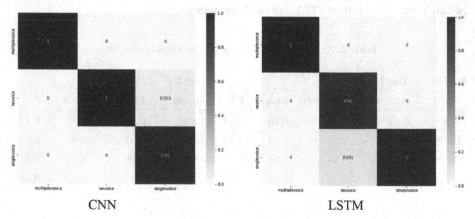

CNN   LSTM

Fig. 3. Confusion Matrix

We displayed the confusion matrices for the best performed 2D CNN and LSTM models in Fig. 3. It almost perfectly spotted the activities in 2D CNN. But occasionally, it seems to mistakenly identify no voice as a single voice. With LSTM, we see that it is challenging to find activities without a voice. Figure 4 shows a comparison of training and testing accuracy over a period of 10 epochs.

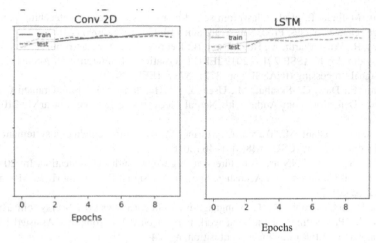

Fig. 4. Accuracy

5 Conclusion

The classification of classroom activities using Mel spectrograms is compared in this research amongst various deep learning frameworks. The extraction of the features from raw audio data is not very effective. The solution can be promising if the sound classification problem is handled as an image classification challenge, for example by transforming the problem into a Mel spectrogram. Using data from two experiments, we can see that a 2D convolutional neural network can classify classroom audio with 97% accuracy, which is a good finding. LSTM gives the best result of 98% accuracy for identifying classroom activities. By identifying the classroom activities properly, we can measure the participation of the student in the classroom which helps for active learning monitoring. In subsequent studies, the concatenation of many feature extraction techniques might be used in place of using only one separate feature. Pre-trained models can be used to learn features more effectively and quickly. This research can yet be improved by using more deep learning architectures or ensemble models.

Acknowledgment. This work was supported by the National Science Foundation under Award No. OIA-1946391(DART), and DCSTEM Seed Grant.

References.

1. Freeman, et al.: Active learning increases student performance in science, engineering, and mathematics. Proc. Nat. Acad. Sci. **111**(23), 8410–8415 (2014)
2. Olson, S., Gerardi, D.: Riordan Engage to excel: producing one million additional college graduates with degrees in science, technology, engineering, and mathematics. Report to the president. Executive Off. President (2012)
3. Wang, Z., Pan, X., Miller, K.F., Cortina, K.S.: Au- tomatic classification of activities in classroom discourse. Comput. Educ. **78**, 115–123 (2014)

4. Owens, Melinda T., et al.: Classroom sound can be used to classify teaching practices in college science courses. Proc. Nat. Acad. Sci. **114**(12), 3085–3090 (2017)
5. Cosbey, R., Wusterbarth, A., Hutchinson, B.: Deep learning for classroom activity detection from audio. In: ICASSP 2019- 2019 IEEE International Conference on Acoustics, Speech and Signal Processing (ICASSP), pp. 3727–3731. IEEE (2019)
6. Slyman, E., Daw, C., Skrabut, M., Usenko, A., Hutchinson, B.: Fine-Grained Classroom Activity Detection from Audio with Neural Networks. arXiv preprint arXiv:2107.14369 (2021)
7. Crocco, M., Cristani, M., Trucco, A., Murino, V.: Audio surveillance: a systematic review. ACM Comput. Surv. (CSUR) **48**(4), 1–46 (2016)
8. Hershey, S., et al.: CNN archi- tectures for large-scale audio classification. In: 2017 IEEE international Conference on Acoustics, Speech and Signal Processing (ICASSP), pp. 131–135. IEEE (2017)
9. Ganek, H., Eriks-Brophy, A.: The Language environment analysis (LENA) system: a literature review. In: Proceedings of the joint workshop on NLP for Computer Assisted Language Learning and NLP for Language Acquisition, pp. 24–32 (2016)
10. Palanisamy, K., Singhania, D., Angela Yao, A.: Rethinking CNN models for audio classification. arXiv preprint arXiv:2007.11154 (2020)
11. Dai, J., Liang, S., Xue, W., Ni, C., Liu, W.: Long short-term memory recurrent neural network based segment features for music genre classification. In: 2016 10th International Symposium on Chinese Spoken Language Processing (ISCSLP), pp. 1–5. IEEE (2016)
12. Lezhenin, I., Bogach, N., Pyshkin, E.: Urban sound classification using long short-term memory neural network. In: 2019 Federated Conference on Computer Science and Information Systems (FedCSIS), pp. 57–60. IEEE (2019)
13. Li, H., Wang, Z., Tang, J., Ding, W., Liu, Z.: Siamese neural networks for class activity detection. In: Bittencourt, I.I., Cukurova, M., Muldner, K., Luckin, R., Millán, E. (eds.) AIED 2020. LNCS (LNAI), vol. 12164, pp. 162–167. Springer, Cham (2020). https://doi.org/10.1007/978-3-030-52240-7_30
14. Li, H., et al.: Multimodal learning for classroom activity detection. In: ICASSP 2020- 2020 IEEE International Conference on Acoustics, Speech and Signal Processing (ICASSP), pp. 9234–9238. IEEE (2020)
15. Khan, A., Sohail, A., Zahoora, U., Qureshi, A.S.: A survey of the recent architectures of deep convolutional neural networks. Artif. Intell. Rev. **53**(8), 5455–5516 (2020). https://doi.org/10.1007/s10462-020-09825-6
16. Albawi, S., Mohammed, T.A., Al-Zawi, S.: Understanding of a convolutional neural network. In: 2017 International Conference on Engineering and Technology (ICET). IEEE (2017)
17. Ranjana Dangol Abeer Alsadoon P W C Prasad Indra Seher Omar Hisham Alsadoon 2020 Speech Emotion Recognition UsingConvolutional Neural Network and Long-Short TermMemory Multimedia Tools and Applications 79 43-44 32917 32934 https://doi.org/10.1007/s11042-020-09693-w
18. Ma, X., Yang, H., Chen, Q., Huang, D., Wang, Y.: Depaudionet: An efficient deep model for audio based depression classification. In: Proceedings of the 6th International Workshop on Audio/Visual Emotion Challenge, pp. 35–42 (2016)
19. Liu, R., Yang, X., Chong, X., Wei, L., Zeng, X.: Comparative study of convolutional neural network and conventional machine learning methods for landslide susceptibility mapping. Remote Sensing **14**(2), 321 (2022)
20. Sepp, H., Schmidhuber, J.: Long short-term memory. Neural Comput. **9**(8), 1735–1780 (1997)
21. Alex Graves 2012 Long short-term memory Alex Graves Eds Supervised sequence labelling with recurrent neural networks Springer Berlin Heidelberg Berlin, Heidelberg 37 45 https://doi.org/10.1007/978-3-642-24797-2_4

22. Stevens, Smith, S., Volkmann, J., Edwin Broomell Newman, E.B.: A scale for the measurement of the psychological magnitude pitch. J. Acoust. Soc. Am. **8**(3), 185–190 (1937)
23. Scarpiniti, M., Comminiello, D., Uncini, A., Lee. Y.-C.: Deep recurrent neural networks for audio classification in construction sites. In: 2020 28th European Signal Processing Conference (EUSIPCO), pp. 810–814. IEEE (2021)
24. Choi, K., Joo, D., Kim, J.: Kapre: On-gpu audio preprocessing layers for a quick implementation of deep neural network models with keras. arXiv preprint arXiv:1706.05781 (2017)
25. Choi, S., Jiang, Z.: Comparison of envelope extraction algorithms for cardiac sound signal segmentation. Expert Syst. Appl. **34**(2), 1056–1069 (2008)
26. Ru-Shan, W., Luo, J., Wu, B.: Seismic envelope inversion and modulation signal model. Geophysics **79**(3), WA13–WA24 (2014)
27. Yang, Y.: A signal theoretic approach for envelope analysis of real-valued signals. IEEE Access **5**, 5623–5630 (2017)

Pain Detection in Biophysiological Signals: Transfer Learning from Short-Term to Long-Term Stimuli Based on Signal Segmentation

Tobias B. Ricken[1]($\boxtimes$) (iD), Peter Bellmann[1], Steffen Walter[2] (iD),
and Friedhelm Schwenker[1] (iD)

[1] Institute of Neural Information Processing, Ulm University,
89081 James-Franck-Ring, Ulm, Germany
{tobias-1.ricken,peter.bellmann,friedhelm.schwenker}@uni-ulm.de
[2] Medical Psychology Group, University Clinic, Ulm, Germany
steffen.walter@uni-ulm.de

Abstract. In this study, we analyze the pain detection transfer learning task from short-term (*phasic*) training stimuli to long-term (*tonic*) test stimuli, based on the X-ITE Pain Database, which consists of recordings of both duration types. To this end, we divide the tonic samples into equally sized chunks of the same length as their phasic counterpart. In our specific case, a tonic sample is then represented by 14 chunks. We evaluate different approaches in which we train a Random Forest model in combination with the provided phasic samples and evaluate it on the created chunk-based representations of the tonic samples. Each strategy is compared to the naive approach in which the model is trained on the phasic stimuli and simply evaluated on the unmodified tonic samples. As the evaluation protocol, we apply the leave-one-subject-out cross-validation approach and measure the performance of each proposed chunk-based transfer learning approach based on accuracy. Our results show that most of our proposed chunk-based methods are able to outperform the naive approach.

Keywords: Transfer Learning · Pain Recognition · Physiological Signals · e-Health · X-ITE Pain Database

1 Introduction

Suffering from pain is always a subjective phenomenon [14], whereby the pain itself is a highly complex arousal [22]. To express the intensity of the perceived pain to a practitioner, in general, a self-report is the most qualified way [8], despite the existence of pain characteristics an expert is able to observe [5].

The work of Peter Bellmann and Friedhelm Schwenker is supported by the Project *Multimodal Recognition of Affect over the course of a tutorial learning experiment* funded by the German Research Foundation (DFG) under Grant SCHW623/7-1.

J.-J. Rousseau and B. Kapralos (Eds.): ICPR 2022 Workshops, LNCS 13643, pp. 394–404, 2023.
https://doi.org/10.1007/978-3-031-37660-3_28

However, a pain self-report is not always possible, for instance, if a patient is unconscious [5]. Furthermore, the observation of pain is a difficult task, even for an expert [5]. A human observer is not able to permanently observe a patient [22]. Moreover, the observer might be affected by different characteristics, such as the patient's attractiveness, which can lead to non-objective assessments of the patient's pain status [7]. In the field of automated pain recognition (APR), the aim is to build robust detection algorithms to address these problems [22,23]. Note that, in general, patients do not only suffer for short-time periods from pain, covering solely a duration of a few seconds, as it is the case in different pain databases. Therefore, in this work, we analyze the knowledge transfer from short-time pain periods to long episodes of pain, based on the physiological signals provided by the X-ITE Pain Database [6] in combination with Random Forests (RFs) [4].

2   Related Work

With the goal to improve classification accuracy in the area of APR, our research group performed many studies over the last years, e.g., [1,2,9,10,12,13,16,18]. For instance, in [17], Thiam et al. obtained outstanding results for the pain detection task in combination with the BioVid Heat Pain Database [21] by applying an end-to-end convolutional neural network for the feature extraction process. For the classification task of no pain vs. the highest pain intensity level in combination with the electrodermal activity signal, an accuracy value of 84.57% is achieved.

Initial results, based on the X-ITE Pain Database [6], are provided in [23], in combination with handcrafted features. In [20], Wally et al. present the first transfer learning task outcomes in combination with the X-ITE Pain Database (also based on handcrafted features), by training RF models and neural networks specific to phasic stimuli and evaluating the models based on tonic stimuli (see Sect. 3). Note that in [20], the authors apply 10-fold and 11-fold cross validation evaluations without any adaptation of the tonic stimuli. Generally, in APR scenarios, the leave-one-subject-out cross-validation is used.

In one of our previous studies, in [3], we analyzed a straightforward approach for the evaluation of tonic stimuli from the test set, given that the classification models are trained in combination with phasic stimuli. To this end, we proposed to simply divide the tonic stimuli into chunks of the same size as the phasic stimuli from the training set. Note that the setting in [3] was artificially generated and evaluated in combination with the BioVid Heat Pain Database [21], which consists of phasic stimuli only. In the current study, we will apply and extend the approach proposed in [3], by evaluating different settings for the aggregation of the chunks obtained from long-term periods.

Note that in [15], we presented baseline results specific to the X-ITE Pain Database, based on handcrafted features. More precisely, we analyzed a set of various feature extraction windows (FEWs), which differed in length and the starting time. The starting time of the FEWs was evaluated in combination with several shifts, in relation to the starting time of the corresponding stimuli.

3 Data Set Description and Feature Extraction

In this work, we analyze the X-ITE Pain Database [6], which was collected at Ulm University. In total, 134 healthy subjects – half male, half female – participated in strictly controlled heat and electric pain elicitation experiments. A personalized calibration phase was used to determine the participant's pain and tolerance levels. The pain level (PL) was defined as the temperature/current value at which the participant started to feel pain, whereas the tolerance level (TL) was defined as the temperature/current value at which the pain became unbearable. An additional pain level was defined as the mean value of PL and TL, for each of the pain sources (heat and electricity). The baseline, i.e. pain-free level, was defined as 32 $°C$. The heat stimuli were induced at the participant's forearm, whereas the electric stimuli were induced using two disposable Ag/AgCl electrodes which were attached at the participant's index finger and middle finger, respectively.

The experimenters defined two types of pain elicitation, i.e. phasic and tonic, based on the stimuli length. Phasic heat pain levels were held for four seconds and phasic electric pain levels were held for five seconds. Tonic stimuli were held for 60 s each. The participants were stimulated 30 times with each of the phasic pain levels, followed by a baseline stimulus with a random duration of 8–12 s. The tonic pain levels were applied once per participant, followed by a baseline stimulus of 300 s. The pain experiments were conducted in one single session.

The experimenters recorded different video, audio and physiological signals. In this study, we focus on the latter, which include electrocardiogram (ECG), electrodermal activity (EDA) and electromyogram (EMG). The signals ECG, EMG and EDA measure a person's heart activity, muscle activity and skin conductance, respectively. The EDA sensors were placed at the participant's ring finger and index finger. The EMG sensors were measuring the muscles zygomaticus major (cheek), corrugator supercilii (eyebrow) and trapezius (shoulder). For a complete description of the X-ITE Pain Database, we refer the reader to [6].

Based on our findings from [15], we use a shift of 3 s and 1 s for the phasic heat and phasic electric stimuli, respectively. The features are extracted from windows of length 4 s each. Moreover, each tonic sample is shifted in the same way as their phasic counterpart. With the application of the same shifts to the tonic samples, we make the first chunks as similar to the phasic stimuli as possible. Since each tonic stimulus has a length of 60 s, we split the tonic sequences into 14 chunks, also each with a length of 4 s, for heat and electric pain stimuli, respectively. The 15-th chunks at the end of each tonic stimulus are shorter than 4 s and therefore simply ignored.

We use the same filters and features as in our previous work [15], with the following minor modifications. In the current study, the filters are applied for each feature extraction window separately, instead of filtering the whole signal at once. Let the area covered between the lowest value and the signal itself be defined by the feature *area*. Moreover, let the feature *area_min_max* represent the area between the lowest and the highest value of the signal. Then, the ratio between these two features ($\frac{area\_min\_max}{area}$) is defined by the feature *areaR*. In this study, the feature *areaR* is computed for each physiological signal, resulting in 5 additional features. Moreover, in addition, the averaged heart rate and the averaged distance rate between the R-peaks within the specific time windows are computed from the ECG signal. In total, we extracted 412 features from each time window. We standardized each phasic feature set by computing the z-score over all phasic samples specific to each subject. We standardized the sliced tonic data sets by computing the z-score over all chunks specific to one tonic sample of one specific subject. In contrast to our previous work [15], we extracted separate baselines for both pain domains, heat and electro.

The domain-specific sample distribution is summarized in Table 1.

Table 1. Domain-specific class label distribution. Baseline: Pain-free stimuli. Tolerance: Pain tolerance level stimuli. P/T: Phasic/Tonic domain.

Label	Baseline (P)	Tolerance (P)	Baseline (T)	Tolerance (T)
Electro	3720	3719	123	123
Heat	3727	3716	121	124

4 Results

In this section, we will first present the experimental setup. Subsequently, we will provide domain-specific baseline results as well as initial transfer learning outcomes, followed by the results of four different chunk-based settings.

4.1 Experimental Setup

In each experiment, we focus on the binary classification task of no pain vs. the highest pain intensity level (pain tolerance), which we simply denote by no pain vs. pain. We use the combined feature vectors (412 features per sample) and apply the RF algorithm [4] with 100 decision trees as the classification model. We limit the maximum depth of each decision tree to 10 nodes. Moreover, each decision tree is constructed in combination with the Gini Index split criterion. This setup was also used in [15,23]. As the evaluation protocol, we apply the leave-one-subject-out cross-validation (LOSO-CV) in which the evaluation is performed on the data of the left out subject. The performance is measured by the mean accuracy value over all LOSO-CV evaluations for each task separately. The RF models are always trained on the phasic pain stimuli, separately for heat and electro pain stimuli, and evaluated on the chunk-based feature sets.

4.2 Domain-Specific Baseline Results and Naive Approach

First, we provide the results in which a model is trained on phasic (tonic) pain stimuli and evaluated on samples from the same pain domain, each in combination with heat and electro pain. In addition, as a reference value for the pain pain duration transfer learning task, we evaluate the naive approach in which we use the phasic pain stimuli to train a RF model and evaluate it on the complete tonic sequences without any modifications. The results are presented in Table 2.

Table 2. Reference values and naive approach results (mean LOSO-CV accuracy and standard deviation in %). Ref.: Reference value. Naive Transfer: Training on phasic data and testing on tonic data without modification.

Domain	Phasic Ref.	Tonic Ref.	Naive Transfer
Electro	95.4 ± 6.1	93.6 ± 17.9	56.4 ± 38.5
Heat	85.9 ± 13.8	86.0 ± 28.7	58.4 ± 33.3

4.3 Decision Average-Based Chunk Approach

In the first non-naive experiments, we use the first n chunks ($n \in \{1, \ldots, 14\}$ is fixed for each LOSO-CV) of a tonic sample to classify a tonic stimulus. The classification model determines the class membership scores for each of the chunks. Therefore, n two-dimensional decision vectors are obtained from each tonic test sample (one score for class *no pain*, one score for class *pain*). The mean value is then computed over the obtained vectors and the class with the highest score is taken as the final output for the corresponding tonic sample.

The results for the decision average approach are depicted in Fig. 1. The highest mean accuracy value of 68.8% for this approach in combination with electro pain stimuli is obtained with the first chunk. For the heat pain domain, the highest mean accuracy value of 60.0% is obtained with the first 10 chunks.

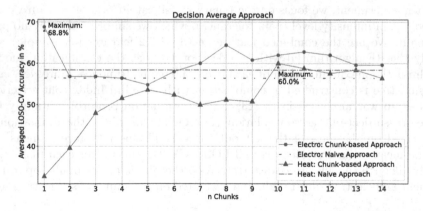

Fig. 1. Decision average approach (mean LOSO-CV accuracy in %). Each tonic test sample is represented by 14 equally sized chunks. The classification of each tonic stimulus is obtained from the averaged decision vector of the first n chunks.

4.4   Feature Average-Based Chunk Approach

Another way to accomplish the transfer learning task from the phasic to the tonic pain domains is to create a feature average chunk representation, based on the first n chunks of a tonic sample. The newly created feature vector represents the corresponding tonic stimulus, which can be then directly classified by the classification model. The resulting label is then taken as the prediction for the corresponding tonic sample.

The results of the feature average approach are depicted in Fig. 2. For the electro pain domain, the highest mean accuracy value of 68.8% is achieved for the first chunk (in which no feature average is computed). The highest mean accuracy value of 53.2% for the heat pain domain is obtained in combination with the first four chunks of a tonic sample.

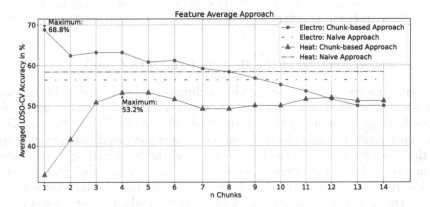

Fig. 2. Feature average approach (mean LOSO-CV accuracy in %). Each tonic test sample is represented by 14 equally sized chunks. The classification of each tonic stimulus is based on the averaged feature vector of the first n chunks.

4.5   Evaluation of Individual Chunks

In addition, we conducted further experiments in which only the k-th chunk is used to classify a tonic sample. The results of this evaluation are depicted in Fig. 3. The outcomes of the individual chunks show that the highest mean accuracy value of 68.8% in combination with electro pain stimuli is achieved when only the first chunk of the tonic samples is used. For the heat pain domain, the highest mean accuracy value of 66.0% is obtained with the third chunk of the tonic samples. Based on these outcomes, we can conclude that a tonic electro sample is best represented by its first chunk, whereas a tonic heat sample is best represented by its third chunk.

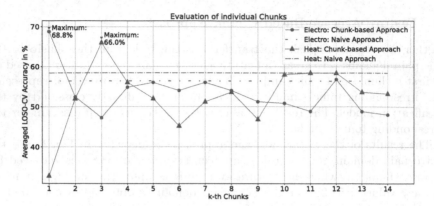

Fig. 3. Evaluation of individual chunks (mean LOSO-CV accuracy in %).
Each tonic test sample is represented by 14 equally sized chunks. Only the k-th chunk
is used for prediction. The obtained label is assigned to the corresponding tonic sample.

4.6   Decision Average of the Best and the k-th Chunk

Following the evaluation of the individual chunks, we conducted additional decision average-based experiments in which we used the best chunk of each domain
in combination with one of the remaining chunks to classify a tonic sample. In
this experiment, the mean value is computed over the two decision vectors (one
for the best chunk, one for the k-th chunk) and the label leading to the highest
mean score is taken as the prediction for the corresponding tonic pain stimulus.

The results are depicted in Fig. 4. For the electro pain domain, the combination of the first and the eighth chunk reached the highest mean accuracy value
of 69.2%. The highest mean accuracy value of 67.6% for the heat pain duration
transfer learning task is achieved with the third chunk in combination with the
eleventh chunk.

The best outcomes for each of the approaches are summarized in Table 3.
Note that the standard deviation values in Table 3 are omitted due to the lack
of space.

Table 3. Results summary (best mean LOSO-CV accuracy in %). Ref.: Training and testing on tonic data. Naive: Training on phasic data and testing on tonic data
without modification. Decision/Feature Average: The numbers in brackets denote the
number of (the first n) chunks leading to the best result. Individual Chunks: Only one
chunk per tonic test sample is used for classification (best chunk).

Domain	Ref.	Naive	Decision Ave	Feature Ave	Ind. Chunks	Best & k-th Chunk
Electro	93.6	56.4	68.8 (1)	68.8 (1)	68.8 (1st)	69.2 (1st & 8th)
Heat	86.0	58.4	60.0 (10)	53.2 (4)	66.0 (3rd)	67.6 (3rd & 11th)

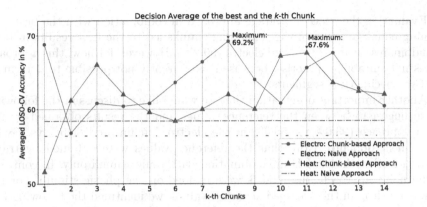

Fig. 4. Decision average of the best and the k-th chunk (mean LOSO-CV accuracy in %). The classification of each tonic stimulus is obtained from the averaged decision vector of the best and the k-th chunk. The first and the third chunks are applied as the best chunks, for the electro and the heat pain domain, respectively (see Fig. 3).

5 Discussion and Future Work

Based on the electro pain domain, for the decision average and feature average approaches, the best results were obtained by focusing solely on the first chunk of the tonic stimuli. Note that in the evaluation of individual chunks, the first chunk was identified as the best performing one, specific to the electro pain domain. Using only the first chunk for the classification of the tonic stimuli improved the mean accuracy value to 68.8% in comparison to the 56.4% arising from the naive approach (see Table 3). From this observation, we can conclude that the first chunk of a long-term electro stimulus constitutes the best representation of a short-term electro stimulus. This confirms the fact that, in contrast to thermal stimuli, the human body reacts immediately to the beginning and ending of electrically induced pain, which was already discussed in [15,23].

Based on the heat pain domain, for the decision average approach, the best result was obtained by averaging over the first ten chunks (see Table 3). The mean accuracy value improved to 60.0% in comparison to the 58.4% arising from the naive approach. No improvement was observed in combination with the feature average approach. The corresponding highest mean accuracy value of 53.2% is outperformed by the naive approach (58.4%). The third chunk was identified as the best individual chunk of a tonic heat stimulus, leading to a mean accuracy of 66.0%. From the observed outcomes, we can conclude that, in contrast to electrical stimuli, there is a delay in the human body's reactions to the beginning of thermally induced pain, which was also confirmed, for instance, in [19]. Moreover, this observation is also confirmed in [15].

Evaluating the decision average approach in combination with the best performing chunk and one of the remaining chunks led to the best results in both pain domains, heat (67.6%) and electro (69.2%). However, for now, this approach seems not suitable in practise, because it is currently not possible to determine the two specific time segments.

Another important observation that we would like to discuss in the following is the huge gap between the reference values and the results obtained by the naive approach (93.6% vs. 56.4% in the electro domain, and 86.0% vs. 58.4% in the heat domain). Note that the reference values were obtained by training and testing the models in combination with tonic stimuli only. In contrast, in the naive approach, the models were trained on the phasic stimuli. For the significant drop in the averaged accuracy values, we identified the following two main reasons. Firstly, the phasic and tonic pain levels were calibrated separately, leading to different individual temperature and current values. Stimulating with unequal thermal and electrical levels can obviously lead to different physiological reactions. Secondly, in contrast to the phasic pain domain, a human body is expected to adapt to continuous pain stimuli, also leading to different physiological reactions over time, as already discussed in one of our previous studies [3].

As a follow-up study, we are currently evaluating the pain duration transfer task, as well as the transfer between the two pain sources (thermal and electrical) in combination with different transfer learning approaches. Another alternative is the application of deep domain adaptation models, as for instance in [11].

References

1. Bellmann, P., Lausser, L., Kestler, H.A., Schwenker, F.: Introducing bidirectional ordinal classifier cascades based on a pain intensity recognition scenario. In: Del Bimbo, A., Cucchiara, R., Sclaroff, S., Farinella, G.M., Mei, T., Bertini, M., Escalante, H.J., Vezzani, R. (eds.) ICPR 2021. LNCS, vol. 12666, pp. 773–787. Springer, Cham (2021). https://doi.org/10.1007/978-3-030-68780-9_58
2. Bellmann, P., Thiam, P., Schwenker, F.: Using a quartile-based data transformation for pain intensity classification based on the senseEmotion database. In: 2019 8th International Conference on Affective Computing and Intelligent Interaction Workshops and Demos (ACIIW), pp. 310–316. IEEE (2019)
3. Bellmann, P., Thiam, P., Schwenker, F.: Pain intensity recognition - an analysis of short-time sequences in a real-world scenario. In: Schilling, F.-P., Stadelmann, T. (eds.) ANNPR 2020. LNCS (LNAI), vol. 12294, pp. 149–161. Springer, Cham (2020). https://doi.org/10.1007/978-3-030-58309-5_12
4. Breiman, L.: Random forests. Mach. Learn. **45**(1), 5–32 (2001)
5. Craig, K.D.: The facial expression of pain better than a thousand words? APS J. **1**(3), 153–162 (1992)
6. Gruss, S., et al.: Multi-modal signals for analyzing pain responses to thermal and electrical stimuli. JoVE (Journal of Visualized Experiments) (146), e59057 (2019)
7. Hadjistavropoulos, H.D., Ross, M.A., Von Baeyer, C.L.: Are physicians ratings of pain affected by patients physical attractiveness? Soc. Sci. Med. **31**(1), 69–72 (1990)

8. Herr, K., Coyne, P.J., McCaffery, M., Manworren, R., Merkel, S.: Pain assessment in the patient unable to self-report: position statement with clinical practice recommendations. Pain Manag. Nurs. **12**(4), 230–250 (2011)
9. Kächele, M., Amirian, M., Thiam, P., Werner, P., Walter, S., Palm, G., Schwenker, F.: Adaptive confidence learning for the personalization of pain intensity estimation systems. Evolving Syst. **8**(1), 71–83 (2017)
10. Kächele, M., Thiam, P., Amirian, M., Schwenker, F., Palm, G.: Methods for person-centered continuous pain intensity assessment from bio-physiological channels. IEEE J. Sel. Top. Sig. Process. **10**(5), 854–864 (2016)
11. Kalischek, N., Thiam, P., Bellmann, P., Schwenker, F.: Deep domain adaptation for facial expression analysis. In: ACII Workshops, pp. 317–323. IEEE (2019)
12. Kessler, V., Thiam, P., Amirian, M., Schwenker, F.: Pain recognition with camera photoplethysmography. In: 2017 Seventh International Conference on Image Processing Theory, Tools and Applications (IPTA), pp. 1–5. IEEE (2017)
13. Mamontov, D., Polonskaia, I., Skorokhod, A., Semenkin, E., Kessler, V., Schwenker, F.: Evolutionary algorithms for the design of neural network classifiers for the classification of pain intensity. In: Schwenker, F., Scherer, S. (eds.) MPRSS 2018. LNCS (LNAI), vol. 11377, pp. 84–100. Springer, Cham (2019). https://doi. org/10.1007/978-3-030-20984-1_8
14. Merskey, H., et al.: Editorial: The need of a taxonomy. Pain **6**(3), 247–252 (1979)
15. Ricken, T., Steinert, A., Bellmann, P., Walter, S., Schwenker, F.: Feature extraction: a time window analysis based on the X-ITE pain database. In: Schilling, F.-P., Stadelmann, T. (eds.) ANNPR 2020. LNCS (LNAI), vol. 12294, pp. 138–148. Springer, Cham (2020). https://doi.org/10.1007/978-3-030-58309-5_11
16. Sellner, J., Thiam, P., Schwenker, F.: Visualizing facial expression features of pain and emotion data. In: Schwenker, F., Scherer, S. (eds.) MPRSS 2018. LNCS (LNAI), vol. 11377, pp. 101–115. Springer, Cham (2019). https://doi.org/10.1007/ 978-3-030-20984-1_9
17. Thiam, P., Bellmann, P., Kestler, H.A., Schwenker, F.: Exploring deep physiological models for nociceptive pain recognition. Sensors **19**(20), 4503 (2019)
18. Thiam, P., Hihn, H., Braun, D.A., Kestler, H.A., Schwenker, F.: Multi-modal pain intensity assessment based on physiological signals: a deep learning perspective. Front. Physiol. **12**, 720464 (2021)
19. Thiam, P., et al.: Multi-modal pain intensity recognition based on the senseEmotion database. IEEE Trans. Affect. Comput. **12**(3), 743–760 (2021)
20. Wally, Y., Samaha, Y., Yasser, Z., Walter, S., Schwenker, F.: Personalized k-fold cross-validation analysis with transfer from phasic to tonic pain recognition on X-ITE pain database. In: Del Bimbo, A. (ed.) ICPR 2021. LNCS, vol. 12666, pp. 788–802. Springer, Cham (2021). https://doi.org/10.1007/978-3-030-68780-9_59
21. Walter, S., et al.: The biovid heat pain database data for the advancement and systematic validation of an automated pain recognition system. In: 2013 IEEE International Conference on Cybernetics (CYBCO), pp. 128–131. IEEE (2013)
22. Werner, P., Lopez-Martinez, D., Walter, S., Al-Hamadi, A., Gruss, S., Picard, R.: Automatic recognition methods supporting pain assessment: a survey. IEEE Trans. Affect. Comput. **13**(1), 1–1 (2019)

23. Werner, P., Al-Hamadi, A., Gruss, S., Walter, S.: Twofold-multimodal pain recognition with the X-ITE pain database. In: 8th International Conference on Affective Computing and Intelligent Interaction Workshops and Demos, ACII Workshops 2019, Cambridge, United Kingdom, 3–6 September 2019, pp. 290–296. IEEE (2019). https://doi.org/10.1109/ACIIW.2019.8925061

Leveraging Sentiment Analysis Knowledge to Solve Emotion Detection Tasks

Maude Nguyen-The[1], Soufiane Lamghari[1(✉)], Guillaume-Alexandre Bilodeau[1], and Jan Rockemann[2]

[1] LITIV Lab., Polytechnique Montréal, Montréal, Canada
{maude.nguyen-the,soufiane.lamghari,gabilodeau}@polymtl.ca
[2] Airudi, Québec, Canada
jan.rockemann@airudi.com

Abstract. Identifying and understanding underlying sentiments or emotions in text is a key component of multiple natural language processing applications. While simple polarity sentiment analysis is a well-studied subject, fewer advances have been made in identifying more complex, finer-grained emotions using only textual data. In this paper, we present a Transformer-based model with a Fusion of Adapter layers that leverages knowledge from more simple sentiment analysis tasks to improve the emotion detection task on large scale datasets, such as CMU-MOSEI, using the textual modality only. Results show that our proposed method is competitive with other approaches. Experiments on the CMU-MOSEI, Emotions and GoEmotions datasets show that the knowledge from the sentiment analysis task can indeed be leveraged for emotion recognition.

Keywords: Emotion recognition · Transformer language models · Fusion models

1 Introduction

Sentiment analysis is a subject that has long interested multiple researchers in the natural language understanding domain. This task aims to identify sentiment polarity (positive, negative, and neutral) for a given signal, which can be of the audio, visual or textual modality. Emotion recognition is a related task which consists of assigning more fine-grained labels, such as anger, joy, sadness, etc.

This work is in the context of a textual chatbot, where the chatbot is an empathetic dialogue agent that should assess the mental state of a user. Therefore, we focus on analyzing textual inputs. The ability to recognize the emotion behind a given sentence or paragraph is essential for this application. While sentiment analysis in the form of assigning polarities to text data is a task that is often studied and for which adequate results have already been obtained for multiple datasets, identifying finer-grained labels such as specific emotions is still a challenge. In

© Springer Nature Switzerland AG 2023
J.-J. Rousseau and B. Kapralos (Eds.): ICPR 2022 Workshops, LNCS 13643, pp. 405–416, 2023.
https://doi.org/10.1007/978-3-031-37660-3_29

addition to the task complexity, in most datasets available for this task, some emotions are much less represented than others, making the training data unbalanced. To address this issue, the model proposed in this work combines knowledge from less complex tasks and is trained using methods to counteract class imbalance. It is a Transformer-based model with a Fusion of Adapter layers to leverage knowledge from the more simple sentiment analysis task.

The results obtained are competitive with state-of-the-art multi-modal models on the CMU-MOSEI dataset [1], while only utilizing the textual modality. Experiments on the CMU-MOSEI, Emotions [2] and GoEmotions [3] datasets show that the knowledge from the sentiment analysis task can indeed be leveraged for emotion recognition. Our main contribution can be formulated as:

- We designed a method that capitalizes on both pretrained Transformer language models and knowledge from complementary tasks to improve on the emotion recognition task, whilst using Adapter layers, that require less training parameters than the conventional fine-tuning approach, and taking into account class imbalance.

2   Prior Works and Background

There are multiple approaches that have been used to solve text-based sentiment analysis and emotion detection tasks, namely rule-based and machine learning approaches. Rule-based approaches consist of creating grammatical and logical rules to assign emotions and use lexicons to assign emotions or polarities to words [4,5]. These methods are limited by the size and contents of the lexicon used and by the ambiguity of some keywords.

Most recent methods are based on the machine learning approach where a network is trained to learn the relationships between words and emotions. Methods such as those proposed by [6,7] use recurrent neural networks to solve sentiment analysis tasks to break down sentences and understand the relationship between the succession of words and sentiments or emotions. Since the release of pretrained models, recent works have been focused on fine-tuning transformer models [8,9], which have consistently outperformed previous methods thanks to the multi-head attention applied on words. To improve previous textual emotion recognition methods, we believe that in addition to transfer learning, multi-task learning and class imbalance should be considered.

2.1   Transfer Learning

Transfer learning is a method where the weights of a model trained on a task are used as a starting point to train a model for another task. The use of transfer learning with pretrained models has been, for the past few years, the way to obtain state-of-the-art results for multiple natural language understanding (NLU) tasks. Transformer-based pretrained models such as BERT [10], RoBERTa [11], XLNet [12], etc. have been dominating the field over previously used methods.

2.2 Multi-task Learning

Multi-task learning is used to train one model to solve multiple tasks instead of fine-tuning separate models. Multiple approaches have been used to solve multi-task learning problems. Liu et al. [13] proposed a Multi-Task Deep Neural Network (MT-DNN) with a shared transformer encoder and task-specific heads. Knowledge distillation was also introduced by [14,15] to improve the performances of the MT-DNN. These approaches allow the model to learn a shared representation between all tasks. Houlsby et al. [16] introduced a new model architecture using task-specific adapter layers and keeping the weights of the pretrained encoder frozen. This method, while preventing task interference and catastrophic forgetting, does not allow to transfer knowledge between tasks. To counter this weakness, AdapterFusion, a way to combine knowledge from multiple adapters, was proposed in [17].

2.3 Class Imbalance

Class imbalance is a challenge in resolving many artificial intelligence tasks. It occurs when one or multiple classes make up significantly less samples of the data than the majority class or classes, often leading to a poor predictive performance for those minority classes. Classic approaches to this problem include re-sampling minority class samples or weighting the loss function according to class frequency. In the field of computer vision, a modified version of the cross-entropy loss called the focal loss was proposed to handle imbalance [18].

3 Proposed Approach

To improve over previous methods, we have based our method on transfer learning, multi-task learning and we specifically considered class imbalance. To capitalize on transfer learning, our method is based on a strong language model, BERT [10]. Our intuition is that identifying emotion requires a good overall understanding of a language, as captured by BERT. The language understanding capability of a model can be evaluated using the GLUE benchmark [19] and BERT obtains very good results [10]. We will see later that our intuition is confirmed for sentiment analysis in Table 7, where the performance in detecting sentiment follows the language understanding capability of a model. Since sentiment analysis and emotion detection are closely related, we propose a model that learns to combine knowledge from multiple tasks of that nature. This allows leveraging datasets that are annotated only with sentiment for the emotion detection task. Finally, our model is designed to consider class imbalance. Our method is described in detail in the following.

3.1 Model

The proposed model is based on the pretrained Transformer encoder BERT [10] and of a fusion of separately trained Adapter layers. The overall architecture of the model can be seen in Fig. 1. We chose the BERT encoder (base size), which consists of a stack of twelve encoder layers, preceded by token, sentence and position embeddings. Following the encoder, the last hidden state corresponding to the special classification token ([CLS]) is fed to a classification head formed by two feed forward layers.

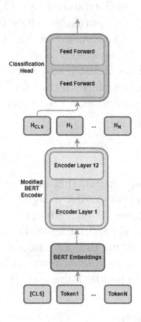

Fig. 1. Architecture of the proposed model.

Adapter layers are inserted in each of the encoder layers and are trained to adapt the encoder pretrained knowledge to a specific task, while the weights of the encoder are kept frozen (see Fig. 2). In this work, each adapter layer trained for a specific task has the same structure, which is the one found to be the best across multiple diverse tasks in [17]. They are composed of a feed forward layer that projects the encoder hidden state to a lower dimension, a nonlinear function and a feed forward layer that projects it back up to the original hidden size. It was also found in [17] that a reduction factor of 16 for the projection down layer adds a reasonable number of parameters per task whilst still achieving good results. All adapters were therefore trained using this reduction factor.

There are as many adapter layers as there are tasks. Figure 2 illustrates that there are several adapter layers that are used in parallel in our model. To combine the knowledge of each adapter, the AdapterFusion method and architecture is used [17]. This method consists of learning a composition of the knowledge of different trained adapters. In this stage of the learning, the weights of the pretrained encoder and of all single adapters are frozen, while the classification and fusion layers are trained. The architecture of the fusion layers is also presented in Fig. 2.

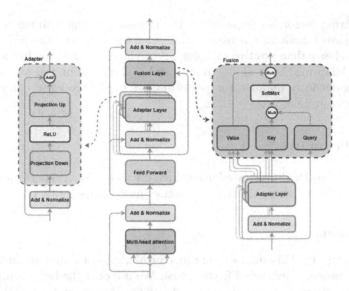

Fig. 2. Modified encoder layer proposed in our method (middle), as defined in [17]. On the left, architecture of an adapter layer. On the right, architecture of a fusion layer.

These layers are similar to attention layers used in Transformer models [20]. They are composed of Query, Key and Value matrices. The output of the feed forward layer of the base encoder is used as the query vector, whereas the outputs of each adapter are used as key and value vectors. A dot product is computed between the query and all the keys, then the result is passed through a SoftMax layer. The output of that layer is then multiplied to the values to weight the knowledge of each adapter.

3.2   Loss Function

The loss function used to counter the imbalance present in emotion detection datasets is a modified version of the classic Binary Cross-Entropy (BCE) Loss used for multi-label classification and can be defined as follows:

$$L = \sum_{n=1}^{N} \sum_{c=1}^{C} -w_c [y_{n,c} \log(\sigma(x_{n,c})) + \\ (1 - y_{n,c}) \log(1 - \sigma(x_{n,c}))] \tag{1}$$

where N is the number of samples in the batch, C is the number of classes, $x_{n,c}$ is the output of the classification layer of the model for class c of sample n, and w_c is the positive answer weighting factor for class c defined as:

$$w_c = \frac{\# \text{ of negative samples of class } c}{\# \text{ of positive samples of class } c}$$

This weighting factor is computed on the statistics of the training set data. It weighs the loss function to increase recall when the data contains more negative samples of class c than positive samples, and to increase precision in the opposite situation. Adapting the focal loss to multi-label classification was also tested but did not significantly improve the performances of the model in comparison to using the classic BCE loss.

4   Experiments

Our proposed method was tested using Five datasets. We also performed several ablation studies to assess the contribution of each component.

4.1   Datasets

CMU-MOSEI [1]: This dataset contains visual, acoustic and textual features for 23,500 sentences extracted from videos. We use only the textual inputs. It is labeled for sentiments on a scale of -3 to 3 and for Ekman emotions [21] on a scale of 0 to 3. For binary sentiment classification, the labels are binarized to negative and non-negative. The emotions are discretized to non-present (label equal to 0) or present (label greater than 0). For performance evaluation, standard binary accuracy (A), F1 scores (F1) for each emotion, and the Macro-F1 score are used.
GoEmotions [3] and Emotion [2]: GoEmotions contains 58K textual Reddit comments in English. It includes both sentiment and emotion annotations. The Emotion dataset is composed of English tweets annotated with emotions. For both datasets, performances are evaluated the same way as CMU-MOSEI.
SST-2 [22] and IMDB [23]: SST-2 contains over 60K sentences extracted from movie reviews. IMDB contains 50K movie reviews. Both are labeled for sentiment analysis in a 2-class split (positive or negative). The models performance on these datasets is measured with the same binary accuracy scores as CMU-MOSEI.

4.2   Experimental Setup

All experiments use BERT$_{base}$ (cased) [10] as the pretrained model, which has 12 encoder layers and a hidden size of 768. Adapter and AdapterFusion layers are added to each of those encoder layers. The classification heads are composed of two fully connected linear layers with sizes equal to the hidden size of the transformer layer (768) and the number of labels (6) respectively, and with $tanh$ activation functions. The input of the first linear layer is the last hidden state of the BERT model corresponding to the classification token ([CLS]) at the beginning of the input sequence. All models were trained using AdamW [24] with a linear rate scheduler, a learning rate of 1e-5, and a weight decay of 1e-2. All models were trained for 10 epochs with early stopping after 3 epochs if the validation metric did not improve. The Adapter-Transformers library [25] was used to incorporate the Adapter and AdapterFusion layers to the model. The results presented in the following section are averaged over 3 runs.

Table 1. Accuracy and F1 scores on CMU-MOSEI for emotion detection. † Accuracy scores obtained from [26]. ⋄ F1 scores computed using the two provided model checkpoints, as the ones presented in the original paper were weighted F1 scores.

Model	Joy		Sadness		Anger		Surprise		Disgust		Fear		Overall	
	A	F1	A	F1	A	F1	A	F1	A	F1	A	F1	A	Macro-F1
TBJE † ⋄	66.0	**71.7**	**73.9**	17.8	**81.9**	17.3	**90.6**	3.5	**86.5**	45.3	**89.2**	0.0	**81.5**	25.9
BERT	66.3	69.0	69.4	42.8	74.2	44.3	85.8	21.9	83.1	**53.1**	83.8	18.7	77.1	41.6
Adapter	67.3	69.4	66.3	**46.1**	70.4	**48.5**	73.4	26.5	77.3	52.3	70.9	**22.7**	70.9	**44.3**
Fusion₃	**67.5**	70.5	66.5	44.4	72.5	47.3	81.4	25.9	79.0	52.9	81.1	21.1	74.7	43.7
Fusion₅	**67.5**	70.7	69.1	44.6	73.1	47.5	81.3	**26.6**	79.9	53.0	82.2	20.3	75.5	43.8

Several types of fusion models were trained. For CMU-MOSEI: one using a fusion of only CMU-MOSEI tasks (Fusion₃: binary sentiment, 7-class sentiment and emotion classification) and one using additional knowledge from the SST-2 and IMDB sentiment analysis tasks (Fusion₅). For GoEmotions: the two GoEmotions tasks are considered, including 4-class sentiment and emotion classification (Fusion₂). The other fusion model integrates additional knowledge from the emotion detection task of the Emotion dataset (Fusion₃). For Emotion: we considered two fusion variants, a pseudo fusion (Fusion₁) based solely on the adapter trained on the same task, and a knowledge augmented model fusing sentiments and emotions from the GoEmotions dataset (Fusion₃).

4.3 Results

The results for the emotion detection task of CMU-MOSEI are presented in Table 1. The performance of the proposed model is compared to that of a fine-tuned BERT model (BERT) and of a BERT-based model using a single task specific adapter (Adapter), both using the same classification head as our proposed model. The results of the current state-of-the art model (TBJE) for this dataset [26] are also presented. Note that this state-of-the-art model is a Transformer-based model that utilizes both textual and audio modalities. All models trained with our proposed loss function achieve better F1 scores than the current state-of-the-art. While a fully fine-tuned BERT model achieves better overall accuracy, the proposed Fusion model is the one that has best accuracy/F1-score trade-off for all emotions. As observed in Table 2, given that all distributions of emotions, except for *joy*, are heavily imbalanced, accuracy is not an appropriate metric for this dataset as it does not fully represent the model ability to identify each emotion. Therefore, it is better to use the F1-score as a measurement basis. Having a high accuracy score is good only if the F1-score is also high. Single Adapter models are able to achieve good F1 scores, but do not reach comparable accuracy scores to Fusion models. Since adapter models achieve both high accuracy and F1-score, it further demonstrates that combining knowledge from multiple tasks improves the model performance. Capitalizing on knowledge from additional sentiment analysis tasks outside of the CMU-MOSEI dataset also allows

Table 2. Positive samples per class for CMU-MOSEI

	Joy	Sadness	Anger	Surprise	Disgust	Fear
Positive samples proportion	52%	25%	21%	10%	17%	8%

the Fusion$_5$ model to perform slightly better than the Fusion$_3$ model, which only includes knowledge from the CMU-MOSEI tasks.

Table 3. Accuracy and F1 scores on GoEmotions dataset for emotion detection.

Model	Joy		Sadness		Anger		Surprise		Disgust		Fear		Neutral		Overall	
	A	F1	A	F1	A	F1	A	F1	A	F1	A	F1	A	F1	A	Macro-F1
BERT	86.7	**82.8**	95.0	60.3	88.9	**52.8**	90.4	57.2	97.9	21.2	**98.9**	67.0	78.3	61.4	90.9	57.5
VAD [27]	–	–	–	–	–	–	–	–	–	–	–	–	–	–	65.7	**61.1**
Adapter	86.0	81.6	94.8	57.2	89.0	50.0	89.7	51.2	98.0	38.9	98.8	63.4	77.9	63.8	90.6	58.0
Fusion$_2$	86.5	81.9	**95.1**	57.5	**89.2**	50.0	90.0	56.1	**98.1**	44.2	**98.9**	68.7	78.6	**66.3**	90.9	60.7
Fusion$_3$	**86.8**	**82.8**	95.0	57.9	89.1	50.0	**90.5**	60.3	**98.1**	43.0	**98.9**	68.0	**78.9**	65.4	**91.1**	**61.1**

We also tested our method on the GoEmotions dataset. Results are reported in Table 3. In addition to a fine-tuned BERT model, we compared our model with VAD [27]. While VAD achieves a good Macro-F1 score, single adapter models get a comparable Macro-F1 score, and surpass VAD with a considerable margin in terms of accuracy. It is to note that VAD is fine-tuning RoBERTa-Large making it a heavier model with over 355M parameters. For fusion models, the conclusions are the same as for CMU-MOSEI. Considering sentiment analysis data allows improving the accuracy and Macro-F1 scores for the emotion recognition task. In addition, when using complementary emotion knowledge from other datasets (i.e., Fusion$_3$), the fusion model performances are enhanced accordingly.

Table 4. Accuracy and F1 scores on Emotion dataset for emotion detection. ◇: F1 score is not available for the six Ekman emotions.

Model	Joy		Sadness		Anger		Surprise		Love		Fear		Overall	
	A	F1	A	F1	A	F1	A	F1	A	F1	A	F1	A	Macro-F1
BERT	**99.1**	**95.0**	97.4	**96.0**	88.0	**92.0**	83.3	76.0	67.2	80.0	82.6	86.0	**92.2**	87.5
CARER [2]	–	83.0	–	82.0	–	74.0	–	**76.0**	–	◇	–	79.0	81.0	◇
Adapter	93.5	93.0	93.1	93.0	90.9	90.0	66.7	69.0	76.1	78.0	84.8	85.0	89.8	84.7
Fusion$_1$	92.4	93.0	91.0	93.0	**91.2**	89.0	78.8	72.0	80.5	77.0	84.3	86.0	89.6	84.9
Fusion$_3$	94.5	94.0	94.5	95.0	90.9	91.0	80.3	**76.0**	**82.4**	**83.0**	**87.9**	**88.0**	91.9	**88.0**

Finally, we also tested our method on the Emotion dataset (See Table 4). In this case, the adapter version does not perform as well when compared to the fine-tuned BERT model. Compared to CARER [2], single adapter models perform better with a considerable margin of overall accuracy. Here, the pseudo-fusion model performs similar to the single adapter model but adapter fusion allows to obtain better results, which again demonstrates the importance of leveraging additional knowledge from other data. Compared to a fine-tuned BERT, adapter fusion models get similar results. However, the proposed model requires a lot less parameters to train compared to fine-tuning BERT, as can be seen in Table 5.

4.4   Comparison of Loss Functions

The choice of loss function greatly impacts the performance of the model, especially on emotions that are less present in the dataset. Three different loss functions were tested: the traditional Cross-Binary Entropy (BCE), the focal loss (FL) adapted to a multi-label classification setting and the loss function proposed in Sect. 3.2 (MBCE). The performance obtained with the different loss functions are presented in the Table 6.

Table 5. Number of parameters per model

Model	All parameters	Trainable parameters
Fine-tuned BERT	108.3 M	108.3 M
BERT + Adapter	109.8 M	1.5 M
Fusion$_3$	132.8 M	21.8 M
Fusion$_5$	134.6 M	21.8 M

The difference in performance between the classic Binary Cross-Entropy loss and the Focal loss is not significant. While the use of the loss function proposed in this paper decreases to some extent the accuracy for most emotions, it greatly improves the F1-score for all emotions with the exception of *joy*.

Table 6. Accuracy and F1 scores on CMU-MOSEI for emotion detection for different loss functions.

Model	Joy		Sadness		Anger		Surprise		Disgust		Fear		Overall	
	A	F1	A	F1	A	F1	A	F1	A	F1	A	F1	A	Macro-F1
BCE	**67.9**	**71.5**	**75.8**	22.2	**78.5**	25.4	**90.5**	1.3	**85.6**	48.5	**91.7**	0.5	**81.7**	28.2
FL	67.7	70.9	**75.8**	24.9	78.4	23.1	**90.5**	0.6	**85.6**	46.1	**91.7**	0.0	81.6	27.6
MBCE	67.5	70.7	69.1	**44.6**	73.1	**47.5**	81.3	**26.6**	79.9	**53.0**	82.2	**20.3**	75.5	**43.8**

4.5   Performance of Single Adapters

This section presents the performance of the single Adapters on the other tasks used for knowledge composition in the Fusion models. We want to assess if the adapters are learning well to solve their specific tasks. This is important as they are combined in our proposed approaches (Fusion$_3$ and Fusion$_5$). If they learn poorly, they will not contribute to improve the performance. Tables 7 and 8 compare the results obtained by BERT trained with task-specific adapters to fully fine-tuned models and state-of-the-art models. Unless stated otherwise, all accuracy values were obtained by averaging the results over 3 runs using the experimental setup described in Sect. 4.2. Base size versions of BERT, RoBERTa and XLNet models were used for a fair comparison.

Table 7. Accuracy on CMU-MOSEI sentiment analysis tasks. † Accuracy scores obtained from [26].

Model	2-class sentiment	7-class sentiment
TBJE †	84.2	45.5
Fine-tuned BERT	**84.3**	**46.8**
BERT + Adapter	83.9	46.5

The performances of the Adapter models are comparable to those of a fully fine-tuned BERT model. For CMU-MOSEI tasks, they performed on par with or better than state-of-the-art results. For SST-2 and IMDB tasks, they slightly underperformed compared to state-of-the-art fine-tuned language models. However, regardless of the dataset, this experiment shows that adapters can capture useful task-specific information at lower training cost. Furthermore, adapter fusion allows to combine the knowledge from these several good performing task-specific adapters. This explains why our proposed adapter fusion model benefits from the related tasks of sentiment analysis to improve emotion recognition (Table 8).

Table 8. Results on SST-2 & IMDB sentiment analysis tasks.

Model	SST-2	IMDB
Fine-tuned RoBERTa	**94.8**	94.5
Fine-tuned XLNet	93.4	**95.1**
Fine-tuned BERT	93.5	94.0
BERT + Adapter	92.6	93.7

5   Conclusion

The proposed model surpasses state-of-the-art results for emotion recognition on CMU-MOSEI even while using only the textual modality. There is still improvement needed for the rarer emotions in the dataset, but at the time of producing this article, the results presented are substantially stronger than other contributions in terms of F1 scores. Experiments on the CMU-MOSEI, Emotions and GoEmotions datasets show that the knowledge from the sentiment analysis task can be leveraged to improve the emotion recognition. We also show that a strong language model helps for both sentiment analysis and emotion recognition.

Acknowledgments. This work was supported by Mitacs through the Mitacs Accelerate program and by Airudi.

References

1. Bagher Zadeh, A., Liang, P.P., Poria, S., Cambria, E., Morency, L.-P.: Multimodal language analysis in the wild: CMU-MOSEI dataset and interpretable dynamic fusion graph. In: Proceedings of the 56th Annual Meeting of the Association for Computational Linguistics (Volume 1: Long Papers). Melbourne, Australia: Association for Computational Linguistics, Jul. 2018
2. Saravia, E., Liu, H.-C. T., Huang, Y.-H., Wu, J., Chen, Y.-S.: CARER: contextualized affect representations for emotion recognition. In: Proceedings of the 2018 Conference on Empirical Methods in Natural Language Processing (EMNLP) (2018)
3. Demszky, D., Movshovitz-Attias, D., Ko, J., Cowen, A., Nemade, G., Ravi, S.: GoEmotions: a dataset of fine-grained emotions. In: 58th Annual Meeting of the Association for Computational Linguistics (ACL) (2020)
4. Udochukwu, O., He, Y.: A rule-based approach to implicit emotion detection in text. In: Biemann, C., Handschuh, S., Freitas, A., Meziane, F., Métais, E. (eds.) NLDB 2015. LNCS, vol. 9103, pp. 197–203. Springer, Cham (2015). https://doi.org/10.1007/978-3-319-19581-0_17
5. Seal, D., Roy, U., Basak, R.: Sentence-Level Emotion Detection from Text Based on Semantic Rules **06**, 423–430 (2019)
6. Abdul-Mageed, M., Ungar, L.: EmoNet: fine-grained emotion detection with gated recurrent neural networks. In: Proceedings of the 55th Annual Meeting of the Association for Computational Linguistics (Volume 1: Long Papers). Vancouver, Canada: Association for Computational Linguistics, Jul. 2017
7. Tang, D., Qin, B., Feng, X., Liu, T.: Target-dependent sentiment classification with long short term memory. arXiv preprint arXiv:1512.01100 (2015)
8. Park, S., Kim, J., Jeon, J., Park, H., Oh, A.: Toward dimensional emotion detection from categorical emotion annotations. arXiv preprint arXiv:1911.02499 (2019)
9. Acheampong, F.A., Nunoo-Mensah, H., Chen, W.: Transformer models for text-based emotion detection: a review of BERT-based approaches. Artif. Intell. Rev. **54**, 5789–5829 (2021)
10. Devlin, J., Chang, M.-W., Lee, K., Toutanova, K.: BERT: Pre-training of deep bidirectional transformers for language understanding. In: Proceedings of the 2019 Conference of the North American Chapter of the Association for Computational Linguistics (NAACL) (2019)
11. Liu, Y., et al.: Roberta: A robustly optimized BERT pretraining approach. arXiv preprint arXiv:1907.11692. (2019)
12. Yang, Z., Dai, Z., Yang, Y., Carbonell, J.G., Salakhutdinov, R., Le, Q.V.: XLNet: Generalized autoregressive pretraining for language understanding. In: Advances in Neural Information Processing Systems (NeurIPS) (2019)

13. Liu, X., He, P., Chen, W., Gao, J.: Multi-task deep neural networks for natural language understanding. arXiv preprint arXiv:1901.11504 (2019)
14. Clark, K., Luong, M.-T., Khandelwal, U., Manning, C.D., Le, Q.V.: BAM! born-again multi-task networks for natural language understanding. In: Proceedings of the 57th Annual Meeting of the Association for Computational Linguistics. Florence, Italy: Association for Computational Linguistics, Jul. 2019
15. Liu, X., He, P., Chen, W., Gao, J.: Improving multi-task deep neural networks via knowledge distillation for natural language understanding. arXiv preprint arXiv:1904.09482 (2019)
16. Houlsby, N., et al.: Parameter-efficient transfer learning for NLP. In: International Conference on Machine Learning (ICML) (2019)
17. Pfeiffer, J., Kamath, A., Rücklé, A., Cho, K., Gurevych, I.: AdapterFusion: non-destructive task composition for transfer learning. In: EACL 2021–16th Conference of the European Chapter of the Association for Computational Linguistics, Proceedings of the Conference, ser. EACL 2021–16th Conference of the European Chapter of the Association for Computational Linguistics, Proceedings of the Conference. Association for Computational Linguistics (ACL), pp. 487–503 (2021)
18. Lin, T., Goyal, P., Girshick, R., He, K., Dollar, P.: Focal loss for dense object detection. IEEE Trans. Pattern Anal. Mach. Intell. **42**(02), 318–327 (2020)
19. Wang, A., Singh, A., Michael, J., Hill, F., Levy, O., Bowman, S.: GLUE: A multi-task benchmark and analysis platform for natural language understanding. In: Proceedings of the 2018 EMNLP Workshop BlackboxNLP: Analyzing and Interpreting Neural Networks for NLP. Brussels, Belgium: Association for Computational Linguistics, Nov. 2018
20. Vaswani, A., et al.: Attention is all you need. In: Guyon, I., et al. (eds.) Advances in Neural Information Processing Systems. vol. 30. Curran Associates Inc (2017)
21. Ekman, P.: An argument for basic emotions. Cogn. Emot. **6**(3–4), 169–200 (1992)
22. Socher, R., et al.: Recursive deep models for semantic compositionality over a sentiment treebank. In: Proceedings of the 2013 Conference on Empirical Methods in Natural Language Processing. Seattle, Washington, USA: Association for Computational Linguistics, Oct. 2013
23. Maas, A.L., Daly, R.E., Pham, P.T., Huang, D., Ng, A.Y., Potts, C.: Learning word vectors for sentiment analysis. In: Proceedings of the 49th Annual Meeting of the Association for Computational Linguistics: Human Language Technologies. Portland, Oregon, USA: Association for Computational Linguistics, Jun. 2011
24. Loshchilov, I., Hutter, F.: Fixing weight decay regularization in adam. arXiv preprint arXiv:1711.05101 (2017)
25. Pfeiffer, J., et al.: Adapterhub: a framework for adapting transformers. In: Proceedings of the 2020 Conference on Empirical Methods in Natural Language Processing: System Demonstrations, pp. 46–54 (2020)
26. Delbrouck, J.-B., Tits, N., Brousmiche, M., Dupont, S.: A transformer-based joint-encoding for emotion recognition and sentiment analysis. In: Second Grand-Challenge and Workshop on Multimodal Language (Challenge-HML). Seattle, USA: Association for Computational Linguistics, Jul. 2020
27. Park, S., Kim, J., Ye, S., Jeon, J., Park, H.Y., Oh, A.: Dimensional emotion detection from categorical emotion. In: Proceedings of the 2021 Conference on Empirical Methods in Natural Language Processing, pp. 4367–4380 (2021)

Analyzing the Prosodic and Lingual Features of Popular Speakers

Bhavin Jethra[1], Rahul Golhar[1], and Ifeoma Nwogu[2]([⊠]) [iD]

[1] Rochester Institute of Technology, Rochester, NY 14623, USA
[2] University at Buffalo, SUNY, Amherst, NY 14260, USA
inwogu@buffalo.edu

Abstract. If the mission of Technology, Entertainment and Design (TED) is to spread "great ideas" via talks, then high viewership of such talks is imperative to their success. But what are some stylistic differences between talks with higher viewership than others? To better understand this, we collect a large number of TED talk audio (N=2,065) from YouTube and create two categories: the lower (N1=402) and higher (N2=398) viewership classes.

Using an explainable classifier (random forest), we find that prosody is not as effective a modality in predicting viewership classes, but augmenting it with linguistic features results in significantly better predictions. The prediction task is not the main objective of this work, rather it is implemented to help understand what prosodic and linguistic cues are important when differentiating between the delivery styles of low versus high viewership speakers.

Although the main prosodic cues between the two classes are statistically significantly different, we found the most influential cue to be the "fraction of all words in the talk captured by LIWC", a linguistic feature that has been shown to strongly correlate with the use of informal, non-technical language.

Keywords: Prosody · LIWC features · TED Talks

1 Introduction

In recent times, Technology, Entertainment, Design (TED) Talks have made their way into pedagogical literature as an improved method for providing complex information to a varied group of listening learners. So much so, that a department at a major institution of higher learning[1] decided to transform some of its courses into TED-style lectures, especially those offered as open access [6].

TED lectures have also been studied from the psychological and AI perspectives. As discussed in Sect. 2, several AI works that have focused on this rich resource have done so more from a language-only perspective, rather than a

---

This material is based upon work supported by the NSF under the Grant #1846076.
[1] Department of Family and Community Medicine at the University of Toronto in Ontario.

© Springer Nature Switzerland AG 2023
J.-J. Rousseau and B. Kapralos (Eds.): ICPR 2022 Workshops, LNCS 13643, pp. 417–427, 2023.
https://doi.org/10.1007/978-3-031-37660-3_30

multimodal one. But according to the Mehrabian's rule [7], also known as '7-38-55' rule of communication, about 7% of communication of feelings and attitudes is expressed via words we use, 38% via tone and voice and the remaining 55% through body language (especially facial expressions). While this is a general model (and not a hard rule) for communication, it is not clear how much this directly translates to TED Talks, where the goal is not necessarily to express the speaker's feelings and attitudes, but rather for the speaker to attempt to influence a large amount of people about a specific message. In a recent study involving TED Talks popularity [8], the number of views/video was treated as one of the dominant popularity measures. Following this, we also use the total number of views per video as our primary measure of popularity for the TED Talks.

To this effect, in this work *we are interested in using computational methods to determine whether prosodic and lingual cues can be used in explaining the difference between TED Talks with higher versus lesser views, and if so, what specific cues can be used to explain these differences.*

Fig. 1. Technology, Entertainment, Design (TED) Talks

2   Related Works

There has been a significant amount of research work over the years, studying the prosodic characteristics of "'good speakers". Some of the earlier methods include Strangert [12] which studied the prosodic features of a politician and a news reporter and compared them to those of non-professional speakers and Rosenberg and Hirschberg [11] studied how lexical and acoustic information affect subjects' perceptions of charisma in politicians. More recently, in 2015 Tsai [14] studied the prosodic characteristics that separated TED speakers from university professors, under the assumption that one set of speakers was engaging while the other was not.

Other recent AI studies involving TED Talks include work by Weninger et al. [15] where 843 transcripts were used to examine the relation between word usage and categorical affective ratings. Viewers rated the talks by 14 affective states (such as *beautiful, confusing, informative, ingenious, etc.*) and machine learning classifiers were used to predict and learn the words most associated with each state. While this work connected the talks to the affective states, it was not necessarily helpful in delineating high from low viewership talks. More recently, using 1,095 TED Talks, a statistical study was performed by Meier et al. [8] to investigate the link between gender and age related language styles with the number of views as well as the ratios of positive and negative ratings.

Using the transcripts from the talks, they found that more female-style language was linked to more talk views and this was even more significant in talks with extremely high views.

Similar to the work done by [15], Tanveer et. al, 2019 [5] developed a neural-network based computational model to predict the extents of the 14 affective states on a larger collection of TED Talks (N=2200 transcripts). In addition to the language features, they also included prosodic ones but found that this did not enhance their classification. Continuing along this trend, [1,13] developed a causality-guided neural-network aimed at removing biases from the dataset. This resulted in a 10% improvement in their prediction accuracy.

Motivated by these previous works, we study the relation between prosodic + lingual features, and the total number of views per talk, in order to determine what cues most influence the viewership extents of TED talks.

3   Dataset

YouTube is an easily accessible platform for searching and viewing videos related to many different topics and has become the second-most popular search engine after Google [2]. Considering that this is more likely to be the first platform presented to a user for viewing a TED Talk, we targeted the talk videos uploaded on YouTube, which has a dedicated TED channel.

We downloaded 2,065 videos from YouTube, where the videos were uploaded any year up until 2018. The talks covered a wide range topics, had a mix of genders and also a large extent of viewership, ranging from about 2,000 to over 80 million views. All videos collected were greater than 10 min, in order to obtain sufficient text words and voice signal for further analysis per speaker.

Figure 2 shows the YouTube TED Talk viewership over the years and there is no clear indication that older videos would be viewed more frequently than the more recent ones.

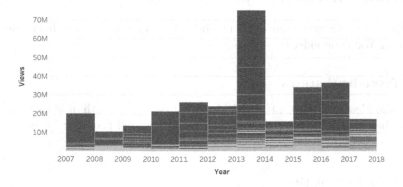

Fig. 2. Number of TED Talk views per year on YouTube

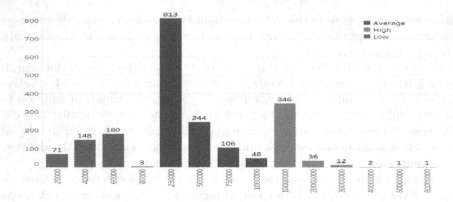

Fig. 3. Distribution of the viewership of the talk videos; The x-axis is # views and y-axis is the frequency. The leftmost red bars are the low viewership talks ($N_l = 402$) and the rightmost orange bars are the high viewership talks ($N_h = 498$). (Color figure online)

Table 1. Statistics of high/low views

Class	Percentile	Count	Threshold	Avg Views
Low	20%	402	< 60,195	36,611
High	80%	398	>994,845	5,519,483

Because we are interested in investigating the characteristics of the more popular talks compared with the less popular ones, to clearly distinguish between these two categories, we split the total videos into the 20th and 80th percentiles, resulting in 402 videos in the low viewership category and 398 in the high viewership category. The viewership distribution is shown in Fig. 3 and the statistics of the two resulting classes are given in Table 1.

4 Feature Extraction and Classifiers

For this work, we extracted both prosodic and lingual features from the *.wav* files from YouTube videos.

4.1 Prosodic Features

The audio files were passed through the MyProsody[2], a Python library for measuring the acoustic features of speech. The 10 essential prosodic features generated are defined in Table 2.

4.2 Language Features

When transcripts were available, we downloaded and used these but unfortunately, not all our selected videos had transcripts provided. For such videos,

---

[2] https://github.com/Shahabks/myprosody.

Table 2. Prosodic features

Feature	Description
Speech time	Total speaking duration (inc. pauses)
Number of pauses	Number of fillers/pauses taken
Pitch Deviation	Fundamental frequency distribution SD
Pitch 25th quantile	25th quantile fundamental frequency
Pitch 75th quantile	75th quantile fundamental frequency
Max pitch	Maximum fundamental frequency
Min pitch	Minimum fundamental frequency
Speech rate	Syllables per second of original duration
Articulation rate	Syllables per second of speaking duration
Speech time ratio	Ratio of speaking over total duration

we used the IBM Watson's speech-to-text API to the generate the additional transcripts.

The Linguistic Inquiry and Word Count (LIWC) text analysis program was applied to the transcribed texts to generate language based features. These included linguistic categories of words used (such as word count, number of words from the dictionary, number of function words, parts-of-speech, and many others); psychological processes associated with the texts (such as positive/negative emotion, insight, uncertainty, and others); spoken categories (such as assenting, filler words, and others); and words concerned with personal living (such as job-related, achievements, religions, and others). The LIWC2015 version [10] that we used for this work produced 70 such lingual features aside from punctuation features which we did not consider.

4.3   Classifiers

We tested two traditional machine learning based classifiers, one for explainability purposes (random forest classifier -RF) and the other as the more flexible sanity checking alternative (neural networks - NN).

Random Forest (RF) Classifier. The RF classifier we implemented here used a number of decision trees spanning from 90 to 1500 depending on the complexity of the input features. We used the Gini impurity criterion to measure the quality of the splits. By computing how much each feature decreased with the impurity and averaging this value across trees, we successfully determined the final importance of each input feature for the classification task.

Multi-layer Neural Network (NN) Classifiers. Fig. 4 summarizes the NN architectures used for this work. The top network alone was used to train on prosody features, the similar bottom network was used on the LIWC lingual features and the overall '"late fusion" network combined the final layers of both networks and simultaneously trained them on both sets of features.

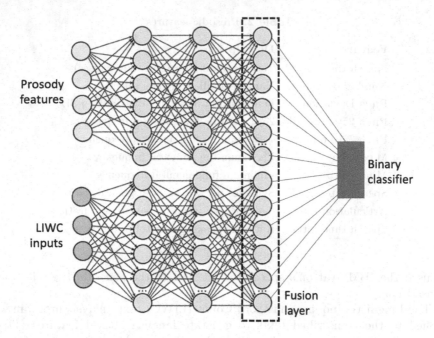

Fig. 4. Multi-layer late fusion neural network on two sets of features

5   Experiments and Results

In this section, we explore the following questions which were also highlighted at the end of Sect. 1:

i Can prosodic or linguistic features be used to distinguish between high and low viewership of TED Talks? If so, which is more effective?
ii What underlying cues are most important for explaining the differences between the 2 classes?

To address these questions, we train two different classifiers in a similar manner on the features extracted from the talks. The dataset is randomly split into 8:2 ratio (we refer to these as training and validation datasets).

The parameters of the two classifiers (RF and NN) are then learned on the training For the NN classifier, we monitor the loss values when the validation data is passed through the network. These values are used in tuning the hyperparameters, such as adjusting the learning rate and regularization. Training subsides when the validation losses become saturated. Similarly, for the RF classifier, the number of trees is adjusted until the best performing model is found.

The model evaluation is performed by applying the best performing classifier on 5 splits of the data (for 5-fold cross-validation). Different sets of inputs (prosodic, lingual or both) are fed to the classifiers and the results are presented. The precision, recall and F1-scores are reported for the best run but the accuracy reported is the mean over 5 splits.

5.1   Prosodic Cues for High and Low Viewership Classification

Using the 10-features prosodic cues, we apply the RF and NN classifiers and the results are presented in Table 3. The order of importance of the prosodic features used during classification is also presented in Fig. 5

Table 3. Classification report using prosody features only

	Precision	*Recall*	F1-score
RF classifier			
Low views	0.66	0.54	0.59
High views	0.61	0.72	0.66
Accuracy	0.63±0.011		
NN classifier			
Low views	0.52	0.66	0.58
High views	0.73	0.60	0.66
Accuracy	0.62±0.00		

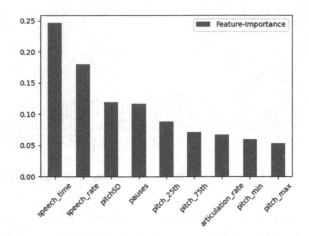

Fig. 5. Order of importance of prosody features from the RF classifier

The most important prosody feature determined by the RF classifier is the overall *speech time*, which includes any pauses and/or fillers in the speech. The other four important features include the speech rate, the standard deviation of the fundamental frequency (f0), number of pauses and the 25th percentile of f0, in that order of importance.

5.2   Lingual Cues for High and Low Viewership Classification

Using the 70 linguistic cues obtained from LIWC, we apply the RF and NN classifiers again and the results are presented in Table 4. The order of importance of the linguistic features is presented in Fig. 6

Table 4. Classification report using lingual features only

	Precision	Recall	F1-score
RF classifier			
Low views	0.75	0.79	0.77
High views	0.77	0.73	0.75
Accuracy	0.74±0.018		
NN classifier			
Low views	0.75	0.78	0.76
High views	0.78	0.75	0.77
Accuracy	0.72± 0.001		

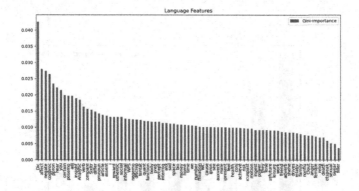

Fig. 6. Order of importance of linguistic features from the RF classifier

The most important lingual feature as determined by the RF classifier, is the *percentage of words used by the speaker that exists in the LIWC dictionary*. Unlike the prosodic results, this feature is significantly more important than the others as seen by the dominant feature in Fig. 6. The next four influential features are *affective processes* (based on words such as happy, cried, abandon, etc.) *negation* (based on words such as no, not, never etc.), *cognitive processes* (based on words such as cause, know, ought, etc.) and *personal pronouns* (based on words such as them, her, I, etc.) in that order of importance. We also ran the NN classifier with the top 5 lingual features and the resulting 5-trial accuracy dropped to 0.668±0.00, hence we did not consider this abbreviated feature list for further processing.

5.3   Combined Cues for Viewership Classification

Lastly, we concatenated the prosodic and lingual features and applied the RF classifier. We also implemented a late fusion NN classifier as shown in Fig. 4. The results from both RF and NN fusion classifiers are shown in Table 5. The order of importance of the combined features is presented in Fig. 7

Table 5. Classification report using combined features; note that the oveall accuracy values are still very close.

	Precision	*Recall*	F1-score
RF classifier			
Low views	0.73	0.86	0.79
High views	0.83	0.67	0.74
Accuracy	0.74±0.014		
NN fusion classifier			
Low views	0.76	0.73	0.74
High views	0.70	0.75	0.73
Accuracy	0.72± 0.00		

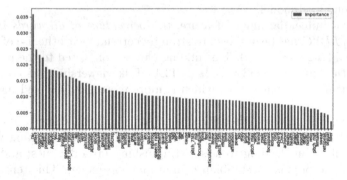

Fig. 7. Order of importance of combined features from the RF classifier. The red bars indicate the importance levels of speech features. (Color figure online)

The interesting finding from this last exercise is the fact that the order of importance is still dominated by the linguistic features where the first 10 most influential features are from LIWC and the single most influential feature is still the same as from the lingual set.

5.4   Statistical Tests of Significance on Prosodic Features

We ran statistical T-tests on the two most influential prosodic features to determine how significant the differences between groups were, and obtained the following results:

Speech time: p-value = 4.10291E-10; T-value = 1.96
Speech rate: p-value = 8.49088E-07; T-value = 1.42

These results indicate that the low and high viewership groups are clearly different when these two prosodic features are considered. Thus, prosody can be used to explain the differences in the viewership classes, but its effect is not as significant as language.

6   Discussion and Conclusion

In this paper, we have studied TED talk popularity as measured by the number of views. It is important to point out that the prediction task is not the main objective of this work, rather it is to help us understand the differences between high and low viewership groups, and what roles prosodic and/or lingual features play in that delineation.

Combining the results from the explainable RF classifier and the statistical tests, we can conclude that although prosody does indeed contribute to the viewership group delineation, it does not play as influential a role in predicting the popularity of the TED talks as language style. This phenomenon was repeatedly demonstrated across the classifier results, evidenced by the fact that the combination models (fusion of prosody and language) only performed on-par with the language-only models. Also, the linguistic features dominated the influence list from the combined model.

The most influential lingual feature, the *percentage of all words in the talk captured by LIWC*, has been shown to strongly correlate with the use of informal, nontechnical language [3,4,9]. This finding can be connected to the recent work [8], where the authors found that high TED Talk viewership was correlated to the use of female-language style, which is more more personal and narrative in style.

Because TED provides extensive presentation-style coaching to its speakers, it is possible that they deviate from their natural ways of speaking when giving TED talks, thus leading to less distinguishing prosodic cues, and a strong violation of the popular Mehrabian communication model. This remains to be explored in the future.

In conclusion, we have shown that although both prosodic and linguistic features are useful in distinguishing between high and low viewership of TED Talks, overall, linguistic features are significantly more effective (17% accuracy jump). Linguistic cues especially the informal, narrative-type style of the talk goes a long way in explaining whether it has high viewership or not. This is probably due to the accessibility of such a talk to a very wide audience.

Going forward, we will be interested in extending the current study to speakers' body movements and gestures to determine if this additional modality provides more evidence in delineating the viewership classes.

References

1. Acharyya, R., Das, S., Chattoraj, A., Tanveer, M.I.: FairyTED: a fair rating predictor for ted talk data. In: AAAI Proceedings of the AAAI Conference on Artificial Intelligence, vol. 34, pp. 338–345 (2020)
2. Arthurs, J., Drakopoulou, S., Gandini, A.: Researching youtube. Convergence **24**(1), 3–15 (2018). https://doi.org/10.1177/1354856517737222
3. Centerbar, D.B., Schnall, S., Clore, G.L., Garvin, E.D.: Affective incoherence: when affective concepts and embodied reactions clash. J. Pers. Soc. Psychol. **94**(4), 560 (2008)
4. Hartley, J., Pennebaker, J., Fox, C.: Abstracts, introductions and discussions: how far do they differ in style? Scientometrics **57**(3), 389–398 (2003)
5. Iftekhar Tanveer, M., Kamrul Hassan, M., Gildea, D., Ehsan Hoque, M.: Predicting ted talk ratings from language and prosody. arXiv e-prints, pp. arXiv-1906 (2019)
6. Masson, M.: Benefits of TED talks. Can. Fam. Physician **60**(12), 1080 (2014)
7. Mehrabian, A., Wiener, M.: Decoding of inconsistent communications. J. Pers. Soc. Psychol. **6**(1), 109 (1967)
8. Meier, T., et al.: Stereotyping in the digital age: Male language is "ingenious", female language is "beautiful"–and popular. PloS one **15**(12), e0243637 (2020)
9. Owen, J.E., Yarbrough, E.J., Vaga, A., Tucker, D.C.: Investigation of the effects of gender and preparation on quality of communication in internet support groups. Comput. Hum. Behav. **19**(3), 259–275 (2003)
10. Pennebaker, J.W., Boyd, R.L., Jordan, K., Blackburn, K.: The development and psychometric properties of liwc2015. Tech. rep. (2015)
11. Rosenberg, A., Hirschberg, J.: Acoustic/prosodic and lexical correlates of charismatic speech. In: INTERSPEECH - Ninth European Conference on Speech Communication and Technology, Lisbon, Portugal, pp. 513–516. ISCA (2005)
12. Strangert, E.: Prosody in public speech: analyses of a news announcement and a political interview. In: Ninth European Conference on Speech Communication and Technology (2005)
13. Tanveer, M.I., Hasan, M.K., Gildea, D., Hoque, M.E.: A causality-guided prediction of the TED talk ratings from the speech-transcripts using neural networks. CoRR abs/1905.08392 (2019). http://arxiv.org/abs/1905.08392
14. Tsai, T.: Are you ted talk material? comparing prosody in professors and ted speakers. In: INTERSPEECH -Sixteenth Annual Conference of the International Speech Communication Association, Dresden, Germany, pp. 2534–2538 (2015)
15. Weninger, F., Staudt, P., Schuller, B.: Words that fascinate the listener: predicting affective ratings of on-line lectures. Int. J. Distance Educ. Technol. (IJDET) **11**(2), 110–123 (2013)

Fairness in Biometric Systems (FAIRBIO)

ICPR 2022 – Workshop Fairness in Biometric Systems (FAIRBIO)

Preface

The ICPR 2022 workshop on fairness in biometric systems was intended to better understand and define the fairness problem in current biometric solutions. In recent years, biometric systems spread worldwide and are increasingly involved in critical decision-making processes, such as in finance, public security, and forensics. Despite their growing effect on everybody's daily life, many biometric solutions perform strongly different on different groups of individuals as previous works have shown. Consequently, the recognition performances of these systems are strongly dependent on demographic and non-demographic attributes of their users. This results in discriminatory and unfair treatment of the user of these systems. However, several political regulations point out the importance of the right to non-discrimination. These include Article 14 of the European Convention of Human Rights, Article 7 of the Universal Declaration of Human Rights, and Article 71 of the General Data Protection Regulation (GDPR). These political efforts show the strong need for analyzing and mitigating these equability concerns in biometric systems. Current works on this topic are focused on demographic-fairness in face recognition systems. However, since there is a growing effect on everybody's daily life and an increased social interest in this topic, research on fairness in biometric solutions is urgently needed.

The contribution of this workshop showed that it is quite important to understand the problem of fairness in biometric systems first, define proper metrics to measure it, and comprehensively analyze the problem before we can effectively mitigate this issue.

We received seven submissions for review. Each paper received at least three independent reviews focusing on the quality of the paper, the scientific novelty of the proposed approach or analysis, the significance of the content, and its applicability to the field of biometrics. This resulted in an acceptance rate of around 57%.

Besides the paper presentations, the workshop was supported by two invited keynote talks focusing on the fairness problem from industrial and academic points of view. Yevgeniy B. Sirotin, the technical director of SAIC's Identity and Data Sciences Laboratory supporting the Department of Homeland Security Science and Technology (DHS S&T) and Principal Investigator at the Maryland Test Facility, was presenting applied research challenges of demographic differentials in face recognition. On the other hand, Ignacio Serna from the Autonomous University of Madrid and the California Institute of Technology presented how biases are encoded in deep networks, the impact on their activations in networks, and how they can be detected in face biometrics and beyond.

Evaluating Proposed Fairness Models for Face Recognition Algorithms

John J. Howard[1] , Eli J. Laird[1]([envelope]) , Rebecca E. Rubin[1] ,
Yevgeniy B. Sirotin[1] , Jerry L. Tipton[1], and Arun R. Vemury[2]

[1] The Identity and Data Sciences Lab at The Maryland Test Facility, Maryland, USA
`{jhoward,elaird,rrubin,ysirotin,jtipton}@idslabs.org`
[2] The U.S. Department of Homeland Security, Science and Technology Directorate,
Washington, USA
`arun.vemury@dhs.gov`

Abstract. The accuracy of face recognition algorithms has progressed rapidly due to the onset of deep learning and the widespread availability of training data. Though tests of face recognition algorithm performance indicate yearly performance gains, error rates for many of these systems differ based on the demographic composition of the test set. These "demographic differentials" have raised concerns with regard to the "fairness" of these systems. However, no international standard for measuring fairness in biometric systems yet exists. This paper characterizes two proposed measures of face recognition algorithm fairness (fairness measures) from scientists in the U.S. and Europe, using face recognition error rates disaggregated across race and gender from 126 distinct face recognition algorithms. We find that both methods have mathematical characteristics that make them challenging to interpret when applied to these error rates. To address this, we propose a set of interpretability criteria, termed the Functional Fairness Measure Criteria (FFMC), that outlines a set of properties desirable in a face recognition algorithm fairness measure. We further develop a new fairness measure, the Gini Aggregation Rate for Biometric Equitability (GARBE), and show how, in conjunction with the Pareto optimization, this measure can be used to select among alternative algorithms based on the accuracy/fairness trade-space. Finally, to facilitate the development of fairness measures in the face recognition domain, we have open-sourced our dataset of machine-readable, demographically disaggregated error rates. We believe this is currently the largest open-source dataset of its kind.

Keywords: Face Recognition · Fairness · Socio-technical Policy

1 Introduction

Facial recognition is the process of identifying individuals using the physiological characteristics of their face [24]. Humans perform such tasks regularly, using

---

J. J. Howard and E. J. Laird and Y. B. Sirotin—First authors contributed equally to this research. Authors listed alphabetically.

© Springer Nature Switzerland AG 2023
J.-J. Rousseau and B. Kapralos (Eds.): ICPR 2022 Workshops, LNCS 13643, pp. 431–447, 2023.
https://doi.org/10.1007/978-3-031-37660-3_31

dedicated neural pathways that are part of the larger human visual system [10]. In 2014 convolutional neural nets were first applied to the face recognition problem, allowing them to achieve near human performance for the first time [29]. Subsequently, public facing deployments of face recognition have been increasing steadily. However, there are also long standing reports of face recognition performance varying for people based on their demographic group membership [4,14,16,21,22,27]. Of particular concern is the notion that false match rates in face recognition may run higher for certain groups of people, namely African Americans [16,22].

In response, there has been considerable work around how to train and subsequently demonstrate a "fair" face recognition algorithm [2,6,12,23,31]. To address the latter, two definitions of "fairness" in face recognition applications were proposed by scientists seeking to quantify the equitability, or lack thereof, of various face recognition algorithms. The first, Fairness Discrepancy Rate (FDR), was proposed by scientists from the Idiap Research Institute, a Swiss artificial intelligence laboratory with a long history of contribution to the field of biometrics [26]. The second, called the Inequity Rate (IR), was proposed by scientists from the U.S. National Institute of Standards and Technology (NIST) [13], a leading scientific body with over 60 years of biometric test and evaluation experience.

However, to date, neither of these techniques has been extensively utilized in practice or audited using a large corpus of actual face recognition error rates. Further, there has been relatively little work to understand the utility of these measures for scoring the fairness of deployed algorithms or for selecting among alternative algorithms during procurement. To address these gaps, we apply these two fairness measures to error rates disaggregated across race and gender demographic groups from 126 commercial and open source face recognition algorithms. We assess their interpretability along three criteria, which we have termed the Functional Fairness Measure Criteria (Sect. 3.4). Finding no current measure meets all three of these criteria, we developed a new technique based on the Gini coefficient and coined the term the Gini Aggregation Rate for Biometric Equitability, or GARBE (Sect. 3.5) to describe it. We show how this measure can be used as part of a down-select protocol that also leverages Pareto optimization (Sect. 3.6). Finally, we discuss the lack of data currently available to developers of fairness measures so that audits of this kind can be executed. As a partial remedy for this, we have open-sourced our dataset of machine-readable, demographically disaggregated error rates. We believe this is currently the largest open-source dataset of its kind.

2   Background

2.1   Face Recognition

Face recognition algorithms operate by generating numerical representations of faces, referred to as templates. Two face templates can then be compared to produce a similarity score s and if s is greater than some discrimination threshold τ the corresponding faces are declared to be a "match" by the algorithm. This process can be used in both identification tasks, where an unknown probe face is matched to a gallery of faces, and face verification tasks, where a single face is matched to a claimed identity. The *false match rate* and the *false non-match rate* are two error rates used to measure the foundational accuracy of face recognition algorithms. The false match rate (FMR) measures the proportion of face comparisons between different identities, or non-mated face pairs, that result in a match. The false non-match rate (FNMR) measures the proportion of face comparisons of the same identity, or mated face pairs, that do not result in a match. FMR and FNMR are specific to a given discrimination threshold τ, which is almost universally set so that FMR $<<$ FNMR. In this paper, we discuss the notion of face recognition fairness with respect to the false match and false non-match rates.

2.2 Fairness in Face Recognition

The fairness of software applications in general has garnered much attention in recent years from organizations across a wide swath of disciplines, including computer science, sociology, policy, and others [3,5,9,17,34]. This focus on algorithmic fairness has been spurred by cases of disparate outcomes for members of different demographic groups in AI-driven software applications. However, until recently there has been relatively little activity on measuring the fairness of face recognition software specifically. One particular challenge in the face recognition domain is that there are numerous ways in which a system can fail, each with different impacts to different users. In the law enforcement use case in particular, a false positive identification has the resulting harm of possible false arrest and imprisonment for a member of the community. A false negative identification, whereby a known suspect in a database is missed, carries the harm of a suspect continuing to be at large in a given community. The favourable outcome in police use of face recognition is therefore a combination of the probability of two distinct error cases, weighted by some social cost of each error case. The fair outcome is that this favourable outcome occurs equally often across demographic groups.

In the absence of other domain specific guidance on fairness, scientists from NIST and the Swiss Idiap Research Institute have proposed two independent measures of fairness with respect to differential error rates. These two methods are known as the Inequity Rate and Fairness Discrepancy Rate, respectively and are discussed in detail in the following sections.

3 Methods

3.1 Fairness Discrepancy Rate

Fairness Discrepancy Rate (FDR) was proposed by scientists at the Idiap Research Institute, a Swiss artificial intelligence laboratory, in November of 2020 [25]. It was subsequently published in a leading IEEE biometrics journal in August, 2021 [26] as the ".. first figure of merit in this field" and highlights that it" consider[s] the FMR and FNMR trade-off in the demographic differential assessment..". Essentially, this metric advocates for calculating the max difference in false match rate (FMR) and false non-match rate (FNMR) performance between any two demographic groups d_i and d_j and a given discrimination threshold τ. Those differences are then weighed by parameters α and $\beta = 1 - \alpha$, which represent the level of concern applied to differences in FMR and FNMR respectively. The resulting FDR metric is on a scale of 0 to 1, with 1 being "fair" and 0 being "unfair" [25]. The exact equations for calculating FDR are shown in Eq. 3.

$$A(\tau) = max(|FMR_{d_i}(\tau) - FMR_{d_j}(\tau)|) \; \forall d_i, d_j \in D \qquad (1)$$

$$B(\tau) = max(|FNMR_{d_i}(\tau) - FNMR_{d_j}(\tau)|) \; \forall d_i, d_j \in D \qquad (2)$$

$$FDR(\tau) = 1 - (\alpha A(\tau) + (1 - \alpha)B(\tau)) \qquad (3)$$

3.2 Inequity Rate

The Inequity Rate (IR) was proposed by scientists at NIST in March of 2021 [13]. Unlike FDR, the IR metric takes ratio differences between min, max FMR and FNMR rates per demographic groups d_i and d_j. It then raises these differences to weighing factors α and $(1 - \alpha)$ and multiplies the results as shown in Eq. 6.

$$A(\tau) = \frac{\max_{d_i} FMR_{d_i}(\tau)}{\min_{d_j} FMR_{d_j}(\tau)} \; \forall d_i, d_j \in D \qquad (4)$$

$$B(\tau) = \frac{\max_{d_i} FNMR_{d_i}(\tau)}{\min_{d_j} FNMR_{d_j}(\tau)} \; \forall d_i, d_j \in D \qquad (5)$$

$$IR = A(\tau)^\alpha B(\tau)^{1-\alpha} \qquad (6)$$

3.3 Data

Evaluating the properties of summative measures of face recognition fairness requires data. In the case of the FDR and the IR, the data required must have false match, and non-match rates across demographic groups at a single threshold. We note this is a non-trivial dataset to develop. Most users and developers of face recognition only have access to a small number of algorithms. There are also a limited number of large datasets with ground truth demographic data. The only source (to our knowledge) of this data in a single, consolidated report is the NIST Face Recognition Vendor Test (FRVT) Part 3. The FRVT evaluation is open to face recognition companies and researchers from around the world. Applicants submit their face recognition algorithm packaged in a NIST defined API. NIST then runs these algorithms over several large corpora of face images where the identity of the individuals in the photo is known (VISA photos, MUGSHOT photos, WILD photos, etc.). From these face comparisons, various metrics are produced such as false match and non-match rates at various thresholds.

Table 1. Data criteria for summative face recognition fairness metric evaluation

Criteria	Description
C.1	False match rates
C.2	False non-match rates
C.3	Criteria C.1 and C.2 at a single threshold per algorithm
C.4	Criteria C.1 and C.2 dis-aggregated by demographic group
C.5	Criteria C.1 - C.4 across a representative number of face recognition algorithms

Part 3 of the FRVT report was released in 2019 and specifically focused on demographic effects [14]. Specifically, Annex 15 of this report contains demographically disaggregated error rates for eight demographic groups, across 126 face recognition algorithms. The demographic groups included in the report consist of two gender groups (Male and Female) paired with four race groups (American Indian, Asian, Black, and White), resulting in eight gender-race pairs. The discrimination threshold τ used to calculate error rates in Annex 15 was set to the value that produced a false match rate of $1e^{-4}$. The face pairs used to generate these metrics are derived from a subset of a dataset known as "Mugshots", which contains images of individuals involved in routine U.S. law enforcement booking procedures. Demographic labels are assigned by law enforcement officers and encoded in a record known as the Electronic Biometric Transmission Specification, or EBTS.

For this work, the values contained in NIST FRVT Part 3, Annex 15 were hand transcribed into a machine readable comma separated value file (CSV). This CSV contains 126 columns (one per algorithm) and 17 rows (algorithm name, 8 false match rates, 8 false non-match rates, one per demographic group). We believe this is currently the largest, machine readable collection of disaggregated face recognition error rates. We have made this dataset available at our organizations GitHub page for the benefit of the ML fairness community (see Acknowledgements Section).

3.4 Functional Fairness Measure Criteria

One primary objective of any proposed fairness measure is to rank classification algorithms by that measure and select the top or "most fair". We argue this objective is aided when the fairness measure has three properties that make the measure intuitive and more easily reasoned about. These properties are listed below. We collectively refer to these three conditions as the Functional Fairness Measure Criteria, or FFMC.

- FFMC.1 - The net contributions of FMR and FNMR differentials to the overall fairness measure should be intuitive when using a normal range of risk parameter weights and operationally relevant error rates.
- FFMC.2 - There should be recognizable points of reference in the domain of the fairness measure. The easiest way to achieve this objective is to have a bounded fairness measure, with a minimum and maximum possible value.
- FFMC.3 - The fairness measure should be calculable when no errors are observed for a demographic group. Particularly in the context of face recognition, as an increasing number of intersectional demographic groups are considered, the likelihood of experiencing a group with a FNMR of zero also increases. Furthermore, in face recognition if cross group FMR numbers are considered, the likelihood of experiencing a group pair with FMR of zero also rises. The fairness measure should be able to be computed in the presence of either one of these conditions.

3.5   The Gini Aggregation Rate for Biometric Equitability

Sections 4.1 and 4.2 examine the properties of the FDR and IR metrics using real, disaggregated face recognition error rates against the FFMC criteria. We find each metric does not fully satisfy the criteria. We thus propose a third fairness aggregation, called the Gini Aggregation Rate for Biometric Equitability (GARBE), inspired by the mathematics of the Gini coefficient. The Gini coefficient is a long-standing measure of statistical dispersion of a set of numbers [11] that is often applied to measure wealth disparity [8]. The formula for the generic Gini coefficient, given n observations of a discrete variable x is shown in Eq. 7. For our purposes, we use a variant that normalizes the upper bound of the sample by $\frac{n}{n-1}$. This corrects for downward bias in Gini coefficient calculations when the number of samples is small, as demonstrated in [7].

$$G_x = \left(\frac{n}{n-1}\right)\left(\frac{\sum_{i=1}^{n}\sum_{j=1}^{n}\mid x_i - x_j\mid}{2n^2\bar{x}}\right) \forall d_i, d_j \in D \tag{7}$$

Given this definition, a simple extension of the Gini coefficient to the face recognition, or general biometric, use case, taking account risk parameters for weighting the impact of a false match versus false non-match error is shown in Eq. 9. We coin the term Gini Aggregation Rate for Biometric Equitability (GARBE) to describe this measure.

$$A(\tau) = G_{FMR_\tau}; \ B(\tau) = G_{FNMR_\tau} \tag{8}$$

$$GARBE(\tau) = \alpha A(\tau) + (1-\alpha)B(\tau) \tag{9}$$

One potential drawback to the approach proposed by Eqs. 7 - 9 is that various studies have documented grouping effects in Gini calculations that can result in underestimation of numeric dispersion [32]. For example, consider calculating the Gini coefficient as shown in Eq. 7 on error counts as experienced across three groups, A, B, and C. For the data $x = \{5, 5, 10\}$, the corresponding $G_x = 0.25$. However, were we to combine the error counts for groups A and B such that $x = \{10, 10\}$ the corresponding would G_x would be 0. It therefore becomes possible to "cheat the system" by grouping the data in such a way that minimizes the Gini coefficient, giving an impression of a "more fair" system that would not exist had data been grouped otherwise. To discourage the intentional use of grouping to bias comparisons involving Gini coefficients, we recommend the specification of grouping variables and group sizes when reporting calculations of the Gini coefficient and derivatives of the metric, such as GARBE.

3.6 The Pareto Curve Optimization with Overall Effectiveness

As others have noted, fairness is often part of a trade space with another optimization criteria, accuracy [33, 35]. For example, one way to achieve "fairness" in a face recognition system is to simply declare every face pair as non-matching. Each demographic group would therefore have precisely equal FNMRs (100%) and precisely equal FMRs (0%). While fair, this solution is less than desirable when one also considers the overall performance of the system.

One common technique for optimization around multiple performance criteria in economics and engineering is Pareto efficiency. One can say a pair of performance measures for a solution is Pareto efficient if it satisfies the following condition. Given a set of performance measures $p_1 = \{p_{1,1}, p_{1,2}...p_{1,m}\}$ and $p_2 = \{p_{2,1}, p_{2,2}...p_{2,m}\}$ for m solutions, a pair $\{p_{1,n}, p_{2,n}\}$ is Pareto efficient if both of the following conditions is met:

$$p_{1,n} < p_{1,x} \forall x \in \{1, .., m\} \mid x \neq n$$
$$p_{2,n} < p_{2,x} \forall x \in \{1, .., m\} \mid x \neq n \tag{10}$$

Similarly, if a pair of performance measures satisfies one condition but not the other then we can say this pair is weakly Pareto efficient.

4 Results

4.1 Properties of Fairness Discrepancy Rate in Practice

When we apply the data described in Sect. 3.3 to the FDR measure (Sect. 3.1) we see the distribution of FDR measures as shown in Fig. 1. We notice that, despite having a theoretical range of 0 to 1, the practical range of the FDR measure, with the alpha and beta set to 0.5, is closer to 0.9 to 1, with over 95% of FDR values falling in that range. This is a straightforward mathematical extension of the fact that, while the act of aggregating error rates makes sense in principle, for the face recognition problem in particular these error rates almost always exist on vastly different scales. For example, using sample data from NIST FRVT part 3 we see FNMRs ranging from 1.29% to 6.54%. Conversely, the false non-match rates are orders of magnitude smaller, ranging from 0.001% ($1e^{-5}$) to approximately 0.05% ($10^{3.3} = 0.000501$). This is generally true of all face recognition error rates found in our dataset (see Fig. 1B, note the log scale of the y axis). This has the effect of limiting the FDR measure, for all practical purposes, to 1 minus the difference in FNMR *only*, hence the practical range from 0.9 to 1.0 (FNMR differences typically vary by <1% to 10%).

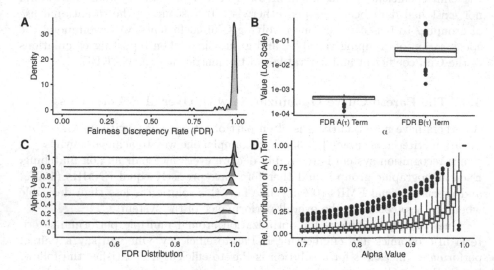

Fig. 1. Fairness Discrepancy Rate values using NIST FRVT Part 3 face recognition error rates. **A.** Overall distribution of FDR values (alpha = 0.5). **B** Magnitude of the alpha and beta terms in Eq. 3. **C.** Minimum and maxiumum values for FDR given an alpha setting. Note the convergence of the range as alpha increases. **D.** Relative contribution of the alpha term to the overall FDR value. Note the truncated x scale (0.7 - 1.0) and that the median contribution of the alpha term does not surpass 50% until alpha is set to 0.99. Error rates used in FDR calculation are across the eight demographic groups described in Sect. 3.3.

Furthermore, this aggregation of error rates that exist on significantly different scales has the extended effect of making the risk parameter α a challenge to configure correctly. Recall from Sect. 3.1 that alpha is the "weight" of the false match discrepancy in the overall FDR calculation. However, because of the small magnitude of FMR differences, these differences only begin to impact the FDR calculation on an equal scale as FNMR differences when alpha is set to greater than 0.99. Indeed, from Fig. 1D we see that the median relative contribution of the FMR difference to the FDR only surpasses 50% when alpha is 0.99 and higher.

4.2   Properties of Inequity Rate in Practice

Because of the ratio rather than aggregation based summative nature of the Inequity Rate (IR) metric, the issues discussed in Sect. 4.1 are largely absent. The distribution of IR values at the default alpha of 0.5 spans a range from 2.4

to 26.38 with lower values representing is more "fair" algorithms in this metric
system (Fig. 2A). The $A(\tau)$ and $B(\tau)$ terms are on more similar scales, with
$A(\tau)$ typically having a value in the 40 - 50 range and the $B(\tau)$ term typically
ranging from 4 to 9. This more congruous relationship between the $A(\tau)$ and
$B(\tau)$ terms means the IR reacts to changes in false match rate weight (α) with
IR distributions continuing to span representative portions of the metric space
at all values of α (Fig. 2C) and the $A(\tau)$ term having more of an impact as alpha
rises (Fig. 2D).

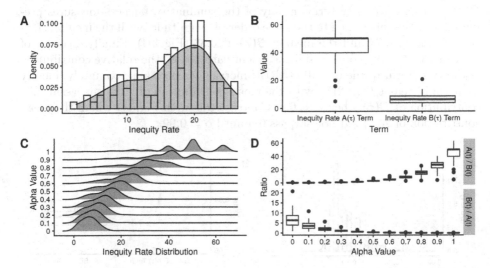

Fig. 2. Inequity Rate (IR) values using NIST FRVT Part 3 face recognition error
rates. **A.** Overall distribution of IR values (alpha = 0.5). **B** Magnitude of the alpha
and beta terms in Eq. 6. **C.** Distribution of IR values given an alpha setting. **D.** Relative
contribution of the alpha term to the overall IR value. Error rates used in IR calculation
are across the eight demographic groups described in Sect. 3.3.

The only challenge to interpreting IR values that arises from this analysis
is the unbounded nature of the metric. Because of its multiplicative nature and
the exponential risk weights, there is no theoretical upper bound on the IR
measure. Although the practical upper limit in this study was 63.1, different face
recognition algorithms could, in theory, give IR results that approach infinity.
Similarly, this ratio property also has the drawback of making IR incalculable
when the min FNMR or FMR for any group is 0.

4.3 Properties of the Gini Aggregation for Biometric Equitability in Practice

The Gini Aggregation for Biometric Equitability (GARBE) measure combines
the positive characteristics of the FDR and IR measures. Namely, it's a summative aggregation, meaning the bound can be reasonably controlled but it does

not add or subtract error rate values that, in practice, exist on markedly different scales. Instead the GARBE calculates the Gini coeffecient as an approximation to the "spread" or dispersion of these error rates and leverages the fact that the resulting coefficient is already scaled from 0 to 1. This coefficient can then be weighed using the same basic, multiplicative weighing technique utilized in the FDR metric. We see that using a default α of 0.5, GARBE metrics for algorithms in [14] span about half of the theoretically usable range (0.165 - 0.618, Fig. 3A). This range continues to span representative portions of the metric space as false match error weight (α) is modulated (Fig. 3C). We also note that the $A(\tau)$ and $B(\tau)$ terms are the only terms in any of the summative fairness measures presented here that are scaled to the same order of magnitude, with the median $A(\tau)$ value found at 0.74 and the median $B(\tau)$ at 0.33 (Fig. 3B). Finally, because of the consistent scaling of the Gini coefficient calculation, the relative contribution of the $A(\tau)$ term to the overall GARBE metric increases approximately linearly as alpha increases (Fig. 2D), with the mean contribution of $A(\tau)$ surpassing the contribution of $B(\tau)$ when $\alpha = 0.4$. Contrast this with Fig. 1D where the mean contribution of $A(\tau)$ did not surpass 0.5 until $\alpha = 0.99$.

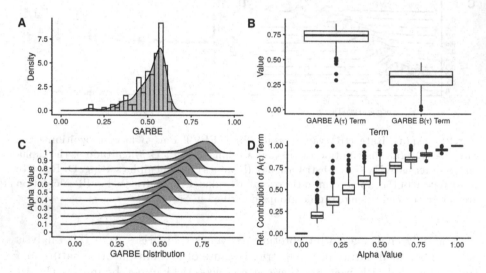

Fig. 3. GARBE values using NIST FRVT Part 3 face recognition error rates. **A.** Overall distribution of GARBE values (alpha = 0.5). **B** Magnitude of the alpha and beta terms in Eq. 9. **C.** Distribution of GARBE values given an alpha setting. **D.** Relative contribution of the alpha term to the overall GARBE value. Error rates used in GARBE calculation are across the eight demographic groups described in Sect. 3.3.

4.4   In Summary of Summative Fairness Measures

Because the FDR metric is bounded, we find it is possible to create reference points in its domain. For example, a perfectly fair algorithm (no differences in group based FNMR or FMR) has a FDR of 1 and an perfectly unfair algorithm (all FNMR or FMR occurring for one group) has a FDR of 0. FDR is also calculable in the presence of zero percent FNMR or FMR. However, the FDR measure's differential terms exist at vastly different scales when using a normal range of risk parameters and operationally relevant error rates (Fig. 1B). In face recognition deployments where false match rate differences across group are of concern, the FDR *alpha* term should be set on the scale from (0.99, 1] in order to allow the contributions from the $A(\tau)$ term to contribute to the overall FDR measure. This is not documented anywhere outside this audit but is an important point should the FDR measure be used to select fair face recognition algorithms in practice.

The IR fairness measure largely rectifies the scaling issues encountered with FDR measure by taking a ratio as opposed to minmax aggregation of FMR and FNMR numbers. This results in the IR measure having a dynamic range that spans from a supposed minimum of 1 ("fair" algorithm) to a practical maximum of 63.1, in this study. Furthermore, the contribution from $A(\tau)$ and $B(\tau)$ are on relatively similar scales when alpha values are set to normal ranges. However, also because of this ratio aggregation, the IR measure can approach ∞ as $\min_{d_j} FNMR_{d_j}(\tau)$ or $\min_{d_j} FMR_{d_j}(\tau)$ approaches 0 and is indeed incalculable should one of these rates reach 0. Its also challenging to interpret and compare IR values both within and across studies. Because of the unbounded nature of the measure, the most direct approach to establishing a "fair" algorithm is to partition the IR space and select algorithms in the Nth quartile. However, this quartile can shift from study to study, depending on the minimum FNMR and FMR's per group encountered. This makes comparing IR values a challenge should the IR measure be used to select fair face recognition algorithm in practice.

Finally, the GARBE fairness measure, proposed in this study, builds on the strength of the FDR and IR measures. Instead of aggregating minmax FNMR and FMR differences, the GARBE measure weighs and aggregates measures of dispersion of these error rates, namely the Gini coefficient (Eq. 7). This has several advantages. One, this measure is calculable in the presence of error rates being 0. Second, this measure first converts two sets of numbers that exist on markedly different scales to a single common metric space before weighing and aggregating. In this fashion we can both avoid the poor relationship between risk ratios and relative contribution of $A(\tau)$ and $B(\tau)$ terms (Fig. 1C-D and 3C-D) and retain a bounded domain (Fig. 2A &C and 3A & C). Because of these properties, the GARBE measure is able to satisfy all the FFMC criteria. Table 2 summarizes the three fairness measures with respect to the FFMC criteria.

Table 2. Summary of Summative Fairness Measures

FFMC Criteria	FDR	IR	GARBE
FFMC.1		✓	✓
FFMC.2	✓		✓
FFMC.3	✓		✓

4.5 Pareto Curve Optimization with the Gini Aggregation Rate for Biometric Equitability

Finally, this study advocates for evaluating face recognition algorithms along multiple axes of performance, namely overall effectiveness and fairness, using the Pareto curve method (Sect. 3.6). This technique requires computing both overall effectiveness and a fairness measure. We select the GARBE fairness measure for the reasons outlined in Sect. 4.4. As a measure of overall performance we select total FNMR across all demographic groups. This value is a weighted average of the error rates as reported in Annex 15 (Sect. 3.3) and the mated comparison counts, also provided in the introductory material to Annex 15 of [14].

This result is shown in Fig. 4, with overall performance (FNMR) plotted on the x axis and the GARBE fairness measure plotted on the y axis. Each point represents an algorithm, while the Pareto efficient algorithms are connected with a red line and have their names printed. We note the Pareto frontier provides a perceptive means of down-selecting which algorithms should be considered in this optimization space. Any algorithm not on the Pareto frontier can be discarded, as there exists another selection that is either mathematically more fair or better performing. This effectively reduces the search space for the "optimal" algorithm from the 126 algorithms tested in [14] to the 9 on the Pareto frontier, a savings of over 90%. Additionally, if we further refine our search to algorithms that had very good performance overall, we only have to consider the six algorithms in the inset of Fig. 4. Algorithm didiglobalface-001 is the highest performing in this space, having achieved the lowest overall FNMR of ∼0.0022. However, it is also the least fair of the Pareto efficient set, having achieved the highest GARBE measure of ∼0.54. Conversely, algorithm intellifusion-001 was the least performative of this set, with a total FNMR of ∼0.0038, but it also had a somewhat improved GARBE fairness measure at ∼0.37. Whether this trade-off of a 0.0016 increase in total performance is worth a decline in fairness of 0.17 is a question that can be posed to system designers. However, the Pareto curve, frontier, and process we have outlined here allow this trade-space to be explored effectively.

5 Discussion

In this study we have executed the first audit of two proposed face recognition fairness measures using demographically disaggregated false match and false non-match error rates from 126 commercial and open source algorithms. We've found that both proposed models have benefits and drawbacks when it comes to interpreting their outcomes on face recognition error rates commonly found in practice. We've attempted to consolidate the benefits of each approach into a set of interpretability criteria, called the FFMC, and hope these can serve as a guide for future development of fairness measures, particularly in the face recognition domain. We've also proposed an alternative fairness measure, the Gini Aggregation Rate for Biometric Equality or GARBE that satisfies all of these criteria and demonstrated a protocol using Pareto efficiency that can rapidly identify optimal algorithms in both the overall performance and fairness domains. The main takeaways and areas of future work are delineated below.

5.1   Audit the Audit

As discussed in Sect. 2.2, there are currently a plethora of definitions for both bias sources and fairness measures propagating throughout the ML fairness space. This increased attention is a positive development. However, in such an environment, it is critical to evaluate the merits of different approaches when applying a given technique to a specific use case. Often times, when analysing the positive outcome in a specific application of a ML decision system, there is not one specific failure case that can cause harm but a set, which requires the aggregation of different error probabilities into a new metric, as we have shown here. As new metrics are developed and proposed, purveyors and evaluators of ML algorithms should strive to ensure the statistical properties of their proposed methods are well documented via the kind of audit we have performed here. In this way they can be of maximum utility to the broader ML fairness community.

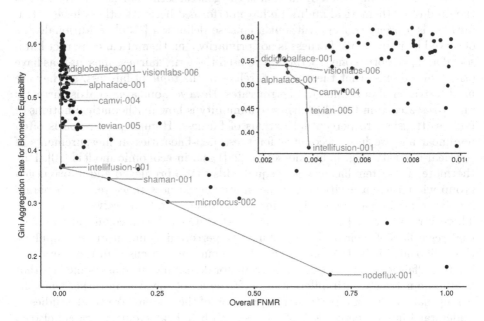

Fig. 4. Pareto curve of Gini Aggregation Rate for Biometric Equitability (GARBE) values plotted against overall performance (Total FNMR) using NIST FRVT Part 3 face recognition error rates. Red line connects algorithms that are Pareto efficient. No algorithms are weakly Pareto efficient. Inset shows zoomed area where total FNMR performance is less than 1% (Color figure online)

5.2   On the Need for Additional Fairness Data

One obvious yet often illusive requirement for auditing fairness measures in any domain is data. This study documented a set of criteria necessary for the evaluation of face recognition fairness measures in particular (Table 1). Access to data of this nature is a necessary for auditing fairness measures, yet datasets of this nature are limited at best. We have attempted to provide one such dataset by open sourcing the error rates used in this research. However, even this dataset has certain drawbacks. For example, our dataset only shows error rates at a single population-wide FMR threshold. FNMR and FMR measures across a range of representative thresholds would allow for a more complete investigation. Additionally, our dataset only includes intra-demographic false match error rates (Male-to-Male and Female-to-Female, for example). However, equatability in the face recognition domain may depend on *inter*-demographic false match rates (Male-to-Female, etc.) [15]. To promote future work in this area, evaluators of face recognition algorithms should consider making more robust datasets available to the community in a readily parsable format.

5.3   Limitations of Mathematical Formulations of Fairness

Finally, we conclude with a discussion of the general term "fairness" in relation to the kind of mathematical audits we have performed here. As others have noted, fairness is a broad concept without a concise definition [1,30]. Additionally, as observed by individuals, fairness is not primarily a mathematical construct but a social and perceptual one [18,19]. We've used the term "fairness measure" as have others in the sense that these metrics relate to the *topic* of fairness, as they are used to reason about differential error rates. However, one area that is currently under-researched in the ML fairness community is how mathematical notions of fairness translate to perceptual notions of fairness. Human perception is often nonlinear and we have accounted for these non-linearities in measurements of physical intensity (e.g. light and sound [28]) and in economic models [20]. Furthermore, if a system has precisely equal odds that a privileged and unprivileged group will receive a positive outcome in a given fairness space (e.g. a disparate impact of 1), does a human observing this system operate perceive it to be fair? There very well may be entire classes of AI systems, face recognition included, that regardless of their performance may be perceived as unfair in some applications. Should this be the case, then, despite current consensus in the literature, the term "fairness" may not be appropriate for describing the class of metrics that deal more narrowly with differential performance of the system rather than the perceptual fairness of a particular application of the system. We think studies to understand human perception of fairness will help bridge current gaps between notions of mathematical fairness based on accuracy and social/perceptual fairness in the ML fairness community.

Acknowlegments. This research was funded by the Department of Homeland Security, Science and Technology Directorate (DHS S&T) on contract number W911NF-13-D-0006-0003. The views presented do not represent those of DHS, the U.S. Government, or the author's employers.

The dataset used in this report is available on the Maryland Test Facility's github: https://github.com/TheMdTF/mdtf-public/tree/master/datasets/nist-frvt-annex15.

Paper contributions: All authors conceived the work; Eli J. Laird and John J. Howard performed the statistical analysis and wrote the paper; Yevgeniy B. Sirotin advised on statistical analysis and edited the paper. Jerry L. Tipton (IDSLabs) and Arun R. Vemury (DHS S&T) also conceived the work.

References

1. Barocas, S., Hardt, M., Narayanan, A.: Fairness and Machine Learning. fairml-book.org (2019). http://www.fairmlbook.org
2. Buolamwini, J., Gebru, T.: Gender shades: Intersectional accuracy disparities in commercial gender classification. In: Conference on fairness, accountability and transparency, pp. 77–91 (2018)
3. Cavazos, J.G., Phillips, P.J., Castillo, C.D., O'Toole, A.J.: Accuracy comparison across face recognition algorithms: where are we on measuring race bias? IEEE Trans. Biometrics Behav. Identity Sci. **3**(1), 101–111 (2021). https://doi.org/10.1109/TBIOM.2020.3027269
4. Cook, C.M., Howard, J.J., Sirotin, Y.B., Tipton, J.L., Vemury, A.R.: Demographic effects in facial recognition and their dependence on image acquisition: an evaluation of eleven commercial systems. Trans. Biometrics Behav. Identity Sci. **1**(1), 32–41 (2019)
5. Danks, D., London, A.J.: Algorithmic bias in autonomous systems. In: Proceedings of the 26th International Joint Conference on Artificial Intelligence, pp. 4691–4697. IJCAI 2017, AAAI Press (2017)
6. Das, A., Dantcheva, A., Bremond, F.: Mitigating bias in gender, age and ethnicity classification: a multi-task convolution neural network approach. In: Leal-Taixé, L., Roth, S. (eds.) ECCV 2018. LNCS, vol. 11129, pp. 573–585. Springer, Cham (2019). https://doi.org/10.1007/978-3-030-11009-3_35
7. Deltas, G.: The small-sample bias of the Gini coefficient: results and implications for empirical research. Rev. Econ. Stat. **85**(1), 226–234 (2003). http://www.jstor.org/stable/3211637
8. Department of Economic and Social Affairs: World economic sitatuon and prospects, monthly briefing. United Nations (2018). https://www.un.org/development/desa/dpad/tag/gini-coefficient/
9. Drozdowski, P., Rathgeb, C., Dantcheva, A., Damer, N., Busch, C.: Demographic bias in biometrics: a survey on an emerging challenge. vol. 1 (03 2020). https://doi.org/10.1109/TTS.2020.2992344
10. Freiwald, W., Duchaine, B., Yovel, G.: Face processing systems: from neurons to real-world social perception. Ann. Rev. Neurosci. **39**, 325–346 (2016)
11. Gini, C.: Variabilità e mutabilità. Reprinted in Memorie di metodologica statistica (Ed. Pizetti E (1912)
12. Gong, S., Liu, X., Jain, A.K.: Jointly De-Biasing face recognition and demographic attribute estimation. In: Vedaldi, A., Bischof, H., Brox, T., Frahm, J.-M. (eds.) ECCV 2020. LNCS, vol. 12374, pp. 330–347. Springer, Cham (2020). https://doi.org/10.1007/978-3-030-58526-6_20
13. Grother, P.: Demographic differentials in face recognition algorithms. EAB Virtual Event Series - Demographic Fairness in Biometric Systems (2021)
14. Grother, P., Ngan, M., Hanaoka, K.: Face Recognition Vendor Test (FRVT) Part 3: Demographic Effects. Tech. rep, United States National Institute of Standards and Technology (2019)
15. Howard, J.J., Sirotin, Y.B., Tipton, J.L., Vemury, A.R.: Quantifying the extent to which race and gender features determine identity in commercial face recognition algorithms. Tech. rep., United States Department of Homeland Security, Science and Technology Directorate, Technical Paper Series (2021)

16. Howard, J.J., Sirotin, Y.B., Vemury, A.R.: The effect of broad and specific demographic homogeneity on the imposter distributions and false match rates in face recognition algorithm performance. In: 2019 IEEE 10th International Conference on Biometrics Theory, Applications and Systems (BTAS), pp. 1–8. IEEE (2019)
17. Hutchinson, B., Mitchell, M.: 50 years of test (un)fairness: lessons for machine learning. In: Proceedings of the Conference on Fairness, Accountability, and Transparency, pp. 49–58. FAT* 2019, Association for Computing Machinery, New York, USA (2019). https://doi.org/10.1145/3287560.3287600
18. Jacobs, A.Z., Wallach, H.: Measurement and fairness. In: Proceedings of the 2021 ACM conference on fairness, accountability, and transparency, pp. 375–385 (2021)
19. Kahneman, D., Knetsch, J.L., Thaler, R.: Fairness as a constraint on profit seeking: entitlements in the market. Am. Econ. Rev. **76**(4), 728–741 (1986)
20. Kahneman, D., Tversky, A.: Prospect theory: an analysis of decision under risk. In: Handbook of the fundamentals of financial decision making: Part I, pp. 99–127. World Scientific (2013)
21. Klare, B.F., Burge, M.J., Klontz, J.C., Bruegge, R.W.V., Jain, A.K.: Face recognition performance: role of demographic information. IEEE Trans. Inf. Forensics Secur. **7**(6), 1789–1801 (2012)
22. Krishnapriya, K., Albiero, V., Vangara, K., King, M.C., Bowyer, K.W.: Issues related to face recognition accuracy varying based on race and skin tone. IEEE Trans. Technol. Soc. **1**(1), 8–20 (2020)
23. Liu, B., et al.: Fair loss: Margin-aware reinforcement learning for deep face recognition. In: 2019 IEEE/CVF International Conference on Computer Vision (ICCV), pp. 10051–10060 (2019). https://doi.org/10.1109/ICCV.2019.01015
24. Organization, I.S., Commission, I.E.: ISO/IEC 2382–37:2015: Information technology - vocabulary - part 37: Biometrics. ISO/IEC, Editor (2015)
25. Pereira, T.D.F., Marcel, S.: Fairness in biometrics: a figure of merit to assess biometric verification systems. arXiv preprint arXiv:2011.02395 (2020)
26. Pereira, T.D.F., Marcel, S.: Fairness in biometrics: a figure of merit to assess biometric verification systems. IEEE Trans. Biometrics Behav. Identity Sci. **4**(1), 1–1 (2021). https://doi.org/10.1109/TBIOM.2021.3102862
27. Phillips, P.J., Jiang, F., Narvekar, A., Ayyad, J., O'Toole, A.J.: An other-race effect for face recognition algorithms. ACM Trans. Appl. Percept. (TAP) **8**(2), 1–11 (2011)
28. Raub, M.: Bots, bias and big data: artificial intelligence, algorithmic bias and disparate impact liability in hiring practices. Ark. L. Rev. **71**, 529 (2018)
29. Taigman, Y., Yang, M., Ranzato, M., Wolf, L.: DeepFace: closing the gap to human-level performance in face verification. In: Proceedings of the IEEE Conference on Computer Vision and Pattern Recognition, pp. 1701–1708 (2014)
30. Verma, S., Rubin, J.: Fairness definitions explained. In: 2018 IEEE/ACM International Workshop on Software Fairness (fairware), pp. 1–7. IEEE (2018)
31. Wang, T., Zhao, J., Yatskar, M., Chang, K.W., Ordonez, V.: Balanced datasets are not enough: Estimating and mitigating gender bias in deep image representations. In: Proceedings of the IEEE/CVF International Conference on Computer Vision (ICCV) (October 2019)
32. Warrens, M.J.: On the Negative Bias of the Gini Coefficient due to Grouping. J. Classif. **35**(3), 580–586 (2018). https://doi.org/10.1007/s00357-018-9267-9
33. Wei, S., Niethammer, M.: The fairness-accuracy pareto front. arXiv preprint arXiv:2008.10797 (2020)

34. Wilson, C., et al.: Building and auditing fair algorithms: a case study in candidate screening. In: Proceedings of the 2021 ACM Conference on Fairness, Accountability, and Transparency, pp. 666–677. FAccT 2021, Association for Computing Machinery, New York, USA (2021). https://doi.org/10.1145/3442188.3445928
35. Zafar, M.B., Valera, I., Rogriguez, M.G., Gummadi, K.P.: Fairness constraints: Mechanisms for fair classification. In: Artificial Intelligence and Statistics, pp. 962–970. PMLR (2017)

Disparate Impact in Facial Recognition Stems from the Broad Homogeneity Effect: A Case Study and Method to Resolve

John J. Howard⊙, Eli J. Laird⁽✉⁾⊙, and Yevgeniy B. Sirotin⊙

The Identity and Data Sciences Lab at The Maryland Test Facility, Upper Malboro, Maryland, USA
{jhoward,elaird,ysirotin}@idslabs.org

Abstract. Automated face recognition algorithms generate encodings of face images that are compared to other encodings to compute a similarity score between the two originating face images. These face encodings, also known as feature vectors, contain representations of various facial features. Some of these facial features, but not all, have been shown to resemble each other across different subjects that happen to share a demographic group assignment, such as having the same race or gender. Recent work has shown that these demographically dependent features can increase similarity scores between different individuals who belong to the same demographic group compared to similarity scores for different individuals in different groups. When one feature vector is compared to many other feature vectors, as in identifications, this effect, referred to as "demographic clustering", can lead to un-equal false positive identification error rates for different demographic groups. In this study, we propose a method of mitigating this clustering effect from face recognition algorithms to reduce these un-equal error outcomes. Our method presumes that feature space patterns shared within demographic groups can be removed while preserving other distinct features of individuals. In this paper, we prove that this is possible, in principle, by applying linear dimensionality techniques to the feature space of two ArcFace face recognition algorithms. We show this method increases four distinct "fairness" measures while preserving useful true match rates.

Keywords: Face Recognition · Demographic Differentials · Disparate Impact · Fairness

1 Introduction

In the 2010s, face recognition algorithms significantly improved in accuracy due to advances in deep learning methods in computer vision. Specifically, the introduction of deep convolutional neural networks (DCNNs) to the face recognition

---

J. J. Howard, E. J. Laird and Y. B. Sirotin—All authors contributed equally to this research. Authors listed alphabetically.

J.-J. Rousseau and B. Kapralos (Eds.): ICPR 2022 Workshops, LNCS 13643, pp. 448–464, 2023.
https://doi.org/10.1007/978-3-031-37660-3_32

task achieved near human performance for the first time in 2014, with an accuracy of 97.35% on the Labeled Faces in the Wild (LFW) dataset [18,26]. The following year, a modified DCNN architecture achieved "better-than-human" performance on the same task (accuracy of 99.63%) [25]. By 2020, government tests of face recognition algorithm performance documented false positive outcomes occurring on 3 out of every 1000 searches, and false negative rates nearing 1 in 1000, when searching galleries of up to of 12 million individuals [10].

These impressive error rates on large galleries may lead advocates of face recognition technology to claim that face recognition is a solved problem. While there are many means to dispute such claims (ageing, gallery size, pose, etc.) [10], one aspect of face recognition regularly receives far less attention than these well-studied problems. Face recognition algorithms have been shown to routinely judge that different individuals, who happen to share gender, race, age, and country of origin designations are more similar than individuals who don't share these categories [11,17]. This group similarity effect has been given different names, first "broad homogeneity" in [15], then "demographically matched individuals" in [11], and "imposter pairs across homogeneous and heterogeneous categories" in [8] (we will use the first term in this manuscript).

Regardless of nomenclature, broad homogeneity was shown in Annex 5 of [11] to exist in *all* of the 138 facial recognition algorithms submitted as part of this global face recognition evaluation in 2019. Furthermore, there seems to be an acceptance, both in the research and commercial communities, that face recognition algorithms *should* behave in this manner, despite these effects being unique to face recognition and decidedly not present in other common biometric modalities, such as fingerprint and iris recognition. Of additional concern are the mathematics first highlighted in [17] and later in [5] that show, in the presence of broad homogeneity effects and imbalanced facial recognition identification galleries, a strong tendency for un-equal identification error rates across demographic groups.

For these reasons, we contend broad homogeneity effects to be an undesirable, but unfortunately, currently universal, characteristic of face recognition algorithms. Additionally, methods to reduce this effect are presently underresearched. This manuscript presents one such method that removes demographically clustered components of the facial biometric feature vector (also known as the face template) that cause broad homogeneity effects. We demonstrate the utility of this approach on two disjoint datasets of test subjects who self reported their gender and race affiliations. We further show that, after applying this technique, each of four currently proposed facial recognition fairness metrics shows an improvement.

2   Background

2.1   Broad Versus Specific Homogeneity Fairness Criteria

A face verification operation involves a one-to-one comparison of two face images. Images are first converted to face feature vectors within a p-dimensional feature space. Two face feature vectors can then be mathematically compared to compute a similarity score that represents the similarity between the two originating face images. If the resulting score is greater than some threshold τ, the algorithm is indicating that the original face images are from the same person. A false match error occurs when an algorithm produces a score greater than τ for two face images that, in fact, were from different people (also known as a non-mated pair). False match rate (FMR) is the frequency with which a false match error occurs in all possible non-mated image pairs within a given evaluation dataset.

When considering the "fairness" of facial recognition systems in regards to FMR, [17] introduced two separate criteria to consider. Briefly, the first, termed "specific homogeneity fairness criteria", stipulated that FMR measured within demographic group should be equal for each group, but that FMR measured between different groups could still take a different (presumably lower) value. For example, the false match rate when Black Males are compared to other Black Males would equal the false match rate when White Females were compared to other White Females ($\mathrm{FMR}_{(WM,WM)} == \mathrm{FMR}_{(BM,BM)}$) but the false match rate between Black Males and White Males may be lower than the false match rate between Black Males ($\mathrm{FMR}_{(WM,BM)} < \mathrm{FMR}_{(BM,BM)}$). That a face recognition algorithm would operate in this way is intuitive to humans because human facial recognition processes behave in this way as well.

However, [17] also demonstrated (along with [5]) that, should specific homogeneity fairness criteria be the goal, disparities in face recognition identification (one-to-N) error rates could still persist, particularly in the presence of demographically imbalanced identification galleries. For this reason [17] advocates for a second criteria for assessing facial recognition systems in regards to FMR, the "broad homogeneity fairness criteria". This criteria states that the false match rate for cross demographic groups should equal the FMR of within demographic groups. Using our previous example, in this model $\mathrm{FMR}_{(WM,WM)} == \mathrm{FMR}_{(BM,BM)} == \mathrm{FMR}_{(WM,BM)}$. This face recognition algorithm would operate in a way that is un-intuitive to humans, as it would confuse White Males for Black Males equally often as it would confuse White Males for other White Males. However, a face recognition algorithm that operated in this fashion may be able to achieve metrically more fair identification outcomes. Graphic descriptions of the specific and broad homogeneity fairness criteria are shown in Fig. 1A and B, respectively.

2.2   Achieving Broad Homogeneity

As stated, demographic clustering effects were found to exist in every face identification algorithm tested in [11]. With such an ubiquitous effect, one might be inclined to think it a natural characteristic of face recognition in general. However, [17] showed that only a small portion of the information content available in a human face appears to be consonant across different people within gender and race categories. On five separate leading commercial face recognition algorithms, [17] found that just 10% of the variation in non-mated similarity score could be attributed to race and gender clustering. This suggests that if a face

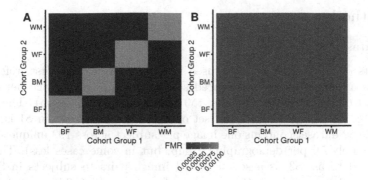

Fig. 1. Examples of cohort matrices that demonstrate fair false match rates (FMR) across demographic groups according to A) the specific homogeneity fairness condition and B) the broad homogeneity fairness condition. Example cohorts are Black Female (BF), Black Male (BM), White Female(WF), and White Male (WM), although the concept applies to categorical demographic groups generally.

recognition algorithm ignored these clustering components, it may be able to achieve broad homogeneity while still maintaining useful levels of performance.

One limitation of [17] was that it measured these grouping effects only in similarity scores between individuals, i.e. the "score space". The researchers achieved this by performing eigenvalue decomposition on a matrix of cross subject similarity scores, as produced by each commercial algorithm. This technique is useful for measuring the magnitude of demographic clustering across algorithms. It could also potentially be useful for removing demographic clustering on a *static* population of identities, such as an access control scenario where every individual attempting to interact with a system is known and the population is relatively stable. However, removing demographic clustering in score space is not practical for algorithms meant to operate on *dynamic* populations, such as a system where new enrolles are frequent or where out-of-gallery or non-mate comparisons are frequent. This is because the specific identities in the database form the basis of score space and correction relies on removing patterns across these identities, not across face features. Furthermore, this correction necessitates establishing demographic group membership of each identity in the sample.

To adapt to the dynamic setting, one must develop a transformation that when computed on one set of subjects can be successfully applied to a disjoint set, i.e. a generalized transformation. Here, we will show that such a transformation can be computed using the p-dimensional feature vectors of face recognition algorithms. We will also show that transformations derived from this space can be applied to the embeddings generated from identities not in the original set and that when error rates and comparison scores generated from the original and transformed features are evaluated, fairness measures consistently improve.

3   Methods

3.1   Dataset

Three sets of images/subjects are used in this research. The first, referred to as 'S1', is a demographically balanced set. S1 contains one image per subject across 600 unique subjects (exactly 150 per demographic group). The second set, referred to as 'S2', is a disjoint set of subjects. No subject in S1 is present in S2. The S2 dataset contains one image per subject across 192 unique subjects (approximately 50 per demographic group, but in some cases less). The third set, referred to as 'S3' is a set of mated image pairs to subjects in S1. The purpose of S3 is to validate that our transforms (see Sect. 3.3) do not corrupt face templates to the point that matching transformed templates to other mated pairs is no longer possible. S3 is not intended to validate transforms that reduce demographic clustering. S3 contains between 1-6 images per subject across 466 unique subjects. Not all subjects in S1 had a corresponding mated image. All datasets were collected by a trained biometric collection operator, minimizing any issues related to image acquisition quality. All samples were collected at biometric scenario evaluations that took place from 2018–2021 [1, 13].

The disjoint property of S1 and S2 is a purposeful and important characteristic. Simply because two subjects identify into the same demographic group, White Male for example, does not signify that they necessarily share similar facial features. S1 and S2 may therefore have legitimately different patterns with respect to face features, despite having the exact same demographic groups.

Table 1. Number of subjects and samples for datasets used in this research.

Dataset	Subjects (Samples)			
	Black Female	Black Male	White Female	White Male
S1	150 (150)	150 (150)	150 (150)	150 (150)
S2	50 (50)	50 (50)	49 (49)	43 (43)
S3	106 (300)	117 (339)	126 (321)	117 (278)

3.2   ArcFace Face Recognition Algorithm

In 2019, Deng et al. [4] proposed and open-sourced a new face recognition loss function named ArcFace that reached the state-of-the-art verification accuracy of 99.83% on the LFW dataset. The ArcFace algorithm belongs to a family of 'margin-based' loss functions that apply margins to their logits to encourage class separability. ArcFace's predecessors, such as SphereFace [21] and CosFace [27], introduced this concept of penalizing class centers in the angular space using margins. ArcFace expanded on these techniques by introducing an additive angular margin loss that improves the compactness of intra-class samples and the separation of inter-class samples in the face embedding space.

A face recognition model trained with ArcFace loss was chosen for this study for three reasons. First, the techniques we outline here require "white-box" algorithms, where the feature space can be interpreted. In many commercial face recognition algorithms, this is not possible. Second, a model trained with Arc-Face has been shown to be one of the highest-ranking, open-source, face recognition algorithms in 1-to-1 comparisons according to NIST's 2021 Face Recognition Vendor Test (FRVT) [10]. Third, the developers of ArcFace open-sourced several pre-trained models [20].

In this work we leverage two pre-trained models obtained from [20]. The first is a ResNet-100 [14], trained on a refined version of the MS-Celeb-1M dataset [12] (referred to here as "ArcFace-MS1MV2"). This is the model that was evaluated in FRVT. We also utilize a second model that is an iResNet-100 [6] trained on the Glint360k dataset [2] (referred to here as "ArcFace-Glint360k"). This model is an improvement over the initial ArcFace-MS1MV2 model submitted to FRVT, both in terms of the training dataset and the architecture used. The Glint360k dataset is much larger and more demographically diverse than MS-Celeb-1M, which when used to train the iResNet architecture led to better performance reported across demographic groups according to [20].

3.3 Identifying and Removing Demographic Clustering in Feature Vectors

The S1 and S2 face samples described in Table 1 were processed using both the ArcFace-MS1MV2 and ArcFace-Glint360k algorithms producing a set of 1584 feature vectors. No failure to process errors occurred. ArcFace feature vectors are 512-dimensional. However, in general the techniques described here apply to any arbitrarily length feature vector $v \in \mathbb{R}^{1 \times p}$.

Identifying Demographic Clustering. We first use the $n = 600$ samples in dataset S1 to identify feature vectors that exhibit demographic clustering using the following approach. First, we normalize the feature vectors such that $\hat{v} = \frac{\bar{v}}{\|\bar{v}\|}$. We then construct a normalized matrix of feature vectors for n subjects $\hat{V}$, where $\hat{V} \in \mathbb{R}^{n \times p}$. This matrix can be decomposed into its subject and feature specific components using singular value decomposition (SVD). The singular value decomposition of feature matrix $\hat{V}$ is defined by $\hat{V} = U \Sigma W^T$, where $U \in \mathbb{R}^{n \times n}$, $\Sigma \in \mathbb{R}^{n \times p}$, and $W^T \in \mathbb{R}^{p \times p}$.

Given the matrix of subject specific components, U, and the demographic labels for each feature vector (see Table 1), we identify which components cluster by demographic group by calculating the clustering index [17] shown in Eq. (1). C_k describes the percent of variance in subject-specific component k that is explained by race and gender features. C_k is calculated by taking the ratio of *within group* variance for a demographic group D $(\sum_D \sum_{i \in D} (u_i - \bar{u}_D)^2)$ and dividing by the *overall* variance in the subject-specific component space $(\sum_i (u_i - \bar{u})^2)$. In this model, if component k had subjects spread over the full space in equal proportion to the variance of that space, both numerator and denominator would be equal and $C_k = 0$. However, if subjects in a group D are spread over less than the full component space, i.e. *cluster* in that space, the numerator becomes less than the denominator and C_k rises.

$$C_k = 1 - \frac{\sum_D \sum_{i \in D}(u_i - \bar{u}_D)^2}{\sum_i(u_i - \bar{u})^2}, \quad k, i \in \{1, ..., n\} \tag{1}$$

Empirically, every C_k is bound to have a non-zero value due to noise in the feature space, therefore we must identify which components have a statistically significant clustering indices. To evaluate the significance of each clustering index we generate a null distribution C_{null} by randomly shuffling each subject's demographic labels and calculating C_k; this is repeated 1000 times to generate the distribution of C_k values. We then define statistically significant features to be those with C_k values greater than the 99th percentile of the C_{null} distribution.

We note that the use of the linear SVD method limits us to only removing clustering based on linear relationships within groups. Removing non-linear clustering will require the use of non-linear decomposition techniques and is the focus of future research.

Removing Demographic Clustering. Once identified, features that exhibit significant demographic clustering in the encoded subject space (U) can be removed from the encoded feature space (W^T). The result of this reduced matrix is $\hat{W}$, where $\hat{W} \in \mathbb{R}^{p \times m}$, and $m = p - r$. The r components are identified from $R = \{U_i...U_r\}$. Using the reduced matrix $\hat{W}$, we can reconstruct a modified feature vector $\dot{v}$ for any arbitrary v by applying the transformation $\dot{v} = v\hat{W}\hat{W}^T$. If the components of R were appropriately selected, the reconstructed feature vector $\dot{v}$ should have reduced demographic clustering and thus reduced overall specific homogeneity effects.

This technique specifically is an extension of the method proposed in [17], in which a similar transformation is performed in the score space using the eigenvalue decomposition of the similarity matrix S. More broadly, this is a modification on a widely used pattern for dimensionality reduction using SVD [24]. Our novel contributions are the application of this approach to biometric feature vectors and the selection mechanism using the clustering index C_k.

3.4   Biometric Fairness Metrics

To evaluate the efficacy of our proposed method, we apply four biometric fairness metrics to quantify the method's ability to reduce demographic bias. The four fairness metrics include the Net Clustering metric from [17], the Gini Aggregation Rate for Biometric Equitability (GARBE) from [16], the Fairness Discrepancy Rate (FDR) from [23], and the NIST Inequity Ratio from [9].

The Net Clustering metric [17], defined in Eq. 2, measures the proportion of total variance in the feature vectors explained by demographic clustering, where C_k is the clustering index defined in Sect. 3.3, σ_k^2 is the variance of the kth feature, and σ_{net}^2 is the total variance in the feature vectors. For the Net Clustering metric, a value closer to zero indicates a more "fair" algorithm.

$$C_{net} = \frac{1}{\sigma_{net}^2} \sum_k \sigma_k^2 C_k \tag{2}$$

The GARBE metric [16] is a fairness measure inspired by the Gini coefficient, a historical measure of dispersion often used in measuring wealth inequality [7]. In [16], the Gini coefficient is applied to biometric error rates, specifically the false match rate (FMR) and false non-match rate (FNMR) across demographic group D, as shown in Eqs. (3) and (5). As an extension of the Gini coefficient, GARBE combines measures of FMR and FNMR dispersion using a weighing factor α as shown in Eq. (5). Similarly to Net Clustering, a value closer to zero indicates a more fair algorithm according to the GARBE metric.

$$G_x = \left(\frac{n}{n-1} \right) \left(\frac{\sum_{i=1}^{n} \sum_{j=1}^{n} |x_i - x_j|}{2n^2 \bar{x}} \right) \; \forall d_i, d_j \in D \qquad (3)$$

$$A(\tau) = G_{FMR_\tau}; \; B(\tau) = G_{FNMR_\tau} \qquad (4)$$

$$GARBE(\tau) = \alpha A(\tau) + (1 - \alpha)B(\tau) \qquad (5)$$

The Fairness Discrepancy Rate (FDR) [23] is made up of two values: the first, shown in Eq. (6), measures the maximum difference in FMR values between demographic groups D for a given threshold τ and the second, shown in Eq. (7), measures the maximum difference in FNMR between demographic groups at the same threshold τ. As in Eqs. (5), (6) and (7) are mixed with the hyper-parameter α and subtracted from 1 to form the Fairness Discrepancy Rate shown in Eq. 8. Unlike other fairness metrics, the FDR metric increases as "fairness" increases, meaning a value closer to 1 is more desirable.

$$A(\tau) = \max(|FMR_{d_i}(\tau) - FMR_{d_j}(\tau)|) \; \forall d_i, d_j \in D \qquad (6)$$

$$B(\tau) = \max(|FNMR_{d_i}(\tau) - FNMR_{d_j}(\tau)|) \; \forall d_i, d_j \in D \qquad (7)$$

$$FDR(\tau) = 1 - (\alpha A(\tau) + (1 - \alpha)B(\tau)) \qquad (8)$$

The NIST Inequity Ratio takes the maximum difference in FMR and FNMR values into account as a ratio as shown in Eqs. (9) and (10). This approach then proposes multiplicative and exponential scaling by risk ratios α and β as opposed to additive scaling as shown in Eq. (11).

$$A(\tau) = \frac{\max(FMR_{d_i}(\tau))}{\min(FMR_{d_j}(\tau))} \; \forall d_i, d_j \in D \qquad (9)$$

$$B(\tau) = \frac{\max(FNMR_{d_i}(\tau))}{\min(FNMR_{d_j}(\tau))} \; \forall d_i, d_j \in D \qquad (10)$$

$$INEQ(\tau) = A(\tau)^\alpha B(\tau)^\beta \qquad (11)$$

We note a special case of the Inequity Ratio is to only calculate this ratio when $i == j \; \forall d_i, d_j \in D$, essentially calculating the ratio across the diagonal of a cohort matrix (see Fig. 1). We refer to this measure as $INEQ(\tau)^\star$.

4   Results

Before applying the transform to the feature vectors, we performed comparisons and calculated false match rates for both the S1 and S2 datasets, resulting in 360,000 and 36,864 comparisons respectively. We found that threshold values of 0.647 and 0.635 produced a false match rate of $1e^{-3}$ globally across the S1 dataset for comparisons performed by ArcFace-MS1MV2 and ArcFace-Glint360k, respectively. We use a global false match rate of $1e^{-3}$ to represent the use case of access control or small gallery matching at border exit and entry sites [22]. For the disjoint S2 set, threshold values of 0.657 and 0.635 produced the same false match rates, again respectively. Cross comparisons between untransformed S1 and S3 sets produced a mated comparison set of 1,238. Of these, one similarity score was below the respective S1 dataset thresholds for the ArcFace-MS1MV2 and ArcFace-Glint360k algorithms ($FNMR = 8.1e^{-4}$).

Two experiments were then performed to evaluate the proposed transform's ability to remove clustering. In Experiment 1, the de-clustering transform is calculated from the S1 dataset and evaluated on the S1 dataset. In Experiment 2, the transform calculated in Experiment 1 is applied to the S2 dataset to test the ability of de-clustering on a disjoint set. In these experiments, when evaluating fairness measure outcomes for metrics with hyper-parameters, we set α to 1 and β to 0. This focuses the measure on variations in false match rate, which are material to broad homogeneity effects.

4.1   Experiment 1 - De-Clustering Learned and Applied to the Same Dataset

The first experiment's purpose is to show that the transform described in Sect. 3.3 is capable of removing demographic clustering effects and increasing fairness from the same dataset the transform is derived from. This is a first-order check that this technique may be useful more broadly. Before applying the de-clustering transformation, at a population FMR of $1e^{-3}$ the Black Female cohort-specific FMR was the largest at $9.75e^{-3}$ and the FMR for the White Male cohort was the smallest at $6.26e^{-4}$. Note the Black Female FMR is roughly 10x larger than the population FMR and the White Male FMR is roughly half of the population FMR. The ratio between the max and min within cohort FMRs, is a factor of roughly 15 ($INEQ(\tau)^{\star} = 9.75e^{-3}/6.26e^{-4} = 15.58$).

Once the transform is applied to the ArcFace-MS1MV2 templates, this dispersion is noticeably reduced, with the highest FMR still belonging to the Black Female cohort but now at a rate of $1.34e^{-3}$ (1.34x larger than the population FMR) and the lowest FMR still belonging to the White Male cohort but now at a rate of $3.58e^{-4}$ (35% of the population FMR). The full FMR spectrum is shown in Fig. 2. Accordingly, every biometric fairness measure introduced in Sect. 3.4 moved in a "more fair" direction after the transform (see Table 2).

A similar effect was observed when applying the de-clustering transformation to the ArcFace-Glint360k templates. Despite being trained on a larger, more diverse dataset, templates generated with this ArcFace model still had a

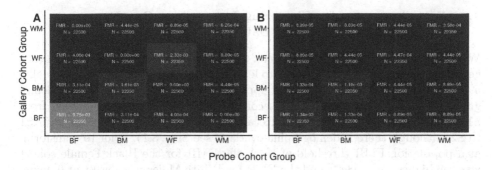

Fig. 2. A) False match rates across demographic groups *before* removing demographic clustering from ArcFace-MS1MV2 templates on S1 dataset. B) False match rates across demographic groups *after* removing demographic clustering from ArcFace-MS1MV2 templates on S1 dataset.

noticeable spread in FMR. At a population FMR of $1e^{-3}$ the FMR of the Black Female cohort was again the highest at $8.66e^{-3}$, 8.6x higher than the disaggregated measure. The FMR for White Males was again the lowest at $5.37e^{-4}$ or roughly half of the disaggregated measure. The ratio between these disaggregated FMRs is on a similar scale to the ratio observed in the MS1MV2 templates $(INEQ(\tau)^* = 8.66e^{-3}/5.37e^{-4} = 16.23)$.

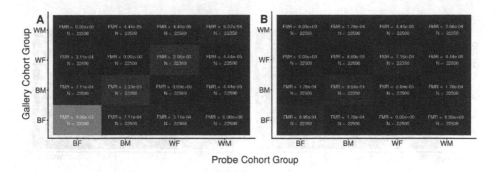

Fig. 3. A) False match rates across demographic groups *before* removing demographic clustering from ArcFace-Glint360k templates on S1 dataset. B) False match rates across demographic groups *after* removing demographic clustering from ArcFace-Glint360k templates on S1 dataset.

After applying the transform described in Sect. 3.3, all within cohort FMR's were within an order of magnitude of each other. The highest FMR now belonged to the Black Male cohort at $9.84e^{-4}$ and the lowest FMR still belonged to White Males at $2.68e^{-4}$. Importantly, this spread is only a factor of roughly 4x. Accordingly, all biometric fairness measures outlined in Sect. 3.4 improved (see Table 2).

4.2   Experiment 2 - De-Clustering Learned on One Dataset and Applied to a Disjoint Dataset

While encouraging, the results in Sect. 4.1 are of limited utility if they do not generalize beyond the subjects used to learn the de-clustering transform. Ideally, a transform $\hat{W}$ (See Sect. 3.3) would apply to other subjects with similar demographics. To test this capability, a second experiment using a $\hat{W}$ learned from S1 was applied to the dataset S2. Recall, there is no subject overlap from S1 to S2, although there is demographic overlap (see Sect. 3.1). Prior to transform, at a population FMR threshold of $1e^{-3}$, the FMR for the Black Female cohort was the highest at $8.98e^{-3}$ and the FMR for White Males was lowest at 0, using the ArcFace-MS1MV2 templates. The FMR for the second lowest cohort, White Females, was $8.5e^{-4}$, making the best calculable spread ratio roughly an order of magnitude $(INEQ(\tau)^\star = 8.98e^{-3}/8.5e^{-4} = 10.56)$.

When the transformation, derived from the S1 dataset, is applied to the disjoint S2 dataset, we again see a decrease in error-rate disparity for FMR as shown in Fig. 4. While the correction is smaller in magnitude than when it was when learned and applied within S1 (as expected), the decrease shows that the transformation can be generalized to an extent to feature vectors derived from unseen faces. After the de-clustering transform, the highest FMR was still for black females at $7.35e^{-3}$. The lowest, non-zero FMR is for White Males, at $1.11e^{-3}$. This factor of $INEQ(\tau)^\star \approx 7$ is an improvement on the spread observed before the transform. All other biometric fairness measures outlined in Sect. 3.4 also improved (see Table 2).

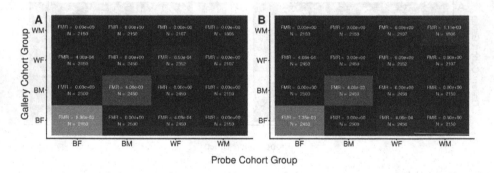

Fig. 4. A) False match rates across demographic groups *before* removing demographic clustering from ArcFace-MS1MV2 templates on S2 dataset. B) False match rates across demographic groups *after* removing demographic clustering from ArcFace-MS1MV2 templates on S2 dataset.

A similar effect was observed when applying the de-clustering transformation, derived from the S1 dataset, to the ArcFace-Glint360k templates in S2. Originally in the S2 dataset, at a population FMR of $1e^{-3}$, the Black Female cohort experienced a FMR of nearly 10x that rate ($1.06e^{-2}$). The lowest FMR was experienced by the White Male group at 0 and the second lowest by the White Female group at $8.5e^{-4}$. The spread ratio between the highest and lowest calculable within cohort FMRs is thus ($INEQ(\tau)^{\star} = 1.06e^{-2}/8.5e^{-4} = 12.5$). After the de-clustering transform is applied all within cohort FMR's were within an order of magnitude of each other. The highest FMR was still for the Black Female cohort at $4.08e^{-3}$ and the lowest non-zero FMR was for White Males at $1.11e^{-3}$, leading to a $INEQ(\tau)^{\star}$ of 4x. All other biometric fairness measures outlined in Sect. 3.4 also improved (see Table 2).

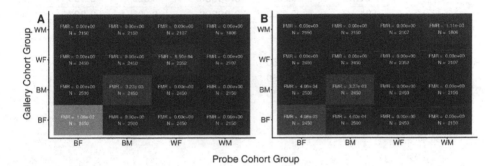

Fig. 5. A) False match rates across demographic groups *before* removing demographic clustering from ArcFace-Glint360k templates on S2 dataset. B) False match rates across demographic groups *after* removing demographic clustering from ArcFace-Glint360k templates on S2 dataset.

The de-clustering transform derived from the S1 dataset, on both algorithms, was also applied to feature vectors in the S3 dataset and mated similarity scores between S1 and transformed S3 were calculated. Of 1,238 mated comparisons, one had a similarity score below the S1 non-transformed threshold, giving an $FNMR = 8.1e^{-4}$. Upon further inspection this one false non-match was for a subject who's clothing had a distractor face, meaning the true FNMR for both the transformed and untransformed templates was likely 0. FNMRs at these levels confirm the feature vector transform documented here both improves fairness (see Table 2) while preserving useful true match rates.

5   Discussion and Conclusions

5.1   Summary

In this research, we've shown that the clustering index metric can be used to measure demographic clustering in the space of face recognition feature vectors. We

Table 2. Fairness metric values calculated on the training (S1) and test (S2) datasets, using the ArcFace-MS1MV2 and ArcFace-Glint360k algorithm, before and after demographic clustering correction. Optimal fairness measures for each experiment are shown in **bold**. Note that fairness measures *universally* move in a "more fair" direction (increasing for FDR, decreasing for Net Clustering, GARBE, and NIST INEQ) once the demographic clustering correction method from Sect. 3.3 is applied.

Algorithm	Fairness	Experiment 1		Experiment 2	
	Metric	S1 Original	S1 Transformed	S2 Original	S2 Transformed
ArcFace-MS1MV2	Net Clustering	0.0163	**0.00549**	0.0252	**0.0207**
	GARBE	0.8540	**0.65000**	0.922	**0.909**
	FDR	0.9900	**0.99900**	0.991	**0.993**
	INEQ	219.00	**30.2000**	22.00	**18.00**
	INEQ*	15.58	**3.74**	10.56	**6.62**
ArcFace-Glint360k	Net Clustering	0.0150	**0.00497**	0.0250	**0.0197**
	GARBE	0.8350	**0.67100**	0.955	**0.881**
	FDR	0.9910	**0.99900**	0.990	**0.996**
	INEQ	199.00	**22.1000**	12.5	**10.20**
	INEQ*	16.23	**3.67**	12.47	**3.68**

then show how we can use this knowledge to form a matrix transformation that removes feature vector components that exhibit demographic clustering from a disjoint test set of feature vectors. Applying this transformation decreases the disparity in false match rates across demographic groups. As evidence of this, we show increases in four published "fairness" metrics. We replicate these findings across two, separately trained biometric algorithms, ArcFace-MS1MV2 and ArcFace-Glint360k. We believe this is evidence of this approaches generalizability and utility.

5.2 Impact on Human and Algorithm Identification Workflows - Why Does This Matter?

When performing face identifications in practice, it is common to use a face recognition algorithm to generate similarity scores between a probe image and a gallery of images. The results are then ranked by decreasing similarity score and down-selected to include only the top n possible matches, referred to here as a "rank-n candidate list". This candidate list is then passed on to a human adjudicator whose task is to choose the image from the list that matches the probe subject.

Broad homogeneity effects in the identification context mean that the candidate list will consist largely of subjects belonging to the same demographic group as the probe subject. This consequently makes the identification task for the human more difficult, which can result in errant outcomes.

To explore the broad homogeneity effect in an identification operation, we performed identifications for the 192 subjects in the S2 dataset against the 600 subjects in the S1 dataset and ranked them by their similarity scores. This process was performed for both the original and transformed ArcFace-MS1MV2 face templates. In Fig. 6 we show two, Rank-4 candidate lists resulting from the identification of two subjects; one list generated using the original face templates, Fig. 6A-B, and the other generated using the transformed templates, Fig. 6C-D. To simulate what the human adjudicator would see in the identification process we embed a mated image amongst the Rank-4 non-mated images in a random position.

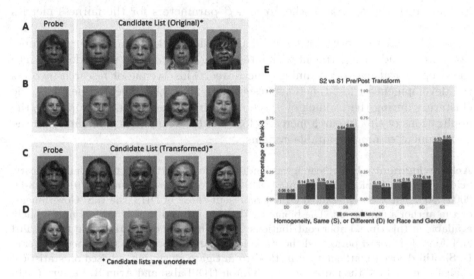

Fig. 6. (A-B) Rank-4 Candidate lists, with mated images included, for two subjects in S2 dataset compared against images in S1 dataset for non-transformed ArcFace-MS1MV2 face templates. (C-D) Rank-4 Candidate lists, with mated images included, for two subjects in S2 dataset compared against images in S1 dataset for transformed ArcFace-MS1MV2 face templates. (E) Percentage of homogeneity in Rank-4 identification results.

For both of the non-transformed candidate lists in Fig. 6A-B, we note that all subjects included in the list are of the same demographic group. After applying the transform, the candidate list for one probe changed from a demographically homogeneous list in Fig. 6A, to demographically diverse list in Fig. 6D. We also note that the demographic homogeneity for the other candidate list, Fig. 6C, did not change after applying the transformation, highlighting that future work in developing more sophisticated transformations is needed. Despite the remaining homogeneity of some candidate lists in this experiment, we do note an 11% decrease in the percentage subjects belonging to the same demographic group within the Rank-4 results, as seen in Fig. 6E.

5.3   Further Research

This research demonstrates that broad homogeneity effects can be reduced by removing components of the face feature vectors that show demographic clustering. However, due to the limited size of the datasets used here, we suggest further analysis is needed to confirm the effectiveness of the proposed method on larger, open-source identification galleries comparable to those used in practice. We also suggest analysis of the proposed method on face recognition models trained with other loss functions, such as CurricularFace [19] or ElasticFace [3], as well as the evaluation of the approach when α and β parameters for the fairness metrics vary.

In addition to the use of larger identification galleries and other loss functions, we intend to experiment with integrating the proposed methodologies into the deep neural network training procedures. This avenue of research involves the development of loss functions designed to limit the effects of demographic clustering during the training of a face recognition algorithm. We hope that the applications of this research increases focus in the biometrics community on the development of more equitable systems.

Acknowlegment. This research was funded by the Department of Homeland Security, Science and Technology Directorate (DHS S&T) on contract number W911NF-13-D-0006-0003. The views presented do not represent those of DHS, the U.S. Government, or the author's employers. The biometric dataset utilized in this work is not publicly available at this time. Paper contributions: All authors conceived the work; Eli J. Laird and John J. Howard performed the statistical analysis and wrote the paper; Yevgeniy B. Sirotin devised mathematical method to mitigate clustering, advised on statistical analysis, and edited the paper. Jerry L. Tipton (IDSLabs) and Arun R. Vemury (DHS S&T) also conceived the work.

References

1. Rally - Maryland Test Facility. https://mdtf.org/Rally2021
2. An, X., et al.: Partial FC: training 10 million identities on a single machine. In: 2021 IEEE/CVF International Conference on Computer Vision Workshops (ICCVW), pp. 1445–1449 (2021). https://doi.org/10.1109/ICCVW54120.2021.00166
3. Boutros, F., Damer, N., Kirchbuchner, F., Kuijper, A.: ElasticFace: elastic margin loss for deep face recognition. CoRR abs/2109.09416 (2021). https://arxiv.org/abs/2109.09416
4. Deng, J., Guo, J., Niannan, X., Zafeiriou, S.: ArcFace: additive angular margin loss for deep face recognition. In: CVPR (2019)
5. Drozdowski, P., Rathgeb, C., Busch, C.: The watchlist imbalance effect in biometric face identification: comparing theoretical estimates and empiric measurements. In: Proceedings of the IEEE/CVF International Conference on Computer Vision, pp. 3757–3765 (2021)
6. Duta, I.C., Liu, L., Zhu, F., Shao, L.: Improved residual networks for image and video recognition. arXiv preprint arXiv:2004.04989 (2020)
7. Gini, C.: Variabilità e mutabilità. Reprinted in Memorie di metodologica statistica (Ed. Pizetti E) (1912)

8. Gong, S., Liu, X., Jain, A.K.: Jointly de-biasing face recognition and demographic attribute estimation. In: Vedaldi, A., Bischof, H., Brox, T., Frahm, J.-M. (eds.) ECCV 2020. LNCS, vol. 12374, pp. 330–347. Springer, Cham (2020). https://doi.org/10.1007/978-3-030-58526-6_20
9. Grother, P.: Face recognition vendor test (FRVT) part 8: summarizing demographic differentials (2022)
10. Grother, P., Ngan, M., Hanaoka, K.: Face recognition vendor test (FRVT) part 2: identification (2018)
11. Grother, P., Ngan, M., Hanaoka, K.: Face recognition vendor test (FRVT) part 3: demographic effects (2019)
12. Guo, Y., Zhang, L., Hu, Y., He, X., Gao, J.: MS-Celeb-1M: a dataset and benchmark for large-scale face recognition. In: Leibe, B., Matas, J., Sebe, N., Welling, M. (eds.) ECCV 2016. LNCS, vol. 9907, pp. 87–102. Springer, Cham (2016). https://doi.org/10.1007/978-3-319-46487-9_6
13. Hasselgren, J.A., Howard, J.J., Sirotin, Y.B., Tipton, J.L., Vemury, A.R.: A scenario evaluation of high-throughput face biometric systems: select results from the 2019 Department of Homeland Security Biometric Technology Rally. The Maryland Test Facility (2020)
14. He, K., Zhang, X., Ren, S., Sun, J.: Deep residual learning for image recognition. In: 2016 IEEE Conference on Computer Vision and Pattern Recognition (CVPR), pp. 770–778 (2016)
15. Howard, J.J., Sirotin, Y.B., Vemury, A.R.: The effect of broad and specific demographic homogeneity on the imposter distributions and false match rates in face recognition algorithm performance. In: 2019 IEEE 10th International Conference on Biometrics Theory, Applications and Systems (BTAS), pp. 1–8 (2019). https://doi.org/10.1109/BTAS46853.2019.9186002
16. Howard, J.J., Laird, E.J., Sirotin, Y.B., Rubin, R.E., Tipton, J.L., Vemury, A.R.: Evaluating proposed fairness models for face recognition algorithms (2022). https://doi.org/10.48550/ARXIV.2203.05051. https://arxiv.org/abs/2203.05051
17. Howard, J.J., Sirotin, Y.B., Tipton, J.L., Vemury, A.R.: Quantifying the extent to which race and gender features determine identity in commercial face recognition algorithms (2020)
18. Huang, G., Mattar, M.A., Berg, T.L., Learned-Miller, E.: Labeled faces in the wild: a database for studying face recognition in unconstrained environments (2008)
19. Huang, Y., et al.: CurricularFace: adaptive curriculum learning loss for deep face recognition. CoRR abs/2004.00288 (2020). https://arxiv.org/abs/2004.00288
20. InsightFace: State-of-the-art 2D and 3D face analysis project. https://github.com/deepinsight/insightface/tree/master/model_zoo
21. Liu, W., Wen, Y., Yu, Z., Li, M., Raj, B., Song, L.: SphereFace: deep hypersphere embedding for face recognition. In: Proceedings of the IEEE Conference on Computer Vision and Pattern Recognition, pp. 212–220 (2017)
22. Manaher, C.: Privacy impact assessment for the traveler verification service (2018). https://www.dhs.gov/publication/dhscbppia-056-traveler-verification-service
23. de Freitas Pereira, T., Marcel, S.: Fairness in biometrics: a figure of merit to assess biometric verification systems. IEEE Trans. Biometrics Behav. Identity Sci 4, 19–29 (2021). https://doi.org/10.1109/TBIOM.2021.3102862
24. Rajaraman, A., Ullman, J.D.: Mining of Massive Datasets. Cambridge University Press (2011)
25. Schroff, F., Kalenichenko, D., Philbin, J.: FaceNet: a unified embedding for face recognition and clustering. In: Proceedings of the IEEE Computer Society Con-

ference on Computer Vision and Pattern Recognition, 07–12-June, pp. 815–823 (2015). https://doi.org/10.1109/CVPR.2015.7298682

26. Taigman, Y., Yang, M., Ranzato, M., Wolf, L.: DeepFace: closing the gap to human-level performance in face verification. In: Proceedings of the IEEE Conference on Computer Vision and Pattern Recognition, pp. 1701–1708 (2014)

27. Wang, H., et al.: CosFace: large margin cosine loss for deep face recognition. In: Proceedings of the IEEE Conference on Computer Vision and Pattern Recognition, pp. 5265–5274 (2018)

The Influence of Gender and Skin Colour on the Watchlist Imbalance Effect in Facial Identification Scenarios

Jascha Kolberg(✉), Christian Rathgeb, and Christoph Busch

da/sec - Biometrics and Internet Security Research Group Hochschule Darmstadt,
Darmstadt, Germany
{jascha.kolberg,christian.rathgeb,christoph.busch}@h-da.de
https://dasec.h-da.de/

Abstract. Nowadays it is well known that artificial intelligence can be biased. In biometric recognition, this is a very sensitive topic since biased algorithms often discriminate against specific demographic groups. This can have severe consequences when searching criminal databases or blacklists. In this context, the watchlist imbalance effect might induce additional performance differentials based on the demographic composition of the target database. In this work, we utilise a fairly distributed subset of the FairFace database to evaluate the watchlist imbalance effect when combining the demographic attributes gender and skin colour. The results show that the skin colour has a huge impact on the differential performance to the disadvantage of dark skin tones.

Keywords: Bias and Fairness · Biometric Face Identification · Watchlist Imbalance Effect · Demographic Inequitity

1 Introduction

With the steadily increasing usage of machine learning and artificial intelligence in all areas of our daily life, concerns regarding fairness and bias in aforementioned techniques rise accordingly [11,25,30]. Consequently, first efforts are made to measure fairness for machine learning methods [2,29], even for already trained black-box models [33].

In the area of biometric recognition, (deep) machine learning methods for different tasks are considered as the state-of-the-art since they already surpassed human recognition performance [27,28]. In this context, algorithmic bias in biometrics is an especially sensitive topic as it can lead to higher arrest rates for specific demographic groups, e.g. in the case of applying facial recognition software [4,13]. In recent years, the problem of demographic bias in biometrics [1,10]

This research work has been funded by the German Federal Ministry of Education and Research and the Hessian Ministry of Higher Education, Research, Science and the Arts within their joint support of the National Research Center for Applied Cybersecurity ATHENE.

J.-J. Rousseau and B. Kapralos (Eds.): ICPR 2022 Workshops, LNCS 13643, pp. 465–478, 2023.
https://doi.org/10.1007/978-3-031-37660-3_33

as well as bias beyond demographics [39] has been studied. More specifically, bias was reported across various sub-modules of face recognition including face detection [26] and face quality estimation [38].

One pioneering work in the area of face recognition was done in 2012, where Klare et al. [22] analysed the role of specific demographic attributes. They concluded that the training data has the biggest influence on the biometric recognition performance of particular demographic groups. More recently, Albiero et al. [3] studied the gender inequality for different facial expressions, forehead occlusions, and make-up usage. Even a balanced training set was not able to achieve unbiased results. Also Serna et al. [34] highlight that the most commonly used face databases for training deep networks are heavily biased in their demographic compositions.

The topic of bias and fairness was pushed even more by the FairFace challenge [36] and quantified in the ongoing face recognition vendor tests [14], which analyse demographic effects on a large scale. In order to measure the fairness in biometric verification systems, a figure of merit was proposed in [6]. In an extensive evaluation, Howard et al. [17] analysed 126 commercial and open source face recognition algorithms in order to propose functional fairness measure criteria and benchmark the accuracy-fairness trade-off. As a result, research is shifting from pure identifying to mitigating bias in biometrics [5]. One possible approach is to utilise synthetic data to reduce the database bias [23]. This could assist the training process of biometric recognition algorithms by including all demographic groups to the same extend. In this regard, Tan et al. [37] improve the fairness of synthetic GAN-generated face images without a time expensive retraining. As requested by multiple experts [31], metrics and criteria need to be standardised for common testing and certification. Hence, the biometric community is currently drafting the standard ISO/IEC 19795-10 [19] to unify the measuring and reporting of demographic fairness.

Drozdowski et al. [9] analysed another form of demographic differentials resulting from an unbalanced database composition in biometric identification systems that is referred to as *watchlist imbalance effect*. They proposed formulas to theoretically estimate the watchlist imbalance effect in biometric identification scenarios. The theoretical model is then compared to empiric results while considering gender or skin colour as demographic attributes. The results show that it is hard to estimate the probability of a false match but the modelled and empiric inequity aligns very well.

Based on this work, our contribution consists of the following steps. We combine the demographic attributes of gender and skin colour to analyse the watchlist imbalance effect on demographic subgroups. While previous works considered either gender or skin colour due to database limitations, we make use of a larger database in order to validate the theoretical estimation on demographic subgroups. The motivation for this is the possibility to utilise the formulas to predict possible biases and adjust the comparison scores accordingly. For this it is necessary to validate the formulas on a different database and additionally test their suitability to estimate the inequity even for demographic subgroups.

dark female   dark male   light female   light male

Fig. 1. Example images for demographic subgroups when combining skin colour and gender attributes.

Since this requires more samples, we take a fairly distributed subset of the Fair-Face database [21], which further prevents additional bias in finding the decision threshold. Furthermore, we focus on the demographic attributes of gender and skin colour to keep the comparability of our results to the original work. Example images of our demographic subgroups are shown in Fig. 1.

The rest of this paper is structured as follows: Sect. 2 introduces terminology and concepts of our approach. The experimental evaluation is discussed in Sect. 3 and Sect. 4 concludes our findings.

2   The Watchlist Imbalance Effect

Generally, biometric systems operate either in verification (1:1 comparison) or identification (1:n comparison) modes. The watchlist imbalance effect focuses on the biometric identification scenario, where one probe is compared to all enrolment records (watchlist). For closed-set identifications we know that the corresponding reference is definitely in the enrolment database. However, this assumption does not hold for most realistic use cases (e.g., suspect list for criminal investigations). In fact, it is a realistic option that the probe sample from a suspect (e.g. individual that was observed on a crime scene) is not yet known to the police, which is called open-set identification. Moreover, an exhaustive identification search comes with two main challenges: i) search time increases for larger databases, and ii) the probability of a false match increases as well. Thus, biometric identifications are generally more challenging than verification scenarios [8]. In this context, false matches are more likely to occur within the own demographic group [14,18] and thus less likely when comparing across demographic groups.

In case of demographically unbalanced galleries, it is always more likely for the dominant demographic group to result in a false match. This is called the *watchlist imbalance effect* [35]. As defined by Drozdowski et al. [9], the probability of at least one false match in biometric identification for a probe of demographic group x against a gallery with exactly two demographic groups x and y can be computed as:

$$P_N(x) = 1 - (1 - P_1(x, x))^{N_x} \cdot (1 - P_1(x, y))^{N_y}. \qquad (1)$$

Here $P_1(x,x)$ is the false match rate (FMR) within the probe's demographic group and $P_1(x,y)$ the FMR across both demographic groups. N_x and N_y are the numbers of enrolled subjects belonging to those demographic groups. This equation was further extended to apply for more than two demographic groups:

$$P_N(x) = 1 - (1 - P_1(x,x))^{N_x} \cdot \prod_{y \in \mathbb{D}} (1 - P_1(x,y))^{N_y}, \qquad (2)$$

with $\mathbb{D}$ being a set of other demographic groups than x. Thus, the relevant factors to estimate the watchlist imbalance effect are: i) the FMRs within one demographic group, ii) the FMRs across demographic groups, and iii) the demographic composition of the gallery.

Furthermore, the inequity between groups can be computed as a ratio between maximum probability divided by the minimum probability:

$$\max_{\forall d \in \mathbb{D}} P_N(d) / \min_{\forall d \in \mathbb{D}} P_N(d). \qquad (3)$$

In the case that no differentials are measurable, this ratio is equal to 1. On the other hand, higher values reflect the inequity of specific demographic groups.

3   Experimental Evaluation

This section provides information about the experimental setup including database preparation and and implementation aspects. Subsequently, the results for all selected demographic groups are presented and discussed.

3.1   Experimental Setup

While previous studies [3,9,24] on demographic differentials were done on the academic UNCW-MORPH dataset [32], it includes only 669 female subjects (4.91% of 13,617 total subjects) with light skin tones as its smallest demographic subgroup. Hence, we make use of the FairFace database [21] (total of 97,698 subjects) to work on larger subgroups and be able to validate the watchlist imbalance effect on those. It should be noted that the FairFace database is not suited to evaluate the general performance of biometric recognition algorithms since it comprises only one sample for each data subject, which prevents the computation of mated comparison scores. However, in our case we do need only non-mated comparisons in order to calculate the probability of a false match in a biometric identification scenario.

Before starting, duplicate images were removed by calculating cryptographic hash values of all images. Additionally, the age group of 0-2 years was excluded for the evaluation. For the feature extraction the well established open-source face recognition system ArcFace[1] [7] was used, which achieves excellent recognition performance in popular large-scale face recognition benchmarks.

---

[1] model: LResNet100E-IR,ArcFace@ms1m-refine-v2
https://github.com/deepinsight/insightface/wiki/Model-Zoo/
6633390634bcf907c383cc6c90b62b6700df2a8e.

For the experiments, we split the FairFace database in smaller sets according to demographic attributes such as gender and skin colour. It should be noted that we did not assign gender and ethnicity to the data subjects but used the available labels, coming with the database, as ground truth. In terms of gender, the database labels were binary, thus only distinguishing between female and male. In order to evaluate the influence of the skin colour, we focused on the ethnicity labels *Black* and *White* to have a clear separation in skin tones in these experiments. We are aware that these limitations do not represent all people, but we selected this setting to analyse the watchlist imbalance effect on demographic subgroups. The idea is that those subgroups consist of a combination of two demographic attributes, thus gender and skin colour. In the following, the ethnic labels are discarded and the terms *dark* and *light* are used to separate the skin tones. The resulting demographic subgroups are therefore: dark female, dark male, light female, and light male.

While FairFace provides nearly equal shares for all subgroups, we want to have a perfectly fair distribution of all four subgroups in our experiments. Thus, we computed the image quality scores for the entire FairFace database using the open-source FaceQnetV1[2] [15, 16]. Subsequently, we took the facial images with the best 4,000 quality scores for each demographic subgroup, which resulted in our experimental dataset of 16,000 subjects in total. This dataset is then used for our experiments. Reproducibility of this dataset is granted by using only publicly available data and algorithms (feature extraction and quality estimation).

The galleries to validate the watchlist imbalance effect were filled with random subjects, following the work in [9]. This includes different shares of each demographic subgroup (as explained in Sect. 2) and different gallery sizes, which were filled incrementally. Meaning, larger galleries contain all subjects of corresponding smaller smaller galleries. Thus, e.g. a gallery for a given demographic split with 2,000 subjects contains all the subjects from the corresponding 1,000-subject gallery plus additional 1,000 subjects. In accordance to [9], this procedure was evaluated using 10-fold cross validation and plotted with 95% confidence intervals. Finally, the results are reported using the standardised metrics of ISO/IEC 19795-1 [20].

3.2 Results

A baseline experiment on our full dataset of all 16,000 subjects was conducted to establish a global decision threshold for a FMR of 0.1% as e.g. recommended for border control [12]. Given this threshold, the verification performances within and across the selected demographic groups are computed. The results are shwon in Table 1 for the groups female, male, dark skin, light skin as well as the subgroups dark female (df), dark male (dm), light female (lf), and light male (lm). Due to the combination of two subgroups to form one demographic group (e.g. female = df + lf), the number of comparisons differ between those two settings, while they are the same within one setting.

---

[2] FaceQnet: https://github.com/uam-biometrics/FaceQnet.

Table 1. Verification performances given the global decision threshold.

(a) within demographic groups

	female	male	dark	light	df	dm	lf	lm
FMR (%)	0.134	0.144	0.347	0.049	0.480	0.431	0.049	0.144

(b) across demographic groups

	gender	skin	df-dm	df-lf	df-lm	dm-lf	dm-lm	lf-lm
FMR (%)	0.061	0.002	0.240	0.004	0.001	0.001	0.001	0.002

The assumption is that false matches are much more likely to occur within a demographic group than across different demographic groups [14,18]. From Table 1a we can see that the FMRs are generally higher than 0.1% (global FMR for this threshold), except for the group with light skin tones (0.049%). Additionally, the FMRs of dark skinned groups are much higher than for light groups. Hence, it is much more likely for demographic groups with dark skin tones to result in a false match. On the other hand, the gender does not influence the verification performance as much as the skin tone. The results in Table 1b support these findings. When comparing across genders, the FMR is 30 times higher (0.061%) than across skin tones (0.002%). Furthermore, the cross comparison between dark female and dark male results in a 120 times higher (0.240%) FMR than for the other subgroups (max 0.002%) and thus is even higher than the FMRs within light demographic groups. This proves even more that the dark skin tone influences the comparison scores much more than the gender, especially since the cross comparison between light female and light male achieves a FMR of 0.002%. Those results generally align with many previous results in this area [10].

When computing the probability of a false match for two demographic groups using Eq. (1), we can generally say that the probability increases with the size of the gallery. However, with the results from Table 1 we also know that this increase will vary in its ascent depending on the demographic composition of the gallery. In this context, we applied five splits to fill the galleries with subjects from corresponding demographic groups: 10-90, 25-75, 50-50, 75-25, and 90-10.

The first experiments mirror those from [9] to apply the procedure on a larger and equally distributed dataset. Hence, only one demographic factor (skin colour or gender) is evaluated at a time. In addition to the false match probability, also the inequity ratio is plotted. Figure 2 shows the calculated model following Eq. (1) next to the empiric 10-fold analysis. As in [9] the model generally overestimates the probability of a false match, thus the curves are ascending much faster. However, computing with Eq. (3) the inequity from the model aligns much better with the empiric results. Thus, we are able to predict the inequity regarding light or dark skin tones by calculating the model based on FMRs of our enrolment database. In the next step, Fig. 3 shows the results for the gender experiment. While the model still overestimates the probability of a false match, the curves do not ascend as fast as those for the skin colour experiment.

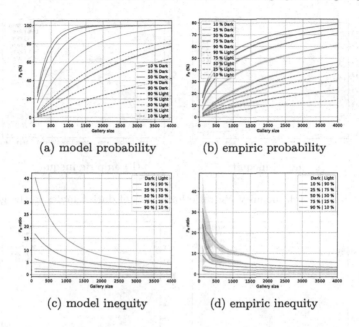

(a) model probability   (b) empiric probability

(c) model inequity   (d) empiric inequity

Fig. 2. False-match probability P_N and false-match inequity P_N ratio for selected shares of skin colour in the gallery.

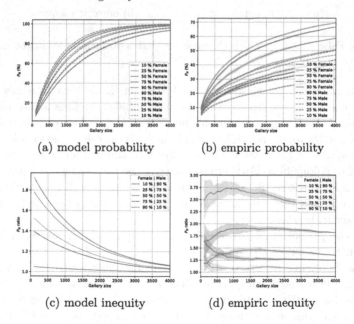

(a) model probability   (b) empiric probability

(c) model inequity   (d) empiric inequity

Fig. 3. False-match probability P_N and false-match inequity P_N ratio for selected shares of genders in the gallery.

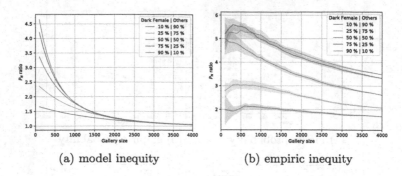

Fig. 4. False-match inequity P_N ratio for shares of dark females in the gallery.

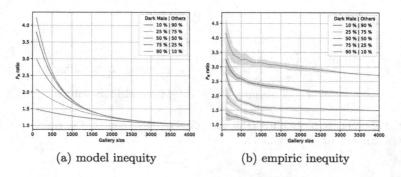

Fig. 5. False-match inequity P_N ratio for shares of dark males in the gallery.

Combining those insights with the FMRs in Table 1 we can say that the gender imbalance is less strong than the skin imbalance. This is also reflected in the inequity plots. The maximum inequity for model and empiric is below 3.0 in the case of gender analysis, while the maximum is over 40 for skin colours. Given that an inequity of 1.0 represents a fair system, the gender bias is less relevant than the skin colour bias. Furthermore, we can see that the gender inequity plots of model and empiric results do not align as nicely as they did for the skin colour. When there is less bias for the analysed groups, the empiric results cannot be modelled accurately anymore.

While the probabilities are required to compute the inequity, they are not well suited to visualise the differences between modelled and empiric results. Hence, the following results on the demographic subgroups focus on inequity plots, which allow better comparisons. The next experiments combine the gender and skin colour attributes to further investigate the watchlist imbalance effect on our demographic subgroups. The experimental galleries are filled by taking one subgroup (e.g., dark female) and split the *other* part of the gallery equally among all other subgroups.

Figure 4 shows the inequity with focus on the dark female subgroup. In contrast the the sole gender results, the order of the empiric results aligns with

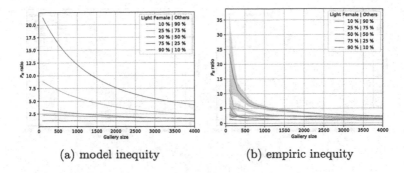

(a) model inequity   (b) empiric inequity

Fig. 6. False-match inequity P_N ratio for shares of light females in the gallery.

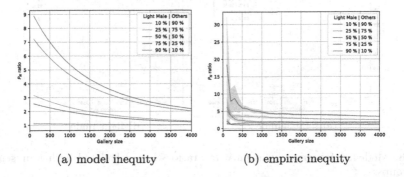

(a) model inequity   (b) empiric inequity

Fig. 7. False-match inequity P_N ratio for shares of light males in the gallery.

the modelled ones. However, the empiric inequity is slightly higher and does not descent as fast as the modelled one. The same observations can be made for the dark male subgroup in Fig. 5. For shares greater than 10% of dark males in the gallery, it appears that there remains a constant inequity that does not decrease for larger gallery sizes.

When looking at the results for the light female subgroup in Fig. 6 we notice that both modelled and empiric inequity start with much higher values for small gallery sizes. On the other hand, the empiric curves descent even faster than the modelled ones, thus opposite than the dark skinned subgroups. Additionally, the empiric inequity diminishes for larger galleries.

Finally, Fig. 7 presents the inequity for the light male subgroup. These plots are very similar to the light female case: we see a high inequity for small galleries, which quickly descents when adding more subjects to the gallery. However, as for the dark male group the curves somehow stop descending at the end of the plot, which implies some constant inequity.

All these models for the demographic subgroups were calculated using Eq. (1), thus for exactly two demographic groups (e.g., dark female vs. others). When using Eq. (2) to compute the inequity for four demographic groups, the resulting inequity is about 10 times higher as can be seen in Fig. 8. Hence,

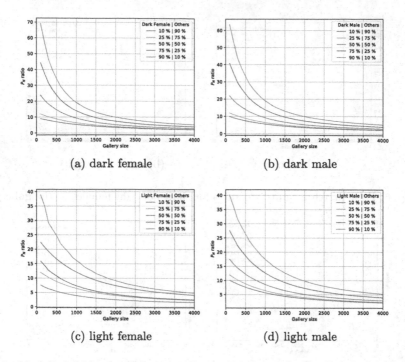

(a) dark female   (b) dark male

(c) light female   (d) light male

Fig. 8. Modelled false-match inequity P_N ratio when calculated with four separate subgroups.

we emphasise that this formula is not suited to model the inequity of the watch-list imbalance effect. In fact, the problem can always be estimated by using two groups: one group vs. all but this group. On the other hand, the inequity range of Eq. (1) fits the empiric results but fails to accurately estimate the descent for increasing galleries. While the model descents too fast for dark skins, its descent is too slow for the light skin tones. Hence, the experiments show that there is only one setting, where the model could precisely predict the empiric inequity: the demographic separation of dark and light skin tones. Furthermore, when reviewing all presented results, we can highlight that for state-of-the-art deep learning face recognition systems, the gender has less bias than skin colours.

4   Conclusions

This paper composed a large scale experimental dataset with fair demographic distributions by selecting face images with specific demographic attributes of the FairFace database. By relying only on publicly available data and algorithms, these steps are fully reproducible. Based on this dataset, an unbiased decision threshold was computed to analyse the FMRs within and across our demographic (sub)groups. It turned out that the FMR is much higher when comparing across genders than comparing across skin colours. This is highly influenced by false matches between dark females and dark males. Thus, the experimental evaluation showed that there is a significant performance difference for dark skin tones in contrast to light skin tones. While demographic groups with light skin have much lower error rates, groups with dark skin have a much higher false match probability.

The second part of experiments analysed the watchlist imbalance effect in terms of inequity in identification scenarios. The results show that the formulas presented in [9] do not accurately predict the inequity of demographic subgroups. Even in our experimental dataset with only two skin colours, the empiric results show significant differences towards the modelled prediction. Since real world data comprises naturally more divers skin tones, we conclude that these formulas are not suited to model the false match probability and compute the inequity.

All in all, it remains an open challenge to predict biased behaviour and adjust comparison scores accordingly. Therefore, every operator of biometric systems should be aware of system bias and interpret the results accordingly.

References

1. Abdurrahim, S.H., Samad, S.A., Huddin, A.B.: Review on the effects of age, gender, and race demographics on automatic face recognition. Vis. Comput. **34**(11), 1617–1630 (2017). https://doi.org/10.1007/s00371-017-1428-z
2. Agarwal, A., Agarwal, H., Agarwal, N.: Fairness score and process standardization: Framework for fairness certification in artificial intelligence systems. AI and Ethics, pp. 1–13 (2022). https://doi.org/10.1007/s43681-022-00147-7
3. Albiero, V., Krishnapriya, K.S., Vangara, K., Zhang, K., King, M.C., Bowyer, K.W.: Analysis of gender inequality in face recognition accuracy. In: Proceedings IEEE/CVF Winter Conference on Applications of Computer Vision Workshops, pp. 81–89 (2020). https://doi.org/10.1109/WACVW50321.2020.9096947
4. Angwin, J., Larson, J., Mattu, S., Kirchner, L.: Machine Bias: there's software used across the country to predict future criminals and it's biased against blacks. ProPublica (2016)
5. Das, A., Dantcheva, A., Bremond, F.: Mitigating bias in gender, age and ethnicity classification: a multi-task convolution neural network approach. In: Leal-Taixé, L., Roth, S. (eds.) ECCV 2018. LNCS, vol. 11129, pp. 573–585. Springer, Cham (2019). https://doi.org/10.1007/978-3-030-11009-3_35
6. de Freitas Pereira, T., Marcel, S.: Fairness in biometrics: a figure of merit to assess biometric verification systems. IEEE Trans. Biometr. Behav. Ident. Sci. **4**(1), 19–29 (2021). https://doi.org/10.1109/TBIOM.2021.3102862
7. Deng, J., Guo, J., Zafeiriou, S.: ArcFace: additive angular margin loss for deep face recognition. In: Conference on Computer Vision and Pattern Recognition (CVPR) (2019). https://doi.org/10.1109/TPAMI.2021.3087709
8. Drozdowski, P., Rathgeb, C., Busch, C.: Computational workload in biometric identification systems: an overview. IET Biometrics **8**(6), 351–368 (2019). https://doi.org/10.1049/iet-bmt.2019.0076
9. Drozdowski, P., Rathgeb, C., Busch, C.: The watchlist imbalance effect in biometric face identification: comparing theoretical estimates and empiric measurements. In: International Conference on Computer Vision Workshops (ICCVW), pp. 1–9. IEEE/CVF (2021). https://doi.org/10.1109/ICCVW54120.2021.00419

10. Drozdowski, P., Rathgeb, C., Dantcheva, A., Damer, N., Busch, C.: Demographic bias in biometrics: a survey on an emerging challenge. Trans. Technol. Soc. (TTS) **1**(2), 89–103 (2020). https://doi.org/10.1109/TTS.2020.2992344
11. Du, M., Yang, F., Zou, N., Hu, X.: Fairness in deep learning: a computational perspective. IEEE Intell. Syst. **36**(4), 25–34 (2020). https://doi.org/10.1109/MIS.2020.3000681
12. eu-LISA: Best practice technical guidelines for automated border control (ABC) systems. Tech. rep. TT-02-16-152-EN-N, European Agency for the Management of Operational Cooperation at the External Borders of the Member States of the European Union (2015)
13. Garvie, C.: The perpetual line-up: Unregulated police face recognition in America. Center on Privacy & Technology, Georgetown Law (2016)
14. Grother, P., Ngan, M., Hanaoka, K.: Ongoing face recognition vendor test (FRVT) part 3: Demographic effects. National Institute of Standards and Technology (NIST), vol. 8280 (2019)
15. Hernandez-Ortega, J., Galbally, J., Fierrez, J., Haraksim, R., Beslay, L.: FaceQnet: quality assessment for face recognition based on deep learning. In: International Conference on Biometrics (ICB), pp. 1–8. IEEE (2019). https://doi.org/10.1109/ICB45273.2019.8987255
16. Hernandez-Ortega, J., Galbally, J., Fierrez, J., L. Beslay, L.: Biometric quality: review and application to face recognition with FaceQnet. arXiv preprint arXiv:2006.03298 (2020). https://doi.org/10.48550/arXiv.2006.03298
17. Howard, J.J., Laird, E.J., Sirotin, Y.B., Rubin, R.E., Tipton, J.L., Vemury, A.R.: Evaluating proposed fairness models for face recognition algorithms. arXiv preprint arXiv:2203.05051 (2022). https://doi.org/10.48550/arXiv.2203.05051
18. Howard, J.J., Sirotin, Y.B., Vemury, A.R.: The effect of broad and specific demographic homogeneity on the imposter distributions and false match rates in face recognition algorithm performance. In: IEEE International Conference on Biometrics Theory, Applications and Systems (BTAS), pp. 1–8. IEEE (2019). https://doi.org/10.1109/BTAS46853.2019.9186002
19. ISO/IEC JTC1 SC37 Biometrics: ISO/IEC 19795–10. Information Technology - Biometric Performance Testing and Reporting - Part 10: Quantifying Biometric System Performance Variation Across Demographic Groups. International Organization for Standardization, unpublished draft
20. ISO/IEC JTC1 SC37 Biometrics: ISO/IEC 19795–1:2021. Information Technology - Biometric Performance Testing and Reporting - Part 1: Principles and Framework. International Organization for Standardization (2021)
21. Karkkainen, K., Joo, J.: FairFace: face attribute dataset for balanced race, gender, and age for bias measurement and mitigation. In: Proceedings of the IEEE/CVF Winter Conference on Applications of Computer Vision, pp. 1548–1558 (2021). https://doi.org/10.1109/WACV48630.2021.00159
22. Klare, B.F., Burge, M.J., Klontz, J.C., Bruegge, R.W.V., Jain, A.K.: Face recognition performance: Role of demographic information. IEEE Trans. Inform. Forensics Secur. (TIFS) **7**(6), 1789–1801 (2012). https://doi.org/10.1109/TIFS.2012.2214212
23. Kortylewski, A., Egger, B., Schneider, A., Gerig, T., Morel-Forster, A., Vetter, T.: Analyzing and reducing the damage of dataset bias to face recognition with synthetic data. In: Proceedings of the IEEE/CVF Conference on Computer Vision and Pattern Recognition Workshops, pp. 2261–2268 (2019). https://doi.org/10.1109/CVPRW.2019.00279

24. Krishnapriya, K.S., Albiero, V., Vangara, K., King, M.C., Bowyer, K.W.: Issues related to face recognition accuracy varying based on race and skin tone. IEEE Trans. Technol. Soc. 1(1), 8–20 (2020). https://doi.org/10.1109/TTS.2020.2974996
25. Mehrabi, N., Morstatter, F., Saxena, N., Lerman, K., Galstyan, A.: A survey on bias and fairness in machine learning. ACM Comput. Surv. (CSUR) 54(6), 1–35 (2021). https://doi.org/10.1145/3457607
26. Menezes, H.F., Ferreira, A.S.C., Pereira, E.T., Gomes, H.M.: Bias and fairness in face detection. In: Proceedings Conference on Graphics, Patterns and Images (SIB-GRAPI), pp. 247–254. IEEE (2021). https://doi.org/10.1109/SIBGRAPI54419.2021.00041
27. O'Toole, A.J., Phillips, P.J., Jiang, F., Ayyad, J., Penard, N., Abdi, H.: Face recognition algorithms surpass humans matching faces over changes in illumination. IEEE Trans. Pattern Anal. Mach. Intell. (TPAMI) 29(9), 1642–1646 (2007). https://doi.org/10.1109/TPAMI.2007.1107
28. O'Toole, A.J., Phillips, P.J., Narvekar, A.: Humans versus algorithms: comparisons from the face recognition vendor test 2006. In: IEEE Intl. Conf. on Automatic Face & Gesture Recognition, pp. 1–6. IEEE (2008). https://doi.org/10.1109/AFGR.2008.4813318
29. Park, S., Kim, S., Lim, Y.: Fairness audit of machine learning models with confidential computing. In: Proceedings of the ACM Web Conference, pp. 3488–3499 (2022). https://doi.org/10.1145/3485447.3512244
30. Pessach, D., E. Shmueli, E.: A review on fairness in machine learning. ACM Comput. Surv. (CSUR) 55(3), 1–44 (2022). https://doi.org/10.1145/3494672
31. Rathgeb, C., Drozdowski, P., Damer, N., Frings, D.C., Busch, C.: Demographic fairness in biometric systems: what do the experts say? arXiv preprint arXiv:2105.14844 (2021). https://doi.org/10.48550/arXiv.2105.14844
32. Ricanek, K., Tesafaye, T.: MORPH: a longitudinal image database of normal adult age-progression. In: Intl. Conference on Automatic Face and Gesture Recognition (FGR), pp. 341–345. IEEE Computer Society (2006). https://doi.org/10.1109/FGR.2006.78
33. Segal, S., Adi, Y., Pinkas, B., Baum, C., Ganesh, C., Keshet, J.: Fairness in the eyes of the data: Certifying machine-learning models. In: Proceedings AAAI/ACM Conference on AI, Ethics, and Society, pp. 926–935 (2021). https://doi.org/10.1145/3461702.3462554
34. Serna, I., Morales, A., Fierrez, J., Cebrian, M., Obradovich, N., Rahwan, I.: Algorithmic discrimination: Formulation and exploration in deep learning-based face biometrics. In: Proceedings of the Workshop on Artificial Intelligence Safety (SafeAI), pp. 146–152 (2020)
35. Sirotin, Y.B., Vemury, A.R.: Demographic variation in the performance of biometric systems: Insights gained from large-scale scenario testing. EAB Virtual Events Series - Demographic Fairness in Biometric Systems (2021)
36. Sixta, T., Jacques Junior, J.C.S., Buch-Cardona, P., Vazquez, E., Escalera, S.: FairFace challenge at ECCV 2020: analyzing bias in face recognition. In: Bartoli, A., Fusiello, A. (eds.) ECCV 2020. LNCS, vol. 12540, pp. 463–481. Springer, Cham (2020). https://doi.org/10.1007/978-3-030-65414-6_32
37. Tan, S., Shen, Y., Zhou, B.: Improving the fairness of deep generative models without retraining. arXiv preprint arXiv:2012.04842 (2020)
38. Terhörst, P., Kolf, J.N., Damer, N., Kirchbuchner, F., Kuijper, A.: Face quality estimation and its correlation to demographic and non-demographic bias in face recognition. In: Proceedings IEEE International Joint Conference on Biometrics (IJCB), pp. 1–11. IEEE (2020). https://doi.org/10.1109/IJCB48548.2020.9304865

39. Terhörst, P., Kolf, J.N., Huber, M., Kirchbuchner, F., Damer, N., et al.: A comprehensive study on face recognition biases beyond demographics. IEEE Trans. Technol. Soc. (TTS) **3**(1), 16–30 (2021). https://doi.org/10.1109/TTS.2021.3111823

Fairness Index Measures to Evaluate Bias in Biometric Recognition

Ketan Kotwal[1]([✉]) [iD] and Sébastien Marcel[1,2] [iD]

[1] Idiap Research Institute, Martigny, Switzerland
{ketan.kotwal,sebastien.marcel}@idiap.ch
[2] University of Lausanne, Lausanne, Switzerland

Abstract. The demographic disparity of biometric systems has led to serious concerns regarding their societal impact as well as applicability of such systems in private and public domains. A quantitative evaluation of demographic fairness is an important step towards understanding, assessment, and mitigation of demographic bias in biometric applications. While few, existing fairness measures are based on post-decision data (such as verification accuracy) of biometric systems, we discuss how pre-decision data (score distributions) provide useful insights towards demographic fairness. In this paper, we introduce multiple measures, based on the statistical characteristics of score distributions, for the evaluation of demographic fairness of a generic biometric verification system. We also propose different variants for each fairness measure depending on how the contribution from constituent demographic groups needs to be combined towards the final measure. In each case, the behavior of the measure has been illustrated numerically and graphically on synthetic data. The demographic imbalance in benchmarking datasets is often overlooked during fairness assessment. We provide a novel weighing strategy to reduce the effect of such imbalance through a non-linear function of sample sizes of demographic groups. The proposed measures are independent of the biometric modality, and thus, applicable across commonly used biometric modalities (*e.g.*, face, fingerprint, etc.).

Keywords: Biometrics · Demographic · Fairness · Fairness Evaluation

1 Introduction

In recent years, algorithmic bias and fairness have emerged as noteworthy challenges for automated biometric systems [2,6,8,15,18]. A biometric system or algorithm is considered to be biased if significant differences in its operation can be observed for different demographic groups of individuals [2]. With growing adoption of various biometric applications, the non-equitable performance of such applications across demographic groups has led to several discussions and debates [7,13,19]. Several institutions have conducted evaluations (w.r.t demographic bias) of popular biometric applications, such as face recognition, developed by commercial vendors [1,6,14,15]. On academic front as well, the

© Springer Nature Switzerland AG 2023
J.-J. Rousseau and B. Kapralos (Eds.): ICPR 2022 Workshops, LNCS 13643, pp. 479–493, 2023.
https://doi.org/10.1007/978-3-031-37660-3_34

research in understanding, estimating, and mitigating demographic bias is gaining significant traction [2,4,17,18].

As the issue of fairness in biometric systems has received attention lately, very few attempts have been made to define fairness measures for generic and/or specific biometric applications. As per Howard *et al.* [8], the fairness of biometric system can be measured using two approaches: differential performance and differential outcome. The former approach refers to the difference in the genuine or imposter distributions between specific demographic groups for a given biometric task, whereas the latter deals with differences in classification error rates among demographic groups. The differential performance is, thus, independent of any classification threshold, while the differential outcomes are functions of a chosen threshold that binarizes scores into match or no-match.

A recently proposed fairness measure- Fairness Discrepancy Rate (FDR)- is based on the differential outcome of biometric verification systems [3]. To compute the FDR, authors first assess the maximum discrepancy in the false match rate (FMR) and false non-match rate (FNMR) of different demographic groups for several score thresholds. The fairness of the system is evaluated through a weighted combination of these maximum discrepancies. The FDR has also been adapted to measure the fairness in detection of face morphing attacks in [16]. Gong *et al.* have considered the area under the ROC (Receiver Operating Characteristic) curve as a proxy to measure demographic differentials [5]. In its special report on demographic effects in face recognition [6], the Face Recognition Vendor Test (FRVT) has employed differential outcome-based strategy where they discuss the impact FMR and FNMR using a global threshold. A demographic-specific score thresholding has been analyzed in [1].

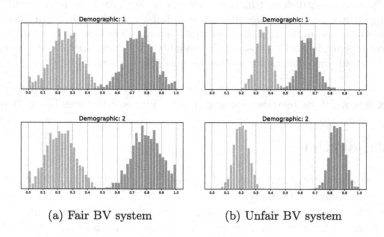

(a) Fair BV system   (b) Unfair BV system

Fig. 1. Score distributions of canonical biometric verification systems with two demographic groups (d_1 and d_2). Distributions of genuine and imposter scores are represented by green and orange bars, respectively. The systems in (a) and (b) exhibit similar overall verification accuracies. However, their score distributions reveal demographic disparity. (Color figure online)

Majority of the existing work in evaluating the fairness or demographic equitability of the biometric system is based on the differential outcome. These measures are easy to calculate, based on well-established error rates, and treat the biometric system as a complete black box. The assessment of demographic fairness of biometric system based on differential performance has received little attention. The use of distributions of genuine and imposter scores of a biometric recognition system towards evaluation of its demographic fairness has several advantages: first, the measures based on differential outcome evaluate fairness of the system entirely from the (number of) samples causing incorrect decisions. While these extremal samples signify the accuracy of the biometric system, we believe that the demographic fairness needs to be evaluated across all samples, irrespective of their recognition outcome. The use of differential performance (score distributions) facilitates consideration of entire sample set towards fairness assessment. Second, the incorrect decisions (characterized by FMR and FNMR) are dependent on a score threshold. This variable is either fixed or computed from probably different set of data. In the former case, one has to evaluate fairness at multiple score thresholds to interpret the equitability of the biometric system. In the latter case, the score threshold is sensitive to, and hence, impacted by the distribution of unseen, disjoint set of data (and underlying demographic) [9]. The measures based on score distributions do not involve such threshold, and thus, can be computed without interference of such external parameters. Third, the score threshold, being external, is often easy to *tune* as per the need of the application. The fairness measures based on differential performance are agnostic to such tuning, and represent the fairness of underlying core mechanism of the biometric system.

Consider two (canonical) biometric verification systems—whose score distributions are shown in Figs. 1a–b. For both systems, the classification accuracy (in terms of FMR and FNMR) is nearly the same. However, the first system (Fig. 1a) is likely to be fair to both demographic groups (top and bottom row), whereas the other biometric system is likely to be unfair to demographic d_1 (top row). We believe that such disparity among demographic groups, beyond the recognition accuracy, needs to be quantified systematically. In this work, we propose three measures based on differential performance for evaluation of demographic fairness of a biometric verification system. The fundamental component of each measure is calculated on distributions of an individual demographic group. Depending on fusion of these components to obtain a final measure, we define three different variants of each measure. We also provide a solution to reduce the effect of demographic imbalance in the test dataset towards fairness evaluation. We explain the behavior of each fairness measure followed by illustration on canonical data (synthetic, yet realistic). Our contributions can be summarized as follows:

- We propose three measures for evaluation of demographic fairness of biometric verification systems.[1] Our measures, being based on scores, consider how well

---

[1] A Python implementation of each evaluation measure is provided at: https://gitlab.idiap.ch/bob/bob.paper.icpr2022_fairness_index_measures2022.

a pair of samples (genuine or imposter) has been matched, rather than just 'whether it has been matched'.

– We propose a weighted fusion strategy to account for demographic imbalance in the benchmarking datasets. Our weighing strategy attempts to provide higher importance to relatively under-represented demographic groups.
– We propose three different variants for each fairness measure to facilitate assessment of fairness from multiple perspectives.
– Being agnostic to the modality, the proposed measures are applicable across various biometric modalities.

In Sect. 2, we formulate the problem of algorithmic fairness in general and biometric verification-specific context. The weighted-fusion strategy and fairness measures are proposed in Sect. 3. Summary is presented in Sect. 4.

2   Problem Formulation

We begin with general definition of algorithmic fairness in biometrics followed by discussion on how the notion of fairness applies to the problem of biometric verification (BV).

2.1   Fairness in Biometrics

In [11], Mehrabi *et al.* provide several definitions for algorithmic fairness in machine learning. The definition related to demographic parity (Def. 3, Sec. 4.1), which is more suitable for the present discussion, suggests that the likelihood of the positive outcome should be the same regardless of whether the person is in the protected group. For a biometric system, the term protected group may be used to refer to different demographics present in data. The demographic division could be based on the factors such as gender, race, or ethnicity. While these factors are often regarded as sensitive issues, the authors discuss these attributes of data purely from technical aspect, and provide solutions (*i.e.* fairness measures) that are generic towards any multi-demographic attribute. In this paper, the term 'demographic' refers to subset(s) of data—where the partitioning is possible due to any demographic attribute.

Let $\mathcal{T}$ be the test dataset, consisting of N samples (biometric presentations), used to benchmark the fairness of a given biometric system. We assume that the presentations are correctly acquired, labelled, and processed to obtain feature descriptors. Let the dataset consist of samples from K demographic groups, such that $\mathcal{D} = \{d_1, d_2, \cdots, d_K\}$. Here, $K > 1$ is a finite, but usually small number (For $K = 1$, the dataset represents homogeneity in terms of demographic variation). Additionally, we assume that each sample can be associated with one and only one demographic from $\mathcal{D}$. That is, demographic subsets $d_1, d_2, \cdots, d_K$ are disjoint. This assumption may not always hold true in some real-world scenarios due to finite number of demographic classes, and (quite often) subjective assignment of these classes to the samples. Notwithstanding with these imperfections, we consider samples in $\mathcal{T}$ to be disjoint in terms of demographic categorization; and therefore, if a demographic d_i, $i = 1, 2, \cdots, K$ consists of N_i samples ($N_i > 0$), we have $\sum_{i=1}^{K} N_i = N$. A biometric system, with predictor function F, is considered to be fair, if $P(\text{F}|d_i) = P(\text{F}|d_j)$ for every pair of d_i, $d_j \in \mathcal{D}$ [3,11]. Thus, parameters of distribution characterizing different demographic groups need to be analyzed for fairness of the system.

2.2 Fairness in Biometric Verification

In this work, we discuss fairness for a BV system which is one of the most important and widely deployed biometric application. The BV system is a 1:1 matching process that compares the features of probe sample with the features of previously enrolled sample of the claimed identity. When both samples belong to the same identity, the match is considered to be *genuine* and a match between features of two different identities is regarded as *imposter*. A score threshold (τ), fixed or computed over different dataset, binarizes the matching scores into decisions (match or no-match). If **e** and **p** represent the feature vectors (generated by the BV system) of enrolled and probe samples, respectively; a matching score is calculated using a score function $s_f(\mathbf{e}, \mathbf{p})$. Most often, the score function comprises Euclidean or cosine distances followed by suitable modifications to ensure that the matching score is a real-valued scalar in [0, 1] with higher values indicating a better match. For an ideal BV system, $s_f(\mathbf{e}, \mathbf{p}) \rightarrow 1$ for a genuine match, and $s_f(\mathbf{e}, \mathbf{p}) \rightarrow 0$ for an imposter pair.

For a BV system, the algorithmic fairness can be defined as the ability of the BV system to exhibit similar performance– in terms of scores, accuracies, or error rates– to different demographic groups in the test data. However, quantitative measurement of the said term is necessary in order to systematically assess the fairness of BV systems. In our work, the fairness test is performed by obtaining the feature vectors or *embeddings* for N pairs from $\mathcal{T}$. The matching scores are obtained for multiple pairs of $(\mathbf{e}, \mathbf{p})$ samples by computing score function s_f. For a genuine match, the features **e** and **p** refer to the same subject, and hence, both samples essentially belong to the same demographic in $\mathcal{D}$. For an imposter match, on the other hand, both identities may or may not belong to the same demographic in $\mathcal{D}$. In this work, however, the imposter matches (and thus, corresponding score distributions) are restricted to the pair of samples from different identities, yet belonging to the same demographic. This experimental setup, thus, evaluates or defines the imposter matches in *intra-demographic* manner. One rationale behind this setup is to analyze the behavior of the BV system, towards each demographic independently. Also, it has been demonstrated that the number of false matches from inter-demographic pairs is much smaller than those from the same demographic [6,8,12]. Therefore, for fairness evaluation, we restrict the choice of sample pairs selected within same demographic group.

3   Proposed Fairness Measures

Prior to the introduction of fairness measures, we discuss strategy to reduce the impact of demographic imbalance in test data.

3.1   Fusion for Demographic Imbalance in Test Datasets

The fairness of a BV system refers to its equitability across different demographic groups. The test or benchmarking dataset acts as a proxy to real-world scenario with a fundamental assumption that these data represent a reasonably similar distribution of real-world data w.r.t. multiple attributes. However, studies have noted that many biometric datasets are highly imbalanced in distributions of their demographic attributes [4,9]. To the best of our knowledge, existing evaluations of fairness do not take into account the fact that, in most cases, the test datasets under-represent some demographic groups. The disparity in sample sizes in the training set is beyond the scope of this work. However, the question: "should the imbalance in sample sizes of different demographic groups be considered during evaluation of fairness?" needs to be addressed. Such a consideration can be helpful while comparing the fairness of a system across datasets (or in dataset-agnostic manner). An intuitive solution would be designing a weighing strategy (weighted-fusion rule) where a weight relative to the cardinality (sample size) of each demographic group can be assigned while computing overall fairness measure. If w_i is the weight assigned to the demographic group d_i, then $w_i = f(N_i)$, $i = 1, 2, \cdots, K$.

For several use-cases, the fusion weights are monotonically non-decreasing functions of (or directly proportional to) the sample size, $i.e.$, $w_i \propto N_i$. The normalized weights are related to the probability of a sample drawn from the test dataset $\mathcal{T}$ belonging to d_i. With this approach, the fairness measure of under-represented demographic groups (where few N_i's are significantly smaller than remaining ones) are assigned smaller weights during the fusion (weighted linear combination). The imbalance in demographic data (training or testing) has adverse impact on the fairness of the biometric system [9]. Unfortunately, the aforementioned approach of computing fusion weights suppresses the measures for those demographic groups—for which the BV system is likely to be unfair. Alternatively, the fusion weights could be inversely proportional to (or monotonically non-increasing functions of) the sample size of the demographic $(w_i \propto \frac{1}{N_i})$. This weighing approach emphasizes the contributions of under-represented demographic groups. While this approach appears to be reasonable for minor variations in sample sizes, it is not robust for highly unbalanced test datasets. If the proportion of the sample size of any demographic group is tiny $\left(\frac{N_i}{N} \to 0\right)$, the corresponding measure will be assigned excessively high fusion-weight. With only few test samples, it is indeed difficult to ascertain whether these samples represent true distribution of the underlying demographic group. Therefore, assigning high weights to such groups may not reflect true fairness of the BV system, either. We propose the following mechanism to compute fusion weights, towards obtaining final fairness measure, for demographic groups in $\mathcal{D}$.

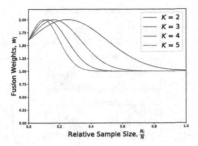

Fig. 2. Fusion weights (without normalization) as a function of relative sample size illustrated for different number of demographic groups (K).

For a test dataset comprising K-demographic groups, the ideal data distribution refers to (nearly) equal sample size of each demographic group (*i.e.*, $N_i \approx N/K$, $\forall i$). A demographic with relatively minor representation than the ideal one should be assigned with higher fusion weights to provide higher attention to its fairness score. However, if the sample size of a particular group is substantially small, the fusion weight should be nominally controlled to avoid a possibility of insufficient samples affecting the fairness score of the BV system. Consequently, we propose a weighing function where the fusion weights are calculated through exponential function of the sample size N_i. The parameters of the exponential are determined from the properties of the test dataset. Equation 1 provides the formula for fusion weights.

$$\hat{w}_i = c + \exp\left(\frac{-1}{2\sigma^2}\left(\frac{N_i}{N} - \frac{1}{2K}\right)^2\right), \tag{1}$$

$$w_i = \frac{\hat{w}_i}{\sum_i \hat{w}_i} \quad i = 1, 2, \cdots K; \tag{2}$$

where, $\sigma = \frac{1}{2K}$ represents the standard deviation of the weighing function. The numeric constant, c set to 1.0, provides numerical stability to the weight calculation, and also limits drastic variations across fusion weights. The unnormalized and normalized fusion weights are represented by $\hat{w}$ and w, respectively. Figure 2 shows the unnormalized fusion weights for $K = 2, 3, 4, 5$. It may be observed that fusion weights (*i.e.* relative importance) are assigned higher values for marginally under-represented demographic groups; however, further reduction in sample size does not encourage similar importance (due to possibly inaccurate representation of underlying demographic data). On the other hand, the over-represented demographic group is assigned relatively lesser importance to avoid its dominance on determining the fairness of the BV system.

3.2   Fairness Measures

A primary component (akin to the building block) of a particular fairness measure is first calculated separately for each demographic group in $\mathcal{D}$. The fairness

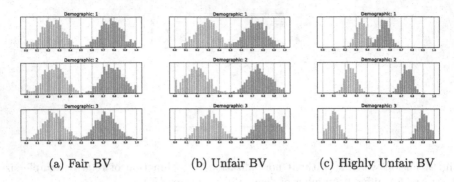

(a) Fair BV   (b) Unfair BV   (c) Highly Unfair BV

Fig. 3. Score distributions of a canonical biometric verification systems with three demographic groups evaluated for SFI measure. Histograms of genuine and imposter scores are represented by green and orange bars, respectively. (Color figure online)

measure for overall test dataset $\mathcal{T}$ is obtained by combining the corresponding resultants (of primary component) for each demographic group. In each case, the output of the scoring function is normalized in the range $[0, 1]$. The values of fairness measures are dependent on the chosen score function (*i.e.*, distance function).

1. Separation Fairness Index (SFI):

We define the Separation Fairness Index (SFI) of the biometric verification system as the measure of its equitability towards separation of expected values of genuine and imposter scores across constituent demographic groups.

Consider a BV system that generates feature vectors for samples of demographic group d_i. The matching scores for pairs of the feature vectors $\mathbf{e}$ and $\mathbf{p}$ are calculated using score function, s_f. Let μ_G be the expected value of matching scores obtained for genuine pairs ($\mathbf{e}$ and $\mathbf{p}$ belong to the same subject), and μ_I be the expected value of imposter pairs ($\mathbf{e}$ and $\mathbf{p}$ belong to different subjects, but within same demographic). Higher separation between μ_G and μ_I generally leads to better verification rates. If we denote the separation between two expected values for demographic group d_i as z_{S_i}, a fair BV system is expected to exhibit similar values of z_{S_i} for each demographic group in $\mathcal{D}$. We define the normal (or absolute) variant of SFI as the following.

$$z_{S_i} = |\mu_{G_i} - \mu_{I_i}|, \quad i = 1, 2, \cdots, K$$

$$z_{S_{\text{mean}}} = \frac{1}{K} \sum_{i=1}^{K} z_{S_i}$$

$$\text{SFI}_{\text{N}} = 1 - \frac{2}{K} \sum_{i=1}^{K} |z_{S_i} - z_{S_{\text{mean}}}|. \tag{3}$$

For a fair BV system, the SFI_{N} reaches a value of 1.0 indicating similar (and hence, fair) separation of expected values of genuine and imposter scores across demographic groups. If the BV system exhibits unequal separation of such scores, the FSI value decreases accordingly with the worst-case value being 0. Figure 3 depicts these scenarios on a canonical (synthetic) data.

Sometimes the performance of overall system is characterized by the worst performing sub-system. Depending on the nature of performance measure, the minimum or maximum fusion rule is applied. Accordingly, we suggest an extremal variant of the FSI measure where maximum value of discrepancy in separation is chosen to represent the fairness of the BV system. The extremal variant of SFI, denoted as SFI_E is provided by Eq. 4.

$$SFI_E = 1 - 2 \max_i \left| z_{S_i} - z_{S_{\text{mean}}} \right|, \tag{4}$$

where intermittent variables computed as described previously in Eq. 3. The normal and extremal variants of SFI do not consider any variations in the sample sizes of demographic groups. We propose a weighted variant of the SFI using the weighing strategy discussed earlier in this section (Eq. 1), and re-using the calculation from Eq. 4 for group-level variables. The resultant fairness measure is given by Eq. 5.

$$SFI_W = 1 - 2 \sum_{i=1}^{K} w_i \left(\left| z_{S_i} - z_{S_{\text{mean}}} \right| \right). \tag{5}$$

Being a linear combination with normalized weights ($\sum_i w_i = 1$), the overall range and behavior of SFI_W is similar to that of normal variant of SFI, however, it *scales* the combination based on sample sizes of demographic groups. Note that a highly accurate BV system may still be considered less fair, if the separation across groups is not uniform. For the canonical BV systems, whose score distributions are depicted in Fig. 3, the FSI values are provided in Table 1.

2. Compactness Fairness Index (CFI):

We define the Compactness Fairness Index (CFI) of the biometric verification system as the measure of its equitability towards compactness (or spread) of genuine scores and imposter scores across constituent demographic groups.

For a BV system, let σ_G and σ_I be the standard deviations of the matching scores obtained for genuine and imposter pairs, respectively. Smaller values

Table 1. The values of the SFI measure on canonical BV systems. For balanced case, 1000 samples were selected for each demographic group. For imbalanced case, the number of samples per demographic group was modified to [100, 1000, 2000].

	Balanced			Imbalanced		
	Fair	Unfair	Highly Unfair	Fair	Unfair	Highly Unfair
SFI_N	0.9489	0.9064	0.6017	0.9833	0.8424	0.5975
SFI_E	0.9233	0.8596	0.4025	0.9750	0.7636	0.3963
SFI_W	0.9489	0.9064	0.6017	0.9846	0.8292	0.6230

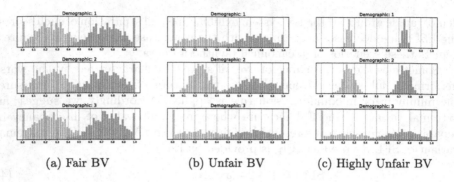

(a) Fair BV   (b) Unfair BV   (c) Highly Unfair BV

Fig. 4. Score distributions of a canonical biometric verification systems with three demographic groups evaluated for CFI measure. Histogram of genuine and imposter scores are represented by green and orange bars, respectively. (Color figure online)

of spread (measured in terms of standard deviation here) for both genuine and imposter scores are desirable, though this characteristic alone does not determine accuracy of verification. Consistency of spread of score distributions across demographic groups simplifies several scaling and normalization procedures– even if applied using global statistics of $\mathcal{T}$.

If we denote the combined spread of both score distributions for demographic group d_i as z_{C_i}, a fair BV system is expected to exhibit similar values of z_{C_i} for each demographic group in $\mathcal{D}$. We define the normal (or absolute) variant of CFI as the following.

$$z_{C_i} = \sigma_{G_i} + \sigma_{I_i}, \quad i = 1, 2, \cdots, K$$

$$z_{C_{\text{mean}}} = \frac{1}{K} \sum_{i=1}^{K} z_{C_i}$$

$$\text{CFI}_N = 1 - \frac{2}{K} \sum_{i=1}^{K} (|z_{C_i} - z_{C_{\text{mean}}}|). \tag{6}$$

Similar to SFI, the best possible value for CFI_N is 1.0—where the combined spread of genuine and imposter score distributions for each demographic group is the same. With disparity in the combined spread of scores across demographics, the CFI_N value decreases, indicating that for some groups the BV system does not generate enough compact representations in feature space than others. The behavior of CFI_N is graphically depicted in Fig. 4. An extremal variant of the CFI measure, as given in Eq. 7, is based on the maximum discrepancy in the spread of scores for a particular demographic group in $\mathcal{D}$.

$$\text{CFI}_E = 1 - 2 \max_i (|z_{C_i} - z_{C_{\text{mean}}}|). \tag{7}$$

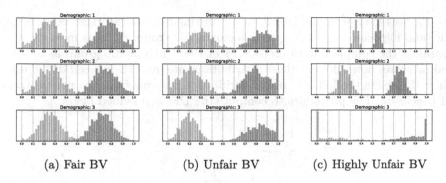

| (a) Fair BV | (b) Unfair BV | (c) Highly Unfair BV |

Fig. 5. Score distributions of a canonical biometric verification systems with three demographic groups evaluated for DFI measure. Histogram of genuine and imposter scores are represented by green and orange bars, respectively. (Color figure online)

The weighted variant of the CFI weighs the spread variables (z_{C_i}) depending on the sample size of the demographic group, d_i. The fusion weights are calculated as discussed earlier in Eq. 1. The expression for CFI_W is given below in Eq. 8. Table 2 provides the values of all variants of CFI computed on balanced as well as imbalanced canonical datasets.

$$CFI_W = 1 - 2 \sum_{i=1}^{K} w_i \left(|z_{C_i} - z_{C_{\text{mean}}}| \right). \tag{8}$$

3. Distribution Fairness Index (DFI):

We define the Distribution Fairness Index (DFI) of the biometric verification system as the measure of its equitability towards overall score distributions across constituent demographic groups.

The literature is enriched with the similarity measures between probability distributions. We consider the Jensen-Shannon divergence [10] to quantify the similarity among score distributions of demographic groups. Unlike previous

Table 2. The values of the CFI measure on canonical BV systems. For balanced case, 1000 samples were selected for each demographic group. For imbalanced case, the number of samples per demographic group was modified to [100, 1000, 2000].

	Balanced			Imbalanced		
	Fair	Unfair	Highly Unfair	Fair	Unfair	Highly Unfair
CFI_N	0.9930	0.9157	0.7921	0.9888	0.9195	0.7901
CFI_E	0.9895	0.8735	0.6882	0.9832	0.8793	0.6851
CFI_W	0.9930	0.9157	0.7921	0.9893	0.9191	0.8052

two fairness measures, the DFI does not distinguish between the scores of genuine and imposter pairs for a given demographic group, d_i. This measure, thus, considers the complete data and scores of the demographic group as a whole, and measures how different these distributions are from their *mean* distribution. Figure 5 depicts the fair and unfair verification systems from the perspective of DFI measure. The procedure to compute the DFI is provided below.

$$z_{D_{\text{mean}}} = \frac{1}{K} \sum_{i=1}^{K} z_{D_i}$$

$$\text{DFI}_{\text{N}} = 1 - \frac{1}{K \log_2 K} \sum_{i=1}^{K} D_{\text{KL}}(z_{D_i} \| z_{D_{\text{mean}}}), \tag{9}$$

where z_{D_i} is the combined (genuine + imposter) score distribution, normalized to yield a unity sum, of the demographic group d_i. To compute the score histogram we empirically consider 100 bins. The Kullback-Leibler (KL) divergence, D_{KL}, has been computed on distributions $A(x)$ and $B(x)$ considering 100-binned score histogram as follows:

$$D_{\text{KL}}(A(x) \| B(x)) = \sum_x A(x) \log_2 \left(\frac{A(x)}{B(x)} \right). \tag{10}$$

The normal variant of the DFI measures the summation of average distance between the score distributions of demographic groups. In the best case scenario, where the BV system generates nearly same score distributions (as a whole) for each demographic group, the value of DFI_{N} approaches to one. The extremal variant of DFI computed using the demographic group with maximum KL divergence from the average distribution.

$$\text{DFI}_{\text{E}} = 1 - \frac{1}{\log_2 K} \max_i D_{\text{KL}}(z_{D_i} \| z_{D_{\text{mean}}}). \tag{11}$$

For the weighted variant of DFI, we replace the relative weights $(1/K)$ from normal variant to the sample size-based weights (w_i) as discussed in the previous section. However, we do not modify the computation of average distribution using fusion weights. The formula for DFI_{W} is provided in Eq. 12.

$$\text{DFI}_{\text{W}} = 1 - \frac{1}{\log_2 K} \sum_{i=1}^{K} w_i D_{\text{KL}}(z_{D_i} \| z_{D_{\text{mean}}}). \tag{12}$$

The values of all variants of the DFI, corresponding to the score distributions in Fig. 5, are provided below in Table 3. It also includes the values for demographically imbalanced datasets where only the weighted variant obtains different values than the balanced scenario.

Table 3. The values of the DFI measure on canonical BV systems. For balanced case, 1000 samples were selected for each demographic group. For imbalanced case, the number of samples per demographic group was modified to [100, 1000, 2000].

	Balanced			Imbalanced		
	Fair	Unfair	Highly Unfair	Fair	Unfair	Highly Unfair
DFI_N	0.9744	0.9206	0.3367	0.9293	0.8763	0.3364
DFI_E	0.9687	0.8930	0.1295	0.8570	0.7820	0.1198
DFI_W	0.9744	0.9206	0.3367	0.9219	0.8622	0.3052

4 Summary

In this work, we have introduced three measures for evaluation of demographic fairness of a generic biometric verification system. The proposed measures determine the fairness of a verification system, towards demographic groups, based on its equitability w.r.t separation, compactness, and distribution of genuine and imposter scores. In addition to mathematical expressions, we have also provided practical meaning and desired behavior of these fairness measures.

We have discussed three variants of each fairness measure based on how the effect of each demographic group contributes towards the final measure. We have also addressed the concern related to the demographic imbalance in test datasets. We have discussed why a simple linear relationship between fusion weights and sample sizes (of demographic groups) is not effective. Our weighted fusion strategy attempts to balance relative importance of under-represented demographic groups without aggravating their contributions towards the final fairness measure. Such fusion strategies could be useful in comparing the fairness of biometric systems on imbalanced datasets.

Our work seeks at decoupling the notion of fairness of a verification system from its accuracy. Since we employ a differential performance-based approach, our measures are dependent on the chosen score function, but not on any external parameters such as score threshold. The proposed measures are not be considered as alternative to the outcome-based fairness measures, rather both evaluation approaches are complementary towards analysis of the demographic fairness of a biometric verification system.

Acknowledgements. Authors would like to thank the Hasler foundation for their support through the SAFER project.

References

1. Cook, C., Howard, J., Sirotin, Y., Tipton, J., Vemury, A.: Demographic effects in facial recognition and their dependence on image acquisition: an evaluation of eleven commercial systems. IEEE Trans. Biometrics Behav. Identity Sci. **1**(1), 32–41 (2019). https://doi.org/10.1109/TBIOM.2019.2897801

2. Drozdowski, P., Rathgeb, C., Dantcheva, A., Damer, N., Busch, C.: Demographic bias in biometrics: a survey on an emerging challenge. IEEE Trans. Technol. Soc. 1(2), 89–103 (2020)
3. de Freitas Pereira, T., Marcel, S.: Fairness in biometrics: a figure of merit to assess biometric verification systems. IEEE Trans. Biometrics Behavior Identity Sci. 4(1), 19–29 (2021)
4. Garcia, R., Wandzik, L., Grabner, L., Krueger, J.: The harms of demographic bias in deep face recognition research. In: International Conference on Biometrics, pp. 1–6. IEEE (2019)
5. Gong, S., Liu, X., Jain, A.K.: Jointly de-biasing face recognition and demographic attribute estimation. In: Vedaldi, A., Bischof, H., Brox, T., Frahm, J.-M. (eds.) ECCV 2020. LNCS, vol. 12374, pp. 330–347. Springer, Cham (2020). https://doi.org/10.1007/978-3-030-58526-6_20
6. Grother, P., Ngan, M., Hanaoka, K.: Face recognition vendor test part 3: demographic effects (Dec 2019). https://doi.org/10.6028/NIST.IR.8280
7. Racial discrimination in face recognition technology. https://sitn.hms.harvard.edu/flash/2020/racial-discrimination-in-face-recognition-technology. Accessed 10 July 2022
8. Howard, J., Sirotin, Y., Vemury, A.: The effect of broad and specific demographic homogeneity on the imposter distributions and false match rates in face recognition algorithm performance. In: International Conference on Biometrics Theory, Applications and Systems, pp. 1–8 (2019). https://doi.org/10.1109/BTAS46853.2019.9186002
9. Hupont, I., Fernández, C.: Demogpairs: quantifying the impact of demographic imbalance in deep face recognition. In: International Conference on Automatic Face and Gesture Recognition, pp. 1–7 (2019). https://doi.org/10.1109/FG.2019.8756625
10. Lin, J.: Divergence measures based on the Shannon entropy. IEEE Trans. Inf. Theory 37(1), 145–151 (1991). https://doi.org/10.1109/18.61115
11. Mehrabi, N., Morstatter, F., Saxena, N., Lerman, K., Galstyan, A.: A survey on bias and fairness in machine learning. ACM Comput. Surv. 54(6), 1–35 (2021)
12. Michalski, D., Yiu, S.Y., Malec, C.: The impact of age and threshold variation on facial recognition algorithm performance using images of children. In: International Conference on Biometrics, pp. 217–224 (2018). https://doi.org/10.1109/ICB2018.2018.00041
13. MIT Technology Review. https://www.technologyreview.com/2016/07/06/158971/are-face-recognition-systems-accurate-depends-on-your-race. Accessed 10 July 2022
14. Raji, I., et al.: Saving face: investigating the ethical concerns of facial recognition auditing. In: Proceedings of the AAAI/ACM Conference on AI, Ethics, and Society, pp. 145–151 (2020)
15. Raji, I., Buolamwini, J.: Actionable auditing: investigating the impact of publicly naming biased performance results of commercial AI products. In: Proceedings of the AAAI/ACM Conference on AI, Ethics, and Society, pp. 429–435 (2019)
16. Ramachandra, R., Raja, K., Busch, C.: Algorithmic fairness in face morphing attack detection. In: Proceedings of the IEEE/CVF Winter Conference on Applications of Computer Vision, pp. 410–418 (2022)
17. Sixta, T., Jacques Junior, J.C.S., Buch-Cardona, P., Vazquez, E., Escalera, S.: FairFace challenge at ECCV 2020: analyzing bias in face recognition. In: Bartoli, A., Fusiello, A. (eds.) ECCV 2020. LNCS, vol. 12540, pp. 463–481. Springer, Cham (2020). https://doi.org/10.1007/978-3-030-65414-6_32

18. Sun, Y., Zhang, M., Sun, Z., Tan, T.: Demographic analysis from biometric data: achievements, challenges, and new frontiers. IEEE Trans. Pattern Anal. Mach. Intell. **40**(2), 332–351 (2018). https://doi.org/10.1109/TPAMI.2017.2669035
19. The Washington Post. https://www.washingtonpost.com/world/2021/09/15/un-ai-moratorium. Accessed 10 July 2022

Indoor Algorithms to Visible Light in Dynamic Recognition

2nd International Workshop
on Artificial Intelligence for Healthcare
Applications (AIHA 2022)

Preface

AIHA is a forum of researchers working on artificial intelligence techniques and applications in healthcare. The increased availability of the medical data, collected from healthcare systems recorded in digital format, has enabled a number of artificial intelligence applications. Specifically, machine learning can generate insights to improve the discovery of new therapeutics tools, to support diagnostic decisions, to help in the rehabilitation process, to name a few. Researchers coupled with expert clinicians can play an important role in turning complex medical data (e.g., genomic data, online acquisitions of physicians, medical imagery, electrophysiological signals, etc.) into actionable knowledge that ultimately improves patient care. In the last years, these topics have drawn clinical and machine learning research which ultimately led to practical and successful applications in healthcare. The scientific objective of the workshop is to present the most recent advances in artificial intelligence techniques for healthcare applications including, but not limited to, automatic diagnosis support systems, automatic disease prediction, assisted surgery, and medical image analysis.

The 2022 edition of the AIHA workshop was held fully virtual in conjunction with the 25th Internal Conference of Pattern Recognition. The format of the workshop includes an introduction of the three sessions and eleven oral presentation of the accepted papers.

This year we received 13 submissions for reviews. After an accurate and thorough single-blind peer review process involving two reviewers for each submission, we selected 11 papers for oral presentation at the workshop. The review process focused on the quality of the papers, their scientific novelty, technical soundness, and relevance with the topics of the workshop. The acceptance of the papers was the result of the workshop organizers' discussion and agreement based on reviewers' reports and their self-assigned expertise rating. Due to the overall high quality of submissions, the acceptance rate was 84%. The accepted articles represent an interesting mix of Machine learning techniques of (i) medical imaging for cancer detection, (ii) deep learning for medical applications, (iii) mental and neurodegenerative disease assessment.

We would like to thank the AIHA 2022 Program Committee, whose members made the workshop possible with their rigorous and timely review process, and ICPR 2022 for hosting the workshop and our emerging community.

Organization

AIHA Chairs

Nicole Dalia Cilia   University of Enna, Kore, Italy
Francesco Fontanella   University of Cassino and Southern Lazio, Italy
Claudio Marrocco   University of Cassino and Southern Lazio, Italy

Program Committee

Berdakh Abibullaev	University of Houston, USA
George Azzopardi	University of Groningen, Netherlands
Jesus G. Cruz-Garza	University of Houston, USA
Vittorio Cuculo	University of Milan, Italy
Claudio De Stefano	University of Cassino and Southern Latium, Italy
Moises Diaz	University of Las Palmas de Gran Canaria, Spain
David Fofi	Université de Bourgogne, France
Adrian Galdran	University Pompeu Fabra, Spain
Donato Impedovo	University of Bari, Italy
Guillaume Lemaître	Inria, France
Xavier Lladó	University of Girona, Spain
Robert Martí	University of Girona, Spain
Murad Mengjhani	University of Columbia, USA
Mario Merone	University Campus Bio-Medico of Rome, Italy
Arnau Oliver	University of Girona, Spain
Antonio Parziale	University of Salerno, Italy
Carlo Sansone	University of Naples Federico II, Italy
Desirè Sidibè	University Evry Val d'Essonne, France
Omar Tahri	University of Burgundy, France
Francesco Tortorella	University of Salerno, Italy
Gennaro Vessio	University of Bari, Italy

Class-Balanced Affinity Loss for Highly Imbalanced Tissue Classification in Computational Pathology

Taslim Mahbub$^{(\boxtimes)}$ (iD), Ahmad Obeid, Sajid Javed, Jorge Dias, and Naoufel Werghi

Department of Electrical Engineering and Computer Science, Khalifa University, Abu Dhabi, United Arab Emirates
{100060836,ahmad.obeid,sajid.javed,jorge.dias,Naoufel.Werghi}@ku.ac.ae

Abstract. Early detection of cancer, and breast cancer in particular, can have a positive impact on the survival rate of cancer patients. However, visual inspection by expert pathologists of whole-slide-images is subjective and error-prone given the lack of skilled pathologists. To overcome this limitation, many researchers have proposed deep learning driven approaches to detect breast cancer from histopathology images. However, these datasets are often highly imbalanced as patches belonging to the cancerous category is minor in comparison to the healthy cells. Therefore, when trained, the classification performance of the conventional Convolutional Neural Network (CNN) models drastically decreases, particularly for the minor class, which is often the main target of detection. This paper proposes a class balanced affinity loss function which can be injected at the output layer to any deep learning classifier model to address the imbalance learning. In addition to treating the imbalance, the proposal also builds uniformly spread class prototypes to address the fine-grained classification challenge in histopathology datasets, which conventional softmax loss cannot address. We validate our loss function performance by using two publicly available datasets with different levels of imbalance, namely the Invasive Ductal Carcinoma (IDC) and Colorectal cancer (CRC) datasets. In both cases, our method results in better performance, especially for the minority. We also observe a better 2D feature projection in multi-class classification with the proposed loss function, making it more apt to handle imbalanced fine-grained classification challenges.

Keywords: Imbalanced Classification · Class-Balanced Affinity Loss · Cluster-based Feature Learning · Histopathology Cancer Diagnosis

1 Introduction

Cancer is a leading cause of death as well as a prominent barrier to increasing life expectancy in every country around the world [1]. Breast cancer alone reports greater than 1,300,000 cases and 450,000 deaths each year worldwide [2]. Histopathological diagnosis, involving a skilled pathologist examining high-resolution histopathology slides, is a key standard for identifying breast cancer

© Springer Nature Switzerland AG 2023
J.-J. Rousseau and B. Kapralos (Eds.): ICPR 2022 Workshops, LNCS 13643, pp. 499–513, 2023.
https://doi.org/10.1007/978-3-031-37660-3_35

[3]. If cancer can be detection at an early stage, it can have a significant impact on the mortality rate [4]. In general, early cancer detection using imaging data has been major trend up to now [5–11].

However, the visual inspection of the histopathological slides requires a pathologist with enriched professional experience, and many hospitals and clinical suffer from the absence of such skilled pathologists [12]. In addition to that, manual diagnoses of these slides is time-intensive and are error-prone with the fatigue because of prolonged work by the pathologist. Hence, various studies introduce the automatic detection of cancer from histopathology images by applying machine learning techniques [12–14]. Typically, these include the use of deep Convolutional Neural Networks (CNNs) to learn features from ground-truth data that are labeled by expert pathologists. While many different CNN models and networks have been researched to assess their compatibility in cancer detection, the issue of data imbalance remains understudied. Due to a natural imbalance in these datasets [13], the performance of many of the existing cancer detection studies is vulnerable for the underrepresented class [15].

In recent literature, many works highlight that the distribution of data in various real-world datasets is often skewed, where most of the data belong to a few dominant/over-represented classes while minority classes have relatively few data points [16,17]. There are two general strategies in machine learning literature that are used to address the problem of class data imbalance: either work on the data-level approaches or algorithmic level approach. In data-level approach, we can re-sample the data by either over-sampling the minority class or under-represent the majority class. Under-sampling the majority class can lead to the loss of very important information from some unique samples. In the medical domain, under-sampling can lead to critical information that is required for generalization being lost, hence it is not a viable option. Meanwhile, oversampling can lead to overfitting [16] and additionally, increase the training time significantly due to the large number of image patches that typically exist in histopathology datasets (see Table 1).

In terms of algorithmic solutions to the class-imbalance challenge, we can introduce cost-sensitive learning by applying weights to each class [16,18] or modify the loss function [17,19,20]. Modifying the loss function essentially changes the way we train the model and has a better theoretical basis to solve specific learning issues with a traditional softmax-based cross-entropy loss function. Some of these loss functions have proven to work well with a skewed dataset from the most popular image datasets, such as CIFAR 10/100. However, with histopathological images, the datasets are fine-grained, where all the objects in the dataset belong to the same major class (cell) and the structural similarity between these images is higher when compared to other generic objects dataset (see Fig. 1). More work is needed to explore the effect of these algorithmic solutions to imbalance datasets when applied to fine-grained digital pathology datasets.

While traditional Softmax loss can suffer when the data is imbalanced, it also does not have any mechanism to optimize the feature embedding to enforce

Similarity of inter-class in fine-grained classification

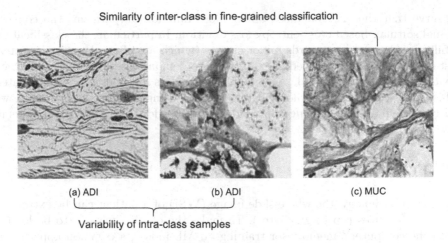

(a) ADI   (b) ADI   (c) MUC

Variability of intra-class samples

Fig. 1. Two of the nine classes from the Colorectal cancer dataset [21] are represented by 3 random image patches where ADI refers to Adipose tissue and MUC is Smooth Muscle tissue. They show the challenge in fine-grained histopathology image classification because of the broad variability of image appearance within the same class and high similarity between other classes.

higher similarity for intra-class samples and diversity for inter-class samples [22]. Note that the term 'Softmax loss' used in various literature refers to softmax activation in the output layer followed by normalized cross-entropy loss. Hence, for robust classification of fine-grained histopathology images, the loss function needs to optimize the feature embeddings learned as well as handle the imbalance within the datasets. This means that loss functions that use class prototypes [19] or impose angular margins [22] without considering the class imbalance can still suffer from the dominance of the majority class during classification. To solve these issues, a loss function that can separate the feature embedding for multiple classes into distinct clusters, aided by a weighting mechanism to ensure minor classes have an equal share of the embedding space, is proposed in this study. To the best of our knowledge, this is the first study that aims to handle the fine-grained class-imbalance issue in histopathology datasets by optimizing the loss-function utilized to train deep CNN models.

In this paper, we propose a class-balanced affinity loss function that allows jointly maximizing the inter-categorical distances and minimizing the intra-categorical differences while using the effective class samples to learn robust and discriminative features from a given imbalanced histopathology dataset. The loss function is designed to tackle both the class imbalance that naturally persists in histopathology datasets as well as the fine-grained classification aspect as the different classes are closely related (Fig. 1). We validate our loss function on two separate public-access datasets by performing an ablation study where we observe that the class-balanced affinity loss function outperforms the conventional softmax-based cross-entropy loss function. In particular, the classification ability of the system towards minor classes (which are often the primary interest of detection) is improved. In addition, we demonstrate that the 2D learned feature projections of the class-balanced affinity loss have better spaced isolated clusters in comparison to floral petals learned using softmax loss. Finally, we discuss the practical challenges introduced by the additional hyperparameters in the proposed loss function.

2   Literature Review

In digital pathology, the whole-slide image (WSI) of a patient can be extremely large in file sizes (up to gigabytes). To make these WSIs feasible to be loaded into the computer's memory for training an ML model, a common approach is to divide them into smaller patches (see Fig. 1). The patches can be labeled either as a patch-based approach where a patch belongs to a specific category or a segmented structure approach where the pathologist draws a well-defined boundary around a region of interest.

In this study, we use patch-level labelled dataset to study the effect of the proposed loss function. One such dataset is the histopathology image dataset of Invasive Ductal Carcinoma (IDC), which is the most common phenotypic subtype of all Breast cancers [13]. The dataset consists of patches which belongs to either class 0 (IDC negative) or class 1 (IDC positive). The researchers in [13] utilize two layers of convolutional and pooling layers with a tanh activation for feature extraction, followed by a fully-connected layer with a softmax activation for output. The cross-entropy loss was utilized and the F1 scored obtained is 0.7180 with a balanced accuracy of 84.23%. The authors in [14] improve this score by utilizing the Alexnet model architecture and achieving an F1-score of 0.7648 and a balanced accuracy of 84.68%. Similar CNN based approaches were also used with the 100,000 H&E stained Colorectal cancer (CRC) dataset which has patches from 9 different tissue classes [21]. A VGG19 model had the best performance in comparison to other smaller models in this dataset, achieving a 94.3% accuracy in an external 7k testing dataset [21]. These studies did not consider addressing the class imbalance issue in the datasets.

Authors in [23] recently propose a novel lesion-level and slice-level cost-sensitive classification loss which reduces the False Negative Rate in the prostate cancer detection network. In another study by [24], researches proposed a weighted focal loss, which makes the model pay more attention to the difficult, underrepresented class. They show that the AUC value when using their proposed loss exceeds the weighted cross-entropy loss by at least 2% on the Chest X-ray 14 database. The dataset used is heavily imbalanced with the smaller class having a share of only 0.161% in the dataset and the most represented class has a share of 14.05%. These studies show that loss function modification to alter the training process of CNNs can have promising improvements for class-imbalanced learning in the medical imaging domain. Hence it is necessary to explore more recent concepts such as affinity loss and effective number of samples, which introduce better discriminative ability to CNNs, with histopathology datasets to address the imbalance learning as well as fine-grained classification challenges.

3 Methodology

3.1 Loss Function Formulation

To improve the performance of class imbalanced datasets, we propose an approach which leverages both cost-sensitive learning and max-margin learning. To introduce cost-sensitivity to the learning process, we adopt the class-balanced loss function paradigm [16]. The idea of this loss function is to remedy the class imbalance by weighting class samples. Additionally, to introduce max-margin learning, we apply affinity loss which fits the condition of improving margins between classes in an imbalanced dataset [17]. In the subsequent paragraphs, we briefly describe these two concepts.

Class-Balanced Loss Function. The authors in [16] introduce the concept of "effective number of samples" which can be defined as the smallest most informative subset of a given class. The effective number can be viewed as the number of actual different representatives in the class, i.e., ignoring duplicated samples or those showing minor differences. For example, naïve data augmentation techniques which add minor noise, or perform slight translations, do not generate more meaningful data for the model to learn, which means the effective number of samples does not directly increase because of data augmentation. In [16], the "effective number of samples" of a specific class y is approximated to:

$$E_{n_y} = \frac{1 - \beta}{1 - \beta^{n_y}} \tag{1}$$

where n_y is the number of samples in the ground-truth class y. $\beta \in [0, 1]$ is a parameter that controls how fast the effective number grows as the number of samples grows. Normally, β should be specific for each class, but for simplicity in parameter tuning, it is assumed to be the same for all the classes. In this work, we experiment with a range of values for β to determine the most suited value for a particular dataset. The class balanced loss function is thus weighted by E_{n_y}, instead of the number of samples in the class y as in the classical class weighting methods, as shown below:

$$CB(\mathbf{p}, y) = \frac{1}{E_{n_y}} \mathcal{L}(\mathbf{p}, y) \tag{2}$$

where CB denotes the class-balanced loss function, $\mathcal{L}$ represents any employed loss function, and $\mathbf{p}$ is the prediction probability for the specific class y.

Affinity Loss Function. The affinity loss function proposed by [17] jointly learns classification and clustering, adopting the max-margin paradigm with Gaussian affinity. Compared to softmax activation which uses the inner vector product $\langle w, f \rangle$ between the class weights w and the feature vectors f at the last fully connected layer, the affinity loss function quantifies the similarity using the Gaussian similarity measure in terms of the Bergman divergence:

$$d(\mathbf{f_i}, \mathbf{w_j}) = exp(-\frac{\| \mathbf{f_i} - \mathbf{w_j} \|^2}{\sigma}) \tag{3}$$

where σ refers to a weighting parameter. Unlike softmax activation, utilizing the above divergence measure allows us to enforce margin maximization constraints, which will subsequently allow the loss function to reduce intra-class variations and increase inter-class distance by margin enforcement between each class. Furthermore, the authors employ diversity regularization and multi-centered partitioning terms in the loss function to intra-class centroid delocalization while mitigating class imbalance. Let $\{X_i, Y_i\}$ denote the input-output pairs, C and N the number of classes and training samples, respectively. The feature space representation from the input samples is denoted by: $f_i, i = 1 : N$ and the class weights by $w_j, j = 1 : C$, is the class vectors. The affinity loss function is expressed as follows:

$$\mathcal{L}_a = \mathcal{L}_{mm} + R(w) \tag{4}$$

$$\mathcal{L}_{mm} = \sum_j max(0, \lambda + d(\mathbf{f_i}, \mathbf{w_j}) - d(\mathbf{f_i}, \mathbf{w_{y_i}})), j \neq y_i \tag{5}$$

$$R(w) = E[(\| \mathbf{w_j} - \mathbf{w_k} \|^2 - \mu)^2], j < k \tag{6}$$

where $i \in [1, N]$, $j \in [1, C]$, $d(\mathbf{f_i}, \mathbf{w_{y_i}})$ is the similarity with its true class, $d(\mathbf{f_i}, \mathbf{w_j})$ is the similarity of the sample with other classes, and λ denotes the enforced margin. The $R(w)$ is a 'diversity regularizer' term that enforces the class centers to spread out in the feature space, which ensures the learned features converge to a class prototype center (the idea behind center loss [19]), but the prototypes are equally spaced out to give a fair representation to all class samples. The μ is the mean distance between all class prototypes.

Proposed Balanced Affinity Loss. We propose a synergic integration between the max-margin constraints with Gaussian affinity and a loss-agnostic modulating factor to yield a class-balanced affinity loss function, denoted as $\mathcal{L}_{cba}$, expressed as follows:

$$\mathcal{L}_{cba} = \frac{1}{E_{n_y}} \mathcal{L}_a(\mathbf{p}, y) \tag{7}$$

In practice, the class-balancing of affinity loss impacts the $\mathcal{L}_{mm}$ which is the max-margin loss function. The class-balancing helps to penalize any misclassification of minor class samples to a greater extent and thus giving more attention to the rare data examples during training from classes that would otherwise perform poorly.

3.2 Model Architectures

The proposed loss ($\mathcal{L}_{cba}$) function can be easily plugged into any deep neural network architecture as a differentiable block. The only impacted segment of the network is the last output layer, where a custom layer block is inserted with the class-balanced affinity loss as the loss function for training the model parameters, as shown in Fig. 2. We implement the proposed loss function in TensorFlow v.2. The final layer weights learn class prototypes for each of the classes present in the dataset and the outputs are computer using the Bergman divergence (Eq. 3), instead of the vector dot product used in softmax loss. To perform the ablation study, other parameters of the CNNs in the previous study were held constant, including the requirement of pretrained ImageNet weights.

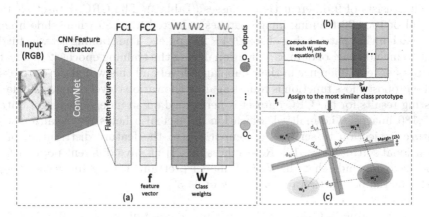

Fig. 2. An overview of the proposed framework. (a) During training phase, the weights (W) representing class prototypes are learnt, where C is the number of classes. The learned hidden features (FC2) in Euclidean space are similar to its class prototype, where similarity is measured using Eq. 3. (b) The feature vector is assigned to an output class by using the similarity measure in Eq. 3 instead of vector dot product commonly used in softmax. (c) By using the class-balanced affinity loss, we ensure intra-class compactness as well as inter-class separation of these class prototypes. Unlike the vanilla affinity loss, margin penalty for misclassification of minor classes are more strict in comparison to the major classes. Best viewed in color.

3.3 Dataset Description

We verify our proposed loss function ($\mathcal{L}_{cba}$) on two separate public-access histopathology datasets as benchmarks. First, is the Invasive Ductal Carcinoma (IDC) dataset introduced by [13]. The dataset is heavily skewed towards IDC negative (non-cancerous) cases (Table 1). The dataset contains a total of 277,524 patches sized 50 × 50 obtained from 162 patients' WSI. We use the study in [14] to serve as a baseline to compare our results against. They use Alexnet for classification obtaining an F1-score of 0.7648 and a balanced accuracy of 84.68%. We perform a split of the full IDC dataset to randomly assign 70% of data to the training set and 30% to the testing set, in accordance with the previous studies.

Table 1. Invasive Ductal Carcinoma (IDC) dataset distribution [13]

Class	Number of Samples	Percentage (%)
IDC Negative	198,738	71.61
IDC Positive	78,786	28.39
Total	*277,524*	*100.00*

Second, we utilize the Colorectal Cancer (CRC) histology slides dataset [21] which consists of 9 different tissue classes (Table 2). The CRC dataset contains a total of 100,000 training image patches collected from 86 whole-slide images, with each image patch being of size 224 × 224 pixels. The training set was further split to include 15% of data as validation during the training epochs [21]. The two datasets have a difference in their imbalance level and this will allow us to assess if the proposed loss function is robust against the various level of data imbalance. Testing results for the CRC dataset is performed on an independent test dataset of 7,180 images. The multi-classification dataset also helps us visualize the 2D feature projection to serve as a comparison to the feature distribution of the traditional softmax loss [17]. Researchers in [21] use five different popular CNN models to conclude that the VGG19 model pretrained using ImageNet weights performs the best with a test accuracy of 94.3%.

Table 2. Colorectal Cancer (CRC) dataset distribution [21]

Tissue Class	Number of Samples	Percentage (%)
ADI (adipose tissue)	10,407	10.41
BACK (background)	10,566	10.57
DEB (debris)	11,512	11.51
LYM (lymphocytes)	11,557	11.56
MUC (mucus)	8,896	8.90
MUS (smooth muscle)	13,536	13.54
NORM (normal colon mucosa)	8,763	8.76
STR (cancer-associated stroma)	10,446	10.45
TUM (colorectal adenocarcinoma epithelium)	14,317	14.32
Total	*100,000*	*100.00*

3.4 Training

The training of the CNNs was done on an NVIDIA Quadro RTX 6000 GPU. Due to the high number of images in both datasets, generators were used to load the images in a batch size of 64. The images in the IDC dataset were resized to 32×32 pixels to match the experiment conducted by [14]. We empirically determine that λ (which denotes the enforced margin in the $\mathcal{L}_{cba}$), σ (weighting parameter in the Gaussian similarly measure), β (controls growth of the effective number of samples), and the choice of optimizer are additional hyperparameters that can affect the performance of the model trained with the proposed $\mathcal{L}_{cba}$). These hyperparameters are application dependant (based on image properties) and need to be fine-tuned based on the application domain and the dataset imbalance level. Table 3 shows the different values/ranges for each hyperparameter in the tuning search space. Early stopping is used with a patience of 5 to prevent any overfitting when the validation loss plateaus.

Table 3. Hyperparameter ranges in the parameter search.

Hyperparameter	Values
Beta (β)	0.9, 0.99, 0.999, 0.9999, 0.99999
Lambda λ	0.1 - 0.9 (increments of 0.1)
Sigma σ	80 - 430 (increments of 50)
Optimizer	Adam, Nadam, Adadelta

4 Results and Discussion

4.1 Model Performance

Table 4 highlights the increase in classification performance by using the proposed class-balanced affinity loss ($\mathcal{L}_{cba}$) in comparison to the regular Alexnet with categorical cross-entropy loss (CCE) and softmax activation used by [14] on the IDC dataset. The best model from their study is used as a baseline for comparison. For this dataset, hyperparameter tuning results in the best parameters as follows: beta (0.999), lambda (0.1), sigma (130), and optimizer (Nadam). The most significant metric on the table is the F1-score since accuracy is not a comprehensive evaluation criterion in imbalanced datasets. We can observe a 5% increase in the F1-score (76% to 81%) with the introduction of the proposed class-balanced affinity loss ($\mathcal{L}_{cba}$), highlighting overall performance increase in the recall and precision of minor class samples. This is further shown in the confusion matrix plot (normalized over true/row values) in Fig. 3. Since the authors of the benchmark paper do not provide their confusion matrix or weights, we recreate their experiment with similar performance, F1-score of 0.77 (+1.3%)

Table 4. Classification results with Invasive Ductal Carcinoma (IDC) dataset with different loss functions.

Model: Alexnet	Cross-entropy Loss [14]	Class-balanced Affinity Loss ($\mathcal{L}_{cba}$)
F1 Macro	0.76	**0.81**
Accuracy	0.85	**0.85**

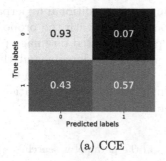
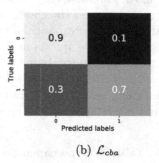

(a) CCE   (b) $\mathcal{L}_{cba}$

Fig. 3. IDC Dataset confusion matrix normalized over true (row) values. Class 1 is the IDC Positive (cancerous) minor class. (a) Alexnet with Categorical cross-entropy (CCE) loss (F1-score 0.77, Accuracy 83.5%). (b) Alexnet with $\mathcal{L}_{cba}$ (F1-score 0.81, Accuracy 85%).

and accuracy of 83.5% (-1.8%), to show the dramatic difference in the minor class (class 1) prediction. Note the metrics presented in Table 4 are reported to 2 significant figures for a fair comparison to the benchmark paper scores.

The results for the ablation study with CRC dataset are shown in Table 5. An independent hyperparameter tuning was performed for this dataset. The lambda and sigma values corresponding to the proposed loss were the same as the Alexnet model with the IDC dataset, which suggests that the aforementioned values for lambda and sigma can be used across various histopathology image datasets. However, the adadelta optimizer was utilized instead of Nadam and the most optimal beta value for this dataset was 0.9999. The F1-macro score was obtained by evaluation done using the trained VGG19 model and code as provided by [21]. As seen in Table 5, a 1.8% increase in the accuracy metric is observed by utilising the class-balanced affinity loss ($\mathcal{L}_{cba}$). Further, the F1-macro score has risen considerably from 0.92 to 0.95 (3% increase), which reinforces the overall improvement of precision and recall metrics across all the classes. In particular, the STR (cancer-associated stroma) class which performs very poorly with softmax loss is shown to have a significant improvement by the class-balanced affinity loss, as seen in the confusion matrix in Fig. 4. In both the experiments, class-balanced affinity loss has also surpassed the vanilla affinity loss implementation by more than 1% improvement in both accuracy and F1-score measures. The result on the CRC dataset further highlight that the higher discriminative ability of the proposed $\mathcal{L}_{cba}$ improves classification of fine-grained classes even with a smaller level of data imbalance.

Table 5. Classification results with Colorectal cancer (CRC) dataset with different loss functions.

Model: VGG19	Cross-entropy Loss [21]	Class-balanced Affinity Loss ($\mathcal{L}_{cba}$)
F1 Macro	0.92	**0.95**
Accuracy (%)	94.3	**96.1**

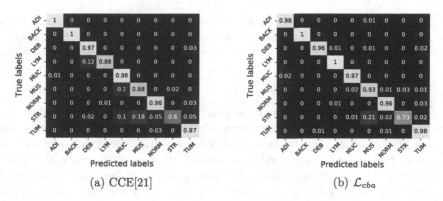

(a) CCE[21]

(b) $\mathcal{L}_{cba}$

Fig. 4. CRC dataset confusion matrix normalized over true (row) values with (a) VGG19 with CCE (F1-score 0.92, Accuracy 94.3%). (b) VGG19 with $\mathcal{L}_{cba}$ (F1-score 0.95, Accuracy 96.1%).

4.2 Role of Hyperparameters

In addition to the already extensive search space in the neural network models, our proposed balanced affinity loss function adds three additional hyperparameters: sigma (σ), lambda (λ), and beta (β). The ranges for each of these hyperparameters must be empirically determined based on the application context (Table 3). Figure 5a shows how the (σ) hyperparameter affected the maximum test accuracy for the IDC dataset with the Alexnet model and $\mathcal{L}_{cba}$. Figure 5b shows how the effective weights assigned to each class in CRC dataset changes as the beta value is altered. For values 0.999 and below, the change is very minimal and close to 1 (standard weight). As the beta value increases, under-represented classes gain more attention to in the learning process as these data samples are likely to be unique samples with important features and not appear again in the dataset.

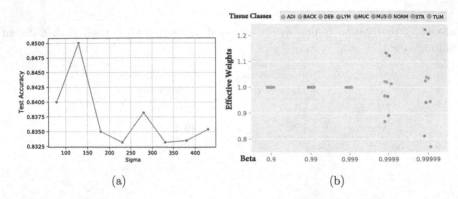

(a)   (b)

Fig. 5. (a) Impact of sigma values on the test accuracy of the IDC dataset with Alexnet. (b) Impact of beta values on the effective weights for each class in the CRC dataset. A higher effective weight results in more attention to the particular class during training.

This means that the proposed loss function ($\mathcal{L}_{cba}$) adds more parameters to the search space for model tuning during the training phase. Further, our experiments show that sigma and lambda values can dramatically change between datasets. For instance, a low value of sigma (10) can work well with MNIST dataset but for the histopathology datasets, a higher value (130) yields better results. Beta controls the growth of effective number as the number of samples become larger, and the ideal value of Beta depends on the extent of imbalance in the dataset. Finally, the choice of optimizer is significant, and it is also dependent on the dataset context. Thus, with a greater control over the loss function, $\mathcal{L}_{cba}$ introduces a bigger search space for the best hyperparameters. For both the histopathology dataset experiments, we obtain the same optimal value for sigma (130) and lambda (0.1) which can serve as reference for other experiments in the same domain.

4.3   Feature Projection for Multi-class Histopathology Dataset

In this section, we compare the 2D feature space projections of the penultimate layer activations between the categorical cross-entropy (CCE) loss (or softmax loss) and the proposed class-balanced affinity loss (see Fig. 6) for CRC dataset with VGG19 model. In comparison to [17], the histopathology dataset classes are more difficult to distinguish as they include very fine-grained classes, which requires many years of experience by pathologists to classify accurately [12].

To keep the comparison between CCE and $\mathcal{L}_{cba}$ losses fair, we used the same model (VGG19) for both with the CRC dataset. The only comparison between the two is based on their feature projections, where a better separation and compact clustering of the features means that they are more robust to class imbalance and more apt to fine-grained classification.

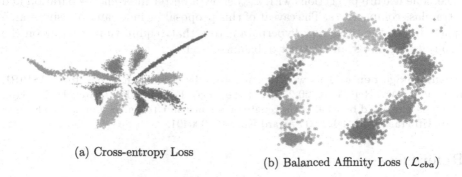

(a) Cross-entropy Loss

(b) Balanced Affinity Loss ($\mathcal{L}_{cba}$)

Fig. 6. The 2D feature space projection of the penultimate layer activations for the validation dataset. Both models are trained on the CRC dataset with VGG19 backbone structure using different loss functions: (a) softmax loss and (b) class-balanced affinity loss ($\mathcal{L}_{cba}$). Each color represents a specific class features where we can notice more compact clusters and a better separation of the classes with $\mathcal{L}_{cba}$. Features rotated for visual clarity and the diagram is best viewed in color.

The balanced affinity loss function ($\mathcal{L}_{cba}$) shows a better distribution of clusters while the cross-entropy loss function has a weaker separation between the feature projections for the different classes (see Fig. 6). This means that between the two loss functions, the proposed $\mathcal{L}_{cba}$ is more robust in handling imbalanced histopathology datasets as each class features have a well-defined feature space projection. There is, however, a noticeable difference in the space between each cluster when compared to the MNIST feature space projections [17]. There is a slight overlap in the feature space between clusters for some data points and the distances are not maximized as much in comparison, which highlights the fine-grained challenging aspect of the histopathology datasets where class samples are very closely related.

5   Conclusion

This paper presented a novel class-balanced affinity loss ($\mathcal{L}_{cba}$) function that improves the performance of imbalanced data distribution in fine-grained histopathology image classification. The key idea is to utilize the proposed class-balanced factor to improve the effectivity of the affinity loss function, enabling it to learn the uniform-sized equidistant clusters in the feature space, consequently improving class separability and reducing intra-class disparities. These features of the loss function are crucial in tackling the fine-grained imbalanced aspect of the histopathology datasets, which conventional softmax loss cannot overcome. We validated our proposed method across two publicly available datasets where it demonstrates a superior performance in comparison to the existing literature. Further, the different extent of imbalance in the two datasets also suggest that the proposed loss function is robust against different levels of data imbalance. The feature projections with $\mathcal{L}_{cba}$ show a better inter-class separation and intra-class compactness. The caveat of this proposal includes an extensive search space due to the three new hyperparameters that require tuning based on the application context and dataset imbalance level.

Acknowledgements. This work is supported by a research grants from ASPIRE Institute, UAE, Ref: AARE20-279, and the Terry Fox Foundation Ref: I1037. Sajid Javed, is supported by Khalifa University of Science and Technology under the Faculty Start Up grants FSU-2022-003 Award No. 8474000401.

References

1. Bray, F., Laversanne, M., Weiderpass, E., Soerjomataram, I.: The ever-increasing importance of cancer as a leading cause of premature death worldwide. Cancer **127**(16), 3029–3030 (2021). https://doi.org/10.1002/cncr.33587
2. Koboldt, D.C., et al.: Comprehensive molecular portraits of human breast tumours. Nature **490**(7418), Art. no. 7418 (2012). https://doi.org/10.1038/nature11412
3. L. SR, E. IO, S. SJ, T. PH, and van de V. MJ, WHO Classification of Tumours of the Breast. Accessed: Mar. 15, 2022. [Online]. https://publications.iarc.fr/Book-And-Report-Series/Who-Classification-Of-Tumours/WHO-Classification-Of-Tumours-Of-The-Breast-2012
4. Smith, R.A., et al.: American Cancer Society guidelines for the early detection of cancer. CA Cancer J. Clin. **52**(1), 8–22 (2002). https://doi.org/10.3322/canjclin.52.1.8
5. Reda, I., et al.: Computer-aided diagnostic tool for early detection of prostate cancer. In: 2016 IEEE International Conference on Image Processing (ICIP), 2016-August, 2016, pp. 2668–2672 (2016). https://doi.org/10.1109/ICIP.2016.7532843
6. El Khatib, A., Werghi, N., Al-Ahmad, H.: Automatic polyp detection: a comparative study. In: Proceedings Annual International Conference of the IEEE Engineering in Medicine and Biology Society, EMBS, 2015, pp. 2669–2672, 7318941. https://doi.org/10.1109/EMBC.2015.7318941
7. Taha, B., Werghi, N., Dias, J.: Automatic polyp detection in endoscopy videos: a survey. In: Proceedings of 13th IASTED International Conference on Biomedical Engineering, BioMed 2017, 2017, pp. 233–240. https://doi.org/10.2316/P.2017.852-031
8. Alkadi, R., Taher, F., El-Baz, A., Werghi, N.: A deep learning-based approach for the detection and localization of prostate cancer in T2 magnetic resonance images. J. Digit. Imaging **32**(5), 793–807 (2019). https://doi.org/10.1109/ACCESS.2019.2943567
9. Alkadi, R., Abdullah, O., Werghi, N.: The classification power of classical and Intra-voxel Incoherent Motion (IVIM) fitting models of diffusion-weighted magnetic resonance images: an experimental study. J. Digit. Imaging **35**(3), 678–691 (2022). https://doi.org/10.1007/s10278-022-00604-z

10. Hassan, T., Javed, S., Mahmood, A., Qaiser, T., Werghi, N., Rajpoot, N.: Nucleus classification in histology images using message passing network. Med. Image Anal. **79**, 102480 (2022). https://doi.org/10.1016/j.media.2022.102480

11. Javed, S., Mahmood, A., Dias, J., Werghi, N.: Multi-level feature fusion for nucleus detection in histology images using correlation filters. Comput. Biol. Med. **143**, 105281 (2022). https://doi.org/10.1109/ACCESS.2022.3155660

12. Han, Z., Wei, B., Zheng, Y., Yin, Y., Li, K., Li, S.: Breast cancer multi-classification from histopathological images with structured deep learning model. Sci. Rep. **7**(1), 4172 (2017). https://doi.org/10.1038/s41598-017-04075-z

13. Cruz-Roa, A., et al.: Automatic detection of invasive ductal carcinoma in whole slide images with convolutional neural networks, San Diego, California, USA, Mar. 2014, p. 904103. https://doi.org/10.1117/12.2043872

14. Janowczyk, A., Madabhushi, A.: Deep learning for digital pathology image analysis: a comprehensive tutorial with selected use cases. J. Pathol. Inform. **7**(1), 29 (2016). https://doi.org/10.4103/2153-3539.186902

15. He, H., Garcia, E.A.: Learning from imbalanced data. IEEE Trans. Knowl. Data Eng. **21**(9), 1263–1284 (2009). https://doi.org/10.1109/TKDE.2008.239

16. Cui, Y., Jia, M., Lin, T.-Y., Song, Y., Belongie, S.: Class-balanced loss based on effective number of samples. In: Proceedings of the IEEE/CVF Conference on Computer Vision and Pattern Recognition, pp. 9268–9277 (2019)

17. Hayat, M., Khan, S., Zamir, S.W., Shen, J., Shao, L.: Gaussian affinity for max-margin class imbalanced learning. In: 2019 IEEE/CVF International Conference on Computer Vision (ICCV), Seoul, Korea (South), Oct. 2019, pp. 6468–6478. https://doi.org/10.1109/ICCV.2019.00657

18. Huang, C., Li, Y., Loy, C.C., Tang, X.: Learning deep representation for imbalanced classification. In: 2016 IEEE Conference on Computer Vision and Pattern Recognition (CVPR), Las Vegas, NV, USA, June 2016, pp. 5375–5384 (2016). https://doi.org/10.1109/CVPR.2016.580

19. Wen, Y., Zhang, K., Li, Z., Qiao, Yu.: A discriminative feature learning approach for deep face recognition. In: Leibe, B., Matas, J., Sebe, N., Welling, M. (eds.) ECCV 2016. LNCS, vol. 9911, pp. 499–515. Springer, Cham (2016). https://doi.org/10.1007/978-3-319-46478-7_31

20. Lin, T.-Y., Goyal, P., Girshick, R., He, K., Dollár, P.: Focal loss for dense object detection. IEEE Trans. Pattern Anal. Mach. Intell. **42**(2), 318–327 (2020). https://doi.org/10.1109/TPAMI.2018.2858826

21. Kather, J.N., et al.: Predicting survival from colorectal cancer histology slides using deep learning: a retrospective multicenter study. PLoS Med. **16**(1), e1002730 (2019). https://doi.org/10.1371/journal.pmed.1002730

22. Deng, J., Guo, J., Xue, N., Zafeiriou, S.: ArcFace: additive angular margin loss for deep face recognition. In: IEEE/CVF Conference on Computer Vision and Pattern Recognition (CVPR) 2019, pp. 4685–4694 (2019). https://doi.org/10.1109/CVPR.2019.00482

23. Min, Z., et al.: Controlling false positive/negative rates for deep-learning-based prostate cancer detection on multiparametric MR images. In: Medical Image Understanding and Analysis, , pp. 56–70. Cham (2021)

24. Qin, R., Qiao, K., Wang, L., Zeng, L., Chen, J., Yan, B.: Weighted focal loss: an effective loss function to overcome unbalance problem of chest X-ray14. IOP Conf. Ser. Mater. Sci. Eng. **428**, 012022 (2018). https://doi.org/10.1088/1757-899X/428/1/012022

Hybrid Approach for the Design of CNNs Using Genetic Algorithms for Melanoma Classification

Luigi Di Biasi[1]([⊠]) [iD], Fabiola De Marco[1] [iD], Alessia Auriemma Citarella[1] [iD],
Paola Barra[2] [iD], Stefano Piotto Piotto[1] [iD], and Genoveffa Tortora[1] [iD]

[1] University of Salerno, Fisciano, Italy
{ldibiasi,fdemarco,aauriemmacitarella,piotto,tortora}@unisa.it
[2] Parthenope University of Naples, Naples, Italy
paola.barra@uniparthenope.it

Abstract. Melanoma is one of the most dangerous and deadly cancers in the world. In this contribution, we proposed a convolutional neural network architecture implemented in its design by using genetic algorithms. The aim is to find the best structure of a neural network to improve melanoma classification. An experimental study has evaluated the presented approach, conducted using a refined subset of images from ISIC, one of the most referenced datasets used for melanoma classification. The genetic algorithm implemented for the convolutional neural network design allows the population to evolve in subsequent generations to achieve fitness optimally. Convergence leads to the survival of a set of neural network populations representing the best individuals designated to optimize the network for melanoma classification. Our hybrid approach for the design of CNN for melanoma detection reaches 94% in accuracy, 90% in sensitivity, 97% in specificity, and 98% in precision. The preliminary results suggest that the proposed method could improve melanoma classification by eliminating the necessity for user interaction and avoiding *a priori* network architecture selection.

Keywords: First keyword · Second keyword · Another keyword

1 Introduction

One of the most dangerous and deadly tumors is skin cancer, and, unfortunately, the rate of skin cancer has been increasing in recent years [13]. Even though different skin lesions exist, it is crucial to focus on melanoma, a malignant subtype of skin cancer, due to two critical characteristics that make it extremely dangerous. First, although melanoma accounts for only a small percentage of all cutaneous malignancies, it is the primary cause of death due to its capability to metastasize and spread rapidly across different tissues. Second, it is hard to recognize melanoma early because, in the first stage, it could look very similar to a benign naevus. Third, the most significant issue for some subtypes of

J.-J. Rousseau and B. Kapralos (Eds.): ICPR 2022 Workshops, LNCS 13643, pp. 514–528, 2023.
https://doi.org/10.1007/978-3-031-37660-3_36

skin cancer is a lack of early detection, which is a limiting factor for first-line therapy. Discovering melanoma at an early stage, when the tumor is thin, can lead to a favourable prognosis, with a 90% chance of therapy [14]. At the biological level, melanoma originates from melanocytes, the pigment-producing cells [1] involved in maintaining epidermal homeostasis: melanin plays a significant role in determining the behavior of skin cancer [5]. In addition, both genetic and environmental risk factors play a role in melanoma development: Caucasian race, light-colored skin, the number and kind of nevi, and a positive family history of melanoma. Among environmental risk variables, there are burns, UV rays exposure which has a genotoxic effect and sunburn history [4]. The physician performs clinical diagnosis by visual inspection and evaluates the presumed morphological criteria of the lesion. To assess the stage of melanoma, it is possible to take into account multiple characteristics: the thickness of the tumor, the presence of ulceration and the presence of metastasis to the lymph nodes or other parts of the body [3]. The most commonly used guideline of dermatological origin is the ABCDE rule, which considers asymmetry, regular or irregular edges, color, diameter, and the evolution of the lesion over time [7]. Early detection of lesions is critical for therapy success: it is possible to consider a detection as "early" if the melanoma is detected when the tumour is *still confined* to the skin without having already metastasized to other sites. Furthermore, the possibility of cure and the reduction of patient mortality is strictly related to the detection time [14]. Several Computer-Aided Decision (CAD) systems have emerged to assist clinical decisions to facilitate the diagnosis of melanoma: using an automatic system in optimal conditions can result in a faster diagnosis and a better standard of accuracy [6]. These CAD systems are designed and implemented following different Computer Vision (CV), Machine Learning (ML) and Deep Learning (DL) techniques applied to images. It is possible to classify the melanoma images into clinical, dermoscopic, and histologic images. Nowadays, it is possible to use any smart device to obtain a clinical image. The dermoscopy, an instrument that allows for image enlargements between 10 to 20 times, is used to perform the dermoscopic examination. Histological images result from suitably treated biological tissue preparation for subsequent microscopic analysis. The histological examination allows us to have information on the morphology and functionality of the tissues and cells that constitute them. As a result, histological images provide the highest informative content at the cellular level. In contrast, dermoscopic images appear to have a higher informative content by applying the "ABCD" rule since they enable the examination of the pigment arrangement in the context of the lesion, the depth of localization, and the presence of subcutaneous patterns not presently visible to the human eye.

Convolutional Neural Networks (CNN) and similar architectures are frequently employed for image analysis and aim for high classification accuracy performances regarding melanoma classification problems [14]. Unfortunately, these performances are strictly related to the optimal training/validation/test conditions: multiple unfortunate situations can drop classifier performances from up to 0.9 to near 0.5 (coin flip)-for example, interclass differences and extra-class similarities [15].

This contribution reports the results we obtained with an Evolutionary-Based CNN Design Strategy for Melanoma Detection (GACNN) based on genetic algorithm operators, extended by adding a *merging* operator. We used ISIC[1] as the training dataset and included new selectable layers such as `Hangout`, `batchNorm` and `chanNorm` in the gene list. Our original working hypothesis is that a neural network population, utilizing a genetic algorithm technique, can converge to a desirable solution (an NN-based classifier with high accuracy), avoiding the need to design *a priori* the network structure.

The paper is organized as follows. In Sect. 2, we present an overview of the current use of neural networks and genetic algorithm approaches for melanoma detection and classification. In Sect. 3, we present the GACNN method used in this work. In Sect. 4, we report the achieved results with a brief comparison with the literature and, finally, in Sect. 5, we draw conclusions and future works.

2 Related Works

There are many melanoma detection and classification approaches, including machine learning techniques.

Already in 2013, *Razmjooy et al.* [16] proposed a new algorithm for hair removal applying canny edge detection and new features based on asymmetry and irregular border quantification to improve Support Vector Machine (SVM). They reached an accuracy of 95%. In 2014, *Ramezani et al.* [17] used SVM employed with a threshold-based method for segmentation after applying noise removal techniques to the images. They used 187 features indicating asymmetry, border irregularity, color variation, dimension, and texture, which are reduced by applying principal component analysis (PCA). The authors obtained an ACC of 82.2%, a specificity of 86.93%, and a sensitivity of 77%.

From 2015 to recent years, several neural network architectures, in particular *Convoutional Neural Networks* (CNNs), have been used for the classification of melanoma.

Kawahara et al. proposed a multitask deep CNN trained on multimodal data using clinical, dermoscopic images and patient metadata. Using several multitask loss functions, each of which takes into account different combinations of input modalities and a seven-point checklist, their neural network generated multimodal feature vectors for image retrieval and detection of clinical discriminant regions [8].

Zhang et al. have constructed an attention residual learning CNN, called ARL-CNN, to avoid the problem of little data available, extra-class similarity and intra-class variation. They based their network on an attention mechanism capable of increasing the possibility of discriminating the information available by focusing on its semantic meaning. The authors do not introduce new extra

---

[1] https://challenge.isic-archive.com/data/.

learnable layers in the network. Still, they delegate the possibility of grasping the semantic meaning to the more abstract feature maps of the higher layers. The authors use the dataset ISIC 2017 with 1320 additionally dermoscopy images, including 466 melanoma. ARL-CNN network consists of 50 layers and has obtained an ACC of 85%, a specificity of 89.6% and a sensitivity of 65.8% [9].

Jinnai et al. use a dataset of over 12.000 skin images to extract 5.846 clinical images of pigmented skin lesions from 3.551 individuals. Among these, the dataset includes 1.611 malignant melanoma images. Because of its consistency in demonstrating strong classification accuracy, robustness, and speed, a faster, region-based CNN (FRCNN) model has been adopted [8].

Alizadeh et al. [19] suggest a method to classify skin cancer on dermoscopy images based on four steps: pre-processing, CNN classification, classification based on feature extraction, and final classification using the ensemble method. They have tested their approach on ISIC datasets.

Kaur et al. [20] have developed a new deep convolutional neural network (DCNN) model for classifying skin lesions by connecting many blocks to allow ample feature information to pass straight through the network. They have named this architecture Lesion Classification Network (LCNet). In order to extract low and high-level feature information from lesions, each block of the network uses distinct parameters such as the number of kernels, filter size, and stride. Furthermore, since ISIC datasets are unbalanced, the authors use data augmentation and oversampling methods.

The application of genetic algorithms has grown in popularity in neural network (NN) optimization. Genetic algorithms can optimize several processes using the notion of biological evolution. The approach iterates through three stages: selection, crossover, and mutation, starting with a random population of network architectures [11]. GAs are used to improve CNN hyperparameters. For example, the number of neurons in each layer and the size and number of filters in each layer can affect the accuracy of a neural network model.

Recently, *Pérez and Ventura* have proposed a CNN architecture designed by a genetic algorithm that finds optimal members of an ensemble learning model. Their work suggests how genetic algorithms can find efficient architectures in the diagnosis of melanoma with performances 11% and 13% better than CNN models used in the literature [10].

3   Methods

3.1   Dataset

The International Skin Imaging Collaboration (ISIC) is an academic-industry collaboration that aims to make it easier to use digital skin imaging to help reduce melanoma mortality. The Memorial Sloan Kettering Cancer Center managed the project with the economic aid of philanthropic contributions (sponsors and partners). As a result, the ISIC dataset is our starting point for building the training, validation, and test set used in this contribution.

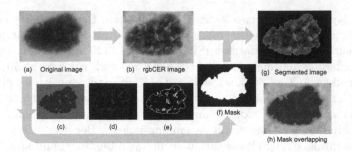

(a) Original image   (b) rgbCER image   (g) Segmented image

(c)   (d)   (e)   (f) Mask

(h) Mask overlapping

Fig. 1. The image segmentation process.

ISIC consists of several image datasets associated with well-founded clinical diagnoses: it contains more than 150.000 dermoscopy images, 7.000 of which are publicly available. Each image is associated with metadata that includes information on the image's status (benign or malignant), approximate location on the body, and demographic factors such as age and gender. ISIC is in development from 2016 to 2020. In addition, the ISIC challenge, an annual competition involving the scientific community to improve dermatologic diagnostic accuracy [2], uses ISIC to compare multiple approaches to skin disease detection.

3.2 Pre-processing

We defined an ISIC refined dataset (*Refined ISIC*) composed of 500 RGB images (250 melanoma images and 250 benign nevi). As the first step, we pre-processed the entire ISIC dataset by executing a *contrast enhancement for coloured images routine (rgbCER)* because many images, such as medical images, suffer from poor contrast. Therefore, it is necessary to enhance such contrast of images before further pre-processing, or analysis can be conducted [18]. The technique of enhancing the perceptibility of an image so that the output image is better than the input image is known as image enhancement.

Figure 1 shows each phase of the segmentation process; it involves the creation of a mask to split the background and the foreground. In Fig. 1 a sample image before (a) and after the *rgbCER application* (b) is shown.

Figure 1(g) shows the result of the segmentation approach regarding a single ISIC image. It applies the mask obtained from the previous process Fig. 1(f) to the image improved by rgbCER (Fig. 1(b)) to exclude the background and obtain only the information relating to the foreground. Figure 1(h) highlights in blue the original image parts considered foreground by the previous routine. The pixels not captured by the blue mask are considered background.

The images given as input to the algorithm are those obtained after the pre-processing phase just described, so all the images have the part of interest in evidence and the black background. To provide a quality training set to our DL approach, we manually extracted 500 images avoiding those still containing imperfections undetected by the pre-processing step. We named this subset of images *Refined ISIC*.

3.3 Training, Validation and Test Sets

The complete *Refined ISIC* dataset was split into three subsets using the splitEachLabel function using 0.5, 0.3 and 0.2 as splitting parameters. In particular, we built three subsets named *training*, *validation* and *test*: training was composed of 250 images, validation of 150 images and test of 100 images. Each subset (training, validation, and test set) was built by randomly picking the images from the Refined-ISIC dataset.

Each network training session used only training and validation subsets. We used the test set to evaluate the network performances by simulating a real case scenario (in which no one of the test images was even seen by the network before).

3.4 Genetic Algorithms

Following our working hypothesis, we do not propose to use the GA to improve the determination of hyperparameters on a defined and static NN. Instead, we suggest using a genetic approach to develop a self-assembling NN population to enhance melanoma classification. GA algorithms replicate the modes of evolution by following the Darwinian premise that the most suitable environment elements have a better chance of surviving and transmitting their features to their descendants. There is a population of individuals (n chromosomes) that evolve from generation to generation using techniques that are similar to natural evolutionary processes. To represent chromosomes, we used the binary string representation; this might be a limitation because the string length limits the final size of the entity. In fact, in our experimentation, we extended classic GA operations with another operation (merging) that allows two genomes (two entities) to concatenate together. In chromosomes, each locus (specific location on a chromosome) has two alleles (different versions of genes): 0 and 1. Therefore, it is possible to consider the chromosomes as discrete points in a solution space [12]. The evolutionary algorithms carry out heuristic exploration for new solutions to issues in which there is no complete knowledge of the search area, and they explore all of it. Then, starting with the first solution, they tweak it, combine it, and evolve until they find a better result. Three fundamental mechanisms are considered in evolution:

- *selection*: the selection indicates the process of selection of the most promising solutions capable of generating individuals who survive in the environment;
- *cross over*: it is a genetic recombination operator which introduces variation in the population;
- *mutation*: it shifts the space of solutions, resulting in the development of new information and the recovery of knowledge that has been lost through time in the population.

As written before, we added another mechanism called merging in our proposal. We permit the merging of two chromosomes to able network structure to grow. We discuss the proposed method in more detail below.

3.5 GA Definition

Population. We used GA terminology to identify our working items. The basic components of evolutionary algorithms used in our research will be described and explained in detail below. For example, the notation $F(t)$ indicates a composition of an object at time t.

Entity E_i is a vector $E_i = \{F_1, \ldots, F_m\}$ of m features. F_j of a generic entity E_i represents a gene of E_i. The Genome of E_i is the entire set of genes. The set $P(t) = \{E_1, \ldots, E_n\}$ is called Population at time t. For the experiment to reach a sufficiently extended network architecture, the start size of the genome was set to ten to allow at least the presence of the minimal layers required to execute a CNN. In addition, we let the genome size grow using the merge operation (not related to the GA fundamental) to make network architecture more complex: the merge operation sticks two different genomes, doubling the size of an entity genome. Each gene represents one of the Matlab CNN network layers: input, dropout, batch norm, cross-chan norm, 2d-convolution, RELU, softmax, and Fully Connected. An array represents each chromosome: each cell indicates whether or not a characteristic (a feature) inside the entity exists. A feature denotes one of the layers used to build a CNN. When a feature (array cell) is active, the related layer becomes part of the network. On the other hand, we consider the feature not expressed if it is not active and the layer does not belong to the network. Please note that a mutation may activate a non expressed feature in the future in some evolutionary cycle. So, each feature F_j can be expressed or not by E_i and, consequently, we can have silent and expressed genes. Furthermore, each chromosome does not have a predetermined length because the merging technique has been implemented and allows the joining of two chromosomes.

Fitness Function. We have addressed the *selection* to the score function and to the capacity of the entity to survive in the execution environment. So, to drive population evolution, we used the global population accuracy as *fitness* function, whose formula is reported in Eq. 1.

$$Accuracy(ACC) = \frac{TP + TN}{TN + FP + FN + TP} \tag{1}$$

This fitness function represents the accuracy of all networks in an evolutionary cycle arranged in a straightforward decreasing order. We determined the highest accuracy from each surviving entity for each evolutionary phase. As a result, for each generation, all entities that expose an accuracy at time t equal to or better than the previous generation at time t-1 will survive. Also, a random 10% of the entities still survive and pass in the next evolution step, regardless of the accuracy reached at time t. The execution of the GA stops if no progress in the accuracy metric (used as a fitness function) occurs for ten consecutive evolution stages.

Euristic, Constraints and Limitations. Unfortunately, due to the physical restrictions of our cloud platform, we were forced to limit the possible crossover, mutation and merging to 10, 100, and 10, respectively. To overcome these limitations, we used an initial randomized population of 10.000 entities in which we randomly generated the genome. In particular, each entity's genome gene was chosen randomly from the allowed gene set and each gene parameter. We were able to set up the experimental environment to run up to 100 iterations to allow the system to evolve correctly. Also, we established the following limitations:

- the initial gene of each entity E_i must be an image input (II) or one of the previously established pre-processing routines;
- if the gene g is a pre-processing routine, the gene $g + 1$ must be an II layer or another pre-processing layer;
- the latest gene of an entity must be a classification layer.

Also, due to hardware limitations, we restrict the network structure to a series of the layer. Therefore, no graph or cycle was possible in this experimentation.

Experiment Execution. To drive the genetic evolution process, we wrote our GA engine (GAE) using C and OpenMP [21]. GAE perform all the task involved in population initialization and management. In particular, each simulation step (SS) is split into three phases: population evolution (P1), Network execution (P2) and fitness evaluation (P3).

- *Phase P1*: for each SS, the GAE performs the GA operations (mutation, crossover and merging) on the current population to obtain new NN candidates;
- *Phase P2*: GAE sends the entire population and training sets to a GRIMD cluster using a map/reduce approach: each NN is associated with a worker; each worker called the MATLAB train function to train the NN on the training datasets. At this point, GAE will hold, waiting for the completion of the "reduce" phase that will return to GAE the survived trained networks with the corresponded accuracy.
- *Phase P3*: GAE sorts all the accuracies in descending order and selects the new candidate for the next evolution, following the rules described before in the fitness section.

Figure 2 shows a simplified overview of the computational environment.

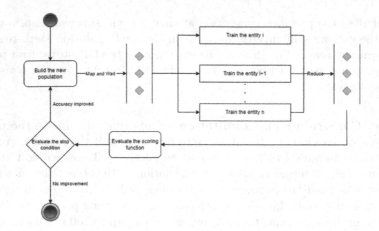

Fig. 2. An overview of the experiment environment architecture.

3.6 Performance Measures

We evaluated the performance of our approach with four metrics, including the accuracy (ACC) in Eq. 1. In particular, we used sensitivity, specificity and precision, as reported in Eqs. 2–4.

$$Sensitivity(SEN) = \frac{TP}{TP + FN} \tag{2}$$

$$Specificity(SPE) = \frac{TN}{TN + FP} \tag{3}$$

$$Precision(PRE) = \frac{TP}{TP + FP} \tag{4}$$

The terms TP, TN, FP, and FN represent the number of true positives, true negatives, false positives, and false negatives, respectively. The fraction of positive entities correctly detected is known as sensitivity. In particular, the specificity measures the fraction of correctly detected negative entities. Finally, the precision represents the positive predictive value, and it is the percentage of retrieved instances relevant to the experiment.

3.7 Experiments Setup

We worked with a hybrid Beowulf/Cloud Computational (GRIDC) architecture setup, designed to run the `Matlab 2021` environment across multiple workstations and cloud workers. In addition, we adapted GRIMD architecture [22] that provides a map/reduce approach to distributing across the "grimd slaves" the working package composed of: training and validation sets and neural networks structure to train.

The Beowulf part of the GRIDC was composed of three high-performance workstations equipped with NVIDIA GPU, high RAM available and multicore capabilities running Windows 10: the SoftMatterLab (University of Salerno - DIFARMA) provided pro-bono the Beowulf part of GRIDC.

The cloud part was composed of three Amazon AWS c5d.metal instances running Centos. However, we shut down the c5d.metal cluster during the experimentation as soon as the number of NN became tractable only via our HPC system. The cloud part was provided pro-bono by Softmining SRL.

Table 1. Work Environment

GRIDC	#Core	RAM	GPU0	GPU1
Beu	64	250 GB	Quadro P400	RTX5000
Beu	20	64 GB	Intel UHD G 770	GeForce RTX 3060 Ti
Beu	12	16 GB	Intel UHD G 630	Quadro P2000
Cloud	96	192 GB	-	-
Cloud	96	192 GB	-	-
Cloud	96	192 GB	-	-

4   Results and Discussion

This section reports and analyzes the preliminary results of our experiments.

Immediately after the initialization phase, at the second iteration, we noticed that the population shrank by a *ratio* of about 1:3. In particular, we observed that incompatible NN structure (NN structure that causes MATLAB train function to crash) or valid NN structure that requires more RAM than the available RAM on workers causes this high death ratio. In particular, we discovered that the second observation is strictly related to our initial choice to avoid pooling layers to be part of the genome. These facts strongly suggest that an improvement in the random initialization approach (better heuristics) is needed. Figure 3 reports the trend of the death *ratio* across the eleven iterations.

However, despite the high death ratio, the execution of the GA led to an improvement in the accuracy metric in every iteration, as we expected, by selecting entities with high-quality criteria as the best option over less desirable alternatives. However, we observed that many NN populations tended to overfit: preliminary observations suggest many dropout layers are needed. Also, it is possible to see that the GA algorithm reached a stable population (a plateau regarding accuracy) after 11 evolutionary cycles, without reaching the limit of 100 iterations; at the 11th iteration, it appears that the loss of diversity of the NN population prevents the exploration of novel solutions because the GA reached a local or global optimum. This behaviour led to drastic computation time and cost-saving because the number of "networks to train" rapidly became tractable

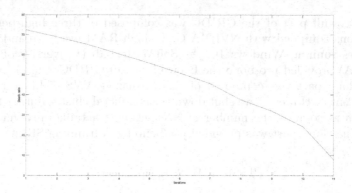

Fig. 3. Trend of death ratio over the 11 iterations

without cloud computational power. Furthermore, it was possible to disable the
c5d.metal (Table 1) instances after the fourth evolutionary cycle: the residual
evolutionary steps needed only up to three days to complete.

The high mortality *ratio* observed may be due to the randomness of the
initial population, where the networks die either because the layers are incompatible with each other or because the structure is incompatible with the working
environment.

Table 2. Evolution during the iterations

#Iteration	#Population	CrossOver	Mutation	Merge	Death Ratio	ACC(Val)	ACC(Test)
1	10000	10	100	10	72,5	0,5	0,41
2	3745	9	95	9	68,9	0,52	0,57
3	1535	8	89	9	64,9	0,56	0,53
4	686	8	83	9	60,3	0,58	0,56
5	336	7	76	8	55,6	0,6	0,60
6	178	7	70	8	50,7	0,62	0,67
7	101	6	62	8	45,5	0,69	0,74
8	60	5	51	8	37,4	0,7	0,81
9	39	4	44	8	31,9	0,74	0,81
10	26	3	33	8	24,2	0,89	0,89
11	18	1	11	8	7,9	0.90	0.94

Table 2 shows the evolution during the 11 iterations.

After the stop of GA routines, 19 NN (19NN set) exposed a validation accuracy less or equal to 0.90, with a final validation loss of 0.2047: due to the high
validation accuracy, we considered all these 19 networks equivalent. Figure 4
shows the training plot of one network picked from the 19NN set. The accuracy
of this network on the test set was 0.94.

Fig. 4. Structure of the best network in the last iteration

Also, Fig. 5 shows the confusion matrix regarding network performance on the test set. We observed that the crossover and the mutation operations tend to decrease following the population size and accuracy.

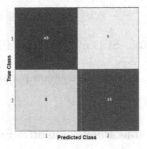

Fig. 5. Confusion matrix of the best NN in the 11th iteration

The preliminary results reported in this work strongly suggest that the GA approach can enable the design of the structure of a neural network driven by the problem to solve, avoiding human interaction. The Table 3 shows the best results for each iteration until convergence is reached (up to the 11th iteration). The last iteration reports excellent performances such as 0.97 and 0.98 of specificity and precision, which show the potential to outperform the method proposed in the literature. However, it is mandatory to perform more experimentation, particularly performance analysis, using larger training and test sets.

4.1 Comparison with the Literature

Table 4 reports the performances of multiple deep-learning techniques performed on ISIC datasets.

For our proposal, we preliminary opted to use a balanced and small refined subset of images of ISIC, composed of 500 images, to provide quality images to the networks. On this refined dataset, our approach, which involves the building of the network guided by the use of genetic algorithms, achieves maximum values

Table 3. Experiments results

#Iteration	TP	FP	FN	TN	ACC	SEN	SPE	PRE
1	36	14	42	8	0,44	0,46	0,36	0,72
2	50	0	43	7	0,57	0,53	1	1
3	50	0	47	3	0,53	0,51	1	1
4	41	9	35	15	0,56	0,53	0,62	0,82
5	10	40	0	50	0,60	1	0,55	0,2
6	34	16	17	33	0,67	0,66	0,67	0,68
7	50	0	26	24	0,74	0,65	1	1
8	44	6	13	37	0,81	0,77	0,86	0,88
9	50	0	19	31	0,81	0,72	1	1
10	43	3	8	42	0,89	0,85	0,93	0,94
11	49	1	5	45	0,94	0,90	0,97	0,98

of ACC of 94%, SEN of 90%, SPE of 97%, and PRE of 98% at the eleventh iteration.

We used this data for a preliminary comparison between our and other approaches.

Table 4. Reference literature

Reference Paper	Dataset	Methods	ACC	SEN	SPE	PRE
Alizadeh et al. [19]	ISIC 2016	CNN + feature extraction	85.2%	52%	93.40%	66%
Alizadeh et al. [19]	ISIC 2019	CNN + feature extraction	96.7%	96.3%	97.1%	95.1%
Kaur et al. [20]	ISIC 2016	LCNet	81.41%	81.3%	80.83%	81.88%
Kaur et al. [20]	ISIC 2017	LCNet	88.23%	87.86%	88.86%	78.55%
Kaur et al. [20]	ISIC 2020	LCNet	90.42%	90.39%	90.39%	90.48%
Our approach	**ISIC 2020**	**GA design**	**94%**	**90%**	**97%**	**98%**

Alizadeh et al. [19] proposed an ensemble method to detect melanoma. Their method consists of two models of CNNs and two texture features, local binary pattern and Haralick features. During ISIC 2016 and ISIC 2019, the authors evaluated the method. The first model has nine layers and employs many batch normalization layers to speed up classification and prevent the problem of over-fitting. The second model used a pre-trained VGG-19. An ensemble approach is used to integrate these two models for the classification task.

In 2022, *Kaur et al.* [20] proposed a deep convolutional neural network, called LCNet, to classify malignant versus benign melanoma images. The deep network is composed of eleven blocks.

5 Conclusion

This contribution proposes using genetic algorithms as a building CNNs method to address the melanoma classification problem, one of the most dangerous skin cancers. The initial hypothesis claims that it is possible to interpret the development of a network as the evolution of a system over time. In the GA context, the entire system adapts, modifying its configuration in response to the dynamic of its interactions with the environment, like reinforcement learning. Finally, the system leads to selecting optimal solutions (local or global) to achieve the goals of the considered task.

The initial generation of NN is stochastic. Consequently, initially, a remarkably low accuracy is observed, while with the advancement of the experiment, there is an attenuation of the error consequent to a better level of fitness of the NN population. A set of equivalent NN with high classification performance was available in the last evolutionary iteration.

According to our preliminary results, allowing GA to assist in designing a NN structure could yield results comparable to traditional NN design (by humans) methods. Furthermore, the proposed approach must be expanded and evaluated on larger or additional melanoma datasets (e.g., clinical or histological). Our future goal is to extend the training set images to improve our understanding of the genetic algorithm in constructing the network as the starting dataset increases.

Also, the evaluation of a new heuristic could reduce the high death ratio, the tendency to overfit and permit fast convergence to a local or global optimum. In future research, we expect to investigate the use of additional criteria to define the initialization of the algorithm and the use of a more targeted population to achieve the desired result. Also, we expect to extend the permitted layer to be part of the entity genome. Finally, We will also plan to improve the selection procedures of individuals to be used for subsequent generations through the fitness function.

References

1. Naik, P.P.: Cutaneous malignant melanoma: a review of early diagnosis and management. World J. Oncology **12**(1), 7 (2021)
2. Skin Lesion Analysis toward Melanoma Detection: A Challenge at the International Symposium on Biomedical Imaging (ISBI) 2016, hosted by the International Skin Imaging Collaboration (ISIC). http://arxiv.org/abs/1605.01397
3. Duncan, L.M., et al.: Melastatin expression and prognosis in cutaneous malignant melanoma. J. Clin. Oncol. **19**(2), 568–576 (2001)
4. Rastrelli, M., et al.: Melanoma: epidemiology, risk factors, pathogenesis, diagnosis and classification. In: vivo 28.6, pp. 1005–1011 (2014)
5. Slominski, R.M., Zmijewski, M.A., Slominski, A.T.: The role of melanin pigment in melanoma. Exp. Dermatol. **24**(4), 258 (2015)
6. Maiti, A., et al.: Computer-aided diagnosis of melanoma: a review of existing knowledge and strategies. Current Med. Imaging **16**(7), 835–854 (2020)

7. Rigel, D.S., et al.: ABCDE-an evolving concept in the early detection of melanoma. Archives Dermatology 141(8), 1032–1034 (2005)
8. Jinnai, S., et al.: The development of a skin cancer classification system for pigmented skin lesions using deep learning. Biomolecules **10**(8), 1123 (2020)
9. Zhang, J., et al.: Attention residual learning for skin lesion classification. IEEE Trans. Med. Imaging **38**(9), 2092–2103 (2019)
10. Pérez, E., Ventura, S.: An ensemble-based convolutional neural network model powered by a genetic algorithm for melanoma diagnosis. Neural Comput. Appl. **34**(13), 10429–10448 (2022)
11. Kramer, O.: "Genetic algorithms" Genetic algorithm essentials 11–19 (2017)
12. Katoch, S., Chauhan, S.S., Kumar, V.: A review on genetic algorithm: past, present, and future. Multimed. Tools Appl. **80**(5), 8091–8126 (2021)
13. Viale, P.H.: The American Cancer Society's facts & figures: 2020 edition. J. Adv. Practitioner Oncol. **11**(2), 135 (2020)
14. Popescu, D., et al.: New trends in melanoma detection using neural networks: a systematic review. Sensors **22**(2), 496 (2022)
15. Di Biasi, L., et al.: A cloud approach for melanoma detection based on deep learning networks. IEEE J. Biomed. Health Inf. **26**(3), 962–972 (2021)
16. Razmjooy, N., et al.: A computer-aided diagnosis system for malignant melanomas. Neural Comput. Appl. **23**(7), 2059–2071 (2013)
17. Ramezani, M., Karimian, A., Moallem, P.: Automatic detection of malignant melanoma using macroscopic images. J. Med. Signals Sensors **4**(4), 281 (2014)
18. Perumal, S., Velmurugan, T.: Preprocessing by contrast enhancement techniques for medical images. Int. J. Pure Appl. Math. **118**(18), 3681–3688 (2018)
19. Alizadeh, S.M., Mahloojifar, A.: Automatic skin cancer detection in dermoscopy images by combining convolutional neural networks and texture features. Int. J. Imaging Syst. Technol. **31**(2), 695–707 (2021)
20. Kaur, R., et al.: Melanoma classification using a novel deep convolutional neural network with dermoscopic images. Sensors **22**(3), 1134 (2022)
21. Dagum, L., Menon, R.: OpenMP: an industry standard API for shared-memory programming. IEEE Comput. Sci. Eng. **5**(1), 46–55 (1998)
22. Piotto, S., et al.: GRIMD: distributed computing for chemists and biologists. Bioinformation **10**(1), 43 (2014)

Transfer Learning in Breast Mass Detection on the OMI-DB Dataset: A Preliminary Study

Marya Ryspayeva[1], Mario Molinara[1(✉)], Alessandro Bria[1], Claudio Marrocco[1], and Francesco Tortorella[2]

[1] University of Cassino and Southern Lazio, 03043 Cassino, Italy
{m.molinara,a.bria,c.marrocco}@unicas.it
[2] University of Salerno, 84084 Fisciano, SA, Italy
ftortorella@unisa.it

Abstract. Early screening for breast cancer is an effective tool to detect tumors and decrease mortality among women. However, COVID restrictions made screening difficult in recent years due to a decrease in screening tests, reduction of routine procedures, and their delay. This preliminary study aimed to investigate mass detection in a large-scale OMI-DB dataset with three Transfer Learning settings in the early screening. We considered a subset of the OMI-DB dataset consisting of 6,000 cases, where we extracted 3,525 images with masses of Hologic Inc. manufacturer. This paper proposes to use the RetinaNet model with ResNet50 backbone to detect tumors in Full-Field Digital Mammograms. The model was initialized with ImageNet weights, COCO weights, and from scratch. We applied True Positive Rate at False Positive per Image evaluation metric with Free-Response Receiver Operating Characteristic curve to visualize the distributions of the detections. The proposed framework obtained 0.93 TPR at 0.84 FPPI with COCO weights initialization. ImageNet weights gave comparable results of 0.93 at 0.84 FPPI and from scratch demonstrated 0.84 at 0.84 FPPI.

Keywords: breast cancer · mass detection · transfer learning · artificial intelligence

1 Introduction

X-ray mammography is a golden standard in the early diagnosis of any abnormality in the breast. Every year a woman from 40 years old should take a mammography screening which is an effective tool to lower mortality [1]. Unfortunately, COVID-19 has made the screening difficult in recent years and women worldwide have felt the impact of quarantine measures on the early diagnosis of breast cancer, which is a valuable step in detecting a common disease among

This work was supported by MIUR (Minister for Education, University and Research, Law 232/216, Department of Excellence).

J.-J. Rousseau and B. Kapralos (Eds.): ICPR 2022 Workshops, LNCS 13643, pp. 529–538, 2023.
https://doi.org/10.1007/978-3-031-37660-3_37

women [2,3]. Radiologists may miss a lesion in image analysis because of physician fatigue, diagnostic errors, artifacts, noise, and time-consuming annotation. Artificial Intelligence (AI) can help speed the detection and diagnosis of disease to overcome these difficulties, which aggravated due to COVID in recent years, and catch up on the delay due to the pandemic. The problem of tumors in women is an important health issue and has been investigated widely with different approaches in the last years [4–6], especially Convolutional Neural Networks (CNN) for the detection of lesions in mammograms [7]. Nevertheless, to successfully train a system based on AI methods, developers demand tens of thousands of snapshots with annotated groundtruths that are difficult to obtain in the medical domain due to the high cost and exhausting labeling and contouring process. Transfer Learning has already established itself as an effective method of AI in the medical domain and is capable of reaching state-of-the-art results.

This preliminary study aimed to investigate how a transfer learning approach affects the performance of a system for breast cancer detection. In particular, we considered a detector based on RetinaNet with two different Transfer Learning settings (ImageNet and COCO) and trained from scratch. Experiments have been performed on the OMI-DB dataset containing mammography images with masses labeled as 'benign' or 'malignant.' The approach is to preprocess mammograms and use the entire images as input to the model in the detection step. The preprocessing step is made up of the downsampling and cropping breast area. It is proved that preprocessing can progress detection performances and generally CNN-based architectures work efficiently also without preprocessing [8,9]. The detection results during the training are evaluated with mean Average Precision (mAP) using IoU (Intersection over Union), in the testing True Positive Rate (TPR) at False Positive per Image (FPPI) with Free-response Receiver Operating Characteristic curve (FROC). The IoU evaluates the overlapping between the predicted and the groundtruth bounding boxes.

2   Dataset and Data Pre-processing

In this research, we used the OMI-DB dataset with a subset of 6,000 cases of 148,461 processed and unprocessed full-field digital mammograms (FFDM) [10] stored in DICOM format. The data were collected by the United Kingdom's National Health Service Breast Screening Programme. DICOM files contained an annotation that reported equipment and screening parameters. We selected Hologic Inc. manufacturer because the majority of the images were taken by its equipment, and defined the dataset as OMI-H. Images were acquired in two views for both breasts: Mediolateral oblique (MLO) and Craniocaudal (CC) in two sizes, $2,560 \times 3,328$ and $3,328 \times 4,048$ pixels. In the dataset, different abnormalities are labeled; however, we analyze only masses without implants. Additionally, we excluded cases with one breast or one view, which were considered the clinical history of a patient. The size of the considered dataset is 3,525 positive and 4,100 negative images split into train, validation, and test subsets with a ratio of 70%, 10%, and 20%, respectively.

Selected images are represented in grayscale DICOM format with a 16-bit range of intensity which we transformed to png format with 8-bit. After that, we downsampled images to the lowest pixel resolution, 70µm, and the black areas around the breast were cropped out [11]. This preliminary study investigates one approach where the entire image acts as an input. It means that downsampled and cropped out mammograms with the common size of 800×800 pixels are fed to the networks which allow us to train the model with the whole breast pictured on the image.

3 Methodology

The main idea of Transfer Learning is to transfer knowledge from one domain to another. Features are learned from such large datasets as ImageNet [12] and COCO [13] datasets with millions of images, and the obtained weights are further applied in different domains, such as breast cancer.

In this research, we propose using RetinaNet [15], a one-stage detector constructed with a ResNet-50-FPN backbone. Comparing two-stage detectors, for instance, R-CNN [15], Faster R-CNN [16], FPN (Feature Pyramid Network) [17], where the first stage is Region Proposal Network (RPN) to straighten the number of the predicted objects, and the second stage is classification to detect objects according to the required class, classification and regression subnets in RetinaNet operate in parallel and simultaneously.

It is recognized that RetinaNet detects objects well with different scales thanks to the FPN approach. This architecture has become useful and essential in the medical domain. For instance, it helps to detect various lesions [18–21]. RetinaNet consists of ResNet-50 and FPN backbones, where the first plays a role as a feature extractor, while the second creates a multi-scale feature pyramid, scale-invariant, and comprises two subnetworks for classification and regression. The regression subnetwork predicts bounding boxes and the classification subnetwork determines the object's class.

The challenging problem in object detection is foreground and background class imbalance. In two-stage detectors, the background classes are narrowed to 1,000–2,000, while RetinaNet enumerates 100,000 predicted objects, spreading densely distributed in the spatial domain and ratios [14]. The imbalance of negative and positive objects is solved with Focal Loss proposed by [14], increasing the training efficiency. Focal Loss is a version of Cross-Entropy Loss. Focal Loss solves the imbalance problem by adding more weights to the foreground and fewer weights to background objects, in other words, Focal Loss down-weights the contribution of easy examples and focuses the model on hard examples.

In this preliminary study, we trained our dataset with the RetinaNet model with ResNet50 backbone with ImageNet and COCO weights initialization, and from scratch. In this case, the ImageNet and COCO weights act as initialization to speed up the training process which are extracted from a large amount of data and transferred to the required small dataset, reaching high effectiveness. Training the model from scratch is a time- and resource-consuming challenge.

However, we trained our model from scratch to compare three variants of the methods. Figure 1 shows the architecture of the network with the training process.

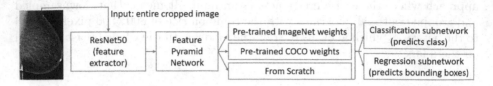

Fig. 1. RetinaNet architecture with ImageNet, COCO weights and from-scratch

4   Experiments and Results

In this section, we present the preliminary results of the mass detection in the OMI-DB dataset. We trained the RetinaNet model with ResNet50 backbone, and the model was initialized with ImageNet, COCO weights, and from scratch. The weights initialization yields advantages in the starting point, training speed, and higher results. The total number of epochs is 100 in each initialization mode, and the batch size is 4 with 676 steps, 1e−5 learning rate with Adam optimizer. The mAP was utilized as a metric to monitor the training process on the validation subset, and a snapshot of each epoch was saved. As a result, ResNet50 with ImageNet weights demonstrated the best mAP 0.704 at 40 epochs, ResNet50 with COCO weights - mAP 0.709 at 14 epochs, and ResNet50 from scratch 0.570 mAP at 57 epochs. Epochs with the highest mAP were saved as the best.

Consequently, initialization with COCO weights gave us faster convergence with fewer epochs and highest metric versus ImageNet weights and from scratch, which took more time to train and worse performance. COCO and ImageNet weights displayed the same comparable mAP. However, we trained all 100 epochs and saved snapshots for all of them to compare the results. The convergence of the models occurs before 20 epochs, and the model ResNet50 with COCO weights reached the convergence in the same way.

The commonly used primary metric in medical detection is TPR, which refers to sensitivity and recall. All predicted masses are categorized as True Positive (TP), True Negative (TN), False positive (FP), and False Negative (FN). Our research follows the same metrics as in Agarwal et al. [11, 22–30] to compare our results.

According to the accepted metric, True Positive masses are detected if the IoU is greater than 10%. It means that the predicted bounding box overlaps its GTs by 10%. False Negatives are considered if the IoU is less than 10%.

We took each 10th epoch and predicted test datasets with 11 different variants from 10 to 100 epochs, including the best epoch. For each chosen epoch, we predicted bounding boxes and calculated the TPR metric for all three models.

Table 1. Performance comparison of mass detection methods in epochs with step 10. The metrics correspond to the TPR at 0.84 FPPI.

Model	TPR at 0.84 FPPI										
Epochs	10	20	30	40	50	60	70	80	90	100	BEST
RetinaNet+ResNet50+ImageNet	0.91	0.91	0.93	0.92	0.91	0.91	0.91	0.90	0.90	0.90	0.90
RetinaNet+ResNet50+COCO	0.90	0.91	0.91	0.92	0.93	0.91	0.91	0.90	0.90	0.90	0.90
RetinaNet+ResNet50+Scratch	0.78	0.82	0.82	0.83	0.84	0.84	0.84	0.84	0.84	0.84	0.83

Table 1 illustrates that in model ResNet50 with ImageNet weights, we reached 0.93 TPR at 0.84 FPPI at 30 epochs. The model with COCO weights demonstrated the 0.93 TPR at 0.84 FPPI at epochs 50. The model from scratch showed the lowest 0.84 TPR at 0.84 FPPI at 50 epochs than in the previous two models. All real masses were predicted better in these epochs than in the best. Though, we can say that models initialized with weights in ranges of epochs indicated comparable and promising results of TPR except for the model from scratch.

Additionally, we plotted the FROC curves from 10 to 100 epochs with a step of 10 epochs with one of the best epochs (Fig. 2). The best epoch was chosen

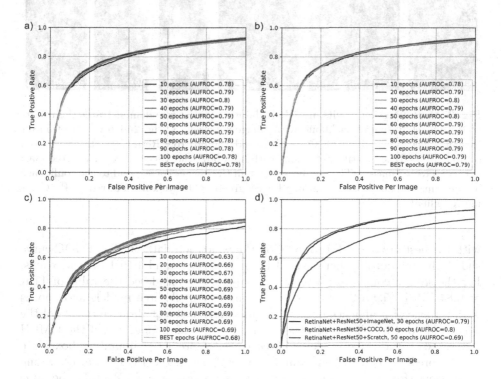

Fig. 2. Free-response Receiver Operating Characteristic curve with Area Under The Curve: a) ResNet50 with ImageNet weights; b) ResNet50 with COCO weights; c) From scratch; d) Comparison of the top three models

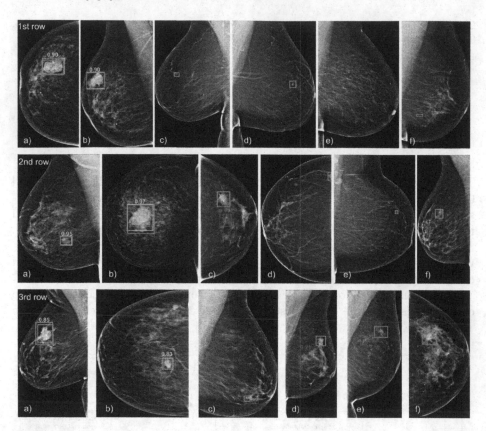

Fig. 3. Mass detection results in OMI-H dataset, the 1st row demonstrates the results of RetinaNet Resnet50 backbone with ImageNet weights, the 2nd row is RetinaNet Resnet50 backbone with COCO weights, and the 3rd row RetinaNet Resnet50 from scratch: a, b - True Positive detections with high objectness score; c, d - FP detections; e, f - undetected masses. The numbers shown in the images correspond to the confidence of being mass. The color of bounding boxes: green - GTs, yellow - TP, red - FP. (Color figure online)

with the best mAP and IoU of 50% on the validation dataset. The FROC curve shows the relationship between TPR on the y-axis and FPPI on the x-axis. For the sake of comparison with other papers, we considered the value of TPR at 0.84 FPPI. Figure 2 contains FROC curves for all three models and epochs with a range of confidence degrees. Figure 3 shows the qualitative results of the predicted bounding boxes of masses on the entire mammograms of the OMI-H dataset with the three models. Three types of predicted bounding boxes are shown: predictions with high confidence (90% and higher) (Fig. 3, a, b), wrong predictions (Fig. 3, c, d), and undetected masses (Fig. 3, e, f). We take the same color parameters of the bounding boxes visualization as Agarwal et al. [11]: green bounding boxes are GTs, yellow - True Positives, and red - False Positives. Above each prediction, the confidence score is displayed.

5 Discussion

Agarwal et al. [11] reached 0.87 TPR at 0.84 FPPI (Table 2), while RetinaNet+ResNet50+ImageNet in this paper shows 0.93 TPR at 0.84 FPPI of 30. The model with COCO weights demonstrates 0.93 TPR at the same FPPI of 50 epochs, and from scratch, 0.84 TPR at 0.84 FPPI with 50 epochs in this model.

The primary model in the paper of Agarwal et al. [11] used Faster Region-based Convolutional Neural Network (Faster-RCNN) with Hologic, General Electric, and Siemens manufacturers. The data distribution in OMI-H subsets consists of 2,042 malignant and 842 benign images. We extracted 3,525 images with masses, 3,162 malignant and 362 benign, which is 90% versus 10% in the percentage ratio in our dataset.

Table 2 compares the methods of mass detection in different datasets of breast cancer. One of our proposed models, RetinaNet with ResNet50 backbone and COCO weights, illustrates the highest 0.93 TPR at 0.84 FPPI, while Agarwal et al. (2019) [30] reported about 0.98 TPR at 1.67 FPPI. Jung et al. [29] reported 0.94 TPR at 1.30 FPPI, Kozegar et al. [22] showed the highest 0.91 TPR at 4.8 FPPI in their investigation. However, in this preliminary study, our results are promising and encouraging to continue work in this field.

Table 2. Comparison between proposed framework and the published results.

Method	TPR at FPPI	Dataset
Kozegar et al. (2013) [22]	0.87 at 3.67/0.91 at 4.8	INbreast/mini-MIAS
Akselrod et al. (2017) [23]	0.93 at 0.56/0.90 at 1.0	INbreast/Private
Shen et al.(2020) [24]	0.8788 at 0.5/0.9479 at 2.0	INbreast/Private
Anitha et al. (2017) [25]	0.935 at 0.62/0.925 at 1.06	mini-MIAS/DDSM
Brake et al. (2000) [26]	0.55 at 0.10	DDSM
Dhungel et al. (2017) [27]	0.90 at 1.3	INbreast
Ribli et al. (2018) [28]	0.90 at 0.30	INbreast
Jung et al. (2018) [29]	0.94 at 1.30	INbreast
Agarwal et al. (2019) [30]	0.98 at 1.67	INbreast
Agarwal et al. (2020) [11]	0.87 at 0.84	OMI-H
Proposed framework		
RetinaNet+ResNet50+ImageNet	0.93 at 0.84	OMI-H
RetinaNet+ResNet50+COCO	0.93 at 0.84	OMI-H
RetinaNet+ResNet50+Scratch	0.84 at 0.84	OMI-H

6 Conclusions and Future Work

This preliminary study demonstrates the first results of the mass detection using the RetinaNet model with ResNet50 backbone, which was initialized with ImageNet and COCO weights. The model was also trained from scratch. We were able to predict benign and malignant masses and extract predicted objects for further tasks. In this study, we applied only one of the planned approaches, using the entire mammogram as input to the models.

Some studies [11, 26, 28] have investigated the evaluation metric TPR depending on the type of malignancy (benign and malignant). In this study, we evaluated the parameters in terms of the whole dataset. Additionally, we utilized TPR with FROC as the main evaluation metric; besides, Receiver Operating Characteristic (ROC) with specificity could help compare the results more robustly. The proposed framework has the potential to be investigated further with different backbones and weights. It was shown that COCO weights yield higher results than ImageNet and from scratch.

In future work, we will add ResNet101 and ResNet152 as backbones with the initialization modes and further classification of the predicted bounding boxes to benign and malignant. Moreover, in this study, we analyzed only one approach, while in future work, we intend to use patches of the mammograms as input. As an additional suggestion of future work, a direct comparison with Agarwal et al. would be essential to compare Faster R-CNN with RetinaNet.

7 Declaration of Competing Interest

The authors declare that they have no known competing financial interests or personal relationships that could have appeared to influence the work reported in this paper.

Acknowledgements. The authors acknowledge the OPTIMAM project and Cancer Research Technology for providing the images used in this study, the staff at Royal Surrey NHS Foundation Trust who developed OMI-DB, and the charity Cancer Research UK which funded the OPTIMAM project.

This work was supported by MUR (Italian Ministry for University and Research) funding to AB, CM, and MM through the DIEI Department of Excellence 2018-2022 (law 232/2016) and to FT through the DIEM Department of Excellence 2023-2027 (law 232/2016). Ruth Kehali Kassahun holds an EACEA Erasmus+ grant for the master in Medical Imaging and Applications.

References

1. Yu, X., Wang, S.-H.: Abnormality diagnosis in mammograms by transfer learning based on ResNet18. Fundam. Inform. **168**, 219–230 (2019). https://doi.org/10.3233/fi-2019-1829

2. Monticciolo, D.L., et al.: Breast cancer screening recommendations inclusive of all women at average risk: Update from the ACR and Society of Breast Imaging. J. Am. Coll. Radiol. **18**, 1280–1288 (2021). https://doi.org/10.1016/j.jacr.2021.04.021

3. Monticciolo, D.L., et al.: Breast cancer screening for average-risk women: recommendations from the ACR commission on breast imaging. J. Am. Coll. Radiol. **14**, 1137–1143 (2017). https://doi.org/10.1016/j.jacr.2017.06.001

4. D'Elia, C., Marrocco, C., Molinara, M., Tortorella, F.: Detection of clusters of microcalcifications in mammograms: a multi classifier approach. In: 2008 21st IEEE International Symposium on Computer-Based Medical Systems. IEEE (2008)

5. Bria, A., Marrocco, C., Karssemeijer, N., Molinara, M., Tortorella, F.: Deep cascade classifiers to detect clusters of microcalcifications. In: Tingberg, A., Lång, K., Timberg, P. (eds.) IWDM 2016. LNCS, vol. 9699, pp. 415–422. Springer, Cham (2016). https://doi.org/10.1007/978-3-319-41546-8_52

6. Marrocco, C., Molinara, M., Tortorella, F.: Algorithms for detecting clusters of microcalcifications in mammograms. In: Roli, F., Vitulano, S. (eds.) ICIAP 2005. LNCS, vol. 3617, pp. 884–891. Springer, Heidelberg (2005). https://doi.org/10.1007/11553595_108

7. Savelli, B., Bria, A., Molinara, M., Marrocco, C., Tortorella, F.: A multi-context CNN ensemble for small lesion detection. Artif. Intell. Med. **103**, 101749 (2020). https://doi.org/10.1016/j.artmed.2019.101749

8. Bria, A., et al.: Improving the automated detection of calcifications using adaptive variance stabilization. IEEE Trans. Med. Imaging **37**, 1857–1864 (2018). https://doi.org/10.1109/tmi.2018.2814058

9. Marchesi, A., et al.: The effect of mammogram preprocessing on microcalcification detection with convolutional neural networks. In: 2017 IEEE 30th International Symposium on Computer-Based Medical Systems (CBMS). IEEE (2017)

10. Halling-Brown, M.D., et al.: OPTIMAM mammography image database: a large-scale resource of mammography images and clinical data. Radiol. Artif. Intell. **3**, e200103 (2021). https://doi.org/10.1148/ryai.2020200103

11. Agarwal, R., Díaz, O., Yap, M.H., Lladó, X., Martí, R.: Deep learning for mass detection in full field digital mammograms. Comput. Biol. Med. **121**, 103774 (2020). https://doi.org/10.1016/j.compbiomed.2020.103774

12. Deng, J., Dong, W., Socher, R., Li, L.-J., Li, K., Fei-Fei, L.: ImageNet: a large-scale hierarchical image database. In: 2009 IEEE Conference on Computer Vision and Pattern Recognition. IEEE (2009)

13. Lin, T.-Y., et al.: Microsoft COCO: common objects in context. In: Fleet, D., Pajdla, T., Schiele, B., Tuytelaars, T. (eds.) ECCV 2014. LNCS, vol. 8693, pp. 740–755. Springer, Cham (2014). https://doi.org/10.1007/978-3-319-10602-1_48

14. Lin, T.-Y., Goyal, P., Girshick, R., He, K., Dollar, P.: Focal loss for dense object detection. In: 2017 IEEE International Conference on Computer Vision (ICCV). IEEE (2017)

15. Girshick, R., Donahue, J., Darrell, T., Malik, J.: Rich feature hierarchies for accurate object detection and semantic segmentation. In: 2014 IEEE Conference on Computer Vision and Pattern Recognition. IEEE (2014)

16. Girshick, R.: Fast R-CNN. In: 2015 IEEE International Conference on Computer Vision (ICCV). IEEE (2015)

17. Lin, T.-Y., Dollar, P., Girshick, R., He, K., Hariharan, B., Belongie, S.: Feature pyramid networks for object detection. In: 2017 IEEE Conference on Computer Vision and Pattern Recognition (CVPR). IEEE (2017)

18. Zlocha, M., Dou, Q., Glocker, B.: Improving RetinaNet for CT lesion detection with dense masks from weak RECIST labels. In: Shen, D., et al. (eds.) MICCAI 2019. LNCS, vol. 11769, pp. 402–410. Springer, Cham (2019). https://doi.org/10.1007/978-3-030-32226-7_45

19. Chen, J., et al.: Detection of cervical lesions in colposcopic images based on the RetinaNet method. Biomed. Sig. Process. Control **75**, 103589 (2022). https://doi.org/10.1016/j.bspc.2022.103589

20. Swinburne, N.C., et al.: for the MSK mind consortium: semisupervised training of a brain MRI tumor detection model using mined annotations. Radiology **303**, 80–89 (2022). https://doi.org/10.1148/radiol.210817

21. Adachi, M., et al.: Detection and diagnosis of breast cancer using artificial intelligence based assessment of maximum intensity projection dynamic contrast-enhanced magnetic resonance images. Diagnostics (Basel) **10**, 330 (2020). https://doi.org/10.3390/diagnostics10050330

22. Kozegar, E., Soryani, M., Minaei, B., Domingues, I.: Assessment of a novel mass detection algorithm in mammograms. J. Cancer Res. Ther. **9**, 592–600 (2013). https://doi.org/10.4103/0973-1482.126453

23. Akselrod-Ballin, A., et al.: Deep learning for automatic detection of abnormal findings in breast mammography. In: Cardoso, M.J., et al. (eds.) DLMIA/ML-CDS -2017. LNCS, vol. 10553, pp. 321–329. Springer, Cham (2017). https://doi.org/10.1007/978-3-319-67558-9_37

24. Shen, R., Yao, J., Yan, K., Tian, K., Jiang, C., Zhou, K.: Unsupervised domain adaptation with adversarial learning for mass detection in mammogram. Neurocomputing (2020)

25. Anitha, J., Peter, J.D., Pandian, S.I.A.: A dual stage adaptive thresholding (DuSAT) for automatic mass detection in mammograms. Comput. Comput. Methods Programs Biomed. **138**, 93–104 (2017)

26. te Brake, G.M., Karssemeijer, N., Hendriks, J.H.C.L.: An automatic method to discriminate malignant masses from normal tissue in digital mammograms1. Phys. Med. Biol. **45**, 2843–2857 (2000). https://doi.org/10.1088/0031-9155/45/10/308

27. Dhungel, N., Carneiro, G., Bradley, A.P.: A deep learning approach for the analysis of masses in mammograms with minimal user intervention. Med. Med. Image Anal. **37**, 114–128 (2017)

28. Ribli, D., Horváth, A., Unger, Z., Pollner, P., Csabai, I.: Detecting and classifying lesions in mammograms with Deep Learning. Sci. Sci. Rep. **8** (2018)

29. Jung, H., et al.: Detection of masses in mammograms using a one-stage object detector based on a deep convolutional neural network. PLoS ONE **13**, e0203355 (2018). https://doi.org/10.1371/journal.pone.0203355

30. Agarwal, R., Diaz, O., Lladó, X., Yap, M.H., Martí, R.: Automatic mass detection in mammograms using deep convolutional neural networks. J. Med. Imaging (Bellingham). **6**, 1 (2019). https://doi.org/10.1117/1.jmi.6.3.031409

On the Applicability of Prototypical Part Learning in Medical Images: Breast Masses Classification Using ProtoPNet

Gianluca Carloni[1,2], Andrea Berti[1,2]([✉]), Chiara Iacconi[3],
Maria Antonietta Pascali[1], and Sara Colantonio[1]

[1] Institute of Information Science and Technologies (ISTI), National Research Council of Italy (CNR), Pisa, Italy
{gianluca.carloni,andrea.berti,maria.antonietta.pascali,
sara.colantonio}@isti.cnr.it
[2] Department of Information Engineering, University of Pisa, Pisa, Italy
{gianluca.carloni,andrea.berti}@phd.unipi.it
[3] UOSD Breast Radiology, Territorial Area of Massa Carrara, Azienda USL Toscana Nord-Ovest, Carrara, Italy

Abstract. Deep learning models have become state-of-the-art in many areas, ranging from computer vision to agriculture research. However, concerns have been raised with respect to the transparency of their decisions, especially in the image domain. In this regard, Explainable Artificial Intelligence has been gaining popularity in recent years. The ProtoPNet model, which breaks down an image into prototypes and uses evidence gathered from the prototypes to classify an image, represents an appealing approach. Still, questions regarding its effectiveness arise when the application domain changes from real-world natural images to gray-scale medical images. This work explores the applicability of prototypical part learning in medical imaging by experimenting with ProtoPNet on a breast masses classification task. The two considered aspects were the classification capabilities and the validity of explanations. We looked for the optimal model's hyperparameter configuration via a random search. We trained the model in a five-fold CV supervised framework, with mammogram images cropped around the lesions and ground-truth labels of benign/malignant masses. Then, we compared the performance metrics of ProtoPNet to that of the corresponding base architecture, which was ResNet18, trained under the same framework. In addition, an experienced radiologist provided a clinical viewpoint on the quality of the learned prototypes, the patch activations, and the global explanations. We achieved a Recall of 0.769 and an area under the receiver operating characteristic curve of 0.719 in our experiments. Even though our findings are non-optimal for entering the clinical practice yet, the radiologist found ProtoPNet's explanations very intuitive, reporting a high level of satisfaction. Therefore, we believe that prototypical part learning offers a reasonable and promising trade-off between classification performance and the quality of the related explanation.

G. Carloni and A. Berti—These authors share the first authorship.

J.-J. Rousseau and B. Kapralos (Eds.): ICPR 2022 Workshops, LNCS 13643, pp. 539–557, 2023.
https://doi.org/10.1007/978-3-031-37660-3_38

Keywords: ProtoPNet · Breast masses · Classification · Deep learning · Explainable Artificial Intelligence

1 Introduction

Today's world of information research is largely dominated by artificial intelligence (AI) technologies. In particular, deep learning (DL) models are being deployed transversely across many sectors, revealing a great added value to humans in many of them. Some examples are autonomous driving [8] and smart agriculture [16]. Although DL models usually outperform humans at many levels, performance is not all we need. Indeed, industrial and research communities demand more explainable and trustworthy DL models. These needs emerge from the user's difficulty in understanding the internal mechanisms of an intelligent agent that led to a decision. Based on this degree of understanding, the user often decides whether to trust the output of a model.

Explainable AI (XAI) plays a pivotal role in this scenario. Research is now focusing on developing methods to explain the behavior and reasoning of deep models. Explanation methods developed so far can be divided into two major classes: *post-hoc* explanations and *ante-hoc* explanations. The first class comprises solutions that are based on separate models that are supposed to replicate most of the behavior of the black-box model. Their major advantage is that they can be applied to an already existing and well-performing model. However, in approximating the outcome, they may not reproduce the same calculations of the original model. Among this family of explanations we find global/local approximations, saliency maps and derivatives. By contrast, the second class of explanation methods, also known as *explaining by design*, comprises inherently interpretable models that provide their explanations in the same way the model computes its decisions. Indeed, training, inference, and explanation of the outcome are intrinsically linked. Examples of such methods are Deep k-Nearest Neighbors [17] and Logic Explained Networks [7].

Regarding the image domain, a substantial body of DL literature concerns classification tasks [11,14]. When it comes to image classification, one of the most familiar approaches humans exploit is to analyze the image and, by similarity, identify the previously seen instances of a certain class. A line of DL research focuses on models that mimic this type of reasoning, which is called prototypical learning [13,20]. The key feature of this class of learning algorithms is to compare one whole image to another whole image. Instead, one could wish to understand what are the relevant parts of the input image that led to a specific class prediction. In other words, parts of observations could be compared to parts of other observations. In the attempt to build a DL model that resembles this kind of logic, Chen et al. [6] proposed prototypical part network (ProtoPNet).

ProtoPNet breaks down an image into prototypes and uses evidence gathered from the prototypes to qualify the image. Thus, the model's reasoning is qualitatively similar to that of ornithologists, physicians, and others on the image classification task. At training time, the network uses only image-level labels without fine-annotated images. At inference time, the network predicts the image class by comparing its patches with the learned prototypes. The model provides an explanation visually by indicating the most informative parts of the image w.r.t. the output class. This allows the user to qualitatively evaluate how reasonable and trustworthy the prediction is according to the user domain knowledge.

ProtoPNet posed brilliant promises in classification domains regarding natural images (e.g., birds and cars classification [6], video deep-fake detection [23]). On the other hand, the applicability of this type of reasoning to medical images is still in its infancy. When presented with a new case, radiologists use to compare the images with previously experienced ones. They recall visual features that are specific to a particular disease, recognize them in the image at hand, and provide a diagnosis. For this reason, medical imaging seems to be suitable for prototypical part-based explanations. Nevertheless, some critical issues can arise when bringing technologies from other domains - like computer vision - into the medical world. Unlike natural images, usually characterized by three channels (e.g., RGB, CYM), conventional medical images feature single-channel gray-scales. For this reason, pixels contain a lower amount of information. Furthermore, x-ray images represent a body's projection and therefore are flat and bi-dimensional. As a result, objects in the field of view could not be as separable and distinguishable as in real-world natural images. Such issues might be detrimental to the application of these methodologies. In addition, the scarcity of labeled examples available for supervised training undermines the generalization capability achievable by complex models. This lack of labeled data is mainly due to the low prevalence of certain diseases, the time required for labeling, and privacy issues. Moreover, additional problems include the anatomical variability across patients and the image quality variability across different imaging scanners.

This work aims to investigate the applicability of ProtoPNet in mammogram images for the automatic and explainable malignancy classification of breast masses. The assessment of applicability was based on two aspects: the ability of the model in facing the task (i.e., classification metrics), and the ability of the model to provide end-users with plausible explanations. The novelty of this work stems from both the application of ProtoPNet to the classification of breast masses without fine-annotated images, and the clinical viewpoint provided for ProtoPNet's explanations.

2   Related Works

Several works in the literature have applied DL algorithms, and convolutional neural network (CNN) architectures in particular, to automatically classify benign/malignant breast masses from x-ray mammogram images. By contrast, only few works explored the applicability of ProtoPNet to the medical domain and, more specifically, on breast masses classification.

Concerning the use of CNNs for this task on the Curated Breast Imaging Subset of DDSM (CBIS-DDSM) [12] dataset some works follow. Tsochatzidis et al. [24] explored various popular CNN architectures, by using both randomly initialized weights and pre-trained weights from ImageNet. With ResNet50 and pre-trained weights they obtained an accuracy of 0.749. Alkhaleefah et al. [1] investigated the influence of data augmentation techniques on classification performance. When using ResNet50, they achieved 0.676 and 0.802 before and after augmentation, respectively. Arora et al. [3] proposed a two-stage classification system. First, they exploited an ensemble of five CNN models to extract features from breast mass images and then concatenated the five feature vectors into a single one. In the second stage, they trained a two-layered feed-forward network to classify mammogram images. With this approach, they achieved an accuracy of 0.880. They also reported the performance obtained with each individual sub-architecture of the ensemble, achieving an accuracy of 0.780 with ResNet18. Ragab et al. [19] also experimented with multiple CNN models to classify mass images. Among the experiments, they obtained an accuracy of 0.722, 0.711 and 0.715 when applying ResNet18, ResNet50 and ResNet101, respectively. Finally, Ansar et al. [2] introduced a novel architecture based on MobileNet and transfer learning to classify mass images. They benchmarked their model with other popular networks, among which ResNet50 led to an accuracy of 0.637.

Regarding the application of ProtoPNet to the medical domain, only few attempts have investigated it to date. Mohammadjafari et al. [15] applied ProtoPNet to Alzheimer's Disease detection on brain magnetic resonance images from two publicly available datasets. As a result, they found an accuracy of 0.91 with ProtoPNet, which is comparable to or marginally worse than that obtained with state-of-the-art black-box models. Singh et al. [21,22] proposed two works utilizing ProtoPNet on chest X-ray images of Covid-19 patients, pneumonia patients, and healthy people for Covid-19 identification. In [22] they slightly modified the weight initialization in the model to emphasize the effect of differences between image parts and prototypes in the classification process, achieving an accuracy of 0.89. In [21] they modified the metrics used in the model's classification process to select prototypes of varying dimensions, and obtained the best accuracy of 0.87.

To the best of our knowledge, the only application of prototypical part learning to the classification of benign/malignant masses in mammogram images was provided by Barnett et al. [4]. They introduced a new model, IAIA-BL, derived from ProtoPNet, utilizing a private dataset with further annotations by experts in training data. They included both pixel-wise masks to consider clinically significant regions in images and mass margin characteristics (spiculated, circumscribed, microlobulated, obscured, and indistinct). On the one hand, annotation masks of clinically significant regions were exploited at training time in conjunction with a modified loss function to penalize prototype activations on medically irrelevant areas. On the other hand, they employed annotations of mass margins as an additional label for each image and divided the inference process into two phases: first, the model determines the mass margin feature and then predicts

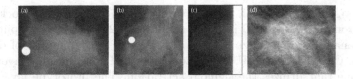

Fig. 1. Examples of images from the original CBIS-DDSM dataset that were removed due to artifacts. (a)–(b): annotation spot next to or within the mass; (c): white-band artifact; (d) horizontal-pattern artifact.

malignancy based on that information. For this purpose, they added a fully-connected (FC) layer to convert the mass margin score to the malignancy score. With that architecture, they managed to achieve an AUROC of 0.84.

3 Materials and Methods

In this work, we trained a ProtoPNet model to classify benign/malignant breast masses from mammogram images on a publicly available dataset. We compared its performance to the baseline model on which ProtoPNet is based. We conducted a random search independently on both models with five-fold cross-validation (CV) to optimize the respective hyperparameters.

3.1 Dataset

In our study, we used images from CBIS-DDSM [12]. The dataset is composed of scanned film mammography studies from 1566 breast cases (i.e., patients). For each patient, two views (i.e., MLO and CC) of the full mammogram images are provided. In addition, the collection comes with the region of interest (ROI)-cropped images for each lesion. Each breast image has its annotations given by experts, including the ground truth for the type of cancer (benign, malignant, or no-callback) and the type of lesion (calcification or mass). Only the ROI-cropped images of benign and malignant masses for each patient were used in this study. As a first step, we performed a cleaning process of the dataset by removing images with artifacts and annotation spots next to or within the mass region (Fig. 1). We then converted DICOM images of the cleaned dataset into PNG files. The training and test split of the cohort was already provided in the data collection. To obtain a balanced dataset, we randomly selected the exceeding elements from the most numerous class and excluded them from the cohort.

3.2 ProtoPNet

Architecture and Functioning. ProtoPNet, introduced in [6], comprises three main blocks: a CNN, a prototype layer, and an FC layer. As for the CNN block, it consists of a feature extractor, which can be chosen from many of the popular models competing on ImageNet challenges (VGGs, ResNets,

DenseNets), and a series of add-on convolutional layers. This block extracts features from an input RGB image of size 224×224. Given this input size, the convolutional output has size $7 \times 7 \times D$, where D is the number of output filters of the CNN block. ReLU is used to activate all convolutional layers, except the last one that utilizes the sigmoid activation. The prototype layer that follows comprises two 1×1 convolutional layers with ReLU activation. It learns m prototypes, whose shape is $1 \times 1 \times D$. Each prototype embodies a prototypical activation pattern in one area of the convolutional output, which itself refers to a prototypical image in the original pixel space. Thus, we can say that each prototype is a latent representation of some prototypical element of an image.

At inference time, the prototype layer computes a similarity score as the inverted squared L^2 distance between each prototype and all patches of the convolutional output. For each prototype, this produces an activation map of similarity score whose values quantify the presence of that prototypical part in the image. This map is up-sampled to the size of the input image and presented as an overlayed heat map highlighting the part of the input image that mostly resembles the learned prototype. The activation map for each prototype is then reduced using global max pooling to a single similarity score. A predetermined number of prototypes represents each class in the final model. In the end, the classification is performed by multiplying the similarity score of each prototype by the weights of the FC layer.

Prototype Learning Process. The learning process begins with the stochastic gradient descent of all the layers before the FC layer (joint epochs). Then, prototypes are projected onto the closest latent representation of training images' patches. Finally, the optimization of the FC layer is carried out. It is possible to cycle through these three stages more than once.

Differences in Our Implementation. Differences exist between the original paper introducing ProtoPNet [6] and our work. Firstly and more importantly, we conceived a hold-out test set to assess the final models' performance, after the models were trained using CV. In the original paper, instead, both the selection of the best model and the evaluation of its performance were carried out on the same set, i.e., validation and test sets were the same.

In addition, since ProtoPNet works with three-channel images, we modified the one-channel gray-scale input images by copying the information codified in the single channel to the other two. Then, we set the number of classes for the classification task to two instead of 200. Finally, to reduce overfitting when training a large model using a limited dataset, we introduced a 2D dropout layer and a 2D batch-normalization layer after each add-on convolutional layer of the model. An overview of our implementation of ProtoPNet architecture and its inference process is depicted in Fig. 2, taking the classification of a correctly classified malignant mass as an example.

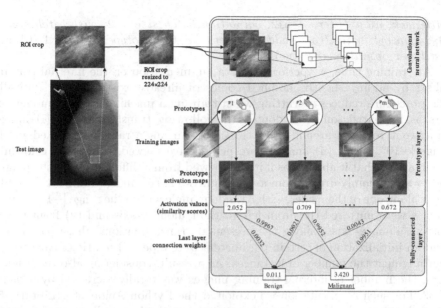

Fig. 2. Inference process through ProtoPNet: classification of a breast mass by means of the activation of pre-learned prototypes within the test image.

3.3   Experiment with ProtoPNet

As for the CNN block of ProtoPNet, the residual network ResNet18 with weights pre-trained on the ImageNet dataset was used in this experiment. Images were resized to a dimension of 224×224 pixels and their values were normalized with *mean* and standard deviation (*std*) equal to 0.5 for the three channels. As a result, image values range between -1 and $+1$ and this helps to improve the training process.

We then performed a random search to optimize the model's hyperparameters. For each configuration, we built a five-fold CV framework for training lesions, creating the internal-training and internal-validation subsets with an 80-20% proportion. We performed the splitting in both class-balanced and patient-stratified fashion; this way, we maintained the balance between the classes and we associated lesions of the same patients to the same subset (internal-training or internal-validation) for each CV fold. We employed the StratifiedGroupKFold function from the scikit-learn library [18] for this purpose.

Given the large number of hyperparameters in ProtoPNet that can be optimized, we investigated only a fraction of them in this work. In particular, we examined the learning rate (LR) at joint epochs, the weight decay (WD), the batch size of the internal-training subset, the coefficients of the ProtoP-Net loss function terms, and the number of prototypes per class. Their possible values are reported in Table 1. Among the resulting 2592 configurations, 30 were randomly selected and used for training. The remaining hyperparameters were chosen with fixed values instead. The ones different from the original ProtoPNet paper follow: *dropout_proportion* = 0.4; *add_on_layers_type* =

bottleneck; $num\_filters = 512$; $validation\_batch\_size = 2$; $push\_batch\_size = 40$; $warm\_optimizer\_lrs = \{add\_on\_layers : 1e\text{-}6, prototype\_vectors : 1e\text{-}6\}$; and $last\_layer\_optimizer\_lr = 1e\text{-}6$.

At training time, we performed data augmentation on the internal-training subset by adding slightly modified copies of already existing data. Typically, this procedure reduces overfitting when training a machine learning model and acts as regularization. We adopted the following transformations: (i) images underwent rotation around their center by an angle randomly picked in the range $[-10°, +10°]$; (ii) images were perspective skewed, that is, transforming the image so that it appears as if it was viewed from a different angle; the magnitude was randomly drawn from a value up to 0.2; (iii) images were stretched by shear along one of their sides, with a random angle within the range $[-10°, +10°]$; images were mirrored (iv) from left to right along y-axis and (v) from top to bottom along x-axis. Among the presented transformations, those based on a random initialization of certain parameters were repeated ten times each to further augment the number of instances. As a result, considering also the original ones, the number of internal-training images was totally increased by a factor of 33. For such augmentation we exploited the Python Augmentor Library [5], which has been designed to permit rotations of the images limiting the degree of distortion.

Differently from the original study, we used fixed LR values instead of an LR scheduler, and we framed the training process within an early stopping (ES) setting rather than a 1000-epochs one. In particular, we checked the trend of the loss function for ES. We exploited a moving average with $window = 5$ and $stride = 5$ to reduce the influence of noise in contiguous loss values at joint epochs. At every push epoch, a discrete derivative was computed on the two averaged values resulting from the ten joint epochs preceding that push epoch. A non-negative derivative was the condition to be checked. If the condition persisted for the following 30 joint epochs (patience), ES occurred, and the training process stopped. The considered model was the one saved before the 30 patience epochs.

Table 1. Values of the ProtoPNet Hyperparameters for the Random Search

Parameter	Domain
$lr\_features$	$[1e\text{-}7, 1e\text{-}6]$
lr_add_on	$[1e\text{-}7, 1e\text{-}6]$
lr_prot_vector	$[1e\text{-}7, 1e\text{-}6]$
WD	$[1e\text{-}3, 1e\text{-}2]$
$train\_batch\_size$	$[20, 40]$
$clst$	$[0.6, 0.8, 0.9]$
sep	$[-0.1, -0.08, -0.05]$
$l1$	$[1e\text{-}5, 1e\text{-}4, 1e\text{-}3]$
$num\_prots\_per\_class$	$[5, 20, 40]$

Following the random search, we chose the best-performing configuration based on the metrics reported in Sect. 3.4. Hence, we re-trained the model on the whole training set with the selected configuration for as many epochs as the average maximum epoch in the CV folds. We then performed a prototype pruning process, as suggested in the workflow of the original paper [6]. We did that to exclude, from the set of learned prototypes, those that potentially regard background and generic regions in favor of more class-specific ones. Finally, we evaluated the final model on test set images.

In the end, we compared ProtoPNet with a simpler, conventional black-box model. Since our ProtoPNet uses ResNet18 as the CNN block, we repeated the classification task with the same pre-processed dataset using a ResNet18 with weights pre-trained on ImageNet.

We conceived the training framework as a fine-tuning of the last convolutional layers. The fine-tuning was performed under the same five-fold CV settings and with the same data augmentation operations. To reduce the overfitting during training, we also inserted a dropout layer before the final FC layer.

Provided that ProtoPNet and ResNet18 have globally different hyperparameters, an independent random search was performed. The subset of investigated hyperparameters follows: number of re-trained last convolutional layers = $[1, 2, 3, 4, 5, 10, 20]$; LR = $[1e\text{-}7, 1e\text{-}6]$; WD = $[1e\text{-}3, 1e\text{-}2, 1e\text{-}1]$; and dropout proportion = $[0, 0.2, 0.4]$. Among the 126 possible configurations, 50 were randomly selected for training.

Following the random search, we selected the top-performing configuration according to the metrics outlined in Sect. 3.4. Accordingly, we re-trained the model on the entire training set with the chosen configuration for a number of epochs equal to the average maximum epoch in the CV folds. Lastly, we evaluated the final model on the test set images.

3.4   Evaluation Metrics

We used both quantitative metrics and a qualitative assessment to evaluate the performance of the models at training time. As for quantitative metrics, we computed the accuracy value and stored it for both the internal training and the internal-validation subsets at each epoch for each CV fold of a given configuration. We then obtained the configuration accuracy with its standard deviation by averaging the best validation accuracy values across the CV folds.

Even though some CV folds might reach high validation accuracy values at some epochs, the overall trend of the validation learning curves could be erratic and noisy over epochs. Hence, we computed the learning curves of accuracy and loss for each configuration and collected them for both internal-training and internal-validation subsets at each CV fold. Then, these curves were averaged epoch-wise to obtain an average learning curve and standard deviation values for each epoch.

We used a qualitative assessment of the average learning curves in combination with quantitative metrics to verify the correctness of the training phase. In this regard, we considered a globally non-increasing or with a high standard deviation trend as unjustifiable. We then selected the best performing configuration of hyperparameters based on both the configuration accuracy and the quality assessment. When evaluating the model on the test set, we assessed its performance through Accuracy, Precision, Recall, F1 score, F2 score, and AUROC.

3.5   Implementation Environment

All the experiments in this study ran on the AI@Edge cluster of ISTI-CNR, composed by four nodes, each with the following specifications: 1× NVIDIA® A100 40 GB Tensor Core, 2× AMD - Epyc 24-Core 7352 2.30 GHz 128 MB, 16 x DDR4-3200 Reg. ECC 32 GB module = 512 GB.

We implemented the presented work using Python 3.9.7 on the CentOS 8 operating system and back-end libraries of PyTorch (version 1.9.1, build py3.9-cuda11.1-cudnn8005). In addition, to ensure reproducibility, we set a common seed for the random sequence generator of all the random processes and PyTorch functions.

4   Results

4.1   CBIS-DDSM Dataset

The original dataset consisted of 577 benign and 637 malignant masses in the training set and 194 benign and 147 malignant masses in the test set. As a result of the cleaning process, we removed 49 benign and 60 malignant masses from the training set and 48 benign and 16 malignant masses from the test set. Next, based on the more prevalent class in each set, we removed 49 malignant masses from the training set and 15 benign masses from the test set to balance the resulting dataset. Therefore, the final number of utilized masses was 528 for each label in the training set and 131 for each label in the test set.

4.2   Experiment with ProtoPNet

As a result of the internal-training and internal-validation split, each CV fold consisted of 844 and 210 original images, respectively. Then, as a result of the data augmentation, the internal-training subset consisted of 27852 images.

The random search with five-fold CV on the specified hyperparameters yielded the results reported in Table 2. There, values in each configuration belong to the hyperparameter domain of Table 1, and are listed in the same order. For each configuration, we reported the values of mean and standard deviation accuracy across the CV folds.

Based on those values, the best-performing model was obtained in configuration 28, which has the following hyperparameter values: $lr\_features = 1e\text{-}6$; $lr\_add\_on = 1e\text{-}6$; $lr\_prot\_vector = 1e\text{-}6$; $WD = 1e\text{-}3$; $train\_batch\_size = 20$; $clst = 0.8$; $sep = -0.05$; $l1 = 1e\text{-}4$; and $num\_prots\_per\_class = 20$. With this model, the validation accuracy was 0.763 ± 0.034.

The selected model also satisfied goodness of the learning curves, according to the quality assessment (Fig. 3). During the training phase, the ES condition was triggered at epoch 30. Nevertheless, 60 epochs are reported in the plot because of the 30 patience interval epochs.

Table 2. Accuracy Results for the Random Search on ProtoPNet's Configurations

Configuration	$mean \pm std$
0 : [1e-6, 1e-7, 1e-7, 1e-3, 40, 0.6, −0.1, 1e-4, 5]	0.718 ± 0.069
1 : [1e-6, 1e-6, 1e-6, 1e-3, 20, 0.8, −0.1, 1e-3, 40]	0.753 ± 0.038
2 : [1e-6, 1e-7, 1e-7, 1e-3, 20, 0.9, −0.05, 1e-4, 20]	0.746 ± 0.043
3 : [1e-6, 1e-6, 1e-6, 1e-3, 20, 0.9, −0.08, 1e-5, 40]	0.743 ± 0.042
4 : [1e-6, 1e-6, 1e-6, 1e-3, 20, 0.9, −0.05, 1e-5, 40]	0.759 ± 0.035
5 : [1e-7, 1e-6, 1e-6, 1e-3, 40, 0.8, −0.08, 1e-3, 20]	0.706 ± 0.056
6 : [1e-7, 1e-6, 1e-6, 1e-2, 20, 0.8, −0.05, 1e-5, 5]	0.624 ± 0.045
7 : [1e-7, 1e-6, 1e-6, 1e-2, 20, 0.8, −0.1, 1e-3, 20]	0.698 ± 0.082
8 : [1e-7, 1e-6, 1e-6, 1e-2, 20, 0.6, −0.08, 1e-3, 5]	0.700 ± 0.037
9 : [1e-7, 1e-6, 1e-7, 1e-3, 20, 0.6, −0.05, 1e-5, 40]	0.713 ± 0.058
10 : [1e-7, 1e-6, 1e-7, 1e-2, 40, 0.9, −0.05, 1e-5, 5]	0.683 ± 0.042
11 : [1e-7, 1e-6, 1e-7, 1e-2, 40, 0.6, −0.08, 1e-3, 40]	0.697 ± 0.057
12 : [1e-7, 1e-6, 1e-7, 1e-2, 20, 0.6, −0.05, 1e-5, 40]	0.697 ± 0.066
13 : [1e-7, 1e-7, 1e-6, 1e-3, 40, 0.6, −0.08, 1e-4, 5]	0.591 ± 0.055
14 : [1e-7, 1e-7, 1e-6, 1e-3, 20, 0.8, −0.08, 1e-4, 20]	0.683 ± 0.067
15 : [1e-7, 1e-7, 1e-6, 1e-2, 20, 0.9, −0.08, 1e-3, 5]	0.668 ± 0.032
16 : [1e-7, 1e-7, 1e-7, 1e-3, 40, 0.6, −0.05, 1e-4, 5]	0.574 ± 0.030
17 : [1e-7, 1e-7, 1e-7, 1e-3, 20, 0.6, −0.1, 1e-4, 5]	0.679 ± 0.045
18 : [1e-7, 1e-7, 1e-7, 1e-2, 40, 0.6, −0.08, 1e-3, 20]	0.668 ± 0.041
19 : [1e-6, 1e-6, 1e-6, 1e-2, 20, 0.8, −0.05, 1e-5, 5]	0.748 ± 0.019
20 : [1e-6, 1e-6, 1e-6, 1e-3, 40, 0.9, −0.05, 1e-4, 20]	0.736 ± 0.039
21 : [1e-6, 1e-6, 1e-7, 1e-3, 40, 0.6, −0.08, 1e-5, 5]	0.757 ± 0.023
22 : [1e-6, 1e-6, 1e-7, 1e-3, 20, 0.8, −0.05, 1e-3, 20]	0.722 ± 0.018
23 : [1e-6, 1e-6, 1e-7, 1e-3, 20, 0.6, −0.1, 1e-3, 40]	0.762 ± 0.036
24 : [1e-6, 1e-6, 1e-7, 1e-2, 40, 0.6, −0.05, 1e-4, 20]	0.757 ± 0.038
25 : [1e-6, 1e-7, 1e-6, 1e-2, 40, 0.9, −0.1, 1e-3, 20]	0.732 ± 0.055
26 : [1e-6, 1e-7, 1e-6, 1e-2, 40, 0.6, −0.1, 1e-3, 40]	0.745 ± 0.028
27 : [1e-6, 1e-6, 1e-6, 1e-3, 40, 0.8, −0.08, 1e-5, 40]	0.743 ± 0.042
28 :[1e-6, 1e-6, 1e-6, 1e-3, 20, 0.8, −0.05, 1e-4, 20]	**0.763 ± 0.034**
29 : [1e-6, 1e-7, 1e-6, 1e-2, 20, 0.9, −0.1, 1e-4, 20]	0.741 ± 0.040

According to the training curves in Fig. 3, we re-trained the selected model on the training set for 30 epochs. After pruning, 9 and 2 prototypes were removed from the benign and the malignant classes, respectively. As a result, 29 final prototypes were retained. Then, we assessed this model on the test set.

Finally, regarding the comparison with ResNet18, we obtained the following results. Among the 50 explored configurations, the best performing model was found with the following hyperparameters: number of re-trained last convolutional layers = 3, LR = 1e-6, WD = 1e-3, dropout rate = 0.4. This model reached an average validation accuracy across the five CV folds of 0.776 ± 0.026. After re-training the model on the whole training set for 20 epochs, we evaluated it on the test set images.

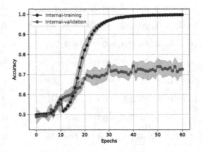

Fig. 3. Average accuracy curves across the five CV folds for the selected ProtoPNet model's configuration. Shaded regions represent $\pm 1 \cdot std$ interval for each epoch.

The test-set metrics yielded by ProtoPNet and ResNet18 in their independent experiments are reported in Table 3. In Fig. 4, we report an example of an explanation provided by ProtoPNet for a test image of a correctly classified malignant mass. Similarities with prototypes recognized by the model are listed from top to bottom according to decreasing similarity score of the activation. Note that the top activated prototypes correctly derive from training images of malignant masses. Instead, towards the lower scores, prototypes originating from other classes might be activated, in this case of benign masses.

5   ProtoPNet's Prototypes: A Clinical Viewpoint

Specific domain knowledge is necessary to understand and interpret explanations provided by models such as ProtoPNet when applied to medical images. The validity of provided visual explanations is hardly evaluable by someone without a background in the specific task. Furthermore, explanations can be misleading or confusing when analyzed by non-experts.

When dealing with explainable models, one of the first concerns is to assure that explanations are based on correct information. Also, for such models to be interpretable and hence helpful in the medical practice, their explanations should use intuitions that somewhat resemble the reasoning process of a physician. In

Table 3. Test Set Metrics With Best-performing Models

Model	Accuracy	Precision	Recall	F1	F2	AUROC
ProtoPNet	0.685	0.658	0.769	0.709	0.744	0.719
ResNet18	0.654	0.667	0.615	0.640	0.625	0.671

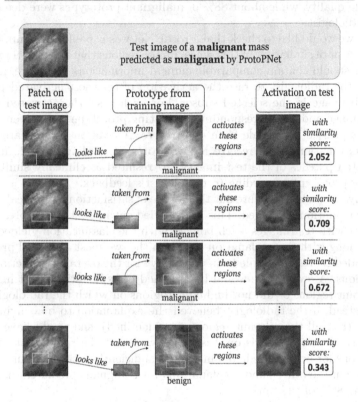

Fig. 4. The test image of a malignant mass is correctly classified as malignant by the model. Each row of this image represents the activation process of a certain prototype. In the first column there is the patch found on the test image, in the second column the activated prototype is shown together with the training image from which it originated, in the third column is shown the activation map with the corresponding similarity score.

this regard, we asked a radiologist with 16 years of experience for a clinical viewpoint on the outputs of the selected model on a random subset of test images (15 benign, 15 malignant). In particular, we conceived three tasks (i.e., Task 1, 2 and 3).

As before stated, ProtoPNet bases the classification outcome and the explanation on patch similarities with a set of learned prototypes. Therefore, we first wish to understand whether good-quality prototypes were learned and used to characterize each class. This was done in Task 1. We presented the radiologist with a series of images representing the learned prototypes from both classes and the images from which they were extracted. We asked her to rate how much each prototype was specific for its corresponding class on a scale from one to five. Lower scores would be assigned to generic, not clinically significant prototypes, while class-specific, meaningful prototypes would receive higher scores. As a result of Task 1, only 50% of the benign prototypes were considered to be of acceptable quality, while about 88% of malignant prototypes were deemed good by the radiologist.

Next, we would like to check that ProtoPNet was capable of learning a meaningful concept of similarity. In this sense, image regions that the model recognized as similar should contain comparable clinical information. Therefore, in Task 2, we asked the radiologist to rate the activation of the most activated prototype w.r.t each image in the selected subset. For each case, the activated patch on the test image and the corresponding activating prototype were given. The rating was expressed on a scale from one to five. Activations that shared mutual clinical information would receive higher scores. Regarding Task 2, among the 30 activated patches of the test images, 20 resulted as clinically similar to the activating prototypes according to radiologist's feedback.

Finally, we wished to figure out the degree of satisfaction in medical end-users for the explanations provided. This was carried out in Task 3. We presented the radiologist with test images, each labeled with the classification yielded by ProtoPNet, along with the explanation based on the two most activated prototypes. She provided scores on a scale from one to five for the overall satisfaction of such explanations. A lower score would be assigned to explanations that highlighted non-relevant regions or did not highlight regions on which the radiologist would focus. Instead, if the radiologist believed the explanation to be convincing and complete (i.e., all the relevant regions are identified), she would have returned a higher score. The analysis on Task 3 showed that the radiologist recognized explanations for benign-predicted masses as sufficiently satisfying only in 50% of the cases. On the other hand, explanations for malignant-predicted masses were convincing 89% of the times.

This investigation of the explanation quality of the proposed method, both on the detection of prototypes and the activations correctness, is preliminary. As a by-product, the expert radiologist's feedback is a precious contribution for the design, in the near future, of other tests to assess both the explanation's correctness and of explanation's acceptance by end-users.

6   Discussion

Historically, not knowing precisely why DL models provide their predictions has been one of the biggest concerns raised by the scientific community. Healthcare, in particular, is one of the areas massively impacted by the lack of transparency of such black-box models. That is especially relevant for automatic medical image classification, which medical practice still strives to adopt. Explainable and interpretable AI might overcome this issue by getting insights into models' reasoning. In this regard, a promising approach is that of ProtoPNet [6], an explainable-by-design model firstly introduced in the natural images domain.

Our work aimed at exploring the applicability of prototypical part learning in medical images and, in particular, in the classification of benign/malignant breast masses from mammogram images. We assessed the applicability based on two aspects: the ability of the model to face the task (i.e., classification metrics) and the ability of the model to provide end-users with plausible explanations. We trained a ProtoPNet model and optimized its hyperparameters in a random search with five-fold CV. Then, we compared its performance to that obtained with an independently optimized ResNet18 model. We selected images from CBIS-DDSM [12], a publicly available dataset of scanned mammogram images. After, came a cleaning and balancing process to obtain the final study cohort. As opposed to the original paper, we utilized a hold-out test independent from the internal-validation subset used at training time to assess the final performance. In addition, we introduced two-dimensional dropout and batch-normalization after each add-on convolutional layer in the ProtoPNet architecture.

Evaluation metrics resulting from the best performing ProtoPNet model seem mostly higher than with the ResNet18 architecture. In particular, we observed the most substantial improvement in the Recall, which is of considerable interest for this specific task. Indeed, it represents the capacity of the model to detect positive cases: a high Recall means that the model correctly identifies the majority of malignant masses. In addition, ProtoPNet provides a level of transparency that is completely missing from ResNet18. That said, it is well known that neural networks often use context or confounding information instead of the information that a human would use to solve the same problem in both medical [25] and non-medical applications [10].

We believe a large amount of prior domain knowledge is necessary to evaluate ProtoPNet's explanations. Without domain knowledge, its results are likely to be misinterpreted. Moreover, such knowledge would be necessary to properly select the number of prototypes for each class, instead of empirically derive it from a hyperparameter optimization. To prevent explanations to be based on irrelevant regions of the images, we asked for the radiologist's viewpoint. In this regard, she provided some helpful insights into the models' outputs. From Task 1, it seems reasonable to assume that ProtoPNet manages to learn more relevant prototypes for malignant masses similar to radiologists. As in actual practice, a suspicious finding (a non-circumscribed contour, whether microlobulated, masked, indistinct, or spiculated), even only in one projection, results easy to detect and justifies a recall for further assessment. On the other hand, a benign judgment requires an accurate bi-dimensional analysis of typical benign findings in both projections and differential diagnoses with overlapping tissue. From Task 2, it appears that the model's mathematical concept of similarity differs from how a radiologist would deem two regions clinically similar. The reason behind this may be that the radiologist recalls specific features from past experience, possibly consisting of other exams aside from mammography and biopsy results alone. This is way broader than the dataset the network uses for training, which strictly consists of image-biopsy label pairs. Finally, from Task 3, results that explanations for images classified as malignant are, in general, more likely to be more convincing to the radiologist. Notably, this behavior goes in the same direction as the low clinical relevance of benign prototypes from Task 1. Overall, the radiologist found ProtoPNet's explanations very intuitive and hence reported a high level of satisfaction. This is remarkably important because we were interested in the right level of abstraction for explanations to foster human interpretability.

Comparing our work with previous studies is not straightforward: no other work with prototypical part learning has been done on the CBIS-DDSM dataset and benign/malignant mass classification task. Nevertheless, we hereafter compare our results with previous works utilizing ResNets on the same dataset and task, albeit some of them in slightly different ways. In the comparison, we report the accuracy as the common performance metric across these studies. In our experiments we achieved an accuracy of 0.654 with ResNet18 and of 0.685 with ProtoPNet. Among the ones using ResNet18, Arora et al. [3] and Ragab et al. [19] achieved an accuracy of 0.780 ad 0.722, respectively. Instead, among the works using different ResNet architectures, Ragab et al. [19] achieved an accuracy of 0.711 and 0.715 when using ResNet50 and ResNet101, respectively. Tsochatzidis et al. [24] deployed ResNet50 obtaining an accuracy of 0.749. Also Alkhaleefah et al. [1] experimented with ResNet50 in different scenarios and achieved accuracy values between 0.676 and 0.802. Finally, Ansar et al. [2] reported an accuracy of 0.637 by using ResNet50. Although performance metrics reported in the previous works are in line with ours, they are, in general, higher.

Regarding previous studies adopting a prototypical part learning scheme to the mass classification task, not much work has been done. To the best of our knowledge, the work by Barnett et al. [4] is the only one, even though the authors utilized a different (and private) dataset and a different novel architecture, derived from ProtoPNet. For these reasons, a fair comparison may not be feasible. Besides, we achieved an AUROC of 0.719 with ProtoPNet, which is lower than theirs (0.840). The authors used images in combination with a dedicated fine-annotation of relevant regions and mass margins, and their model heavily exploits that information for its conclusions. We point out that this is different from our work, where ProtoPNet uses only image-level labels without annotated images to resemble the experimental setup of the original work on bird classification [6]. This is probably one of the reasons for the performance discrepancies between the two studies. However, fine-annotated images needed in their methodology require a massive intervention by clinical experts. Also, intending to deploy such models to fast assist radiologists in the classification of a new image, we believe their approach to be too dependent on annotations, therefore, our approach may be preferable. We likely obtained acceptable results without the complexity of the model and of the dataset of [4].

Interestingly, the performance in [4] is somewhat similar to that obtained on the bird classification task of the original work introducing ProtoPNet [6]. The inclusion of information regarding relevant regions and mass margins annotations might have been the key to achieve such high results on the mass classification task. However, our work shows that, by taking the same annotation-free approach of [6], lower results might be obtained for this task. According to our results, without additional information to complement images, the task to be solved is more challenging, and the problem covers a higher level of complexity. Specifically, in images acquired by projection, planes at different depths are fused in a single bi-dimensional representation. That makes object separation especially hard for these images. This implies that answering our research question may not be as straightforward as for the ornithology task.

Our work comes with limitations. Firstly, given the large number of hyper-parameters in ProtoPNet, we selected a subset of them for the optimization process. Moreover, of all the possible configurations obtainable with the chosen subset of hyper-parameters, we evaluated the model only on a random selection of them. That likely had an impact on the discovery of the optimal configuration. Secondly, due to the limited size of the utilized dataset, our models were prone to overfitting, which affects the generalization capabilities on new images. That is particularly true for ProtoPNet, where the entire architecture has to be re-trained. That happened even though we took several actions to counteract the issue. Specifically, we selected a shallower ResNet architecture, deployed WD, and introduced dropout and batch-normalization layers. In addition, we provided the clinical viewpoint of a single radiologist. We are aware that this clashes somewhat with the subjective nature of such views: a group of differently experienced radiologists should have been included to reach more robust conclusions.

7   Conclusion and Future Work

Our research question was to investigate the applicability of ProtoPNet to the automatic classification of breast masses from mammogram images. Although a clear-cut answer might not have been provided, this exploratory work allowed us to assess the advantages and the weak points of this kind of approach. The two aspects we considered to evaluate the applicability of this approach were the classification capabilities and the validity of explanations. Classification results were acceptable but insufficient for this method to enter the clinical practice. Based on the clinical assessment, we may say that explanations provided for malignant masses were highly plausible, valuable, and intuitive to a radiologist. However, this is not true for benign masses yet, and this currently invalidates the applicability of ProtoPNet in real clinical contexts. On the other hand, this behavior is comparable to that of a radiologist, who, typically, finds it easier to recognize malignant masses' characteristics. Nevertheless, our findings are promising and suggest that ProtoPNet may represent a compelling approach that still requires further investigation. We believe that training this model on more images or performing a more extensive optimization of the model's architecture may bring improved classification performance. That might also increase the ability of the model to deliver plausible explanations for benign cases.

Future work would include combining several ProtoPNet models with different base architectures together in an ensemble fashion or choosing a Vision

Transformer architecture [9] instead of a CNN model at the core of ProtoPNet. In addition, a different initialization for the filter values could be adopted, for example, with values learned on the same dataset using the corresponding base architecture instead of those pre-trained on ImageNet. Moreover, in addition to geometrical transformations, one could also exploit intensity-based transformations to try improving the networks' generalization capabilities on images possibly obtained with different acquisition settings. These may include histogram equalization and random brightness modification. Also, one could utilize a combination of different mammogram images datasets to augment diversity in the data cohort. On top of that, a dataset comprising digital breast tomosynthesis images instead of conventional digital mammogram images could be used. That is a pseudo-3D imaging technique based on a series of low-dose breast acquisitions from different angles, which has the potential to overcome the tissue superposition issue and thus improve the detection of breast lesions. From a broader point of view, we see the customization of ProtoPNet functioning to produce explanations grounded in causality, instead of correlation, as a promising future work.

Acknowledgment. The research leading to these results has received funding from the Regional Project PAR FAS Tuscany - PRAMA and from the European Union's Horizon 2020 research and innovation programme under grant agreement No 952159 (ProCAncer-I). The funders had no role in the design of the study, collection, analysis and interpretation of data, or writing the manuscript.

References

1. Alkhaleefah, M., Chittem, P.K., Achhannagari, V.P., Ma, S.C., Chang, Y.L.: The influence of image augmentation on breast lesion classification using transfer learning. In: 2020 International Conference on Artificial Intelligence and Signal Processing (AISP), pp. 1–5. IEEE (2020)
2. Ansar, W., Shahid, A.R., Raza, B., Dar, A.H.: Breast cancer detection and localization using MobileNet based transfer learning for mammograms. In: Brito-Loeza, C., Espinosa-Romero, A., Martin-Gonzalez, A., Safi, A. (eds.) ISICS 2020. CCIS, vol. 1187, pp. 11–21. Springer, Cham (2020). https://doi.org/10.1007/978-3-030-43364-2_2
3. Arora, R., Rai, P.K., Raman, B.: Deep feature-based automatic classification of mammograms. Med. Biol. Eng. Comput. **58**(6), 1199–1211 (2020)
4. Barnett, A.J., et al.: A case-based interpretable deep learning model for classification of mass lesions in digital mammography. Nat. Mach. Intell. **3**(12), 1061–1070 (2021)
5. Bloice, M.D., Stocker, C., Holzinger, A.: Augmentor: an image augmentation library for machine learning. arXiv preprint arXiv:1708.04680 (2017)
6. Chen, C., Li, O., Tao, D., Barnett, A., Rudin, C., Su, J.K.: This looks like that: deep learning for interpretable image recognition. In: Advances in Neural Information Processing Systems, vol. 32 (2019)
7. Ciravegna, G., et al.: Logic explained networks. arXiv preprint arXiv:2108.05149 (2021)

8. Cui, Y., et al.: Deep learning for image and point cloud fusion in autonomous driving: a review. IEEE Trans. Intell. Transport. Syst. (2021)
9. Dosovitskiy, A., et al.: An image is worth 16x16 words: transformers for image recognition at scale. arXiv preprint arXiv:2010.11929 (2020)
10. Hu, S., Ma, Y., Liu, X., Wei, Y., Bai, S.: Stratified rule-aware network for abstract visual reasoning. arXiv preprint arXiv:2002.06838 (2020)
11. Ismail Fawaz, H., Forestier, G., Weber, J., Idoumghar, L., Muller, P.-A.: Deep learning for time series classification: a review. Data Min. Knowl. Disc. **33**(4), 917–963 (2019). https://doi.org/10.1007/s10618-019-00619-1
12. Lee, R.S., Gimenez, F., Hoogi, A., Miyake, K.K., Gorovoy, M., Rubin, D.L.: A curated mammography data set for use in computer-aided detection and diagnosis research. Sci. Data **4**(1), 1–9 (2017)
13. Li, O., Liu, H., Chen, C., Rudin, C.: Deep learning for case-based reasoning through prototypes: a neural network that explains its predictions. In: Proceedings of the AAAI Conference on Artificial Intelligence, vol. 32 (2018)
14. Minaee, S., Kalchbrenner, N., Cambria, E., Nikzad, N., Chenaghlu, M., Gao, J.: Deep learning-based text classification: a comprehensive review. ACM Comput. Surv. (CSUR) **54**(3), 1–40 (2021)
15. Mohammadjafari, S., Cevik, M., Thanabalasingam, M., Basar, A.: Using protopnet for interpretable Alzheimer's disease classification. In: Proceedings of the Canadian Conference on Artificial Intelligence, vol. 10 (2021)
16. Pandey, C., Sethy, P.K., Behera, S.K., Vishwakarma, J., Tande, V.: Smart agriculture: technological advancements on agriculture - a systematical review. In: Deep Learning for Sustainable Agriculture, pp. 1–56 (2022)
17. Papernot, N., McDaniel, P.: Deep k-nearest neighbors: towards confident, interpretable and robust deep learning. arXiv preprint arXiv:1803.04765 (2018)
18. Pedregosa, F., et al.: Scikit-learn: machine learning in Python. J. Mach. Learn. Res. **12**, 2825–2830 (2011)
19. Ragab, D.A., Attallah, O., Sharkas, M., Ren, J., Marshall, S.: A framework for breast cancer classification using multi-DCNNs. Comput. Biol. Med. **131**, 104245 (2021)
20. Rudin, C., Chen, C., Chen, Z., Huang, H., Semenova, L., Zhong, C.: Interpretable machine learning: fundamental principles and 10 grand challenges. Stat. Surv. **16**, 1–85 (2022)
21. Singh, G., Yow, K.C.: An interpretable deep learning model for COVID-19 detection with chest x-ray images. IEEE Access **9**, 85198–85208 (2021)
22. Singh, G., Yow, K.C.: These do not look like those: an interpretable deep learning model for image recognition. IEEE Access **9**, 41482–41493 (2021)
23. Trinh, L., Tsang, M., Rambhatla, S., Liu, Y.: Interpretable and trustworthy deep-fake detection via dynamic prototypes. In: Proceedings of the IEEE/CVF Winter Conference on Applications of Computer Vision, pp. 1973–1983 (2021)
24. Tsochatzidis, L., Costaridou, L., Pratikakis, I.: Deep learning for breast cancer diagnosis from mammograms-a comparative study. J. Imaging **5**(3), 37 (2019)
25. Wang, H., Wu, Z., Xing, E.P.: Removing confounding factors associated weights in deep neural networks improves the prediction accuracy for healthcare applications. In: BIOCOMPUTING 2019: Proceedings of the Pacific Symposium, pp. 54–65. World Scientific (2018)

Deep Learning for Remote Heart Rate Estimation: A Reproducible and Optimal State-of-the-Art Framework

Nelida Mirabet-Herranz[1]([✉]), Khawla Mallat[2]([✉]), and Jean-Luc Dugelay[1]([✉])

[1] EURECOM, 450 Route des Chappes, 06410 Biot, France
{mirabet,dugelay}@eurecom.fr
[2] SAP Labs, 805 Avenue du Dr Donat– Font de l'Orme, 06259 Mougins, France
mallat@eurecom.fr

Abstract. Accurate remote pulse rate measurement from RGB face videos has gained a lot of attention in the past years since it allows for a non-invasive contactless monitoring of a subject's heart rate, useful in numerous potential applications. Nowadays, there is a global trend to monitor e-health parameters without the use of physical devices enabling at-home daily monitoring and telehealth. This paper includes a comprehensive state-of-the-art on remote heart rate estimation from face images. We extensively tested a new framework to better understand several open questions in the domain that are: which areas of the face are the most relevant, how to manage video color components and which performances are possible to reach on a public relevant dataset. From this study, we extract key elements to design an optimal, up-to-date and reproducible framework that can be used as a baseline for accurately estimating the heart rate of a human subject, in particular from the cheek area using the green (G) channel of a RGB video. The results obtained in the public database COHFACE support our input data choices and our 3D-CNN structure as optimal for a remote HR estimation.

Keywords: Remote HR estimation · 3D-CNN · G channel · ROI

1 Introduction

Heart rate (HR) is an important physiological signal that reflects the physical and emotional status of an individual. Monitoring physiological parameters, such as heart rate is of great importance to address an individuals' health status and it is beneficial not only for patients in critical situations, but also for high-risk patients in home-care and outdoor areas [2]. Photoplethysmography (PPG) is a low-cost and noninvasive means of sensing the cardiovascular blood volume pulse through subtle color variations in reflected light of human skin [1]. Although PPG is typically implemented using dedicated light sources, Verkruysse *et al.* [32] showed that using ambient light as illumination source it is sufficient to capture a person's vital signs from RGB videos. Remote PPG technologies (rPPG), allow for non-intrusive measurements, highly relevant when

© Springer Nature Switzerland AG 2023
J.-J. Rousseau and B. Kapralos (Eds.): ICPR 2022 Workshops, LNCS 13643, pp. 558–573, 2023.
https://doi.org/10.1007/978-3-031-37660-3_39

contact has to be prevented (e.g. skin-damage) or users' cooperation cannot be required (e.g. surveillance). Some studies showed that a laptop camera is enough to capture the subtle changes on skin color that lead to a successful HR estimation [21,22,24], making it accessible to every individual with a webcam-equipped laptop or a mobile phone.

In the past years, there has been a growing number of studies dedicated to remote HR estimation via rPPG using data extracted from face videos [5,12,21,34]. Most of those rPPG algorithms are based on handcrafted features and consist of a two-stage pipeline which first extract the rPPG signals from the face, and then perform a frequency analysis to estimate the corresponding average HR from a peak detection algorithm. They also require different preprocessing techniques such as skin segmentation, color space transformation, signal decomposition and filtering steps among others. Some filters require parameter adjustment and tuning according to the data that is being used, making those approaches nearly impossible to replicate as shown in [7]. Nowadays deep learning is successfully used in many tasks related to computer vision and medical analysis, such as body mass index (BMI) estimation from face images [25]. End-to-end deep neural models have out-performed traditional multi-stage methods that require hand-crafted feature manipulation being as well possible to replicate. Therefore, recent works have been focused on implementing deep learning techniques for the rPPG extraction when a large amount of labeled data is available [4,17,20,28,29]. Its performance can be also improved by the increasing of the training set size, unlike previous hand-crafted methods.

The main contributions of this work are the following: 1) We aim to respond the most common unanswered questions on remote HR estimation by proposing the first study, to our knowledge, of the influence of different inputs on a 3D-CNN based HR estimation network, particularly the selection of face region and the channel choice of a video source. 2) We propose a benchmark for HR estimation by assembling an optimal and reproducible 3D-CNN that directly estimates the HR from face videos. 3) The method is evaluated on the publicly available database COHFACE, allowing comparability with future works, and evaluated against other learning-based HR estimators.

The rest of this paper is organized as follows. In Sect. 2 a review of the state-of-the-art methods for HR estimation is presented. Section 3 describes the selected neural network that extracts the heart rate from facial videos. The database description, experimental setup and results are presented in Sect. 4. Finally, we conclude with future research directions in Sect. 5.

2   Related Work

In this Section, we give an overview of the state-of-the-art methods for pulse rate estimation presented in two categories: Hand-crafted approaches and learning-based models. The hand-crafted methods aim to estimate the rPPG signal from which the HR is later extracted, while the learning-based models are able to recover the rPPG signal as well as to directly estimate the HR value. In earlier studies, some claims regarding the optimal input unit to use in order to estimate the HR from skin patches were made. Those claims were proved for hand-crafted approaches but not exhaustive study was done for the latest works that include deep learning structures. We aim to identify the most important not-verified statements and to provide an answer to those open questions in Sect. 4.

2.1 Hand-Crafted rPPG Signal Estimation

Traditional measurement approaches for extracting human physiological signals such as HR involve devices that require physical contact. In 2008, Verkruysse et al. [32] showed that natural light photo-plethysmography could be used for medical purposes such as remote sensing of vital signs for triage or sport purposes. They also claimed that the G channel of a video contains the strongest plethysmographic signal due to the fact that hemoglobin absorbs green light better than red or blue.

Since small variations in reflected light from the skin can be used to estimate the HR, in the past years, traditional methods studied rPPG measurement from videos taken with digital cameras by analyzing the color changes on facial regions of interest (ROI). In 2010, Poh et al. [22] presented a non-contact low-cost method for remotely measuring the HR of a subject using a basic webcam. They extracted the blood volume pulse from the selected facial ROI by spatially averaging the value of the ROI for each color channel and then applying independent component analysis to recover the underlying PPG signal. To compute the average HR value of a video, they applied Fast Fourier Transform (FFT) on the estimated signal to find the highest power spectrum. In [21], they extended their work by adding several temporal filters to prune the PPG recovered signal.

Due to the promising results that previous researchers have obtained, several studies focused on overcoming the problems on rPPG signal recovery. Hann et al. [5] highlighted the limitations of blind source separation when motion problems are present in the videos and propose a chrominance-based method that combines two orthogonal projections of the RGB space. Li et al. [12] approached the problem of rigid movements by implementing face tracking techniques using facial landmarks. Their research focused as well on the illumination variation problem, which influence was rectified with adaptive filters and by comparing background and foreground illumination. Other authors claimed that the state-of-the-art approaches were not robust enough in natural conditions and tried to improve the quality of the rPPG signal. Tulyakov et al. [30] divided the face into multiple ROI regions and introduced a matrix completion approach to prune rPPG signals. Wang et al. [34] proposed a projection plane orthogonal to the skin tone for rPPG pulse extraction and afterwards they expanded their research in [38] proposing a joint face detection and alignment model followed by an adaptive patch selection method which chooses the best size-variable triangular patches to exclude undesired facial motions. Later, Niu et al. presented one of the first real-time rPPG method for continuous HR measurement which included a multi-patch region selection to remove outlier signals and a distribution-based model to link the rPPG signal to their best HR estimation [16]. Recent works have persisted in the use of hand-crafted methods trying to improve the recovered rPPG signal with band-pass filters [11], adding intermediate steps such as feature points generation for optimum masking and Variational Mode Decomposition (VMD) based filtering [14] or by combining Ensemble Empirical Mode Decomposition (EEMD) with Multiset Canonical Correlation Analysis (MCCA) [27].

The main drawback of the presented methods is that they are partly based on denoising algorithms that do not require any type of training but a complex parameter tuning, making them extremely difficult to reproduce as pointed out in previous researches [7]. They include a spatially averaging of the image color values per ROI which helps in reducing Gaussian noise but fails when the different pixels in the ROI do not follow the same distribution. This average operation is also highly sensitive to different types of noise; motion, lightning and/or sensor artifacts.

2.2   HR Estimation via Learning-Based Models

The first research, to our knowledge, that introduces machine learning techniques for pulse estimation was presented by Monkaresi et al. [15] in 2013. They proposed a modification of [22] to improve the accuracy of HR detection by adding machine learning classification techniques in the last step of the pipeline. After a power spectrum analysis, they explore machine learning techniques to find the cardiovascular pulse frequency. In 2018, Qiu et al. approached the problem in a similar way. They applied spatial and temporal filtering to extract the rPPG signal and then they estimated the corresponding HR using a Convolutional Neural Network (CNN) [23].

In the recent years, deep-learning models, especially convolutional networks, have gained more importance in the task of HR estimation. Some of those research works have focused on extracting the rPPG signal from face videos, similarly to the traditional methods. In 2018, Chen et al. [4] proposed Deep-Phys, the first end-to-end system for recovering physiological signals using a CNN. DeepPhys was trained to learn at the same time the most appropriate mask for ROI selection and to recover the Blood-Volume Pulse (BVP) signals. Yu et al. [39] proposed the first known approach that includes the use of 3D-CNN for reconstructing rPPG signals from raw facial videos. In their first research, the whole video frame is passed as an input of the network and the output is expected to be the rPPG estimated signal. In a more recent publication [40], they proposed a two-stage method to extract the rPPG signal in which the 3D-CNN is used for video enhancement to counter video compression loss. Similar to [39], Perepelkina et al. [20] developed HeartTrack, a two-stage method that uses a 3D-CNN that recovers the rPPG signal from face frames and a 1D-CNN to map the signals to their corresponding HR values.

Other works have focused on the task of estimating the HR in beats per minute (bpm) from face videos, without an intermediate signal estimation step. In 2018, Spetlik et al. [29] proposed their two-step CNN to directly estimate a heart rate from a face video. This network consisted on a pipeline of two CNNs, the first one extracted a 1D embedding from face images and the second one mapped this embedding to the estimated HR of a subject. Later on, Wang *et al.* [37] proposed a double feature extraction stream by adopting first a low-rank constraint to guide the network to learn a robust feature representation and second a rPPG extraction stream. Combining both, they were able to develop a unified neural network to learn the feature extraction and to estimate HR simultaneously. Niu *et al.* [17] introduced a new data transformation to represent both, the temporal and the spatial information in a 2D manner from face videos as input of a deep heart rate estimator. In future researches, they refined this approach by using multiple ROI volumes as its input [18] and by performing data augmentation [19]. Song *et al.* created their own version of spatio-temporal maps constructed from pulse signals extracted from existing rPPG methods to feed their CNN [28]. In [8], Hu *et al.* compared the effectiveness of extracting spatial-temporal facial features using 2D-CNN against 3D-CNN and in [13] Lokendra *et al.* experimented with the utilization of Action Units (AUs) and Temporal Convolutional Networks (TCN) for denoising temporal signals and improve the HR estimation. Other deep learning methods considering the temporal information of a video for direct HR estimation have been explored. Huang *et al.* [9] proposed a deep neural network consisting in 2D convolutional layers and long short-term memory (LSTM) operations. The first to propose a 3D deep learning architecture were Bousefsaf *et al.*, who presented in [3] a method relying on 3D networks with embedded synthetic signals in real videos. This 3D network outputs values recorded in a histogram composed by intervals of 2.5 bpm producing HR predictions per intervals. The model also ensures concurrent mapping by producing a prediction for each local group of pixels which, as already highlighted by some users and confirmed by the authors in their git repository, makes the framework slow since the processing time of one testing sample is on the order of days. As a way to decrease the number of parameters to leverage the tasks of the network, the authors used as input of the 3D structure a random shuffle of the group of pixels in the selected regions of a single channeled frame, and the G-frame was chosen without any further study supporting this choice.

As stated in this Section many researches have work on the task of extracting the rPPG signal and/or the HR of a person from facial videos but little attention has been given on stating an unified criteria for input data choice, specially for the learning based approaches. We aim to verify some claims by providing a study on some choices that an author has to make when implementing a deep learning HR estimator. For this purpose, an overview of recent and relevant works that use deep learning structures for a direct HR estimation from face videos is presented in Table 1. The table presents the model structure chosen in each approach, the type of input data passed to the network, the ROI selected and the public database (if any) in which their results were reported. As reported in Table 1 no comparison between input data or ROI is done when the selection of those needs to be made. The only comparative study made, to the knowledge of the authors, concerned the performance of a HR when a 2D or a 3D CNN is selected as network [8]. We aim to enlarge the state of the art by covering studies such as comparison of different facial areas to be selected as ROI (full face, cheeks and forehead) and which channels of the input video give the more valuable information for a CNN-based HR estimator. We will also report our results in one of the most popular public database for direct HR estimation from face videos using deep learning based approaches, the COHFACE [7] dataset.

3   Method

3.1   ROI Selection

A region of interest (ROI) is a subset of a dataset particularly relevant for a specific purpose. In our study, a ROI is a part of a video frame that contains relevant information for our HR task. The right selection of the ROI on a subject's face is critical to perform an efficient HR estimation. Despite several research works have analyzed the facial region leading to the most accurate estimation, these regions have been tested only with hand-crafted methods [10,33]. In Sect. 4, we aim to contribute to this choice by performing an evaluation comparison between the most commonly used ROIs for remote HR estimation.

We extract the cheek area from the face videos as described in Fig. 1. First we divide our videos in 5 s sequences of images creating sub-videos. We detect from every frame in the sub-video the location of the 68 (x, y)-coordinates of the dlib landmark detector to map the shape of the face on the image. Then, we obtain the average landmark points per sub-video and based on those, we compute a 40×40 pixels sized region of each of the two cheek areas for every frame of the sub-video. Most of the HR measurement methods tend to average the color values in the entire ROI and use them as the original rPPG signal. By performing this step, we loose the local information within each ROI, therefore, we choose to pass it entirely as input to our neural network.

video sequence   average landmarks   ROI extraction
                        detection

Fig. 1. Diagram of the proposed ROI extraction approach from a video sequence.

3.2   Green Channel Selection

In early studies, the strength of the plethysmographic signal in the G channel of a face video was proved sufficent [32]. This is consistent with the fact that

Table 1. Overview of the most relevant deep learning structures aiming for a direct HR estimation from face videos. The table includes the model structure, the type of input data, the ROI selected, and the public database in which the results were reported.

Paper	Year	Structure	Input data	ROI	Databases	Metrics	Code available
HR-CNN [29]	2018	CNN	RGB	Full frame	COHFACE MAHNOB PURE ECG-Fitness	MAE RMSE ρ	Yes
SynRhythm [17]	2018	ResNet18	Spatial-temporal maps	Nose and cheeks	MAHNOB MMSE-HR	Me STDe RMSE MER	No
2-stream CNN [37]	2019	Two layer LSTM	Spatial-temporal maps	Full frame	COHFACE PURE	MAE RMSE ρ	No
RhythmNet [18]	2019	ResNet18	Spatial-temporal maps	Full face	MAHNOB MMSE-HR	Me STDe MAE RSME MER ρ	Yes but trained model not shared
3D-Mapping [3]	2019	3DCNN	Shuffled G pixels	Full frame	UBFC-RPPG	Me STDe MAE RMSE	Yes but trained model not shared
Visual-CNN [9]	2020	CONV2D with LSTM	RGB	Full face	-	STDe MAE RSME MER ρ	No
Robust-CNN [19]	2020	CNN	Spatial-temporal maps	Full face	MMSE-HR	STDe MAE RSME MER ρ	No
HR-CNN [28]	2020	ResNet18	Spatial-temporal maps	Nose and cheeks	MAHNOB ECG-FITNESS	Me STDe MAE RSME MER ρ	No
AND-rPPG [13]	2021	Temporal Convolution Networks	RGB	Full face	COHFACE UBFC-rPPG	STDe MAE RSME ρ	No
rPPGNet [8]	2021	**2DCNN vs 3DCNN**	RGB	Full frame	COHFACE PURE	Me STDe MAE RSME	No
Ours	2022	3D-CNN	**RGB vs R vs G vs B**	**Full face vs cheeks vs forehead**	COHFACE	Me STDe MAE RSME MER ρ	Yes, upon request

hemoglobin absorbs green light better than red and blue [31] light. However, in [32] the fact that the R and B channels may contain complementary information is highlighted, this is why in Sect. 4 we perform an evaluation of the effectiveness of the G channel selection for our method compared to the choice of R and B channels and the use of the three RGB channels as originally provided in the video. Other deep learning approaches [3] used as input of their structures just the G channel of the face videos although our approach differs from theirs in a crucial point: they consider the selection of the G channel as a way to leverage the tasks of a CNN, reducing the number of parameters of the network without any study that justifies the selection.

3.3   Neural Network

Convolutional neural networks (CNN) are a type of deep learning models that usually act directly on raw inputs such as images to extract patterns for various tasks. CNNs have been proved very efficient, particularly for classification tasks with which we are dealing in this paper. Those models are often limited to handling 2D inputs. A three dimensional CNN is a network of processing layers used to reduce three dimensional data to its key features so that it can be more easily classified. We model our input data in a three dimensional representation, where the first two dimensions correspond to the 2D images while the third dimension represents time.

Recent works on the literature have proved that 3D-CNN structures successfully handle 3D data such as videos [35,36]. We believe in the potential of 3D-CNN for extracting the rPPG information embedded in human faces in the same way that we suspected that this type of network has not been exploited yet. Two other works have intended a HR estimation using a 3D-CNN but in our view major drawbacks from those approaches encourage us to propose our optimal and reproducible option. In [3] the authors presented a 3D-CNN that produces a prediction for every pixel present in a video stream leading to a heavy network that leads to a processing time of days for one test video. In [8] a comparison between 2D-CNN and 3D-CNN is performed being the rough implementation of 3D-CNN proved to be more suitable for the HR estimation task. In this work, Hu *et al.* apply several techniques to improve the performance of both networks but their main focus lays on adding modules to the 2D-CNN structure leading to a lack of exploitation of their 3D-CNN.

The architecture of the selected 3D-CNN is shown in Fig. 2. The input video patch samples are of the size $(300, 40, 40, 1)$ being 300 the number of frames, $(40, 40)$ the ROI size defined in the Sect. 3.1 and 1 representing the G channel. This input data is passed to the first *convolution layer*, where the video patch is transformed by kernels, sets of learnable filters. The *convolution layers* are followed by *pooling layers*, where filters evaluate small sections at a time to abstract the values to maps. We use *maxpooling layers*, that act as noise suppressant by taking the highest value of an area. After an alternated use of *convolution layers* and *pooling layers* our network has two *dense layers*, resulting from flattening the last *maxpooling layer*. Our last *dense layer* implements a *softmax function* which assigns decimal probabilities to each class to solve the multi-classification problem. Those decimal probabilities add up to 1 for a faster convergence. We decided to exploit the softmax function at the output layer of our network as a way to handle outliers for a better estimation of the HR. By leveraging classification over regression, our network is more resilient to outliers.

When the probabilities are identified and analyzed, the output is assigned to a value, in our case, a *one hot encoding* representation of the HR. The output of our network is then a vector of length l, being l the number of classes. In this case, $l = 52$ classes from 48 to 100 bpm with a step of one. Finally, after a conversion from *one hot encoding* vectors to scalar, we perform an average for all the predictions per sub-video for both cheeks, computing the final HR prediction.

All the results in this paper are reproducible using open source tools. The trained model will be publicly available upon request to the authors.

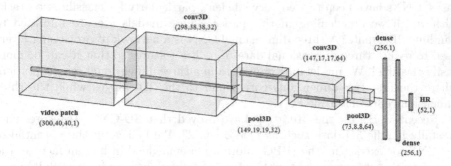

Fig. 2. Model architecture. The network takes the data as a 3D input, then alternates between 3D Convolutional layers and 3D MaxPool layers, ending with two fully connected layers that output the estimated HR.

3.4   Implementation Details

The 3D-CNN structure was implemented in TensorFlow and Keras using a standard chain of conv3D layers, maxpool3D layers and activation functions. After each maxpool3D layer, a batch normalization was applied. Batch normalization was initialized with weights randomly sampled from a Gaussian and their values were scaled with a value γ and shifted with a value β, parameters learnt during training. This was performed to avoid a linear activation of the inputs. A dropout of 0.5 was applied after each batch normalization to ensure a good training process by preventing model overfitting. Rectified linear activation functions were used in every conv3D and dense layer.

The size of the kernels was set to $3 \times 3 \times 3$ for the convolutional layers and to $2 \times 2 \times 2$ for the max pooling layers. The weights of the kernels were initialized sampled from a normal distribution with a mean of zero and a standard deviation of $\sqrt{\frac{\alpha}{n}}$ with n equal to the number of input samples. The model was trained for 10 epochs, Adam optimizer was selected with learning rate set to 0.001 and the loss function chosen was categorical cross-entropy.

4   Experiments

4.1   Experimental Settings

Many existing methods reported their results in private self-collected datasets making difficult a performance comparison of the individual approaches. We want to demonstrate whether our method is capable of performing under different illumination conditions when sometimes part of the subject's face is barely illuminated, i.e. the light source comes from one side and not frontal. To validate those hypothesis and enable a fair comparison with other approaches, we evaluated our method on the public and challenging dataset COHFACE. The COHFACE dataset [7] is composed of 160 facial videos captured at 20 fps with a resolution of 640×480 collected from 40 healthy individuals and their physiological signals. The database includes 12 female and 28 male subjects between 19 and 67 years old. Each video has a length of 60 s. Physiological readings were taken by a BVP sensor, which measures changes in skin reflectance to near-infrared lighting caused by the varying oxigen level in the blood due to heart beating. We converted the BVP signals to HR measurement using a function from the Bob package `bob.db.cohface` [26]. The videos in this database have realistic illumination conditions, the subjects are recorded under two different lighting conditions as shown in Fig. 3: (a) Studio, closed blinds, avoiding natural light, and using extra light from a spot to homogeneously illuminate the subject's face, (b) Natural, all the lights turned off and open blinds. The daylight videos (b) represent one of the main challenges of this research since the right side of the subject's face is not well illuminated, being the value of the pixels for every channel close to 0. This will generate dark ROI videos that might act as disturbance to the network in the learning process. But as discussed in [6], a varied training data, that is representative of realistic conditions, enables deep learning models to extract information that is independent of the acquisition scenario. We take advantage of the self-leaning characteristic of neural networks to face the challenges presented in COHFACE.

Different metrics have been used in the literature for reporting the HR estimation performance of an approach. Evaluating a deep learning algorithm with different evaluation metrics is an essential part of its validation because it gives an overall assessment of a model's performance. We present the mean and standard deviation (Me, STDe) in bpm of the HR error, the mean absolute HR error (MAE) in bpm, the root mean squared HR error (RMSE) in bpm, the mean of error rate percentage (MER) in bpm, and Pearson's correlation coefficients (ρ).

(a)   (b)

Fig. 3. Example video frames of two videos from a subject of the COHFACE dataset. Frame (a) shows the subject's face illuminated with studio light and frame (b) with daylight coming form a left source.

4.2   HR Estimation Results

In this study, we will compare our method with other deep learning based methods for direct HR estimation. Similar to [29], we performed a subject-exclusive split of the videos for training and testing subsets. The training set is composed of 24 subjects and a testing set of the remaining 12.

The results in Table 2 show that the proposed 3D CNN structure presents a competitive performance achieving the lowest STD in the COHFACE dataset. It achieves higher performance compared to [29] confirming that a sequential processing of the spatial and afterwards the temporal information of a video as proposed in [29] cannot capture the HR information as well as our network, which processes both spatial and temporal information simultaneously. It also overperforms, for every metric reported [37] whose double stream cannot beat the power of simultaneous 3D convolutions among all input video patches. Furthermore, by using as input the cheek area of the video we acheive lower MAE and RMSE compared to the denoising patches obtained by the full face in [13]. We prove here that the selection of an optimal face region outperforms the denoising of the full face. Finally, our model surpasses for almost every metric the two networks proposed by [8], which aimed for a CNN-based feature maps extractor from full faces. In their work they implemented a rough version of 2D and 3D-CNN and then they improve both structures by adding aggregation functions. The performance of those networks is presented in Table 2. Their further promote improvements in the 2D model putting on the side the 3D model. The results highlight the optimal performance of our 3D-CNN indicating how an end-to-end 3D CNN can overperform a 2D structure in accurately estimating a subject's HR directly from the cheek area without the need of any other intermediate face representation. This provides a new way to capture the rPPG information without compromising the model accuracy.

In addition, the processing time of one 60s video with 20 fps for our 3D-CNN is of 0, 1 ms. The proposed 3D network does not require any extra pre or post processing step, making it highly efficient and convenient for online estimation.

Table 2. Comparison between our model and other neural network based approaches on COHFACE.

Method	STD	MAE	RMSE	MER	ρ
HR-CNN [29]	–	8.10	10.78	–	0.29
2-STREAM CNN [37]	–	8.09	9.96	–	0.40
3D-rPPGNet [8]	8.98	5.86	9.12	–	–
2D-rPPGNet [8]	8,08	5.59	8.12	–	**0.63**
AND-rPPG [13]	7.83	6.81	8.06	–	**0.63**
Ours	**7.23**	**5.5**	**7.74**	**7.12**	0.62

4.3 Effectiveness of Input Choice Selection

We also perform a study of the effectiveness of different video input choices: ROI and input channel selection. As a baseline experiments, we trained and tested our 3D-CNN on full face 3 channeled videos. For the consequent experiment, each of the RGB channels was used to train the network on the full face videos, and the results are reported in Table 3. The experiments suggest that even though no clear choice between the use of RGB vs G as input can be made, the selection of just the R or B channels clearly decreases the network's performance. As a next step, we trained and tested the 3D-CNN by feeding it with a 40×40 and 30×80 ROI for the cheeks and forehead experiments respectively. Those areas detected and cropped using the 68 (x, y)-coordinates of the dlib landmark detector as explained on Sect. 3.1. The results presented in Table 3 indicate that taking as input a smaller and more specific area than the full face is particularly beneficial to perform an accurate HR estimation especially in the case of the cheeks region. The cheek area is less affected by nonrigid motion such as smiling or talking and can yield better results since in some cases the forehead can be occluded by hair or other monitoring devices. However they can be equally

Table 3. Evaluation of the proposed network using different input video channels and ROI on the COHFACE dataset.

Method	Me	STD	MAE	RMSE	MER	ρ
Full face RGB	2.43	9.55	8.22	9.86	11.32	0.28
Full face R	4.05	11.08	9.82	11.80	12.87	0.11
Full face G	1.44	10.35	8.23	10.45	11.54	0.29
Full face B	−0.29	10.47	8.95	10.47	12.79	0.23
Forehead RGB	−1.22	10.61	8.35	10.68	12.13	0.42
Forehead G	−3.17	8.80	7.84	9.35	11.71	0.52
Cheeks RGB	**0.01**	7.99	5.78	7.99	7.99	0.46
Cheeks G	2.75	**7.23**	**5.5**	**7.74**	**7.12**	**0.62**

affected by difficult illumination conditions explaining why in both areas, the results are specially promising for the G channel, highlighting how in adversarial illumination conditions (e.g. natural light sources that do not distribute the light equally on the face skin areas) the proposed 3D-CNN predicts successfully the HR only passing the G channel.

5   Conclusion and Future Works

Remote HR estimation allows a pulse rate extraction from the skin regions in face videos without any type of physical contact with the subject. In this study, we presented a review on the most relevant SoA methods for a remote rPPG and HR estimation from RGB face videos. For the learning based approaches, we summarized some of the choices regarding the structure and the data that those models use and we extract some key experiments that, in our view, are lacking from the current literature. More specifically, we perform a comparison of the most common ROI for remote HR estimation obtaining best results using the cheek area and we evaluate the choice of the G channel as input against using the three channels of RGB videos. We highlight how some other deep learning based models, require a pipeline of different techniques that can be costly in terms of memory and time, therefore, non suitable for real-time usage with affordable devices such as mobile phones. Our 3DCNN has a processing time of 0, 1 ms for a 60 s video with 20 fps. We propose a competitive, fast and reproducible HR estimation method based on a 3D-CNN structure and we evaluate the network against similar deep learning state-of-the-art structures on the publicly available dataset COHFACE.

Future challenges include the evaluation of the G channel as input against using the three channels of RGB videos. A 3 stream 3D-CNN for the R, G and B channels will be further explored as well as an adaptive ROI selection for forehead skin areas that can be more equally illuminated in natural light conditions.

References

1. Allen, J.: Photoplethysmography and its application in clinical physiological measurement. Physiol. Measur. **28**(3) (2007)
2. Blazek, V.: Ambient and unobtrusive cardiorespiratory monitoring. In: 2016 ELEKTRO. IEEE (2016)
3. Bousefsaf, F., Pruski, A., Maaoui, C.: 3d convolutional neural networks for remote pulse rate measurement and mapping from facial video. Appl. Sci. **9**(20) (2019)
4. Chen, Weixuan, McDuff, Daniel: DeepPhys: video-based physiological measurement using convolutional attention networks. In: Ferrari, Vittorio, Hebert, Martial, Sminchisescu, Cristian, Weiss, Yair (eds.) ECCV 2018. LNCS, vol. 11206, pp. 356–373. Springer, Cham (2018). https://doi.org/10.1007/978-3-030-01216-8_22
5. De Haan, G., Jeanne, V.: Robust pulse rate from chrominance-based RPPG. IEEE Trans. Biomed. Eng. **60**(10), 2878–2886 (2013)

6. Hernandez-Ortega, J., Fierrez, J., Morales, A., Diaz, D.: A comparative evaluation of heart rate estimation methods using face videos. In: 2020 IEEE 44th Annual Computers, Software, and Applications Conference (COMPSAC). IEEE (2020)

7. Heusch, G., Anjos, A., Marcel, S.: A reproducible study on remote heart rate measurement. arXiv preprint arXiv:1709.00962 (2017)

8. Hu, M., Qian, F., Wang, X., He, L., Guo, D., Ren, F.: Robust heart rate estimation with spatial-temporal attention network from facial videos. IEEE Trans. Cognit. Dev. Syst. (2021)

9. Huang, B., Chang, C.M., Lin, C.L., Chen, W., Juang, C.F., Wu, X.: Visual heart rate estimation from facial video based on CNN. In: 2020 15th IEEE Conference on Industrial Electronics and Applications (ICIEA). IEEE (2020)

10. Kwon, S., Kim, J., Lee, D., Park, K.: Roi analysis for remote photoplethysmography on facial video. In: 37th Annual International Conference of the IEEE Engineering in Medicine and Biology Society (EMBC) (2015)

11. Lamba, P.S., Virmani, D.: Contactless heart rate estimation from face videos. J. Stat. Manage. Syst. 23(7), 1275–1284 (2020)

12. Li, X., Chen, J., Zhao, G., Pietikainen, M.: Remote heart rate measurement from face videos under realistic situations. In: Proceedings of the IEEE Conference on Computer Vision and Pattern Recognition, pp. 4264–4271 (2014)

13. Lokendra, B., Puneet, G.: And-RPPG: a novel denoising-RPPG network for improving remote heart rate estimation. Comput. Biol. Med. 105146 (2021)

14. Mehta, A.D., Sharma, H.: Heart rate estimation from RGB facial videos using robust face demarcation and VMD. In: 2021 National Conference on Communications (NCC), pp. 1–6. IEEE (2021)

15. Monkaresi, H., Calvo, R.A., Yan, H.: A machine learning approach to improve contactless heart rate monitoring using a webcam. IEEE J. Biomed. Health Inform. 18(4), 1153–1160 (2013)

16. Niu, X., Han, H., Shan, S., Chen, X.: Continuous heart rate measurement from face: A robust rppg approach with distribution learning. In: 2017 IEEE International Joint Conference on Biometrics (IJCB), pp. 642–650. IEEE (2017)

17. Niu, X., Han, H., Shan, S., Chen, X.: Synrhythm: learning a deep heart rate estimator from general to specific. In: 2018 24th International Conference on Pattern Recognition (ICPR). IEEE (2018)

18. Niu, X., Shan, S., Han, H., Chen, X.: Rhythmnet: end-to-end heart rate estimation from face via spatial-temporal representation. IEEE Trans. Image Process. 29 (2019)

19. Niu, X., et al.: Robust remote heart rate estimation from face utilizing spatial-temporal attention. In: 2019 14th IEEE International Conference on Automatic Face & Gesture Recognition (FG 2019) (2019)

20. Perepelkina, O., Artemyev, M., Churikova, M., Grinenko, M.: Hearttrack: Convolutional neural network for remote video-based heart rate monitoring. In: Proceedings of the IEEE/CVF Conference on Computer Vision and Pattern Recognition Workshops, pp. 288–289 (2020)

21. Poh, M.Z., McDuff, D.J., Picard, R.W.: Advancements in noncontact, multiparameter physiological measurements using a webcam. IEEE Trans. Biome. Eng. 58(1), 7–11 (2010)

22. Poh, M.Z., McDuff, D.J., Picard, R.W.: Non-contact, automated cardiac pulse measurements using video imaging and blind source separation. Optics Express 18(10), 10762–10774 (2010)

23. Qiu, Y., Liu, Y., Arteaga-Falconi, J., Dong, H., El Saddik, A.: EVM-CNN: real-time contactless heart rate estimation from facial video. IEEE Trans. Multimedia **21**(7) (2018)

24. Rahman, H., Ahmed, M.U., Begum, S., Funk, P.: Real time heart rate monitoring from facial rgb color video using webcam. In: The 29th Annual Workshop of the Swedish Artificial Intelligence Society (SAIS), 2–3 June 2016, Malmö, Sweden. No. 129, Linköping University Electronic Press (2016)

25. Siddiqui, H., Rattani, A., Kisku, D.R., Dean, T.: AI-based BMI inference from facial images: an application to weight monitoring. preprint arXiv:2010.07442 (2020)

26. Soleymani, M., Lichtenauer, J., Pun, T., Pantic, M.: A multimodal database for affect recognition and implicit tagging. IEEE Trans. Affect. Comput. **3**(1) (2012)

27. Song, R., Li, J., Wang, M., Cheng, J., Li, C., Chen, X.: Remote photoplethysmography with an EEMD-MCCA method robust against spatially uneven illuminations. IEEE Sens. J. **21**(12), 13484–13494 (2021)

28. Song, R., Zhang, S., Li, C., Zhang, Y., Cheng, J., Chen, X.: Heart rate estimation from facial videos using a spatiotemporal representation with convolutional neural networks. IEEE Trans. Instrument. Measur. **69**(10) (2020)

29. Špetlík, R., Franc, V., Matas, J.: Visual heart rate estimation with convolutional neural network. In: Proceedings of the British Machine Vision Conference, Newcastle, UK (2018)

30. Tulyakov, S., Alameda-Pineda, X., Ricci, E., Yin, L., Cohn, J.F., Sebe, N.: Self-adaptive matrix completion for heart rate estimation from face videos under realistic conditions. In: Proceedings of the IEEE Conference on Computer Vision and Pattern Recognition, pp. 2396–2404 (2016)

31. Van Kampen, E., Zijlstra, W.G.: Determination of hemoglobin and its derivatives. Adv. Clin. Chem. **8** (1966)

32. Verkruysse, W., Svaasand, L.O., Nelson, J.S.: Remote plethysmographic imaging using ambient light. Optics Express **16**(26) (2008)

33. Wang, G.: Influence of roi selection for remote photoplethysmography with singular spectrum analysis. In: 2021 IEEE International Conference on Artificial Intelligence and Industrial Design (AIID), pp. 416–420. IEEE (2021)

34. Wang, W., den Brinker, A.C., Stuijk, S., De Haan, G.: Algorithmic principles of remote PPG. IEEE Trans. Biomed. Eng. **64**(7) (2016)

35. Wang, X., Xie, W., Song, J.: Learning spatiotemporal features with 3DCNN and convgru for video anomaly detection. In: 2018 14th IEEE International Conference on Signal Processing (ICSP), pp. 474–479. IEEE (2018)

36. Wang, Y., Dantcheva, A.: A video is worth more than 1000 lies. comparing 3DCNN approaches for detecting deepfakes. In: 2020 15th IEEE International Conference on Automatic Face and Gesture Recognition (FG 2020), pp. 515–519. IEEE (2020)

37. Wang, Z.K., Kao, Y., Hsu, C.T.: Vision-based heart rate estimation via a two-stream CNN. In: 2019 IEEE International Conference on Image Processing (ICIP), pp. 3327–3331. IEEE (2019)

38. Wang, Z., Yang, X., Cheng, K.T.: Accurate face alignment and adaptive patch selection for heart rate estimation from videos under realistic scenarios. PLoS ONE **13**(5), e0197275 (2018)

39. Yu, Z., Li, X., Zhao, G.: Remote photoplethysmograph signal measurement from facial videos using spatio-temporal networks. arXiv preprint arXiv:1905.02419 (2019)
40. Yu, Z., Peng, W., Li, X., Hong, X., Zhao, G.: Remote heart rate measurement from highly compressed facial videos: an end-to-end deep learning solution with video enhancement. In: Proceedings of the International Conference on Computer Vision (2019)

Automatic Bowel Preparation Assessment Using Deep Learning

Mahmood Salah Haithami[1]([✉]) [iD], Amr Ahmed[2] [iD], Iman Yi Liao[1] [iD],
and Hamid Jalab Altulea[3,4] [iD]

[1] School of Computer Science, University of Nottingham, Semenyih, Malaysia
{hcxmh1, Iman.Liao}@nottingham.edu.my
[2] School of Computer Science, University of Nottingham, Nottingham, UK
Amr.Ahmed@nottingham.ac.uk
[3] Department of Computer System and Technology, Faculty of Computer Science, and
Information Technology, Universiti Malaya, Kuala Lumpur, Malaysia
hamidjalab@um.edu.my
[4] Information and Communication Technology Research Group, Scientific Research Center,
Al-Ayen University, Dhi Qar, Iraq
hamid.a@alayen.edu.iq

Abstract. Bowel preparation is considered a critical step in colonoscopy. Manual
bowel preparation assessment is time consuming and prone to human errors and
biases. Automatic Bowel evaluation using machine/deep learning is a better and
efficient alternative. Most of the relevant literature have focused on achieving
high validation accuracy, where private handy-picked dataset does not reflect real-
environment situation. Furthermore, treating a video dataset as a collection of
individual frames may produce overestimated results. This is due to the fact a video
contains nearly identical consecutive frames, hence, dividing them into training
and validation sets yields two similar distributed datasets. Given a public dataset,
Nerthus, we show empirically a significant drop in performance when a video
dataset is treated as a collection of videos (depicting the real environment/context),
instead of a collection of individual frames. We propose a model that utilizes both
sequence and none-sequence (spatial) information within videos. The proposed
model achieved on average 83% validation accuracy across 4 validation sets,
whereas, the state-of-the-art models achieved on average a range of 66%–72%
validation accuracy.

Keywords: Bowel preparation · assessment · deep learning · colonoscopy
videos · individual frames

1 Introduction

In the US, colorectal cancer is considered the third most common type of cancer and the
second leading cause of all cancer deaths [22]. It is well known in the endoscopy field
that detecting lesions at early stages would significantly increase the survival rate [7, 8].
The gold standard method for colon screening is colonoscopy. However, the quality of

© Springer Nature Switzerland AG 2023
J.-J. Rousseau and B. Kapralos (Eds.): ICPR 2022 Workshops, LNCS 13643, pp. 574–588, 2023.
https://doi.org/10.1007/978-3-031-37660-3_40

colonoscopy screening heavily determines the prevention of colorectal cancers which can be evaluated -among other terms- by the withdrawal time (i.e., time spent during the withdrawal phase) and the rigorous investigation of the colonic mucosa [17].

The quality of bowel preparation determines the diagnostic accuracy of colonoscopy [13, 17]. Although some existing work attempted to optimize cleansing methods, inappropriate cleansing was found in 75% of patients in randomized controlled trials [16]. Therefore, the diagnostic accuracy of colonoscopy may be degraded due to a poor quality of the bowel preparation [3]. As a result, bowel preparation is a critical preprocessing stage before starting colon screening. Consequently the American Society for Gastrointestinal Endoscopy (ASGE) and American College of Gastroenterology (ACG) Taskforce on Quality in Endoscopy suggested to attach a colonoscopy report that includes the bowel preparation's quality [17].

However, those institutions (i.e., ASGE and ACG) did not provide evaluation metrics [15, 19]. Accordingly, Boston Bowel Preparation Scale (BBPS) quantized the quality from 0 (poor) to 3 (excellent) depending on the clarity of the mucosa [15]. However, such quantization is still subject to human bias. It is appealing to develop an automatic system to identify the clarity degree of the mucosa which could eliminate any human subjectivity and lessen the documentation efforts.

2 Literature Review

Bowel preparation assessment using computer aided systems is not a new research problem. The earliest works used image processing methods or conventional machine learning models (e.g., Support Vector Machine SVM) [13, 17]. In [13], an image was divided into blocks and color features were extracted from each block to train SVM. Meanwhile [17] employs color to determine the classification class. Stool pixels are projected to a 3D-space (i.e., Red, Green, and Blue) "Cube" [17]. Finally, the 3D-space is divided into planes and used as an index for detecting stool pixels. Both methods [13, 17] achieved high Sensitivity results with 99.25% and 92.9%, respectively. However, the model in [13] had a major misclassification problem when it comes to learn new instances, meanwhile, the model in [17] would work only under the assumption that stool pixels are different from mucosa pixels. However, in reality this assumption is hard to meet due to lighting variations, field of view, bubbles, water, and residual liquid.

Recently, methods based on deep learning have been proposed [1, 6, 18, 25, 26]. DenseNet [12] was employed in [25] and achieved 89.04% classification accuracy when it was tested on 20 colonoscopy videos, though a significant drop in performance was reported when images with bubbles were incorporated in the experiments. The work in [18] used convolutional neural networks (CNN) and transfer learning (TL). They compared the obtained results from deep learning method with that of other machine learning methods such as Logistic Model Tree method [9]. The goal of [18] is to create a baseline performance for their public dataset Nerthus [18]. Both works [6, 26] used deep learning methods to evaluate bowel cleansing degree on Nerthus dataset. The latter used a simple CNN containing four convolutional blocks, whereas the former employed pretrained ResNet50 [10] appended with relational mapping [20] followed by Long Short-Term Memory LSTM [11] and 3 fully-connected layers. In [6], ResNet50 is employed to only extract representative features from middle layers and fed to the other parts. Both works [6, 26] achieved high validation accuracy of 100% and 97.7%, respectively. In [1], Nerthus dataset have been used to test their proposed model which consists of pre-trained ResNet50 combined with Bayesian inference [14], and similarly achieved 100% validation accuracy.

In conclusion, the existing works have either used private datasets such as in [13, 17, 25] or public dataset (i.e., Nerthus [18]) such as in [1, 6, 18, 26]. Using private datasets would prevent reproducibility and analysis of the published work. Furthermore, the published work in [13, 17, 25] depends on high quality handy-picked images which are hard to comply with in real life. On the other hand, those which used the public dataset Nerthus achieved high validation accuracy [1, 6, 18, 26]. However, we argue that the high accuracy achieved is inflated due to a mistreatment of the video dataset. Nerthus videos, as well as any other videos, consist of nearly identical consecutive frames. Dividing video frames randomly between training and validation set would yield similar, if not nearly identical, data distribution for both datasets. As a result, the actual performances of the models are over estimated. This issue is discussed in detail in the Experiment section.

3   Methodology

In this section, we first illustrate the Nerthus dataset and then present our proposed model. We also discuss a simple sampling method that represents videos with a smaller number of frames due to the limited capacity of the used GPU.

3.1   Nerthus Dataset

The Nerthus dataset has a collection of videos in which each video is labeled based on the clarity degree of the colon. Following the BBPS [15], the Nerthus dataset is divided into four classes as depicted in Fig. 1 and Fig. 2. The description along with its corresponding examples for each of the classes are shown in Fig. 1. The length of each video is between 10 to 11 s with a frame rate around 24 frames/s, hence, a video contains approximately 225–275 frames.

The class-distribution of these videos are not balanced, as shown in Table 1 and Table 2. The authors of Nerthus datasets divided the videos into sub-videos and applied holdout cross validation (i.e., half for training and the other half for validation) [18]. Although the dataset consists of videos, the literature that employed Nerthus dataset treated it as a collection of individual unrelated images [6, 18, 25, 26]. It has led to high validation accuracy that does not reflect the actual performance of a trained model, as illustrated in the experiments.

3.2   Proposed Model

The proposed model has four main components, as shown in Fig. 3. Firstly, an encoder is used to map frames to vectors, followed by two branches. One branch is a sequence-based layer to capture the temporal information. In this layer we opt to use Gated Recurrent

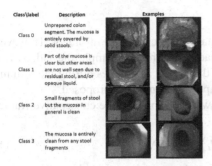

Fig. 1. Nerthus dataset labels with a description and examples for each corresponding label.

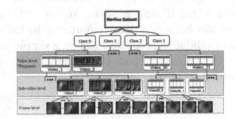

Fig. 2. Hierarchy of Nerthus dataset. Nerthus dataset can be viewed as a collection of Videos, Sub-videos, or Frames. Considering this hierarchy, tested models would achieve different results as shown in Fig. 4.

Unit (GRU) [4]. The other branch is a non-sequence based layer to select a key vector that signifies the video class. As opposed to the sequence-based layer, the order of frames is not considered in this layer. Finally, a fully-connected layer is applied to the output vectors from both Sequence and None-Sequence layers. SoftMax is used to generate probabilities for each class.

In order to increase the stability and enhance the overall performance of a model, temporal frames should be utilized [2]. We employ Gated Recurrent Unit [4] to incorporate temporal information, though different RNN models such as Long Short Term Memory (LSTM) can be applied as well.

In general, most of the frames within a video are consistent and would indicate the actual label of that video. However, there are also frames within the video which are distorted due to factors such as blurring, out of focus, bubbles, etc. Furthermore, some frames within a video may have varying amount of stool, despite the entire video is labelled according to the overall clarity degree. Consequently, it is likely to degrade the performance of the sequence-based layer (i.e., GRU). To compensate for this effect, a non-sequence based layer is proposed to select a representative feature-vector that indicates the corresponding video label. The underlying assumption is that there is at least one frame within the video that can be used to indicate the label of the overall video.

This representative frame is called a "key frame" and the corresponding feature-vector r_i is passed to support the information obtained from the sequence-based layer (i.e., GRU). We name the non-sequence based layer as Multiplexer. This name is inspired by a combinational gate in digital circuits called Multiplexer that selects between several input signals and passes the selected input to a single output.

The detailed architecture of the branch of GRU sequence and that of the branch of Multiplexer are shown in Fig. 3. Employing the proposed Multiplexer to support GRU layer has shown its efficiency in enhancing the overall performance of the proposed model as suggested in Table 4.

3.3 Sampling Videos

In this section we propose to treat Nerthus dataset as a collection of videos. However, due to the limitation of the current GPU capacity, we had to sample the videos into smaller but representative frames to be fed to the model as batches during the training and validation processes. Hence, a simple sampling technique is proposed.

For a set of videos $D = \{V_1, V_2, ..., V_I\}$, we can represent the consecutive frames within a video as follows:

$$V_i = \{f_{i,n} : 1 \le n \le N_i\}, n \text{ and } N_i \in \mathbb{N} \tag{1}$$

where N_i represents the number of frames in the corresponding video V_i.

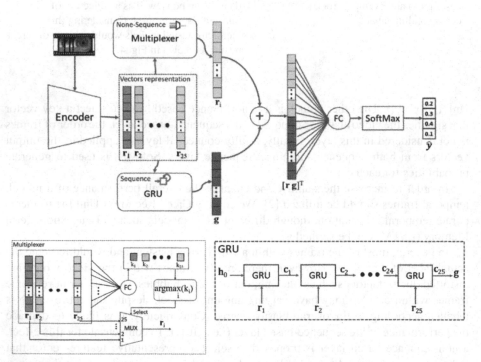

Fig. 3. Proposed model has mainly four components; namely, 1) An encoder that represents frames as vectors, 2) Sequence based layer (GRU), 3) None-Sequence based layer (Multiplexer), and 4) fully-connected layer. The vectors produced by both Sequence and None-Sequence models are concatenated before being fed to the fully-connected layer. Finally, SoftMax is applied to the output to generate probabilities for each class.

The idea is to take one frame from different location within the video to form a representative sample. For a fixed sampling size of m = 25 frames/sample, we can create multiple samples from each video. Let C_i represent a set of all samples that can be created from V_i and let the set $S_{i,j}$ represents the j-th sample. The sets C_i and $S_{i,j}$ can be defined as follows:

$$C_i = \{S_{i,j} : 1 \le j \le \tau_i\}, j \text{ and } \tau_i \in \mathbb{N} \tag{2}$$

$$S_{i,j} = \{f_{i,j+k\tau_i}\}, \; for \; k = 0, 1, 2, ..., m-1 \tag{3}$$

$$\tau_i = \left\lceil \frac{N_i}{m} \right\rceil \tag{4}$$

Note that the sets C_i and $S_{i,j}$ will always have the following properties:

$$|S_{i,j}| = m = 25 \tag{5}$$

$$|C_i| = \tau_i \tag{6}$$

$$\bigcap_j S_{i,j} = \varnothing \tag{7}$$

$$\bigcup_j S_{i,j} = C_i \subseteq V_i \tag{8}$$

In general, each video will be sampled into shorter videos, each having the same number of frames m = 25. The new samples will have distinctive frames. According to this sampling technique a few trailing frames in some videos will be discarded if the number of frames in the videos are not divisible by m. However, the size of all videos in Nerthus dataset is divisible by 25, hence, no frames had been discarded in the experiments. The number of newly created samples based on the proposed sampling method along with the corresponding videos is illustrated in Table 1 and Table 2. Note that the training and validation sets have been created according to the set D (i.e., videos level). However, we will use the corresponding samples $S_{i,j}$ as mini-batches.

Table 1. Validation dataset videos with their corresponding samples are listed. All videos have been shuffled randomly to create dataset1

Dataset1 (Shuffle1)						
Class	Validation set 1			Validation set 2		
	Video number	Video samples	Total frames	Video number	Video samples	Total frames
Class 0 (stool)	V_1	9	225	V_2	11	275
Class 1	V_3, V_5, V_6, V_8, V_9	59	1475	$V_4, V_7, V_{10}, V_{11}, V_{12}$	49	1225
Class 2	$V_{13}, V_{16},$	17	425	V_{14}, V_{15}	22	550
Class 3 (clear)	V_{17}, V_{20}	24	600	V_{18}, V_{19}, V_{21}	30	750
Total	10	109	2725	11	112	2800

Table 2. Validation dataset videos with their corresponding samples are listed. All videos have been shuffled randomly to create dataset2

Dataset2 (Shuffle2)						
Class	Validation set 1			Validation set 2		
	Video number	Video samples	Total frames	Video number	Video samples	Total frames
Class 0 (stool)	V_2	11	275	V_1	9	225
Class 1	$V_3, V_4, V_5,$ V_7, V_9	50	1250	$V_6, V_8, V_{10},$ V_{11}, V_{12}	58	1450
Class 2	$V_{15}, V_{14},$	22	550	V_{16}, V_{13}	17	425
Class 3 (clear)	V_{18}, V_{17}	21	525	$V_{20}, V_{19},$ V_{21}	33	825
Total	10	104	2600	11	117	2925

4   Experiments

This section contains 3 sections including **1)** the parameters and metrics, **2)** demonstration of the inflated results reported by the framework in the current literature (i.e., due treating videos as collection of frames), and **3)** comparisons between the proposed model and the state-of-the-art SOTA models.

We train our proposed model in two phases. In the first phase, the encoder was trained on Nerthus individual frames. ResNet50 [10] have been used as an encoder to provide feature-vector for each frame. The trained encoder was used to generate feature vectors but was not involved in the training process in the second phase. In the second phase, only the GRU, the Multiplexer, and the fully-connected layer were trained.

4.1   Parameters and Metrics

For the experiments, PyTorch have been used with a Tesla P100-PCIE (16 GB) GPU. The learning rate is set as $lr = 0.001$ and 4 video samples/sub-videos are used in each batch (see Table 1 and Table 2). To create more than 2 validation sets, the dataset was shuffled twice and for each shuffle we created 2-fold cross validation as listed in Table 1 and Table 2. The metrics for evaluating the model performance are F1-score, Precision, Recall, and Accuracy. Weighted average is used to combine the metrics of all classes.

4.2   Overestimation Due to Treating a Video Dataset as a Collection of Individual Frames

Nerthus dataset consists of videos consisting of nearly identical consecutive images. In the literature, the dataset was treated in different manners. To demonstrate that, a hierarchy of Nerthus dataset is depicted in Fig. 2. Nerthus videos were divided into a smaller 5-s sub-videos that were further divided into training and validation set in [18]. Notice that two sub-videos may have in common nearly identical frames, as seen in Fig. 2. For instance, frames found at the end of "Video2_0" is nearly identical to the frames found at the beginning of "Video2_1" and similarly for "Video2_2", as shown in Fig. 2. Therefore, if a model is trained on "Video2_0" and "Video2_2", then it will classify frames in "Video2_1" with high accuracy.

On the other hand, the Nerthus dataset was also treated as a collection of individual frames which were randomly divided into training and validation sets [6, 25, 26]. Since each video has nearly identical consecutive frames, the distribution of the training and validation would be nearly identical as well. This has led to near 100% validation accuracy.

From Fig. 2, we can conclude that Nerthus dataset can be treated as a collection of frames, a collection of sub-videos, or a collection of videos. To the best of our knowledge, the Nerthus dataset has not been treated as a collection of videos in the literature. This has led to inflated validation accuracy as we mentioned earlier. To further confirm this pitfall, we conducted extensive experiments with various models and the results are summarized in Table 3 and in Fig. 4. The SOTA models have been tested on Nerthus dataset with different configurations (i.e., Nerthus as a collection of frames, sub-videos, and videos, respectively). A model would achieve different validation accuracies depending on the way the Nerthus videos are treated. For the same model, the highest validation accuracy was achieved when the dataset was treated as a collection of frames, whereas when it was treated as a collection of videos the model produced the lowest validation accuracy. A significant drop in performance have been observed across different types of models when videos have been used as means for creating training and validation sets, as shown in Fig. 4.

Table 3. Various models are tested with different level configurations. Notice the difference in performance between frames level and videos level

Model	Validation Accuracy		
	Frames	Sub-videos	Videos
ResNet50 [10]	0.9982	0.8241	0.6837
ViT [5]	0.9982	0.8213	0.7218
MLP_Mixer [24]	0.9973	0.8353	0.6462
VGG11 [21]	1	0.8526	0.7156
InceptionV3 [23]	0.9982	0.8241	0.6899
DenseNet [12]	0.9991	0.8673	0.6683

4.3 Results of the Proposed Model vs SOTA Results

In this section we compare the proposed model with the state-of-the-art models (SOTA) such as ResNet50 [10] and Vision Transformer (ViT) [5]. Since we have limited videos,

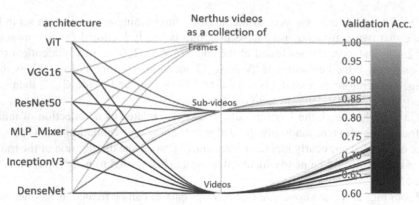

Fig. 4. This Parallel Coordinates conveys the information listed in Table 3. Notice the drop in performance between Frame level and Videos level for each model.

we shuffled all videos twice to create Dataset1 and Dataset2 as listed in Table 1 and Table 2, respectively. For each dataset, 2-fold cross validation was applied. Notice that it is impossible to create more than 2 folds for each dataset (i.e., Dataset1 & Dataset2) since we have only two videos for Class0. Therefore, if video1 is used for training then video2 will be used for validation and vice versa.

Table 4 lists the average performance of the SOTA models over all validation sets. The standard deviations were also shown across the validation folds for each metric. In Table 4, the best two results are highlighted in bold font. A graphical representation of Table 4 is depicted in Fig. 5.

It is evident from Table 4 and Fig. 5 that the proposed model had a better performance than the SOTA. Particularly, the F1-score of the proposed model is higher than all other models. This indicates that designing a model that considers videos as an input would produce better results than individual frames. Regardless of the used encoder (i.e., ResNet50 and VGG11), still the proposed model achieved better than other models. In fact, the proposed model with a better encoder model (i.e., VGG11) achieved the highest results.

Generally, colonoscopy videos may contain non-informative frames (e.g., frames that are blurred, out of focus, saturated, etc.) and, in some cases, some frames in a video may not belong to the same class of the video. However, it is unlikely that a sampled video based on our simple sampling method contains only non-informative or conflicting frames. Consequently, utilizing informative temporal frames can mitigate issues caused by non-informative frames found within videos. Videos in Nerthus dataset are not an exception. Therefore, it is noticed that the proposed model with only GRU layer achieved relatively better than all the other models that are frame-based.

We assume that there is at least one frame that can indicate the label of a video. Hence, a Multiplexer is proposed to select such frame. Employing only the Multiplexer component achieved lower than the conventional models. When the Multiplexer is used along with the GRU, the output of the proposed model was significantly enhanced. The features produced by Multiplexer layer complement the one produced by the GRU layer. This can be seen in both Table 4 and Fig. 5.

The variance in F1-scores over all validation folds is depicted using whisker plot as in Fig. 6. It is noticed that the proposed model with VGG11 [21] as an encoder has the least variance across all models followed by ResNet50 [10]. In contrast, the proposed model without either the Multiplexer component or GRU presented the largest variance in F1-score. This indicates that more stable results are achieved when both the Multiplexer and GRU are used.

Table 4. The average and standard deviation are calculated over all validation folds. The two best results are highlighted in bold

Model	Average and Std			
	Precision	Recall	F1-score	Accuracy
DenseNet [12]	0.7139 ± **0.0436**	0.6874 ± 0.0446	0.6706 ± 0.0470	0.6874 ± 0.0446
VGG11 [21]	0.721 ± 0.0465	0.7065 ± 0.0545	0.6945 ± 0.0567	0.7065 ± 0.0545
Inception [23]	0.7386 ± 0.0456	0.7336 ± 0.0477	0.7204 ± 0.0487	0.7336 ± 0.0477
ResNet50 [10]	0.6884 ± **0.0094**	0.6987 ± **0.0406**	0.6699 ± **0.0321**	0.6987 ± **0.0406**
MLP_Mixer [24]	0.7049 ± 0.0458	0.6675 ± 0.0478	0.6699 ± 0.0480	0.6675 ± 0.0478
ViT [5]	0.7321 ± 0.0528	0.7213 ± 0.0464	0.7127 ± 0.0564	0.7213 ± 0.0464
Proposed w/o GRU	0.7463 ± 0.0787	0.7055 ± 0.0936	0.7084 ± 0.0936	0.7055 ± 0.0936
Proposed w/o Multiplexer	0.7812 ± 0.1007	0.7758 ± 0.0949	0.7511 ± 0.0982	0.7758 ± 0.0949
Proposed-Encoder (VGG11)	**0.8635** ± 0.0517	**0.862 ± 0.0147**	**0.8514 ± 0.0314**	**0.862 ± 0.0147**
Proposed-Encoder (ResNet50)	**0.7916** ± 0.0925	**0.8017** ± 0.0609	**0.7792** ± 0.0632	**0.8017** ± 0.0609

4.4 The Proposed Model with Different Video Size

We have explained in the sub-Sect. 3.3 Sampling Videos) that entire videos in Nerthus dataset is not used directly for training due to the limitation of the used GPU, therefore, we have illustrated that a video can be sampled into smaller, representative sub-videos. The default size of each sub-video is 25 frames (i.e. frames m = 25) taken from different locations within the video. The choice of 25 frames for sampling sub-videos is convenient

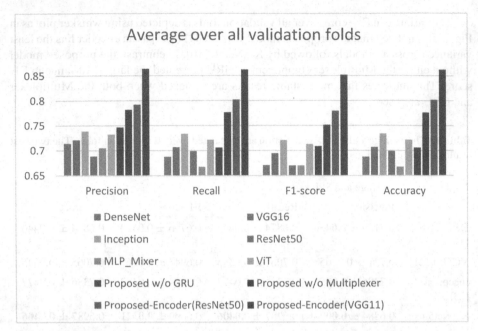

Fig. 5. The average over all validation folds is depicted. The proposed model which contains both the Sequence and none-Sequence components (i.e., GRU and Multiplexer, respectively) achieved the best results across all employed metrics. Regardless the encoder type, still the proposed model achieved the highest results compared with other methods

due to the current sizes of Nerthus videos (i.e. 25 is a common factor across all the Nerthus videos).

In this section, experiments are conducted to examine the effect of different sampling sizes (i.e., m = {5, 15, 25, 35, 45}). The average performance, across various metrics, is listed in Table 5. The best results achieved with sample size of m = 25 and m = 45, meanwhile, the lowest results achieved when the sample size m = 5. It is noticeable that the proposed model (with ResNet50 as encoder) achieved higher than the SOTA models when the sample/video size m >= 25, as shown in Table 4.

Nevertheless, considerable drop in performance is noticed when the sub-video size is m = 5 (i.e., 5 frames were selected to represent entire video). Given variations within a video, we suspect that 5 frames would capture all the necessary information that determine the video class/label. Furthermore, with such low frame rate (i.e., 5 frames/video) key frames may get missing in some sub-video samples which would harm the learning process. Adequate sub-video size should be considered given the current dataset.

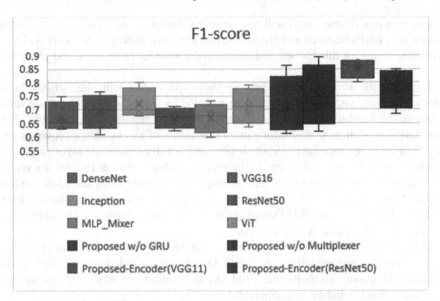

Fig. 6. Whisker plot created based on the F1-score. Total of 4 folds are considered (i.e., 2-fold of Dataset1 & 2-fold of Dataset2).

Table 5. The effect of Different sampling sizes (i.e., sub-video size) for the proposed model is listed. The proposed model with ResNet50 as encoder was used. Metrics for two-fold cross validation of Dataset1 are listed.

Average and Std over the two-fold cross validation of Dataset1				
Sub-video sizes	Precision	Recall	F1-score	Accuracy
m = 5	0.6979 ± 0.0849	0.6933 ± 0.0603	0.6651 ± 0.0608	0.6933 ± 0.0603
m = 15	0.7317 ± 0.0876	0.7361 ± 0.0587	0.7086 ± 0.0564	0.7361 ± 0.0587
m = 25 (Default)	**0.771** ± 0.0986	**0.768** ± 0.0620	**0.753** ± 0.0699	**0.768** ± 0.0620
m = 35	0.7272 ± 0.1234	0.7487 ± 0.0536	0.704 ± 0.0668	0.7487 ± 0.0536
m = 45	**0.7774** ± 0.0871	**0.7612** ± 0.0597	**0.7352** ± 0.0535	**0.7612** ± 0.0597

5   Conclusion and Limitations

In this paper we discussed the motivation behind automating the bowel preparation assessment. Most of the literature evaluated their methods on a private dataset which contains high quality handy-picked images. The literature in general treated their dataset as a collection of individual frames. We have shown that such arrangement yields inflated results that could be misleading and impractical. A significant drop in performance (i.e., from 100% to 68% accuracy) was observed when the Nerthus dataset was treated as a collection of videos instead of individual frames. We demonstrated that this is not due to a specific architecture of a model but rather due to mis-treatment of the video dataset. Achieving almost 100% validation accuracy might discourage other researchers to approach this dataset. And with the current scarcity of datasets in the endoscopy domain, this limits research and progress in this area. We hope that this work will avoid this issue, removing this barrier, and opens up the way for more work and progress to be achieved.

Based on the above arrangements, we proposed to deal with the Nerthus dataset videos as videos, instead of individual frames. We proposed a four-component model to handle the Nerthus dataset as a collection of videos including the inherit temporal information as well as spatial information. It consists of an encoder, a sequence layer (GRU), a non-sequence layer (Multiplexer), and a fully-connected layer to generate probability distribution of the output. The encoder converts frames into feature vectors, followed by two parallel branches, i.e., the sequence layer of GRUs and a non-sequence layer of Multiplexer. The GRU utilizes the temporal information in the videos, whereas the Multiplexer supports GRU feature space by selecting a feature vector corresponds to a representative frame within a video.

Due to the limited capacity of the GPU, a simple sampling method was proposed to create fixed-size representative sub-videos. Depending on video size, multiple frames are selected (maintaining their order) from various locations across the video to represent the entire video (including its temporal information).

The average performance over all validation sets has shown that the proposed model, regardless of the used encoder, outperformed SOTA methods with an average F1-score of 81.5%. Meanwhile the highest SOTA model (i.e., Inception) achieved F1-score of 72.0%. The GRU and Multiplexer layers in the proposed model have been tested separately. The proposed model achieved the best performance when both components were employed together. This supports the hypothesis that video datasets need to be dealt with as videos, i.e., with both temporal and spatial information being utilized, instead of individual unrelated images.

Adequate sampling size (i.e. sub-video size) should be considered carefully. A sub-video with only 5 frames wouldn't be able to represent the main features in a video. Hence, the proposed model will negatively get affected.

The encoder layer in the proposed model is considered as the base that both the GRU and the Multiplexer layers depend on. Hence, a better encoder would be expected to enhance the overall performance. There is a room for enhancement since augmentation and transfer learning have not been used in the current proposed method. We anticipate that empowering the encoder by using transfer learning might be more useful than augmentation given the tremendous variations naturally presented in the Nerthus dataset videos.

It is hard to conclude on the generalizability of the proposed model as well as that of the SOTA. Nerthus is the only public dataset available, and it has a limited number of videos for "Class0". Nevertheless, it is paramount to clarify the inflated results reported in the literature due to treating videos as collection of individual unrelated frames.

References

1. Amin, J., et al.: 3D-semantic segmentation and classification of stomach infections using uncertainty aware deep neural networks. Complex Intell. Syst. 0123456789 (2021). https://doi.org/10.1007/s40747-021-00328-7
2. Boers, T., et al.: Improving temporal stability and accuracy for endoscopic video tissue classification using recurrent neural networks. Sens. (Switzerland). **20**(15), 1–11 (2020). https://doi.org/10.3390/s20154133
3. Cappell, M.S., Friedel, D.: The role of sigmoidoscopy and colonoscopy in the diagnosis and management of lower gastrointestinal disorders: endoscopic findings, therapy, and complications (2002). https://doi.org/10.1016/S0025-7125(02)00077-9. http://www.medical.thecli nics.com/article/S0025712502000779/fulltext
4. Cho, K., et al.: On the properties of neural machine translation: encoder–decoder approaches. Presented at the (2015). https://doi.org/10.3115/v1/w14-4012
5. Dosovitskiy, A., et al.: An image is worth 16x16 words: transformers for image recognition at scale (2020)
6. Gammulle, H., Denman, S., Sridharan, S., Fookes, C.: Two-stream deep feature modelling for automated video endoscopy data analysis. In: Martel, A.L., et al. (eds.) MICCAI 2020. LNCS, vol. 12263, pp. 742–751. Springer, Cham (2020). https://doi.org/10.1007/978-3-030-59716-0_71
7. Haithami, M., et al.: An embedded recurrent neural network-based model for endoscopic semantic segmentation. In: CEUR Workshop Proceedings, pp. 59–68 (2021)
8. Haithami, M., et al.: Employing GRU to combine feature maps in DeeplabV3 for a better segmentation model. Nord. Mach. Intell. **1**(1), 29–31 (2021). https://doi.org/10.5617/nmi. 9131
9. Hall, M., et al.: The WEKA data mining software. ACM SIGKDD Explor. Newsl. **11**(1), 10–18 (2009). https://doi.org/10.1145/1656274.1656278
10. He, K., et al.: Deep residual learning for image recognition. In: 2016 IEEE Conference on Computer Vision and Pattern Recognition (CVPR), pp. 770–778. IEEE (2016). https://doi.org/10.1109/CVPR.2016.90
11. Hochreiter, S., Schmidhuber, J.: Long short-term memory. Neural Comput. **9**(8), 1735–1780 (1997). https://doi.org/10.1162/neco.1997.9.8.1735
12. Huang, G. et al.: Densely connected convolutional networks. In: Proceedings - 30th IEEE Conference on Computer Vision and Pattern Recognition, CVPR 2017 (2017). https://doi.org/10.1109/CVPR.2017.243
13. Hwang, S., et al.: Stool detection in colonoscopy videos. In: Proceedings of the 30th Annual International Conference of the IEEE Engineering in Medicine and Biology Society, EMBS 2008 - "Personalized Healthcare through Technology" (2008). https://doi.org/10.1109/iembs.2008.4649835
14. Krizhevsky, A., et al.: Learning multiple layers of features from tiny images (2009)
15. Lai, E.J., et al.: The Boston bowel preparation scale: a valid and reliable instrument for colonoscopy-oriented research. Gastrointest. Endosc. **69**(3), 620–625 (2009). https://doi.org/10.1016/j.gie.2008.05.057
16. Levenstein, S., et al.: Predictors of inadequate bowel preparation for colonoscopy. Am. J. Gastroenterol. **96**(6), 1797–1802 (2001). https://doi.org/10.1016/S0002-9270(01)02437-6
17. Muthukudage, J., Oh, J.H., Tavanapong, W., Wong, J., de Groen, P.C.: Color based stool region detection in colonoscopy videos for quality measurements. In: Ho, Y.-S. (ed.) PSIVT 2011. LNCS, vol. 7087, pp. 61–72. Springer, Heidelberg (2011). https://doi.org/10.1007/978-3-642-25367-6_6

18. Pogorelov, K., et al.: Nerthus: a bowel preparation quality video dataset. In: Proceedings of the 8th ACM Multimedia Systems Conference, MMSys 2017, pp. 170–174 ACM (2017). https://doi.org/10.1145/3083187.3083216

19. Rex, D.K., et al.: Quality indicators for colonoscopy. Gastrointest. Endosc. **63**(4 SUPPL.), S16–S28 (2006). https://doi.org/10.1016/j.gie.2006.02.021

20. Santoro, A. et al.: A simple neural network module for relational reasoning. In: Advances in Neural Information Processing Systems. Neural Information Processing Systems Foundation, pp. 4968–4977 (2017)

21. Simonyan, K., Zisserman, A.: Very deep convolutional networks for large-scale image recognition. In: 3rd International Conference on Learning Representations, ICLR 2015 - Conference Track Proceedings (2015)

22. Society, A.C.: Colorectal Cancer Facts and Figures (2005). https://www.google.com/url?sa=t&rct=j&q=&esrc=s&source=web&cd=&cad=rja&uact=8&ved=2ahUKEwj_5L-vy9P0AhULUGwGHUstD_MQFnoECAgQAQ&url=https%3A%2F%2Fwww.cancer.org%2Fcontent%2Fdam%2Fcancer-org%2Fresearch%2Fcancer-facts-and-statistics%2Fcolorectal-cancer-facts-

23. Szegedy, C., et al.: Rethinking the inception architecture for computer vision. In: Proceedings of the IEEE Computer Society Conference on Computer Vision and Pattern Recognition (2016). https://doi.org/10.1109/CVPR.2016.308

24. Tolstikhin, I., et al.: MLP-Mixer: An all-MLP Architecture for Vision (2021)

25. Zhou, J., et al.: A novel artificial intelligence system for the assessment of bowel preparation (with video). Gastrointest. Endosc. **91**(2), 428-435.e2 (2020). https://doi.org/10.1016/j.gie.2019.11.026

26. Zhu, Y. et al.: A CNN-based cleanliness evaluation for bowel preparation in colonoscopy. In: Proceedings - 2019 12th International Congress Image Signal Processing Biomedical Engineering and Informatics, CISP-BMEI 2019, pp. 1–5 (2019). https://doi.org/10.1109/CISP-BMEI48845.2019.8965825

A Hierarchical 3D Segmentation Model for Cone-Beam Computed Tomography Dental-Arch Scans

Francesco Rundo[1] , Carmelo Pino[1]([✉]) , Riccardo E. Sarpietro[1] ,
Concetto Spampinato[2] , and Federica Proietto Salanitri[2]

[1] STMicroelectronics ADG, R&D Power and Discretes, Catania, Italy
{francesco.rundo,carmelo.pino,riccardoemanuele.sarpietro}@st.com
[2] Università degli Studi di Catania DIEEI - PeRCeiVe Lab, Catania, Italy
cspampin@dieei.unict.it, federica.proiettosalanitri@phd.unict.it

Abstract. In this paper we define a deep learning architecture, for automated segmentation of anatomical structures in Craniomaxillofacial (CMF) CT images that leverages the recent success of encoder-decoder models for semantic segmentation of medical images.

The aim of this work is to propose an architecture capable to perform the automated segmentation of the dental arch from CBCT scans Cranio-Maxillo-Facial, offering a fast, efficient and reliable method of obtaining images labeled.

A deep convolutional neural network was applied by exploiting the deep supervision mechanism with the aim of train a model for the extraction of feature maps at different levels of abstraction, to obtain an accurate segmentation of the images passed in input.

In particular, we propose a 3D CNN-based architecture for automated segmentation from CT scans, with a 3D encoder that learns to extract features at different levels of abstraction and send them hierarchically to four 3D decoders that predict intermediate segmentation maps used to obtain the final detailed binary mask.

The automated segmentation model is tested with an error, on average, of 0.2%.

Keywords: 3D segmentation · Hierarchical architecture · Deep network

1 Introduction

Computed tomography (CT) and cone beam computed tomography (CBCT) are the most common imaging methods for the diagnosis and treatment of Craniomaxillofacial (CMF) disorders. Usually the standard clinical procedures include visual inspection and manual annotation of CT images in order to have a detailed segmentation of CMF bones (e.g., mandible, dental arch) and other structures (e.g., paranasal sinus and pharyngeal airway).

© Springer Nature Switzerland AG 2023
J.-J. Rousseau and B. Kapralos (Eds.): ICPR 2022 Workshops, LNCS 13643, pp. 589–601, 2023.
https://doi.org/10.1007/978-3-031-37660-3_41

The segmentation task is very time-consuming for physicians, in addition is a method error-prone and subject to inter-user variability. Therefore, there is a great unmet need for the development of highly accurate and efficient segmentation methods to support clinical analysis Fig. 2.

There are three main segmentation techniques. The first is the manual one, which represents the standard clinical procedure in the context of visual inspection, for then switch to manually annotate the entire dental arch from the CT scans. This approach is actually a challenging job, which it takes a long time and the result is strongly influenced by the actual experience of the medical expert. It usually takes 5-6 h to finalize the manual segmentation of the entire dental-arch region of a single patient.

The second type of segmentation is the semi-automatic one (SAS), which extends the selection of voxels of the Region of Interest (ROI) through different slices of the scan, requiring further manipulation to correct the procedure and appropriate knowledge in the anatomical field. For this reason, the research is going concentrating as much as possible on the third and last type, or automatic segmentation (AS), with the aim of finding the most reliable and promising method, although it is not an easy task.

There are many challenges in developing automated methods for CMF structure segmentation:

- due to the limited radiation dose used to obtain the slice, they are characterized by high noise, inhomogeneity, low contrast and artifacts.
- the extreme proximity between the teeth and other surrounding objects, including the jawbones, which can lead to so many boundaries that are complicated to delineate.
- the presence of several structures characterized by irregular and complex shape patterns.
- the lack of contrast in joints, and the significant morphological differences between different patients.

These elements make the task of automatic segmentation of anatomical structure a major challenge and facilitates the use of commercial software which still relies on manual or semi-automated segmentation.

The application of deep learning networks to CT segmentation has opened the way to general-purpose approaches.

Actually the CMF segmentation task is performed by encoder-decoder fully-convolutional networks [13], the *Tiramisu* fully-convolutional network [8] (based on DenseNet [7]).

Leveraging these recent results, our work focuses on improving the network architecture by automatically modeling and identifying the most meaningful spatio-temporal features, in order to improve segmentation performance and enhance generalization capabilities to multiple CMF structures (e.g., mandible, sino-nasal cavity, pharyngeal airways, dental arch), while reducing the need of large annotated datasets.

To do this, we propose a model that consists of a 3D encoder that learns to extract volume features at different scales;

Features taken at different level of the encoder hierarchy are then sent to multiple 3D decoders that predict intermediate segmentation maps. Finally, all segmentation maps are combined to obtain a detailed segmentation mask.

Unlike classic encoder-decoder schemes with a single path of decoding, 4 decoders are used in parallel at different abstraction levels by using low-level and high-level features. The decoding hierarchical is also different from the skip connections present in the UNet architecture [19], as the latter have the purpose of facilitating the descent of the gradient and transmit the low-level features for the reconstruction of the output, while instead multiple decoders aim to extract local and global dependencies (Fig. 1).

The performance results of the models are compared with other models: MobileNet and S3D proposed in [17] and with U-Net (3D) (using both basic version and with residual layers version).

The remainder of the paper is as follows: in the Sect. 2 is reported the state of the art about segmentation model in medical domain. in the Sect. 3 the architecture of the proposed system is discussed. In the Sect. 4 an experimental results with details about dataset and metrics are shown. Finally, in the last section conclusion and future work are, presented.

2   Related Works

Before the advent of deep learning, CMF bone segmentation and landmarking were mainly addressed through atlas-guided methods [5,6], which however required a preliminary, and often not precise, registration step. Although these methods nominally report high accuracy on standard benchmarks, they fail in case of high variability in CT scans.

Deep learning has revolutionized the medical images analysis domain, although with several key differences from the general images domain, including the difficulty to train medical-purposed models due to the lack of large datasets of annotated data, which are, instead, easily obtainable in the case of natural images.

The U-Net architecture has played the leading role for anatomical structure segmentation. It generally consists of two processing paths: the *encoder* or *down-sampling path*, which aims at extracting the global context using a sequence of convolutional layers, and — symmetrically — the *decoder* or *upsampling path*, which, instead, employs transposed convolutions to recover the original image size, with skip connections between corresponding layers in the encoder and the decoder, for feature re-use and detailed reconstruction. Since its introduction, the original architecture was improved by: a) combining segmentation maps created at different scales [10], b) integrating 3D convolutions [22], c) devising new loss functions [21] and computing losses as different layers through deep supervision [20]. In order to reduce the difference between the aggregation of low-level visual features extracted by the encoder and high-level semantic concepts derived from the decoder, introduced a series of nested, dense skip pathways to connect the two sub-networks. In addition to changes to the basic U-NET architectures,

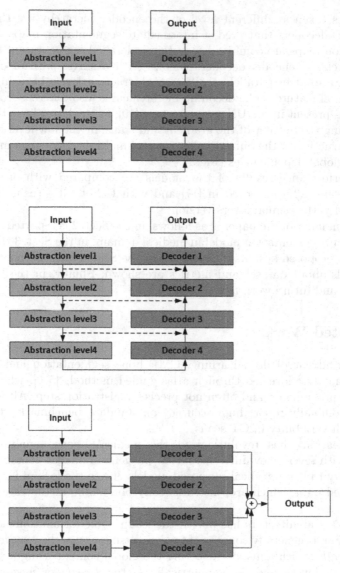

Fig. 1. Segmentation architecture comparison. Encoder-decoder(first), skip-connection (second), hierarchical decoding (last).

recurrent modules have increased the complexity of the models in order to capture the inter-slices spatial dependencies: recurrent GRU [16] or bi-directional Convolutional-LSTM (C-LSTM) [2] have been applied to the output of the bottleneck layer, to the feature maps produced by multiple decoding networks [3], or to all layers [1].

Usually the anatomical structures of the dental bones are segmented manually by medical experts, requiring a lot of time. Therefore, the automated segmentation of dental structures starting from CranioMaxillo-Facial scans, despite being a very demanding task, assumes a role fundamental in many clinical applications. In the literature there are several approaches that have been proposed in recent years for treat in the appropriate way the problems of the automated segmentation of dental structures from CT or CBCT scans. In [15] a convolutional network is proposed which combines the advantages of the Tiramisu encoder-decoder architecture, with squeeze-and-excitation blocks for the recalibration of the features, integrated with LSTM levels for modeling space-time correlations between consecutive sections.

In [11] a point-based network of tooth localization is proposed that is able to distinguish individual teeth based on a Gaussian objective function of dissolution, which performs a regression heatmap jointly with a box regression for all teeth.

In [4] a two-stage network is proposed, where in the first stage they are extracted the edges to improve the contrast of the image along the borders of the shape they are passed to the second stage, that is to a 3D RPN model with a matrix of similarity.

In [9] a robust algorithm based on morphological operators is proposed, which uses a marker-controlled watershed for teeth and a global threshold for it nail varnish.

In [14] a dense mixed-scale network is proposed for the segmentation of scans CBCT affected by metal artifacts, to which the masks of segmentation created by an experienced medical engineer who tried to remove the noise.

In [12] a convolutional network is proposed with preprocessing performed with a histogram-based method, and multiphase training using sub-volumes of different sizes and dense convolutional blocks.

In [18] a 3D convolutional network is proposed which obtains the distribution of probability from features, which is then redefined by a CRF algorithm that it removes redundant information making the results more accurate.

3 Segmentation Model

The proposed model is based on a hierarchical decoding, the downsampling path coincides with a single 3D encoder composed of four processing sub-levels that process the input data (i.e. CT scans) decreasing the spatial resolution of the image and the number of feature maps through a sequence of convolutional levels. For each encoding step, the features are sent to upsampling path with four 3D decoders to reconstruct a segmentation map. The four intermediate maps obtained are finally combined along the dimension of the channels and passed to a convolutional layer in order to obtain a detailed segmentation mask (Fig. 3).

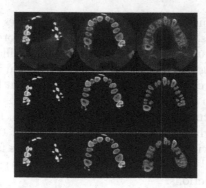

Fig. 2. Example of 3D semantic segmentation of dental crowns and roots.

4   Experimental Results

4.1   Dataset and Annotations

Our dataset includes 32 CT scans acquired with the patient's head in a natural position without perform any preprocessing.

Each CT scan was annotated by experts who tagged manually the different anatomical dental structures to identify the different ones regions in a segmented mask on each slice of the dataset. Each ground truth consists of two labels, where the 0 (black) label corresponds to the background, while label 1 (black) corresponds to the teeth, in this way became easy a comparison with segmentation results.

All images in the dataset have a size of 576×576 pixels (resized 128×128).

4.2   Split and Metrics

Dataset is split into two parts: CT images (32) are used for model training, selection and ablation studies; CBCT images (20 CT scans) are instead used for testing generalization capabilities. Among the CT images, we select 25 CT scans as training set and the remaining 7 CT scans as a validation set, which is employed to perform model selection through ablation studies.

For segmentation assessment, we adopt the standard Dice similarity coefficient (DSC), defined as follows:

$$DSC = \frac{2\sum_{i}^{N} p_i g_i}{\sum_{i}^{N} p_i^2 + \sum_{i}^{N} g_i^2} \tag{1}$$

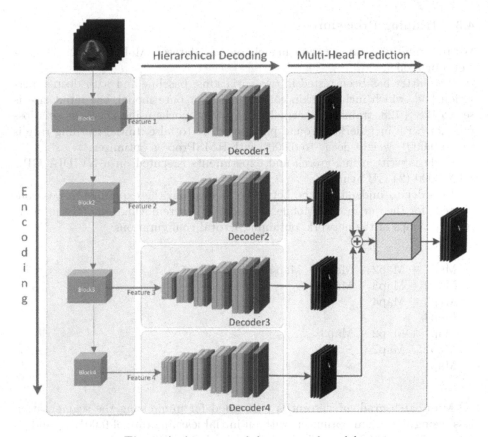

Fig. 3. Architecture of the proposed model.

where N is the number of pixels, while p_i and g_i are, respectively, the output computed by the model and the ground truth at pixel i.

For performance evaluation, commonly employed metrics for semantic segmentation are used. Accuracy, precision, recall and F1 score are computed according to their definition, by using true positives, true negatives, false positives and false negatives. More in detail:

$$Accuracy = \frac{TP + TN}{TP + FP + TN + FN}$$

$$Precision = \frac{TP}{TP + FP}$$

$$Recall = \frac{TP}{TP + FN}$$

$$F_1 = \frac{2 * Precision * Recall}{Precision + Recall} = \frac{2 * TP}{2 * TP + FP + FN}$$

4.3 Training Procedure

We test multiple segmentation models on our dataset: MobileNetV2, S3D, U-Net, our model.

The latter has been tested in two variations: baseline and with deep supervision [19], which includes skip connections. For oure model, the input size is set to 128 × 128, training is carried out for 500 epochs using DiceLoss as a loss function with includeBackground parameter set to false. Initial learning rate is set to 0.0001, weight decay to 0.0001 with RMSProp as optimizer.

Code is written in Pytorch and experiments executed on a NVIDIA GPU RTX 3090 (24 GB memory).

In order to understand the better configuration, the experiments was conducted (for the our model, MobileNet and S3d) by removing some of the intermediate maps of the network, obtaining 7 total configurations:

- Map1 + Map2 + Map3 + Map4 (full model)
- Map2 + Map3 + Map4
- Map3 + Map4
- Map4
- Map1 + Map2 + Map3
- Map1 + Map2
- Map1

Mini-batch gradient descent is performed for minimizing the segmentation loss, using the Adam optimizer, with an initial learning rate of 0.001, β_1 and β_2 set to 0.5 and 0.999, respectively, and a mini-batch size of 8.

Table 1. Performance MobileNetV2

	Maps 1,2,3,4	Maps 2,3,4	Maps 3,4	Maps 4	Maps 1,2,3	Maps 1,2	Maps 1
Epochs	500	500	500	500	500	500	500
Dice score	0,694	0,570	0,392	0,167	0,663	**0,7040**	0,688
Hausdorff distance	138,228	97,697	**70,077**	112,210	101,558	124,184	89,847
Sensitivity	**0,845**	0,739	0,510	0,318	0,764	0,793	0,791
Specificity	0,895	**0,899**	0,898	0,897	0,899	0,892	0,892
Accuracy	0,892	0,898	0,897	0,896	**0,899**	0,8992	0,899
Precision	0,595	0,469	0,299	0,111	0,610	**0,652**	0,624
F1-Score	0,698	0,571	0,374	0,163	0,675	**0,714**	0,698

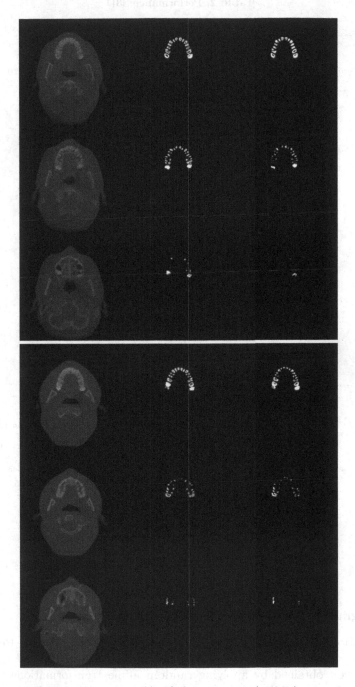

Fig. 4. Output segmentation maps: (left) input image, (middle) ground truth mask, (right) prediction mask.

Table 2. Performance S3D

	Maps 1,2,3,4	Maps 2,3,4	Maps 3,4	Maps 4	Maps 1,2,3	Maps 1,2	Maps 1
Epochs	500	500	500	500	500	500	500
Dice score	0,406	0,382	0,295	0,289	**0,535**	0,500	0,464
Hausdorff distance	97,454	19,762	86,253	181,42	16,891	**15,270**	175,671
Sensitivity	0,629	0,527	0,321	0,536	0,541	0,531	**0,693**
Specificity	0,898	0,898	0,898	0,897	0,899	0,899	0,898
Accuracy	0,897	0,898	0,897	0,896	**0,898**	0,897	0,898
Precision	0,290	0,323	0,236	0,204	**0,564**	0,484	0,360
F1-Score	0,396	0,399	0,271	0,291	**0,543**	0,501	0,468

Table 3. Performance U-Net3D

	No residual	Residual
Epochs	500	500
Dice score	0,702	**0,784**
Hausdorff distance	143,812	**109,838**
Sensitivity	**0,9111**	0,857
Specificity	0,898	**0,899**
Accuracy	0,895	**0,898**
Precision	0,601	**0,746**
F1-Score	0,722	**0,798**

Table 4. Performance Our model

	Maps 1,2,3,4	Maps 2,3,4	Maps 3,4	Maps 4	Maps 1,2,3	Maps 1,2	Maps 1
Epochs	1000	1000	1000	1000	1000	1000	1000
Dice score	**0,662**	0,564	0,511	0,363	0,474	0,386	0,326
Hausdorff distance	134,458	131,826	**130,804**	146,616	138,716	148,445	157,736
Sensitivity	0,760	0,772	0,810	0,699	0,866	**0,905**	0,701
Specificity	**0,899**	0,898	0,898	0,897	0,897	0,896	0,897
Accuracy	**0,899**	0,898	0,898	0,897	0,897	0,896	0,896
Precision	**0,584**	0,466	0,384	0,262	0,342	0,262	0,227
F1-Score	**0,656**	0,573	0,518	0,378	0,482	0,400	0,339

4.4   Segmentation Results

Segmentation accuracy is reported in terms of the Dice coefficient. Results are computed (with 5-fold cross-validation) in terms of pixel error and using data augmentation obtained by applying random affine transformations (rotation, translation, scaling and shearing) to input images. The obtained results are reported in Tables 2, 3, 4. As we can see from the values reported, use the full model equipped with all 4 intermediate encoding-decoding flows, not always warrant the best performance. The worst performance is almost always achieved when it is used only the last map, the reason is that the features that are extracted from the latter encoding step are at a very high level, causing the loss of most of the basic details.

Using MobileNet at the encoding level, the best configuration results is the one that only uses the first two maps. While using S3D instead at the encoding level, we have too many parameters, and the model overfitted with any learning rate after a few hundred epochs.

With U-Net we get better performance than just the two multi-scale models are mentioned, but there are many false positives in the slices where not there should be teeth. While in the particular case of the our network, the higher value Dice Score and the F1-Score comes after 500 epochs of training achieved when using all 4 maps. The Fig. 4, shown the segmentation results, in particular in the first column we have the input slice, in the middle column the ground truth and in the last column the prediction.

5 Conclusions

In this paper we propose a learning-based approach for automated segmentation. In particular, the segmentation network is based on hierarchical decoding, capable to obtain a detailed segmentation map by combine the results from the single decoding steps powered up from a 3D encoding. The architecture is inspired by U-Net but was modified to suit a multi-scale architecture based on hierarchical decoding and deep supervision mechanisms. Our model demonstrates quite high generalization skills, overtaking the performances offered by U-Net with residual levels or the multiscale network that uses MobileNet at the encoding level.

The combination of good generalization performance in segmentation proposed approach suitable for being used in the clinical practice.

References

1. Alom, M.Z., Yakopcic, C., Hasan, M., Taha, T.M., Asari, V.K.: Recurrent residual U-Net for medical image segmentation. J. Med. Imaging **6**(1), 1–16 (2019). https://doi.org/10.1117/1.JMI.6.1.014006
2. Bai, W., et al.: Recurrent neural networks for aortic image sequence segmentation with sparse annotations. In: Frangi, A.F., Schnabel, J.A., Davatzikos, C., Alberola-López, C., Fichtinger, G. (eds.) MICCAI 2018. LNCS, vol. 11073, pp. 586–594. Springer, Cham (2018). https://doi.org/10.1007/978-3-030-00937-3_67
3. Chen, J., Yang, L., Zhang, Y., Alber, M., Chen, D.Z.: Combining fully convolutional and recurrent neural networks for 3D biomedical image segmentation. In: NIPS (2016)
4. Cui, Z., Li, C., Wang, W.: ToothNet: automatic tooth instance segmentation and identification from cone beam CT images. In: Proceedings of the IEEE/CVF Conference on Computer Vision and Pattern Recognition, pp. 6368–6377 (2019)
5. Daisne, J.F., Blumhofer, A.: Atlas-based automatic segmentation of head and neck organs at risk and nodal target volumes: a clinical validation. Radiat. Oncol. **26**, 154 (2013)

6. Fritscher, K.D., Peroni, M., Zaffino, P., Spadea, M.F., Schubert, R., Sharp, G.: Automatic segmentation of head and neck ct images for radiotherapy treatment planning using multiple atlases, statistical appearance models, and geodesic active contours. Medical Phys. **41**, 051910 (2014)
7. Huang, G., Liu, Z., Van Der Maaten, L., Weinberger, K.Q.: Densely connected convolutional networks. In: CVPR, vol. 1, p. 3 (2017)
8. Jégou, S., Drozdzal, M., Vazquez, D., Romero, A., Bengio, Y.: The one hundred layers Tiramisu: Fully convolutional DenseNets for semantic segmentation. In: CVPRW 2017, pp. 1175–1183. IEEE (2017)
9. Kakehbaraei, S., Seyedarabi, H., Zenouz, A.T.: Dental segmentation in cone-beam computed tomography images using watershed and morphology operators. J. Med. Sig. Sensors **8**(2), 119 (2018)
10. Kayalibay, B., Jensen, G., van der Smagt, P.: CNN-based segmentation of medical imaging data. arXiv preprint arXiv:1701.03056 (2017)
11. Lee, J., Chung, M., Lee, M., Shin, Y.G.: Tooth instance segmentation from cone-beam CT images through point-based detection and Gaussian disentanglement. Multimedia Tools Appl. **81**(13), 18327–18342 (2022)
12. Lee, S., Woo, S., Yu, J., Seo, J., Lee, J., Lee, C.: Automated CNN-based tooth segmentation in cone-beam ct for dental implant planning. IEEE Access **8**, 50507–50518 (2020)
13. Long, J., Shelhamer, E., Darrell, T.: Fully convolutional networks for semantic segmentation. In: Proceedings of the IEEE Conference on Computer Vision and Pattern Recognition, pp. 3431–3440 (2015)
14. Minnema, J., et al.: Segmentation of dental cone-beam CT scans affected by metal artifacts using a mixed-scale dense convolutional neural network. Med. Phys. **46**(11), 5027–5035 (2019)
15. Murabito, F., et al.: Deep recurrent-convolutional model for automated segmentation of craniomaxillofacial CT scans. In: 2020 25th International Conference on Pattern Recognition (ICPR), pp. 9062–9067. IEEE (2021)
16. Poudel, R.P.K., Lamata, P., Montana, G.: Recurrent fully convolutional neural networks for multi-slice MRI cardiac segmentation. In: Zuluaga, M.A., Bhatia, K., Kainz, B., Moghari, M.H., Pace, D.F. (eds.) RAMBO/HVSMR -2016. LNCS, vol. 10129, pp. 83–94. Springer, Cham (2017). https://doi.org/10.1007/978-3-319-52280-7_8
17. Proietto Salanitri, F., Bellitto, G., Irmakci, I., Palazzo, S., Bagci, U., Spampinato, C.: Hierarchical 3D feature learning forpancreas segmentation. In: Lian, C., Cao, X., Rekik, I., Xu, X., Yan, P. (eds.) MLMI 2021. LNCS, vol. 12966, pp. 238–247. Springer, Cham (2021). https://doi.org/10.1007/978-3-030-87589-3_25
18. Rao, Y., et al.: Multi-feature fusion 3d-CNN for tooth segmentation. In: Twelfth International Conference on Graphics and Image Processing (ICGIP 2020), vol. 11720, p. 1172010. International Society for Optics and Photonics (2021)
19. Ronneberger, O., Fischer, P., Brox, T.: U-Net: convolutional networks for biomedical image segmentation. In: Navab, N., Hornegger, J., Wells, W.M., Frangi, A.F. (eds.) MICCAI 2015. LNCS, vol. 9351, pp. 234–241. Springer, Cham (2015). https://doi.org/10.1007/978-3-319-24574-4_28
20. Zhou, Z., Rahman Siddiquee, M.M., Tajbakhsh, N., Liang, J.: UNet++: A nested U-net architecture for medical image segmentation. In: Stoyanov, D., Stoyanov, et al. (eds.) DLMIA/ML-CDS -2018. LNCS, vol. 11045, pp. 3–11. Springer, Cham (2018). https://doi.org/10.1007/978-3-030-00889-5_1

21. Zhu, Q., Du, B., Turkbey, B., Choyke, P.L., Yan, P.: Deeply-supervised CNN for prostate segmentation. In: 2017 International Joint Conference on 184 Neural Networks (IJCNN), pp. 178–184. IEEE (2017)
22. Zhu, W., et al.: AnatomyNet: deep learning for fast and fully automated whole-volume segmentation of head and neck anatomy. Med. Phys. **46**(2), 576–589 (2019)

SARS-CoV-2 Induced Pneumonia Early Detection System Based on Chest X-Ray Images Analysis by Jacobian-Regularized Deep Network

Francesco Rundo[1]([envelope])[iD], Carmelo Pino[1][iD], Riccardo E. Sarpietro[1][iD],
and Concetto Spampinato[2][iD]

[1] STMicroelectronics ADG, R&D Power and Discretes, Catania, Italy
{francesco.rundo,carmelo.pino,riccardoemanuele.sarpietro}@st.com
[2] Università degli Studi di Catania DIEEI - PeRCeiVe Lab, Catania, Italy
cspampin@dieei.unict.it

Abstract. SARS-CoV-2 induced disease (Covid-19) was declared as a pandemic by the World Health Organization in March 2020. It was confirmed as severe disease which induces pneumonia followed by respiratory failure. Real-Time Polimerase Chain Reaction (RT-PCR) is the de-facto standard diagnosis for Covid-19 but due to the cost and processing-time it is inapplicable for large screening programs. By contrast, Chest X-Ray (CXR) imaging analysis offers a fast, sustainable and performing approach for the early detection of Covid-19 disease. The proposed solution consists of a novel end-to-end intelligent system for CXR analysis embedding lung segmentation and an innovative 2D-to-3D augmentation approach in order to provide a robust classification of input CXR as viral (no Covid-19 pneumonia), Covid-19 pneumonia and healthy subject. Furthermore, in order to make a robust classification process we have implemented a compensation mechanism for adversarial attacks phenomena on CXR images using Jacobian regularization techniques. The collected performance results confirmed the effectiveness of the designed pipeline.

Keywords: SARS-CoV-2 detection · Jacobian regularization · Deep network

1 Introduction

Real-Time Polimerase Chain Reaction (RT-PCR) is the standard medical approach for Covid-19 diagnosis but the poor economic sustainability, the technical detection times and the presence of a - although limited - percentage of false negatives make this system inefficient for mass screening [22]. On the other hand, less invasive and more sustainable techniques based on the analysis of medical images of subjects potentially affected by SARS-CoV-2 seem to find significant interest in the medical scientific community. Among these, Chest X-Ray (CXR) analysis is faster and cost effective and becomes particularly efficient when it is combined

J.-J. Rousseau and B. Kapralos (Eds.): ICPR 2022 Workshops, LNCS 13643, pp. 602–616, 2023.
https://doi.org/10.1007/978-3-031-37660-3_42

with the experience of examining radiologists or with the automatic processing performed by artificial intelligence algorithms (so-called Radiomics) [2].

The weakness and lack of disease-knowledge of the Covid-19 outbreak poorly supported the rapid evolution of the disease, leading to the collapse of global health systems towards the treatment of the most serious cases. Supporting data were limited and reflected in quality of the analysis through machine learning techniques that have been combined with the extraction of hand-crafted features [7]. Furthermore, often the data, even in sufficient quantity, turned out to be not very discriminating and affected by distortions, noise or other.

This paper handled the reduced size of discriminating data as well as the presence of noise and distortion in the imaging data collected by the various medical centers around the world, by implementing a novel end-to-end imaging pipeline embedding an innovative 2D-to-3D data augmentation block (instead of classical augmentation approaches) [2,11] including a spatio-temporal feature generator. Ad hoc Jacobian-regularization enhancement of the learning process will be applied in order to compensate the noise and distortion embedded in the input medical images [12]. As input images of the proposed pipeline, the authors propose the usage of chest X-Ray (CXR) of the subject to be analyzed.

Finally, the designed deep architecture has been deployed to an embedded system [6] using commercially available devices as a cost-effective Point-of-Care for disadvantaged areas of the world.

2   Related Works

Due to the growing application of Deep Learning approaches, this paper focused on methods for Covid-19 detection using CXR images. Traditional Deep learning architectures sometimes suffer from a limited availability of CXR images and this produces overfitting originated mainly by class imbalance [2].

In literature different approaches have been exploited. The authors tried to classify these approaches following a methodological criterion as follow.

- **"Transfer Learning" based solutions**. Transfer learning allows deep models previously trained on a different dataset (e.g. ImageNet or others) to leverage learned features to improve the performance of a new classification task (i.e. CXR Classification), this is the case of [11,14] which use a combination of state-of-the-art architecture with a downstream shallow classifier or [21] that uses ensemble of models to improve classification performance while [4] enhance the Sigmoid activation function to guarantee good classification in imbalanced dataset. Alternatively, instead of using pre-trained models some authors have preferred to pre-train their models on such CXR dataset and then performed ad-hoc fine-tuning of the pipeline to CXR Covid-19 assessment. Similar solutions have been proposed in [1] based on the usage of CapsuleNet or [23] based on the usage of Siamese deep architectures.
- **"Trained from scratch" based solutions**. Such authors have preferred to design their deep models to be trained from scratch (i.e. without any pre-training of the architecture). The developed deep models although based on

state-of-the-art architectures exploited a complete training on X-Ray images dataset to find discriminative features to be used for performing downstream classification. This is the case of [31] where two Convolutional Neural Networks were used to discriminate between Covid-19 and no-Covid-19 CXR image. The authors of [13] proposed a deep architecture optimization between network complexity accuracy maximization using Evolutionary Algorithms.

– **"End-to-End" based solutions**. The aforementioned Deep Learning approaches, both Transfer Learning or Pre-trained from scratch, showed solutions which processed the entire CXR images although Covid-19-induced pneumonia disease patterns are predominantly found in the lung parenchymas. Several studies confirmed that an end-to-end solution embedding a preliminary segmentationof the lung parenchymas of the CXR improve significantly the classification performances of deep classifier as reported in [25,29]. In these contributions the authors proposed an architecture based on U-NET for CXR lungs segmentation followed by a deep Covid-19 classifier previously pre-trained (transfer learning approach).

– **"X-Ray based imaging solutions with Adversarial-Attacks compensation"** As introduced, researchers have analyzed security vulnerabilities in deep learning based solutions to adversarial perturbations. In [15] the authors validated different Covid-19 diagnostic innovative approaches by adding adversarial perturbation. The collected outcomes confirmed that their developed deep learning systems remain significantly vulnerable to adversarial attacks. In [9] the authors studied the vulnerability issue of deep models used for performing advanced Covid-19 screening. Deep neural architectures are remarkably vulnerable to perturbation of the input data. As reported in [3] the CXR imaging have been used for properly assessment of the Covid-19 disease. Anyway a more accurate evaluation of the artificial intelligence based solutions confirmed that influence of adversarial attacks on deep model functionality leads to going wrong in most of the classification problems. In [9] the authors experimented and evaluated the performance of several deep architectures used to provide Covid-19 risk assessment against two types of adversarial attack: non targeted and targeted. The authors detected that the implemented deep models are highly vulnerable to adversarial attack. In [32] the authors analyzed both adversarial attacks and defense solutions in deep learning solutions. They proposed interesting compensation approaches for adversarial examples on deep models. In [12] the authors discovered a novel and robust algorithm to improve the networks' robustness on adversarial attacks. The implemented method applies regularization using the Frobenius norm of the Jacobian of the deep network, which is applied as post-processing, after regular training has finished. They validated the implemented approach confirming the effectiveness on adversarial compensation.

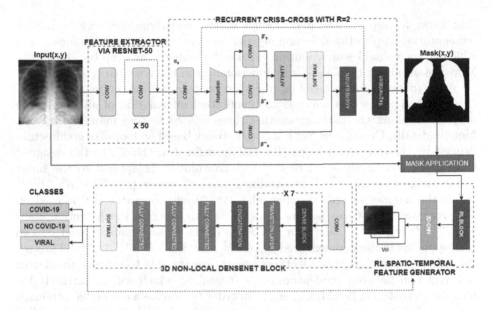

Fig. 1. The Proposed end-to-end deep pipeline

3 Proposed Architecture

The proposed architecture combining different stand-alone deep learning blocks enabling an end-to-end solution for SARS-CoV-2 early detection. The proposed solution embeds ad-hoc robust non local deep segmentation pipeline suitable to extract lungs from input CXR of the subject to be analyzed. The so generated segmented 2D images will be augmented with an innovative 2D-to-3D augmentation block which will generate a Volume of Interest (VOI) of augmentated features finally classified by a downstream Non-Local Dense Convolutional Neural Network. An overall representation of the proposed pipeline is reported in Fig. 1. Each block reported in the designed pipeline (Fig. 1) is going to be discussed separately in the next sections.

3.1 CXR Feature Extractor

A slightly modified implementation of ResNet-50 deep backbone removing down-sampling layers is used as feature extractor of the 224×224 CXR input images $I(x, y)$ of the subjects to be analyzed. The output of that deep model will be a feature maps α_s of size $H_s \times W_s$. That feature map will be fed as input of the Lung Segmentation block implemented in the Recurrent Criss-Cross block.

3.2 Recurrent Criss-Cross Block: The Lungs Segmentation

The Feature map α_s was fed to the designed Recurrent Criss-Cross deep model [10] generating an enhanced and more discriminative feature map β_s. Criss-Cross deep networks are architectures recently proposed in scientific literature that allow to improve the performance of the underlying network mainly in segmentation applications, leveraging the concept of "contextual information" which actually enables an attention mechanism embeds the deep backbone [10]. More details about the Criss-Cross functionality in the next paragraphs.

As introduced, the received input feature map α_s will be processed by Criss-Cross deep model which harvests the contextual information of all the feature map pixels along the path, generating three related feature maps β'_s, β''_s β'''_s. More in details, Criss-Cross Net is a deep network based on loop-like architecture defined by the number of loops (R) usually defined as "R=2". In the designed Criss-Cross Net firstly a set of two 1×1 convolution is applied to the input feature maps $\alpha_s \in R^{C \times W \times H}$ generating β'_s and β''_s where $\{\beta'_s, \beta''_s\} \in R^{C' \times W \times H}$ (C' is the number of reduced channels). An Affinity operator [10] is used on the processed Criss-Cross feature maps (β'_s, β''_s) to generate the Attention maps $\gamma \in R^{(H+W-1) \times (W \times H)}$. For each position v of the feature maps β'_s and β''_s two corresponding vectors are extraced $\beta'_{sv} \in R^{C'}$ and $\beta''_{sv} \in R^{(H+W-1) \times C'}$. Through the Affinity operator applied to those vectors we are able to retrieve the degree of correlation between the feature maps β'_s and β''_s which will be furtherly fed into the downstream SoftMax operator in order to provide a correlated attention map γ_s. Finally, another convolutional layer with a 1×1 kernel will be applied on the feature map α_s to generate the re-mapped feature $\vartheta \in R^{C \times W \times H}$ to be used for spatial adaptation. At each position v in the spatial dimension of ϑ, we can define a vector $\beta'''_{sv} \in R^C$. Finally, we define the Aggregation operator as a weighted sum of the collected feature maps in order to provide the so called "contextual information" for each pixel of the so processed feature maps.

$$H'_s = \sum_{i=0}^{H+W-1} A_M^{i,s} \gamma_{i,s} + \beta'''_{sv} \tag{1}$$

where $A_M^{i,s}$ is a learnable scalar factor while H'_s is a feature vector which will be added to the given input feature map α_s to augment the pixel-wise representation and aggregating context information. More detail about Criss-Cross Attention enhancement in [10]. At the end, the enhanced feature map will be fed as input to the Segmentation layer providing the segmentation mask $M(x,y)$ required to lung segmentation. $M(x,y)$ will be applied to the source input image $I(x,y)$ (through the 'Mask Application block') extracting only the lungs of the source CXR images. A bicubic resizing to 256×256 will be furtherly applied. The so enhanced and segmented lungs of the input CXR will be fed as input of the RL Spatio-Temporal Feature generator block.

3.3   The RL Spatio-Temporal Feature Generator Block

In order to improve the discriminative capability of the proposed solution as well as of the retrieved CXR based feature maps, (which usually bring to a misleading classification and accuracy of models) ad-hoc and innovative data augmentation technique has been designed. Specifically, the designed features generator block aims to generate discriminating feature from input segmented

CXR lungs through the usage of ad-hoc modified Cellular Nonlinear Networks architectures configured with a custom version of a reinforcement learning system. In details, the designed feature generator works with a grid of 2D Cellular Nonlinear Network cells (2D-CNN) where pixels of the segmented CXR lungs are fed as input and state of each 2D-CNN cell. The 2D-CNN we have implemented works in transient mode [17]. Each 2D-CNNs cell (pixel) is connected directly with its neighbors and can interact with them, with the exception of the cells that are outside the neighborhood. The transient dynamic evolution of the cell is defined by its initial state and the converged steady-state equilibrium which however will not be achieved as the designed 2D-CNN works in transient mode [20]. For the sake of mathematical modeling, the designed 2D-CNN can be presented as follow:

$$
\frac{dx_{ij}(t)}{dt} = -\frac{1}{\phi}x_{ij} + \sum_{Cell(k,l)\in N_r(i,j)} A_1(i,j;k,l)y_{kl}(t)+
$$

$$
+ \sum_{Cell(k,l)\in N_r(i,j)} A_2(i,j;k,l)u_{kl}(t) + \sum_{Cell(k,l)\in N_r(i,j)} A_3(i,j;k,l)x_{kl}(t)+
$$

$$
+ \sum_{Cell(k,l)\in N_r(i,j)} A_4(i,j;k,l)(x_{ij}(t),x_{kl}(t))+
$$

$$
+ \sum_{Cell(k,l)\in N_r(i,j)} D_1(i,j;k,l)(y_{ij}(t),y_{kl}(t))+
$$

$$
+ K_b
$$

$$
1 \leq i \leq M, 1 \leq j \leq N \tag{2}
$$

$$
y_{ij}(t) = \frac{1}{2}(|x_{ij}(t)+1| - |x_{ij}(t)-1|) \tag{3}
$$

$$
N_r(i,j) = \{Cell_r(k,l); (max(|k-i|,|i-j|) \leq r)\}
$$

$$
(1 \leq k \leq M, 1 \leq l \leq N) \tag{4}
$$

where x_{ij} is the state, u_{ij} is the input, $N_r(i,j)$ is the neighborhood of each cell $Cell(i,j)$ with a radius r. The 2D grid size of the 2D-CNN corresponds to the input CXR resolution 256×256 cells. The 2D-CNN output $y_{ij}(t)$ is computed as PWL processing of the state x_{ij} (see Eqs. (3)) while $A_i, i = 1..4$ and D_1 are the cloning templates suitable to configure the 2D-CNN which were arranged as a 3×3 matrices with a 1×1 K_b scalar defined as bias coefficient. Both the cloning templates and the bias will be randomly initialized. We have enhanced the previous 2D-CNN architecture designed to assess Covid-19 disease from CXR and reported in [17]. Specifically, we have added a new innovative cloning template A_4 which will be used to properly characterize the weighted correlation between the state of the neighboring cells. This further correlation allowed better performance in terms of Covid-19 disease classification as the generated augmented feature map seems more discriminative with respect to previous version [17].

The so designed spatio-temporal generator feature generator block embeds a Reinforcement Learning (RL) stage suitable to find the dynamic setup of the 2D-CNN model (specifically the coefficient of the cloning templates as well as the bias). By taking into consideration the computational cost to generate them, the authors implemented 32 different configurations of the 2D-CNN model (cloning templates coefficients and bias) in order to provide a 3D VOI of $32{\times}256{\times}256$ dimension. During the training of the downstream deep architecture, an embedded RL algorithm search an optimal configuration of the 2D-CNN cloning templates and biases for all the defined 32 configuration. The reward function associated to the RL algorithm is defined as follow:

$$R = -(\frac{\partial L(A_m^v(\cdot), D_1^v(\cdot), K_b^v(\cdot), \xi_v, v, t)}{\partial t})^2$$
$$m = 1, 2, 3, 4; v = 1, 2, ..., 32 \tag{5}$$

where $L(.)$ represents the loss of the downstream deep classifier (see next paragraph) which depends of the 2D-CNN configuration i.e. the coefficients of the cloning templates $A_m; m = 1, 2, 3, 4$ and biases K_b for each of the defined $v = 32$ setup. The variable ξ_v represents a binary mask [17]. More in detail, at each epoch the defined binary mask ξ_v is generated randomly as bit-stream of length 32. All the 2D-CNN setup corresponding to the bit set to 1 in the binary mask ξ_v will be selected and updated randomly (both cloning templates coefficients and biases). For each training epoch and 2D-CNN setup update as described, the loss $L(.)$ will be computed. If the so computed loss will be worse than the previous one, the corresponding 2D-CNN setup will be discarded otherwise it will be stored and will become the current 2D-CNN architecture setup. The so augmented feature map will be fed as input of the downstream deep classifier.

3.4   3D Non-Local DenseNet Block: The Deep Classifier

The final input CXR classification will be performed by the designed 3D Non-local DenseNet. More in details, the input augmented $32{\times}256{\times}256$ are fed into a $3{\times}3{\times}3$ convolution layer and then through a set of 7 Embedded Gaussian Non-local layers [30] followed by a densely connected and Transition layers. More details about the backbone configuration of the classifier, in Table 1. The implemented Dense layer is composed by a Batch Normalization and a ReLU activation function as well as by a $3{\times}3{\times}3$ depth-wise convolution followed by a point-wise $1{\times}1{\times}1$ convolution [19]. The transition layer is composed by a $1{\times}1{\times}1$ convolution and a $2{\times}2{\times}2$ Max pooling operator. The Non-local blocks are suitable to exploit hierarchically deep dependencies and correlation along the backbone, weighting feature maps as a custom self-attention mechanism. Non-local blocks was firstly introduced by [30]. The Non-Local attention processing can be defined as follow: given as input the feature map x from the $s - th$ densely connected block α_s, the output of the Non-local block β_s at location s is the weighted sum of all the input data within the all position $r \neq s$:

Table 1. The Non-Local deep backbone specification

Block	Output Size	Layer(s) Description	Layers Numbers
Convolution	$32 \times 16 \times 256 \times 256$	$3 \times 3 \times 3$ conv.	1
Dense Block	$128 \times 16 \times 256 \times 256$	Batch Normalization ReLU $3 \times 3 \times 3$ depth-wise conv. $1 \times 1 \times 1$ point-wise conv.	6
Transition Layer	$128 \times 8 \times 128 \times 128$	$1 \times 1 \times 1$ conv. $2 \times 2 \times 2$ maxpool	1
Dense Block	$256 \times 8 \times 64 \times 64$	[...]	8
Transition Layer	$256 \times 4 \times 32 \times 32$	$1 \times 1 \times 1$ conv. $2 \times 2 \times 2$ maxpool	1
Dense Block	$384 \times 4 \times 32 \times 32$	[...]	8
Transition Layer	$384 \times 2 \times 16 \times 16$	$1 \times 1 \times 1$ conv. $2 \times 2 \times 2$ maxpool	1
Dense Block	$512 \times 2 \times 16 \times 16$	[...]	8
Transition Layer	$512 \times 1 \times 8 \times 8$	$1 \times 1 \times 1$ conv. $2 \times 2 \times 2$ maxpool	1
Dense Block	$640 \times 1 \times 8 \times 8$	[...]	8
Transition Layer	$640 \times 1 \times 4 \times 4$	$1 \times 1 \times 1$ conv. $2 \times 2 \times 2$ maxpool	1
Dense Block	$736 \times 1 \times 4 \times 4$	[...]	8
Transition Layer	$768 \times 1 \times 2 \times 2$	$1 \times 1 \times 1$ conv. $2 \times 2 \times 2$ maxpool	1
Dense Block	$864 \times 1 \times 2 \times 2$	[...]	6
Transition Layer	$864 \times 1 \times 1 \times 1$	$1 \times 1 \times 1$ conv. $2 \times 2 \times 2$ maxpool	1
Fully Connected	350	FC, ReLU	1
Fully Connected	250	FC, ReLU	1
Fully Connected	250	FC, ReLU	1
Classification	2	FC, Softmax	1

$$\beta_s = \frac{1}{\theta(\alpha)} \sum_{\forall r} \phi(x_s, \ x_r)\eta(x_r) \qquad (6)$$

where the function $\phi(.)$ defines the relationship of data spatial positions r and s while η represents a non-linear function modulating ϕ according to input data. The whole computation is then normalized by θ. The parameters for performing Non-Local computation will be learned and configured in the Embedded Gaussian setup as described in [30]. At the end of the implemented deep network, there is a stack embedding three fully connected layers followed by ReLU activation function and lastly a SoftMax operator to discriminate input CXR in three different classes i.e. "Covid-19 induced pneumonia **[COVID-19 class]**", "No-Covid-19 healthy subject **[NO COVID-19 class]**" and "Viral (No Covid-19) or Bacterical pneumonia **[VIRAL class]**". More details about the designed deep architecture in Table 1.

3.5   The Adversarial Compensation: Jacobian Regularization

As introduced, the authors have integrated the proposed pipeline with a mechanism to compensate [9,15,32] a possible adversarial attack problem due to the presence of intrinsic noise in the CXR images. Such noise leads with imaging device, the CXR digitization process, a voluntary adversarial attack, or acquisition distortions. Among the different approaches cited in the scientific literature, the authors implemented the method based on the regularization of the Jacobian associated with the Non-Local DenseNet used as downstream classifier [12]. Basically, we have checked if the designed Non-Local deep classifier can be susceptible to a adversarial phenomenas where very small changes to an input CXR can cause it to be misclassified. As reported in [9,15] these changes are often imperceptible to humans. Concretely, consider a the designed Covid-19 supervised assessment modeled by the implemented Non-Local Deep Network trained with the classical SGD approach. At each iteration, a mini-batch β consists of a set of labeled examples $(I_a(x,y), C_a)$ where C_a is the label of input image $I_a(x,y)$. Those example were used to optimize the loss ℓ_{JR} in the field of network parameters ψ which we have enhanced with a factor related to jacobian, as follow:

$$\ell^{\beta}_{JR}(I_a(x,y), C_a, \psi)_{a \in \beta} = \ell(I_a(x,y), C_a, \psi)_{a \in \beta} +$$

$$+ \frac{\xi_{JR}}{2} \left[\frac{1}{|\beta|} \sum_{a \in \beta} ||J(I_a(x,y))||^2_F \right] \tag{7}$$

where ξ_{JR} is a learnable hyper-parameter to weight the Jacobian regularization process while $\ell(.)$ is the classic loss of the deep model, $J(.)$ is the Jacobian matrix of the Non-Local deep network and $||.||_F$ is the Frobenius norm. By minimizing the joint loss ℓ^{β}_{JR} with a properly chosen ξ_{JR}, we expected the deep model to learn both correctly and robustly compensating the adversarial distortion embedded in the input CXR images. More details about the Jacobian regularization model can be found in [12]. Considering that, the Jacobian can be expensive to compute, (it requires such backward passes through the network during the training) such authors proposed an approximation method [8].

4   Experiment Results

This section will describe and report the collected experimental results related to the validation of the proposed pipeline on a large CXR dataset by integrating benchmarks against other deep models in order to provide enough elements of comparison.

4.1   Dataset

The testing and validation sessions have been done on the "COVID-QU-Ex dataset" which consists of 33.920 chest X-ray (CXR) images including: 11.956

COVID-19 CXR images, 11.263 Non-COVID infections (Viral or Bacterial Pneumonia), and 10.701 Normal CXR images (healthy subjects without pneumonia). Ground-truth lung segmentation masks are provided for the entire dataset [5,16,26,27].

4.2 Training Details

The input CXR images have been resized and fed as input to the Criss-Cross based blocks which segmented the images extracting the lungs. The training phase of that sub-pipeline consisted of 200 epochs of SGD optimized learning with a learning rate of $1e-4$ and dropout of 10%. After the lungs were segmented from input CXR image, the resized output (256×256) will be fed into the RL Spatio-Temporal Feature Generator block for performing the RL-driven augmentation with associated classification made by the downstream 3D Non-local DenseNet. We trained the designed pipeline with 1200 SGD optimized epochs with a mini-bath of 10 samples and a learning rate of $1e-4$. During the classification of the input CXR images, we have emulated adversarial attacks by adding gaussian noise to the input CXR images and checking the classification rate of the implemented deep network with and without the jacobian regularization block as previously described. All the training sessions have been executed on a SERVER MultiCores INTEL with RTX 3080 GPU having 48 Gbyte of memory video.

In order to train and test the proposed full pipeline, we have splitted the input dataset as follow: 70 % for training (8369 images of COVID-19 class; 7884 of VIRAL class; 7491 of No-COVID-19 class) and the remaining 30 % for validation and testing of the deep pipeline. Moreover, we have tested the released system both with augmentation performed by the RL features generator block and with classical augmentation methods. Finally, we have validated the improvement of the proposed pipeline with respect to our previous solution reported in [17]. A k-fold (k=5) cross validation has been applied on test-set.

4.3 Performance Results

In order to provide a robust benchmarking of the proposed approach, such common metrics have been used: Accuracy, Sensitivity and Specificity as shown in the following tables. In Table 2, we reported the compared performance of the proposed pipeline against such other deep architectures both leveraging the designed RL spatio-temporal features generator (as augmentation method) and without that block (by classical augmentation method). In Table 3 we reported a benchmark comparison between same deep architectures with respect to their ability to classify the input CXR with and without a Jacobian regularization applied to the training phase. As shown in the mentioned Tables, our proposed architecture outperformed the compared ones. The determining role of the features generator system based on 2D-CNN is showed from the comparisons reported in

Table 2. Performance Benchmark (in %) for CXR based Covid-19 Assessment (three classes)

Schemes	Models	Accuracy	Sensitivity	Specificity
w/o Augmentation	SqueezeNet	94.85	96.93	95.62
	MobileNetv2	92.86	94.73	93.33
	ResNet-18	95.51	96.95	96.67
	InceptionV3	92.76	94.03	93.85
	ResNet-101	96.84	98.01	97.11
	DenseNet-201	97.04	97.12	96.90
	VGG-19	95.17	96.10	94.75
With Augmentation	SqueezeNet	95.10	94.85	96.01
	MobileNetv2	94.22	95.25	94.82
	ResNet-18	96.94	96.98	96.90
	InceptionV3	93.17	94.01	93.50
	ResNet-101	96.95	98.72	97.50
	DenseNet-201	97.89	97.85	97.94
	VGG-19	96.30	96.35	96.25
	Previous [24]	98.32	98.69	97.95
	Proposed	**98.76**	**98.95**	**99.40**

Table 2 which confirm a significant increase in performance of all the deep backbones tested including the proposed one. The latter outperforms the previous architectures thus confirming the effectiveness of the implementing method.

As scheduled, we have tested and compared the proposed pipeline by emulating an adversarial attack on the input dataset. Specifically, we have added a Gaussian noise to the input CXR images before to be fed to the input of the deep network to be tested as classifier (three class classification as per Fig. 1). In Tables 3 and 4, we have reported the results comparing the designed pipeline against the best performing architectures according to Table 2 data, namely ResNet-101, DenseNet-201 and the previous version of our pipeline. We have tested the performance also foreseeing the application of the Jacobian regularization to the comparable architectures.

Table 3. Performance Benchmark (in %) against Adversarial Attacks of the input dataset (without JR)

Models	Accuracy	Sensitivity	Specificity
DenseNet-201 w/o JR	84.23	82.25	86.96
ResNet-101 w/o JR	83.41	83.51	84.22
Previous w/o JR [24]	86.96	87.01	86.48
Proposed with JR	**96.30**	**95.52**	**96.82**

In Table 3 were reported the benchmark comparison of the implemented pipeline against the others by emulating the adversarial attack of the input CXR dataset. As confirmed, the compared architectures tested without Jacobian Regularization (w/o JR) dropped significantly in performance (see the same results reported in Table 2). For instance, the DenseNet-201 dropped in sensitivity (from previous 97.85% to 82.25%), specificity (from 97.94% to 86.96%) while the proposed pipeline maintains in average an excellent level of performance with a decrease within the limits of the acceptability range (Accuracy dropped from 98.76% to 96.30%). The same performance benchmarks have been extended to the same architecture but with Jacobian Regularization (with JR). The results have been reported in the following Table 4. Although there is a significant increase in performance in the comparison architectures, our pipeline continues to outperform the others thus confirming the effectiveness of the underlying methodology.

Table 4. Performance Benchmark (in %) against Adversarial Attacks of the input dataset (with JR)

Models	Accuracy	Sensitivity	Specificity
DenseNet-201 with JR	93.37	93.71	94.12
ResNet-101 with JR	92.96	94.51	93.01
Previous with JR [24]	94.22	95.36	94.62
Proposed with JR	**96.30**	**95.52**	**96.82**

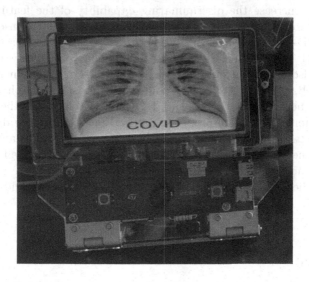

Fig. 2. The proposed Point-of-Care embedded system

4.4   Embedded CXR Point-of-Care

To complete the designed pipeline, we are deploying the developed full pipeli-jne into an hybrid embedded system resulting in a stand-alone Point of Care to be used for Covid-19 early assessment from CXR. The designed embedded system consists of a NVIDIA Jetson TX2 platform connected with an STA1295 Accordo5 Dual ARM A7 with GFX accelerator [24] (shown in Fig. 2) delivered by STMIcroelectronics and embedding a graphic accelerator for this kind of applications. As shown in Fig. 2, the display of the STA1295 board will show in few secs (average response time: 20 secs to retrieve a CXR classification) the classification results of the input CXR.

5   Conclusion and Discussion

The target of the proposed pipeline is to deliver a practical and efficient system to Covid-19 early diagnosis also including a differential diagnosis of the induced pneumonia. At the same time we have implemented a method that was sustainable for mass screening of the population avoiding the problems of costs and exposure to ionizing radiation that instead present the classic methods based on RT-PCR and CT-scan. For this reason we have developed a pipeline that highlights high performance in classification based on CXR images that can be easily extended to the entire population worldwide. Besides this, foreseeing adversarial attack problems of CXR images due both to the presence of intrinsic noise in the images and to voluntary attacks, we have designed a compensation approach of the adversarial distortion through a Jacobian regularization technique. To increase the discriminating capability of the features extracted from the previously segmented CXR image, we implemented an extended version of the 2D-CNN-based features generator block already used in previous applications [17]. Therefore, the proposed pipeline is placed on end-to-end systems which also include attention mechanisms both in the segmentation phase of the lung lobes (Criss-Cross layers) and in the classification phase (Non-local Blocks). The performance reported in Tables II-IV highlights the effectiveness and high performance of the proposed method on a large-scale dataset and in adversarial attacks conditions. Both the excellent performance and the current deploying of the full pipeline on a hybrid embedded system make this system an excellent diagnostic tool for physicians and radiologists. Future works aims to integrate further discriminative features also by using such hand-crafted landmarks [18,28].

References

1. Afshar, P., Heidarian, S., Naderkhani, F., Oikonomou, A., Plataniotis, K.N., Mohammadi, A.: COVID-CAPS: a capsule network-based framework for identification of COVID-19 cases from x-ray images. Pattern Recogn. Lett. **138**, 638–643 (2020)

2. Alghamdi, H.S., Amoudi, G., Elhag, S., Saeedi, K., Nasser, J.: Deep learning approaches for detecting COVID-19 from chest X-ray images: a survey. IEEE Access **9**, 20235–20254 (2021)
3. Basu, S., Mitra, S., Saha, N.: Deep learning for screening COVID-19 using chest x-ray images. In: 2020 IEEE Symposium Series on Computational Intelligence (SSCI), pp. 2521–2527 (2020)
4. Bridge, J., Meng, Y., Zhao, Y., Du, Y., Zhao, M., Sun, R., Zheng, Y.: Introducing the GEV activation function for highly unbalanced data to develop COVID-19 diagnostic models. IEEE J. Biomed. Health Inform. **24**(10), 2776–2786 (2020)
5. Chowdhury, M.E.H., et al.: Can AI help in screening viral and COVID-19 pneumonia? IEEE Access **8**, 132665–132676 (2020)
6. Florea, A., Fleaca, V.: Implementing an embedded system to identify possible COVID-19 suspects using thermovision cameras. In: 2020 24th International Conference on System Theory, Control and Computing (ICSTCC), pp. 322–327. IEEE (2020)
7. Genovese, A., Hosseini, M.S., Piuri, V., Plataniotis, K.N., Scotti, F.: Acute Lymphoblastic Leukemia detection based on adaptive unsharpening and Deep Learning. In: Proceedings of the 2021 IEEE International Conference on Acoustics, Speech and Signal Processing (ICASSP), pp. 1205–1209. IEEE (2021)
8. Goodfellow, I.J., Shlens, J., Szegedy, C.: Explaining and harnessing adversarial examples. arXiv:1412.6572 (2021)
9. Hoque, M.A., Haque, S., Debnath, S.K., Ahiduzzaman, M.: Investigating the robustness of deep neural network based COVID-19 detection models against universal adversarial attacks. In: 2021 3rd International Conference on Sustainable Technologies for Industry 4.0 (STI), pp. 1–6. IEEE (2021)
10. Huang, Z., Wang, X., Wei, Y., Huang, L., Shi, H., Liu, W., Huang, T.S.: CCNet: Criss-cross attention for semantic segmentation. IEEE Trans. on Pattern Analysis and Machine Intelligence (2020)
11. Ismael, A.M., Şengür, A.: Deep learning approaches for COVID-19 detection based on chest x-ray images. Expert Syst. Appl. **164**, 114054 (2021)
12. Jakubovitz, D., Giryes, R.: Improving DNN robustness to adversarial attacks using jacobian regularization. CoRR abs/1803.08680 (2018)
13. Louati, H., Bechikh, S., Louati, A., Hung, C.C., Ben Said, L.: Deep convolutional neural network architecture design as a bi-level optimization problem. Neurocomputing **439**, 44–62 (2021)
14. Ohata, E.F., et al.: Automatic detection of COVID-19 infection using chest X-ray images through transfer learning. IEEE/CAA J. Automatica Sinica **8**(1), 239–248 (2021)
15. Rahman, A., Hossain, M.S., Alrajeh, N.A., Alsolami, F.: Adversarial examples-security threats to COVID-19 deep learning systems in medical IoT devices. IEEE Internet Things J. **8**(12), 9603–9610 (2021)
16. Rahman, T., et al.: Exploring the effect of image enhancement techniques on COVID-19 detection using chest x-rays images. https://arxiv.org/abs/2012.02238 (2020)
17. Rundo, F., Genovese, A., Leotta, R., Scotti, F., Piuri, V., Battiato, S.: Advanced 3D deep non-local embedded system for self-augmented x-ray-based COVID-19 assessment. In: Proceedings of the IEEE/CVF International Conference on Computer Vision, pp. 423–432 (2021)
18. Rundo, F., Spampinato, C., Conoci, S.: Ad-hoc shallow neural network to learn hyper filtered photoplethysmographic (ppg) signal for efficient car-driver drowsiness monitoring. MDPI Electron. **8**, 890 (2019)

19. Rundo, F., Banna, G.L., Prezzavento, L., Trenta, F., Conoci, S., Battiato, S.: 3D non-local neural network: a non-invasive biomarker for immunotherapy treatment outcome prediction. case-study: metastatic urothelial carcinoma. J. Imaging **6**(12), 133 (2020)

20. Rundo, F., et al.: Advanced non-linear generative model with a deep classifier for immunotherapy outcome prediction: a bladder cancer case study. In: Del Bimbo, A., et al. (eds.) ICPR 2021. LNCS, vol. 12661, pp. 227–242. Springer, Cham (2021). https://doi.org/10.1007/978-3-030-68763-2_17

21. Shamsi, A., et al.: An uncertainty-aware transfer learning-based framework for COVID-19 diagnosis. IEEE Trans. Neural Networks Learn. Syst. **32**(4), 1408–1417 (2021)

22. Shi, F., et al.: Review of artificial intelligence techniques in imaging data acquisition, segmentation, and diagnosis for COVID-19. IEEE Rev. Biomed. Eng. **14**, 4–15 (2021)

23. Shorfuzzaman, M., Hossain, M.S.: MetaCOVID: a siamese neural network framework with contrastive loss for n-shot diagnosis of COVID-19 patients. Pattern Recogn. **113**, 107700 (2021)

24. STMicroelectronics: STMicroelectronics ACCORDO 5 Automotive Microcontroller. https://www.st.com/en/automotive-infotainment-and-telematics/sta1295. html (2018)

25. Tabik, S., et al.: COVIDGR dataset and COVID-SDNet methodology for predicting COVID-19 based on chest x-ray images. IEEE J. Biomed. Health Inf. **24**(12), 3595–3605 (2020)

26. Tahir, A.M., et al.: COVID-QU-Ex. Kaggle (2021)

27. Tahir, A.M., et al.: COVID-19 infection localization and severity grading from chest x-ray images. Comput. Biol. Med. **139**, 105002 (2021)

28. Trenta, F., Conoci, S., Rundo, F., Battiato, S.: Advanced motion-tracking system with multi-layers deep learning framework for innovative car-driver drowsiness monitoring. In: 2019 14th IEEE International Conference on Automatic Face Gesture Recognition (FG 2019), pp. 1–5. IEEE (2019)

29. Vidal, P.L., de Moura, J., Novo, J., Ortega, M.: Multi-stage transfer learning for lung segmentation using portable x-ray devices for patients with COVID-19. Expert Syst. Appl. **173**, 114677 (2021)

30. Wang, X., Girshick, R., Gupta, A., He, K.: Non-local neural networks. In: 2018 IEEE/CVF CVPR, pp. 7794–7803. IEEE (2018)

31. Wang, Z., et al.: Automatically discriminating and localizing COVID-19 from community-acquired pneumonia on chest x-rays. Pattern Recogn. **110**, 107613 (2021)

32. Yuan, X., He, P., Zhu, Q., Li, X.: Adversarial examples: attacks and defenses for deep learning. IEEE Trans. Neural Networks Learn. Syst. **30**(9), 2805–2824 (2019)

SERCNN: Stacked Embedding Recurrent Convolutional Neural Network in Detecting Depression on Twitter

Heng Ee Tay(✉)[ID], Mei Kuan Lim[ID], and Chun Yong Chong[ID]

Monash University Malaysia, 47500 Selangor, Malaysia
{Heng.Tay,Lim.MeiKuan,Chong.ChunYong}@monash.edu

Abstract. Conventional approaches to identify depression are not scalable and the public has limited awareness of mental health, especially in developing countries. As evident by recent studies, social media has the potential to complement mental health screening on a greater scale. The vast amount of first-person narrative posts in chronological order can provide insights into one's thoughts, feelings, behavior, or mood for some time, enabling a better understanding of depression symptoms reflected in the online space. In this paper, we propose SERCNN, which improves the user representation by (1) stacking two pretrained embeddings from different domains and (2) reintroducing the embedding context to the MLP classifier. Our SERCNN shows great performance over state-of-the-art and other baselines, achieving 93.7% accuracy in a 5-fold cross-validation setting. Since not all users share the same level of online activity, we introduced the concept of a fixed observation window that quantifies the observation period in a predefined number of posts. With as minimal as 10 posts per user, SERCNN performed exceptionally well with an 87% accuracy, which is on par with the BERT model, while having 98% less in the number of parameters. Our findings open up a promising direction for detecting depression on social media with a smaller number of posts for inference, toward creating solutions for a cost-effective and timely intervention. We hope that our work can bring this research area closer to real-world adoption in existing clinical practice.

Keywords: Depression detection · Social media · Deep learning

1 Introduction

Depression is a serious, yet common mental disorder that affects more than 264 million people worldwide. The number is projected to grow amid the war against the pandemic of COVID-19. Unlike the usual mood fluctuations and emotional responses, long-lasting sadness, emptiness, or irritation in one's day-to-day life is usually accompanied by somatic and cognitive changes that heavily disrupt an individual's functioning capacity. Hence, depression is often associated with

© Springer Nature Switzerland AG 2023
J.-J. Rousseau and B. Kapralos (Eds.): ICPR 2022 Workshops, LNCS 13643, pp. 617–631, 2023.
https://doi.org/10.1007/978-3-031-37660-3_43

suicide at its worst. In the latest Word Health Statistics 2021 [25], there is a 28% increase in the suicide rate in the United States in this period.

Often, people who suffer from depression tend to be unaware of their mental condition, as there is no specific feedback from the body, like common physical injuries do. Furthermore, existing depression screening approaches through self-reporting questionnaires and clinical interviews are expensive and not scalable. Currently, many countries, especially developing countries, are suffering from a shortage of provisions and services to identify, support, and treat mental health issues. Therefore, there is a dire need to promote mental health awareness and create technologies to help complement existing screening or diagnosis approaches to help reach a wider community. Patients are required to disclose truthful information during clinical interviews [1]. Until now, global provision and services to identify, support, and treat mental health problems are insufficient despite the disruption of essential health services, community mistrust, and fears of COVID-19 infections.

Meanwhile, social media has become part and parcel of everyday life. The availability of a large volume of data has motivated research to utilize social media data for depression detection. Social media data can serve as a life log that records user activities in text, image, audio, or video. In addition, the enormous amount of first-person narrative posts can provide insight into one's thoughts, behavior, or mood in the temporal dimension.

Previous studies have demonstrated the great potential of social media posts in detecting mental disorders, such as depression [4,11,16], anxiety [7,10], and eating disorders [26]. In existing depression diagnostics using DSM-5 [1], a 14-day observation period is required. However, using machine learning-based models, Hu et al. [12] and Tsugawa et al. [22] have suggested that two months of posting data are used to detect depression. Lately, Shen et al. [20] have constructed a depression dataset from users' one-month posting history. Shen et al. [20] and Gui et al. [8,9] have demonstrated that a single month of posting history is sufficient to classify depression online. However, there is still a lack of evidence on the number of posts required for efficient and cost-effective detection in the online space.

In this paper, we propose SERCNN - Stacked Embedding Recurrent Convolutional Neural Network, to perform early depression detection based on their one-month social media posts. Our SERCNN improves the overall user representations in two ways: (1) stacking representation vectors from pretrained embeddings from both the general and social media domains and (2) allowing the MLP classifier to exploit the context by co-learning the CNN context with the recurrence of the embedding context. We also trained SERCNN on different lengths of posting history measured in the number of posts (fixed observation windows) to offer a unique perspective on optimizing the amount of data required for early depression detection. We further assessed the robustness of the observation window by comparing the performance differences trained on the subsets extracted from the earliest (head) and latest (tail) of a user-posting history. Despite having a fraction of the BERT [5] classifier's size (in terms of the number of parameters), SERCNN is on par, if not better than our BERT baseline, confirming that depression can be identified even if we have only 10 posts for a given user. This discovery sheds light on the adoption of social media analytics to complement existing clinical screening practices without a substantial investment in computational resources.

The contributions of this paper can be summarized below:

1. We show that it is possible to improve the feature representation of social media text by stacking features from two low-dimensional pretrained embeddings. As a result, the number of feature dimensions is also reduced.
2. We propose the concept of a fixed observation window that quantifies the observation period in a predefined number of posts and provide insights into the potential for early depression detection using the observation window with SERCNN.
3. We highlight the performance and advantage of SERCNN over the fine-tuned BERT classifier in early depression detection for its fraction of BERT's size in terms of number of parameters.

The rest of the paper is organized as follows: Sect. 2 covers the related work in this domain and Sect. 3 describes the problem statement and motivation of this research. The dataset used in the experiments is elaborated in Sect. 4 and the proposed method is discussed in Sect. 5. In Sect. 6, we present the experiment settings and discuss the experimental results in Sect. 7. Finally, Sect. 8 summarizes the main findings of this work and some perspectives for future research.

2   Related Work

Various natural language processing (NLP) techniques have been applied to extract relevant features from social media data. Modeling feature representations is a crucial task in machine learning; features that are not discriminative will result in poor and faulty model performance. Hence, earlier research works are mainly focused on feature extraction techniques. Choudhury et al. [3] and Tsugawa et al. [22] have found that depressed users tend to be emotional. [23] have found that using sentiment analysis in depression detection can achieve about 80% accuracy. Resnik et al. [18] extracted topics distribution with Latent Dirichlet Allocation (LDA) [2] to differentiate depressed individuals from the healthy controls. Researchers have also extracted features based on the industry standard, the Diagnostic and Statistical Manual of Mental Disorders (DSM), such as the insomnia index derived from the user posting time [20]. Linguistic Inquiry and Word Count (LIWC) [21] is a widely used word matching-based feature extraction tool that builds on top of previous findings [6, 19] discovered decades ago. Both Choudhury et al. [3, 20] found that depressed users tend to have a high focus on self-attention, increased medical concerns, and increased expression of religious thoughts. These findings are consistent with previous work [19], in which depressive indicators are identifiable from human-generated content. Furthermore, Shen et al. [20] have also attempted to identify sparse features of their multimodal handcrafted features with dictionary learning. Their studies have discovered that depressed users tend to post tweets at midnight, which could be a result of insomnia. Furthermore, depressed users tend to use emotional words and depression-related terms (antidepressants and symptoms) more often than the controls.

However, the aforementioned feature extraction approaches are often ineffective due to the nature of noisy and unstructured social media text. An extensive data cleaning and preprocessing are required for the feature extraction to work as intended. Recent advancements in deep learning have shown its robustness without needing manual annotation and label supervision. Word embedding approaches are introduced to learn disentangled representations by learning a mapping function that takes all the embeddings as input and outputs a compact representation of the words. Deep neural networks, such as the recurrent neural network (RNN) and convolutional neural network (CNN) [13], can further leverage and exploit these disentangled text representations to reach to state-of-the-art performance. The learned representation can be used as a discriminative classifier for downstream tasks. With the policy gradient agent implemented alongside, authors in [8] have leveraged word embedding learned from the depression dataset and deep learning models (RNN and CNN) to achieve state-of-the-art depression detection results. These works have shown that deep learning models can outperform shallow models in accuracy and sensitivity with minimal preprocessing effort.

3   Problem Statement and Motivation

Depression in developing countries has always been under-addressed. Many NGOs, local governments, and clinics in these countries do not have ample computing power resources to train and deploy a fully automated screening model that utilizes cutting-edge deep learning, such as BERT. Therefore, there is a dire need for a cost-effective, efficient, and robust early depression detection solution.

4   Depression Dataset

We train and evaluate our proposed method using the Shen Depression Dataset [20], D, which comprises two labeled user groups: (D_1) self-declared depressed users and (D_2) controls. We formed a balanced dataset by drawing 1,401 samples from D_1 and D_2, resulting in 2,802 samples and 1.35 million posts made within a month to eliminate bias in our results which may be caused by an imbalanced dataset. On average, a depressed user tends to post lesser at 165 posts as compared to 799 posts for the control user. An overview of the dataset is presented in Table 1.

We have also performed a statistical analysis on the dataset to better understand how the majority of the users behave online in terms of the posting frequency, which is displayed in Table 2. We can observe that 75% of the users in

Table 1. Overview of the dataset

Dataset	Number of users	Number of posts	Average posts
D_1 Depressed	1,401	231,494	165
D_2 Controls	1,401	1,119,080	799
D ($D_1 + D_2$)	2,802	1,350,574	482

the dataset have at least 34 posts (first quartile) and a midspread of more than 400 posts (interquartile range). The dataset also has users with only one post; the longest posting history is 11,127.

Table 2. Statistics of the number of posts per user

Statistics	Number of posts
First quartile	49
Median	154
Third quartile	479
Interquartile range	430
Minimum	1
Maximum	11127

5 Proposed Method

5.1 Background

Given that our dataset, $\mathcal{D}$, consists of N_1 number of social media users $\mathbf{u}$, where each user's N_2 number of social media posts, $\mathbf{p}$, within a month were collected, and each post has N_3 words, w, we denote the dataset as $\mathcal{D} = \{(u_1, y_1), ..., (u_{N_1}, y_{N_1})\}$, where $y \in [0,1]$ is the label in which 0 represents the *control user* and 1 for the *depressed user*. For a random social media user u_i, it can be formulated as $u_i = \{p_1^i, ..., p_{N_2}^i\}$, and a random social media post as $p_j = \{w_1^j, ..., w_{N_3}^j\}$.

5.2 SERCNN

We propose a Stacked Embedding Recurrent Convolutional Neural Network (SERCNN), which is made up of a stacked embedding (SE) and recurrent convolutional neural network (RCNN) [15]. The overall architecture of SERCNN is simple, consisting of a SE layer, TextCNN [13], a mean-pooling layer, and two fully connected layers, with the latter one being as an output layer with Softmax function, as visualized in Fig. 1.

For the input of the SERCNN, we model our user representation by first concatenating N_2 social media posts in chronological order. For a random user

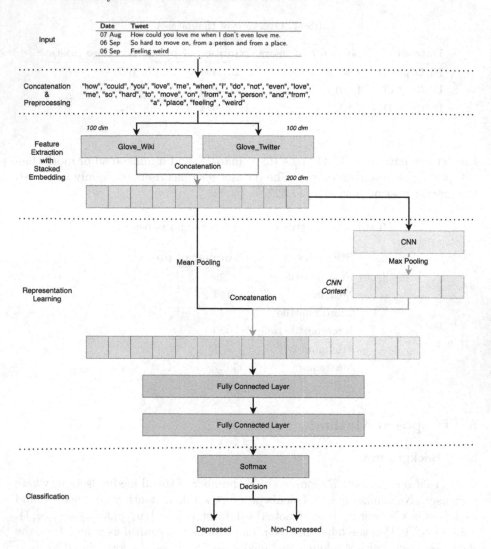

Fig. 1. The overall architecture of SERCNN.

u_i, it can be formulated as (padded where necessary):

$$u_i = \{p_1^i \oplus ... \oplus p_{N_2}^i\} \tag{1}$$

$$u_i = \{w_1^1 \oplus ... \oplus w_{N_3}^1 \oplus ... \oplus w_{N_3}^{N_2}\} \tag{2}$$

where $\oplus$ is the concatenation operator.

The concatenated text can be viewed as a single unique "monthly diary", journal, or large document that characterizes the user. By concatenating the user-generated text, it allows the deep learning model to take advantage of the context across different time frames (global context) without losing much information throughout the time span.

Then, we extract the distributed text representation of each word with Stacked Embedding (SE); an ensemble embedding technique commonly falls under the category of Meta-embedding. The concept of Meta-embedding was first introduced by [28] to utilize and learn the meta of existing well-trained pretrained embeddings and extend the vocabulary. Meta-embedding formed from pre-trained embeddings trained on heterogeneous datasets allows for an improved vocabulary coverage and reduces out-of-vocabulary words. As the name suggests, SE is formed by stacking a collection of dense vectors (pretrained weights) $\mathbf{E} = \{\mathbf{E}_1, ..., \mathbf{E}_{N_4}\}$ extracted from N_4 number of pretrained embeddings trained on heterogeneous datasets. SE can be formulated with:

$$\mathbf{E}_{SE} = \mathbf{E}_1 \oplus ... \oplus \mathbf{E}_{N_4} \tag{3}$$

where the embedding context, $\mathbf{c}_{SE}$, of a given user u can be obtained via:

$$\mathbf{c}_{SE} = \mathbf{E}_{SE}(u) \tag{4}$$

The vocabulary of the stacked embedding, $\mathbf{V}_{SE}$, is now considered as the union of the N_4 number of pretrained embeddings' vocabularies ($\mathbf{V}$), resulting in an extensive vocabulary than a single domain embedding as shown in Formula 5.

$$\mathbf{V}_{SE} = \bigcup_{n=1}^{N_4} \mathbf{V}_n \tag{5}$$

In this study, the following pre-trained embeddings are used:

1. **Glove Twitter (100 dimensions)** is trained using global word co-occurrences information by Pennington et al. [17] under an uncased setting, using 2 billion tweets, with 27 billion tokens. The resulting vector consists of 1.2 million vocabularies learned from the corpus.
2. **Glove Wikipedia 2014 + Gigaword 5 (100 dimensions)**, similarly, Pennington et al. [17] have pretrained a word embedding from the corpus made up of Wikipedia 2014 and Gigaword 5 datasets using their proposed global word co-occurrences information. The embedding covers approximately 400 thousand words.

The recurrent neural network (RNN) is capable of capturing contextual information over a long sequence. However, the RNN model favors the latter words over words in the earlier sequence. Since we are interested in identifying words that associate with depression throughout the posting history, therefore, the bidirectional Long Short Term Memory (BiLSTM) of the original RCNN [15] implementation is replaced with Kim's [13] TextCNN. The TextCNN is implemented to learn the context representation from the stacked embedding vector, $\mathbf{c}_{SE}$. The formulation of the CNN includes the convolution operation of a filter, which is applied to a window of N_5 words to produce a new feature.

We have defined three filters $\mathbf{w} = \{1, 2, 3\} \in \mathbb{R}$, which are used to extract $N_5 \in \{$unigram, bigram, and trigram$\}$ of feature maps. A max-pooling layer is then applied to capture the most significant features from the generated feature maps, resulting in context $\mathbf{c}_{\text{CNN}}$.

$$\mathbf{c}_{\text{CNN}} = \max\{\mathbf{c}_{\mathbf{w}_1}, \mathbf{c}_{\mathbf{w}_2}, \mathbf{c}_{\mathbf{w}_3}\} \tag{6}$$

Here, the context of the stacked embedding is reintroduced in the form of mean pooled,

$$\mathbf{c}_{\text{SE\_mean}} = \text{mean}\{\mathbf{c}_{\text{SE}}\} \tag{7}$$

and is then concatenated with the $\mathbf{c}_{\text{CNN}}$, forming a rich SERCNN context $\mathbf{c}_{\text{SERCNN}}$ as shown in Formula 8.

$$\mathbf{c}_{\text{SERCNN}} = \{\mathbf{c}_{\text{CNN}} \oplus \mathbf{c}_{\text{SE\_mean}}\} \tag{8}$$

$\mathbf{c}_{\text{SERCNN}}$ is then fed to two fully connected layers that have the following formulation (o),

$$o = W\mathbf{c} + b \tag{9}$$

where W is the trainable weight and b is the bias term. The final output $\hat{y}$ presents as the classification output in probabilities using softmax:

$$\hat{y} = softmax(o_2) \tag{10}$$

where o_2 is the output of the second fully connected layer.

5.3   Early Depression Detection

From the statistics of our dataset (as tabulated in Table 2), we found that not all users are active on social media. There are 75% of users who have at least 49 posts, and the median of the dataset is 154 posts. This indicates that more than 50% of the users have at least 154 posts (refer to Table 2). Here, we propose to look into the viability of utilizing fixed observation windows, which are measured in the number of posts, to detect depression on social media. In this study, three observation windows: $\{10, 30, 100\}$ posts are evaluated.

Since Shen et al.'s [20] dataset consists of a single month of posts before the ground truth tweet, we further assess the robustness of our proposed observation windows by training our model on two subsets of the posting history, denoted by a suffix of **-E** and **-L**. Given that the number k is one of the observation windows we experimented with, the model with the suffix -E is trained with the k number of posts retrieved from the earliest k posts. Similarly, models with the suffix -L are trained with the k number of posts from the latest k posts. An example is presented on Fig. 2. Do note that for some users with k number of posts or less, the earliest k^{th} and latest k^{th} posts are the same, but this happens for several users only, as 75% of the users have at least 49 posts and a median of 154 posts (refer to Table 2).

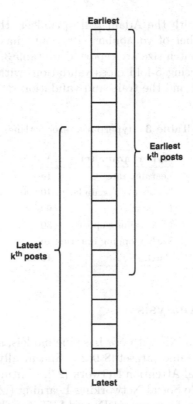

Fig. 2. Assuming the user has 14 posts, model with the suffix -E is trained with the earliest k^{th} posts while the one with the suffix -L is trained with the latest k^{th} posts as illustrated.

6   Experiments

6.1   Preprocessing

To ensure a fair comparison with previous papers, we do not expand the dataset and use the data included in the dataset only. The following preprocessing steps have been applied:

1. removes ground truth (anchor tweet),
2. lowercasing,
3. removes URL,
4. ensures only English healthy controls are included.

6.2   Experiment Settings

We trained our model using the PyTorch library. All models are implemented with a cross-entropy function as the loss function and the overall objective function is optimized with the Adam [14] optimizer. Hyperparameters including learning rate, number of vocabulary, dropout, max training epochs, early stopping criteria, and batch size are reported in Table 3. SERCNN and baseline models are evaluated using 5-fold cross-validation, with each fold of the train and test ratio being 4:1 and the train and validation ratio of 9:1.

Table 3. Hyperparameter settings

Hyperparameter	Value
Learning rate	1e−3
Number of vocabulary	10,000
Dropout	0.5
Max training epochs	30
Early stopping criteria	10
Batch size	120

7   Results and Analysis

We benchmark our SERCNN with our baseline models, as well as previous work that was trained on the same dataset [8,9,20]. Specifically, we compare SERCNN with LSTM, Hierarchical Attention Network [27], Multimodal Dictionary Learning (MDL) and Multiple Social Networking Learning (MSNL) by [20] (which is trained with handcrafted features), CNN and LSTM with Policy Gradient Agent (PGA) by [8], and Gated Recurrent Unit + VGG-Net + Cooperative Misoperation Multi-Agent (GVCOMMA) policy gradients by [9]. The performance of the models is evaluated with precision, macroaverage precision, macroaverage recall, and macroaverage F1 measure, which are tabulated in Table 4.

Table 4. Performance comparison against baselines

Model	Features	Accuracy	Precision	Recall	F1
Shen et al.'s MSNL [20]	Handcrafted	0.818	0.818	0.818	0.818
Shen et al.'s MDL [20]	features	0.848	0.848	0.85	0.849
Gui et al.'s CNN + PGA [8]	Text	0.871	0.871	0.871	0.871
Gui et al.'s LSTM + PGA [8]		0.870	0.872	0.870	0.871
Gui et al.'s GVCOMMA [9]	Text + image	0.900	0.900	0.901	0.900
Our LSTM	Text	0.900	0.921	0.900	0.910
Our HAN		0.900	0.920	0.906	0.913
Our SERCNN		**0.937**	**0.929**	**0.941**	**0.933**

From Table 4, we can observe that the SERCNN outperformed all baseline models and previous works [8,9,20]. Overall, we have the following observations:

1. The baseline LSTM model has better performance than Gui et al.'s LSTM variant [8], which suggests that using pretrained embedding for depression detection on social media is an effective method for mitigating the effects of over-fitting using embedding trained from the dataset.
2. The performance of the baseline LSTM and HAN models is about the same indicating the hierarchical representation of the data does not necessarily represent the intrinsic structure of the data.
3. SERCNN outperforms other models, which can be due to the richer and more robust representation generated from the stacked embedding and the reintroduction of the embedding context, allowing the model to have a second chance to understand the context better.

For early depression detection using our proposed observation windows, we have also trained a classifier with the pretrained *bert-base-uncased* model (Bert-ForSequenceClassification) from Hugging Face[1] [24] as a baseline, since the concatenated text is much shorter now. The performance is presented in Table 5.

Table 5. Performance comparison using the earliest posts and the latest posts based on fixed observation windows.

Model	Number of posts	Accuracy	Precision	Recall	F1
BERT-E	10	**0.878**	**0.872**	**0.882**	**0.873**
BERT-L	10	0.863	0.851	0.835	0.832
SERCNN-E	10	0.865	0.858	0.871	0.860
SERCNN-L	10	0.870	0.861	0.872	0.864
BERT-E	30	**0.907**	**0.902**	**0.909**	**0.902**
BERT-L	30	0.903	0.883	0.874	0.872
SERCNN-E	30	**0.907**	0.899	0.910	0.903
SERCNN-L	30	0.900	0.892	0.902	0.895
BERT-E	100	0.904	0.899	0.904	0.899
BERT-L	100	0.901	0.882	0.874	0.871
SERCNN-E	100	**0.922**	**0.914**	**0.926**	**0.918**
SERCNN-L	100	0.915	0.907	0.919	0.911

Based on the results shown in Table 5, we observed that the BERT-E models for all observation windows performed better than their BERT-L, while the discrepancies between the SERCNNs are less than 1% for all measured metrics. Comparing the performance of SERCNN with BERT, our proposed model shows competitive performance if not better than the finetuned BERT model despite using about a fraction of the number of parameters (about 2%) as shown in Table 6.

In addition, these models also outperformed previous work that used the entire posting history. These findings suggest that depression symptoms are reflected in social media data throughout the month, which is consistent with the depression criteria stated in DSM-5 [1] where symptoms persist over time. Therefore, our empirical results indicate that not all posts in the user history are required to predict depression online.

---

[1] https://huggingface.co/.

Table 6. Comparison of BERT and SERCNN in the number of parameters

Model	Number of parameters
BERT	109,482,240
SERCNN	2,095,452

8   Conclusion

Empirical results have suggested that SERCNN has the advantage of achieving state-of-the-art accuracy and, at the same time, requires less computational cost and, most importantly, fewer posts for depression detection. This is crucial as different users may have different posting behaviors, ranging from less active to more active users. Concatenating social media posts into a single diary (document) allows the deep learning model to take advantage of the relationship of words in a different time frame, resulting in a generalized global context for a user. Adopting embeddings from general and social media domains allows better vocabulary coverage, thus reducing the out-of-vocabulary words for much more robust classification. Taking advantage of the rich representation, SERCNN achieved 93.7% accuracy, outperforming previous works and baselines. Besides that, our experiment demonstrates that SERCNN can achieve 86.6% accuracy using 10 posts only and 92.2% accuracy using only 100 posts, instead of utilizing the whole dataset. We also show that SERCNN is neck-and-neck with fine-tuned BERT classifier across the three different observation window settings while having only 2% of the BERT size in terms of parameter numbers. For our future work, we plan to explore incorporating transformer models into the architecture and looking into the transferability of the models on different datasets.

Acknowledgment. This work was carried out within the framework of the research project FRGS/1/2020/ICT02/MUSM/03/5 under the Fundamental Research Grant Scheme provided by the Ministry of Higher Education, Malaysia.

Ethics Statement. Early screening of depression can significantly increase the discoverability of depression symptoms, allowing timely intervention to reduce symptoms. Our work provides novel insight into the potential of using a lesser number of posts that simulate the existing screening observation window of 14 days and reduce the cost of acquiring and storing data despite the limited number of real patient data and privacy concerns. However, our subjects are often sensitive and vulnerable; hence, additional measures have been taken to preserve their privacy. This study has received ethics approval from the *Institutional Review Board* with review reference number: 2020-22906-40238. Essential measures have been taken to exclude identifiable information from the data before it is used in this study. In addition, datasets obtained from their respective authors are stored in an encrypted repository. None of the users in the datasets is contacted throughout the study.

References

1. American Psychiatric Association: Diagnostic and statistical manual of mental disorders (DSM-5®). American Psychiatric Pub (2013)
2. Blei, D.M., Ng, A.Y., Jordan, M.I.: Latent Dirichlet allocation. J. Mach. Learn. Res. **3**, 993–1022 (2003). https://doi.org/10.5555/944919.944937
3. Choudhury, M.D., Gamon, M., Counts, S., Horvitz, E.: Predicting depression via social media. In: ICWSM (2013). https://ojs.aaai.org/index.php/ICWSM/article/view/14432
4. Coppersmith, G., Dredze, M., Harman, C., Hollingshead, K., Mitchell, M.: CLPsych 2015 shared task: Depression and PTSD on twitter. In: Proceedings of the 2nd Workshop on Computational Linguistics and Clinical Psychology: From Linguistic Signal to Clinical Reality, pp. 31–39 (2015). https://doi.org/10.3115/v1/W15-1204. https://aclanthology.org/W15-1204
5. Devlin, J., Chang, M.W., Lee, K., Toutanova, K.: BERT: pre-training of deep bidirectional transformers for language understanding. In: Proceedings of the 2019 Conference of the North American Chapter of the Association for Computational Linguistics: Human Language Technologies, Volume 1 (Long and Short Papers), pp. 4171–4186. Association for Computational Linguistics, Minneapolis, Minnesota (2019). https://doi.org/10.18653/v1/N19-1423. https://aclanthology.org/N19-1423
6. Gortner, E.M., Rude, S.S., Pennebaker, J.W.: Benefits of expressive writing in lowering rumination and depressive symptoms. Behav. Therapy **37**(3), 292–303 (2006). https://doi.org/10.1016/j.beth.2006.01.004. https://www.sciencedirect.com/science/article/pii/S0005789406000487
7. Gruda, D., Hasan, S.: Feeling anxious? perceiving anxiety in tweets using machine learning. Comput. Human Behav. **98**, 245–255 (2019). https://doi.org/10.1016/j.chb.2019.04.020. http://www.sciencedirect.com/science/article/pii/S0747563219301608
8. Gui, T., Zhang, Q., Zhu, L., Zhou, X., Peng, M., Huang, X.: Depression detection on social media with reinforcement learning. In: Sun, M., Huang, X., Ji, H., Liu, Z., Liu, Y. (eds.) CCL 2019. LNCS (LNAI), vol. 11856, pp. 613–624. Springer, Cham (2019). https://doi.org/10.1007/978-3-030-32381-3_49
9. Gui, T., Zhu, L., Zhang, Q., Peng, M., Zhou, X., Ding, K., Chen, Z.: Cooperative multimodal approach to depression detection in twitter. In: Proceedings of the AAAI Conference on Artificial Intelligence, vol. 33, pp. 110–117 (2019). https://doi.org/10.1609/aaai.v33i01.3301110. https://ojs.aaai.org/index.php/AAAI/article/view/3775
10. Guntuku, S.C., Preotiuc-Pietro, D., Eichstaedt, J.C., Ungar, L.H.: What twitter profile and posted images reveal about depression and anxiety. In: Proceedings of the International AAAI Conference on Web and Social Media, vol. 13, pp. 236–246 (2019). https://doi.org/10.48550/arXiv.1904.02670. https://ojs.aaai.org/index.php/ICWSM/article/view/3225
11. Holleran, S.: The early detection of depression from social networking sites, Ph. D. thesis, The University of Arizona (2010). https://repository.arizona.edu/handle/10150/196085
12. Hu, Q., Li, A., Heng, F., Li, J., Zhu, T.: Predicting depression of social media user on different observation windows. In: 2015 IEEE/WIC/ACM International Conference on Web Intelligence and Intelligent Agent Technology (WI-IAT), vol. 1, pp. 361–364 (2015). https://doi.org/10.1109/WI-IAT.2015.166

13. Kim, Y.: Convolutional neural networks for sentence classification (2014). https://doi.org/10.48550/arXiv.1408.5882. https://arxiv.org/abs/1408.5882
14. Kingma, D.P., Ba, J.: Adam: A method for stochastic optimization. CoRR abs/1412.6980 (2015). https://doi.org/10.48550/arXiv.1412.6980. https://arxiv.org/abs/1412.6980
15. Lai, S., Xu, L., Liu, K., Zhao, J.: Recurrent convolutional neural networks for text classification. In: Proceedings of the Twenty-Ninth AAAI Conference on Artificial Intelligence, pp. 2267–2273. AAAI'15, AAAI Press (2015). https://doi.org/10.5555/2886521.2886636
16. Losada, D.E., Crestani, F., Parapar, J.: eRISK 2017: CLEF Lab on early risk prediction on the internet: experimental foundations. In: Jones, G.J.F., et al. (eds.) CLEF 2017. LNCS, vol. 10456, pp. 346–360. Springer, Cham (2017). https://doi.org/10.1007/978-3-319-65813-1_30
17. Pennington, J., Socher, R., Manning, C.D.: Glove: global vectors for word representation. In: Empirical Methods in Natural Language Processing (EMNLP), pp. 1532–1543 (2014). https://doi.org/10.3115/v1/D14-1162. http://www.aclweb.org/anthology/D14-1162
18. Resnik, P., Armstrong, W., Claudino, L., Nguyen, T., Nguyen, V.A., Boyd-Graber, J.: Beyond LDA: exploring supervised topic modeling for depression-related language in twitter. In: Proceedings of the 2nd Workshop on Computational Linguistics and Clinical Psychology: From Linguistic Signal to Clinical Reality, pp. 99–107 (2015). https://doi.org/10.3115/v1/W15-1212. https://aclanthology.org/W15-1212/
19. Rude, S., Gortner, E.M., Pennebaker, J.: Language use of depressed and depression-vulnerable college students. Cogn. Emotion 18(8), 1121–1133 (2004). https://doi.org/10.1080/02699930441000030. https://www.tandfonline.com/doi/abs/10.1080/02699930441000030
20. Shen, G., et al.: Depression detection via harvesting social media: a multimodal dictionary learning solution. In: IJCAI, pp. 3838–3844 (2017). https://doi.org/10.24963/ijcai.2017/536. https://www.ijcai.org/proceedings/2017/0536
21. Tausczik, Y.R., Pennebaker, J.W.: The psychological meaning of words: LIWC and computerized text analysis methods. J. Lang. Soc. Psychol. 29(1), 24–54 (2010). https://doi.org/10.1177/0261927x09351676. https://journals.sagepub.com/doi/abs/10.1177/0261927x09351676
22. Tsugawa, S., Kikuchi, Y., Kishino, F., Nakajima, K., Itoh, Y., Ohsaki, H.: Recognizing depression from twitter activity. In: Proceedings of the 33rd Annual ACM Conference on Human Factors in Computing Systems, pp. 3187–3196. CHI 2015, Association for Computing Machinery, New York, NY, USA (2015). https://doi.org/10.1145/2702123.2702280. https://dl.acm.org/doi/10.1145/2702123.2702280
23. Wang, X., Zhang, C., Ji, Y., Sun, L., Wu, L., Bao, Z.: A depression detection model based on sentiment analysis in micro-blog social network. In: Li, J., et al. (eds.) PAKDD 2013. LNCS (LNAI), vol. 7867, pp. 201–213. Springer, Heidelberg (2013). https://doi.org/10.1007/978-3-642-40319-4_18
24. Wolf, T., et al.: Transformers: State-of-the-art natural language processing. In: Proceedings of the 2020 Conference on Empirical Methods in Natural Language Processing: System Demonstrations, pp. 38–45. Association for Computational Linguistics (2020). https://doi.org/10.18653/v1/2020.emnlp-demos.6. https://aclanthology.org/2020.emnlp-demos.6
25. World Health Organization.: World health statistics 2021. World Health Organization (2021). https://www.who.int/publications/i/item/9789240027053

26. Yan, H., Fitzsimmons-Craft, E.E., Goodman, M., Krauss, M., Das, S., Cavazos-Rehg, P.: Automatic detection of eating disorder-related social media posts that could benefit from a mental health intervention. Int. J. Eating Disorders **52**(10), 1150–1156 (2019). https://doi.org/10.1002/eat.23148. https://onlinelibrary.wiley.com/doi/10.1002/eat.23148

27. Yang, Z., Yang, D., Dyer, C., He, X., Smola, A., Hovy, E.: Hierarchical attention networks for document classification. In: Proceedings of the 2016 Conference of the North American Chapter of the Association for Computational Linguistics: Human Language Technologies, pp. 1480–1489. Association for Computational Linguistics, San Diego, California (2016). https://doi.org/10.18653/v1/N16-1174. https://aclanthology.org/N16-1174

28. Yin, W., Schütze, H.: Learning word meta-embeddings. In: Proceedings of the 54th Annual Meeting of the Association for Computational Linguistics (Volume 1: Long Papers), pp. 1351–1360 (2016). https://doi.org/10.18653/v1/P16-1128. https://aclanthology.org/P16-1128/

Predicting Alzheimer's Disease: A Stroke-Based Handwriting Analysis Approach Based on Machine Learning

Nicole Dalia Cilia[1,3], Tiziana D'Alessandro[2], Claudio De Stefano[2], Francesco Fontanella[2(✉)], and Emanuele Nardone[2]

[1] Department of Computer Engineering, University of Enna "Kore", Cittadella Universitaria, Enna, Italy
[2] Department of Electrical and Information Engineering (DIEI), University of Cassino and Southern Lazio, Via G. Di Biasio 43, 03043 Cassino, FR, Italy
fontanella@unicas.it
[3] Institute for Computing and Information Sciences, Radboud University, Toernooiveld 212, 6525 Nijmegen, EC, The Netherlands

Abstract. Alzheimer's disease (AD) causes most of dementia cases. Although currently there is no cure for this disease, predicting the cognitive decline of people at the first stage of the disease allows clinicians to alleviate its burden. Recently, machine learning based approaches have been developed to automatically analyze handwriting to support early diagnosis of AD. In this context, features are extracted from the coordinates of the handwriting traits, recorded using digital devices. For a given task used for data collection, typically these features take into account the whole handwriting making up the task. In this paper, we present a novel approach to predict Alzheimer's Disease based on machine learning that analyses the single elementary traits making up handwriting, named strokes. The experimental results confirmed the effectiveness of the proposed approach.

1 Introduction

Alzheimer's Disease (AD) is the most common neurodegenerative disease. Although currently there is no cure for this disease, predicting the cognitive decline of people at the first stage of the disease allows clinicians to alleviate its burden. Recently, machine learning based approaches have been developed to automatically analyze handwriting to support early diagnosis of AD, since handwriting is one of the first skills affected by the onset of cognitive disorders which represent the first set of symptoms of AD. For this reason, recently there has been a growing interest in analyzing handwriting to evaluate the compromised motor planning skills caused by AD [8,11]. To this aim, researchers typically record the coordinates of the handwritten traces and extract specifically devised features which characterize the movements of people while performing a given

© Springer Nature Switzerland AG 2023
J.-J. Rousseau and B. Kapralos (Eds.): ICPR 2022 Workshops, LNCS 13643, pp. 632–643, 2023.
https://doi.org/10.1007/978-3-031-37660-3_44

"task". A task may consist in handwriting letters, words, simple sentences, etc. or drawing objects or figures. Once extracted, the features are given in input to machine learning (ML) based systems. In this framework, it is crucial to define the concept of stroke. A stroke is defined as an elementary trait of handwriting, performed with a single movement, or a single motor act, in which a person plan a part of the ink trace, move muscles to the direction planned and stop it to reset motor execution. Typically, strokes are split using as segmentation points pen-down/pen-up movements and/or changes of direction on the Cartesian axis (vertical or horizontal). A task is composed by several or even many strokes, then the features can be extracted either from each single stroke or applying a preliminary statistical analysis to calculate mean, standard deviation, minimum, maximum etc., over all strokes of a single task [2,5,15]. In the following, we will refer to the first and second approach with the terms "stroke-based" and "task-based", respectively.

In this paper, we present the results of a preliminary study in which we have tested the effectiveness of the stroke-based approach to characterize the handwriting of people affected by AD, on the basis of their ability to accomplish nine well-defined task related to handwriting. Those tasks were introduced in [6], and are described later in this paper. To test the proposed approach, we compared its results with those achieved by a task-based approach.

The remaining of the paper is organized as follows: in Sect. 2 we describe the data acquired, and procedures used to extract the engineered features. In Sect. 3 we explain the two methodologies used for the classification step, whereas in Sect. 4 we present and discuss the experimental results. Finally, Sect. 5 is devoted to some final remarks.

2   Data Collection

With the support of the geriatric ward, Alzheimer unit, of the "Federico II" hospital in Naples, we recruited 174 participants equally balanced between AD patients and healthy people. Participants were recruited according to clinical tests (such as PET, TAC and enzymatic analyses) and standard cognitive tests (such as MMSE and FAB). In order to have a fair comparison of the two groups of participants, demographic as well as educational characteristics were considered and matched. Finally, for both patients and controls, it was necessary to check whether they were on therapy or not, excluding those who used psychotropic drugs or any other drug that could influence their cognitive abilities. The data were collected by using the graphic tablet BAMBOO Folio, which allows the recording of pen tip movements in terms of (x,y) coordinates during the handwriting process. During the trial, we also used images and sound stimuli to guide each participant in the execution of the handwriting tasks. Finally, participants were also asked to follow the indications provided by the experimenter.

In this experiment we analyze the performance of nine tasks, included in the protocol presented in [6]. We considered these tasks because the copy tasks are the most studied in the literature for the handwriting analysis of AD. The nine tasks are detailed in the following.

(1) As in [16] or in [21], in the first task the participant have to copy three letters which have different graphic composition and presented ascender and descender in the stroke.

(2) The second task consists in copying four letters on adjacent rows. The aim of the cues is to test the spatial organization abilities of the subject [18].

(3-4) Tasks 3 and 4 require participants to write continuously for four times, in cursive, a single letter ('l') and a bigram ('le'), respectively [14,20]. These letters have been chosen because they can be written with a single continuous stroke and contain ascenders, descenders and loops. These characteristics allow us the testing of the motion control alternation.

(5-8) Tasks 5, 6, 7 and 8 imply word copying, which is the most explored activity in the analysis of handwriting for individuals with cognitive impairment [14,17,21]. Moreover, to observe the variation of the spatial organization, we have introduced a copy of the same word without or with a cue.

(9) In the ninth task, participants were asked to write, above a line (the cue), a simple phrase, dictated them by the experimenter. The phrase had a complete meaning, and described an action easy to memorize. As in [13], the hypothesis is that the movements can be modified because of the lack of visualization of the stimulus.

2.1 Feature Engineering

The features extracted during the handwriting process have been used to predict AD through ML-based algorithms. As mentioned in the Introduction we extracted the features from single strokes using the raw data recorded by the tablet, i.e. (x, y) coordinates, pressure and timestamps. We used the MovAlyzer® tool to process the handwriting data recorded. It also allowed us to segment handwriting movement patterns into a sequence of discrete movements (strokes). We used as segmentation points both pen up and pen down, as well as the zero crossings of the vertical velocity profile. Figure 1 shows an example of handwriting segmented by Movalyzer®.

MovAlyzer® allowed us to extract several features, obtaining a value for each stroke for the 26 features calculated. In practice, for the stroke-based approach we obtained 26 values for each stroke for each task for each participant. For the task-based approach, instead, the feature values for each stroke were averaged over all strokes form a single task, for each participant.

The 26 features extracted belong to two categories, namely static and dynamic. The first were computed taking into account the shape or the position of the strokes, whereas the second were related to quantities like velocity and acceleration. Table 1 shows the list of the extracted features. Note that, as suggested in [21], we separately computed the features over on-paper and in-air traits, because the literature shows significant differences in motor performance in these two cases. An in-air traits were computed when the pen tip was lifted up from the paper sheet. Note that in this case we extracted 25 features because pressure (feature #21) was zero in this case.

We also considered two additional feature types:

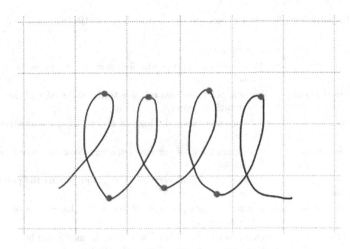

Fig. 1. Stroke Segmentation with Movalyzer®

(1) the first called All in which each sample was represented by a feature vector containing both in-air and on-paper features, i.e. by merging the vectors of in-air and on-paper features. Note that in this case the total number of features extracted was forty-seven (personal features and pressure were not repeated).

(2) In-air and on-paper: these features were computed without distinguishing between in-air and on-paper traits. In practice, for each task, each of the 26 features listed in Table 1 was extracted averaging the values on both in-air and on-paper traits. This represented a different way of providing all the information to the classification systems.

In order to take into account the differences due to age, education and work, we have also added the following "personal" features: gender, age, type of work, and level of education. Summarizing, we used four groups of features, each represented by nine datasets (one for each task), each containing 174 samples, each represented by a number of features dependending on the feature type. In particular, we extracted: 26 both for on-paper (P) and in-air and on-paper features (AP); 25 (no pressure) in-air features (A); forty-four for the category All (AL).

3   Methods and Features

As mentioned in the introduction, we compared two different approaches for feature extraction from handwriting, i.e. task-based and stroke-based. On one hand, in the task-based approach for each participant, we used the data obtained by computing mean and standard deviation of all strokes from a given task. The aim of the task-based approach is, indeed, to evaluate the whole movement performed by a participant in one task and analyze whether this type of movement, represented by the features chosen, allows us distinguishing the handwriting of

Table 1. Feature list. Feature types are: dynamic (D), static (S), and personal (P).

#	Name	Description	Type
1	Duration	Time interval between the first and the last points in a stroke	D
2	Start Vertical Position	Vertical start position relative to the lower edge of the active digitizer area	S
3	Vertical Size	Difference between the highest and lowest y coordinates of the stroke	S
4	Peak vertical velocity	Maximum value of vertical velocity among the points of the stroke	D
5	Peak vertical acceleration	Maximum value of vertical acceleration among the points of the stroke	D
6	Start horizontal position	Horizontal start position relative to the lower edge of the active tablet area	S
7	Horizontal size	Difference between the highest (right most) and lowest (left most) x coordinates of the stroke	S
8	Straightness error	It is calculated estimating the length of the straight line, fitting the straight line, estimating the (perpendicular) distances of each point to the fitted line, estimating the standard deviation of the distances and dividing it by the length of the line between beginning and end	D
9	Slant	Direction from the beginning point to endpoint of the stroke, in radiant	S
10	Loop Surface	Area of the loop enclosed by the previous and the present stroke	S
11	Relative initial slant	Departure of the direction during the first 80 ms to the slant of the entire stroke.	D
12	Relative time to peak vertical velocity	Ratio of the time duration at which the maximum peak velocity occurs (from the start time) to the total duration	D
13	Absolute size	Calculated from the vertical and horizontal sizes	S
14	Average absolute velocity	Average absolute velocity computed across all the samples of the stroke	D
15	Road length	length of a stroke from beginning to end, dimensionless	S
16	Absolute y jerk	The root mean square (RMS) value of the absolute jerk along the vertical direction, across all points of the stroke	D
17	Normalized y jerk	Dimensionless as it is normalized for stroke duration and size	D
18	Absolute jerk	The Root Mean Square (RMS) value of the absolute jerk across all points of the stroke	D
19	Normalized jerk	Dimensionless as it is normalized for stroke duration and size	D
20	Number of peak acceleration points	Number of acceleration peaks both up-going and down-going in the stroke	S
21	Pen pressure	Average pen pressure computed over the points of the stroke	D
22	#strokes	Total number of strokes of the task	S
23	Sex	Subject's gender	P
24	Age	Subject's age	P
25	Work	Type of work of the subject (intellectual or manual)	P
26	Instruction	participant's education level, expressed in years	P

people affected by AD from that of healthy people. On the other hand, in the stroke-based approach, we focused directly on the data obtained from with all the single strokes by every participant in every task. The aim of the stroke-based approach is to evaluate if the single movement, captured by a stroke, is more informative than the task-based to distinguish an AD patient from a healthy person.

For both methods, we performed a Grid search for classifier hyperparameter optimization. Grid Search build and evaluate a model for each combination of algorithm hyperparameter specified in a grid exhaustively. In our case we obtained the best parameters for every task for each of the chosen classifier.

After the grid search, the classifier hyperparameters used to train and test the specific task was chosen using the *best score criteria* on the accuracy values. Grid search, as well as classification training and prediction, have been implemented with Scikit-learn functions in python.

For the stroke-based approach, in every dataset, each sample represented a single stroke of a participant, each identified by a unique ID number. In order to test the ability of the learned classifiers to correctly classify the condition of people never seen before, we split the train and test sets in such a way that all strokes of a participant were included only in one of these sets. To this aim, for each dataset (one per task) we shuffled the samples according to the IDs and executed the train-test split using the Scikit-learn function *GroupShuffleSplit*, with the train set containing the 80% of the 174 participants, and the test set the remaining ones. Furthermore, since each participant wrote a variable number of strokes to perform a given task, each train (and test) set contained a different number of samples (strokes). Once the classifiers was been trained, we predicted every single stroke label. To decide the final predicted label for the specific ID, we applied a *Majority Vote* on the strokes label.

To obtain statistically significant results, we performed 20 runs, generating the train and test sets according to the procedure described above.

4   Experimental Results

As mentioned above, two different groups of data were considered in the experiments: the data obtained by task-based approach and the data of stroke-based approach, as better explained in the previous section. For each method we used the four feature types presented in Sect. 2. The data were produced by 174 participants, each performing the nine tasks detailed in Sect. 2. As for the classification stage, we used five different classification schemes: Random Forest (RF) [1], Decision Tree (DT) [19], Multi Layer Perceptron (MLP), Support Vector Machines (SVM) [3], and XGboost (XGB) [4]. The lists of hyperparameters used for the grid search are shown in Table 2. For the performance evaluation we used the five-fold cross-validation strategy.

Table 2. Classifiers and their hyperparameters involved in the Grid search process

Classifier	Hyperparameters	constraits
XGB	min child weight	1, 5, 10
	gamma	0.5, 1, 1.5, 2
	subsample	0.6, 0.8, 1
	colsample bytree	0.6, 0.8, 1
	max depth	3, 4
RF	bootstrap	True, False
	max depth	10, 20, 50
	mas features	auto, sqrt
	min samples leaf	1, 2, 4
	min samples splir	2, 5, 10
	n estimators	100, 200
DT	criterion	gini, entropy
	min samples split	2, 10
	max depth	2, 5, 10
	min samples leaf	1, 5, 10
	max leaf nodes	2, 5, 10
SVM	C	0.1, 1, 10, 100
	gamma	1, 0.1, 0.01, 0.001
	kernel	rbf
	class weight	balanced, None
MLP	hidden layer sizes	50, 100, 200
	activation	tanh, relu
	solver	lbfgs, sgd
	alpha	0.0001, 0.05
	learning rate	constant, adaptive

The tables in the following summarize the values of accuracy of every classifier for each task. The first four tables refer to the task-based approach, whereas the other three refer to the stroke-based approach.

From the first table we can observe that the best value of accuracy, 86.30%, was achieved by DT on task 8. However, the best performing classifier was XGB that outperformed the others seven times out of nine. The all feature type achieved good performances, which were around 80% of accuracy. SVM and MLP, instead, did not reach a satisfactory classification performance. For the in-air Feature the XGB classifier and DT achieved similar results. In fact, XGB and DT were the best classifiers for four tasks each. Compared to the all

Table 3. Grid search results for the task-based approach.

All

Task #	XGB	RF	DT	SVM	MLP
6	**82.31**	79.23	81.54	57.69	65.38
7	80.00	78.33	**84.17**	67.50	60.83
8	78.80	78.93	**86.30**	64.20	62.53
9	**77.68**	71.56	75.11	67.17	60.25
10	**78.93**	76.53	77.97	69.07	65.97
11	**77.43**	75.87	71.03	63.67	72.67
12	**83.57**	78.57	75.17	67.77	74.33
13	**84.80**	76.00	76.00	65.60	70.40
20	**80.69**	79.82	75.65	66.38	68.12

In-air

Task #	XGB	RF	DT	SVM	MLP
6	**84.77**	80.67	79.13	71.00	72.60
7	**83.20**	76.67	81.17	62.55	60.52
8	76.00	**81.16**	80.21	61.47	64.37
9	75.79	74.74	**81.05**	64.21	61.05
10	**86.05**	82.24	**86.05**	64.52	75.19
11	81.38	71.23	**85.65**	57.94	64.47
12	78.00	74.05	**79.71**	73.19	73.14
13	**85.36**	82.79	79.28	68.22	69.89
20	**82.07**	80.62	77.07	72.75	75.36

feature type, it seems that only the in-air features allowed us to achieve satisfactory classification results. Furthermore, best result was obtained on task 10. Once again with the on-paper features the most performing classifier was the XGB which reached the peak of accuracy in task 13, followed by the DT which achieved good results on task 7, 8 and 9. To conclude the discussion about the results of the task-based approach, we can observe that the in-air and on-paper features allowed us to reach the best mean results with XGB and the peak on task 13. The on-paper data achieved on average the worst performance. We can therefore say that the information of the in-air traits is relevant for the detection of the disease. The best classifier is the XGB, followed only by the DT (Tables 3 and 4).

As for the stroke-based approach, the results are very different. Wit the all features, for example, we achieved the peak accuracy in task 9 with the DT but, on average, the highest accuracy value per task is lower than the stroke-based approach. Also, there is no classifier that performed better than the others.

Table 4. Grid search results for the task-based approach.

On-paper

Task #	XGB	RF	DT	SVM	MLP
6	**82.72**	77.72	80.15	72.94	65.37
7	81.05	81.05	**84.21**	62.11	73.68
8	78.10	69.52	**79.05**	63.81	62.86
9	79.70	80.65	**82.25**	67.66	74.98
10	**77.27**	75.45	74.55	75.45	71.82
11	**83.16**	77.63	77.63	69.64	74.98
12	**81.90**	78.34	73.91	69.37	73.87
13	**87.28**	81.45	84.64	71.96	71.01
20	**81.39**	81.26	80.30	71.99	75.76

In-air and on-paper

Task #	XGB	RF	DT	SVM	MLP
6	81.54	80.77	**83.08**	65.38	70.77
7	**81.67**	77.50	80.00	74.17	68.33
8	**83.73**	74.77	78.10	73.27	69.10
9	**80.98**	76.78	75.07	72.43	72.46
10	**78.90**	74.07	75.73	67.60	73.17
11	**83.93**	76.53	77.40	69.33	74.17
12	**85.13**	77.70	82.73	70.30	67.70
13	**86.40**	81.60	82.40	72.80	72.80
20	**83.95**	78.19	78.08	71.56	72.28

Indeed, MLP and SVM achieved the best result in three tasks. From Table 5 we can observe that no classifier outperformed the others and the MLP never achieved the best result. However, from this table we can also observe that the stroke-based approach achieved the highest accuracy value in absolute terms, even with respect to the task-based approach. In fact, on tasks 8 and 9 we achieved an accuracy value near to 90% with the RF classifier. Once again the in-air data proved that it contains information really useful for AD detection by handwriting analysis. For the on-paper features, the trend of the stroke-based approach is confirmed: there is no classifier that is more performing than others and, on average, the accuracy results are lower than the other types of features.

Table 5. Grid search results for the stroke-based approach.

All

Task #	XGB	RF	DT	SVM	MLP
6	64.16	61.60	56.87	59.72	**65.70**
7	72.95	**77.10**	71.69	64.01	64.18
8	79.26	**80.90**	73.26	71.46	73.74
9	80.72	81.14	**82.64**	72.66	75.87
10	63.18	66.76	**68.17**	66.80	67.23
11	69.17	70.42	66.03	70.95	**71.11**
12	**66.38**	64.11	61.13	59.09	60.53
13	75.64	73.95	71.48	**77.03**	76.80
20	70.22	71.59	**73.26**	61.46	61.05

In-air

Task #	XGB	RF	DT	SVM	MLP
6	76.67	77.17	**77.81**	70.88	74.58
7	84.75	82.26	**88.21**	70.12	72.80
8	87.98	**89.92**	89.48	83.47	81.12
9	87.94	**89.80**	79.37	78.90	75.96
10	**80.07**	78.95	75.60	78.16	75.50
11	**83.40**	82.06	82.88	78.41	79.90
12	74.13	74.13	68.53	**76.00**	75.20
13	84.08	**85.37**	78.92	76.55	80.00
20	**72.89**	72.03	66.82	64.83	66.12

On-paper

Task #	XGB	RF	DT	SVM	MLP
6	64.80	63.10	55.96	64.65	**69.61**
7	72.33	70.88	59.36	**77.07**	76.86
8	62.19	64.72	67.07	63.63	**67.32**
9	**68.35**	65.26	64.33	64.70	65.57
10	**71.44**	71.04	65.45	68.67	70.97
11	**73.15**	72.60	67.44	67.99	72.05
12	67.11	67.02	65.58	**69.67**	65.35
13	69.21	**70.30**	63.95	69.42	69.76
20	65.63	69.20	58.33	**69.33**	67.30

5   Conclusions

In this paper we presented a novel approach to predict Alzheimer's Disease based on machine learning that analyses strokes, i.e. the single elementary traits making up handwriting. The experimental results showed that the proposed approached achieved a classification performance comparable with that achieved by the task-based approach, which processes the handwriting data as a whole. These results are important since they prove that analyzing the entire movement or single movements during handwriting is equally informative. Furthermore, the stroke-based results showed a high variability, with the classification performance depending on the task, the classifier and the feature type. On the contrary, for the task based approach the XGB is more performing than the others. Finally, it is also worth noticing that in-air features allowed us to achieve the best performance on both approaches. This result confirms the effectiveness of the proposed approach. Furthermore, since this approach does not take into account the average between the strokes of a task, but analyzes the traits individually, can be advantageous for cross language studies.

As feature perspective, we will try to: (i) increase classification performance by combining for each participant the responses from the tasks making up the protocol, following the methods proposed in [9, 10, 12]; apply deep learning based approaches to classify the single strokes [7].

References

1. Breiman, L.: Random forests. Mach. Learn. **45**(1), 5–32 (2001)
2. Carmona-Duarte, C., Ferrer, M.A., Parziale, A., Marcelli, A.: Temporal evolution in synthetic handwriting. Pattern Recogn. **68**(Supplement C), 233–244 (2017)
3. Chang, C.C., Lin, C.J.: LIBSVM: A library for support vector machines. ACM Trans. Intell. Syst. Technol. **2**, 1–27 (2011)
4. Chen, T., Guestrin, C.: XGBoost: A scalable tree boosting system. In: Proceedings of the 22nd ACM SIGKDD International Conference on Knowledge Discovery and Data Mining, pp. 785–794. KDD2016, ACM, New York, NY, USA (2016)
5. Cilia, N.D.: Understand me or duplicate me? levels of explanation in artificial methodology. In: Cilia, N.D., Tonetti, L. (eds.) Wired Bodies. New Perspectives on the Machine-Organism Analogy. CNR Edizioni (2017)
6. Cilia, N.D., De Stefano, C., Fontanella, F., Scotto Di Freca, A.: An experimental protocol to support cognitive impairment diagnosis by using handwriting analysis. In: Procedia Computer Science, Proceeding of The 8th International Conference on Current and Future Trends of Information and Communication Technologies in Healthcare (ICTH), pp. 1–9. Elsevier (2019)
7. Cilia, N.D., D'Alessandro, T., De Stefano, C., Fontanella, F., Molinara, M.: From online handwriting to synthetic images for Alzheimer's disease detection using a deep transfer learning approach. IEEE J. Biomed. Health Inform. **25**(12), 4243–4254 (2021)
8. Cilia, N.D., De Stefano, C., Fontanella, F., Freca, A.S.D.: Feature selection as a tool to support the diagnosis of cognitive impairments through handwriting analysis. IEEE Access **9**, 78226–78240 (2021)
9. Cordella, L.P., De Stefano, C., Fontanella, F., Marrocco, C., Scotto di Freca, A.: Combining single class features for improving performance of a two stage classifier. In: 20th International Conference on Pattern Recognition (ICPR 2010), pp. 4352–4355. IEEE Computer Society (2010)

10. De Stefano, C., Fontanella, F., Folino, G., di Freca, A.S.: A Bayesian approach for combining ensembles of GP classifiers. In: Sansone, C., Kittler, J., Roli, F. (eds.) MCS 2011. LNCS, vol. 6713, pp. 26–35. Springer, Heidelberg (2011). https://doi.org/10.1007/978-3-642-21557-5_5

11. De Stefano, C., Fontanella, F., Impedovo, D., Pirlo, G., Scotto di Freca, A.: Handwriting analysis to support neurodegenerative diseases diagnosis: a review. Pattern Recogn. Lett. **121**, 37–45 (2018)

12. De Stefano, C., Fontanella, F., Marrocco, C., di Freca, A.S.: A hybrid evolutionary algorithm for Bayesian networks learning: an application to classifier combination. In: Di Chio, C., et al. (eds.) EvoApplications 2010. LNCS, vol. 6024, pp. 221–230. Springer, Heidelberg (2010). https://doi.org/10.1007/978-3-642-12239-2_23

13. Hayashi, A., et al.: Neural substrates for writing impairments in Japanese patients with mild Alzheimer's disease: a spect study. Neuropsychologia **49**(7), 1962–1968 (2011)

14. Impedovo, D., Pirlo, G.: Dynamic handwriting analysis for the assessment of neurodegenerative diseases: a pattern recognition perspective. IEEE Reviews in Biomedical Engineering, pp. 1–13 (2018)

15. Impedovo, D., Pirlo, G., Barbuzzi, D., Balestrucci, A., Impedovo, S.: Handwritten processing for pre diagnosis of Alzheimer disease. In: Proceedings of BIOSTEC 2014, pp. 193–199. SCITEPRESS, Portugal (2014)

16. Lambert, J., Giffard, B., Nore, F., de la Sayette, V., Pasquier, F., Eustache, F.: Central and peripheral agraphia in Alzheimer's disease: From the case of Auguste d. to a cognitive neuropsychology approach. Cortex **43**(7), 935–951 (2007)

17. Onofri, E., Mercuri, M., Archer, T., Ricciardi, M.R., F.Massoni, Ricci, S.: Effect of cognitive fluctuation on handwriting in Alzheimer's patient: a case study. Acta Medica Mediterranea **3**, 751 (2015)

18. Onofri, E., Mercuri, M., Salesi, M., Ricciardi, M., Archer, T.: Dysgraphia in relation to cognitive performance in patients with Alzheimer's disease. J. Intell. Disability-Diagnosis Treat. **1**, 113–124 (2013)

19. Quinlan, J.R.: C4.5: Programs for Machine Learning (Morgan Kaufmann Series in Machine Learning). Morgan Kaufmann, San Francisco, CA, USA (1993)

20. Slavin, M.J., Phillips, J.G., Bradshaw, J.L., Hall, K.A., Presnell, I.: Consistency of handwriting movements in dementia of the Alzheimer's type: a comparison with Huntington's and parkinson's diseases. J. Int. Neuropsychol. Soc. **5**(1), 20–25 (1999)

21. Werner, P., Rosenblum, S., Bar-On, G., Heinik, J., Korczyn, A.: Handwriting process variables discriminating mild Alzheimer's disease and mild cognitive impairment. J. Gerontol. Psychol. Sci. **61**(4), 228–36 (2006)

Unsupervised Brain MRI Anomaly Detection for Multiple Sclerosis Classification

Giovanna Castellano[1], Giuseppe Placidi[2], Matteo Polsinelli[3],
Gianpiero Tulipani[1], and Gennaro Vessio[1(✉)]

[1] Department of Computer Science, University of Bari Aldo Moro, Bari, Italy
gennaro.vessio@uniba.it
[2] Department of Life, Health & Environmental Sciences, University of L'Aquila,
L'Aquila, Italy
[3] Department of Computer Science, University of Salerno, Fisciano, Italy

Abstract. Supervised deep learning has been widely applied in medical imaging to detect multiple sclerosis. However, it is difficult to have perfectly annotated lesions in magnetic resonance images, due to the inherent difficulties with the annotation process performed by human experts. To provide a model that can completely ignore annotations, we propose an unsupervised anomaly detection approach. The method uses a convolutional autoencoder to learn a "normal brain" distribution and detects abnormalities as a deviation from the norm. Experiments conducted with the recently released OASIS-3 dataset and the challenging MSSEG dataset show the feasibility of the proposed method, as very encouraging sensitivity and specificity were achieved in the binary health/disease discrimination. Following the "normal brain" learning rule, the proposed approach can easily generalize to other types of brain diseases, due to its potential to detect arbitrary anomalies.

Keywords: Multiple sclerosis · Computer-aided diagnosis · Deep learning · Anomaly detection · Convolutional autoencoder · MRI · OASIS

1 Introduction

Multiple sclerosis (MS) is a chronic autoimmune disease of the central nervous system that usually affects young adults [13]. The course of the disease can be highly variable among individuals, but inflammation, demyelination, and axonal loss are typical signs, even in the early stages of the disease [16]. The causes of MS are still not fully understood and there is no cure. However, early treatments can help slow the course of the disease and manage symptoms. This is particularly important considering that manifestations of MS are increasingly recognized in childhood and adolescence [9]. Although several diseases share similarities with MS, one of the primary diagnostic tools is magnetic resonance imaging (MRI)

© Springer Nature Switzerland AG 2023
J.-J. Rousseau and B. Kapralos (Eds.): ICPR 2022 Workshops, LNCS 13643, pp. 644–652, 2023.
https://doi.org/10.1007/978-3-031-37660-3_45

of the brain and/or spinal cord, due to its ability to show areas of demyelination in the form of plaques or lesions.

In recent years, deep learning-based methods have been widely applied to medical imaging to detect signs of abnormalities and lesions in the brain, thus aiding in the diagnosis of the disease. Most of these are supervised learning methods that rely on the availability of large, high-quality annotated datasets that must be manually produced by human experts [23,25]. However, due to the constraints of time, cost, and experience in clinical practice, manual annotations are not always accurate. Although consensus is generally sought between different annotators, intra- and inter-rater variability are known to cause ambiguity and uncertainty [8,17]. Furthermore, this phenomenon is exacerbated by the heterogeneity of the scanners used and the similarity between the lesions and healthy tissues. As a result, deep learning models trained on images whose annotations are inherently imprecise may fail to generalize in several cases and, at best, may reflect annotation bias and inaccuracies.

A different way of approaching the problem of automatic detection of MS based on brain MRI is to take a completely unsupervised approach, totally unaware of labels that could be inaccurate and ambiguous. Indeed, there is a recent stream of papers in the literature attempting to model healthy brain distribution and use an anomaly detection approach so that pathologies can be detected as deviations from the norm. By reconstructing the MRI of the brain, for example with an autoencoder, the lesions can be detected/segmented based on erroneous reconstructions (for a recent survey see [2]). However, although promising, the problem is still challenging due to the high variability of voxel intensities and image contrast that creates ambiguity even in healthy brains, where similar patterns can also occur. In other words, the question is still open.

In this paper, we contribute to this research challenge by introducing an unsupervised deep learning method that learns a robust MS classification model while avoiding the use of potentially inconsistent annotations. The method relies on a convolutional autoencoder and, unlike many works, leverages the recently released OASIS-3 dataset [14] as a data source to model the healthy distribution. Experimental tests have been conducted on the challenging MSSEG dataset [12] and promising results have been obtained in the binary health/disease classification based on some peculiar hyperparameter choices.

The rest of this paper is structured as follows. Section 2 reviews related work. Sections 3 and 4 describes materials and methods. Section 5 reports and discusses the results obtained. Section 6 concludes the paper and outlines future developments of our research.

2 Related Work

Recently, many studies have shown the negative effects of training deep learning models with noisy annotations, e.g. [24]. Existing methods use conditional random fields [21] and neural networks [15] to correct annotation noise. Other approaches, such as [1,10], apply resampling methods to the training samples and evaluate the importance of each sample during training to obtain a more robust model. In [26], the authors provide RetinaNet with an additional attention module to perform high-quality lesion detection. Another strategy is to combine different sources of information to compensate for missing or low-quality annotations. In [23], different CT lesion data are combined to jointly train a mixture-of-expert system with multiple detection networks. In [22], 3D context information in the form of multiple neighboring slices from CT scans is fed into a 2D convolutional neural network to generate separate feature maps which are then aggregated for final prediction. In this article, to address the annotation noise in brain MRI for MS detection, we place ourselves in a recent stream of articles that follow a completely unsupervised approach.

Seminal papers on unsupervised anomaly detection in medical imaging are the work of Schlegl et al. [18] and Baur et al. [3]. In the former, a generative adversarial network is used to learn the normal anatomical variability of retinal images; in the latter, the idea is taken up, and the authors propose a variational autoencoder specifically aimed at reconstructing the brain MRI of individuals with or without MS (private data were used). Since then, some other papers, such as [4–6,11], have developed this idea by experimenting with combinations of data, preprocessing, and training techniques. The unsupervised anomaly detection approach better mimics the way radiologists analyze MRI scans, as even non-experts can detect abnormalities after seeing what a healthy brain looks like. Furthermore, the use of unsupervised learning in this domain has the potential to detect arbitrary anomalies—not necessarily related to a specific disease—without knowing their a priori appearance [2].

Despite the work done so far, as reviewed in [2] there is still no method capable of perfectly detecting and segmenting pathological lesions. In other words, sufficiently conclusive results have not already been obtained. One of the main reasons is that the fidelity of healthy tissue reconstruction is far from perfect. In this perspective, we are contributing here with a new experience to investigate potentially promising directions.

3   Materials

For our study, we needed a training dataset comprising MRI scans of healthy brains. To this end, we used the recently released OASIS-3 dataset [14], which represents a new benchmark for mental health studies. OASIS-3 is a longitudinal neuroimaging, clinical, cognitive, and biomarker dataset for normal aging and Alzheimer's disease. Participants include 609 cognitively normal adults and 489 individuals at various stages of cognitive decline ranging in age from 42 to 95 years. The dataset contains over 2000 MR sessions including, among others, T1w and FLAIR. For our purposes, we only considered axial FLAIR data from cognitively normal people. We focused on FLAIR sequences as they are a common choice in clinical practice for identifying white matter lesions due to MS. Additionally, as we found that some scans have areas of hyperintensity, despite being classified as healthy, and considering that MS primarily affects young people, we further limited our attention to subjects no older than 55, resulting in 69 scans. As a necessary preprocessing, we stripped the skull from each image and, to

this end, we co-registered T1w and FLAIR by resampling them via BRAINSRe-
sample[1] to obtain spatially matching images with the same voxel size; then, for
skull-stripping, we used the DeepBrain tool,[2] which is based on a convolutional
neural network and required T1w data to extract a brain tissue mask.

For the evaluation of the brain anomaly detection method only, we also used
the MSSEG dataset [12], which was used in the MICCAI 2016 MS lesion segmentation challenge. Data from 15 subjects are available in this dataset, the
hyperintense lesions of which were manually delineated by seven trained radiologists. However, as previously mentioned, we only used the diagnosis information
to distinguish MS patients from healthy people, but we did not use the lesion
annotation to train the model. It is worth noting that MSSEG data are already
provided with skull-stripping.

Finally, all images from both datasets were normalized to the interval $[0, 1]$;
furthermore, for each patient, we extracted 40 consecutive 2D axial slices around
the midline, with a resolution of 176×176. The latter choice was motivated by
the need to focus on white matter tissue and by computational reasons.

4   Methods

We assume that a training set $\{\mathbf{X}_i\}_{i=1}^N$ of N samples is available, each of which
is a 2D brain slice $\mathbf{X} \in \mathbb{R}^{176 \times 176}$ of a healthy brain. The main idea is to learn a
model of healthy brain anatomy with unsupervised deep representation learning.
To this end, we propose the use of a convolutional autoencoder. An autoencoder
is a type of neural network that learns a low-dimensional representation of data
without supervision. It consists of two components: an encoder and a decoder.
The encoder $\mathrm{ENC}(\mathbf{X})$ learns to map the input data $\mathbf{X}$ to a small representation, in our case $\mathbf{Z} \in \mathbb{R}^{22 \times 22 \times 32}$. Contrary to other works, we are therefore
compressing the input image into a three-dimensional space, rather than a one-
dimensional vector, to try to retain more information. The decoder $\mathrm{DEC}(\mathbf{Z})$
learns to reconstruct the original input from the low-dimensional representation,
i.e. $\hat{\mathbf{X}} = \mathrm{DEC}\left(\mathrm{ENC}\left(\mathbf{X}\right)\right)$. The goal of training is to minimize the reconstruction
error, which is the difference between the input data $\mathbf{X}$ and the reconstructed
output $\hat{\mathbf{X}}$. The rest of the architecture, as schematized in Fig. 1, is completed as
follows. A convolutional layer with 32 filters, kernel size 3, and stride 2 transforms the input image into a three-dimensional volume. Two residual blocks with
16 filters, kernel size 3, stride 2, and a batch normalization layer in the middle
further downsample the volume in the latent space $\mathbf{Z}$. Residual blocks have been
added to help the encoder not lose much information when compressing the original image. The decoder uses transposed convolutional layers to restore the data
to its original size. ReLU has been chosen as non-linearity.

Through training the autoencoder on healthy data, it learns a reconstruction
model that may work well for normal brains (i.e., returning a low reconstruction error) and may work poorly for abnormal brains (i.e., returning a high

---

[1] https://www.slicer.org/wiki/Modules:BRAINSResample.

[2] https://pypi.org/project/deepbrain/.

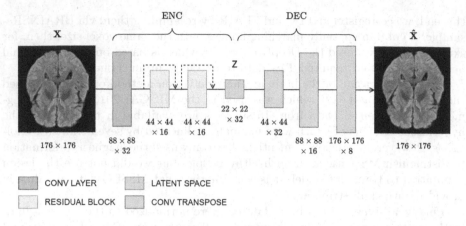

Fig. 1. Scheme of the autoencoder.

reconstruction error). In other words, the main hypothesis is that the presence of lesions causes a higher reconstruction error. We can then classify a scan as belonging to an MS patient if the reconstruction error exceeds a threshold.

As a reconstruction error to drive model optimization, we used both squared error (SE) and structural dissimilarity (DSSIM). Squared error is a classical reconstruction loss, defined as follows:

$$ SE = \left\| \mathbf{X} - \hat{\mathbf{X}} \right\|^2, $$

where $\|\cdot\|$ is the Euclidean norm. DSSIM, on the other hand, can be derived from the so-called structural similarity index measure (SSIM) as follows:

$$ DSSIM = 1 - SSIM, $$

where:

$$ SSIM = \frac{(2\mu_x\mu_y + c_1)(2\sigma_{xy} + c_2)}{(\mu_x^2 + \mu_y^2 + c_1)(\sigma_x^2 + \sigma_y^2 + c_2)}, $$

with x and y windows of common size of $\mathbf{X}$ and $\hat{\mathbf{X}}$ respectively (the index is calculated on various windows), μ_x and σ_x^2 the average and variance of x, μ_y and σ_y^2 the average and variance of y, σ_{xy} their covariance, and c_1 and c_2 two stabilizing variables. SSIM is a measure of the structural similarity between two images. It is not generally used in similar studies but may be better suited to our reconstruction goal since, unlike squared error, it takes structural brain information into account.

5   Experiments

The experimental study was performed on Google Colab, which provides a free GPU. The code was written in Python, while the model was implemented using the TensorFlow library. The autoencoder was trained from scratch for 50 epochs with RMSProp and mini-batch size 64.

We split the data subject-wise into a training and testing set, thus preventing slices of the same subjects from appearing in both sets. 80% of the OASIS-3 dataset was used for training, of which 20% was further separated to form a validation set. This validation set was used to monitor for validation loss and implement an early stopping strategy. The remaining 20% of the overall OASIS-3 formed, together with the MSSEG data, the test set, used to evaluate the ability to discriminate between MS and healthy brains. To overcome the data limitation and therefore improve the model reconstruction capacity, we have augmented the training set with the following transformations: horizontal flipping; center crop to allow the model to focus on finer details; addition of Gaussian noise; and rotation between -25 and $+25$ degrees, to compensate for head rotations.

Finally, by imposing a threshold on the absolute difference between the reconstruction error of a test instance and the average reconstruction error calculated on the training set, we can transform the problem into a binary classification task. This allows us to measure standard classification metrics, such as true and false positives, true and false negatives, and therefore precision and recall. Precision expresses the percentage of correct positive predictions; recall expresses the proportion of true positives that have been correctly predicted. By varying the threshold, we can adjust the trade-off between precision and recall.

Figure 2 shows the results obtained by the model using SE or DSSIM as a loss function, in terms of precision-recall curve and confusion matrix at the best threshold, i.e. the one that simultaneously maximizes precision and recall. From the results it is quite evident that, as expected, DSSIM represents a better option to measure the reconstruction error, confirming what has already been observed in other domains, such as [7]. This loss, in fact, better considers the inter-dependencies between local image regions, rather than simply comparing the values of individual pixels. In particular, the confusion matrix at the best threshold with DSSIM reveals that very encouraging results can be obtained with the proposed method, as a true positive rate (sensitivity) of 97.8% and a true negative rate (specificity) of 94.1% were achieved. As recently reviewed in [19], these results are in line with performance recently reported in the literature obtained with deep learning-based methods applied to private or public MRI data. However, the main point is that our results were obtained without supervision.

It is worth noting that we have also experimented with a version of the deep autoencoder that substantially doubles the number of hyperparameters, thus increasing the capacity of the model; however, we have found that this model is much more prone to overfitting.

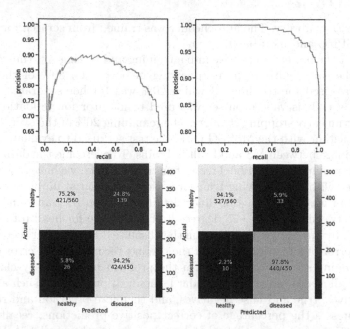

Fig. 2. Precision-recall curves and confusion matrices, when using SE (left) or DSSIM (right) as the loss function, at the best threshold (in both cases around 0.01).

6   Conclusion and Future Work

Unsupervised anomaly detection in medical imaging is an active area of research that is generating growing interest. In this paper, we have contributed to this research effort by proposing a model that discriminates between multiple sclerosis patients and healthy individuals based on their MR images. The accuracy shown by the model is very encouraging, considering that it was obtained without any prior knowledge, despite what was perceived "visually", that is, without relying on a ground truth that may be inherently inaccurate and ambiguous.

However, it should be emphasized that the experimental study reported here has an exploratory and preliminary character. The binary classification addressed may be just the first step in a more complex pipeline, in which lesions are precisely detected and segmented from the rest of the brain. Many questions also remain about which preprocessing and postprocessing techniques should be applied to improve performance. For example, we have not considered potentially confounding factors related to the scanner or protocol used, and we have not yet designed a specific strategy for the final diagnosis of the patient, as the method now only classifies individual slices. Furthermore, in this study we have focused only on 2D slices; feeding the model with 3D brain volumes, as initially done in some recent work [5,20], can retain much more information and further improve performance. Finally, a natural extension of the proposed approach is its application to other neurological diseases, in addition to MS, due to its potential to detect arbitrary anomalies.

References

1. Arazo, E., Ortego, D., Albert, P., O'Connor, N., McGuinness, K.: Unsupervised label noise modeling and loss correction. In: International Conference on Machine Learning, pp. 312–321. PMLR (2019)
2. Baur, C., Denner, S., Wiestler, B., Navab, N., Albarqouni, S.: Autoencoders for unsupervised anomaly segmentation in brain MR images: a comparative study. Med. Image Anal. **69**, 101952 (2021)
3. Baur, C., Wiestler, B., Albarqouni, S., Navab, N.: Deep autoencoding models for unsupervised anomaly segmentation in brain MR images. In: Crimi, A., Bakas, S., Kuijf, H., Keyvan, F., Reyes, M., van Walsum, T. (eds.) BrainLes 2018. LNCS, vol. 11383, pp. 161–169. Springer, Cham (2019). https://doi.org/10.1007/978-3-030-11723-8_16
4. Baur, C., Wiestler, B., Albarqouni, S., Navab, N.: Fusing unsupervised and supervised deep learning for white matter lesion segmentation. In: International Conference on Medical Imaging with Deep Learning, pp. 63–72. PMLR (2019)
5. Bengs, M., Behrendt, F., Krüger, J., Opfer, R., Schlaefer, A.: Three-dimensional deep learning with spatial erasing for unsupervised anomaly segmentation in brain MRI. Int. J. Comput. Assist. Radiol. Surg. **16**(9), 1413–1423 (2021). https://doi.org/10.1007/s11548-021-02451-9
6. Bercea, C.I., Wiestler, B., Rueckert, D., Albarqouni, S.: FedDis: disentangled federated learning for unsupervised brain pathology segmentation. arXiv preprint arXiv:2103.03705 (2021)
7. Bergmann, P., Löwe, S., Fauser, M., Sattlegger, D., Steger, C.: Improving unsupervised defect segmentation by applying structural similarity to autoencoders. arXiv preprint arXiv:1807.02011 (2018)
8. Carass, A.: Longitudinal multiple sclerosis lesion segmentation: resource and challenge. Neuroimage **148**, 77–102 (2017)
9. Casalino, G., Castellano, G., Consiglio, A., Nuzziello, N., Vessio, G.: MicroRNA expression classification for pediatric multiple sclerosis identification. J. Ambient Intell. Humanized Comput. 1–10 (2021). https://doi.org/10.1007/s12652-021-03091-2
10. Chen, P., Liao, B.B., Chen, G., Zhang, S.: Understanding and utilizing deep neural networks trained with noisy labels. In: International Conference on Machine Learning, pp. 1062–1070. PMLR (2019)
11. Chen, X., Konukoglu, E.: Unsupervised detection of lesions in brain MRI using constrained adversarial auto-encoders. arXiv preprint arXiv:1806.04972 (2018)
12. Commowick, O., et al.: Multiple sclerosis lesions segmentation from multiple experts: The MICCAI 2016 challenge dataset. Neuroimage **244**, 118589 (2021)
13. Dobson, R., Giovannoni, G.: Multiple sclerosis-a review. Eur. J. Neurol. **26**(1), 27–40 (2019)
14. LaMontagne, P.J., et al.: OASIS-3: longitudinal neuroimaging, clinical, and cognitive dataset for normal aging and Alzheimer disease. MedRxiv (2019)
15. Lee, K.H., He, X., Zhang, L., Yang, L.: CleanNet: transfer learning for scalable image classifier training with label noise. In: Proceedings of the IEEE Conference on Computer Vision and Pattern Recognition, pp. 5447–5456 (2018)

16. Oh, J., Vidal-Jordana, A., Montalban, X.: Multiple sclerosis: clinical aspects. Curr. Opin. Neurol. **31**(6), 752–759 (2018)

17. Placidi, G., Cinque, L., Mignosi, F., Polsinelli, M.: Multiple Sclerosis lesions identification/segmentation in Magnetic Resonance Imaging using ensemble CNN and uncertainty classification. arXiv preprint arXiv:2108.11791 (2021)

18. Schlegl, T., Seeböck, P., Waldstein, S.M., Schmidt-Erfurth, U., Langs, G.: Unsupervised anomaly detection with generative adversarial networks to guide marker discovery. In: Niethammer, M., et al. (eds.) IPMI 2017. LNCS, vol. 10265, pp. 146–157. Springer, Cham (2017). https://doi.org/10.1007/978-3-319-59050-9_12

19. Shoeibi, A., et al.: Applications of deep learning techniques for automated multiple sclerosis detection using magnetic resonance imaging: a review. Comput. Biol. Med. **136**, 104697 (2021)

20. Simarro Viana, J., de la Rosa, E., Vande Vyvere, T., Robben, D., Sima, D.M., Investigators, C.E.N.T.E.R.-T.B.I.P.: Unsupervised 3D brain anomaly detection. In: Crimi, A., Bakas, S. (eds.) BrainLes 2020. LNCS, vol. 12658, pp. 133–142. Springer, Cham (2021). https://doi.org/10.1007/978-3-030-72084-1_13

21. Vahdat, A.: Toward robustness against label noise in training deep discriminative neural networks. In: Advances in Neural Information Processing Systems 30 (2017)

22. Yan, K., Bagheri, M., Summers, R.M.: 3D context enhanced region-based convolutional neural network for end-to-end lesion detection. In: Frangi, A.F., Schnabel, J.A., Davatzikos, C., Alberola-López, C., Fichtinger, G. (eds.) MICCAI 2018. LNCS, vol. 11070, pp. 511–519. Springer, Cham (2018). https://doi.org/10.1007/978-3-030-00928-1_58

23. Yan, K., Cai, J., Harrison, A.P., Jin, D., Xiao, J., Lu, L.: Universal lesion detection by learning from multiple heterogeneously labeled datasets. arXiv preprint arXiv:2005.13753 (2020)

24. Yi, K., Wu, J.: Probabilistic end-to-end noise correction for learning with noisy labels. In: Proceedings of the IEEE/CVF Conference on Computer Vision and Pattern Recognition, pp. 7017–7025 (2019)

25. Zhang, H., Oguz, I.: Multiple sclerosis lesion segmentation - a survey of supervised CNN-based methods. In: Crimi, A., Bakas, S. (eds.) BrainLes 2020. LNCS, vol. 12658, pp. 11–29. Springer, Cham (2021). https://doi.org/10.1007/978-3-030-72084-1_2

26. Zlocha, M., Dou, Q., Glocker, B.: Improving RetinaNet for CT Lesion detection with dense masks from weak RECIST labels. In: Shen, D., et al. (eds.) MICCAI 2019. LNCS, vol. 11769, pp. 402–410. Springer, Cham (2019). https://doi.org/10.1007/978-3-030-32226-7_45

Multimodal Data for Mental Disorder Recognition (MDMR)

Preface

Mental disorder is a worldwide disease. According to the report of WHO in 2017, there were at least 300 million people suffering from mental disorder. The research on mental disorder recognition has great value for early mental disorder diagnosis, including depression, schizophrenia, bipolar disorder, etc. This is significant for protecting the mental health of the public.In recent years, the superiority of machine learning in multimedia analysis has been validated in a wide range of real-world applications. With more and more attention paid to humanity's mental health, many researchers try to use multimedia technologies to assist or replace the traditional face-to-face diagnosis manner. Recently, with the development of deep learning technology, there are many breakthroughs achieved in multimedia analysis, including audio, video, EEG, etc. These latest advances have offered enormous opportunities in improving mental disorder diagnosis.

We organized the first workshop on this year's ICPR conference. There were finally eight submissions since we published call-for-paper about one month ahead of the deadline. We invited 15 experts in this research field worldwide to take the program commitee roles. After one month of peer review, four papers were accepted and they all presented virtually their works on the workshop. Prof. Emily Cross from University of Glasgow accepted our invitation and gave a keynote on "social robots for facilitating self-disclosure in mental hearl intervention". This workshop was fully sponsored by Anhui Association of Artificial Intelligence, China.

August 2022

Richang Hong
Marwa Mahmoud
Bin Hu

Dep-Emotion: Suppressing Uncertainty to Recognize Real Emotions in Depressed Patients

Gang Fu, Jiayu Ye, and Qingxiang Wang[✉]

School of Computer Science and Technology Qilu University of Technology
(Shandong Academy of Sciences), Jinan 250353, China
wangqx@qlu.edu.cn

Abstract. In depression, affective and emotional dysfunction are important components of the clinical syndrome. At present, doctors mainly judge the real emotions of depressed patients through the naked eye, with a strong subjective consciousness. We collected images of seven expressions voluntarily imitated by 168 subjects, and then recruited 9 raters to recognize these images. The study found that depressed patients have deficits in Facial Emotion Expression, resulting in great uncertainty in their facial expressions. Therefore, we propose the Dep-Emotion to solve this problem. For the depression expression dataset with uncertainty, we use Self-Cure Network to correct the sample label to suppress the uncertainty. At the same time, the input part and downsampling block of ResNet18 are adjusted to better extract facial features. The input image is regularized by Cutout, which enhances the generalization ability of the model. The results show that Dep-Emotion achieves the best accuracy of 40.0%. The study has important implications for automatic emotion analysis and adjunctive treatment of depression.

Keywords: Dep-Emotion · Depression · Uncertainty · Facial expression

1 Introduction

In depression, emotional dysfunction is an important component of the clinical syndrome. Expression is one of the most powerful, natural, and universal signals of human expression of emotion and intention [5,36]. In the 20th century, Ekman and Friesen defined six basic emotions that contain human emotions, namely anger, disgust, fear, happiness, sadness and surprise [14,15]. Humans tend to reflect the emotional state through facial expressions. Therefore, through various emotion-specific facial features, the cognitive process of human emotion can be studied. Emotions are equally important in the diagnosis and treatment of psychiatric disorders [42]. At present, doctors mainly analyze the emotional state

Supported by Qilu University of Technology (Shandong Academy of Sciences).

J.-J. Rousseau and B. Kapralos (Eds.): ICPR 2022 Workshops, LNCS 13643, pp. 655–667, 2023.
https://doi.org/10.1007/978-3-031-37660-3_46

of depressed patients by observing facial expressions of patients with naked eye, which has a strong subjective consciousness and high rate of misjudgment, making it difficult to accurately recognize the real emotions of depressed patients. Therefore, it is necessary to use other means to assist doctors in emotion recognition, so as to solve the potential emotion recognition barriers.

In the field of computer vision, various Facial Expression Recognition (FER) systems have been explored to encode expression information from facial features [32]. With the development of deep learning, significant progress has also been made in the related algorithms of FER as well as facial expression datasets, which are mainly collected from the Internet. Due to the subjectivity of annotators and the uncertainty caused by ambiguous face images, the presence of incorrect labels in datasets severely hinders the progress of deep learning-based FER [41].

In order to observe the facial emotion expression (FEE) deficits of depressed patients, we designed an experiment to collect seven basic expression images voluntarily imitated by 102 depressed patients and 128 healthy people, and recruited 9 raters to recognize the collected images. Then we count all recognition results and build facial expression dataset. Next, we screened the data and performed statistical analysis based on the experimental results, quantified the differences in expression mimicry between two groups. We found that depressed patients have deficits in FEE. This defect is manifested as inconsistent or uncertain labels in the dataset, which will lead to the FER model learning the features of uncertain samples, or even overfitting. This is detrimental to automatic FER.

Aiming at the uncertainty problem in depression expression dataset, we refer to the implementation of Self-Cure Network (SCN) [41], which successfully suppresses the uncertainty of samples. In order to further improve the model performance, we refer to the adjustment of the input part of the network in ResNet-C [35] and the adjustment of the downsampling block in ResNet-D [23] to improve the network structure. To prevent the network from overfitting, we refer to the implementation of the regularization method-Cutout [7], which randomly masks the square regions of the input during training, further improving the model performance.

Overall, our contributions can be summarized as follows,

Firstly, compared with previous depression studies, the number of subjects involved in this study is the largest, ensuring a sufficient sample size.

Secondly, we found through statistical analysis that depressed patients have deficits in FEE, which leads to facial expression uncertainty problem.

Thirdly, for the uncertainty problem, we refer to the implementation of SCN. By looking for uncertain samples and modifying the given label to the maximum predicted label, the label uncertainty problem in the dataset is effectively suppressed.

Fourthly, in order to further improve the model performance, we combine adjusted ResNet-C and ResNet-D, and then added the Cutout regularization method during training, we got the best accuracy of 40.0%.

2   Related Work

2.1   Facial Emotion Expression (FEE)

FEE is the way humans express emotional state through facial expressions, which can be measured by voluntary facial expression mimicry (VFEM). Facial expression mimicry is a perceptual movement after emotion perception, which is described as a general process from emotion recognition to emotion expression [1]. Previous studies have measured emotion recognition in depressed patients and have not found any difference between patients and normal people [18, 19, 37]. Depressed patients retain the basic emotional perception ability, and have no emotional cognitive bias. Dimberg [11] showed subjects images containing happy and angry expressions, and measured facial electromyographic activity (EMG) at the same time . He found that happy faces evoked increased activity in the zygomatic region, while angry faces evoked increased activity in the wrinkled region. Based on this study, Wexler [42] observed by measuring EMG that depressed patients responded insufficiently to both negative and positive emotion-evoking stimuli, and had reduced sadness responses when seeing happy, neutral, and sad faces. But there was no stronger sadness response to seeing sad faces, whereas sadness responses were significantly reduced when seeing happy faces.

2.2   Facial Expression Recognition (FER)

Due to FER's practical importance in social robotics, smart medical care, satisfaction surveys, and other human-computer interaction systems, a great deal of research has been done on FER. For example, the Facial Action Coding System (FACS) [39] is thought to represent a wider range of emotions. FER systems are mainly divided into static image-based and dynamic sequence-based according to features, where static image-based features are encoded using only spatial information from a single image [31]. Most traditional methods use handcrafted features or shallow learning (Local Binary Patterns (LBP) [31], Three Orthogonal Planes (LBP-TOP) [45], Non-negative Matrix Factorization (NMF) [46] and sparse learning [47]) for FER. With the development of emotion recognition competitions such as FER2013 [21] and emotion recognition in the wild (EmotiW) [8–10], sufficient training data has been collected from real-world scenarios, and deep learning techniques have been increasingly used to process FER challenges.

Facial expression datasets containing enough training data are important for the design of deep FER systems, among which widely used public datasets include CK+ [26], FER2013 [21], FERPLUS [4] and so on. Given a batch of data, the first step of the FER system is face detection, which removes background and non-face regions. The Viola-Jones (V&J) [40] face detector is widely used, which is robust and computationally simple to detect near-frontal faces. Multi-task Convolutional Neural Networks (MTCNN) [25] have also been used for face detection in complex scenes, leveraging multi-task learning to improve performance. The detected faces can be further subjected to face alignment, data augmentation and face regularization. For feature extraction, studies [16, 17] found that CNNs are robust in facing position and scale changes, and can be used to solve the subject independence and translation, rotation and scale invariance problems in FER [27]. Ji et al. [20] proposed 3D-CNN to capture motion information encoded in multiple adjacent frames, followed by 3D convolution for action recognition. In the study [20], Faster R-CNN [24] was used to perform FER by generating high-quality region proposals. After learning deep features, the FER system needs to perform emotion classification on the input face. The cross-entropy between the estimated class probability and the true distribution can be minimized by adding a softmax loss function at the end of the CNN to adjust the back-propagation error. Then the network can directly output the predicted probability for each sample [32]. There are also studies [12,33] that use deep neural networks as a feature extraction tool, and then apply additional independent classifiers, such as support vector machines or random forests, to the extracted features.

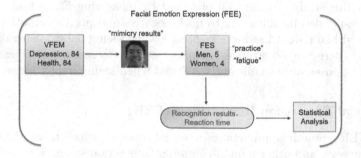

Fig. 1. Complete experimental design process.

2.3 Uncertainty Research

In the FER task, uncertainty mainly manifests as ambiguous expressions, incorrect labels and inconsistent labels (noisy labels). Dehghani et al. [6] pretrain the neural network by using a large amount of data with noisy labels, then use a small amount of data with real labels to fine-tune the parameters and evaluate the quality of the labels during training. Sukhbaatar and Fergus [34] adapted the network output to the distribution of noisy labels by adding an extra noise layer into the network and then estimated it. Azadi et al. [3] used mislabeled samples to train a deep CNN model for image classification and encouraged the model to select reliable images for robust learning. Veit et al. [38] proposed a multi-task network that jointly learns to clean up noisy labels and accurately classify images, which can effectively use a large number of uncertain images and a small subset of clean images to learn features. Instead of using clean data, Hinton et al. [29] set additional constraints on uncertain samples, such as a specific loss for randomly flipping labels [30]. Zeng et al. [44] considered the problem of inconsistent labels across different datasets and proposed exploiting these uncertainties to improve FER. In contrast, our work focuses on suppressing label uncertainty to learn reliable facial features to better recognize the real emotions of depressed patients.

3 Facial Emotion Expression

The complete FEE consisted of VFEM, Facial Expression Scoring (FES) and statistical analysis. VFEM means that subjects were asked to imitate seven facial expressions, and the mimicry results were recorded. FES refers to the raters performing FER on the mimicry results of subjects, and recording the recognition results and reaction time. As shown in Fig. 1.

3.1 VFEM

Valid data on 168 subjects were involved in this study, including 84 depressed patients and 84 healthy people, who were similar in age, sex, education, and marital status. All subjects were Chinese. The depression group met the screening rules of the Diagnostic and Statistical Manual of Mental Disorders (DSM-IV) [2], had a score of more than 20 on the Hamilton Depression Scale (HAMD-24) [22], and had no other mental disorders or serious illnesses. The healthy group had a score of less than 8 on the HAMD-24 score, and had no previous history of mental disorders or family history.

Before the experiment, all subjects were informed of the experimental content, participated voluntarily, and signed an informed consent form. During the experiment, the researchers sequentially played computer-generated static images of seven basic emotions (anger, disgust, fear, neutrality, happiness, surprise, and sadness), which proved to be more effective stimuli [43]. Subjects were required to stare at computer screen, imitate expressions under the guidance of doctor, and keep it for as long as possible. When subject's facial movement was stable, the researchers controlled the camera to take a frontal shot of it and save it by the corresponding emotion category.

3.2 FES

Before the experiment, we use the Haar classifier that comes with OpenCV to perform face detection on collected images, and then crop the part of the image that contains complete face into a 224×224 (unit is pixel) square image. We recruited 9 graduate students (5 men, 4 women) as raters at a local graduate school to participate in the scoring. All raters had no previous history of mental disorders or family history, and the HAMD-24 score was less than 8 points. During the experiment, the collected images were randomly displayed on computer screen, and the raters were asked to choose an emotion category they thought was correct for each image. Images of the depressed group were mixed with images of the healthy group. There is no limit to the reaction time of raters, but they are encouraged to make a choice as soon as possible. The experimental

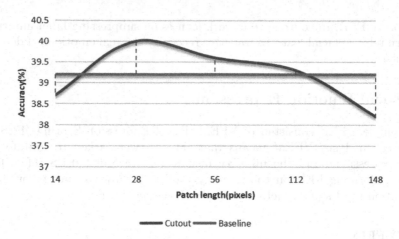

Fig. 2. The effect of different patch length on accuracy.

program automatically records the recognition results as well as the reaction time. Before the experiment, a random sample of 15% of the collected images was practiced to quickly familiarize the raters with this task. To reduce the effect of fatigue, the experiment was divided into 4 stages, with a 15-minute rest after each stage was completed. After the experiment is over, all recognition results are counted and aggregated into a new dataset. Each image corresponds to 10 labels, representing the subject's emotion category and the recognition results of the 9 raters.

3.3 Statistical Analysis

Table 1 provides descriptive information for two groups of subjects. There were no significant differences in gender, age, education level and marital status between the two groups, which were in line with the conditions of the control experiment. As expected, there was a significant difference in HAMD-24 scores between the depressed and non-depressed groups.

We conducted a detailed analysis of the difference in scores of the seven expressions imitated by two groups of subjects. The results showed that compared with healthy people, depressed patients had lower accuracy in imitating anger, fear, happiness and neutrality. Sadness, surprise, fear and disgust imitated by depressed group had higher neutral bias, among which sadness and surprise had lower bias of happiness. Happiness imitated by depressed patients had higher biases of anger, disgust, fear, neutrality and surprise. Neutrality imitated by depressed patients had higher biases of disgust and sadness, and lower bias of happiness.

Table 1. Descriptive information for two groups of subjects. *Represents independent sample t-test. &Represents chi-square test.

Categories	Depression	Health controls	t/F	p
Gender(female)&	52.38%	48.80%	0.214	0.643
Age(year, x±s)*	38.50±14.50	38.51±14.54	0.002	0.965
University entrance Diploma(yes)&	47.62%	54.76%	0.858	0.354
Marital status marriage Certificate(yes)&	64.29%	66.67%	0.105	0.746
HAMD-24*	29.15±6.80	0.56±0.87	38.22	**<0.001**

We also analyzed the reaction time of the raters. The results showed that the raters had longer reaction time to recognize the happiness imitated by depressed group than the healthy group. Combining the scores of happiness imitated by subjects, it can be concluded that compared with the healthy group, depressed patients are difficult to be recognized when expressing happy emotion, and are more easily recognized as other expressions.

Regarding the relationship between FEE and depression severity (HAMD-24 score), the study found that the accuracy of subjects imitating happiness was negatively correlated with depression severity. The neutral bias of the surprise imitated by subjects was positively correlated with depression severity. the reaction time of raters to recognize the happiness imitated by subjects was positively related to the depression severity of the subjects.

In conclusion, depressed patients have deficits in FEE, which leads to facial expression uncertainty problem.

4   Dep-Emotion

We propose Dep-Emotion to solve label uncertainty in depression facial expression dataset. It mainly contains 3 parts. The first part is Self-Cure Network, the second part is ResNet Adjustments, and the third part is Cutout. The pipeline of Dep-Emotion is shown in Fig. 3.

4.1   Self-Cure Network (SCN)

SCN contains three main modules. They are Self-Attention Importance Weighting (SAIW), Rank Regularization (RR) and Relableling [41]. First, given a batch of images, use ResNet18 to extract facial features. The SAIW module learns a sample weight for each input feature, some samples have higher importance weights, while uncertain samples have lower importance weights. Let $F = [x_1, x_2, ...x_N] \in R^{D \times N}$ denotes the facial features of N images. The

SAIW module consists of linear fully connected layer and sigmoid activation function, which can be expressed as,

$$\alpha_i = \sigma \left(W_a^T x_i \right), \tag{1}$$

where α_i is the importance weight of the i-th sample, w_a is the parameters of the fully connected layer used for attention, and σ is the sigmoid function.

The RR module sorts the sample weights in descending order and divides them into high and low importance groups with a ratio β. Regularization is done by placing a margin between the average weights of the two groups. A ranking regularization loss (RR-Loss) was defined for this purpose, as shown below,

$$\mathcal{L}_{RR} = max[0, \delta_1 - (\alpha_H - \alpha_L)], \tag{2}$$

$$\alpha_H = \frac{1}{M} \sum_{i=0}^{M} \alpha_i, \alpha_L = \frac{1}{N-M} \sum_{i=M}^{N} \alpha_i, \tag{3}$$

where δ_1 is a margin, which can be a fixed hyperparameter or a learnable parameter, α_H and α_L are the average values of the high importance group with $\beta * N = M$ samples and the low importance group with $N - M$ samples respectively.

The Relableling module works by comparing the maximum predicted probability with the probability of the given label, and then relabeling these samples in a low importance weights group. If the maximum predicted probability is higher than one of the given labels with a threshold, the sample is assigned to a new pseudo-label. The relabelling module can be defined as,

$$\mathcal{y}' = \begin{cases} \ell_{\max} & \text{if } P_{\max} - P_{\text{gtInd}} > \delta_2 \\ \ell_{\text{org}} & \text{otherwise} \end{cases} \tag{4}$$

where $\mathcal{y}'$ represents the new label, δ_2 is the threshold, $P_{\max}$ is the maximum predicted probability, and P_{gtInd} is the predicted probability of the given label. ℓ_{max} and ℓ_{org} are the maximum predicted index and the original given label, respectively.

4.2   ResNet Adjustments

Next, we revisit two popular ResNet adjustments, ResNet-C and ResNet-D.

ResNet-C [35]. Replace one 7×7 convolution in the input part with three 3×3 convolutions significantly reduces the amount of parameters and computation. Because the computational cost of convolution is quadratic with the kernel width or height. At the same time, the output channel of the first convolution is 32 and the stride is 2. The output channel of the second convolution is 32 with a stride of 1. The output channel of the last convolution is 64 with a stride of 1.

ResNet-D [23]. Modify the downsampling block of ResNet. A 2×2 average pooling layer is added before the 1×1 convolution on the identity map with a

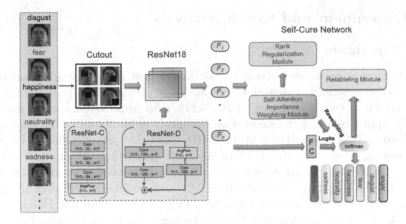

Fig. 3. The pipeline of Dep-Emotion.

stride of 2, and then the stride of the 1×1 convolutional layer is changed to 1. Because information loss occurs when 1×1 convolution and downsampling are performed at the same time.

4.3 Cutout

Cutout [7] mainly targets the overfitting problem of CNNs by regularizing by randomly masking square regions of the input during training, effectively augmenting the dataset with partially masked versions of existing samples. This approach is able to force the FER model to consider the complete image context more than focusing on individual visual features. It is worth noting that objects removed from the input image are also removed in all subsequent feature maps. This approach is close to data augmentation, it does not generate noise, but generates images that look novel to the network.

Table 2. Acc represents Accuracy. Ang, Dis, Fea, Hap, Neu, Sad and Sur represent the F1-score of anger, disgust, fear, happiness, neutrality, sadness and surprise respectively.

Model	Acc	Ang	Dis	Fea	Hap	Neu	Sad	Sur
Deep-Emotion [28]	0.308	0.280	**0.337**	0.226	0.307	0.333	0.043	0.461
SCN [41]	0.387	**0.290**	0.327	0.208	0.407	0.447	0.475	0.466
ViT [13]	0.395	0.225	0.125	0.200	0.483	0.467	**0.535**	0.529
Dep-Emotion	**0.400**	0.203	0.275	**0.227**	**0.506**	**0.500**	0.457	**0.582**

5   Experiment and Result Analysis

5.1   Experiment

The depression expression dataset consisted of 588 images evenly distributed across seven emotional categories. In order to implement Dep-Emotion, we first adjusted the network structure of ResNet18, and improved its input part and downsampling block at the same time. We use it as the baseline for implementing Cutout. GPU is NVIDIA 2070 (8GB). Next, we set parameters for SCN. The training images are divided into 70% high importance group and 30% low importance group at each iteration. The margin δ_1 between two groups is set to 0.07. The learning rate is initialized to 0.01 and divided by 10 after 15 epochs and 30 epochs respectively. A total of 120 epochs were trained. Batch_size is set to 32. From the 10th epoch, the Relabeling module starts to optimize. The optimizer is SGD. Accuracy was used as the evaluation metric for all expressions, it can be defined as,

$$Accuracy = \frac{TP + TN}{TP + TN + FP + FN} \tag{5}$$

where TP and TN represents the number of samples judged correct. FP and FN represents the number of samples judged wrong. The higher the accuracy, the better the classification performance of the model.

F1-score was used as the evaluation metric for single expression, it can be defined as,

$$F1 - score = 2 * \frac{Precision * Recall}{Precision + Recall} \tag{6}$$

where $Precision$ represents the proportion of positive samples judged by the classifier to be positive examples. $Recall$ represents the proportion of predicted positive examples to the total positive examples. Similar to accuracy, the higher the F1-score, the better the classification performance of the model.

To implement Cutout, we experimented with the size of the masked square region. Knowing that the size of the input image is 224×224 pixels, images are first zero-padded with 13 pixels on each side to get a 250×250 pixels image, and then a 224×224 pixels crop Cutout is randomly extracted. We verify the model classification performance with masked regions of 14×14 pixels, 28×28 pixels, 56×56 pixels, 112×112 pixels, and 148×148 pixels in Fig. 2. Finally, we choose a Cutout size of 28×28 pixels for training.

5.2   Result Analysis

After adjusting the network structure of ResNet18, the accuracy of SCN on depression expression dataset is increased by 0.5%. The reason is that ResNet-C significantly reduces the parameters and computational complexity, and ResNet-D effectively avoids the information loss of downsampling, so that more facial features can be extracted and the model performance is improved.

As shown in Table 2, our Dep-Emotion achieves the best accuracy of 40% on depression expression dataset after implementing Cutout. A further increase of 0.8%. Compared with SCN, the accuracy is improved by 1.3%. Deep-Emotion [28] classifies sadness abnormally, but has the highest recognition rate for disgust. SCN [41] has the highest recognition rate for anger. ViT [13] has the highest recognition rate for sadness. Our Dep-Emotion improves the recognition rate of fear by 1.9%, happiness by 9.9%, neutrality by 5.3% and surprise by 11.6%, but anger, disgust and sadness has decreased. We speculate that these three expressions are sensitive to the masked region, which affects feature extraction and leads to a decline in the recognition rate. We hope to collect more data to make sample features more diverse and further improve the model generalization ability.

6 Conclusion

In this paper, we measure facial emotion expression deficits in depressed patients and propose Dep-Emotion to address the uncertainty of facial expressions. The uncertainty is suppressed by correcting the sample labels, and the ResNet network structure is adjusted to better extract facial features, and the input image is regularized to enhance the generalization ability of the model. This study has effectively improved the accuracy of recognizing the real emotions of depressed patients, which is of great significance for automatic emotion analysis and adjuvant treatment of depression.

Acknowledgements. This work was supported by the Shandong Provincial Natural Science Foundation, China (Grant No: ZR2021MF079, ZR2020MF039). The National Natural Science Foundation of China (Grant No: 81573829). The 20 Planned Projects in Jinan (No.2021GXRC046). The Key Research and Development Program of Shandong Province (Grant No.2020CXGC010901).

References

1. Arnold, A.J., Winkielman, P.: Smile (but only deliberately) though your heart is aching: loneliness is associated with impaired spontaneous smile mimicry. Soc. Neurosci. **1**, 1–13 (2020)
2. Association, A., American, P.A.: Diagnostic and statistical manual of mental disorders. Essentials Pain Med. **51**(1), 4–8 (1980)
3. Azadi, S., Feng, J., Jegelka, S., Darrell, T.: Auxiliary image regularization for deep CNNs with noisy labels. arXiv preprint arXiv:1511.07069 (2015)
4. Barsoum, E., Zhang, C., Ferrer, C.C., Zhang, Z.: Training deep networks for facial expression recognition with crowd-sourced label distribution, pp. 279–283 (2016)
5. Darwin, C.: The expression of emotions in man and animals. Tredition Classics **123**(1), 146 (2009)
6. Dehghani, M., Severyn, A., Rothe, S., Kamps, J.: Avoiding your teacher's mistakes: training neural networks with controlled weak supervision. arXiv preprint arXiv:1711.00313 (2017)

7. DeVries, T., Taylor, G.W.: Improved regularization of convolutional neural networks with cutout. arXiv preprint arXiv:1708.04552 (2017)
8. Dhall, A., Goecke, R., Ghosh, S., Joshi, J., Hoey, J., Gedeon, T.: From individual to group-level emotion recognition: Emotiw **5**, 524–528 (2017)
9. Dhall, A., Goecke, R., Joshi, J., Hoey, J., Gedeon, T.: Emotiw 2016: video and group-level emotion recognition challenges, pp. 427–432 (2016)
10. Dhall, A., Ramana Murthy, O., Goecke, R., Joshi, J., Gedeon, T.: Video and image based emotion recognition challenges in the wild: Emotiw **2015**, 423–426 (2015)
11. Dimberg, U.: Facial reactions to facial expressions. Psychophysiology **19**(6), 643–647 (1982)
12. Donahue, J., et al.: Decaf: a deep convolutional activation feature for generic visual recognition, 647–655 (2014)
13. Dosovitskiy, A., et al.: An image is worth 16×16 words: transformers for image recognition at scale. arXiv preprint arXiv:2010.11929 (2020)
14. Ekman, P.: Strong evidence for universals in facial expressions: a reply to Russell's mistaken critique. Psychol. Bull. **115**(2), 268–287 (1994)
15. Ekman, P.: Constants across culture in the face and emotion. J. Pers. Soc. Psychol. 17 (1971)
16. Fasel, B.: Head-pose invariant facial expression recognition using convolutional neural networks. In: Proceedings of the Fourth IEEE International Conference on Multimodal Interfaces, pp. 529–534. IEEE (2002)
17. Fasel, B.: Robust face analysis using convolutional neural networks **2**, 40–43 (2002)
18. Gaebel, W., WöLwer, W.: Facial expression and emotional face recognition in schizophrenia and depression **242**(1), 46–52 (1992)
19. Gessler, S.: Schizophrenic inability to judge facial emotion: a controlled study. British J. Clin. Psychol. 28 (2011)
20. Girshick, R., Donahue, J., Darrell, T., Malik, J.: Rich feature hierarchies for accurate object detection and semantic segmentation, pp. 580–587 (2014)
21. Goodfellow, I.J., et al.: Challenges in representation learning: a report on three machine learning contests. In: Lee, M., Hirose, A., Hou, Z.-G., Kil, R.M. (eds.) ICONIP 2013. LNCS, vol. 8228, pp. 117–124. Springer, Heidelberg (2013). https://doi.org/10.1007/978-3-642-42051-1_16
22. Hamilton, M.: The Hamilton rating scale for depression. Springer (1986). https://doi.org/10.1007/978-3-030-22009-9_826
23. He, T., Zhang, Z., Zhang, H., Zhang, Z., Xie, J., Li, M.: Bag of tricks for image classification with convolutional neural networks, pp. 558–567 (2019)
24. Li, J., et al.: Facial expression recognition with faster R-CNN. Procedia Comput. Sci. **107**, 135–140 (2017)
25. Li, S., Deng, W., Du, J.: Reliable crowdsourcing and deep locality-preserving learning for expression recognition in the wild, pp. 2852–2861 (2017)
26. Lucey, P., Cohn, J.F., Kanade, T., Saragih, J., Ambadar, Z., Matthews, I.: The extended cohn-kanade dataset (ck+): a complete dataset for action unit and emotion-specified expression, pp. 94–101 (2010)
27. Matsugu, M., Mori, K., Mitari, Y., Kaneda, Y.: Subject independent facial expression recognition with robust face detection using a convolutional neural network. Neural Netw. **16**(5–6), 555–559 (2003)
28. Minaee, S., Minaei, M., Abdolrashidi, A.: Deep-emotion: Facial expression recognition using attentional convolutional network. Sensors **21**(9), 3046 (2021)
29. Mnih, V., Hinton, G.E.: Learning to label aerial images from noisy data, pp. 567–574 (2012)

30. Natarajan, N., Dhillon, I.S., Ravikumar, P., Tewari, A.: Learning with noisy labels. In: Advances in Neural Information Processing Systems, vol. 26, pp. 1196–1204 (2013)
31. Shan, C., Gong, S., Mcowan, P.W.: Facial expression recognition based on local binary patterns: a comprehensive study. Image Vis. Comput. 27(6), 803–816 (2009)
32. Shan, L., Deng, W.: Deep facial expression recognition: a survey. IEEE Trans. Affect. Comput. (99) (2018)
33. Sharif Razavian, A., Azizpour, H., Sullivan, J., Carlsson, S.: CNN features off-the-shelf: an astounding baseline for recognition, pp. 806–813 (2014)
34. Sukhbaatar, S., Fergus, R.: Learning from noisy labels with deep neural networks. arXiv preprint arXiv:1406.2080 2(3), 4 (2014)
35. Szegedy, C., Vanhoucke, V., Ioffe, S., Shlens, J., Wojna, Z.: Rethinking the inception architecture for computer vision. IEEE, pp. 2818–2826 (2016)
36. Tian, Y.I., Kanade, T., Cohn, J.F.: Recognizing action units for facial expression analysis. IEEE Trans. Pattern Anal. Mach. Intell. 23(2), 97–115 (2001)
37. Tracy, A., Weightman, M.J., Baune, B.T.: Symptom severity of depressive symptoms impacts on social cognition performance in current but not remitted major depressive disorder. Front. Psychol. 6, 1118 (2015)
38. Veit, A., Alldrin, N., Chechik, G., Krasin, I., Gupta, A., Belongie, S.: Learning from noisy large-scale datasets with minimal supervision, pp. 839–847 (2017)
39. Vick, S.J., Waller, B.M., Parr, L.A., Smith Pasqualini, M.C., Bard, K.A.: A cross-species comparison of facial morphology and movement in humans and chimpanzees using the facial action coding system (facs). J. Nonverbal Behav. 31(1), 1–20 (2007)
40. Viola, P., Jones, M.: Rapid object detection using a boosted cascade of simple features 1, I-I (2001)
41. Wang, K., Peng, X., Yang, J., Lu, S., Qiao, Y.: Suppressing uncertainties for large-scale facial expression recognition, pp. 6897–6906 (2020)
42. Wexler, B.E., Levenson, L., Warrenburg, S., Price, L.H.: Decreased perceptual sensitivity to emotion-evoking stimuli in depression. Psych. Res. 51(2), 127 (1994)
43. Wood, A., Rychlowska, M., Korb, S., Niedenthal, P.: Fashioning the face: sensorimotor simulation contributes to facial expression recognition. Trends Cogn. Sci. 20(3), 227–240 (2016)
44. Zeng, J., Shan, S., Chen, X.: Facial expression recognition with inconsistently annotated datasets, pp. 222–237 (2018)
45. Zhao, G., Pietikainen, M.: Dynamic texture recognition using local binary patterns with an application to facial expressions. IEEE Trans. Pattern Anal. Mach. Intell. 29, 915–928 (2007)
46. Zhi, R., Flierl, M., Ruan, Q., Kleijn, W.B.: Graph-preserving sparse nonnegative matrix factorization with application to facial expression recognition. IEEE Trans. Syst. Man Cybern. B Cybern. 41(1), 38–52 (2011)
47. Zhong, L., Liu, Q., Yang, P., Liu, B., Huang, J., Metaxas, D.N.: Learning active facial patches for expression analysis, pp. 2562–2569 (2012)

EEG-Based Joint Semi-supervised Learning for Major Depressive Disorder Detection

Tao Chen[1,2(✉)] [iD], Tong Zheng[2], Jinlong Shi[2], and Yanrong Guo[1,2]

[1] Key Laboratory of Knowledge Engineering with Big Data, Hefei University of Technology, Hefei, China
[2] School of Computer Science and Information Engineering, Hefei University of Technology, Hefei, China
chentao.hfut@mail.hfut.edu.cn

Abstract. Major Depressive Disorder (MDD) has been a major mental disease in recent years, imposing huge negative impacts on both our society and individuals. The current clinical MDD detection methods, such as self-report scales and interviews, often suffer from their subjectiveness. In contrast, electroencephalography (EEG) signals reflect brain activity and can be used as an effective information source for MDD detection. However, the learning-based MDD detection methods with EEG data usually neglect the valuable information contained in the unlabeled data, therefore possibly suffering from the label scarcity issue. In this context, we propose a simple EEG-based Joint Semi-supervised Learning (JSL) model for the MDD detection task, which fully leverages the information from unlabeled data. Specifically, by equipping the unlabeled samples with the intermediately predicted pseudo labels, the accurate position of the class-specific centroids in the feature space can be gradually refined. Based on that, the auxiliary labels based on a heuristic centroid-based classifier can be obtained, which plays an effective complementary role in predicting the sample labels. The experiments on a public dataset demonstrate the effectivenes s of our method, showing an obvious performance gain via using the proposed semi-supervised strategy.

Keywords: Semi-supervised learning · class-specific centroids · MDD detection

1 Introduction

MDD is a prevalent mental illness that significantly impacts one's life, even causing suicidal behaviors. Nowadays, what is worse, the spread of COVID-19 has intensified the MDD sufferings throughout the world [20, 28].

Researches [41, 47] show that a timely and accurate diagnosis can effectively prevent further deterioration of MDD. Clinically, MDD is diagnosed according to face-to-face interviews or self-report measures such as Beck's Depression Inventory (BDI) [11], Patient Health Questionnaire 9-item (PHQ-9), Self-rating

© Springer Nature Switzerland AG 2023
J.-J. Rousseau and B. Kapralos (Eds.): ICPR 2022 Workshops, LNCS 13643, pp. 668–681, 2023.
https://doi.org/10.1007/978-3-031-37660-3_47

Depression Scale (SDS), or a combination of these measurements in most cases. However, some subjective factors, such as doctors' proficiency and patients' participation, tend to fundamentally affect diagnostic accuracy. As a solution to this issue, many objective technical roadmaps have been proposed, which utilize various sensors to capture useful cues from individuals, such as camera [52], Magnetic Resonance Imaging (MRI) [40], Heart Rate Variability (HRV) [44] and even social media [25]. However, these works can still be limited, due to the unreliable data acquisition process or the expensive costs. Differently, electroencephalography (EEG) has been solidly applied in analyzing brain-behavior of many mental conditions [1,10,22]. In neuroscience and cognitive science studies [37,51], EEG refers to the cerebral cortex's spontaneous and rhythmic bioelectrical impulses, which show subtle changes in brain neurons and reflect mental activity and cognitive behavior [19,34]. Some studies [6,31] have proven that there is a connection between MDD and EEG, demonstrating that EEG can be utilized as a useful indicator.

MDD detection methods based on EEG data have achieved much progress in recent years. However, as for the model-driven methods, they still need an ad hoc feature engineering procedure before the classifiers. However, due to EEG signals' inherent complexity, many feature extraction techniques cannot effectively generalize their characteristics [30]. In contrast, data-driven methods are drawing growing attention due to their powerful feature extraction and representation capacity. Despite the great progress made in the current research, there is still one major obstacle to overcome. It is difficult to collect EEG data from a large number of individuals with accurate labels, which may introduce huge expenses. Therefore, the label scarcity issue is preventing the advance of the data-driven MDD detection research. Second, samples belonging to the same class are relatively close in the feature space.

To overcome these challenges, we design the EEG-based Joint Semi-supervised Learning (JSL) model, aiming to achieve the MDD detection task via jointly considering labeled and unlabeled data. The rationality comes from the assumption that samples belonging to the same class are relatively close in the feature space. The Euclidean distance between samples and the class-specific centroids can reveal useful cues in many classification tasks [42]. Based on that, by combining labeled and unlabeled data, we intend to obtain some auxiliary information at the label prediction level through progressively optimizing the centroid positions in the feature space. The experimental results on a public dataset validate the effectiveness of our technical roadmap. The technical contributions of our model can be concluded as follows.

- We design a semi-supervised learning model that enhances the prediction accuracy by jointly utilizing the labeled data and the unlabeled data.
- We propose to locate the class-specific centroids with the aid of the mean feature of the unlabeled data, aiming to improve the robustness against outliers during the updating process.

The structure of this paper is organized as follows. Section 2 briefly introduces the relevant works. We present the details of our method in Sect. 3. Experimental results and analysis are reported in Sect. 4. Finally, Sect. 5 concludes the paper.

2   Related Work

Since we conduct research on the EEG-based MDD detection task via introducing the semi-supervised learning strategy, we provide a general overview of the research progress made in these two fields.

2.1   EEG-Related Work

Cai *et al.* [7] propose a case-based reasoning model for MDD detection, which extracts features of EEG signals and uses multiple classifiers to obtain the best MDD detection performance. Peng *et al.* [32] use the phase lag index to construct a functional connectivity matrix and adopt the Kendall rank correlation coefficient to classify the samples. Furthermore, Azizi *et al.* [4] explore the nonlinear feature extraction methods to discriminate the MDD individuals and the Normal Control (NC) group. Shi *et al.* [36] use linear and nonlinear hand-crafted features of the EEG signals to perform the MDD classification task under different classifiers (KNN, LR, SVM). The results show that the selected three-channel EEG and features are able to tell depressed subjects from normal ones. DepHNN [35] decomposes the multi-channel EEG signals into multiple frequency bands and applies it to kernel principal component analysis to obtain the low-dimensional vector and perform the classification task on them. These model-driven methods mainly rely on the handcrafted features specifically designed for the MDD detection task, which can be less reliable and difficult for model extension.

Benefiting from the learning ability of deep learning, researchers have resorted to the data-driven roadmap for EEG-based MDD detection. Betul *et al.* [3] propose a deep hybrid model, which adopts CNN and LSTM to detect depression. The method [39] combines the CNN and LSTM architecture to design an MDD depression detection model, while the former learns the local features and the latter captures the sequential features, respectively. The model [27] uses the distance-based and non-distance projection method to construct EEG signals as the input. Aiming at the challenge brought by a small EEG depression dataset, the architecture [33] proposes a hybrid deep learning model, which combines CNN with Gated Recursive Unit (GRU). In contrast, the proposed network is shallower and smaller than the LSTM network. Jiang *et al.* [16] construct a four-layer LSTM network, which extracts EEG features through Wavelet Transform (WT), obtaining promising performance. Li *et al.* [24] extract the functional connectivity matrices of the five EEG bands and convert them into three-channel images, aiming to model the EEG-signal classification task into the image classification task. Hui *et al.* [13] combine Short Time Fourier Transform (STFT) with the CNN model for computer-aided depression detection. From the above methods, we can see that the handcrafted features are still used in them. In addition, few methods pay attention to the problem of insufficient labeled samples, which can often be encountered in the real-world MDD detection scenario. As for our method, different from the above methods, we target at solving the label scarcity issue via introducing the semi-supervised learning strategy.

2.2 Semi-supervised Learning

Semi-supervised learning aims to fully leverage labeled and unlabeled data in extensive tasks, which typically considers the situations when labeled data is insufficient, such as computer-aided diagnosis [49], drug manufacturing [21] and molecular property prediction [12].

Tang et al. [38] propose a semi-supervised self-training framework for mass detection that iteratively refines the model using the image-level soft marker. Kamran et al. [17] propose a new conditional imaging network that can predict fundus lesions. The proposed system is helpful in solving the problem of retinal angiography in a non-invasive way and predicting the existence of retinal abnormalities. Ji et al. [14] predict the potential miRNA disease via integrating disease semantic similarity, miRNA functional similarity and their Gaussian interaction profile similarity in a semi-supervised manner. Liu et al. [26] propose a novel semi-supervised medical image classification method that encourages the prediction consistency of a given input under disturbance and uses the self-scrambling model to generate high-quality consistency targets for unlabeled data. In addition, a new sample relationship consistency paradigm is introduced to model the relationship information between multiple samples. Xia et al. [43] propose a multi-view collaborative training framework for uncertain perception to achieve the accurate segmentation of medical images, which applies joint training via exploring the multi-view consistency across unlabeled data. In addition, the uncertainty estimation of each view is employed and achieves promising performance. You et al. [48] proposes a simple contrast extraction strategy that constructs two independent dropout layers as masks and predicts their symbolic distance map of the decision boundary in the contrast target. Zhou et al. [53] propose a collaborative learning method to improve disease classification performance and lesion segmentation in a semi-supervised manner. Li et al. [23] propose a semi-supervised end-to-end variational reasoning method to generate medical dialogue. It uses the variational Bayesian generation method to approximate the posterior distribution of patient state and expert behavior. Andres et al. [2] train a semi-supervised retinal image synthesizer on slight glaucoma labeled database and an extensive unlabeled database for automatic glaucoma assessment.

Hao et al. [12] propose an active semi-supervised graph neural network, which combines labeled and unlabeled molecules, aiming to combine the information of molecular structure and distribution. Ding et al. [8] propose a semi-supervised locally-preserving dense graph neural network, which uses the auto-regressive moving average filter and context-aware learning to extract useful local information. Yan et al. [46] propose a method to predict drug-drug interaction based on integrated similarity and semi-supervised learning, which integrates drug chemistry, biology, and phenotypic data in a unified framework. Zhu et al. [54] propose

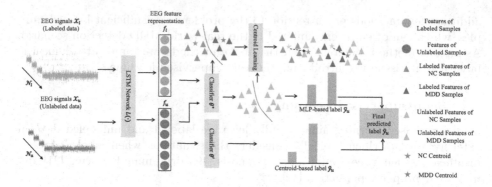

Fig. 1. The overall framework of the proposed model.

a semi-supervised model based on a graph convolution network to detect compact subgraphs effectively. Xu *et al.* [45] propose a shadow consistent learning method in a semi-supervised fashion that uses shadow enhancement and the specifically designed loss to solve the challenges of low-quality medical images. To fully use labeled and unlabeled pixels in training images, Kumar *et al.* [18] design a hyperspectral imaging pixel classification method for dimensionality reduction and pixel clustering. Jiang *et al.* [15] integrate graph learning and graph convolution into a unified architecture to learn an optimal graph structure, which is applied to promote the graph convolution operation of the unlabeled data.

The above research progress shows that the semi-supervised learning strategy can be subtly realized at different levels or starting points in many real-world applications. As for our research, we introduce the semi-supervised learning strategy at the decision level, which combines the predicted pseudo labels to guide the incorporation of the unlabeled data.

3   Method

In this section, we first introduce the overall framework proposed in this paper. Then we introduce the stages of feature extraction and joint semi-supervised learning. The adopted loss function is introduced at last.

3.1   Overall Framework

The overall framework is depicted in Fig. 1, which can be formed as a typical two-class classification problem. The inputs contain a set of labeled subjects $\mathcal{X}_l$ and a set of unlabeled subjects $\mathcal{X}_u$:

$$\mathcal{X}_l = \{x_l^i, y_l^i\}_{i=1}^{\mathcal{N}_l}$$
$$\mathcal{X}_u = \{x_u^i\}_{i=1}^{\mathcal{N}_u}, \tag{1}$$

Specifically, $x^i \in \mathcal{R}^{E \times T}$ denotes the EEG signals, where E and T represent the channel and the time stamp numbers.

Generally, the whole model seeks an optimal mapping between $\{\mathcal{X}_l, \mathcal{X}_u\}$ and the class label k. Here k refers to normal control (NC, $k = 0$) or major depression disorder (MDD, $k = 1$). Specifically, the task-specific features from EEG signals are firstly extracted by using the LSTM-based network for both $\{x_l^i\}$ and $\{x_u^i\}$. Then, the pseudo labels $\overline{y}_u$ are produced based on the classifier θ^*. Equipped with $\overline{y}_u$, $\mathcal{X}_l$ and $\mathcal{X}_u$ can be merged into a large set with the label partition. Based on this, centroid learning is used to optimize the centroid positions of the two classes, producing the auxiliary labels $\tilde{y}_u^i$ by a heuristic centroid-based classifier θ'. The final prediction is jointly determined with $\overline{y}_u$ and $\tilde{y}_u^i$.

3.2 Feature Extraction Based on LSTM

LSTM is usually used to deal with sequence data [5,9,50], which can be effective in exploring the temporal cues. In our model, an LSTM network $L(\cdot)$ is trained to extract task-oriented features for labeled and unlabeled data:

$$f_l = L(x_l)$$
$$f_u = L(x_u) \tag{2}$$

in which x_l and x_u denote raw EEG signals for the labeled and unlabeled data, and f_l and f_u are the extracted features.

3.3 Joint Semi-supervised Learning

Based on the feature extracted from the LSTM network, an MLP classifier θ^* can be obtained based on the labeled data:

$$\theta^* = \arg\max_{\theta} \sum_{(X_l, Y_l)} \log p(Y_l \mid X_l; \theta) \tag{3}$$

The MLP classifier θ^* can be used to predict the labels of EEG data, producing the pseudo labels for the originally-unlabeled subjects:

$$\overline{y}_u = p(x_u, \theta^*) \tag{4}$$

where $\overline{y}_u$ denotes the soft label probability of the unlabeled data x_u. The pseudo labels enable the combination of all the labeled and unlabeled data together.

Based on the labeled data, we initialize class-specific centroids c_k as:

$$c_k = \frac{1}{\mathcal{N}_k} \sum_{i=1}^{\mathcal{N}_k} \{f_{lk}^i, f_{uk}^i\} \tag{5}$$

in which c_k is the initialized centroids for the whole data, and $\mathcal{N}_k$ is the subject number of the k-th class. $\{f_{lk}^i, f_{uk}^i\} \in \mathcal{R}^{\mathcal{N}_k \times d}$ is the collection of feature vectors from class k, and d is the feature dimension.

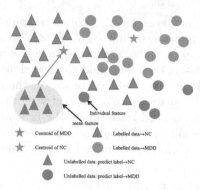

Fig. 2. The update of the centroid is determined by the centroid obtained in the previous epoch and the unlabeled sample.

In the following, we build a heuristic centroid-based classifier θ' to produce the auxiliary labels $\tilde{y}_u^i$ for the unlabeled data. It is built based on the following assumption: two subjects belonging to the same class should be close in their feature space, while two subjects from different classes should be far away from each other. Based on this assumption, we calculate the Euclidean distance between the features from the unlabeled data and the initialized centroids $ED(f_u^i, c_k)$, which is then used to estimate its soft label:

$$s_{i,k} = 1 - \frac{ED(f_u^i, c_k)}{\sum_{k=1}^{K} ED(f_u^i, c_k)} \tag{6}$$

in which $s_{i,k}$ represents the distance between the i-th unlabeled subject and the k-th class. As a step further, the centroid-based classifier θ' can be parameterized as the possibility that the subject f_u^i belongs to the k-th classes:

$$\tilde{y}_u^i = \frac{s_{i,k}}{\sum_{k=1}^{K} s_{i,k}}, \tag{7}$$

in which $\tilde{y}_u^i$ is the desired auxiliary label. Typically, $K = 2$ in our MDD detection task.

With $\overline{y}_u^i$ and $\tilde{y}_u^i$ at hand, the final predicted label $\hat{y}_u^i$ can be directly obtained as:

$$\hat{y}_u^i = \frac{\overline{y}_u^i + \tilde{y}_u^i}{2} \tag{8}$$

3.4   Centroid Learning

In the above process, it is clear that the centroids can be gradually refined to produce more accurate auxiliary labels. To this end, we adopt a simple but effective centroid learning strategy.

Algorithm 1. The pseudocode of the proposed JSL model.

Input:

    The labeled data $\mathcal{X}_l = \{x_l^i, y_l^i\}_{i=1}^{\mathcal{N}_l}$ and the unlabeled data $\mathcal{X}_u = \{x_u^i\}$.

1: **while** *epoch* < *total_epoch* **do**

2: Extract the features of the labeled/unlabeled data f_l and f_u with LSTM according to Eq. (2);

3: Train a classifier θ^* based on the labeled data according to Eq. (3);

4: Use the classifier to predict the MLP-based label $\overline{y}_u^i$ of the unlabeled data according to Eq. (4);

5: Calculate the centroid-based label $\tilde{y}_u^i$ according to Eq. (7);

6: Update the centroids c_k according to Eq. (10);

7: **end while**

Output:

    After the training process, the final label prediction of the unlabeled data can be obtained according to Eq. (8).

The traditional centroid learning updates the centroids $\{c_k\}_{k=1}^K$ based on the individual feature during the forward propagation procedure:

$$c_k \leftarrow \omega \cdot c_k + (1 - \omega) \cdot \sum_{i=1}^{\mathcal{N}_{uk}} f_{uk}^i \tag{9}$$

in which ω is a trade-off parameter and $\mathcal{N}_{uk}$ denotes the subject number of unlabeled data with the k-th class. However, in our application, noisy samples and outliers tend to make the above update procedure less effective. The reason is that Eq. (9) updates centroids based on the individual feature, which may mislead the optimization process.

To solve the above issue, we perform centroid adjustment and optimization based on the mean feature. As shown in Fig. 2, different from the above optimization strategy, we employ the mean feature to update the class-specific centroid, which can be robust against outliers:

$$c_k \leftarrow \omega \cdot c_k + \frac{1}{\mathcal{N}_{uk}} \sum_{i=1}^{\mathcal{N}_{uk}} (1 - \omega) \cdot f_{uk}^i \tag{10}$$

The above centroid learning process is conducted in each training epoch, which drives the previously obtained centroids towards a more accurate location in the feature space. Finally, our whole method is summarized in Algorithm 1.

3.5   Loss Function

To train the whole model, the labeled data play a key role in building the loss function. In our model, we use a simple but effective loss function:

$$\mathcal{L} = \mathcal{L}_{ce}(\hat{Y}_l, Y_l) \tag{11}$$

where $\mathcal{L}_{ce}(\cdot,\cdot)$ means the cross-entropy between $\hat{Y}_l = \{\hat{y}_l^i\}$ and $Y_l = \{y_l^i\}$. With this loss term, the whole model is expected to be optimized when $\hat{Y}_l$ and Y_l become more and more similar.

4   Experiment

4.1   Dataset

We use a publicly available EEG-based Depression Dataset [29] to evaluate our model. The EEG-signal data were collected with different paradigms[1], such as eyes-closed, eyes-open and task-ready (P300). In our research, we only use the eyes-closed part.

Since two of the eye-closed subjects have different channel numbers from other samples, they were removed as outliers in all the experiments. Therefore, there are in total 28 patients with depression and 28 healthy individuals used in our experiments. We conduct experiments in 5-fold cross-validation to evaluate our method. During the training process, the Adam Optimizer was used, and the learning rate was set as 5e-4. The epoch number is empirically set as 120 ($total\_epoch = 120$).

4.2   Evaluation Metrics

In the experiments, we adopt several commonly used metrics to evaluate the classification performance: ACCuracy (ACC), RECall (REC), PREcision (PRE), SPEcifity (SPE) and F1-score, which are defined in the following:

$$ACC = \frac{TP + TN}{TP + FN + FP + TN}$$

$$PRE = \frac{TP}{TP + FP}$$

$$REC = \frac{TP}{TP + FN} \tag{12}$$

$$SPE = \frac{TN}{FP + TN}$$

$$F1 - score = \frac{2 \times PRE \times REC}{PRE + REC}$$

Here, TP, FN, FP and TN represent the true positive, false negative, false positive and true negative, respectively. A higher value of these indicators indicates better performance.

---

[1] https://figshare.com/articles/dataset/EEG_Data_New/4244171.

Table 1. The classification results (ACC, PRE, REC, SPE, F1-score) of EEG signals with different methods. The best results are in bold.

	ACC	PRE	REC	SPE	F1-score
CNN (1 Layer)	0.72 ± 0.15	0.72 ± 0.17	0.85 ± 0.08	0.58 ± 0.37	0.76 ± 0.09
CNN (2 Layers)	0.80 ± 0.10	0.78 ± 0.15	0.86 ± 0.12	0.73 ± 0.18	0.81 ± 0.09
CNN (3 Layers)	0.79 ± 0.07	0.73 ± 0.07	$\mathbf{0.92 \pm 0.08}$	0.66 ± 0.14	0.81 ± 0.05
LSTM (2 Layers)	0.84 ± 0.10	0.84 ± 0.10	0.83 ± 0.12	0.85 ± 0.10	0.84 ± 0.11
JSL	$\mathbf{0.86 \pm 0.06}$	$\mathbf{0.86 \pm 0.07}$	0.88 ± 0.05	$\mathbf{0.85 \pm 0.08}$	$\mathbf{0.87 \pm 0.06}$

4.3 Results and Analysis

In the experiment, we adopt several comparison algorithms to demonstrate the effectiveness of our model. Specifically, we adopt a simple LSTM (2 Layers) and multiple CNN architectures under different experiment settings, such as CNN (1 Layer), CNN (2 Layers) and CNN (3 Layers). Of note, LSTM (2 Layers) indicates the LSTM module has two bi-directional LSTM units. CNN (1 Layer) indicates the CNN module has only one convolution layer. CNN (2 Layers) indicates the CNN module has two convolution layers. CNN (3 Layers) indicates the CNN module has three convolution layers.

The quantitative classification results are shown in Table 1. Based on that, we have the following observations. As a general trend, JSL achieves the best (ACC, PRE, SPE, F1-score) or the second best (REC) performance under all evaluation metrics, which demonstrates the effectiveness of our model. Specifically, on the one hand, LSTM performs better than those using CNNs in terms of task-specific feature extraction, showing the rationality of treating EEG signals as sequential data. On the other hand, more importantly, JSL further outperforms LSTM under all evaluation metrics. As the LSTM model can be seen as the incompleted version without using the semi-supervised learning, the result comparison can be seen as an ablation study to show the usefulness of introducing the semi-supervised learning strategy. Obviously, as the unlabeled data subtly participates in the learning process, some performance gain can be therefore obtained.

5 Conclusion

In this paper, we propose a novel MDD detection method based on joint semi-supervised learning, aiming to fully utilize the unlabeled EEG data. The backbone of our method is the feature extraction module and the MLP-based classifier. To further enhance the performance, we also utilize the unlabeled data to improve the feature distribution. Specifically, pseudo labels are firstly obtained from the unlabeled samples with the classifier, aiming to tentatively complete their label information and merge them into the training set. Then, the unsupervised centroid learning is performed on the merged set to improve the accuracy of the class centroids, which is able to provide effective auxiliary information for the final classification. In the future, we plan to strengthen the experiments by using more experimental data based on the other two paradigms, i.e. eyes-open and task-ready. In addition, considering the label scarcity issue widely exists in multimodal data, we also consider extending our method into multimodal MDD detection research.

Acknowledgements. This work was supported by the National Key Research and Development Program (Grant No. 2019YFA0706200), the National Nature Science Foundation of China under Grant No. 62072152, and the Fundamental Research Funds for the Central Universities under Grant No. PA2020GDKC0023.

References

1. Abásolo, D., Hornero, R., Escudero, J., Espino, P.: A study on the possible usefulness of detrended fluctuation analysis of the electroencephalogram background activity in Alzheimer's disease. IEEE Trans. Biomed. Eng. **55**(9), 2171–2179 (2008)
2. Andres, D.P., Colomer, A., Naranjo, V., Morales, S., Xu, Y., Frangi, A.F.: Retinal image synthesis and semi-supervised learning for glaucoma assessment. IEEE Trans. Med. Imaging **38**(9), 2211–2218 (2019)
3. Ay, B., et al.: Automated depression detection using deep representation and sequence learning with EEG signals. J. Med. Syst. **43**(7), 1–12 (2019)
4. Azizi, A., Moridani, M.K., Saeedi, A.: A novel geometrical method for depression diagnosis based on EEG signals. In: 2019 IEEE 4th Conference on Technology in Electrical and Computer Engineering (2019)
5. Bappy, J.H., Simons, C., Nataraj, L., Manjunath, B.S., Amit, R.C.: Hybrid LSTM and encoder-decoder architecture for detection of image forgeries. IEEE Trans. Image Process. **28**(7), 3286–3300 (2019). https://doi.org/10.1109/TIP.2019.2895466
6. Bocharov, A.V., Knyazev, G.G., Savostyanov, A.N.: Depression and implicit emotion processing: an EEG study. Neurophysiol. Clin/Clin. Neurophysiol. **47**(3), 225–230 (2017)
7. Cai, H., et al.: A pervasive approach to EEG-based depression detection. Complexity (2018)
8. Ding, Y., Zhao, X., Zhang, Z., Cai, W., Yang, N., Zhan, Y.: Semi-supervised locality preserving dense graph neural network with ARMA filters and context-aware learning for hyperspectral image classification. IEEE Trans. Geosci. Remote Sens. **60**, 1–12 (2022)
9. Gao, L., Guo, Z., Zhang, H., Xu, X., Shen, H.: Video captioning with attention-based LSTM and semantic consistency. IEEE Trans. Multimedia **19**(9), 2045–2055 (2017). https://doi.org/10.1109/TMM.2017.2729019
10. Ghorbanian, P., Devilbiss, D.M., Hess, T., Bernstein, A., Simon, A.J., Ashrafiuon, H.: Exploration of EEG features of Alzheimer's disease using continuous wavelet transform. Med. Biol. Eng. Comput. **53**(9), 843–855 (2015)
11. Gilbody, S., Richards, D., Brealey, S., Hewitt, C.: Screening for depression in medical settings with the patient health questionnaire (PHQ): a diagnostic meta-analysis. J. Gen. Intern. Med. **22**(11), 1596–1602 (2007)
12. Hao, Z., et al.: ASGN: an active semi-supervised graph neural network for molecular property prediction. In: Proceedings of the International Conference on Knowledge Discovery & Data Mining, pp. 731–752 (2020)

13. Hui, W.L., Ooi, C.P., Aydemir, E., Tuncer, T., Acharya, U.R.: Decision support system for major depression detection using spectrogram and convolution neural network with EEG signals. Expert Syst. **39**(1), e12773 (2021)
14. Ji, C., Wang, Y.T., Gao, Z., Li, L., Ni, J.C., Zheng, C.H.: A semi-supervised learning method for MiRNA-disease association prediction based on variational autoencoder. IEEE/ACM Trans. Comput. Biol. Bioinform. **19**(4), 2049–2059 (2022)
15. Jiang, B., Zhang, Z., Lin, D., Tang, J., Luo, B.: Semi-supervised learning with graph learning-convolutional networks. In: Proceedings of the IEEE/CVF Conference on Computer Vision and Pattern Recognition, pp. 11313–11320 (2019)
16. Jiang, H., Jiao, R., Wang, Z., Zhang, T., Wu, L.: Construction and analysis of emotion computing model based on LSTM. Complexity **2021**(1), 1–12 (2021)
17. Kamran, S.A., Hossain, K.F., Tavakkoli, A., Zuckerbrod, S.L., Baker, S.A.: VTGAN: semi-supervised retinal image synthesis and disease prediction using vision transformers. In: Proceedings of the IEEE/CVF International Conference on Computer Vision, pp. 3235–3245 (2021)
18. Kumar, N., et al.: Hyperspectral tissue image segmentation using semi-supervised NMF and hierarchical clustering. IEEE Trans. Med. Imaging **38**(5), 1304–1313 (2018)
19. Lachaux, J.P., Axmacher, N., Mormann, F., Halgren, E., Crone, N.E.: High-frequency neural activity and human cognition: past, present and possible future of intracranial EEG research. Prog. Neurobiol. **98**(3), 279–301 (2012)
20. Lakhan, R., Agrawal, A., Sharma, M.: Prevalence of depression, anxiety, and stress during COVID-19 pandemic. J. Neurosci. Rural Pract. **11**(04), 519–525 (2020)
21. Lee, K., et al.: Adverse drug event detection in Tweets with semi-supervised convolutional neural networks. In: Proceedings of the 26th International Conference on World Wide Web, pp. 705–714 (2017)
22. Leuchter, A.F., Cook, I.A., Hunter, A.M., Cai, C., Horvath, S.: Resting-state quantitative electroencephalography reveals increased neurophysiologic connectivity in depression. PloS one **7**(2), e32508 (2012)
23. Li, D., et al.: Semi-supervised variational reasoning for medical dialogue generation. In: Proceedings of the International ACM Conference on Research and Development in Information Retrieval, pp. 544–554 (2021)
24. Li, X., La, R., Wang, Y., Hu, B., Zhang, X.: A deep learning approach for mild depression recognition based on functional connectivity using electroencephalography. Front. Neurosci. **14**, 192 (2020)
25. Lin, C., Hu, P., Su, H., Li, S., Mei, J., Zhou, J., Leung, H.: SenseMood: depression detection on social media. In: Proceedings of the 2020 International Conference on Multimedia Retrieval, pp. 407–411 (2020)
26. Liu, Q., Yu, L., Luo, L., Dou, Q., Heng, P.A.: Semi-supervised medical image classification with relation-driven self-ensembling model. IEEE Trans. Med. Imaging **39**(11), 3429–3440 (2020)
27. Mao, W., Zhu, J., Li, X., Zhang, X., Sun, S.: Resting state EEG based depression recognition research using deep learning method. In: International Conference on Brain Informatics, pp. 329–338 (2018)
28. Mazza, M.G., et al.: Anxiety and depression in COVID-19 survivors: role of inflammatory and clinical predictors. Brain Behav. Immun. **89**, 594–600 (2020)
29. Mumtaz, W.: MDD patients and healthy controls EEG data (new). figshare. Dataset. MDD Patients and Healthy Controls EEG Data generated by https://doi.org/10.6084/m9. figshare 4244171, v2 (2016)
30. Mumtaz, W., Qayyum, A.: A deep learning framework for automatic diagnosis of unipolar depression. Int. J. Med. Inf. **132**, 103983 (2019)

31. Neto, D.A., Soares, F., Rosa, J.L.G.: Depression biomarkers using non-invasive EEG: a review. Neurosci. Biobehav. Rev. **105**, 83–93 (2019)
32. Peng, H., Xia, C., Wang, Z., Zhu, J., Zhang, X., Sun, S., Li, J., Huo, X., Li, X.: Multivariate pattern analysis of EEG-based functional connectivity: a study on the identification of depression. IEEE Access **7**, 92630–92641 (2019)
33. Qayyum, A., Razzak, I., Mumtaz, W.: Hybrid deep shallow network for assessment of depression using electroencephalogram signals. In: International Conference on Neural Information Processing, pp. 245–257 (2020)
34. Schacter, D.: EEG theta waves and psychological phenomena: a review and analysis. Biol. Psychol. **5**(1), 47–82 (1977)
35. Sharma, G., Parashar, A., Joshi, A.M.: DepHNN: a novel hybrid neural network for electroencephalogram (EEG)-based screening of depression. Biomed. Sig. Process. Control **66**, 102393 (2021)
36. Shi, Q., Liu, A., Chen, R., Shen, J., Zhao, Q., Hu, B.: Depression detection using resting state three-channel EEG signal. arXiv preprint arXiv:2002.09175 (2020)
37. Siddharth, Jung, T.P., Sejnowski, T.J.: Utilizing deep learning towards multi-modal bio-sensing and vision-based affective computing. IEEE Trans. Affect. Comput. **13**(1), 96–107 (2022). https://doi.org/10.1109/TAFFC.2019.2916015
38. Tang, Y., et al.: Leveraging large-scale weakly labeled data for semi-supervised mass detection in mammograms. In: Proceedings of the IEEE/CVF Conference on Computer Vision and Pattern Recognition, pp. 3855–3864 (2021)
39. Thoduparambil, P.P., Dominic, A., Varghese, S.M.: EEG-based deep learning model for the automatic detection of clinical depression. Phys. Eng. Sci. Med. **43**(4), 1349–1360 (2020)
40. Wen, B., Ravishankar, S., Pfister, L., Bresler, Y.: Transform learning for magnetic resonance image reconstruction: from model-based learning to building neural networks. IEEE Sig. Process. Mag. **37**(1), 41–53 (2020)
41. Wheidima, C.M., Granger, E., Miguel, B.L.: MDN: a deep maximization-differentiation network for spatio-temporal depression detection. IEEE Trans. Affect. Comput. **14**(1), 578–590 (2021)
42. Xia, S., et al.: A fast adaptive k-means with no bounds. IEEE Trans. Pattern Anal. Mach. Intell. **44**(1), 87–99 (2022)
43. Xia, Y., et al.: Uncertainty-aware multi-view co-training for semi-supervised medical image segmentation and domain adaptation. Med. Image Anal. **65**, 101766 (2020)
44. Xing, Y., et al.: Task-state heart rate variability parameter-based depression detection model and effect of therapy on the parameters. IEEE Access **7**, 105701–105709 (2019)
45. Xu, X., Sanford, T., Turkbey, B., Xu, S., Wood, B.J., Yan, P.: Shadow-consistent semi-supervised learning for prostate ultrasound segmentation. IEEE Trans. Med. Imaging **41**(6), 1331–1345 (2022)
46. Yan, C., Duan, G., Zhang, Y., Wu, F.X., Pan, Y., Wang, J.: Predicting drug-drug interactions based on integrated similarity and semi-supervised learning. IEEE/ACM Trans. Comput. Biol. Bioinform. **19**(1), 168–179 (2022)
47. Yang, Y., Fairbairn, C., Cohn, J.F.: Detecting depression severity from vocal prosody. IEEE Trans. Affect. Comput. **4**(2), 142–150 (2012)
48. You, C., Zhou, Y., Zhao, R., Staib, L., Duncan, J.S.: SimCVD: simple contrastive voxel-wise representation distillation for semi-supervised medical image segmentation. IEEE Trans. Med. Imaging **41**(9), 2228–2237 (2022). https://doi.org/10.1109/TMI.2022.3161829

49. Zhang, E., Seiler, S., Chen, M., Lu, W., Gu, X.: BIRADS features-oriented semi-supervised deep learning for breast ultrasound computer-aided diagnosis. Phys. Med. Biol. **65**(12), 125005 (2020)

50. Zhang, S., Zhao, X., Tian, Q.: Spontaneous speech emotion recognition using multiscale deep convolutional LSTM. IEEE Trans. Affect. Comput. **13**(2), 680–688 (2022). https://doi.org/10.1109/TAFFC.2019.2947464

51. Zheng, W.L., Zhu, J.Y., Lu, B.L.: Identifying stable patterns over time for emotion recognition from EEG. IEEE Trans. Affect. Comput. **10**(3), 417–429 (2019). https://doi.org/10.1109/TAFFC.2017.2712143

52. Zhou, X., Jin, K., Shang, Y., Guo, G.: Visually interpretable representation learning for depression recognition from facial images. IEEE Trans. Affect. Comput. **11**(3), 542–552 (2018)

53. Zhou, Y., et al.: Collaborative learning of semi-supervised segmentation and classification for medical images. In: Proceedings of the IEEE/CVF Conference on Computer Vision and Pattern Recognition, pp. 2079–2088 (2019)

54. Zhu, J., Zheng, Z., Yang, M., Fung, G.P.C., Huang, C.: Protein complexes detection based on semi-supervised network embedding model. IEEE/ACM Trans. Comput. Biol. Bioinform. **18**(2), 797–803 (2019)

Subject-Aware Explainable Contrastive Deep Fusion Learning for Anxiety Level Analysis

Michael Briden[1]([⊠]) [iD] and Narges Norouzi[2] [iD]

[1] Baskin Engineering, UC Santa Cruz, Santa Cruz, CA, USA
mbriden@ucsc.edu
[2] Electrical Engineering and Computer Sciences Department, UC Berkeley,
Soda Hall, Berkeley, CA 94709, USA
norouzi@berkeley.edu

Abstract. We propose a contrastive learning deep fusion neural network for effectively classifying subjects' anxiety levels. The framework, called *WaveFusion*, is composed of lightweight convolutional neural networks for per-lead time-frequency analysis and an attention network for integrating the lightweight modalities for final prediction. To facilitate the training of *WaveFusion*, we incorporate a subject-aware contrastive learning approach by ensuring subject representation within the training phase to boost self-supervised cross-subject feature learning and classification accuracy. The *WaveFusion* framework demonstrates high accuracy in classifying anxiety levels by achieving a classification accuracy of 97.67% while also identifying influential brain regions.

Keywords: Electroencephalogram · Deep Learning · Multi-modal · Fusion · Machine Learning

1 Introduction

Electroencephalography (EEG) measures brain activity by collecting electric potential differences. EEG is often used for understanding cognitive tasks through Machine Learning (ML) models [8]. A common task includes analyzing motor-imagery using Deep Learning (DL) architectures [9,10,20]. DL models have been used to learn representations of EEG signals and generate written textual descriptions of visual scenery for decoding purposes [16,18]. EEG is also commonly used to analyze the neurodynamics of patients suffering from neurological disease and mental disorders [6,7].

Analyzing mental well-being from EEG recordings is an essential task in the medical field. Given that anxiety and fear are associated with specific neurological patterns, Bualan et al. investigated various ML approaches to detect fear level [2,15]. Likewise, Yang et al. use a multi-modal DL approach to measure depression level [19]. Given that most DL approaches lack explainability, we have previously used a multi-modal deep architecture to infer anxiety level and localize the regions of the brain contributing most to prediction [5].

J.-J. Rousseau and B. Kapralos (Eds.): ICPR 2022 Workshops, LNCS 13643, pp. 682–690, 2023.
https://doi.org/10.1007/978-3-031-37660-3_48

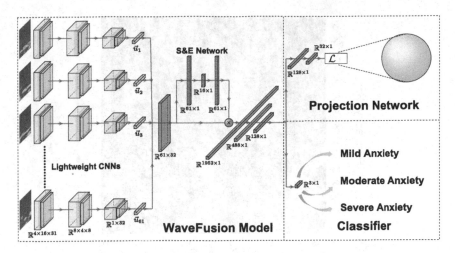

Fig. 1. The WaveFusion architecture contains 61 lightweight CNNs to learn time-frequency features of a specific EEG lead. During a Subject-Aware Contrastive Learning (SAC) training phase, 128×1 feature maps are forwarded to the projection network and embedded onto the unit hyper-sphere via SAC loss. During classification, the learned embeddings are sent to a classification layer for final anxiety level classification.

While DL has been effectively employed in many neuroscience applications, challenges remain with the quality and availability of the data [4,13]. As a result, contrastive learning self-supervised frameworks have been developed for learning representations from EEG data. Banville et al. use contrastive learning to extract similar features in windowed EEG data [3]. Noting subject-invariant representations of emotion, Shen et al. explore the use of contrastive learning to train a DL model to extract cross-subject emotion representations [17]. Han et al. also use self-supervised contrastive learning to label EEG data for the motor imagery classification task [11].

In this work, we propose a multi-modal contrastive learning framework, *WaveFusion Squeeze and Excite (WaveFusion SE)* to learn EEG features in a self-supervised manner (Fig. 1). The model first extracts relevant Complex Morlet Wavelet Transform (CMWT) features by clustering latent embeddings of CMWT scalograms to a 32-dimensional hyper-sphere using a *WaveFusion with a Projection Network (WFP)*. WFP's weights are then transferred to a *Wave-Fusion Classifier (WFC)* where the data is classified as low, moderate, or high anxiety level.

2   Dataset

We demonstrate the effectiveness of the framework on a subset of the Max Planck Institute Leipzig Mind-Brain-Body (LEMON) dataset. The study was conducted to learn the relationship between mental and somatic well-being [1]. The dataset contains the results of six psychological tests, MRI, and EEG readings for 227 patients. The subjects' anxiety levels are labeled as "Mild", "Moderate", and

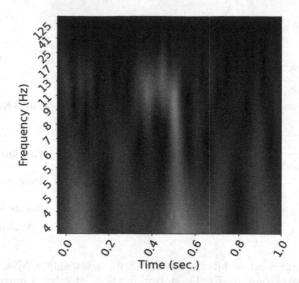

Fig. 2. An "inferno" sequential colormap of a scalogram generated by the CMWT.

"Severe" based upon the State-trait anxiety inventory X2 score (a test taken by the subject before the experiment). The EEG recordings are 16-minute long with 61 leads arranged in the 10-20 comprehensive localization system. Amplitude resolution is 0.1 μV, and recordings are made with a bandpass filter between 0.015 Hz and 1 kHz and a 2500 Hz sampling rate. We select 200 1-second long readings from ten subjects for each class. 75% of each subject's readings are allocated to the training set, while the remaining 25% are assigned to validation set. The readings are further down-sampled to 125 Hz and bandpass filtered to 1-45 Hz with a Butterworth filter.

CMWT is applied to each EEG reading with 32 scales, a Gaussian width of 0.4 Hz, and a center frequency of 1 Hz. The absolute value of the CMWT coefficients are computed to give 61 32 × 125 scalograms per sample. Figure 2 shows an "inferno" sequential colormap example of a 32 × 125 scalogram with scales converted to frequency. The scalograms are concatenated to create 61 × 32 × 125 tensors for inference.

3   Models and Algorithms

We employ a WaveFusion framework that contains 61 individual Convolutional Neural Networks (CNNs) trained on the CMWT data specific to a single EEG lead (Fig. 1). The feature maps from the CNNs are combined using a lightweight Squeeze and Excite Attention Network (SEN) before being embedded onto the unit hyper-sphere or passed to the classifier. This section describes WaveFusion framework, including WaveFusion Projection (WFP) network and WaveFusion Classifier (WFC), and the Subject-Aware Contrastive Learning (SAC) framework.

3.1 WaveFusion Projection Network

Lightweight Convolutional Neural Networks. The WaveFusion models take in spectrogram tensors where each spectrogram is forwarded to 1 of the 61 Lightweight 2D-CNNs (LWCNNs). Each LWCNN learns features of a spectrogram generated by one EEG lead using three convolution layers. The first two layers are followed by batch normalization, ReLU activation, and 2×2 max-pooling. The last convolution layer is followed by batch normalization and global pooling and outputs a feature map of size 1×32.

Squeeze and Excite Network. The 61 LWCNN outputs are combined to form the tensor of feature maps $U = [u_1, u_2, ...u_{61}] \in \mathbb{R}^{61 \times 32}$, which SEN uses to generate attention weight, π_i, for each map [12]. SEN consists of a global pooling layer that reduces U to a 61×1 tensor of averages which are sent to an encoder-decoder model that contains two dense layers. The dense encoder layer condenses the 61×1 input to 16×1 and is followed by ReLU activation. The dense decoder layer expands the output back to 61×1 where sigmoid activation computes attention weights, π_i. The SEN, along with the lightweight CNNs, can lead to the localization of neural activities in the human brain.

Subject-Aware Constrastive Learning Framework. We make use of three components commonly used to facilitate contrastive learning:

Data Augmentation, Aug(): for each x in a batch, two augmentations, $\tilde{x}$ (called "views" of x), are generated by augmenting x with Gaussian pink noise, input dropout, and random Gaussian noise.

Encoder Network, Enc(): the WaveFusion encoder model is a combination of LWCNNs, SEN, a flattening layer, and two dense layers to map inputs $\tilde{x}$ to a vector $r = Enc(\tilde{x}) \in \mathbb{R}^{128}$.

Projection network, Proj(): A multi-layer perceptron specific to WFP that contains a single hidden layer of size 128 and an output layer of 32. Representations, r, are embedded to the tensor $z = Proj(r) \in \mathbb{R}^{32}$, which are normalized for measuring cosine similarity between projections.

We define a multi-label batch of N randomly sampled pairs as $\mathcal{B} = \{x_k, y_{1,k}, y_{2,k}\}_{k=1,...,N}$ where $y_{1,k} \in \{0, 1, 2\}$ denotes the anxiety label and $y_{2,k} \in \{1, 30\}$ is a unique subject ID-label. Augmentation is applied to each CMWT tensor in $\mathcal{B}$ to create the new batch of views $\mathcal{B}_s = \{\tilde{x}_k, \tilde{y}_{1,k}, \tilde{y}_{2,k}\}_{k=1,...,2N}$ where $\tilde{y}_{1,2k-1} = \tilde{y}_{1,2k} = y_{1,k}$ and $\tilde{y}_{2,2k-1} = \tilde{y}_{2,2k} = y_{2,k}$. Letting $i \in I_s = \{1, ..., 2N\}$ be the index of an arbitrary sample in $\mathcal{B}_s$, we use Khosla et al.'s loss function as the SAC loss:

$$\mathcal{L} = -\sum_{i \in I_s} log \left(\frac{1}{\|P(i)\|} \sum_{p \in P(i)} \frac{exp(z_i \cdot z_p / \tau)}{\sum_{s \in S(i)} exp(z_i \cdot z_s / \tau)} \right) \tag{1}$$

where z_i serves as the anchor with $\tau \in \mathbb{R}^+$ as a temperature parameter [14]. The set of positives, $P(i) = \{q \in I_s - \{i\} : \tilde{y}_{1,q} = \tilde{y}_{1,i}\}$, contains all samples of the same class distinct from i. The set $S(i) = P(i) \cup N(i)_o$ is the set of views distinct from i with $N(i)_o = \{s \in I_s - \{i\} : \tilde{y}_{1,s} \neq \tilde{y}_{1,i} \text{ and } \tilde{y}_{2,s} \neq \tilde{y}_{2,i}\}$ containing the samples with class labels different from the anchor's. To facilitate the contrastive learning process, we enforce $||P(i)|| = 0.5N$ and $P(i)$ to contain an equal number of samples from each of the 10 subjects represented within the class. Likewise, we enforce $N(i)_o$ to contain an equal amount of negative samples from each of the other anxiety classes and an equal number of samples from each subject represented in each class. One training epoch is completed when each sample in the training set serves as the anchor.

3.2   WaveFusion Classification Network

After WFP has been trained, the learned embeddings are sent to a classification layer for final anxiety level classification. A dense classification layer with three nodes is used to generate the logits required for softmax classification.

4   Experiments and Results

We studied the classification accuracy and localization effects of the subject-aware contrastive learning WFC on the LEMON dataset. WFP is trained for 25 epochs with stochastic gradient descent with a fixed learning rate of 0.05, and a grid search is performed over all combinations of hyperparameters. We then transferred the learned embeddings to WFC and performed a grid search over the weight decay hyperparameter with Adam optimizer with a learning rate of 10^{-4} and trained each model for 150 epochs.

4.1   Classification Results

A WFP model using a batch size of 500 with 250 subject-aware positives, 250 subject-aware negatives, SAC loss temperature of 0.25, and weight decay of 7×10^{-3} led to the best overall classification accuracy of 96.7%, an improvement compared to training the WaveFusion in a supervised manner (by removing the WFP network). (See Table 1).

4.2   Localizing Neurological Activities

To understand the impact of the contrastive learning training scheme in localizing neurological activities, we used the 61 attention weights, π_i, generated during the inference phase and interpolated them onto brain and scalp models.

Figure 3a illustrates the interpolation of attention weights corresponding to Mild, Moderate, and Severe recordings generated from the subject-aware contrastive learning WFC. In the Mild example, we see a considerable amount of influence from leads C3 to CP3 as well as FC6 and TP8. In the Moderate example, influence is generated largely from FP1 and the F3-C3 leads. Lastly, CP2 contributes a high amount of activation in the Severe example. Figure 3b shows

Table 1. F1 score and accuracy per class for the Contrastive WaveFusion and Supervised WaveFusion classifier models are displayed in columns 2 to 7. Overall F1 score and overall accuracy is displayed in column 8.

	Mild		Moderate		Severe		Overall
Model	F1	Acc.	F1	Acc.	F1	Acc.	Acc.
WaveFusion Contrastive Classifier	**0.98**	**98.0**	**0.978**	**97.4**	**0.972**	97.6	**97.67**
WaveFusion Supervised Classifier	0.979	97.4	0.976	96.6	0.971	**98.6**	97.53

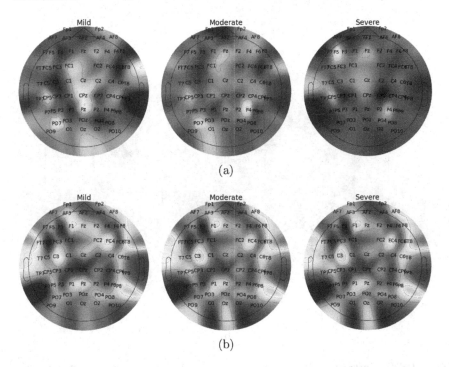

(a)

(b)

Fig. 3. Interpolation of most influential modalities onto a 2D topology map. The interpolation of attention weights learned from (a) subject-aware contrastive learning WFC and (b) supervised WFC.

the interpolation from the supervised WaveFusion classifier. Note that there are only minor differences in the Moderate and Severe maps suggesting that the subject-aware contrastive learning framework learns richer representations of neurological events.

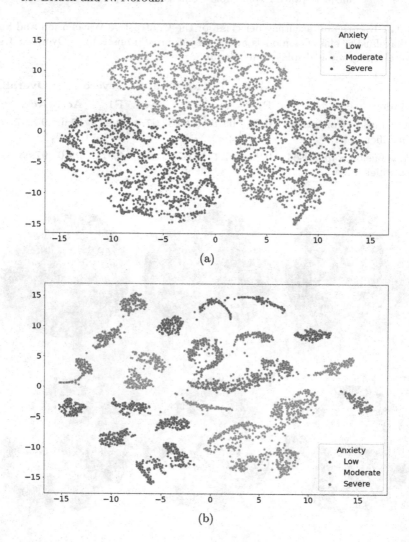

Fig. 4. t-SNE illustrations of the representation vectors generated by WaveFusion models. (a) illustrates the representations generated from the *WFC* architecture. (b) shows the representations generated *WaveFusion SE architecture*.

4.3   Visualization of Learned Representations

Figure 4 illustrates the t-SNE visualization of learned representations, r, of the training dataset. Figure 4a shows the representations generated through the SAC training scheme. The distinct class clusters are a result of enforcing representation likeness through contrastive learning. Figure 4b shows that the representations learned through a supervised training scheme appear in numerous clusters suggesting that the representations contain less class similarity than those generated through a contrastive learning approach.

5   Conclusion

The WaveFusion framework combined with the SAC training scheme is an important step toward 1) multi-modal EEG analysis through an attention-based fusion technique and 2) using an SAC training scheme to classify EEG signals while expanding explainability. Moreover, we show that contrastive learning can boost representation likeness for multi-modal EEG recognition tasks. Additionally, WaveFusion learns EEG features using lead-specific lightweight CNNs, leading to the localization of neural activities.

References

1. Babayan, A., et al.: A mind-brain-body dataset of MRI, EEG, cognition, emotion, and peripheral physiology in young and old adults. Sci. Data **6**(1), 1–21 (2019)
2. Bălan, O., Moise, G., Moldoveanu, A., Leordeanu, M., Moldoveanu, F.: An investigation of various machine and deep learning techniques applied in automatic fear level detection and acrophobia virtual therapy. Sensors **20**(2), 496 (2020)
3. Banville, H., Albuquerque, I., Hyvärinen, A., Moffat, G., Engemann, D.A., Gramfort, A.: Self-supervised representation learning from electroencephalography signals. In: 2019 IEEE 29th International Workshop on Machine Learning for Signal Processing (MLSP), pp. 1–6. IEEE (2019)
4. Banville, H., Chehab, O., Hyvärinen, A., Engemann, D.A., Gramfort, A.: Uncovering the structure of clinical EEG signals with self-supervised learning. J. Neural Eng. **18**, abca18 (2021)
5. Briden, M., Norouzi, N.: WaveFusion squeeze-and-excitation: towards an accurate and explainable deep learning framework in neuroscience. In: 2021 43rd Annual International Conference of the IEEE Engineering in Medicine & Biology Society (EMBC), pp. 1092–1095. IEEE (2021)
6. Chen, D., Wan, S., Bao, F.S.: Epileptic focus localization using EEG based on discrete wavelet transform through full-level decomposition. In: 2015 IEEE 25th International Workshop on Machine Learning for Signal Processing (MLSP), pp. 1–6. IEEE (2015)
7. Coutin-Churchman, P.E., Wu, J.Y., Chen, L.L., Shattuck, K., Dewar, S., Nuwer, M.R.: Quantification and localization of EEG interictal spike activity in patients with surgically removed epileptogenic foci. Clin. Neurophysiol. **123**(3), 471–485 (2012)
8. Craik, A., He, Y., Contreras-Vidal, J.L.: Deep learning for electroencephalogram (eeg) classification tasks: a review. J. Neural Eng. **16**(3), 031001 (2019)
9. Dai, M., Zheng, D., Na, R., Wang, S., Zhang, S.: EEG classification of motor imagery using a novel deep learning framework. Sensors **19**, 551 (2019)
10. Deng, X., Zhang, B., Yu, N., Liu, K., Sun, K.: Advanced tsgl-eegnet for motor imagery eeg-based brain-computer interfaces. IEEE Access **9**, 25118–25130 (2021)
11. Han, J., Gu, X., Lo, B.: Semi-supervised contrastive learning for generalizable motor imagery eeg classification. In: 2021 IEEE 17th International Conference on Wearable and Implantable Body Sensor Networks (BSN), pp. 1–4. IEEE (2021)
12. Hu, J., Shen, L., Sun, G.: Squeeze-and-excitation networks. In: Proceedings of the IEEE Conference on Computer Vision and Pattern Recognition, pp. 7132–7141 (2018)

13. Huang, G., Ma, F.: ConCAD: contrastive learning-based cross attention for sleep apnea detection. In: Dong, Y., Kourtellis, N., Hammer, B., Lozano, J.A. (eds.) ECML PKDD 2021. LNCS (LNAI), vol. 12979, pp. 68–84. Springer, Cham (2021). https://doi.org/10.1007/978-3-030-86517-7_5

14. Khosla, P., et al.: Supervised contrastive learning. Adv. Neural. Inf. Process. Syst. **33**, 18661–18673 (2020)

15. Klados, M.A., Paraskevopoulos, E., Pandria, N., Bamidis, P.D.: The impact of math anxiety on working memory: a cortical activations and cortical functional connectivity eeg study. IEEE Access, p. 15027 (2019)

16. Palazzo, S., Spampinato, C., Kavasidis, I., Giordano, D., Schmidt, J., Shah, M.: Decoding brain representations by multimodal learning of neural activity and visual features. IEEE Trans. Pattern Anal. Mach. Intell. **43**(11), 3833–3849 (2020)

17. Shen, X., Liu, X., Hu, X., Zhang, D., Song, S.: Contrastive learning of subject-invariant eeg representations for cross-subject emotion recognition. IEEE Transactions on Affective Computing (2022)

18. Willett, F.R., Avansino, D.T., Hochberg, L.R., Henderson, J.M., Shenoy, K.V.: High-performance brain-to-text communication via handwriting. Nature **593**(7858), 249–254 (2021)

19. Yang, L., Jiang, D., Xia, X., Pei, E., Oveneke, M.C., Sahli, H.: Multimodal measurement of depression using deep learning models. In: Proceedings of the 7th Annual Workshop on Audio/Visual Emotion Challenge, pp. 53–59 (2017)

20. Zhang, X., Yao, L.: Deep Learning for EEG-Based Brain-Computer Interfaces: Representations. World Scientific, Algorithms and Applications (2021)

MMDA: A Multimodal Dataset for Depression and Anxiety Detection

Yueqi Jiang, Ziyang Zhang, and Xiao Sun(✉)

Hefei University of Technology, Hefei, China
{jiangyueqi,zzzzzy}@mail.hfut.edu.cn, sunx@hfut.edu.cn

Abstract. In recent years, with the development of artificial intelligence, the use of machine learning and other methods for mental illness detection has become a hot topic. However, obtaining data on mental disorders is very difficult, limiting the development of this field. In this paper, we provide a Multimodal dataset for Depression and Anxiety Detection(MMDA). All subjects in the dataset were diagnosed by professional psychologists, and the subjects' disorders were determined by combining HAMD and HAMA scores. The dataset includes visual, acoustic, and textual information extracted after de-identification of the original interview videos, for a total of 1025 valid data, which is the largest dataset on mental disorders available. We detail the correlations between each modal and symptoms of depression and anxiety, and validate this dataset by machine learning methods to complete the two tasks of classification of anxiety and depression symptoms and regression of HAMA and HAMD scores. We hope that this dataset will be useful for establishing an automatic detection system for mental disorders and motivate more researchers to engage in mental disorders detection.

Keywords: Multimodal Dataset · Mental Disorders Detection · Clinical Interview

1 Introduction

Depression and anxiety are the two most common mental disorders in the global population. According to the WHO report [1], more than 280 million people worldwide suffer from depression. Another investigation [2] revealed that the lifetime prevalence of anxiety disorders in China is at a maximum of 7.6% and depression disorders at 6.8%. These two diseases are often co-morbid and have a serious impact on the quality of life and the physical or mental health of patients. When symptoms are severe, patients may develop suicidal tendencies. Therefore, more attention needs to be provided to the promotion, prevention

---

Y. Jiang and Z. Zhang are equally-contributed authors.

J.-J. Rousseau and B. Kapralos (Eds.): ICPR 2022 Workshops, LNCS 13643, pp. 691–702, 2023.
https://doi.org/10.1007/978-3-031-37660-3_49

and treatment of depression and anxiety disorders. Presently, the main common treatment methods are self-rating scales and clinical interviews. Due to the lack of emotional guidance from professional psychologists and subjectivity of the subjects, the scale's assessment results are not comprehensive. Clinical interviews are currently the most effective way to diagnose depression and anxiety, however, they also suffer from time-consuming, low identification rates and high underdiagnosis rates. In addition, more than 70% of patients do not receive psychological diagnostic services due to lack of medical resources, ignorance or shame about their symptoms, which cause an aggravation of the condition [3]. Furthermore, due to the lack of medical resources and specialized psychologists and psychiatrists in some less developed countries, patients with depression and anxiety disorders are often untreated. For all these reasons, depression and anxiety have become a global burden of mental disorders.

Table 1. Datasets Comparison

	Modal	Language	Sample size	Triggering method	Quantification standards
DAIC	A, V, T	English	189	Interview (by avatar)	PHQ-8
E-DAIC	A, V, T	English	275	Interview (by avatar)	PHQ-8
Pittsburgh	A, V	English	130	Interviews (by specialist practitioners)	HAMD
MODMA	A, EEG	Chinese	-	Interviews, readings and picture descriptions	PHQ-9
BD	A, V	Turkish	-	Interviews (by specialist practitioners)	YMRS, MADRS
Ours	**A, V, T**	**Chinese**	**1025**	**Interviews (by specialist practitioners)**	**HAMD, HAMA**

The increasing number of people suffering from depression and anxiety disorders has caused widespread concern in the international community. In the field of artificial intelligence, the detection of mental illnesses by extracting audio, visual and other physiological signals from patients and using methods such as machine learning and deep learning has become a hot research topic in recent years. A portion of these research efforts had been based on unimodality, such as text [4], speech audio [5] and visual [6]. Unimodal information does not provide a thorough representation of all characteristics of the patient, so another group of researchers concerned with multimodal disorder detection [7,8], aiming at combining complementarities between different modalities to improve performance.

All of the work mentioned above has made great progress in the detection of depression and anxiety disorders. However, methods such as machine learning and deep learning tend to rely on large amounts of clean, high-quality data. As mental disorders cannot be fully assessed by self-rating scales and clinical interviews are time-consuming and require a high level of cooperation from the subject, making it difficult to obtain a large amount of clean, high-quality data on patients with depression and anxiety disorders.

Based on the above concerns, we created a multimodal dataset designed to detect depression and anxiety disorders. All subjects in our dataset had a communication with a professional physician and completed an assessment for HAMD [9] or HAMA [10]. The physician will combine the content and psychological condition of patients' answers to score each question on the scale, then obtain the degree of the patients' illness based on the total score. We recorded the whole process by camera and microphone, and extracted the de-identified visual features, acoustic features as well as text features. This dataset contains 501 valid data of HAMA, including 108 normal samples and 393 diseased samples, and 524 valid data of HAMD, including 186 normal samples and 338 diseased samples. We have demonstrated the validity of this dataset through basic experiments, and expect that it will help build an automatic detection system for mental disorders, and will inspire more researchers to focus on and engage in this field. Details of the dataset will be presented in the following sections.

2 Background

The topic of affective computing has attracted a lot of enthusiasm as a hot topic in recent years. In affective computing tasks, the primary focus is on the way in which emotional information is represented. In everyday life, we express emotions naturally, mainly through expressions, tones and the content of words, but there are also details that are difficult to actually perceive. Numerous studies have shown that the detailed information obtained through processing helps to learn emotional features [11]. There are already many high-quality unimodal datasets available, such as IMDb dataset [12], ExpW [13], etc. However, emotional information is not expressed in only one modality, but is often expressed in a multimodal manner. As a result, several datasets collect multimodal information to better capture affective feature information, such as AMIGOS [14], MAHNOB-HCI [15], SEMAINE [16], etc.

However some specific fields require more granular data. In recent years the prevalence of mental disorder and its increasing risk to public health has led researchers to look at the use of artificial intelligence techniques to provide solutions to mental health problems. In 2017, Gong et al. [17] proposed a topic modeling approach for depression detection based on multimodal data. The experimental results show that the application of artificial intelligence techniques to psychological problem detection is fully feasible. In 2020 Zhang et al. [18] proposed a novel solution for the task of mental problem recognition, and the framework achieved a promising result for both bipolar disorder recognition and depression detection tasks. Effective mental disorder monitoring and recognition algorithms require meaningful real data to support them [19], and several researchers created excellent datasets for mental disorder detection and recognition.

[20] is a bipolar disorder corpus proposed by Elvan Çiftçi et al. in 2018. Bipolar disorder is a common psychiatric disorder with symptoms of both mania and depression. The content of this corpus is in Turkish and the data of the interviewed volunteers are labelled with the BD state. The data of the corpus were collected from 46 patients and 49 volunteers without BD. Video and audio data were collected.

Gratch et al. [21] presented a dataset of mental issues containing 3 modalities of information, the DAIC includes audio data and video data, some of

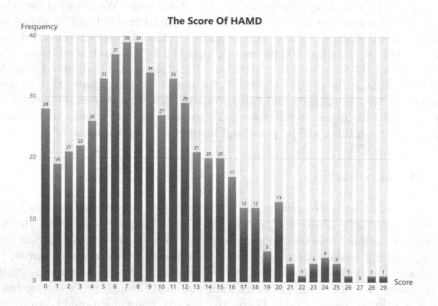

(a) Distribution of HAMD Scores

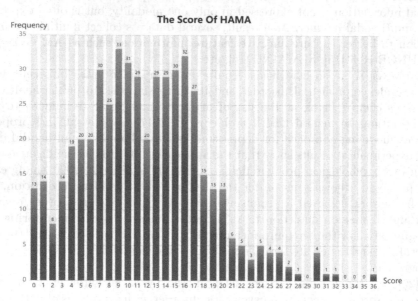

(b) Distribution of HAMA Scores

Fig. 1. Distribution of HAMD and HAMA Scores 0–6:Normal, 7–16:Possible Depression, 17–24:Definite Depression, 25–52:Major Depression 0–6:Normal, 7–13:Possible Anxiety, 14–20:Significant Anxiety, 21–28:Definite Anxiety, 29–56:Severe Anxiety

which are also transcribed with tagged text content and extracted data features. DAIC contains four types of data, face-to-face interviews, interviews conducted remotely using teleconferencing software, interviews conducted by virtual moderators under human control and interviews conducted by virtual moderators in a fully automated mode. The DAIC corpus was further extended by [22]. 351 participants were included in the E-DAIC dataset.

A depressive disorder dataset based on the HAMD was proposed by [23] in 2018. The researchers collected data from 57 volunteers, but for a variety of reasons, data from 49 participants were ultimately used for analysis. The participants were interviewed by a professional doctor based on the HAMD. During the interview, the researcher collected data on three modalities: dynamic facial expressions, head movements, and vocal rhythmic information.

In 2020, Cai et al. [24] launched the MODMA dataset. The participants consisted of patients with mental disorders who had been diagnosed by a medical professional and a normal control group. The researchers recorded the Electroencephalogram signals(EEG) of the participants using a contact device. In addition the researchers interviewed the participants in a quiet and noise-free environment and collected audio data from the participants. The interviews were designed according to the PHQ-9 scale [25].

In the currently available mental disorder datasets, the data collected from real patients are authentic and rigorous, but the sample size is small; the datasets constructed by collecting information from social media have a large amount of data, but are not suitable for tasks such as primary screening of real mental disorders, as they are mostly collected by judging keywords in tweets and cannot guarantee authority.

Based on the above two points, we constructed a multimodal Chinese mental disorder dataset based on clinical interviews. We compared our dataset with the above-mentioned datasets, as shown in Table 1.

3 Dataset Details

3.1 Data Collection

All subjects in our dataset are Chinese, between 13 and 85. Before the doctor starts the conversation with the participant, basic information such as the participant's name, age and relevant medical history will be recorded, and the participant will be informed of the procedure and the non-invasive nature of

Table 2. Statistic of Data

	gender		avg. / min / max of age
	male	female	
Depression	183	313	40.34 / 13 / 85
Anxiety	167	299	40.53 / 13 / 83

the experiment, have any possible psychological concerns removed and sign an informed consent form. The physician then interviewed each subject and completed the HAMD or HAMA, which are widely used in psychiatry to assess depression and anxiety and their severity, and which have good reliability in clinical practice. The HAMD uses a 14-item version with a total score range of 0 to 52. HAMA uses a 17-item version with a total score range of 0 to 56. The distribution of the subjects' HAMD and HAMA scores are shown in Fig. 1. The physician made a diagnosis based on the subject's answers and mental status. After all questions were answered, the degree of illness was obtained from the total score of the scale. The detailed statistical information of dataset is shown in Table 2.

The majority of the data collected from clinical interviews were diseased samples, and a small number of volunteers were recruited from the community in order to balance the data set categories. These volunteers are without depressive and anxiety symptoms, or have low levels of depressive and anxiety symptom expression, which could effectively complement some normal samples. The collection process and scenario remained the same as in the clinical interviews, and the questioner is a trained psychology graduate students. We show the setup of the volunteer data collection scenario in Fig. 2.

During the conversation, the subject was in a sitting position facing the camera, and the camera was able to capture a video of the subject's upper body movement. All interviews were conducted in a noise-free room without interference from others, and the audio of the conversation was captured clearly through a microphone. In total, 501 HAMA data with an average duration of 202s and 524 HAMD data with an average duration of 137s were collected by the two collection methods. Here we provide some samples from our dataset.[1]

Fig. 2. Scenario for collecting volunteer data

---

[1] https://pan.baidu.com/s/1b1qygk1d_kYX0bTbx_JbSA?pwd=0qgx.

3.2 Modality Introduction

Vision Modality. In recent years, there have been many attempts by researchers to use physiological signals such as heart rate [26,27] and EEG [28,29] for depression and anxiety detection. Although the physiological signals are objective and realistic, the requirement to obtain data through a wearable device makes the implementation process difficult and is not conducive to building large-scale datasets. Depression and anxiety can alter a wide range of non-verbal behaviours in people [30]. Patients' faces are often dull, disoriented, depressed, they avoid looking directly at others and blink more frequently than normal. With the development of computer vision, the above symptoms can be analyzed by computer. The acquisition of visual features only requires a camera, which is simple to operate and has been widely used.

In our data set, the subjects' facial key points, head posture, direction of vision and blink frequency change when they answer the doctor's questions. Therefore, we used the OpenFace toolkit [31] to extract the visual features associated with each video, which includes 2D and 3D facial landmark, gaze direction vector and gaze angle of both eyes, euler angles of head posture and facial action units. These basic features can effectively differentiate visual variation between patients and normal subjects.

Audio Modality. In addition to facial features and physical movements, researchers have been trying to obtain valid information from voice signals for the detection of mental disorders. In 2013, Yang et al. [32] demonstrates the usefulness of signal features in speech information, other than semantic features, for depression detection. Studies [33–35] have shown that rhythmic features, acoustic spectrogram-related features, and acoustic quality-related parameters are useful when identifying depression in information in speech.

In this dataset, the audio data is the complete audio of the participant's interview or the recording of the same scale content performed by a volunteer under the supervision of a professional psychology graduate student. The original audio clips include, in addition to clips of the participant's or volunteer's words, the doctor's interview and additional response clips from the participant's accompanying family members. We intercepted the speech segments of the attendee or volunteer based on manually annotated timestamps and extracted the fundamental frequency features, MFCC features, RMS features, etc. of the speech segments using openSMILE [36].

Table 3. Text Data Sample

P.ID	R.ID	R.Name	S.T	E.T	Content
3	2	doctor	6.63	16.36	Feel like you're a light sleeper? Or is it just slumber when you fall asleep and awake when you wake up, rather than the kind of situation where it's like you know there's a noise outside but your eyes aren't actually open.
4	1	patient	16.39	19.54	Well, that's not so much,(I) fell asleep is completely asleep, eh

Text Modality. Data from visual and acoustic modalities exhibit many features that are less easily observed intuitively, while information from text modalities most directly brings out valid information. Much of the work in previous research [37,38] has been on how to mine effective textual feature information from social media for mental disorder detection. [39] analysed the differences between people with mental health problems and normal people by processing text for a range of textual information. [40] concluded that sentiment and thematic information of texts can be used as valid indicators for the detection of mental disorders.

In this dataset, our texts were collected under the guidance of professionals in response to the HAMA and the HAMD. The textual content in this dataset is more specific to the participants' own mental disorder-related realities than the social media data, which contains a lot of invalid and redundant information. We consider that the participants' responses contain more valid semantic information. The specific text data style is shown in Table 3. The text of each sample contains information such as order of the current phrase in the entire speech(P.ID), role identification(R.ID, R.Name), the start(S.T) and end(E.T) of a particular sentence, and the content of the utterance (in Chinese). We also collated both audio and text data from the professional practitioners in the interviews, and the data from the professional practitioners could provide contextual information for the participants' responses.

4 Experiment

To validate our dataset, we used a machine learning approach to train each modal feature and evaluate it on two tasks: (1) classification of depression and anxiety symptoms (2) regression of HAMD and HAMA scores. Given the long-tailed distribution of HAMD and HAMA scores for our data, we combined the last two categories of HAMD and the last three categories of HAMA, classifying both depression and anxiety symptoms as normal, mildly symptomatic and severely symptomatic.

The visual features used the mean value of gaze angle in all frames. The audio features used the MFCC features, fundamental frequency features, RMS features and other base features of the speech data, and the text features used the TF-IDF features. All baselines were implemented through the Scikit-Learn toolkit.

We choose models such as support vector machine, Decision Tree, Random Forest and AdaBoost. The experimental results are shown in Table 4 and Table 5. For svm, we choose the kernel function of rbf, sigmoid and poly for audio, text and visual respectively. AdaBoost and Random Forest use Decision Tree as the base estimator, and the maxnum of base estimator is set to 50. In addition, we use grid search to find the other best parameters. Finally, we choose the svm with the best results for each modality, and use a simple score fusion to complete the multimodal experiment. For evaluation metrics, we report F1, Recall, and Precision with weighted average for the classification task and Mean Absolute Error metrics for the regression task.

Table 4. Depression Detection Baselines

	Classification				Regression
Method	Modalities	F1	Precision	Recall	MAE
SVM	A	54.1	60.8	58	4.01
DT	A	48.5	49	48	4.82
SVM	V	46.8	53.1	56	4.35
DT	V	52.1	49.3	56	4.54
SVM	L	53	60.8	54	4.37
AB	L	50.4	47.4	55	4.28
SVM	AL	58.9	58.4	64	3.84
SVM	AVL	56.5	56.4	62	3.81

Table 5. Anxiety Detection Baselines

	Classification				Regression
Method	Modalities	F1	Precision	Recall	MAE
SVM	A	52.8	54.4	54.0	4.45
DT	A	47.7	48.9	48.0	5.78
SVM	V	40.9	46.2	38.0	5.02
AB	V	42.2	62.1	43.0	5.08
SVM	L	57.9	58.2	58.0	5.11
RF	L	42.1	51.3	45.0	5.10
SVM	AL	60.2	60.7	60.0	4.08
SVM	AVL	59.3	60.5	59.0	4.30

5 Discussion

Before using this dataset for further research, we must point out that this dataset was collected under the guidance of professionals, but it cannot be used for formal, specific psychological diagnosis. This dataset is aimed more at primary or rapid screening for psychological problems in order to save time, labour costs and medical resources.

As a result of this baseline experiment, we are considering the following directions for improvement in future studies: we will consider athematic keyword, volume, gender, blink frequency, facial landmark, etc. It is also planned to add temporal features of text data and speech data to the feature set; there is a category imbalance problem in the current depression data, which affects the accuracy and error to some extent. In the future, how to deal with category imbalances in datasets will be one of the priorities of our work. Last but not least, this dataset is a multimodal dataset, so it is our focus to explore the potential associations between multiple modalities and to use the information from multiple modalities to identify psychological problems.

In conclusion, we propose a multimodal mental disorder Chinese dataset, which includes visual data, speech data and text data. All subjects in the dataset were diagnosed by professional psychologists, and the subjects' disorders were determined by combining HAMD and HAMA scores. We hope that this dataset will be able to supplement the current multimodal Chinese data related to mental disorder and will be useful for establishing an automatic detection system for Depression and Anxiety.

Acknowledgement. This work was supported by the National Key R&D Programme of China (2022YFC3803202), Major Project of Anhui Province under Grant 202203a05020011 and General Programmer of the National Natural Science Foundation of China (61976078).

References

1. Organization, W.H.: Depression key facts [EB/OL]. https://www.who.int/news-room/fact-sheets/detail/depression/. Accessed 13 Sept 2021
2. Huang, Y., et al.: Prevalence of mental disorders in China: a cross-sectional epidemiological study. Lancet Psychiatry **6**(3), 211–224 (2019)
3. Shen, G., et al.: Depression detection via harvesting social media: a multimodal dictionary learning solution. In: IJCAI, pp. 3838–3844 (2017)
4. Xezonaki, D., Paraskevopoulos, G., Potamianos, A., Narayanan, S.: Affective conditioning on hierarchical attention networks applied to depression detection from transcribed clinical interviews. In: INTERSPEECH, pp. 4556–4560 (2020)
5. Ye, J., et al.: Multi-modal depression detection based on emotional audio and evaluation text. J. Affect. Disord. **295**, 904–913 (2021)
6. Guo, W., Yang, H., Liu, Z.: Deep neural networks for depression recognition based on facial expressions caused by stimulus tasks. In: 2019 8th International Conference on Affective Computing and Intelligent Interaction Workshops and Demos (ACIIW), pp. 133–139. IEEE (2019)
7. Haque, A., Guo, M., Miner, A.S., Fei-Fei, L.: Measuring depression symptom severity from spoken language and 3D facial expressions. arXiv preprint arXiv:1811.08592 (2018)
8. Alghowinem, S., et al.: Multimodal depression detection: fusion analysis of paralinguistic, head pose and eye gaze behaviors. IEEE Trans. Affect. Comput. **9**(4), 478–490 (2016)
9. Hamilton, M.: A rating scale for depression. J. Neurol. Neurosurg. Psychiatry **23**(1), 56 (1960)
10. Hamilton, M.: The assessment of anxiety states by rating. Br. J. Med. Psychol. **32**(1), 50–55 (1959)
11. Gaudi, G., Kapralos, B., Collins, K.C., Quevedo, A.: Affective computing: an introduction to the detection, measurement, and current applications. In: Virvou, M., Tsihrintzis, G.A., Tsoukalas, L.H., Jain, L.C. (eds.) Advances in Artificial Intelligence-based Technologies. LAIS, vol. 22, pp. 25–43. Springer, Cham (2022). https://doi.org/10.1007/978-3-030-80571-5_3

12. Maas, A.L., Daly, R.E., Pham, P.T., Huang, D., Ng, A.Y., Potts, C.: Learning word vectors for sentiment analysis. In: Proceedings of the 49th Annual Meeting of the Association for Computational Linguistics: Human Language Technologies, pp. 142–150. Association for Computational Linguistics, Portland (2011), http://www.aclweb.org/anthology/P11-1015
13. Zhang, Z., Luo, P., Loy, C.C., Tang, X.: Learning social relation traits from face images. In: Proceedings of the IEEE International Conference on Computer Vision, pp. 3631–3639 (2015)
14. Miranda-Correa, J.A., Abadi, M.K., Sebe, N., Patras, I.: Amigos: A dataset for affect, personality and mood research on individuals and groups. IEEE Trans. Affect. Comput. 12(2), 479–493 (2018)
15. Soleymani, M., Lichtenauer, J., Pun, T., Pantic, M.: A multimodal database for affect recognition and implicit tagging. IEEE Trans. Affect. Comput. 3(1), 42–55 (2011)
16. Mckeown, G.: The semaine database: annotated multimodal records of emotionally colored conversations between a person and a limited agent. IEEE Trans. Affect. Comput. 3(1), 5–17 (2013)
17. Gong, Y., Poellabauer, C.: Topic modeling based multi-modal depression detection. In: Proceedings of the 7th Annual Workshop on Audio/Visual Emotion Challenge, pp. 69–76 (2017)
18. Zhang, Z., Lin, W., Liu, M., Mahmoud, M.: Multimodal deep learning framework for mental disorder recognition. In: 2020 15th IEEE International Conference on Automatic Face and Gesture Recognition (FG 2020), pp. 344–350. IEEE (2020)
19. Garcia-Ceja, E., Riegler, M., Nordgreen, T., Jakobsen, P., Oedegaard, K.J., Tørresen, J.: Mental health monitoring with multimodal sensing and machine learning: a survey. Pervasive Mob. Comput. 51, 1–26 (2018)
20. Çiftçi, E., Kaya, H., Güleç, H., Salah, A.A.: The turkish audio-visual bipolar disorder corpus. In: 2018 First Asian Conference on Affective Computing and Intelligent Interaction (ACII Asia), pp. 1–6. IEEE (2018)
21. Gratch, J., et al.: The distress analysis interview corpus of human and computer interviews. In: Proceedings of the Ninth International Conference on Language Resources and Evaluation (LREC'14), pp. 3123–3128 (2014)
22. DeVault, D., et al.: Simsensei kiosk: A virtual human interviewer for healthcare decision support. In: Proceedings of the 2014 International Conference on Autonomous Agents and Multi-Agent Systems, pp. 1061–1068 (2014)
23. Dibeklioğlu, H., Hammal, Z., Cohn, J.F.: Dynamic multimodal measurement of depression severity using deep autoencoding. IEEE J. Biomed. Health Inform. 22(2), 525–536 (2017)
24. Cai, H., et al.: Modma dataset: a multi-modal open dataset for mental-disorder analysis. arXiv preprint arXiv:2002.09283 (2020)
25. Spitzer, R.L., Kroenke, K., Williams, J.B., Group, P.H.Q.P.C.S., Group, P.H.Q.P.C.S., et al.: Validation and utility of a self-report version of PRIME-MD: the PHQ primary care study. JAMA 282(18), 1737–1744 (1999)
26. Xing, Y., et al.: Task-state heart rate variability parameter-based depression detection model and effect of therapy on the parameters. IEEE Access 7, 105701–105709 (2019)
27. Byun, S., et al.: Detection of major depressive disorder from linear and nonlinear heart rate variability features during mental task protocol. Comput. Biol. Med. 112, 103381 (2019)
28. Cai, H., et al.: A pervasive approach to EEG-based depression detection. Complexity 2018, 1–13 (2018)

29. Sun, S., et al.: Graph theory analysis of functional connectivity in major depression disorder with high-density resting state EEG data. IEEE Trans. Neural Syst. Rehabil. Eng. **27**(3), 429–439 (2019)
30. Fiquer, J.T., Moreno, R.A., Brunoni, A.R., Barros, V.B., Fernandes, F., Gorenstein, C.: What is the nonverbal communication of depression? assessing expressive differences between depressive patients and healthy volunteers during clinical interviews. J. Affect. Disord. **238**, 636–644 (2018)
31. Baltrusaitis, T., Zadeh, A., Lim, Y.C., Morency, L.P.: Openface 2.0: facial behavior analysis toolkit. In: 2018 13th IEEE International Conference on Automatic Face & Gesture Recognition (FG 2018), pp. 59–66. IEEE (2018)
32. Yang, Y., Fairbairn, C., Cohn, J.F.: Detecting depression severity from vocal prosody. IEEE Trans. Affect. Comput. **4**(2), 142–150 (2012)
33. Taguchi, T., et al.: Major depressive disorder discrimination using vocal acoustic features. J. Affect. Disord. **225**, 214–220 (2018)
34. Low, L.S.A., Maddage, N.C., Lech, M., Allen, N.: Mel frequency cepstral feature and gaussian mixtures for modeling clinical depression in adolescents. In: 2009 8th IEEE International Conference on Cognitive Informatics, pp. 346–350. IEEE (2009)
35. Low, L.S.A., Maddage, N.C., Lech, M., Sheeber, L.B., Allen, N.B.: Detection of clinical depression in adolescents' speech during family interactions. IEEE Trans. Biomed. Eng. **58**(3), 574–586 (2010)
36. Eyben, F., Wöllmer, M., Schuller, B.: Opensmile: the munich versatile and fast open-source audio feature extractor. In: Proceedings of the 18th ACM International Conference on Multimedia, pp. 1459–1462 (2010)
37. Ive, J., Gkotsis, G., Dutta, R., Stewart, R., Velupillai, S.: Hierarchical neural model with attention mechanisms for the classification of social media text related to mental health. In: Proceedings of the Fifth Workshop on Computational Linguistics and Clinical Psychology: From Keyboard to Clinic, pp. 69–77 (2018)
38. Sekulić, I., Strube, M.: Adapting deep learning methods for mental health prediction on social media. arXiv preprint arXiv:2003.07634 (2020)
39. Weerasinghe, J., Morales, K., Greenstadt, R.: "Because... I was told... so much": linguistic indicators of mental health status on twitter. Proc. Priv. Enhancing Technol. **2019**(4), 152–171 (2019)
40. Ji, S., Li, X., Huang, Z., Cambria, E.: Suicidal ideation and mental disorder detection with attentive relation networks. Neural Comput. Appl. **34**(13), 1–11 (2021)

Author Index

A

Agam, Gady 124
Agudo, Antonio 7
Ahmed, Amr 574
Altulea, Hamid Jalab 574
Amadi, Lawrence 124
Amat, Ashwaq Zaini 193
Auriemma Citarella, Alessia 514

B

Baillie, Mark 384
Barra, Paola 514
Bellmann, Peter 394
Berti, Andrea 539
Beyerer, Jürgen 79
Bilodeau, Guillaume-Alexandre 152, 405
Bischl, Bernd 373
Bria, Alessandro 529
Briden, Michael 682
Busch, Christoph 465

C

Cai, Qi 313
Carloni, Gianluca 539
Castellano, Giovanna 644
Ceccaldi, Eleonora 240
Celiktutan, Oya 167
Chalasani, Tejo 359
Chen, Tao 668
Chong, Chun Yong 617
Cilia, Nicole Dalia 632
Clavel, Chloé 225
Colantonio, Sara 539
Corbellini, Nicola 240
Cristani, Marco 49
Cunico, Federico 49

D

D'Alessandro, Tiziana 632
de Belen, Ryan Anthony 178
De Marco, Fabiola 514
De Stefano, Claudio 632

Di Biasi, Luigi 514
Dias, Jorge 499
Dugelay, Jean-Luc 558

E

Estevez, Pablo 7

F

Fink, Gernot A. 256
Fontanella, Francesco 632
Fu, Gang 655
Fu, Nihang 21
Fujii, Keisuke 210
Fujita, Tomohiro 139

G

Georgescu, Alexandra L. 167
Golhar, Rahul 417
Goossens, Ilona 273
Greco, Antonio 95
Guo, Yanrong 668

H

Haithami, Mahmood Salah 574
Hajlaoui, Rihab 152
Heublein, Lucas 373
Hosen, Md Imran 37
Howard, John J. 431, 448
Huang, Xiaofei 21
Hulcelle, Marc 225

I

Iacconi, Chiara 539
Islam, Md Baharul 37

J

Javed, Sajid 499
Jethra, Bhavin 417
Ji, Qiang 109
Jiang, Yueqi 691
Jung, Merel M. 273

J.-J. Rousseau and B. Kapralos (Eds.): ICPR 2022 Workshops, LNCS 13643, pp. 703–705, 2023.
https://doi.org/10.1007/978-3-031-37660-3

K

Kawanishi, Yasutomo   139
Kephart, Jeffery O.   109
Keshtmand, Nawid   330
Kestler, Hans A.   349
Kolberg, Jascha   465
Kotwal, Ketan   479
Kuang, Chenyi   109

L

Laird, Eli J.   431, 448
Lamghari, Soufiane   405
Larsen, Mark   178
Lawry, Jonathan   330
Li, Shiqi   64
Li, Xun   178
Liao, Iman Yi   574
Liebregts, Werner   273
Lim, Mei Kuan   617
Lin, Jingyang   289
Liu, Shuangjun   21
Long, Fuchen   302

M

Mahbub, Taslim   499
Mallat, Khawla   558
Marcel, Sébastien   479
Marrocco, Claudio   529
Milanova, Mariofanna   384
Mirabet-Herranz, Nelida   558
Modayur, Bharath   21
Molinara, Mario   529
Mou, Afsana   384
Moya Rueda, Fernando   256
Mutschler, Christopher   373

N

Nair, Nilah Ravi   256
Nardone, Emanuele   632
Nguyen-The, Maude   405
Norouzi, Narges   682
Nwogu, Ifeoma   417

O

Obeid, Ahmad   499
Onal Ertugrul, Itir   273
Onie, Sandersan   178
Ostadabbas, Sarah   21
Ott, Felix   373

P

Pascali, Maria Antonietta   539
Pino, Carmelo   589, 602
Pino, David Li   21
Piotto Piotto, Stefano   514
Placidi, Giuseppe   644
Plunk, Abigale   193
Polsinelli, Matteo   644

Q

Qian, Yurui   289
Qiu, Zhaofan   302

R

Rathgeb, Christian   465
Reining, Christopher   256
Ricken, Tobias B.   394
Rockemann, Jan   152, 405
Rollet, Nicolas   225
Rubin, Rebecca E.   431
Rügamer, David   373
Rundo, Francesco   589, 602
Ryspayeva, Marya   529

S

Salanitri, Federica Proietto   589
Saldutti, Stefano   95
Santos-Rodriguez, Raul   330
Sarkar, Nilanjan   193
Sarpietro, Riccardo E.   589, 602
Schwenker, Friedhelm   349, 394
Shi, Jinlong   668
Sirotin, Yevgeniy B.   431, 448
Smolic, Aljosa   359
Sowmya, Arcot   178
Spampinato, Concetto   589, 602
Stadler, Daniel   79
Sun, Xiao   691

T

Takeda, Kazuya   210
Tay, Heng Ee   617
Thiam, Patrick   349
Tipton, Jerry L.   431
Toaiari, Andrea   49
Tortora, Genoveffa   514
Tortorella, Francesco   529
Tsutsui, Kazushi   210
Tulipani, Gianpiero   644

V
Varni, Giovanna   225, 240
Vemury, Arun R.   431
Vento, Bruno   95
Vessio, Gennaro   644
Vogeley, Kai   167
Volpe, Gualtiero   240

W
Walter, Steffen   394
Wan, Michael   21
Wang, Qingxiang   655
Wang, Yu   289

Werghi, Naoufel   499
Wilkes, D. Mitchell   193
Wu, Weiyang   167

X
Xiang, Xiang   64

Y
Ye, Jiayu   655

Z
Zhang, Ziyang   691
Zheng, Tong   668